Studies in the Social and Cultural Foundations of Language No. 10

Ku Waru

Studies in the Social and
Cultural Foundations of Language

The aim of this series is to develop theoretical perspectives on the essential social and cultural character of language by methodological and empirical emphasis on the occurrence of language in its communicative and interactional settings, on the socioculturally grounded 'meanings' and 'functions' of linguistic forms, and on the social scientific study of language use across cultures. It will thus explicate the essentially ethnographic nature of linguistic data, whether spontaneously occurring or experimentally induced, whether normative or variational, whether synchronic or diachronic. Works appearing in the series will make substantive and theoretical contributions to the debate over the sociocultural–functional and structural–formal nature of language, and will represent the concerns of scholars in the sociology and anthropology of language, anthropological linguistics, sociolinguistics, and socioculturally informed psycholinguistics.

1. Charles L. Briggs: *Learning how to ask: a sociolinguistic appraisal of the role of the interview in social science research*
2. Tamar Katriel: *Talking straight: Dugri speech in Israeli Sabra culture*
3. Bambi B. Schieffelin and Elinor Ochs (eds.): *Language socialization across cultures*
4. Susan U. Philips, Susan Steele, and Christine Tanz (eds.): *Language, gender, and sex in comparative perspective*
5. Jeff Siegel: *Language contact in a plantation environment: a sociolinguistic history of Fiji*
6. Elinor Ochs: *Culture and language development: language acquisition and language socialization in a Samoan village*
7. Nancy C. Dorian (ed.): *Investigating obsolescence: studies in language contraction and death*
8. Richard Bauman and Joel Sherzer (eds.): *Explorations in the ethnography of speaking*
9. Bambi B. Schieffelin: *The give and take of everyday life: language socialization of Kaluli children*

Ku Waru

Language and segmentary politics in the western Nebilyer Valley, Papua New Guinea

Francesca Merlan and **Alan Rumsey**

Department of Anthropology
University of Sydney

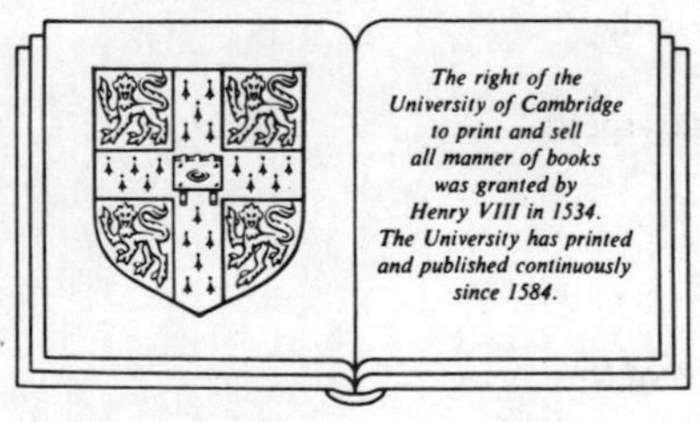

Cambridge University Press
Cambridge
New York Port Chester Melbourne Sydney

Published by the Press Syndicate of the University of Cambridge
The Pitt Building, Trumpington Street, Cambridge CB2 1RP, UK
40 West 20th Street, New York, NY 10011, USA
10 Stamford Road, Oakleigh, Melbourne 3166, Australia

First published 1991

Printed in Hong Kong by Colorcraft Ltd

National Library of Australia cataloguing-in-publication data:

Merlan, Francesca.
Ku Waru: language and segmentary politics in the western Nebilyer Valley, Papua New Guinea.
Bibliography.
Includes index.
ISBN 0 521 32339 8.
1. Anthropological linguistics – Papua New Guinea – Nebilyer Valley. 2. Nebilyer Valley (Papua New Guinea) – Politics and government. 3. Nebilyer Valley (Papua New Guinea) – Social conditions. I. Rumsey, Alan. II. Title. (Series: Studies in the social and cultural foundations of language; no. 10).
306.4409956

British Library cataloguing-in-publication data:

Merlan, Francesca
Ku Waru: language and segmentary politics in the western Nebilyer Valley, Papua New Guinea. – (Studies in the social and cultural foundations of language; 10)
1. Papua New Guinea. Languages. Sociolinguistic aspects
I. Title II. Rumsey, Alan III. Series
409'.95'3
ISBN 0-521-32339-8

Library of Congress cataloguing-in-publication data applied for

ISBN 0 521 32339 8

Contents

List of illustrations viii
List of tables ix
List of abbreviations x
Preface and acknowledgments xii

1 Introduction 1
1.1 Towards an anthropology of events 1
1.2 Who conducts exchange? Problems of representation and agency in some Highlands exchange systems 8
1.3 Summary argument 17

2 The setting 20
2.1 Location, geography and regional populations 20
2.2 European exploration and post-contact 'development' 23
2.3 Indigenous and introduced orders 28
2.4 Ethnographic sources 30
2.5 Talk in the public domain: an introduction 31

3 Some aspects of Ku Waru segmentary sociality 34
3.1 The nature of Ku Waru segmentary structures 34
3.2 Structure and history of some western Nebilyer *talapi* ('tribes') 45
3.3 Conclusion 55

4 Ceremonial exchange and marriage in the western Nebilyer Valley 57
4.1 Structure and history of western Nebilyer ceremonial exchange 57
4.2 Nebilyer marriage, exchange and segmentary politics in comparative perspective 67

5 Some linguistic structures of segmentary politics 88
5.1 Forms of reference and address and their relevance for social action 89
5.2 The grammar of segmentary person 95
5.3 *El ung* ('fight talk') 98
5.4 *Ung eke* ('bent speech') 102
5.5 Speech genres, tropes and remarks on interpretation 109
5.6 Rhetorical questions 111
5.7 Pairing 113
5.8 Talk about talk 116

6 Warfare compensation payment to Laulku: an analysis 122
6.1 Immediate background and synopsis of the event 123
6.2 Topical analysis 129

7 Compensation at Palimung and the Kulka women's club 156
7.1 Western Nebilyer women's clubs 158
7.2 Unfolding of the event 160
7.3 Interlude on a subsequent event at Kopola 185
7.4 The accomplishment of the Kulka women's club 187

8 The events in perspective 198
8.1 Structures and processes of segmentation and exchange 198
8.2 The segmentary order and the Kulka women's club 210
8.3 Action and representation, structure and event 214

9 Perspectives on 'event' 221
9.1 The concealed and the revealed in persons and events 224
9.2 Contingent juxtaposition 236
9.3 Active disposition 238
9.4 Concluding remarks: action and meaning 239

Appendix A: Transcript of proceedings at Kailge on July 24, 1983 245

Appendix B: Grammatical sketch of *Bo Ung*, Ku Waru dialect 322
B.1 Introduction 322
B.2 Phonology and phonetics 323
B.3 Words and phrases 325
B.4 Syntax 337

Appendix C: The conduct of warfare 344

Appendix D: Ku Waru metalinguistic expressions 347
Chapter notes 350
Glossary 367
References 373
Index 381

Illustrations

FIGURES

3–1	Alternative structurings of Araim and Wiyal Kopia	47
4–1	Some marriages between Kopia\Galka and Poika\Lopanuyl	65
8–1	Some overlapping types of relationships among *talapi*	207

MAPS

Map 1	The Nebilyer Valley and environs	xv
Map 2	The Ku Waru region and nearby tribes in the western Nebilyer Valley	xvi
Map 3	The Kailge area and territorial distribution of *talapi*	xvii

PLATES

The plates follow page 174

Plate 1	The Kailge school ground with the *ku waru* in the background
Plate 2	View from Kopia territory to Kubuka territory
Plate 3	Bridewealth negotiation on Kàilge display ground
Plate 4	Kopia Councillor Noma
Plate 5	Kopia-Kubuka march to Palimung
Plate 6	Display of kina notes at Palimung
Plate 7	Kopia-Kubuka charge into Palimung
Plate 8	Kulka Councillor Pokea introducing his daughter at Palimung
Plate 9	Warfare in the lower Nebilyer Valley

Tables

TABLES

3–1	Segments of Wiyal Kopia	46
3–2	Segments of Araim Kopia	46
3–3	Palimi segments resident at Kailge/Ibumuyl	52
4–1	Phases of a Nebilyer *makayl* exchange cycle	58
4–2	Kopia-Kubuka external exchange transactions	60
4–3	Kopia\Tolab contributions to the 1975 *makayl* payment to Kubuka	61
4–4	Kopia\Galka to Poika\Lopanuyl *yi pengi* payment, 1984	64
4–5	Bridewealth offers and payments	72
4–6	Rank order of current Kopia, Kubuka and Palimi men's marriages	76
4–7	Rank order of current Kopia, Kubuka and Palimi women's marriages	79
4–8	Marriages between Kopia-Kubuka and Tea-Dena	84
5–1	Plural references in *el ung* vs. elsewhere	101
6–1	Phases of speech-making at the Kailge compensation event	128
6–2	Alternative constructions of some enchained inter-*talapi* relationships	143
8–1	Orders of relevant segmentary difference at the Kailge and Palimung exchange events	199
8–2	Types of transactional relationship at issue in the Kailge and Palimung exchange events	202

Abbreviations

GRAMMATICAL ABBREVIATIONS AND SYMBOLS USED IN CHAPTER 5 AND APPENDICES

Abs	absolutive
Ben	benefactive
Col	collective
Com	comitative
Csv	causative
Dat	dative
Def	definite
du	dual number (on verb)
Du	dual or 'salient pair' (on NP)
Erg	ergative
Fut	future
Gen	genitive
Hab	habitual
Hrt	hortative
Igv	interrogative
Imt	imminent
Imp	imperative
Ins	instrumental
Jus	jussive
Loc	locative
NF	non-final
Opt	optative
NP	noun phrase
pl	plural
Ppl	participle
Prf	perfective
PPr	present progressive
RP	remote past
sg	singular
Sjv	subjunctive
S/I	singular/indefinite
SR1	switch reference 1

SR2	switch reference 2
1	first person
2	second person
3	third person
2/3	second or third person (see Appendix B.3.1.)
/ /	phonemic or underlying form
→	'is realized as'
[ ]	phonetic form

OTHER ABBREVIATIONS

M	mother('s)
F	father('s)
B	brother('s)
Z	sister('s)
S	son('s)
D	daughter('s)
H	husband('s)
W	wife('s)
SP	segmentary person (see section 5.2)
: : : :	homologous relationship, e.g. A:B::C:D: 'A is to B as C is to D'
	between segmentary names indicates coordinate relation, e.g. Kopia-Kubuka 'the pair of Kopia and Kubuka'
	between segmentary names indicates superordinate–subordinate relations, e.g. Kopia\Kaja 'the Kaja segment of Kopia'
K-M-E-A-L	the congeries of tribes consisting of Kusika, Midipu, Epola, Alya, and Lalka (see section 3.1.3)

Preface and acknowledgments

This book presents an extended, ethnographically-based argument concerning the relationship between social structures and action, focusing upon speech as a salient aspect of the latter. Evidence for our argument is drawn from seventeen months of fieldwork which we conducted jointly between June 1981 and November 1983 in the Nebilyer Valley, Western Highlands Province of Papua New Guinea.

Even before going to New Guinea, we had always felt acutely the lack of successful integration of language-focused studies into mainstream ethnography. We sensed that this lack was due, not to the irrelevance of such material to ethnographic description and social theory, but to the much more fundamental problem of treating situated social *action* (including speech) as an object of ethnographic description and analysis. Our field time in the Nebilyer Valley not only strengthened our general conviction that there is a need to develop analyses of social action (integrating its linguistic and other aspects), but also provided us the opportunity to be present at many kinds of events which seemed to demand analysis in terms which could better reveal the relationship between structures and action. This volume is our attempt to provide such an analysis.

The research on which the book is based was undertaken during a first, exploratory trip during June to August, 1981, and then for 14 months between 1981 and the end of 1983. Two interruptions were necessitated by our involvement in Aboriginal land claims in Australia. These rapid transitions from the New Guinea Highlands to Aboriginal Australia and back were unsettling, but also had the positive effect of making differences between the two situations stand out in even greater relief than they otherwise might have. Alan Rumsey made a three-week return visit to our field site, Kailge, in January 1986, during which he worked mainly on mapping, and checking ethnographic information relating to the analyses in Chapters 6 and 7.

During our first field trip of 1981 we received support from the Australian Research Grants Council (ARGC). During the longer period of our fieldwork we were supported by a National Science Foundation Research Grant (No. BNS-8024174). We wish to express our gratitude for this support, and our particular thanks to Dr Paul Chapin of the National Science Foundation, Washington, DC.

We are also grateful to Professor Stefan Wurm, then Professor in the Department of Linguistics, Research School of Pacific Studies of the Australian National University, who facilitated Alan Rumsey's visiting fellowship at that institution during the first half of 1981.

Both Andrew Strathern and Marilyn Strathern, whose joint and separate anthropological work in the Mt Hagen area now spans well over two decades, were from the first supportive of our plan to work in the region. We thank them for their generosity, and for continuing discussion and scholarly exchange. Our debt to the richness and depth of their work in the Hagen area will be apparent throughout this book.

We also wish to acknowledge with gratitude the suggestions of Daryl Feil and the late Ralph Bulmer in the planning and early stages of our work.

In Papua New Guinea, we owe thanks to many people and are unable to mention them all here. We were affiliated with the Language Department at the University of Papua New Guinea, and are grateful to Professor John Lynch and Dr Terry Crowley for their assistance.

In Ukarumpa, we visited Rob and June Head, Summer Institute of Linguistics workers of many years' experience in the Kaugel area, who generously provided us with copies of their linguistic analyses of that dialect, closely related to Ku Waru. In Mt Hagen, Bruce Blowers also gave us the benefit of discussion of linguistic matters.

In our early search for a suitable field site, and also subsequently, we received much assistance from Catholic priests stationed in the Nebilyer and on the western side of the Tambul Range, who offered us transportation, hospitality and introductions to local people. In particular, we want to thank Father Sigmund Kruczek (Kuruk), Father Paul (Togoba), Father Don O'Connor and Father George (Ulga), and Father John Roelfs (Tabuga) who introduced us to Kailge, our eventual field site. We also thank Bishop Bernarding for discussing with us the Catholic mission in the Nebilyer.

In Mt Hagen, for advice, hospitality and other assistance we wish to thank Roey Berger, Susan Bonnell (then in the Office of Provincial Planning), Kenn Logan, Lois Logan (secretary to Nambuga Mara, former Western Highlands Premier), John Pun (Provincial Secretary), Thomas Nakinch (National Parliamentary Member), and Paias Wingti (National Parliamentary Member). Woytek Dumbrowski and Paul Gorecki, each doing research in the Hagen area, facilitated our trips to the northern 'last Melpa' area, adjacent to the Jimi Valley. The late John Watts and his wife Edith showed us great hospitality on several of our trips into Mt Hagen from the Nebilyer Valley. Dennis and Susan Malone, Summer Institute of Linguistics literacy workers at Tambul, invited us to visit them on their side of the range. We warmly remember Betty Harding at the Mapang Hostel in Mt Hagen who – we hope it may now be said – allowed us to stay there on trips to Mt Hagen at the 'missionary rate'.

We feel a continuing commitment to those who helped us in the Nebilyer Valley, and we look forward to an extended return trip there. At Kailge, Kopia *ada* Yaya took us in and invited us to build our house on his land. We became good friends with him and his family: his daughters Noma, Kin, Jingaba and their children. We enjoyed the company and assistance of Kopia Councillor Noma and his wife Nulya, the late Kopia Kajipu and his wives Yuni and Rami and their large households; Kopia Owa and his family; our close neighbors

Kopia Opa, his wife Rltim and their daughter Tong; Kopia *ada* Yapu and his wife Pilya and their family; Kopia Magistrate Waima; Sirku and his wife Porltap and their family; Palimi Lkuraya, wife Lam and family. Our most assiduous assistants in language transcription were young Kopia men whom we thank here for their persistence at an exacting task, and their general high spirits: Wai Andrew Kajipu, Ambak Owa, Simon Mek, Pai Kajipu, Don Kajipu, and Kerim Koi.

Kubuka Magistrate Unya and his wife Maria were hospitable and helpful to us in many ways, as were Lalka Peace Officer Kewa and his wife Pepu. We gained much from our association with Tilka Councillor Dop (including an unforgettable lesson, early on, in how to ford the River Luip at its height!), Dena Councillor Numje, Midipu Councillor and Magistrate Kujilyi, and Kulka Councillor Pokea. We also thank Epola Koluwa and Midipu Lkerim at Palimung for their assistance.

We made occasional trips to more distant localities in the Nebilyer Valley and beyond. At Ulga, we want to thank Otto Keruwa and Lewa Uwa, and once again, especially Thomas Nakinch for his invitation to visit there. We also want to thank the many people at Togoba, Kemangl, Koibega and Suruk who assisted us with information concerning their perspectives on regional political history and relations.

Even further from Kailge, we gratefully remember our hospitable reception by Mapuke people at Kumai near the Jimi Valley, and especially the companionship of Rafael Rul; the hospitality extended to us by Sister Beverly Wickham of the Bible Mission at Pabarabuk, who put us up on a walking trip to and from West Kambia; Mr and Mrs Jack Taylor at West Kambia who had us and Wai Andrew to Christmas dinner of 1982; and the Opika-Milyaka people who entertained us there, particularly Yobi and his son Damian Yok, and also Naba, Nunya and Kobiki.

For comments on portions of intermediate drafts of this book we thank Daryl Feil, Bill Hanks, Bruce Rigsby and Jimmy Weiner. For their detailed comments on the entire manuscript we are greatly indebted to Larry Goldman, Rena Lederman, Jay Lemke, Neil Maclean, Andrew Strathern and Marilyn Strathern. Our thanks also go to Penny Carter at Cambridge University Press for editorial advice and patience, and to Jean Cooney for her careful reading and skilled copy-editing.

This book is for our sons, the pair of James and Jesse: we look forward to taking them to Papua New Guinea.

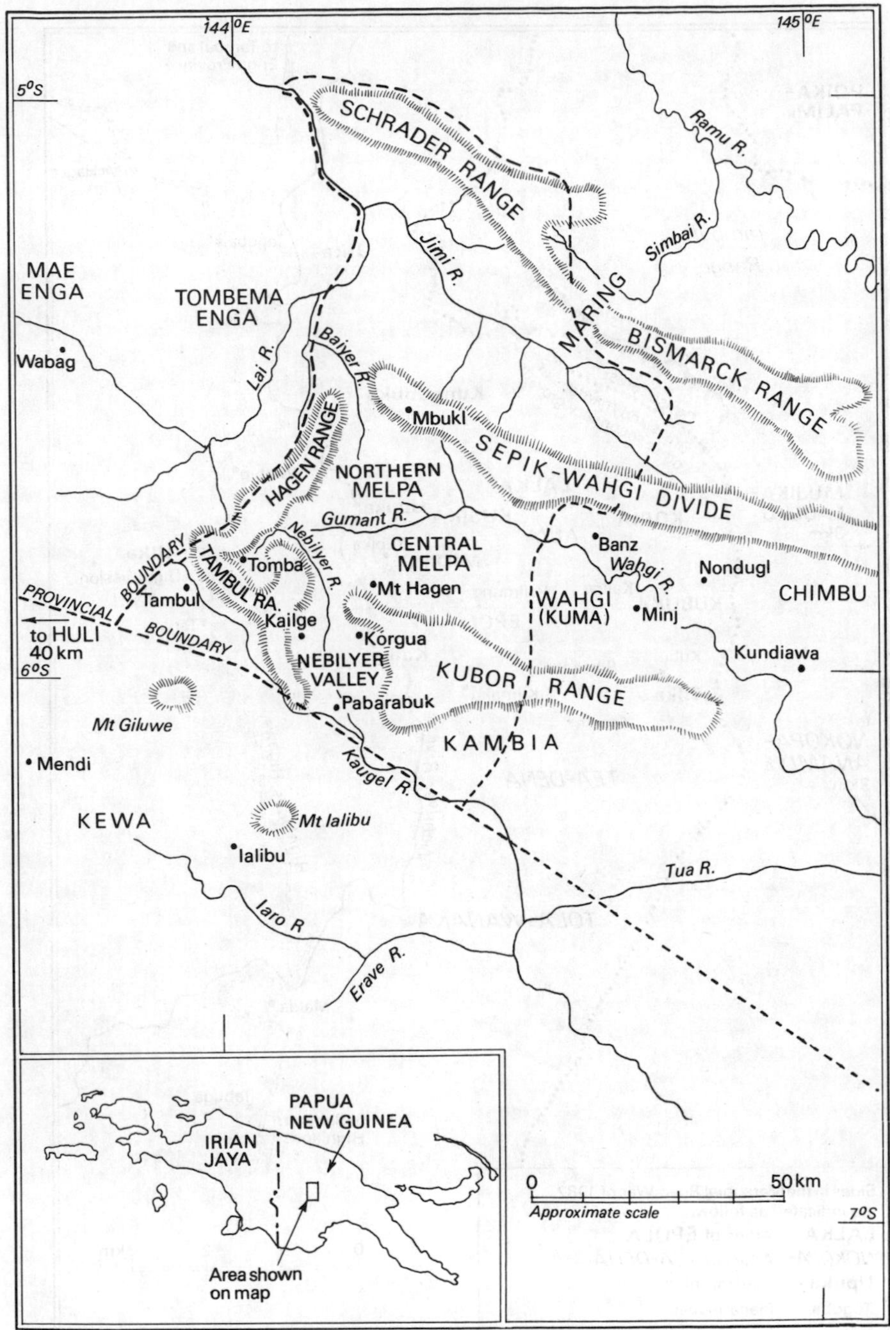

Map 1. The Nebilyer Valley and environs
This map is adapted from Map 1 in A.J. Strathern 1971, *The Rope of Moka*, with some alterations based on more recent 1:100,000 maps by the Royal Australian Survey Corps, series T601, T683.

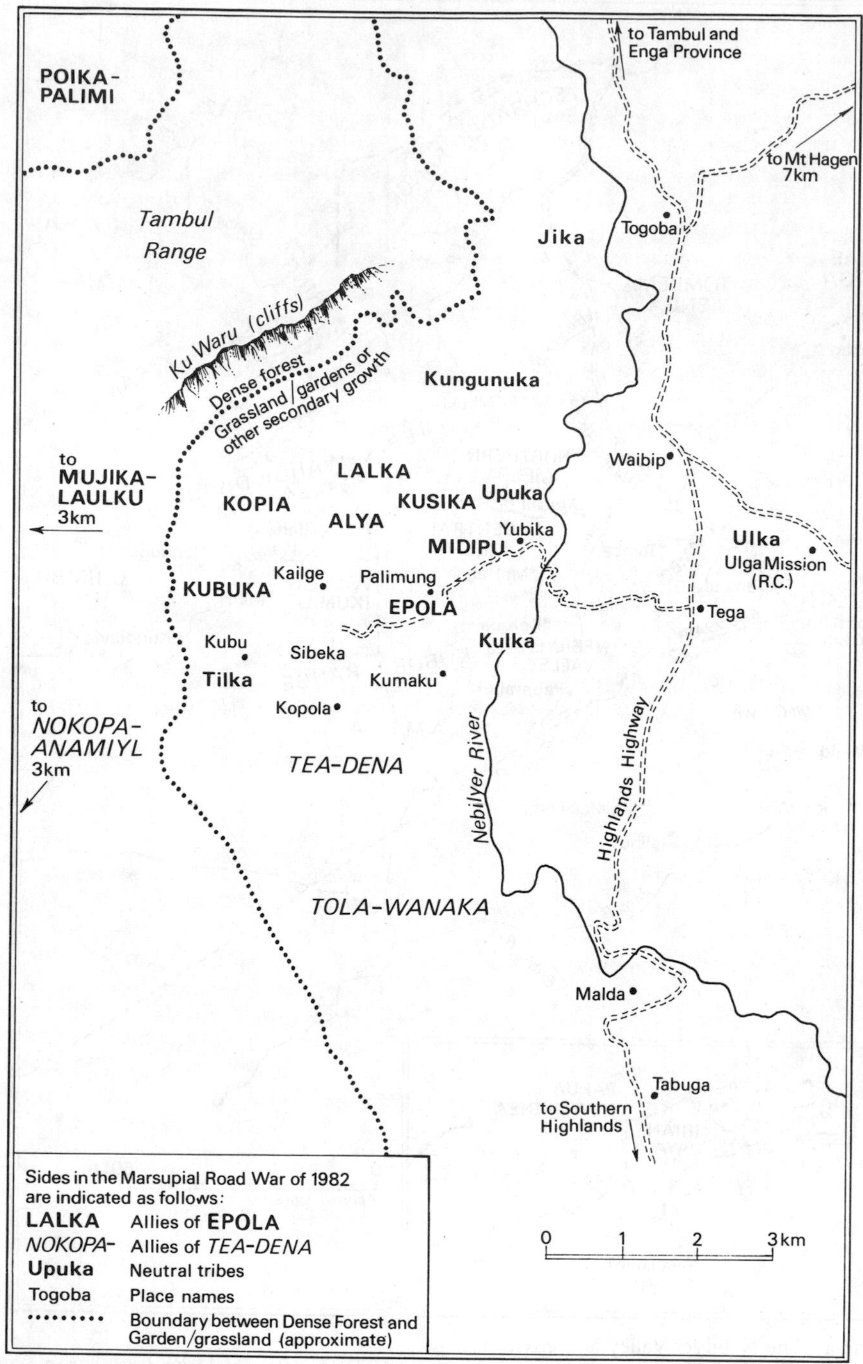

Map 2. The Ku Waru region and nearby tribes in the western Nebilyer Valley

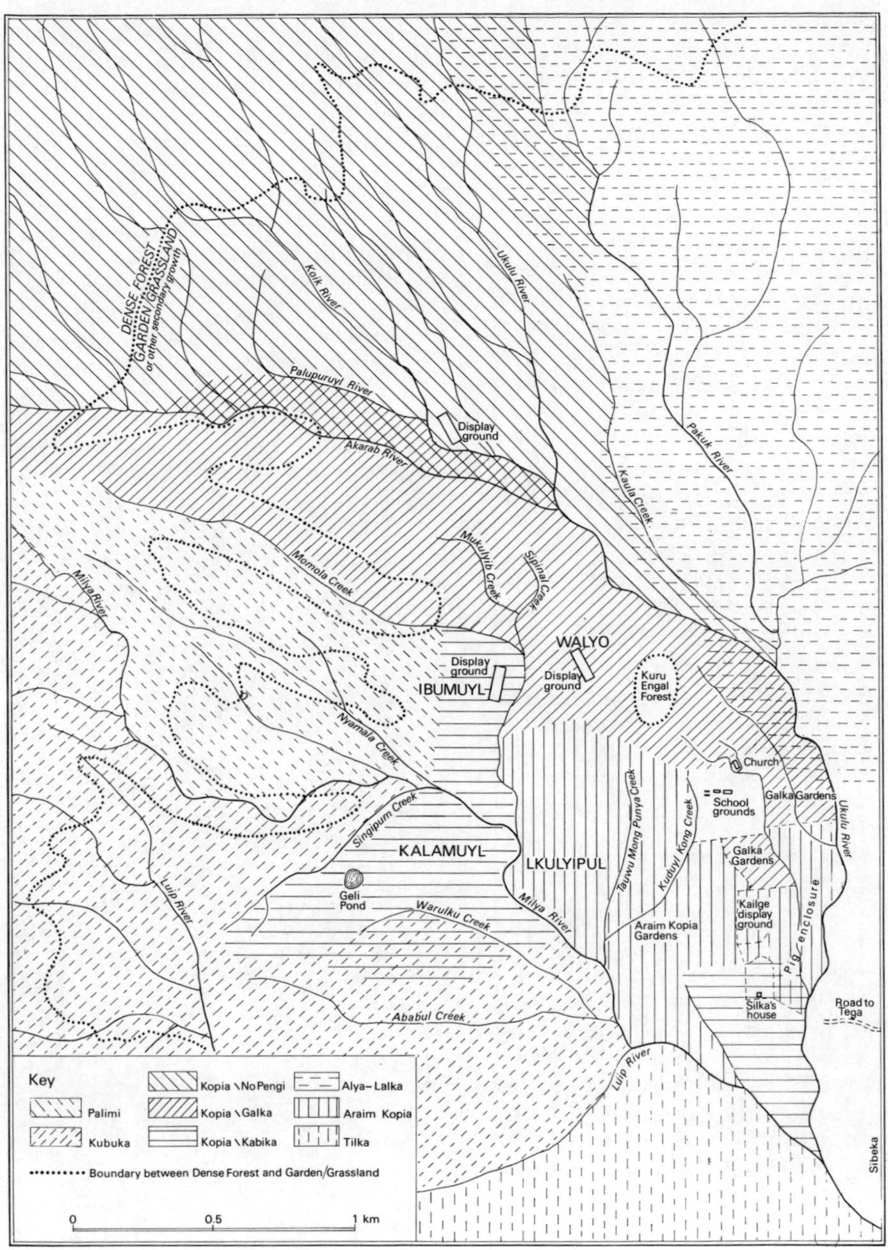

Map 3. The Kailge area and territorial distribution of *talapi*

1. Introduction

Near the middle of the western Nebilyer Valley, in the Highlands of Papua New Guinea, there is a large expanse of grassland locally known as Sibeka Sweet Potato Garden. Though the ground there remains fertile even after thousands of years of cultivation, almost all of it has lain fallow since 1979, when it was used as a battleground between people living to the northeast and south of it. We heard about that fighting when we first visited the area in 1981 and settled at Kailge, immediately to the northwest (see Map 2). The Kailge people told us they themselves had not got into the fight. Fighting commenced at Sibeka again in 1982. This time our hosts at Kailge did join in, on the side of their eastern neighbors. The opposing side called in their allies from further south, and the Kailge people, in turn, called in their allies from over the Tambul Range to the west.

The way in which the 1982 battle ended was remarkable, to us and our hosts. On September 13, onto the battlefield marched the members of a local women's group, one of several that had grown up in this area since around the beginning of 1982. Dressed in identical T-shirts which bore the national insignia, and carrying the Papua New Guinea flag, the women marched into the no-man's-land between the opposing lines and exhorted the men on both sides to lay down their arms. They carried with them onions, cabbages, money, cigarettes and bottled soft drinks, and offered these to the combatants if they would desist. Both sides accepted the offer, the goods were divided equally between them, and they dispersed.

In the following year, 1983, each of the acts of recruitment which brought people into the 1982 war, and the bold act by which the women stopped it, were duly 'paid for' by public, ceremonial presentations of wealth. As is usual at such occasions, there was extensive speech-making at each event.

1.1 TOWARDS AN ANTHROPOLOGY OF EVENTS

Those events of 1982 and 1983 are what this book is largely about. We will be discussing them in sometimes microscopic detail, not so much to provide a record of what happened (though that will be a leading source of interest for people at Kailge), as to advance the understanding of Nebilyer social life, and within it, the relation of certain social structures to specific historical events. By doing so we hope open up new ways of pursuing the general issue of the relations between *structure* and *practice, history* or *event* (cf. e.g. Bourdieu 1977; Sahlins 1981, 1985; Kelly 1977).

The ascent to general theory is not an end in itself. For, among its other uses, theory enables observation: it is only within the context of some set of general assumptions about what can happen, that we are able even to 'describe' certain basic aspects of what did happen (cf. Popper 1959).[1] Consider, for example, the events described in the opening paragraphs above. Though that description may serve as an introduction to the events in question, it is in many respects beside the point. It may be (as coroners say) consistent with what happened, but much of what it includes is incidental to the events as such (even to what made them remarkable), and most of what constitutes them as social action is left out (cf. Sapir 1949 on 'pattern'). We can get a little further by proceeding from an assumption commonly made by 'civilized' folks (some of them anthropologists) that warfare among peoples such as the New Guinea Highlanders is commonly organized in terms of 'tribes' (or 'clans'). Indeed, soon after settling at Kailge we learned that the people grouped themselves into named units they called *talapi*, which did figure centrally in their accounts of the events described above (and of warfare in general). Thus, the principal combatants in the 1979 war had not fought as 'people living to the northeast [of Sibeka]' vs. people to the south of it. Rather, they had fought as Kusika, Midipu, Epola, Alya, and Lalka (hereafter K-M-E-A-L), on the one side, and, on the other, Tea and Dena. And in the 1982 battle, our hosts had not joined in as 'people to the northeast of Sibeka', but as Kopia and Kubuka (see Map 2). Exactly how that is to be construed is far from transparent, as we shall see below. But it should also become clear that social units such as the ones we have just named do figure crucially in the events in question: we cannot begin to understand what happened without including them in the picture. Thus our received notions of 'tribe' are of some use, however modified they may be by the encounter.

Insofar as we think of tribes as 'proto-nations' (see e.g. Radcliffe-Brown 1965: 32–48), we think of them not only as discrete groupings of people, but also as territorial groupings of some kind. This will also get us a certain amount of mileage in understanding what happened in the events we describe here, insofar as Kopia, Kubuka, etc. are identified with discrete blocs of land (as shown in Map 2).

So far, we are within the realm of Western common sense understanding of events such as the above – the kind of understanding common among European expatriates living in the Highlands. This was, after all, a 'tribal fight', so what could the belligerents have been but 'tribes'?

Other aspects of what happened do not conform to established common sense (and therefore are unlikely to have been noticed by most Westerners) but are readily comprehended within the terms of standard anthropological theories about how certain kinds of tribes are organized. These include concepts such as: *segmentation*, which directs us to notice the fact that, for example, the Kopia 'tribe' comprises lower-level divisions (as in section 3.2.1 below), each of which made its own separately-identified contribution as part of the compensation payment by 'Kopia' to the allies they had recruited for the fighting;

agnation, which inclines us to notice that the cooperation within each 'tribe' was enjoined partly on the basis that all male personnel were said to be 'brothers' or 'fathers and sons'; *complementary opposition*, which inclines us to notice that a dispute between men from particular segments of the Epola and Dena tribes respectively, rapidly escalated to include, among others, all segments of Epola on one side and all of Dena on the other; or that a dispute which in 1982 had been escalating towards open warfare between two segments of the Kopia 'tribe' quickly faded into the background when Kopia joined the multi-tribe alliance against Tea-Dena and Tola-Wanaka.

All of this is readily recognized in terms of these anthropological concepts from segmentary lineage theory. That – as we shall argue below – some of this is actually misrecognition is here beside the point, which is that, here as elsewhere, theory directs our attention to things which otherwise we might not have noticed.[2]

Besides these general anthropological concepts, there are a number of others which have been developed or adapted specifically within the context of Melanesianist anthropology, which direct our attention to yet other aspects of what happened at the events in question. Foremost among these are concepts of *reciprocity* or *exchange* as developed by writers such as Mauss (1954), Malinowski (1922), Sahlins (1972), Wagner (1967, 1974), and, for the Hagen-Nebilyer area in particular, by A. Strathern (1971, 1979a) and M. Strathern (1972a, 1988).

In its application to this part of the New Guinea Highlands, exchange theory has provided a valuable corrective to segmentary lineage theory. The latter included the presupposition that what 'holds together' the segmentary system – the principle by which social groups are defined – is 'descent', i.e., common connection through more or less extended series of parent-child (read: father-son) links to common ancestors. Initial assumptions to the contrary, no such principle is evident here (see section 3.1.2).

Conversely, to a much greater extent than in classical 'segmentary lineage' societies, what delimits and/or relates social segments in the Hagen-Nebilyer area is exchange transactions. Thus we shall see, for example, that what links Kopia and Kubuka together as a tribe-pair, and predisposed them to enter the 1982 war together (if at all) is, in large part, the fact that both of them have been involved in a single long series of ceremonial prestations to another tribe-pair: Poika and Palimi. This is something we would have been less likely to notice (instead perhaps searching in vain for a notion of common ancestry for Kopia and Kubuka) if we had not been equipped with concepts of exchange such as those mentioned above, especially Wagner's provocative claim (1967, 1974) that, in the Highlands, exchange *defines* social units whereas descent relates them.

The above examples should suffice to demonstrate the value of theory for noticing what happens (or, if you prefer, for 'constructing' it). So far, the theoretical tools which have been most successfully developed by anthropology have been concepts of structure or institutions, such as exemplified above. All such theory is based upon the positing of general *types* such as 'tribe', 'segment', 'alliance', 'alternating disequilibrium', to which concrete instances or 'tokens' (e.g. 'Kopia\Kabika', 'Kopia-Kubuka-cum-Laulku', the prestation of July 24, 1983) arguably belong.

In order to understand particular events such as those described above, it is not enough just to be able to identify the relevant type of action or actions concerned. Doing so does carry us a step beyond the naivety of our initial description of those events as, for example, in the additional information that *talapi* ('tribes') were involved, and about the segmentary lines along which the conflict escalated.

But a description in terms of social structures alone is of limited use for understanding the detail of what happened. For that, we need to have recourse to the history of concrete *tokens* of the structural types. In the present case, for example, we have not gone very far towards understanding what happened until we know that it involved a dramatic shift in the alignments of *talapi* in the area: the belligerents in the 1979 fight – K-M-E-A-L and Tea-Dena – had previously been allies; in particular, they had been allied against the Kopia-Kubuka, with whom they had fought a bloody war in the period just before the area was pacified by the Australian Colonial Administration in the 1950s. This being so, the 1982 battle marked an equally dramatic realignment from the Kopia-Kubuka viewpoint, in that they were now fighting on the side of their erstwhile major enemies.

Nor can we begin to understand the way in which the women stopped the fighting without knowing about how the area was pacified in the first place; about subsequent colonial and post-colonial economic and political 'development'; about the recent history of women's work cooperatives in the area, the history of the particular club involved here, its relation to the Kulka tribe, and the relationships between its female leaders and particular big-men in the area.

Historical and structural modes of description or understanding have sometimes been seen as antithetical or mutually exclusive. Though this may be advanced as a matter of principle, in practice, neither mode can ever be used in isolation from the other. Anthropologists, for example, would never have been able to formulate general theoretical concepts such as *segmentary lineage* or *alternating disequilibrium* without having known of historically particular entities or cases, such as the Nuer or Kawelka and Tipuka.[3] Conversely, historians, however atheoretical they may proclaim themselves to be, could not begin to narrate 'what really happened' without such general concepts as *state, king, peasants, landed gentry* etc.

The account we wish to develop of the relation *between* structure and history is not one which can replace either of these two modes. On the contrary, we must begin by pushing both to their limits by developing both a maximally explicit account of the structural and actional types – the medium in which action takes place – and an equally detailed account of particular past actions and relationships among historically specific tokens of the types.

Having done so, what additional mileage can we gain by focusing explicitly on the relation between structure and history? Would theory here again enable us to see things we might otherwise have ignored? To see how it might do so, consider some of the complications we will later introduce into our account of what happened at Sibeka on September 13, 1982.

Consider, for example, the question of who it was that was recruited by the Kopia and Kubuka to fight on their side. In the skeletal account above, we have described the recruits merely as 'their allies from over the Tambul Range'. Most of the men who came from over the range are people who in most contexts are identified as of the Laulku *talapi* ('tribe'), but it was by no means all of the men of Laulku – in fact, only a minority of them. And conversely, several men also joined in from the *talapi* which is normally thought of as Laulku's paired tribe – the Mujika. At least two of these Mujika were injured in the fighting. But did the Laulku participate as a *talapi* in the fighting? Did the Mujika?

Similarly, several men who joined in the fighting were identified as Poika, the paired tribe of Palimi. Many people identified with the latter live on a pocket of land which was ceded to them by the Kubuka, and which borders on Kubuka and Kopia territory. But did *Poika* participate?

Another man who joined in the fighting was Bai, who by most accounts is a Laulku man, having been born in Laulku country to a Laulku father. But from an early age, Bai has been living with the Kubuka, his father's mother's tribe. So in which of these two capacities had he participated in the fighting?

For the people involved in each of these cases, the issues at stake are far from from the hair-splitting they may seem to the reader. Each is a matter of very real material consequence. For, as M. Strathern (1985a) has recently emphasized, warfare in this area is an integral aspect of the larger complex of exchange relationships in terms of which social life (including economic production) is largely organized. The 'exchange of blows' is a transaction which, if it is not to precipitate further belligerence, must instead be followed by an exchange of wealth items. In the present case, for example, if the Kopia-Kubuka are to retain their western recruits as allies, they must pay them ample compensation for the blood they have shed in their cause. So the question of whether the Mujika participated as such will in principle determine future exchange obligations between them and the Kopia-Kubuka. During the compensation staged in 1983 by the Kopia-Kubuka, the roles of the Mujika and Poika in the fighting were not presupposed, but were actively contested as a part of the larger process by which some Kopia were attempting to convert this relatively new military alliance with Laulku (or Mujika and Laulku?), to a major *makayl* (ceremonial exchange) relationship, to follow upon the imminent completion of a thirty-year cycle of payments to their older, established allies, the Poika-Palimi.

What are we to make of such apparent indeterminacies and ambiguities about 'what really happened'? In most structural anthropological accounts, they are apparently just ignored. Warfare and other exchange transactions are discussed and tabulated as if there were no such complications about them.

To say this is not necessarily to accuse the ethnographers of distorting their data. In most cases, the account is probably quite true to the data they have gathered. For, in the first instance, it is not just anthropologists who simplify and schematize 'what happened' in order to produce authoritative accounts. This also happens (in the Nebilyer and presumably elsewhere) within the social life of the people concerned in the events, and even more so among their descendants who inherit the traditions.

No anthropologist who wants to be able to generalize about what happens in ceremonial exchange or warfare, for example, can possibly do so entirely on the basis of events she or he has directly observed. In order to have a sufficiently large sample of cases, the researcher must rely on what she or he is told about many other events of the same sort, many of which happened before she or he (or even the informants) came on the scene. This allows for a kind of synoptic or *post festum* view (Bourdieu 1977), in which all indeterminacy, ambiguity, the radical sense of contingency of lived experience, is completely effaced. This effacement is not an obstacle to structural analysis, but an essential precondition for it (ibid.). Accordingly, in order to provide a background for our analysis of the main events, our own discussion of the structure and history of exchange and warfare in the Kailge area will partake amply of the synoptic view provided for us by informants' accounts. But by explicitly posing the question of the relation between structure and history, we are also able to go beyond the synoptic view and focus in detail on the way in which issues such as the above are actively contested, and given instantiations of the structural types ('tribe pair', 'alliance', etc.) are more or less problematically reproduced in the event.

The limits of a purely structural approach – the 'objective limits of objectivism' (ibid.) – are even more evident when we turn to the question of how it is that the 'structural types' may change. Although it is obvious that they do so everywhere, accounts of 'social structure', even in New Guinea under conditions of rapid post-contact transformation, usually do not focus upon those aspects of social life that have been most altered by the recent changes, but rather attempt to (re-)construct an 'ethnographic present' which is as much like the pre-contact traditional social order as possible. This is – no doubt – partly due to the retrospective nature of case material provided by informants.[4] But it is also determined by the nature of structural accounts, which are inherently synoptic or synchronic.

In such an account of the events of 1982 and 1983, we would probably give short shrift to what was at the time generally regarded as one of their most remarkable features – the intervention and subsequent exchange role of the Kulka women's group. This is even less amenable to a purely structural account than the ambiguities and indeterminacies described above. For in the former cases, the structural types themselves are not at issue – only their instantiation in this or that particular token. But in the case of the Kulka women's actions, we are confronted with a challenge to the existing types of political transaction. This is, for instance, a social order in which it had previously been regarded as unthinkable for women to constitute themselves as a group or groups which could transact as such, either on the battlefield or the display ground; or for women to stand up and speak (much less on behalf of such a group) at a public exchange event (cf. M. Strathern 1972a, Lederman 1980). Their performance did not merely instantiate or enact existing structures; it 'made history' in such a way as to alter those structures.

Thus it is only by explicitly posing the question of the relation between structure and history that we are able to avoid banishing the women's actions from our 'ethnographic present' and instead take them as a central part of our analysis.

What other aspects of what happened are opened up to us by this theoretical perspective? Besides the contested character of transactional tokens and of structural types, there is one very concrete aspect of these events which it motivates us to take up as our central subject matter: in order to show *how* they are contested, we must give detailed consideration to the form and content of the many speeches that were made at both compensation events. That might seem an obvious thing for any anthropologist to do, since oratory was the main thing that almost everyone attended to for most of the time at both of the events. But that alone would probably not have led us to notice what the orators were saying. This is apparent from the fact that, although Highland ethnographers have often remarked upon the importance of oratorical skills for big-man status, and alluded to the enormous amount of time, energy and attention given to oratory at public exchange events (see section 2.5), very few of them have reported on what was said in any of the speeches, or offered extensive analysis of them as central evidence for the understanding of Highlands politics and exchange (but cf. M. Strathern 1972b, A. Strathern 1975, Goldman 1983). Instead, it is common to remark on the 'conventional' character of what is said (Meggitt 1965:14), and/or to claim that the speeches merely announced decisions or states of play between groups that had been reached behind the scenes in private discussions (Reay 1959:120 ff, A. Strathern 1975). The reader gets the impression that oratory itself is mere window-dressing, often tedious, long-winded, and the orators 'harangue-utans' (Sahlins 1963:290).

Thus, if we have been led to focus in detail on what is said in the oratory, it cannot be because its importance is self-evident.[5] Rather, it is probably because, to the extent that the observer's perspective is limited to the synoptic, the content of the speeches *does* become superfluous – mere 'harangue'. Insofar as it deals in ambiguities and transformations such as those discussed above, it introduces complications which are not only irrelevant to the synoptic perspective, but a positive hindrance to it.[6] But precisely the same qualities turn it into crucially important data for an investigation into the relation between structure and event.

These in brief are some of the ways in which we think our theoretical perspective may supplement the structural and historical ones in such a way as to enable us to register otherwise obscure aspects of what happened at the events in question, and others like them. We hope that our linguistically-informed way of investigating the relation between structure and history will be widely applicable. Though the instances we examine are specific to a small, long-isolated corner of the world, the problem of structure and history is of far more general importance, both within social theory and elsewhere. If social structures and historical events are related to each other in a mutually-constitutive way, this is not a fact about the Nebilyer Valley alone, but about human social life in general. If it is true, for example, of complementary opposition and warfare on the relatively microscopic scale on which it is fought in that corner of the world, it is equally true of comparable, potentially catastrophic processes on a world scale.

Nor is our motivation for studying these instances strictly theoretical or academic. The question of the relation between structure and history has indeed become a central one within recent social theory (see Ortner 1984), but this is no doubt related at least in part to pressing concerns extending far beyond the walls of academe. The history of the twentieth century has made it increasingly clear that the fate of humankind is bound up in global politico-economic structures which, for all our rationality of means, seem to propel us helplessly toward catastrophic ends, as chillingly foreshadowed in 1905 by Max Weber (1958:181), who saw the modern economic order as having unwittingly built itself into an 'iron cage'. While it would be foolish to imagine that we alone could change all that with an attack upon the problem of structure and event, we do share with such seminal social theorists as Marx and Durkheim the conviction that the attempt to understand social structures and process in general can and should be pursued as a step toward improving our own in particular. If theory can help us bring to light that which would have otherwise remained invisible (as we have argued above), it might also empower us – like the Kulka women's group – to act where we must otherwise have remained immobile.

1.2 WHO CONDUCTS EXCHANGE? PROBLEMS OF REPRESENTATION AND AGENCY IN SOME HIGHLANDS EXCHANGE SYSTEMS

In order to provide for those without specialist knowledge a fuller picture of the anthropological context from which our central problem emerges, we now turn to a brief review of some of the main trends in recent (western) Highlands studies; this is followed by a close exegesis of some recent polemics over the question of whether exchange is conducted by groups or individuals. This will show the kind of impasse that can result from attempting to describe 'what happens' without reference to the 'representational' aspects of social action, including, in this case, what is *said* in the course of it. This will motivate our own approach to the problem, which focuses closely upon what has otherwise been largely ignored: the form and content of Highlands oratory.

Detailed ethnography began to emerge from the central Highlands at a time when descent theory dominated social anthropology. Much of Highlands ethnography was initially concerned largely with group structure and its relation to patterns of residence, marriage, ceremonial exchange, political leadership, dispute settlement, warfare, and so on. Following the Africanist tradition, descent was usually seen as *the* key organizing principle of Highlands societies, and agnation was thought to account well enough for group membership, including both recruitment and lasting affiliation.

After Barnes (1962), however, there was an increased emphasis on differences between the Highlands and Africa, and among various Highlands societies. In most of the latter, genealogical memory is very short, and there is little or no emphasis on extended agnatic (or even cognatic) pedigrees as a basis for full group membership. The idiom of social co-identity is often one of shared substance or 'siblingship' (Weiner 1982), from which common 'descent' is assumed, rather than vice versa. In place of descent, some writers (e.g. Langness 1964, de Lepervanche 1967–8), increasingly identified co-residence and consociality as the actual basis of group solidarity or recruitment or both. By comparison with the presumed African ideal of fully solidary segmentary lineages, Highlands New Guinea was sometimes characterized as having 'loosely structured' societies (Pouwer 1960, Brown 1962). More often (and sometimes concurrently), the relation of patrilineal descent to co-residence in the Highlands was treated as that of ideology to practice. In other words (those of Sahlins 1965) co-residence provided the sociological 'matters of fact' upon which patrilineal descent was more or less artificially or arbitrarily imposed as an ideological construct – ideology here serving its 'usual Mannheimian function of keeping people from knowing what's going on in the world' (Sahlins 1965:105). In a somewhat modified version of the same position, A. Strathern (1972), following Scheffler (1964), argued that for the Highlands a distinction must be made between 'descent constructs' as bases or 'idioms' of segmentary group identity, and the principles by which people are *recruited* to the groups, and that descent was relevant for the former but not the latter.

Although it cannot be said to have been settled (see Feil 1984 and Scheffler 1985 for recent discussion), the issue of the role of descent in the Highlands has been a less hotly contested one during the 1970s and 1980s, as the earlier emphasis on descent as a key organizing principle has been replaced by an emphasis among Melanesianists in general on reciprocity or exchange (see e.g. Wagner 1967, Forge 1972, Schwimmer 1973, A. Weiner 1976, Sillitoe 1979). Theorists who are otherwise as different as Wagner and Sillitoe in the ways they go about characterizing social life have argued that early Highlands accounts over-emphasized the role of solidary agnatic groups as units of social interaction. For example, as part of his general objection to the imposition upon the people studied of Western presumptions that society has determinate form, Wagner (1974) has argued that the anthropological problem should rather be posed as that of discovering how those people 'create themselves socially'. In this vein he (and others, e.g. M. Strathern 1987) have argued that rather than segmentary units participating in exchange as entities defined in advance by descent, the segmentary categories can themselves be precipitated out of exchange transactions. For example, in Daribi society, a condition of children being fully identified with their father's clan is that their mother's brothers be given wealth objects. This establishes a difference between a person and his or her mother's people which is proportional with the similarity or identification between that person and his or her father's people. The aggregate of such differences 'defines' a clan (Wagner 1967).

Others, such as Sillitoe (1979) and Feil (1984), while also arguing that exchange is a fundamental organizing principle in the Highlands, have downplayed its relation to segmentary social structure (and the importance of the latter overall), and stressed the *individual* (within his kin network) as the relevant unit in exchange activities. (Cf. Lawrence 1984 for a similarly individual-based approach in his description of the Garia people of the coastal province, Madang.)

We concur in the emphasis on exchange which is common to all these recent writers, and suggest that, properly developed, the concept of exchange provides an even more powerful organizing principle for the understanding of Highlands societies than does that of descent for African societies. This is because, unlike descent, which is principally a structural notion, the concept of exchange is, as we hope to demonstrate, equally useful for analysis in terms of *structure* and *process* or *event* (cf. A. Weiner 1976: 219–20).[7]

Thus, albeit for different reasons, we agree with Forge's (1972) claim that in his pioneering studies of exchange, Malinowski (1922) procured for Melanesianist studies a 'golden fleece', the full value of which has not yet been fully realized. But, unlike Forge, we consider that one of the major obstacles to its full realization was already created by Malinowski himself, in that, even while providing a mass of interesting details concerning the conduct of particular *Kula* transactions, he explicitly aimed at what he called a 'synoptic' view of exchange as the ultimate goal of a truly 'scientific' account of the phenomena in question (Malinowski 1922:11–17). With but few exceptions (e.g. A. Strathern 1979a, Lederman 1980, Gewertz 1984) this emphasis still prevails in studies of exchange.

As a recent example of the problems that can result from this, and as background for our own analysis of exchange events in the Nebilyer Valley, we turn now to detailed consideration of two accounts of ceremonial exchange among the nearby Enga people – accounts which draw diametrically opposed conclusions concerning the question of who conducts exchange.

The Enga are a language group of some 160,000 people (making them New Guinea's largest), who occupy a large area (now a distinct province) to the northwest of the Kaugel people, extending to within 40km of our Nebilyer field site at Kailge (see Map 1). In terms of its degree and scale of areal integration, their *tee* exchange system is the most highly developed in the Highlands. The central Enga, called Mae, are well known through the work of Meggitt, whose most detailed accounts have been of lineage structure (1965) and warfare (1977), while his most explicit description of ceremonial exchange (1974) is brief. Most recently, a 'fringe' Enga group, the Tombema, have been extensively described by Feil (1984 and refs. therein), whose greatest emphasis has been upon exchange.

Meggitt's ethnography stresses 'the significance of agnatic affiliations in determining the identities of actors and the compositions of groups in recurring and more or less stereotyped social situations' (1965:263). He sees most kinds of ceremonial prestations among the Mae as intergroup transactions, and claims that the prestation types are ranked in a 'hierarchy of social importance and precedence which in turn parallels the hierarchical struction of Mae patrilineal groups, such that particular kinds of prestations are the responsibility of groups at different levels in the descent system' (Meggitt 1974:169). Thus, for example, marriage payments (bridewealth, etc.) are made by patrilineages, while the more 'important', death payments (to matrilateral kinsmen of the deceased), are made by the sub-clan. *Tee* exchanges – more important still – are transacted among clans. Success in the *Te*[8] is crucial to the clan's survival, since 'Prestige achieved through prestations helps a clan maintain its territorial boundaries by attracting both present military allies and wives who produce future warriors. The basic preoccupation of the Mae . . . is with the possession and defense of clan land. Participation in the *Te*, as in other prestations, is but a means to this end' (Meggitt 1974:171).

Feil paints a very different picture. He down-plays the importance of descent ideology for Enga social life in general, especially in matters of exchange. He claims: 'At least in Tombema[9] clans are not "responsible" for making *tee* . . . lineages for bridewealth, and so on. All Tombema transactions are individual ones, without overall planning, and without group concerns or coordination in mind' (Feil 1984:71). *Tee* networks are 'composed of ego-centred, maximizing individuals' (Feil 1984:10,fn.3), who pursue it as an end in itself. Far from seeking to enhance the prestige of their clan as a whole, *tee* participants compete with their fellow clansmen for individual prestige, in the struggle for which they are entirely dependent upon the cooperation of exchange partners from other clans. Since those other clans are often enemy clans, *tee* interests cannot be seen as subservient to, or even consonant with, those of clan strength or security. On the contrary, they inhibit individual clansmen from joining in the fighting, thus serving to 'mute and control intergroup hostilities' (Feil 1984:30).

How is it that two such experienced ethnographers can disagree so fundamentally about apparently similar social systems?[10] One strongly suspects that no amount of new field investigation by either of them could settle the matter. The lesson that can usually be learned from deadlocks of this kind is that what is needed is not a new answer to the question, but rather a new way of posing it. For help along these lines, we will turn, below, to a recent alternative formulation in the work of Lederman (1980, 1986a). First, however, let us conclude the examination of the positions of Meggitt and Feil by considering their (apparent) criteria for the attribution of agency. For despite the great difference between their (nonetheless equally categorical) conclusions about who conducts *tee* exchanges (as cited above), their ethnography contains passages which suggest that the matter is problematic among the Enga.

Consider the following example from Meggitt (italics added):

> Clans regarded by the Mae as being elements of the *Te* cycle are those *which actually participate as corporate units* in the sequential public prestations of main gifts (primarily of pigs) and of return gifts (primarily of pork). There are, however, some clans . . . that do not act this way. Their members are connected with men of the participating groups by filaments of individual, personal exchanges . . . (1974:174)

But what does it take for a given transaction to count as one in which clans 'actually participate as corporate units'? Is it that there be full participation by all its members, or at least its adult male ones? Not so, for this is apparently only an 'ideal':

> Ideally, among the Mae Enga clans that engage corporately in the *Te* cycle . . . every clansman is a potential exchange partner. In fact, however, there are obvious differences in the extent to which individuals participate . . . (Meggitt 1974:182)

Nor does the clan's participation *as a corporate group* entail that the valuables to be given are first contributed to a common fund[11] and then turned over *en masse* to some recipient group. Rather, as already suggested by Meggitt's phrase 'every clansman is a potential exchange partner', each group payment comprises multiple individual payments, each of which has a separate identity as transaction between individual exchange partners.

Nor do the individual partners on the receiving end all belong to the same group:

> At any point in the sequence of prestations . . . it is not a matter of men, for instance of clan 16 . . . receiving valuables only from men of clan 15 and passing them on only to clan 17, which distributes them to clan 18, and so on. Instead, men of 16 receive valuables directly from a number of the clans preceding them in the sequence (for instance of clans 13, 14, and 15) and give them directly to men of several clans (say, 17, 18, 19, 20) [etc.]. (Meggitt 1974:173)

Given such complex, overlapping sets of transactions, even Meggitt is at times inclined to regard individuals as the *real* actors in the system: '. . . in the last analysis, individuals are giving and receiving the valuables . . .' (Meggitt 1974:169).

What then is the difference between clans which are 'regarded by the Mae as being elements in the *Te* exchange cycle' and those which are not? In what sense can a clan ever be said to 'participate as a corporate unit'?

Paradoxically enough, these questions can best be addressed by turning to the individual-centered account of Feil.

Whatever their differences concerning its physiology, Feil and Meggitt are in essential agreement concerning the gross anatomy of the *tee*. A key feature of the system is that Enga clans over a large area are ordered within a single, linear sequence such that in a given cycle of main or return gifts,[12] the prestation of e.g. Meggitt's 'clan 15' must precede that of 'clan 16', 16 that of 17, etc. Feil's work shows that, among the Tombema Enga, this segmentary-group basis extends down to the level of the sub-clan, so that within each clan, there is a set order in which each of its sub-clans must make its prestations. Like Meggitt, Feil shows that not all of the individual payments made on a given day by a given sub-clan go to (members of) another single clan or sub-clan. But Feil's detailed data on individual *tee* partnerships shows that 'The cumulative effect of a sub-clan's *tee* is that partners in the clan that will make the *tee* next receive the largest portion of pigs and other gifts' (Feil 1984:60). That is, in terms of Meggitt's example, when clan 16 makes its prestation, it is true that members of clan 17 do not receive all of the goods, but they do receive 'the largest portion'.

Or so it works in areas along the main *tee* 'roads', where the *tee* is coordinated on a clan or sub-clan basis. Feil agrees with Meggitt that in some parts of Enga country, this does not happen. He disagrees with Meggitt as to whether the 'cumulative effect of a sub-clan's [or clan's] *tee*' is ever such as to warrant the claim that the clans or sub-clans 'participate as corporate units'.

Although they differ in emphasis, it is apparent that Feil and Meggitt are operating in terms of some of the same key assumptions about the nature of social life. Both of them start with 'individual' and 'group' as basic units: actors whose existence is ontologically prior to any of the activities in which they engage. For both of these analysts, the individual is *more* basic than the group, as the latter is composed of the former. Groups may function as actors just insofar as they are 'corporate', i.e. just insofar as they can act *as* a single individual is supposed to act.

But how is that? And what does it mean for a group to act that way? Neither Feil nor Meggitt addresses these questions explicitly, but their arguments evince at least three different implicit criteria for corporate action which we can distinguish as *motivationist, synchronist*, and *representationist* criteria.

The *motivationist* strand, implicit in the main arguments of Meggitt 1974, runs as follows. People do not participate in the *tee* as an end in itself, nor simply for personal prestige. Rather, their main motive is to enhance the prestige of their clan, so that it can 'maintain its territorial boundaries by attracting both present military allies and wives who produce future warriors. The basic preoccupation of the Mae is, it seems to me, with the possession and defense of clan land. Participation in the *Te*, as in other prestations, is but a means to this end' (Meggitt 1974:171).

According to this way of looking at the matter, people are acting as a corporate group when they act out of a perceived common interest which is limited to that group. Another obvious example of such an activity among the Mae Enga is warfare, the main motive for which Meggitt also attributes to 'defense of clan land' (in the face of an acute shortage).

The second of Meggitt's implicit criteria for corporate action is that the individual actions of the group's members be *synchronized* in such a way as to make it obvious to Enga and anthropologist alike that they are all part of the same group action. Thus, for example, in contrast to the initial phase of the *tee*, when payments are made in a fairly uncoordinated way between individuals, Meggitt describes the final phase as one in which the clan '. . . acting as a corporate group, publicly distributes its pork . . .' (1974:177).

A necessary (and perhaps sufficient) condition of 'corporateness' in this final phase is presumably the fact that various members of the group all make their prestations on the same day, and in the same or adjacent display grounds.

A third way in which action becomes corporate for Meggitt is by being *represented* as such. Consider, for example, the fuller context of a line we have already quoted:

> Even though, in the last analysis, individuals are giving and receiving the valuables, the proceedings are mediated through the actions of Big Men who represent the groups concerned. (Meggitt 1974:169)

Since Meggitt elsewhere describes these proceedings as 'corporate', we assume that this activity of representation is supposed to be part of what makes them so.

Note that these three criteria for corporateness are logically independent of each other:[13] each could be met without either of the other two being met, or any combination of two or three of them could be met together. Meggitt does not specify which of them he sees as necessary or sufficient conditions or both, and presents little evidence to show which of them, if any, actually is met. It would appear from his argument that *synchronization* is a necessary condition, for he presents no examples of corporate actions which do not meet it, and one example of a kind of transaction which he considers not to be corporate, presumably just *because* it is not synchronized, viz. the initiatory payments made in phase one of the *tee*. As for their motivation, there is no reason to think these initiatory payments could *not* be done for clan prestige, so the *motivationist* criterion is perhaps a less crucial one for Meggitt than is the *synchronist* one. The *representationist* criterion would seem to be regarded by Meggitt as the least important of all, since he says little or nothing about how the big-men actually go about constructing themselves as representatives of the groups, or representing the exchange transactions as inter-group ones.

Now what are Feil's criteria for corporate action? For him (as perhaps for Meggitt) synchronization is a necessary condition. This can be seen from his discussion of warfare, which he says is 'thought to be a clan activity, but rarely, if ever, can be' (Feil 1984:26). The reason he thinks it cannot be is that cross-cutting ties of individual *tee* partnerships inhibit some clansmen from joining in. The implication is that for warfare to be truly a 'clan activity', every clansmen would have to fight on each of the opposing sides.

But though this strong form of synchronization is a necessary condition of corporateness for Feil, it is not a sufficient one. For in the case of *te* transactions, he claims that every adult male clansman *does* participate, and that, in phases two and three, they all make their payments on the same day and in the same place. Feil's main *empirical* disagreement with Meggitt is over the issue of *corporate motivation*, which he takes as a second necessary condition of corporate action. He claims that, among the Tombema Enga at least, the prestige which men transact in order to advance is not their clan's but their own, which they promote at the expense of (rather than in cooperation with) their fellow clansmen.

As for Meggitt's third implicit criterion of corporateness – the *representational* – Feil disagrees with Meggitt over the extent to which big-men play a part in 'mediating' anybody else's *tee* transactions besides their own, and, furthermore, claims that Tombema Enga people 'do not even speak as if groups are responsible [for making *tee* payments]' (Feil 1984:72). This formulation leads us to suspect that even if the Tombema did speak that way, Feil would not accept this as a criterion for corporate action. This is suggested by his claim that even warfare – which he says the Tombema *do* talk about as being a 'clan activity' – 'rarely if ever, can be', simply because not all clansmen actually participate.

We turn now to Lederman's work (1980, 1986a), which clearly indicates that the scope of the representational is far too narrowly circumscribed in these accounts, and that when its role is adequately recognized, many of the issues between Meggitt and Feil can be resolved or obviated.

Lederman's fieldwork has been in the Mendi area of the Southern Highlands (see Map 1). Ceremonial exchange in this area is conducted according to ground rules quite different from those among the Melpa, Nebilyer, and Enga peoples to the north (cf. Ryan 1961 with A. Strathern 1971, Meggitt 1974, Feil 1984). It is, however, similar in that both individuals and named segmentary groups or categories are locally slated as contenders in the game. Lederman (1980, 1986a) distinguishes between two different, partially contradictory bases on which Mendi exchange is organized: 1) the public arena of *sem onda* (segmentary groups), to which women contribute as producers and as affinal and matrilateral points of linkage – M. Strathern's (1972a) 'women in between' but into which they are not permitted to enter as transactors; and, 2) the personal sphere of *twem* – ego-centered relational networks of affines, cognatic kinsmen and unrelated exchange partners – within which women transact on a potentially equal footing with men. Lederman (1980) shows that not all transactions (if any) belong unambiguously to one or the other of these two spheres, and that a crucial part of what goes on at public exchange events is the struggle for control of the attribution of relevant agency, and of the significance of the event for various spheres of social relations (cf. Rumsey 1986, Merlan and Rumsey 1986).

Lederman (1980) illustrates the character of these processes by reference to a public meeting which was held in order to decide whether the Suolol *sem onda* was going to participate in a parade leading up to the culmination of a 12-year cycle of exchanges in which Suolol had been participating in conjunction with an allied tribe called Surup. At the meeting, a leading Suolol big-man called Olanda spoke against their participation, arguing that they should wait and hold their own parade at a later date, after the expected arrival of another, distant Suolol sub-group. Olanda's speech seemed to carry the day, being followed by general agreement among the Suolol that they would not participate in this parade. However, Lederman was surprised to find when the parade was held a few days later that many of the men from Suolol did in fact participate, at considerable financial expense.[14] Her first conclusion from this was that:

> Olanda's well received speeches had had no practical effect, and that the meeting had had no practical importance, despite all the fanfare. People had acted as individuals and had taken matters into their own hands as events of the moment moved them – a practice perfectly in keeping with the ethos of autonomy I had come to appreciate in Mendi. (1980:487)

But, as Lederman tells it, she later came to realize that the meeting had had an important effect: it had assured that those Suolol men who participated in the parade could only do so 'as individuals' (inverted commas in original) – that the Suolol *sem onda* was not participating *qua sem onda*. The difference was by no means an insignificant one for Mendi social life, for the understandings reached at the meeting:

> had many practical effects on the lives of both those who paraded that week with the Surup and those who did not. At the least, the timing and the general importance of Suolol's own [parade] at Senkere two months later (in which most Suolol men participated, including most of those who paraded the first time with Surup) created problems of resource allocation for many people. Men with Surup exchange partners and affines had to manage their debts and credits very carefully in order to be able to participate in two separate parades. Personal exchange relationships were strained, and a few appeared to break down as a result. (Lederman 1980:489)

At the time of the first parade, one man from Suolol, Pua, gave some kina shells to some of his exchange partners in Surup. This was apparently prompted by the fact that those men had been some of the most militant advocates of Suolol participation in the parade, threatening to block the road to Ialibu (whence the distant Suolol allies were to come) if Suolol did not join in. Lederman suggests that, although the meeting had the effect of assuring that this man's gift of kina shells could only be seen *by other Suolol men* as a 'personal' transaction with his exchange partners, there was some room for the Surup, or Pua at least, to construe it otherwise. For she says that it did 'create enough ambiguity to save the face of his Surup big-men exchange partners, and thereby enable them to back down from their threats to close the road' (1980:488).

What we find most useful in Lederman's account is the way in which it invites us to formulate the question of who it is that is conducting these exchange transactions. Rather than assuming 'group' and 'individual' as concrete, self-evident, mutually exclusive loci of agency, which constitute the *a priori* ground of social interaction, Lederman shows that locally relevant attributions of agency are constructed and contested in the practice of exchange.

It is clear from her account that the alternative possibilities among the Mendi people are neither Meggitt's mechanically solidary 'corporate' entity, confronting other corporate groups nor Feil's (1984:10, fn.3) 'maximising individual' who 'alone makes decisions relevant to *tee* performance' (Feil 1984:36). Rather, particular transactions may belong to one or the other of two distinct, partially incompatible spheres of social relations: *twem*, the ego-centered sphere of personal relationships, in which affinal links may come between brothers; and *sem*, the public, exclusively male arena in which brothers are identified together, and segmentary social categories are prime loci for attributions of agency. And indeed, as some of our citations above from Meggitt's and Feil's accounts indicate, similar ambiguities appear to exist and are explicitly contested in Enga ceremonial exchange, to an extent that even the categorical positions of the ethnographers on 'who conducts exchange?' do not entirely subvert.

It is true that Lederman generally glosses *sem onda* as 'group' or 'corporate group' (e.g. 1980:488), and that she contrasts exchange within the spheres of *sem onda* vs. *twem* as 'group action' vs. 'individual action'. However, it is clear from her account that 'group' and 'individual' cannot be taken as directly observable empirical realities of the order of Radcliffe-Brown's (1965:190) 'actually existing relations'. Which of these spheres any particular transaction belongs to is not a matter which can be unproblematically 'read off' from the 'texts' of social life, or from informants' *post festum* exegeses of them (the latter providing the usual 'data' of ethnographic description). Rather, as Lederman shows, it is a matter which is chronically *contested* in the public arena, a contest whose outcome is indeterminate and subject to continuing ambiguity, as in the case of Pua's gift of kina shells. Even where the outcome is more decisive, as in the case of Olanda's speech, events are always open to retrospective reinterpretation, or reconstruction, in such a way as to alter their current transactional 'meaning' for the distinct spheres of exchange.

Lederman shows that how an exchange event is indigenously 'represented' is not something that can be considered apart from what is 'really going on' in the exchange, as might be determined by the ethnographer from probing people's motivations, or observing the extent to which their activities appear synchronized. Rather, the 'representation' figures crucially in *constituting* the event as an exchange transaction of one kind or another. In the case Lederman describes, no amount of independent ethnographic inquiry concerning people's motivations or physical coordination could have established whether the exchange was between groups or individuals. For a cluster of transactions, which from that viewpoint could have been described in one way only, was nonetheless open to being construed indigenously as either a matter of *sem onda* or *twem*. In short, the nature of the social identities involved in the transactions is under-determined by the motivations and apparent synchronicity of the donors. These identities cannot be established without careful study of the way in which the exchange events are 'represented',[15] both at the moment of transaction and in the ongoing social life of the people concerned.

Though her analysis is suggestive in the ways we have described, Lederman provides very little empirical evidence for the processes of meaning-making which she claims to be taking place. Though recognizing the importance of talk as a medium for the construction of exchange events, she presents us with no examples of what people actually said. Thus, though we are left with a more urgent sense that there are important connections between speech and other moments of social action, these continue to receive independent descriptions, the 'other' moments related to speech-making possibly as effects, and descriptively as summaries of apparent outcomes.

By examining closely the various dimensions of social process – including speech-making – at major Nebilyer exchange events in Chapters 5 to 7 below, we aim to pursue enquiry into how speech as an actional type is *integrated with* other aspects of social action, and together with other action, contributes to the constitution of events in ways that reproduce (and may alter) segmentary and other structures. As anticipated by Lederman, that examination will show that the question of who transacts with whom is hotly contested, not only in anthropological accounts such as those of Feil and Meggitt, but in the practice of exchange itself. But, as we shall see, the alternative answers to the question are, in practice, quite different from, and far more complex than, those assumed by Feil and Meggitt. Their complexity cannot be comprehended without due regard for the formulation of social relations partly within the exchange events themselves, as Lederman suggests. Thus these relations cannot be viewed independently of the recurrent events which continually refashion them (and of which public exchange transactions are only one type). By examining these interdependencies, we seek to overcome the separation of structure and action which Lederman's treatment still leaves in place, moving, we hope, towards clearer definition of the constitutive properties of social action, and of speech as one of its most significant and subtle moments.

1.3 SUMMARY ARGUMENT

Having probed some other approaches to exchange in order to demonstrate the relevance of our own, we conclude this introductory chapter with a brief overview of the argument of the book as a whole.

The heart of the book is a detailed analysis of the exchange events arising out of the fighting at Sibeka in 1982, as summarized at the beginning of this chapter. This analysis comes in Chapters 6 and 7. In order to lay the groundwork for it, we provide some necessary background in Chapters 2 to 5 concerning the people involved, and socio-semiotic structures entailed in those events. This begins in Chapter 2 with some details concerning the Ku Waru locale, the people's encounter with the outside world over the last fifty-five years, and what they have made of it.

Chapter 3 deals with what we call 'segmentary' sociality among Ku Waru people. This is a rather contentious notion among anthropologists – especially Highlands specialists – so in order to make clear what we do and do not mean by it, our account of Ku Waru segmentary structures (section 3.1) is organized around a series of comparative questions arising from the demise of classical segmentary lineage theory and, in particular of 'African Models in the New Guinea Highlands' (as adumbrated in section 1.2 above; see also Barnes 1962). This description of Ku Waru segmentary structures is followed in section 3.2 by some details concerning the ethnohistory and demography of the particular segmentary groupings which figure most centrally in the exchange events of 1983: viz. the various historically disparate segments comprising the Kopia 'tribe', and others involved in the Marsupial Road War of 1982.

In Chapter 4 we describe other dimensions of social life with which the segmentary order is partly consistent, partly opposed. The first of these is ceremonial exchange. In section 4.1, we discuss its form and recent history in the western Nebilyer Valley. We show how transactions can belong simultaneously to the sphere of segmentary social relations and to that of network or interpersonal ones. Essential elements of the latter are links made through marriage. Its patterning in the Ku Waru area is discussed in section 4.2. The main thrust of Chapter 4 as a whole is to demonstrate the interrelationships among marriage patterns, wealth exchange and warfare – the segmentary transaction *par excellence*. The war of 1982 marked a watershed in this respect, because of the radical shift of alliances, and because of the new possibilities for inter-group exchange which were opened up by that shift and related shifts in the direction of Kopia marriages over the previous generation. An understanding of those prior developments provides necessary background for our analysis of the relation between historically given structures and the exchange events of 1983.

In Chapter 5 we turn to a discussion of another order of structures which were in place for those events: namely, linguistic structures. These include not only the entire array of grammatical and lexical resources of everyday Ku Waru (as summarized in Appendix B), but also certain specialized oratorical devices, including distinctive prosodies, imagery, and particular uses of the singular and dual number categories to construct actors as segmentary ones.

In Chapter 6 we examine the large-scale event which was staged as compensation payment by Kopia-Kubuka to the Tambul allies they had recruited to the Marsupial Road War of 1982. Our aim is to reveal the semiotic construction of social identities and of transactions among them in the male-dominated sphere of inter-group political relations, including warfare and wealth exchange. Within the context provided by Chapters 3 to 5, the analysis in Chapter 6 is based upon a full verbatim transcript of the speeches made at this event (available to the reader as Appendix A) and our observations concerning other, non-discursive aspects of the staging of the event, such as audience focus, and movement from one display ground to another. We argue that, even though the reproduction of the segmentary structures (as 'types') proceeds fairly smoothly at this event, the outcome of the event is in many ways indeterminate at the level of tokens: the game remains the same but it is not always clear who the players are or what moves are being made.

In Chapter 7 we examine the second major exchange event to arise out of the Marsupial Road War, in which compensation is presented to the Kopia-Kubuka by the Kusika-Midipu and their allies, Epola, Alya and Lalka. This compensation event differs from the previous one in that here not even the structural types are unproblematically reproduced: this time *women* – namely, the Kulka women's cooperative – act as if according to *new* rules, speaking in the previously all-male arena associated with that sphere of exchange, a possibility which they opened for themselves by their bold intervention on the battlefield in 1982. We focus closely upon their participation at this exchange event, again basing our analysis on speech transcripts (here incorporated within the chapter itself). We show how the women create for themselves throughout this event, and at a subsequent one, a spectrum of voices or positions which increasingly draw upon familiar male, segmentary transactor models, at the same time that they praise themselves and their actions as exemplary of dedication to the new, centralizing political-economic order, and opposed to the segmentary one. That is, their performance as exchange transactors draws upon structures which were already in place, but which had previously been regarded as irrelevant to that sphere of activity, or antithetical to it.

In Chapter 8 we bring together the various strands of our analysis from the previous two, and consider the two events together as phases of the same cycle. Taking warfare and wealth exchange together as alternative moments within a single sphere of segmentary transactions, we argue for the importance of *pairing* as the basic form of relationship within that sphere, and distinguish among three interchangeable variants of it which we call serial, compositional and oppositional parity. In the light of this model, we reconsider the actions of the Kulka women's group, and show what it can contribute to our understanding of the group's relationship to the segmentary order. Drawing upon the analysis in Chapters 6 and 7, and the above, we argue for the crucial role of language in the reproduction and transformation of Nebilyer segmentary relationships, and of the practice of pairing itself.

The sphere of segmentary social relationships is by no means the whole of Nebilyer social life. We focus this book mainly on that sphere in order to demonstrate the sociological relevance of our linguistically-oriented approach by aiming our investigation at a single well-defined question emerging from previous ethnography: Who conducts exchange? But the results bear closely upon other, more quotidian aspects of Ku Waru sociality. In our concluding chapter (Chapter 9), we try to show how they do, by describing some of the latter, and relating them to the former. This helps to elucidate indigenous Ku Waru understandings of what constitutes an event as such, and to motivate a critique of some widely current anthropological notions concerning the relationships between structure and event, meaning and action.

2. The Setting

2.1 LOCATION, GEOGRAPHY AND REGIONAL POPULATIONS

Our field site at Kailge lies in the western Nebilyer Valley, on the eastern slopes of the Tambul Range (see Map 1). Varying in elevation from 1500 to 1900m, the Kailge area is frost-free and suitable for cultivation of a wide variety of staples and specialty foods: many varieties of sweet potato, bananas, cane, greens, maize, pandanus, peanuts, beans and winged beans, and taro. Tobacco is cultivated, usually in small mixed-vegetable or other plots near homesteads. Introduced specialty foods which are grown to a limited extent include tomatoes, carrots and cabbage. The higher locations across the Tambul Range to the west, though disadvantageous in their being subject to periodic frosts, are known to be more suited to cultivation of cabbage and European potatoes. Coffee, which grows well throughout the Nebilyer Valley, was introduced as a cash crop from the mid-1960s. The Tambul-side people with whom residents of Kailge have many close social ties cannot raise coffee at their higher elevations, a factor which appears to be related to notable imbalance between the two areas in women's marital destinations – that is, that more Tambul women marry into the Nebilyer than Nebilyer women do into Tambul (see section 4.2).

The Nebilyer Valley (see Maps 1 and 2) is bisected by the Nebilyer [Napilya] River, which rises on the south slopes of Mt Hagen and flows southwards, joining the Kaugel River at the Southern Highlands border (i.e. the old border between New Guinea and Papua). Until recently, the Nebilyer River was a formidable natural barrier which people crossed east of the Kailge area (in Kulka territory) over vine bridges, to which access could easily be restricted. A vehicular suspension bridge was built across the Nebilyer on the road between Tega(/tela/)Administration Centre on the Highlands Highway and Kailge in 1972. This has done a great deal to expand and expedite travel connections in the western Nebilyer area – though during the time of our fieldwork, the nearest vehicle to Kailge which regularly plied the road, as both PMV (Public Motor Vehicle, licensed to carry paying passengers) and supply vehicle, belonged to the Palimung trade-store, about 25–30 minutes' walk east of Kailge (see Map 2). A visiting priest drove in from Tabuga (/tapula/) on the Highlands Highway to hold mass every two or three weeks at Kailge. During our stay, no one at Kailge owned a vehicle, and normal daily travel throughout the area was on foot, for us and everyone else, though the road was usually in good enough condition for four-wheel drive travel right from Tega to within one kilometer of Kailge.

The largest river which runs through the Kailge area is the Ukulu (see Map 3). It constitutes a natural boundary between Kailge and Sibeka *ga punya* (Sibeka sweet potato garden) to the south-east. There is a log bridge across the Ukulu between Kailge and Sibeka. Though flat, fertile, and potentially of great economic significance to the slope-dwelling Kopia-Kubuka and their neighbors, the use of Sibeka for gardening is nevertheless somewhat discontinuous, as it has been overrun in past times of conflict, and was again the scene of the confrontation of 1982. During that conflict Kailge people did not venture to work in or harvest from their Sibeka gardens. Many of these were eventually trampled in the fighting, and Kailge people suffered an especially severe shortage of sweet potato over the following seven dry season months. By that time they dared to frequent Sibeka, and were driven to harvest even the few scrawny sweet potatoes that remained. During the shortage, neighboring people to the east of Kailge (e.g. some wives of Midipu men) took the opportunity to regularly market their sweet potato surpluses on the road. It is unusual for the sweet potato staple to be put on sale in this area, although it is common for greens and specialty items such as tobacco and betel nut (the latter brought in from Hagen or directly from the coast) to be marketed around Kailge. Those at Kailge who could responded to the shortage which resulted from the destruction of gardens partly by making extra purchases of rice, though not everyone had enough cash or could obtain enough credit to do this.

The road from Tega to Kailge currently stops at the Ukulu. Periodically the proposal is made that the road should be continued: Kailge people would be keen to see a vehicular bridge built over the Ukulu, and access established directly to Tambul over the mountains. (The present road to Tambul is the one which goes north from Togoba(/tokopa/) as shown on Map 2.) Though we heard this proposition discussed during the 1982 election, the roughness of the mountain range makes it seem unlikely that any such project will be feasible in the foreseeable future.

From the Kailge perspective, the people of the region belong to wider territorial-political-dialectal groupings, of which four are regularly mentioned. Some peoples to the north-east towards Hagen are known by a general designation, Lama (literally, 'forest'). This is applied to people of some Jika-Kungunuka segments and other tribes towards Mt Hagen town, but not certain others (such as Jika\Nungupiyl, with whom Kailge people have a small number of marriage ties) whose territory lies closer to Kailge. An important diacritic of the Lama identity seems to be dialect. Jika segments closer to Kailge speak a dialect variant more similar to that of the western Nebilyer and are referred to as Meam (see below); but those Jika and others who speak something more similar to the Mt Hagen dialect are called Lama.

Further towards Mt Hagen and beyond are the Melpa. Since much political and social prestige now emanates from the area of Mt Hagen town, connections with provincial offices and politicians are strategically cultivated by

Kailge magistrates and others. With the development of the Tega-Kailge road and rapid connections via the Highlands Highway to Mt Hagen town, the latter is clearly the major center of political and administrative influence for the Kailge area, as well as a place to which Kailge people commonly make day trips for shopping, visiting, medical attention, court cases, for selling coffee, and for other purposes. When a difficult, Kailge-internal land dispute arose during our stay in 1982 (see section 3.2.3), our local Councillor repaired to town to attempt to arrange adjudication of the matter. Our Kailge Councillor had spent much of his youth in Mt Hagen, had worked with European patrol officers and so had learned Tok Pisin (Neo-Melanesian Pidgin, the lingua franca of Papua New Guinea), an accomplishment rare among men in his age-range; this no doubt contributed greatly to his original selection as Councillor in 1963 when this system of offices began, and to the continuing popular view of him at Kailge as one who, whatever his faults and foibles, adequately represented 'government law' (see section 2.3). The women's cooperative groups which began to form in Kailge in 1982–3 received much of their impetus from contacts with provincial government offices located in Mt Hagen. The political, administrative and cultural dominance of the Hagen area is exemplified by the fact that all speakers of our Nebilyer Valley dialect variants can understand Hagen-area Melpa, and most of them can speak it. The reverse, however, is not true: though many people of Mt Hagen town seem able to understand Nebilyer dialects, not as many can reproduce them as successfully as Nebilyer people can speak Melpa. The Melpa call Nebilyer Valley people 'Temboka' (cf. A. Strathern 1971:6).

The people who live against the eastern Tambul slopes, including the Kopia-Kubuka, are locally known as *Kulyur* or *Ku Waru* ('steep stone', 'cliff'), after the imposing limestone cliffs just to the north of Kailge, which on clear days are visible over much of the valley (see Map 3). In more specific usage, however, this designation is limited to those who have closer social ties and linguistic affinities with Tambul and Kaugel-side people, over the Tambul Range to the west. Thus, Kopia-Kubuka distinguish some neighboring tribes by the term 'Meam', despite the fact that some of these tribes live up against the Tambul slopes. For instance, the neighboring Tilka to the south are considered Meam. They are a small tribe, paired with the large Kulka group (also Meam) of the Nebilyer Valley floor. Both social and linguistic affinities again seem to be important diacritics of the difference between Ku Waru and neighboring Meam tribes. When asked the difference, people often respond in terms of linguistic diacritic features: Ku Waru speakers say *tai tekim*, Meam *oi tekim*, 'he/she laughs', and the like. Such diacritics go along with other recognized differences in overall social – political, military and marital – orientation. Most of the valley-floor tribes are designated Meam by Kailge people: Tilka-Kulka, Ulka, Upuka, Kusika-Midipu, etc. Thus, terms like 'Meam' can by no means be taken as summary designations of political alliance, for 'Meam' is used to designate a large number of tribes among whom political relations vary considerably, and with whom Kailge people have quite variable relations.

Finally, Kailge people designate as 'Kakuyl' those who live on the Kaugel side of the Tambul Range. A special term, based on a linguistic diacritic, is sometimes used to designate people towards the Kaugel-Nebilyer junction: they are characterized as people who say *nuga-naga* 'your/mine' (instead of *nunga-nanga* as in our dialect). Alternatively, they are referred to as speakers of *ibogu*, the western Nebilyer equivalent of which is *bo ung* 'native language'. That is, there is recognition of a major isogloss, south-west of which one finds in place of our velar nasal *ng* the corresponding pre-nasalized stop [ŋg] (*g* in our orthography). The Ibogu ('Imbonggu') dialects extend to the south-west as far as Ialibu in the Southern Highlands Province.

As discussed in section 4.2, Kailge people, and especially Kopia of the Wiyal sub-division, and Kubuka, have strong affinal and matrilateral ties to people they generally designate 'Kakuyl', and indeed, from the Kailge perspective, the term is usually used with positive connotations. There is no sense of Kakuyl being the locus of current major enemies. But ways of typifying the region include references to the less favorable climate, and to generally lesser economic development on the Tambul side.

Kailge people have fewer contacts to the south than within the western Nebilyer, with Tambul, and with Hagen. Their access to the south within the Nebilyer Valley is limited by the fact that Tea-Dena, Tola-Wanaka, and other peoples they consider enemies live in that direction. In general (with the exception of relatively nearby Tabuga, home of the priest who visits Kailge, and where Kailge people have some contacts), the area towards the Southern Highlands is relatively less known and less visited by Kailge people, and is typified as fraught with danger and inhabited by relatively hostile people. But a few Kailge marriage connections extend into the Southern Highlands (see in Tables relating to section 4.2, a few wives are listed as originating from Mendi), so that specific sets of Kailge people travel to these places.

The preceding designations – Lama, Meam, Kakuyl, Ku Waru – are used suggestively in public talk by orators to give a sense of the social orientations which inform statements and actions. For example, in the transcript in Appendix A, it is said repeatedly (e.g. lines 1140, 1215, 1235, 1281) that 'Meam and Kakuyl are different' (cf. also Merlan and Rumsey 1986, lines 146–53 regarding Meam vs. Kulyur).

2.2 EUROPEAN EXPLORATION AND POST-CONTACT 'DEVELOPMENT'

The European discovery of the Hagen area is briefly summarized in Sinclair (1971:20–1), A. Strathern (1971:7), and perhaps most vividly, in Connolly and Anderson (1987), among other sources. The Mt Hagen patrol led by Assistant District Officer J. L. Taylor (March-October 1933, see 13/26 item 218) traveled from BenaBena in the eastern Highlands, through Chimbu and the Wahgi Valley into the Mt Hagen area, where the expedition built a base camp and airstrips in what is now Hagen township, in Mokei territory, and at Kelua, within Jika territory. The early years of European occupation center upon continuing exploration, entrepreneurial efforts, and entrance into the area, not far behind the first explorers, of Catholic and Lutheran missionaries.

Father W. A. Ross of the Catholic Mission first visited Mt Hagen in 1934, and the first residential Catholic station was built at Wilya (near the Mokei airstrip) from June to September 1934 (Ross 1969:321–322). The main Catholic residential station at Mt Hagen was transferred to its present site south of the township at Rebiamul in 1938 (Ross 1969:325). The first Catholic residential station in the Nebilyer was built at Ulga (/ulka/) in 1934 (see Map 2). The Lutherans opened a mission station at Ogelbeng north of (present) Mt Hagen town in 1934 (Strauss 1962:viii). The Catholics and Lutherans have honored early division of the area into domains – the Nebilyer Valley has always been a largely Catholic preserve – and clerics of both denominations appear to view with some resentment the explosion of other, mainly Protestant and strongly proselytizing sects into the Mt Hagen area in recent years.

After years of use of local-style bush buildings, a permanent church building – the first sizable European-style building in Kailge, with partial cement floor and metal roof – was constructed at Kailge in 1982. Church-related activities, including night-time 'fellowship', constituted an important part of Kailge community life during our stay (see section 2.5 for reference to aspects of this).

The first Kailge children to go to school went down the valley to Tabuga, where the priest lives, and where a Kailge man took up residence for a time in order to mind the children. Later, in 1972, a community school was started at Kailge. The Catholics, in this area at least, seem to have employed a policy of not encouraging rapid conversion, but rather emphasizing long-term exposure to Catholic teaching. If and when people become confirmed, it can be seen to be on the basis of familiarity with and acceptance of the teaching. They also do not seem to have advocated that local customs such as large-scale exchange be abolished, while Catholics and local people seem to have handled the problem of what to say or do about what the Church might see as indigenous religion by a policy of mutual avoidance of the subject. The one practice which the priests overtly condemned, by refusing to confirm those engaged in it, was polygyny. A prominent local man, a polygynist who was also a *katakiumen* ('catechumen'), in training for confirmation, explained how he would handle this problem: he was in no hurry, he said; he would wait awhile until he was a bit older (he already had seventeen children), then put his first wife aside – in many respects, she had a relatively independent life anyway – and be confirmed. This illustrates that the policy of slow conversion may not fulfill the need for *éclat* that people often require to throw themselves into new projects and new ends: conversion sooner or later did not make much difference to this man. On the other hand, intense enthusiasms might be short-lived, and the clerics appeared to fear this more. We noticed the priest and local catechist-translator who worked for him were the people's main contact with the Catholic Church. There seemed to be little effort made to promote other sorts of contact with the Church, though on a couple of occasions Kailge people themselves took the initiative in getting together with other 'fellowship' groups in the Valley.

In the early period of exploration of the Hagen area, members of the Taylor expedition made trips to the Sepik-Wahgi divide, into the Jimi, Baiyer, and Lai Valleys, and, relevant here, into the Nebilyer too. Taylor described the Nebilyer Valley as 'grass-covered and undulating', 'well populated and timbered' (1933:222). Reconnoitering from Hagen, members of the expedition flew over the Kaugel (p.142). Later they traveled through Yamka and Penambe country near Hagen to that of the 'Melaga' [Milyaka], to the Nebilyer and 'Durugu' [Trul?] Rivers. Taylor reports contact on July 20, 1933 with the 'Kuger' people of the Nebilyer Valley – no doubt the Kulka. The party proceeded to the Kaugel junction, where already many steel axes were in evidence (entry of July 21, 1933).

Post-war patrol reports (late 1940s, early 1950s) indicate that a considerable number of patrols passed through or near the Nebilyer Valley, but that most of these did not go as far west as the Kailge area. Many of them were passing through to the Southern Highlands to establish an airstrip and other facilities at Mendi, passing through towards Enga, or going to investigate reports of tribal fighting in Tambul/Kaugel, an area which seems to have been of much greater concern to the Administration than our part of the Nebilyer Valley in these years. In general, the establishment of control in the Tambul area seems to have been slow, and facilities remained few. By 1955 there were still no aid posts in Kaugel; there was one mission station (East and West Indies Bible Mission, a mile from Tambul Station); and one airstrip (13/26. No. 4 of 1955).

Patrol reports of 1950 (e.g. 13/26 item 148) mention construction of a leprosarium at Togoba (see Map 2), and a vehicular road linking it with the Mt Hagen sub-district office was completed in that year.

An early-established route through to Tambul was from Hagen to Togoba, along the 'Wabag road', across the Trugl, Iu and Waip, via Tomba to Tambul. This is the approximate route of that section of the present Highlands Highway (see Map 2).

A second patrol route, which also skirted around the western Nebilyer, went south from Hagen to Kuta and Korgua (where Danny Leahy of the original Taylor expedition established himself, see below), to Pabarabuk (now the site of a Bible Mission) south-southwest of Korgua, and onwards to the Kaugel River, whence patrols often continued to Mt Giluwe, Ialibu, Mendi (see Map 1) and Lake Kutubu. The all-weather Highlands Highway link from Hagen to Mendi, which partly follows the original patrol route, was not completed until 1976 (Lederman 1986a:5), and is still almost entirely unpaved.

Having built an airstrip at Wilya, near present Mt Hagen town, in 1934 the Leahy brothers shifted their camp to Kuta (known in English as Ewunga Creek) where they established a gold-mining operation and campsite, from which they carried out explorations west into Enga. (See Connolly and Anderson 1987:159, for an account of the warfare between the Hagen-area tribes Mokei and Elti-Penambe, which had left this area a no-man's-land, and thus open to occupation by the Europeans.) Like the missionaries, the Leahys left during the Second World War, but Danny Leahy returned in 1948, and by 1958 had established a coffee plantation at Korgua (see Map 1). Two sons of his brother Mick Leahy, Joe and Clem, also have establishments in the Nebilyer Valley: Joe a plantation and coffee-processing plant located at Waibip on the Highlands Highway, and Clem a plantation further south along the highway at Malda (see Map 2).

The influence of the Leahy mining and trading establishment at Kuta and Korgua seems to have been considerable, even for people such as the Kopia-Kubuka on the other side of the valley. Before European arrival, the trade routes from Mendi, via which pearl shells were transferred into the Hagen area, had been along the Nebilyer Valley (A. Strathern 1971:107,111). These trade routes would appear to have been affected soon after European contact both by the Leahy establishment, and generally by the Administration's bringing in of large quantities of shells to pay for labor and food supplies. Pearl shell inflation occurred all over the Hagen region (though increase in shell in circulation would have been less dramatic in the Nebilyer than in parts of the immediate Mt Hagen area). The Leahy establishment was apparently the chief source of early trade goods entering our part of the valley, and people still talk today of having gone to the place of 'Ten-Mek-sil' ('Dan-Mick-pair'), the two Leahy brothers, in order to try to obtain goods. However, we were not aware of anyone from our part of the valley who had actually worked at the mine; jobs there may have been largely taken up by people from the Korgua area.

Pearl shells may have retained their currency slightly longer in areas somewhat more remote from Hagen (see Connolly and Anderson 1987:224 for mention of how, after a time, local people in the Korgua area raised their demands for supplying the Leahy establishment). In our part of the western Nebilyer, the last bridewealth payments in which pearl shells constituted a major item were made in the early 1970s. By that time, payments which included up to 25 shells seem to have been considered normal. (Taylor 1933:64, 65, records that when he first came to Hagen, one kina shell was the equivalent of a large pig, and a marriage payment might include three kina shells and 'many' pigs. At that time, he reports, the bailer was even more valuable than the kina shell: one bailer was the equivalent of two large pigs.)

Kailge men told us how, observing the introduction of new wealth objects, they decided to burn their kina shells (see section 9.3). It is difficult to establish exactly when they may have done this, but it would appear to have coincided approximately with the kina's falling into disuse as a bridewealth valuable. They gathered them together and heaped them on fires, thus dramatically proclaiming their interest in a new era of objects and associated meanings, rather than passively accepting what outside observers might consider to be the kina's 'devaluation'.[1] However, there is no doubt that some men cautiously stashed away some of their prized shells, for we observed that some fine specimens were still available when some collectors from the Museum of Brussels passed through our part of the valley in 1982.

However complete destruction of the shells may have been, the main concomitant of their being superseded was undoubtedly the introduction of coffee into the Nebilyer Valley by agricultural officers from the mid-1960s. (As we mentioned above, Danny Leahy had established a plantation across the valley from the late 1950s.) At first, local people were given small numbers of trees gratis, and some instruction about their planting and growth. By the early 1970s these trees were starting to mature. At Kailge, by the mid-1970s major exchange payments started to include significant amounts of cash. A few exceptional years of high coffee prices established coffee as a seasonal source of cash income, large amounts of which could be channeled into exchange. Around this time, the kina and bailer, though they are still valued and used as decoration today, definitely fell out of use as currency in this area.

The planting of coffee small-holdings was taken up by people in our part of the Valley. We knew of no Kailge families who were without some coffee-holdings. Major garden areas were not converted to coffee, which for the most part was planted on steeper slopes and in areas which were not under cultivation, or, more frequently, in the small plots near men's houses that had previously been given over to 'men's crops'), i.e., non-staple 'luxury' items such as bananas, sugar cane, red pandanus, and taro (cf. A. Strathern 1982).

Coffee is now most commonly picked (largely by women) and carried out (by men) in large bags, either all the way to Tega, or to some point along the Tega-Kailge road where coffee buyers regularly come at the height of the coffee season. There is some local buying of small amounts of coffee cherry (i.e. in the husk), generally by those who run trade-stores. Trade-store owners tend to have bought, or have shares in, a coffee-huller. Local buyers may thus process the coffee and resell it to larger buyers from Hagen. But local sale of coffee cherry to trade-stores is a favorite method of raising small amounts of quick cash which people may want for car fares from Tega to Hagen, a small trade-store purchase, or the like. Though people will generally accept any price for a small sale, it is not unusual for a seller to refuse to accept an amount of money offered by a traveling buyer for a larger bag of processed coffee, preferring to take the coffee in to Hagen or at least to the highway in the hopes of a higher offer.

In talking about the fall of the kina as wealth object (the standard phrase is *manya purum*, 'it went down') and their dramatic welcoming of *ku moni* ('money'), Kailge people observe that shells 'just lay there' (*we lirim*), while money circulates. They thus appear to fix upon and value the multi-purpose character of money, which, while still not necessary to daily life from a strictly subsistence perspective, is now required for payment of school fees, minor expenses such as transport to town (80 toea was the fare from Palimung), and in some places, for medical expenses (though certain institutions, such as the Seventh Day Adventist one at Togoba, allow patients to bring food in order to contribute to the running of the hospital); and money is a major form of contribution to bridewealth payments and to large and small exchange events. Thus, the current form of life presupposes some access to cash in order to participate in certain kinds of activities, and correspondingly, not everyone handles money with the same frequency, and certainly not in the same amounts. Avid card-playing – in fair weather, there is usually a group of players somewhere to be seen near the trade-stores or on the Kailge display ground – is one of the few occasions for all involved (even children) to handle money, even if some of the time, these are stakes supplied by other players or onlookers. If one were to call the local economy a dual one, it would have to be in the sense that money now occupies a major place as a valuable in ceremonial and other traditional prestige activities, and a relatively minor place in day-to-day subsistence, which is still largely provisioned through the domestic work effort – not in the sense that one may neatly distinguish an indigenous and an introduced economy.

Only one coffee grower and processor was attempting to establish himself on a large scale in our portion of the valley during our stay. This was a young, married Midipu man who had an interest in the Palimung trade-store (see Map 2). He had parlayed small-scale investments in cabbage and tobacco into a fair-sized coffee venture. The Palimung trade-store bought, dried and resold coffee to Hagen buyers. He was in the process of establishing a coffee plantation on Midipu land. In 1983 he got help from local residents by encouraging communal clearing and planting of winged beans on a large hillside area he intended to later plant with coffee. Once those who had cooperated had harvested their winged beans (which are known to improve the soil), he got assistance in planting coffee seedlings interspersed with casuarina (which also improve the soil and provide necessary shade for the coffee seedlings). It will be some years before these mature and it remains to be seen whether the business venture (a partnership with several other men) can stay afloat. So far, the enterprise has managed to deal successfully with the many local demands on time and money, which, to some extent, seem contrary to the running of the business according to Western notions of economic rationality. Rather, as the example of large-scale planting of coffee by communal effort shows, the enterprise has succeeded in making use of the potentially demanding community around it. Can it continue to do so? It has done so for several years, developing along with other local ventures, including the trade-store, and spawning some others, including a PMV business (which usually manages to collect from most beneficiaries for rides to town from Palimung, using the same Toyota with which the store supplies are fetched), coffee-buying, hulling and resale in bulk. There are three other trade-stores on the road in the immediate Palimung area (one of these operated by a local Councillor), but this one is the largest, most enterprising and, most telling of all, it operates continuously rather than sporadically. There are a few small trade-stores in the Kailge area, but none which so far has operated as continuously or successfully as the main Palimung store.

Other valley-floor facilities which Kailge people make use of, but in which they do not themselves have any organizational involvement, include the coffee-processing plant at Waibip, the produce market at Tega, and beer clubs along the Tega-Kailge road. During our stay there were two of these: one at Tega itself, and a more recent one at Yubika, nearer to Kailge (see Map 2). Enclosed by wire fencing, these clubs seem to assume a certain image of drinking as a potentially animal activity, to be cordoned off from others. There were recurrent proposals to start a beer club near Kailge – but as would-be entrepreneurs always said, on the other side of the Ukulu River, for everyone expected it could be a place of trouble (especially if 'enemies' came together there), and for this reason there was always some opposition to such schemes. In the coffee season, much cash goes towards buying large beer supplies (and, sometimes, remarketing in places like Kailge, at some mark-up).

Selling of produce at the Tega market (two days a week) by Kailge people was an occasional, not a regular activity. People might go to market when they had some other business in Tega on the day, such as a case to attend at the court sitting there. There might be an occasional household surplus of some product, such as greens or tobacco, or a supply of betel brought back from the coast, which women would be asked to market. No large sums of money appeared to be garnered by the marketing activity itself. However, near Tega, there were some families that raised specialty products, such as pineapples, explicitly for sale: these were not a surplus of an ordinary local product. Until women's clubs started to form in 1982–3, produce was not raised specifically for sale.

2.3 INDIGENOUS AND INTRODUCED ORDERS

People of the Kailge area strongly assert the significance of 'government law' (*gavman lo*), relating it to the European advent and the resulting imposition of centralized administration. On many public occasions orators allude to the harsh times of warfare before *gavman lo*, and declare that times have changed, and they too are different people now. But how exactly are we to understand the ways in which they interpret those changes, and the concept of *gavman lo*?

People recall with special interest the methods of the *kiaps* (patrol officers), the arm of the Australian Administration with which they were most familiar before Independence. They talk of corvée labor – many locals were impressed into work on the Waibip section of the road, or jailed for refusing to work. They talk of the suppression of tribal fighting, and the jailing of offenders, which went on into the 1960s in the Kailge area. In all of this talk, there is a certain admiration of perceived strength, and even of violence successfully used to accomplish ends.

Certain institutions developed under the Australian Administration are seen by local people as continuing mechanisms of *gavman lo*, foremost among these perhaps the village *kot* (court) system, local offices decided by election (Magistrate, Councillor), the system of regional and national elections, and the maze of provincial bodies at Mt Hagen with which some local people at least come to develop a certain familiarity.

For most Kailge people at present, coffee small-holding has been the major mode of direct involvement in the cash economy and, seasonal and tenuously related to daily subsistence as it is, money is now clearly tied to some fundamental aspects of their current lifestyle. *Bisnis* – the development of relations with the cash economy – is greatly desired by many local people, and seen as possible only in an environment of *gavman lo*, incompatible with the segmentary politics of warfare. The new order is conceived as a new political-economy, not one and the other, but parts of a whole. Yet, the segmentary order still constitutes a major basis of organization and fund-raising for entry into many forms of commercial enterprise – trade-stores, PMVs, purchase of coffee-hullers, and so forth.

The conduct of the village *kot* serves to illustrate concepts of the relation between what went before and what is emergent. The courts are supposed to be run according to principles of fairness, and to be directed towards achieving resolutions, at least in the form of making decisions, fixing fines, passing sentence, and re-establishing good relations. Hence, court officials warn against favoritism (*wantok sistem*), and make efforts to focus hearings on issues which might be capable of resolution, and thus must often discourage participants' tendencies to bring many related complexities under consideration. It is in regard to such contrasts – resolution as opposed to irresolute talk which goes 'round and round' (see e.g. Merlan and Rumsey 1986, lines 52–4) – that participants may claim that one is typical of *kewa* 'foreign, European' procedure, the other of *bo ul* 'indigenous affairs'.

But it is important to observe that even invidious contrast in such a situation as this does not amount to categorizing particular activities as *kewa* or *bo*. People do not consider, for example, that holding *kot* or conducting exchange belongs to one category or the other. For rather than demarcating or substantivizing activities, the *kewa-bo* contrast is used much more subtly to characterize modes of generating and conducting activities.

In Chapter 9, we develop the idea that a crucial dimension which underlies many domains of Nebilyer activity is a tension between the revealed and the concealed: a disposition people bring to events to imagine that they may harbor unrevealed significance. New ends and even new conceptions of ends, and new ways of pursuing them, may exist, presently unknown but perhaps discoverable. Such a concept of the possible unfolding of significance is not only compatible with the local people's notion of *bo ul*, indigenous ways of carrying on, but is fully part of it: witness the active and recurrent response to the introduction of new weath items and the political order mentioned above, the burning of kina shells and of weapons.

Consistent with this active disposition is the possibility that what is newly revealed may present ways of seeing what went before in a new light. As we will show in Chapter 7, some of the ends of large-scale exchange are seen as compatible with *gavman lo*, but also as continuous and compatible with aspects of the segmentary order, which is thereby brought into partial relationship with the new order.

Thus, perhaps paradoxically, the inculcated disposition to suspect disparity between what is apparent and what may be latent in events is part of a mode of approaching them which makes it possible to interpret their significance as partly continuous with what went before. It fosters reinterpretation of ways of doing things and the reinvesting of them with significance, rather than the demarcating of substantive activities as belonging to the old order, or to the new.

In some following chapters, especially in Chapters 6 to 9, we explore in detail the ways in which the relation of the introduced order, *gavman lo*, to the order of segmentary politics is formulated in particular events, and in Chapter 8 we propose in a somewhat more formal manner the different sorts of structural relations these orders presuppose.

2.4 ETHNOGRAPHIC SOURCES

There exists a relative wealth of ethnographic material for the Hagen area, much of it extending back to the early years of European contact. The early Lutheran missionaries resident in the central and northern Melpa area were particularly prolific writers. Georg Vicedom was *Stationsleiter* at Ogelbeng from 1935, and with H. Tischner (a collaborator on the write-up in Germany who never visited New Guinea), published the large, general ethnographic monograph *Die Mbowamb* (1943–8). Already in this work he acknowledged the research of Hermann Strauss, a missionary who came to Ogelbeng in 1936, and who returned after the disruption of the war years to work in the Hagen area. With Tischner, Strauss produced another monumental work, *Die Mi-Kultur der Hagenbergstaemme* (1962), largely a study of Hagen religious and cult practices. But this work also contains close observations of other aspects of Hagen life, including domestic and productive life, and ceremonial exchange (*moka*). Strauss left a large manuscript Melpa grammar, written in the classical pedagogical tradition. Still unpublished (and in need of systematization in some respects), the work is a valuable resource and indicates the excellent knowledge Strauss had of the language. In fact it seems clear that Strauss's depth of observation and understanding far exceeded that of Vicedom, most of whose work seems less based on detailed observation and less in touch with the quotidian Melpa realities. *Die Mbowamb* is, however, massive (three large volumes), and of considerable value if read with a critical eye (for example, to its full-blown master race theory, see Merlan 1988, fn.11).

The Catholic corpus is much smaller. Father Ross published some notes on the Hagen tribes (1936), and a brief article on the founding of the Catholic Mission (1969). Gitlow (1947), an American military officer stationed in Mt Hagen during the war, seems to have relied on Ross for much of his knowledge of Hagen 'economy'.

Much more recently, Brandewie (1981) has published a general ethnographic account of Melpa of the immediate Mt Hagen area, with particular focus on marriage and exchange. Brandewie's fieldwork was done in 1963–5 and 1968.

From 1964, A. and M. Strathern undertook fieldwork concentrated again in Central and Northern Melpa. From their studies have come works too numerous to list here, except for the major volumes (see also References section for many shorter publications): *The Rope of Moka* (1971, a study of ceremonial exchange); *One Father, One Blood* (1972, a study of group structure and ideology); *Self-Decoration in Mount Hagen* (1971, a joint work, a study of the pre-eminent visual art of the Hagen area, facial and body decoration); *Women in Between* (1972a, a study of Melpa marriage, largely from the female perspective); *Official and Unofficial Courts* (1972b, a study of indigenous and introduced dispute procedures); *No Money on Our Skins* (1975, a study of Hagen migrants in Port Moresby); *Ongka: a Self-account by a New Guinea Big-man* (1979b, translated by A. Strathern).

It would be difficult to overestimate the extent to which the combined Strathern corpus provided a comprehensive background on the basis of which we began fieldwork among the closely-related Nebilyer Valley people. Our view was that these accounts constituted a largely structurally-oriented corpus, with the help of which we could go on much more rapidly than would have otherwise been possible to examine what was of special interest to us, the role of events in the reproduction of social forms in a neighboring social setting, in many ways similar and in others somewhat different from the one described by the Stratherns.

2.5 TALK IN THE PUBLIC DOMAIN: AN INTRODUCTION

Given our focus throughout this book on speech as a form of social action, and its relation to others, it is appropriate to introduce the reader here to certain aspects of the salience of speech in Nebilyer life.

Perhaps the most striking indication of the emphasis upon talk in the Hagen/Nebilyer region is the ubiquity of medium and large-scale events held on display grounds, or elsewhere in public view – disputes, marriage negotiations and prestation events of all kinds – at which there is extensive speech-making (cf. beginning of Chapter 1 above and Merlan and Rumsey 1986). European observers noticed such events from earliest contact, and took special note of the volume and salience of talk at them. Patrol officers in the Hagen/Nebilyer region who were responsible for local 'pacification' and subsequently for the maintenance of 'law and order' frequently commented on public political discussion. One report of 1950, for example, notes that orators near Hagen 'harangued the assembly for hours regarding the non-payment of debts incurred' for assistance in tribal fighting; and, more colloquially, that the 'local orators poured on a session while debating the pros and cons of the recent internecine warfare' (AS 13/26, item 148, ADO Timperley).

As is widely reported of other areas of the central Highlands (e.g. Reay 1959, A. Strathern 1971, Goldman 1983), participation in and a reputation for public speaking is an important criterion of male social prominence, and one of the qualities always mentioned in the Nebilyer region if one asks what makes someone a *yi nuim*, a 'big-man': *ung nyilym* 'he speaks'. In later chapters, particularly in Chapter 9, we try to define, within the broader discussion of social action there, what sort of accomplishment this is, and why it is highly regarded.

Here we will simply give some further indications of the high valuation of public speaking, and of it as a form of male achievement. At Kailge, we noticed that young men in their late teens and early twenties were expected to begin to take a minor part in the public conduct of events, and on two occasions we happened to be present when young men of locally prominent families made their first public remarks. Neither event was of particularly great moment, nor were the remarks especially long or confidently expressed. But what was noticeable was that the gathered public, largely local Kailge people, immediately burst into applause – something not normally done for the best recognized and most accomplished speakers – clearly not so much for their content as for the fact that these speeches were made at all. This reaction showed collective sensitivity to the debut of new speakers in the public arena.

During the years 1982–3, fellowship activity involving mainly local Kopia-Kubuka people gathered momentum at Kailge. This was seen locally as a Catholic fellowship. The stimulus for its formation had been local, and had not come from the priest who visited Kailge every two to three weeks from Tabuga: he told us he had not known of these meetings until we mentioned them to him. In its heyday, the fellowship sometimes met several nights a week, in local houses. Most of those who attended were married women (of all ages) and their children; but noteworthy here is the fact that the fellowship activities were conducted by younger men. The master of ceremonies was usually one of several young, yet-unmarried men in his late teens or early twenties, mostly an elder son of some of the women who regularly came. He assumed the functions of orchestrating the singing, and later in the evening, delivering a kind of sermon (and, for those who were literate, also reading from the Tok Pisin Bible *Niupela Testamen na Ol Sam*).

These young men were ones who did not yet participate in public oratory, but who would shortly be expected to begin to do so. The fellowship seemed to be a kind of proving-ground for them, though the matter was never put this way. The speeches to the fellowship audience were often delivered in what seemed to us an unnecessarily harsh and abusive style, complete with questions ('What does Jesus want you to do?' and the like), which the women would usually answer rather timidly, and for which they would often be corrected. It was also noticeable that there was no overlap between the young men who led the fellowship, and those who had taken their place as active participants in public events of the *pena*, the display ground. All of this is evidence of the importance attributed to male participation in the public domain, and of particular emphasis upon public speaking as a valued kind of action there.

3. Some Aspects of Ku Waru Segmentary Sociality

3.1 THE NATURE OF KU WARU SEGMENTARY STRUCTURES

As already suggested by our opening vignette in Chapter 1, social action among the Ku Waru people (as in many other parts of the New Guinea Highlands) is structured partly in terms of named, quasi-agnatic social identities which bear some formal similarities to the segmentary lineages of classical descent theory (as in, e.g. Fortes 1953). Among Nebilyer people, those social identities are known generically as *talapi*. *Talapi* figure centrally in the events analyzed in Chapters 6 to 8, and so it is important here to provide full background details concerning the nature of these identities in general, and the history and structure of some of the particular *talapi* which are involved in those events.

In most respects, Ku Waru segmentary structures are similar or identical to those which have been extensively discussed in the Melpa ethnography mentioned in section 2.4 above. In view of this similarity, and given the extraordinarily high quality and thoroughness of the Strathern corpus, the present account of *talapi* will not be offered as a general introduction to the subject (for which, see A. Strathern 1972), but as an attempt to explicate aspects of *talapi* structure which are particularly relevant for our analysis of the events in Chapters 6 and 7, and for the model to be developed out of it in Chapter 8. To that end, and given the sort of controversies we have already reviewed concerning *talapi*-like social identities among the neighboring Enga and elsewhere in the Highlands (section 1.2), what is required here is less a matter of new empirical detail, than of how to construe certain largely familiar details in relation to existing anthropological models. Accordingly, the present account of Ku Waru *talapi* as structural type, will be organized around the following vexed issues:

To what extent or in what sense if any are Ku Waru *talapi*:

- segmentary
- based on descent
- hierarchically structured

- corporate
- territorial

This will be followed in section 3.2 by a detailed account of one particular tribe, the Kopia – which will provide substantive background for Chapters 6 and 7, and preliminary evidence for what we will later argue in detail: that *talapi* are at once problematical semiotic constructions and of very real material consequence for Nebilyer social life.

3.1.1 In what sense are *talapi* segmentary?

Following Durkheim (1964), Smith (1956), Sahlins (1961), Fortes (1979), and Dresch (1986), we consider the concept 'segmental' or 'segmentary' to be far more general and widely applicable than 'segmentary lineage'. The notion of segmentary social organization long predates segmentary lineage theory per se, going back at least as far as Durkheim, from whom Fortes and Evans-Pritchard first borrowed it (Fortes 1953). Durkheim's original image of the segmental or segmentary (*segmentaire*) is not of a hierarchically ramified, tree-like organism, but of a very different creature who lives closer to the ground: 'We say of these [Iroquois, etc.] societies that they are segmental in order to indicate their formation by the repetition of like aggregates in them, analogous to the rings of an earthworm . . .' (1964:175). This he contrasts with 'organically solidary' societies which, to complete the analogy, are composed of different, internally differentiated organs, which moreover, 'are not juxtaposed linearly as are the rings of an earthworm, nor entwined, but coordinated and subordinated to one another around the same central organ, which exercises a moderating influence over the rest of the organism' [i.e. the nervous system] (1964:181).

While we do not accept Durkheim's vision of societies as organisms, we follow him in using *segmentary* to refer to social differentiation by the multiplication of (or division into) like parts. As Durkheim emphasizes in his contrast between segmentary and centralized hierarchical organization (ibid.), the difference between the two hinges not only upon whether the relevant parts are alike or different, but also upon the kind of relationships we find among the parts. In structuralist terms, we can be more precise about this latter aspect of the distinction by saying that segmentary structures comprise homologous parts. That is, there is a likeness, not only among the parts, but in the relationships among the parts. So, to revert to Durkheim's biological analogy, given an earthworm with rings a, b, c, d, . . ., ring a is to b as b is to c, as c is to d, etc. It is this homologous relationship among social parts which for us is what defines the segmentary.

There is a second, related but more specific sense which the term segmentary has taken on in anthropological theory since Durkheim's day. In this more restricted sense, which we will for now call *segmentary*$_2$, the term refers to internally ramified structures, where two or more segments at one level comprise a single segment at a higher level, etc. Our usage of the term does not presuppose such ramification, although most of the social identities which we call segmentary do in fact exhibit it. For us, what makes such structures segmentary is not their multi-leveled ramification, but the fact that there is still a homologous relationship among parts, in this case of the form a is to b as a_1 is to a_2 as b_1 is to b_2, etc.

We are *not* using the term *segmentary* in the sense which it has sometimes taken on through its association with 'lineage system' and 'descent' in segmentary lineage theory, as for example in Keesing's (1975:151) textbook definition of 'segmentary' as: 'Of descent systems, defining descent categories with reference to more and more remote apical ancestors so that the descent categories form a tree-like structure (including successively wider ranges of descendants)'. This African-derived notion of 'segmentary lineage system' involves concepts of 'descent' and 'apical ancestor' which are analytically distinct from the notion of 'segmentarity' per se,[1] either in our general sense or in the sense we distinguished as *segmentary*$_2$. It is important to keep these features separate if we want to develop useful ways of comparing, not only the range of societies found in Africa but societies as different as those of Africa and Highland Papua New Guinea.[2] For, as we shall argue in section 3.1.2 below, notions of descent and apical ancestor are of little or no relevance in the Nebilyer area.

But descent is not the only possible basis for a segmentary$_2$ structure (much less a segmentary one *tout court*). Even in the classic Nuer case, Evans-Pritchard distinguished between the lineage system and the territorial system, which was itself segmentary$_2$ in that it comprised contiguous local groups which together formed a single unit vis-à-vis other such groupings, etc. This was in practice related to the lineage system, via the institution of the 'dominant lineage', but that is only a contingent relationship, as exemplified by the case of the (linguistically related) Mursi people, to the west of the Nuer, who have a segmentary territorial system but no lineage system (Turton 1979; cf. Fortes 1979, and note 2 above).

Likewise, Nebilyer *talapi* are segmentary$_2$ in the simple sense that, within a single *talapi*, distinctions are made among multiple, homologous, named sub-groupings, each of which is further subdivided in the same way, etc. Thus within the overarching category of Kopia, people regularly make a primary distinction between Araim and Wiyal, within each of which they draw distinctions among various named men's houses (*lku tapa*), etc. (cf. section 3.2.1). These groupings tend to be territorially localized, as we shall see in section 3.1.5.

3.1.2 Are *talapi* based on descent?

The most literal sense of the term *talapi* is something like 'line', 'row', or 'column'. (This trope is widespread in New Guinea languages, and has been carried over into Tok Pisin, where the word *lain* has the same pair of senses.) Suggestive as this image might be for descent theorists, in Ku Waru discourse the point of contact between the more and less literal senses of *talapi* is not – as they might assume – in some notion of a line of descent by which each member of a group is linked to its apical ancestor. What is locally relevant is not a vertical, genealogical line, but a horizontal, tactical one: the line of men who form a single flank on the battlefield and dance as a single row at ceremonial exchange events.[3]

Talapi is a broad generic term. Nowadays it is used for provincial, national, and even geopolitical identities insofar as these are known: the 'line of China', etc. It seems to have been the only indigenous generic lexeme for the social units which, in established anthropological usage for this area, are called 'tribes'

(A. Strathern 1972) or *Staemme* (Vicedom and Tischner 1943–8), i.e. individually named social identities of the most inclusive segmentary order.

While there is no indigenous generic term which refers only to the 'tribe', there is a hyponym of *talapi*, which refers only to identities included within (i.e., less inclusive than) a tribe. That term is *lku tapa* (=Melpa *manga rapa*), 'men's house'. This term has two senses.

First, it can refer to an actual house built to be occupied primarily by men and boys. These houses are oblong, with a single entrance at one end. That end is rectangular, whereas the back end, where people sleep, is rounded. As a term for houses of this type, *lku tapa* has a synonym *tapa lku*, which contrasts with *ab lku*, 'woman's house'. The latter differ from the former in being rounded at both ends, with the entrance or entrances on one of the long sides.[4]

In its other sense – which is more relevant here – *lku tapa* (but not *tapa lku*) is used as a generic term for a certain order of segmentary sub-groupings within the *talapi*. The relevant groupings are not of men who actually live or sleep in the same house, nor can each 'men's house' as social unit be identified with any actual building. Rather, the term refers to groupings of a size such that most of the men so grouped can meet together in a single *tapa lku* (however crowded!) to discuss matters of common concern. Such meetings seldom involve all or only the members of a single *lku tapa*, but there is a statistically significant and socially salient correlation between that segmentary level and patterns of hearth-centered sociability among men (cf. Langlas 1974, Weiner 1988).

Neither the *talapi* ('line'), nor the *lku tapa* (men's house), nor any other social unit in the Nebilyer entails descent as a structural basis. As already suggested by the horizontal reference of *talapi*, Nebilyer people do not relate themselves to or distinguish themselves from each other, as Keesing has it, 'with reference to more and more remote apical ancestors so that the descent categories form a tree-like structure'. As in most other Highland societies (and modern Western society, for that matter), their known genealogical ancestry is very shallow (three generations at most). Moreover, the sharing of a common apical ancestor is not even imputed as a notional principle of 'group identity'[5] among people who share a common segmentary identity (are of 'one line'), at least not at the level of 'tribe' (i.e., named segmentary identity of the most inclusive order). Rather, where common ancestry is explicitly posited by origin myths, these almost always involve *pairs* of ancestors who are related as brothers (Epri and Apri for the Kopia, Linguwa and Panguwa for the Kubuka, etc.). Though we assume such pairs of brothers would have had a common father, he is not named or even mentioned in most such stories. From this and other evidence (section 3.1.5 below), we conclude that the image of relatedness which they project is not one of 'common descent', or even filiation to a common stock, but brotherhood per se. The same no doubt holds for other areas of Melanesia as well, as many recent ethnographies attest (e.g. Wagner 1967, Kelly 1977, J. Weiner 1988). What is perhaps more specific to the Nebilyer area (and Hagen as well) is the salience of the brother *pair* as epitome of such unity (cf. sections 5.7 and 8.1 below, on pairing and 'compositional parity').

For most of the tribes in the area we surveyed, we were able to elicit such 'brother pair' stories, although they were sometimes not widely known even among men of the tribe in question. At lower and higher levels of segmentation (e.g. within the various Kopia *Iku tapa*, 'men's houses', or among the K-M-E-A-L alliance) there are usually not even notional apical ancestors, brother pairs or otherwise.

3.1.3 Are *talapi* hierarchically structured?

In early accounts of Highlands social structure, an attempt was made to distinguish analytically among various levels of the segmentary hierarchy and to establish a standardized set of terms for units at each: 'great-tribe', 'tribe', 'clan', 'subclan', 'sub-subclan', etc. In trying to do this in the Hagen-Nebilyer area, one immediately runs up against the fact that the maximally inclusive named units ('tribes') differ greatly in size: from under 100 to over 7000 people, with a corresponding variation in the number of named sub-units. One can try to distinguish levels according to 'functional' criteria, such as whether or not co-members occupy contiguous tracts of land, whether they intermarry, conduct ceremonial exchange, fight as major enemies, etc. But these criteria do not allow for categorical, step-wise distinctions among segmentary levels. Rather, they define a cline or sliding scale of increasing vs. decreasing likelihood that certain features will be present, or positively valued or both. Other things being equal, the lower the segmentary node at which persons are grouped together, the less appropriate it is for them to: fight against each other in organized hostilities (especially with lethal weapons); transact with each other in *makayl* ceremonial exchange; live and work in widely separated localities; intermarry. For people so grouped are 'the same' or 'one' (*tilupu*), and these activities are only appropriate for people who are in some way 'different' (*lupu-lupu*) from each other.

To some extent, this sliding scale of sameness vs. difference can be calibrated demographically in a fairly consistent way across the Hagen-Nebilyer area, irrespective of the variation in the size of the 'tribes' and in number of levels of named segmentary groupings. Consider, for example, the Palimung-Yubika area – heartland of one of the combatant sides in the fighting described in Chapter 1 – as compared with the neighboring Ulka (see Map 2). In the former, there is no named unit larger than about 150 people. There are five tribes in the area – Epola, Alya, Lalka, Kusika and Midipu, within none of which are distinctions made among more than three levels of named segmentary subgroupings. These five tribes are allies of long standing, do not regularly intermarry, do not conduct *makayl* ceremonial exchange with each other, and all occupy a single compact region, of approximately four square kilometers.

The neighboring Ulka tribe, occupying a much larger region of the fertile Nebilyer Valley floor, numbers about 4000 people, with at least six levels of named segmentary sub-divisions. At the first segmentary level, the Ulka are divided into two groupings, members of which intermarry freely. At the second level of segmentation there are some Ulka segments which have been involved in major hostilities with each other in the past, and now conduct *makayl* with each other. Below the third level of segmentation, there is generally stable alliance, strict exogamy, and no *makayl*.

In other words, relations among people within Ulka segments which have 300 to 600 people are similar to relations among the (approximately) 500 people at Palimung-Yubika, although the latter belong to five different tribes with no single over-arching hierarchy.[6]

There is, however, a tendency among Nebilyer people (and among the Melpa) for allied tribes to become paired in such a way as to create higher (i.e. supra-tribal) levels of de facto segmentation without monolexemic names for the bipartite identities thus constructed. At Palimung-Yubika, for instance, the Kusika are paired with the Midipu and the Alya with the Epola or the Lalka. If the alliance among these tribes remains fairly stable, it would be easy to imagine the development over the next few generations of a single 'tribal' identity with five levels of named segments, with the present names at level three. Before this could happen, there would have to be a resolution of the present ambiguity over the hierarchical relations among Epola-Alya-Lalka. (Interestingly, people already speak of the whole set of five tribes as a pair of pairs, conveniently ignoring either Epola or Lalka.) One can presently see a similar process occurring at a more advanced stage on the fringes of the Ulka 'tribe', where there is some disagreement about whether the Wapika, Tona, and Lanika are segments of Ulka or distinct allied 'tribes'.[7]

If segmentary identities of the kind we have been discussing are not structured 'with reference to more and more remote apical ancestors', how and to what extent are they really hierarchical? The matter deserves careful consideration in light of Lederman's (1986:44–52) revisionist arguments regarding comparable social identities among the Mendi. Though she seems to accept the claim in earlier Mendi ethnography (Ryan 1959) that such entities may, at least to some extent, 'be arranged hierarchically as a series of progressively more inclusive groups' (Lederman 1986a:41) she is at pains to demonstrate that 'segmentary relationships are not hierarchical'. This may appear contradictory, but becomes less so when we examine her evidence and the following amplification of what she means by 'hierarchical' in the latter remark:

> In Mendi, the parts of a *sem onda* are not conceived to be subordinate to the whole any more than group members are thought to be subordinate to a leader. Rather than being a hierarchically organized structure, a *sem onda* is an affiliation of equivalent segments, each with strong (and diverging) loyalties and interests outside the group. Nor do the functions (or interests) of *sem onda* necessarily override those of its components as they do among the Mae Enga . . . (Lederman 1986a:52)

As suggested by her contrastive reference to Mae Enga, the notion of 'hierarchy' from which Lederman wants to distance herself (or the Mendi) is the functionalist one which reached its Melanesianist apotheosis in Meggitt's (1965) account of the Mae Enga 'lineage system' (see section 1.2 above). Meggitt portrayed this as a descent-based, segmentary lineage system, comprising a 'structural hierarchy of descent groups [clan, subclan, lineage, etc.]' which is:

> paralleled by a ranking both of the kinds of public prestations in which the social units should participate and of the valuables appropriate to each occasion . . . The basic assumption is that normally the commitments of higher-order units override those of their constituent elements. (Meggitt 1965:121–2)

This kind of *functional* hierarchy is no more evident in the Nebilyer Valley than in Mendi. As we shall see below, Ku Waru people do not even espouse in principle the idea that commitments to 'higher order units' override those to lower, or that, in Lederman's terms 'the parts are subordinate to the whole'.

Rather, the part-whole relations which figure in some Ku Waru segmentary structures are hierarchical in the purely formal sense which is entailed in our definition of segmentary$_2$ above, i.e., relations of the form $a{:}b{::}a_1{:}a_2{::}b_1{:}b_2$. We do not claim that the 'parts' are 'subordinate' except in the limited sense that, for example, all men of the Tolab *lku tapa* ('men's house') are of the Kopia *talapi* ('line'), but not all Kopia are of Tolab; or, in general, that there are some segmentary relations in the Nebilyer Valley which are of the form $a_1 \cup a_2 \equiv a$, a form which we will exemplify and discuss below under the rubric *compositional parity* (section 8.1).

This is not to say that it is always clear whether a given actual relationship *is* of this form, as opposed to the other locally relevant alternatives which we will call *serial parity* or *oppositional parity* (section 8.1 below). On the contrary, this is a matter which is chronically contested in the public arena, as we shall see (e.g. in sections 6.2.4 and 7.2.3). The point is rather that the 'compositional' or formally 'hierarchical' relation is one of the possible alternatives within the traditional Ku Waru segmentary order – one of the relevant relation types to which actual relations *may* belong.

3.1.4 Are *talapi* corporate?

Anthropologically trained readers who are used to thinking in terms of a fundamental distinction between social *groups* and cultural *categories* will no doubt have noticed that we have tended to avoid both of those terms, and often have spoken instead of Ku Waru segmentary 'identities'. This is deliberate, for, common-sensical as that distinction may appear to be, and useful as it is for certain purposes, we have found it to be a hindrance to the kind of understanding of the relation between structure and events which we are trying to develop. Ultimately, it is yet another variant of the Western antinomy, which we wish to avoid, between action and representation: between things in the world and things in the mind. The kinds of impasse to which this antinomy can lead should have become evident already from our discussion of the Feil-Meggitt controversy in section 1.2, where both accounts are shown to suffer from the assumption that social groups are not also essentially contested cultural representations.

Nor can we accept, for the Nebilyer anyway, an apparently opposite conclusion by Roy Wagner (1974:187), that the segmentary social identities exist *only* as representations – as mere 'names'. Most of them certainly do exist as names: Kopia, Kubuka, Tea, Dena, etc. But, as we shall see, they also figure crucially in Nebilyer social life as 'things named': as historically specific social actors (or aggregates of them), who speak, exchange wealth, and sometimes fight and die *qua* Kopia, Kubuka, etc. We would even go so far as to call these corporate entities, in something like the limited sense in which Lederman (1986:22) applies that term to Mendi *sem onda*, i.e., that Nebilyer *talapi* are recognized as enduring beyond the lifetimes of their present incumbents, who nonetheless accept common liability (or credit) for past actions of the *talapi*. But it is important to bear in mind (as Lederman does) that this is a matter of *principle*, which does not fully determine social practice or its outcome in specific cases, since there is always room for disagreement as to how the principle is to be applied. To extend the argument we have already made about transactors in section 1.2, 'groups' in general, and 'corporate' ones in particular, should not be taken as preconstituted entities, but as contested ones, which are more-or-less problematically instantiated or reproduced in social action (cf. section 5.1 regarding 'individuals'). It is because the terms 'corporate' and 'group' tend to be taken in the former way that we have shied away from using them here, in favor of the active participle 'grouping', which better suggests the latter characteristics. As we shall see, much of what goes on at public exchange events can be understood as the reproduction or contestation of specific segmentary groupings, largely through various modes of pairing, or 'making twos'.

3.1.5. Are *talapi* territorial?

Another set of social identities with which the segmentary ones intersect are those concerned with locality. Among the typical characteristics of segments which are structurally closely related is that of close co-residence. As elsewhere in the western Highlands, Ku Waru people live not in villages, but in relatively isolated houses or hamlets which are interspersed among their gardens. *Talapi* (and persons) are spoken of as being 'planted' in particular localities (see e.g. Appendix A, line 474), and conversely, all places – except for deepest forest hinterlands and certain interstitial or contested no-man's-lands – are said to be the *kolya* ('region') of some particular *talapi*. This identification is subject to the same hierarchical gradation as is the identification of persons, so that any place identified with a particular segment is also identified with all higher-level segments which subsume it (see Map 3 for Kopia examples).

Aside from their being associated with segmentary identities, places within the Nebilyer region also have names in their own right. Particularly within settled areas, these names are quite thick on the ground, including names for all creeks, streams, rivers, nearly all hilltops or other striking natural features, large clearings, and isolated pockets of dense forest. (See Map 3 for some – but by no means all – place names in the Kailge area). Some of these names have clear etymologies (e.g. *no kuduyl kong* 'red pig creek'; *taina engal suku* 'forest of the engal spirit'), while others apparently do not. Nearly all the place names are thought to be archaic, predating present-day associations of particular segmentary identities with the places. A direct identification between particular people and places is sometimes made in personal reference, e.g. *kalyka kupena* 'Kupena of Kailge', *walyo pai* 'Pai of Walyo'. This is always done instead of rather than in addition to the compounding of a personal name with a segmentary name. For example, Pai who lives at Walyo and belongs to the Kopia tribe is called either Kopia Pai or Walyo Pai, not Kopia Walyo Pai, or Walyo Kopia Pai. The contexts for use of the two sorts of names do not overlap much: segmentary names are used mainly in discourse among or about people who belong to different tribes, while place-identifying names are used more in intra-tribal contexts.

The close identification in the Nebilyer between the *talapi* and places is not just an ideal one. Unlike in some areas of the Southern Highlands (see, e.g. Goldman 1983, Sillitoe 1979, Glasse 1968, Lederman 1986a, A. Strathern 1984), Nebilyer people tend to reside mainly with their fellow tribesmen. Men of each *lku tapa* tend to live and work on land which is identified with their own particular named segment of Kopia (for further discussion, see section 3.2 below.

In other words, in terms of Hogbin and Wedgwood's (1953) distinction between 'monocarpellary' and 'multicarpellary' parishes (which is useful if taken as an ideal-typic continuum rather than as a categorical opposition), Nebilyer peoples approximate the former type. This observable feature of Ku Waru residence patterns is matched by a tendency for Ku Waru people to accord a special status to people such as the Palimi immigrants at Kailge and Ibumuyl (see Map 3; section 3.2.4): they differ from the Kailge Kopia and the Owamul Palimi (Map 2, upper left hand corner) in that they are living apart from the main body of their tribesmen. They are not presently regarded as a segment of the Kopia, but their descendants might well be so regarded if they remain co-residents of the Kopia (cf. section 3.2.4 regarding Kopia-Palimi relations). That things generally work out that way is suggested by the fact that all such pockets of immigrants known to us in the Ku Waru region have well-known histories which place their immigration into the territories of their present hosts at a time depth of two generations or less. These are not *kange* 'myths', but historical accounts of events which are remembered by presently-living people. That some such immigrant pockets have, after a longer time-span, become converted to segmentary sub-groupings, is suggested by the fact that some present-day *lku tapa* 'men's house' units have names which end in *-ka* (perhaps etymologically the word *ka*, 'vine', 'rope') which is otherwise much more common as a final element of 'tribe' names (cf. A. Strathern 1972:239, fn.1).

Of course, not all such immigrant pockets become assimilated in this way. But is seems that no such pocket can remain indefinitely as acknowledged immigrants within the territory of their hosts: they either get expelled or assimilated as segmentary sub-groupings. This is true despite the fact that co-resident immigrants are highly desirable as trading partners among the Ku Waru people, for reasons similar to those described for the Tombema Enga by Feil (1978c). For, however that may be, people who live, work, and eat together among the Ku Waru become like siblings, and the effect multiplies over the course of generations, since in time it is irrelevant whether ancestors were brothers or merely 'like brothers': descendants of co-resident men are 'siblings' in either case (cf. A. Strathern 1972, Watson 1983).

In order to understand why this should be the case, or how the process works, it is useful to know a little about Ku Waru discourse concerning bodily substance. Like the Melpa (A. Strathern 1972), Ku Waru people speak of *kopong* (Eng. 'grease, fat', Tok Pison *gris*) as the essential matter of living organisms, both animal and vegetable. The ultimate source of *kopong* is *ma*, the soil, which is recognized to vary in grease content, or as we would say, fertility. Horticulture is talked about as a way of making the grease available in concentrated form, both for human consumption and also – in the case of sweet potato cultivation – for pig fodder. In the latter case, the grease undergoes further concentration before being made available to humans in the form of cooked pork, of which the fatty tissue is especially valued as virtually pure *kopong*.

In the Ku Waru project of human (and animal) reproduction, *kopong* figures (in different forms) at several distinct stages. First, in the process of procreation, the developing foetus is said to be built up of the bodily *kopong* of both father and mother. The father's contribution comes during the early part of the pregnancy, especially crucially during the first months, when, through repeated acts of intercourse, he must build up sufficient semen (which is called *kopong*) to stop the flow of menstrual blood, allowing the latter to contribute also to the development of the foetus. The mother also contributes *kopong,* which is said to be present in her breast milk. After parturition, the baby's growth at first depends entirely on the grease still provided by mother's milk, until weaning, when the child begins to be able to absorb *kopong* directly from garden produce.[8] It is against the background of this sort of conception ideology that 'siblingship' takes on its particular cast in Ku Waru.

In Western ideologies 'real' siblingship is determined entirely by prenatal influences: by the fact that the corporeal existence of each sibling began with an event of conception at which genetic substance was contributed by the same two individuals. Insofar as we also treat the children of siblings as consubstantial, this is entirely determined by two sets of pre-natal influences, one giving rise to the senior generation and one to the junior, who thereby get at least half of their genetic substance from the former.

Ku Waru discourse about reproduction appears not to entail any such notion of genetic substance.[9] Rather, *kopong* figures at every stage in the reproductive process as a kind of *nutritive* substance, whether extracted directly from the gardens, channeled through a man's reproductive organs, woman's breast, or stored and consumed in the flesh of a pig. In contrast to the western one, there is in this view no essential difference between pre-natal and post-natal influences in their power to make us what we are.[10]

Much as in the materialism of Feuerbach (*Der Mensch ist, was er isst*) what one is among the Nebilyer people, as elsewhere in Melanesia (cf. e.g. Wagner 1967, Young 1971, A. Strathern 1977a, Meigs 1984), is to a great extent a matter of what one eats.

To the extent that siblings are treated as consubstantial among the Nebilyer people, this is not only because they took their pre-natal *kopong* from the same parents, but, equally importantly, because they suckled from the same breast, eat produce from the same gardens, and otherwise share food together. Thus, siblingship is not just a matter of immutable pedigree, but something which requires work to sustain and develop.

Provided that work is done, the pre- and post-natal influences have a compounding effect upon each other from one generation to the next. That is, the offspring of commensal siblings are consubstantial at birth, not only because their parents took pre-natal *kopong* from a common parent, but also because those parents took post-natal *kopong* from the same soil.

The fact that Nebilyer people do not maintain lengthy genealogies (cf. section 3.1.2) can be related to the fact that, over two or three generations, the compounding effect of common *kopong* is such that it ceases to matter whether that which our remote 'ancestors' (*tara*) had in common was pre-natal, post-natal, or both. The well-known ability of Highlanders to absorb non-agnates – and even non-'kinsmen' – into 'agnatic' groupings should not (in the Nebilyer area anyway) be thought of as a case of ideological repression of the genealogical 'facts', since it is clear that the relevant dimensions of consubstantiality are by no means strictly agnatic, nor even strictly genealogical.[11]

Having discussed Ku Waru notions concerning the relation between land, cultivation, and human reproduction, we now return to the question of the relationship between specific persons or segmentary groupings, and particular territories.

At the lowest, most specific level, there are associations between people or households, and plots of land. In particular, much of the garden land has a specific *pul yi-yl* ('base man') or *pulu yab* ('base people'), whose relationship to the land is of the kind which is generally glossed by non-indigenes in the area (anthropologists as well as those with a more practical interest in the subject) as 'ownership'. They are owners insofar as they have control in the first instance over the disposition of the land, but their rights in it are by no means absolute. They are in practice not free to alienate it of their own volition to men of another *talapi* (cf. A. Strathern 1972:97). Furthermore they are expected to let certain other people plant crops on some of the land, and the right to harvest and dispose of crops of all kinds belongs to the person who planted them (cf. M. Strathern 1972a; A. Strathern 1982:96). In the case of 'base men' who are married men, the most notable beneficiaries of this usufruct are, of course, their wives, who are assigned plots for the cultivation of sweet potatoes (cf. section 4.2). But the base man typically assigns bits of land for use by many other people besides his wife or wives, usually for the planting of luxury crops such as sugar cane, taro, and beans. The beneficiaries include, pre-eminently, his affines (male and female) and maternal kin, whose plantings he not only may not harvest, but must guard for them (against theft, damage by pigs, etc.) in their absence.

The result of this disposition is that the land of nearly every *pul yi* ('base man') is a complex patchwork of plots – some large, some minuscule – assigned to a wide variety of other people, some living nearby and some far away.

This is apparently also true of many other areas of the Highlands. But an important difference between Ku Waru and some of the others is that, in Ku Waru (as in Melpa) there are also fairly exclusive associations between portions of territory and this or that segmentary social identity (as above concerning 'monocarpellary' parishes).

These associations are clearest and most nearly categorical for segmentary identities of the most inclusive sort, such as Kopia and Kubuka. Thus, a look at Map 3 will show that there is a single, continuous stretch of territory identified with Kopia, which is filled in on the map with parallel solid (as opposed to dotted) lines (or left blank). That region is not completely well bounded, in that there are, on its southern and eastern edges, border regions which are shared with neighboring *talapi*: Kubuka and Alya-Lalka respectively. But these are relatively small (and in any case mainly uncultivated) areas, the existence of which does not undercut the conceptual and practical discreteness of Kopia territory as a whole. Within that territory, there are many plots with plantings belonging to people who are not Kopia, but there is no land with a base man who is not either a Kopia man or the son of a Kopia woman.

Not all of that land *has* a clearly-agreed-upon base man. As can be seen from Map 3, there some large sections of it which are generally regarded as being common to Kopia at large, or certain segments thereof. These include Kuru Engal Suku, a patch of thick forest which is maintained (in the middle of an otherwise densely settled area) for the use of all Kopia people, and a large expanse of land east of the Ukulu River and north of Sibeka (both left blank on the map, as parallel solid lines are for specific Kopia segments).

Other areas within Kopia territory (most of it in fact) are associated, not just with Kopia, but with particular lower-level segments of Kopia (see section 3.2 and Map 3). The extent to which this is so is correlated with the extent to which contiguous plots of land within those areas have base men who are uniformly of the segment in question (cf. section 3.2). Those particular men and their sons are just the people who are most likely to eat consistently throughout their lifetimes the produce of that land – a commensality which, for reasons which should now be clear, is ideologically salient as a basis of essential linkage among them, and between them and the land in question.

3.2 STRUCTURE AND HISTORY OF SOME WESTERN NEBILYER *TALAPI* ('TRIBES')

Having talked in general terms about the nature of Ku Waru segmentary identities as structural types, we now turn to a detailed account of the historical and structural constitution of particular tokens of those types: *talapi* in the western Nebilyer Valley, with particular emphasis on Kopia and neighboring *talapi*.

This account is based on extensive ethnohistorical information we gathered, upon our participant observation of day-to-day events in the Kailge area, and also upon census data and genealogies we collected of approximately 1500 people within the area shown on Map 2. This included all living Kopia and Palimi in the Ku Waru area as of 1983 and 1986 respectively, almost all Kubuka, and several hundred people from the other *talapi* shown on the map.

3.2.1 The internal structure and ethnohistory of the Kopia *talapi*

The Kopia at Kailge distinguish two large internal sub-divisions, Wiyal and Araim. The name Wiyal designates a mountain peak of the upper Tambul range, supposedly shaped like a dog's ear. The Wiyal division may be characterized as 'upper Kopia' in that its land holdings and settlements now lie mainly in the foothills of the eastern side of the Tambul range, along the upper tributaries of the Ukulu. Wiyal segments are commonly agreed to have also formerly occupied the adjacent lower regions now inhabited by Araim Kopia, who regard themselves as having acquired land rights from the Kabika (a segment of Wiyal Kopia) when they first moved into the Kailge area. Araim now connotes 'lower Kopia' territory, that which extends furthest towards the Nebilyer Valley floor. It seems that 'Araim' is a place-name within the (current) Tola-Wanaka area from which these present segments emigrated to Kailge; and as often happens, this sub-division is named in its current location for its place of provenience (cf. Watson 1983: Ch.5).

Below the level of the *wiyal/araim* split (which is itself evoked only in certain contexts), it is not possible to give any single authoritative account of Kopia segmentary structure, for historical reasons which should become clear below.

At the time of our census, the *wiyal* division included 293 people, of the five segments (*lku tapa*) shown in Table 3–1.

Table 3–1: *Segments of Wiyal Kopia*

Lku Tapa (Men's House)	Living Members in 1983
Galka	62
Kabika	88
Kopil	81
Waipiyl	10
Ukulupiyl	52

The Ukulupiyl segment was, by common agreement, a recent creation, having split off from Kabika within the last generation. As the story goes, two Kabika brothers (both of whom are still living) quarreled, after which one of them was offered land by friends from the Kopil segment around the head-waters of the Ukulu River, well to the north of Kabika territory. Rather than allowing their anger with each other to fester, they both decided it would be best for one of them to leave and settle there. Panguwu did so, taking several other Kabika with him, and there they founded a new *lku tapa* known as Ukulupiyl, 'the Ukulu-dwellers'. Then and now, the Waipiyl segment has been diminishing in size, to the point where it is, for most purposes, lumped together with Kopil as a single *lku tapa*. There is also a tendency for Ukulupiyl, Waipiyl and Kopil all to be lumped together as *no pengi* (i.e., upper Ukulu River) people. (This is how they are shown on Map 3.)

Kabika and Galka are considered paired segments, Kabika-Galka-*sil*, ('Kabika-Galka-pair'), but increasingly this is becoming a mere figure of speech, as Galka have avoided alliance with Kabika in the recent feud between the latter and the Araim division (see section 3.2.3 below).

Within the Araim division, the maximum number of next-level segments (*lku tapa*) that is ever distinguished is four, as shown on Table 3–2.

Table 3–2: *Segments of Araim Kopia*

Lku Tapa (Men's House)	Living Members in 1983
Kupena	53
Kaja	18
Kidi	1
Tolab	78

It is mainly in reference to the past that all four of these segments are distinguished. The formerly dominant way of construing the four of them was as a pair of pairs: Kupena-Kaja and Kidi-Tolab. This is now difficult, for obvious reasons. The one Kidi man who remains at Kailge is old and unmarried. At least two of his brothers were killed in earlier fighting between Kopia-Kubuka and Tea-Dena. During the period of prolonged fighting when he was a boy, he took refuge in his mother's territory among Jika.[12] Two other male members of Kidi who also took refuge during the fighting never returned, and have identified themselves with Jika segments, within which they have both become major 'big-men'.

The Kaja segment too has recently been tending to lose its identity as a distinct 'men's house', and tends to be construed as transacting jointly with

Kupena or Tolab. Indeed, the entire Araim division, which formerly comprised the four *lku tapa*, is increasingly being understood as Kupena-Tolab 'the pair of Kupena and Tolab'; this is understood to subsume what had formerly been distinguished as Kidi and Kaja as well.

In sum, neither the Wiyal division nor the Araim can be said to have *a* structure of further internal subdivisions. Rather, there are various competing structurings of them, including at least the alternatives shown in Figure 3–1.

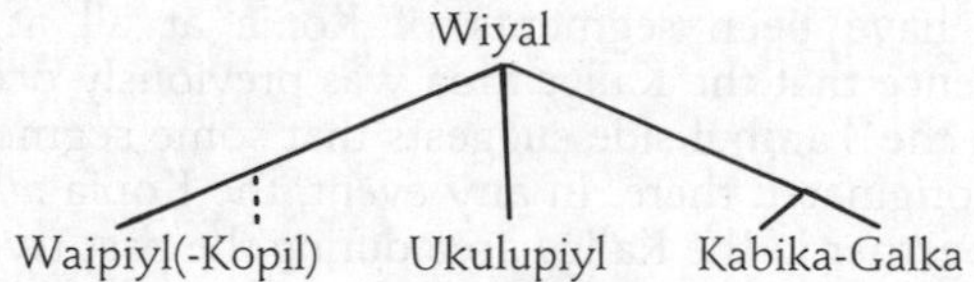

or:

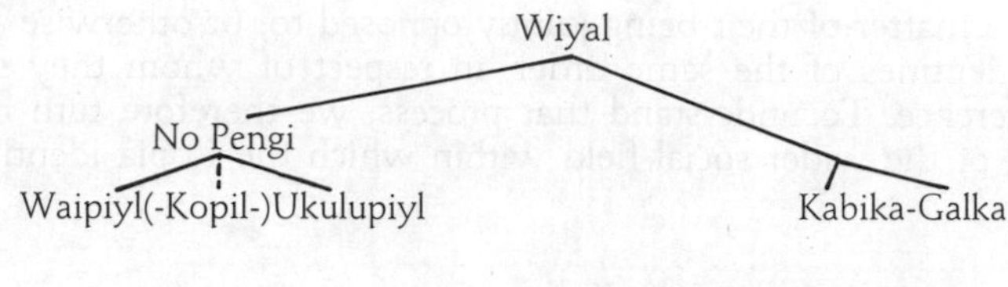

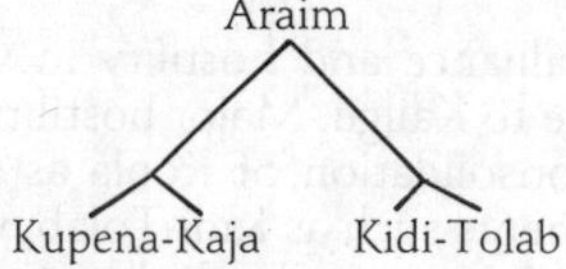

or:

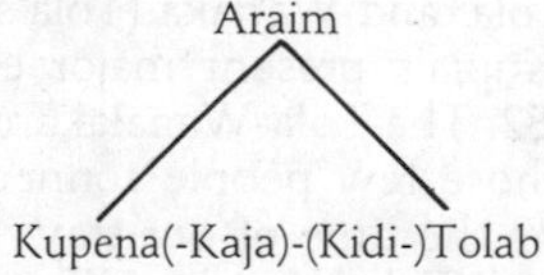

Figure 3–1: *Alternative structurings of Araim and Wiyal Kopia*

Map 3 shows the territories associated with Araim Kopia, and with three divisions of Wiyal Kopia (Kabika, Galka, and No Pengi). Lower level segmentary territorial blocs are less clear-cut (cf. section 3.1.5), but within Araim, we can say that, in general, Tolab is identified with the area around the main Kailge *pena* ('display ground'), Kaja with Kuduyl Kong Creek and with lower Kailge, and Kupena with Lkulyipul.

Of the Wiyal segments, Kabika currently shows the greatest geographical discontinuity: some Kabika reside in lower Kailge between the Luip and Ukulu Rivers, while others live higher up at Ibumuyl and Kalamuyl (see Map 3). Aside from this, in general the Araim segments are associated with lower Kailge, the Wiyal with the upper reaches of the Ukulu and Akarab.

The present relative locations of Araim and Kabika seem to reflect the more recent arrival of the former in the Kailge area from various parts of the Nebilyer Valley floor. At least Kabika and Galka were already represented at Kailge when the Araim arrived, and the area now occupied by the latter is universally agreed to have been ceded to them by the Kabika.

These and other details of oral history suggest that, fifty or sixty years ago, people of the various segments that now comprise the Kopia *talapi* at Kailge were living in different places. Possibly some of them, such as Kabika and Galka, may not have been segments of Kopia at all at that time. The fragmentary evidence that the Kailge area was previously occupied by people who now live on the Tambul side suggests that some segments of the Kailge Kopia may have originated there. In any event, the Kopia *talapi* in its present form has come together in the Kailge area during the past two generations (cf. section 3.2.2 below for further evidence to this effect).

In order to understand how that took place, one cannot look at this emerging *talapi* in isolation: what confers upon the Kailge Kopia their shared identity is, in large part, a matter of their being jointly opposed to, or otherwise aligned with, other identities of the same order, in respect of whom they share a common difference. To understand that process, we therefore turn now to consideration of the wider social field within which the Kopia identity was precipitated.

3.2.2 External relations of the Kopia *talapi*

The external relations of alliance and hostility in which Kopia are currently engaged postdate the move to Kailge. Major hostilities early this century seem to have encouraged the consolidation of Kopia as it is now constituted, and hastened the move of segments such as Kidi-Tolab, which had been located on the valley floor at Wakipul (in present-day Kulka territory), inside 'one fence' at Kailge.

Before the move 'up', Kopia is supposed (at least according to some accounts) to have been allied with Tola, and Wanaka (Tola's present paired tribe) with Poi. Tola-Wanaka aided Kopia's present major enemies, Tea-Dena, in the Marsupial Road War in 1982. The Tola-Wanaka are now considered hostile to Kopia-Kubuka, and only those few people connected by affinity visited between the two areas during the time of our stay. No other Kopia or Kubuka would normally walk through Tola-Wanaka or Tea-Dena territories. However, when there was a major exchange event, members of all these *talapi* would attend in force, confining their movements strictly to the display ground and paths leading out of the more densely settled area.[13]

One index of the state of current relations between Kopia and Wanaka is the paucity of marriages. We recorded only two: one marriage of a Wiyal Kopia man to a Wanaka woman, and one of a Wiyal Kopia woman to a Tola man (cf. section 4.2 regarding Kopia-to-Tea-Dena marriages). In sum, whatever may have been the earlier situation, any previous alliance of Kopia with Tola is now superseded by relatively hostile relations between them, largely based upon the fact that Tola is an ally of Kopia's proximate major enemies, Tea-Dena.

Kopia remember a period of intense conflict after the move to Kailge. This was when some of the men now in their sixties were small children, and so would have predated the arrival of Europeans in this area. In these hostilities, which involved a number of Nebilyer Valley-floor tribes allied against Kopia-Kubuka, the latter seem to have been almost entirely routed. Many who had Tambul-side connections fled over the mountains to the west. Some Araim Kopia who had links with people of the Valley floor and towards Mt Hagen retreated there. The Kopia Councillor Noma spent years in the Hagen area and his children grew up there. (He returned with the advent of European *lo* and has been Councillor at Kailge since 1963.) It was around this time that the Kidi segment was decimated, and most of its few survivors fled (as mentioned above). The entire Kailge area was supposedly burnt to the ground. When the Kopia returned after their rout, they found only bush.

In the more recent fighting, as adumbrated in Chapter 1, the older alliances had shifted so that some formerly hostile *talapi* – Kusika-Midipu and Epola-Alya – have assumed a more-or-less friendly attitude towards Kopia-Kubuka, recruiting them as allies. This has come about because of shifts in alliances among Kopia-Kubuka's former enemies. Why have those shifts occurred?

Already by the time of the compensation events of 1983 (which comprise the subject matter of Chapters 5 and 6), there was a fairly widely agreed-upon account of why the 1982 war had happened: an account which was well-known enough that it could simply be assumed as background knowledge by orators at those compensation events. Thus, while there were frequent allusions to it, especially at the second compensation event (Chapter 7), no one rehearsed it at length. In order to provide the reader with some of the assumed background details, we will now review some aspects of 'what happened' which are widely agreed upon, at least by people on the Kopia-Kubuka-K-M-E-A-L side.

Ultimately, the fighting was all due to the actions of a Dena man, Peam, who had left Dena territory some years ago under a cloud of accusation that he had poisoned another Dena, Paki. The Epola, at that time evidently linked by more relevant ties of alliance to Dena rather than Tea, accused a Tea man, Nyab, of the poisoning instead and succeeded in having him put in jail. The Epola demanded money for their help in the resolution of this affair, but since this occurred at a time when money was not widely used in compensation payments, they received none.

Another incident to which Peam's exodus is also attributed (for which the war was later named) is the following. Peam is said to have built and maintained a track into the Dena hinterland on the Tambul range, which he used for hunting marsupials (highly prized for their meat and fur). A Tea man called Sisip secretly used Peam's 'marsupial road', and succeeded in killing a large number of animals. Peam got wind of this, went up the road one night and, catching the poacher in the act, shot him with an arrow through the thigh. The Tea demanded compensation, which the outraged Peam refused to pay.

Whatever relationship there might have been between these two incidents, the upshot was that Dena Peam moved in to Epola territory with his affines, and resentment between Epola and Dena apparently continued to smolder. In September 1982, a group of Tea-Dena which included a certain Tea Anginua, was attacked by some (mainly younger) Epola and Alya men as he brought home some store-bought foodstuffs, rice and tinned fish. There were efforts by former allies of both Tea-Dena and Epola-Alya to make peace: the Midipu Councillor, Kujilyi, offered to replace the food out of his own pocket (presumably, by collecting money from his supporters), but his efforts were rejected.

These events, made especially bitter by the fact that they involved members of nominally allied *talapi*, in fact broke up the alliance, at least temporarily. Kusika-Midipu sided with Epola-Alya-Lalka, and Kopia-Kubuka were recruited as allies (though only a minority of their men actually participated). They in turn were aided by allies from over the Tambul range. The Tea-Dena recruited the neighboring Tola-Wanaka, who in turn recruited allies from the lower Tambul ranges (Nokopa-Anamiyl, Walima-Laima). Most of the fighting took place over a period of a few days in September 1982. There were a few woundings on both sides, but no deaths, either on the battlefield or attributed to injuries sustained in the fighting.

By the time of Alan Rumsey's return to Kailge in 1986 (although not before our departure in 1983), this fighting of 1982 had in retrospect become known as the Marsupial Road War (*lopa ka el*), a reference to the incident involving Dena Peam. It was clear that this war had marked a considerable, cumulative change in the tenor of relations between Epola and Kopia-Kubuka, in that they were now no longer major enemies. Kopia-Kubuka relations with Epola-Alya-(Lalka) are not stable, but are clearly overall less hostile than formerly.

What has remained stable through both rounds of fighting (i.e., both against the Kusika-Midipu in the 1950s and as their allies in the 1980s) has been the alliance between Kopia and Kubuka, and the internal integrity of those *talapi* groupings vis-à-vis others. As in the classical theory of complementary opposition, this is a *relative* integrity, which by no means precludes internal opposition among Kopia. In order to exemplify the relation between external and internal oppositions, we now turn to an example of the latter.

3.2.3. Kabika versus Kupena-Tolab

As reviewed above, the Kabika and Galka segments are recognized to have been the original Kopia occupants of Kailge, and to have ceded to Kidi-Tolab and Kupena-Kaja land rights over the present territory of those Kopia segments in the Kailge area. The present Ukulupiyl segment is a recent creation, having originated as a Kabika segment which left the Kabika heartland and settled further north. Although this is said to have resulted from a quarrel between two Kabika brothers, it would have had the effect of partially mitigating any land shortage which may have been developing among Kopia\Kabika as a result of their earlier cession to the incoming Araim Kopia.

By 1982, due partly to again-increasing land shortage there, the brother who had stayed behind at Kalamuyl, Kopia Silka, had declared his intention to build a house at lower Kailge, in an area which had not been occupied since the cession of Kailge to the Araim, but had been used by Kopia of all segments (but principally Araim, because of their greater proximity) as a pig pasture (cf. section 3.1.5). Later, he also declared his intention to build a *kung pala* ('pig fence'), and despite vehement opposition from Araim, he did so in January 1983. (See Map 3.) This was even more provocative than his building a house, as it in effect removed from common (Kopia) usage a sizable chunk of pig pasture, and re-established as 'Kabika' a fenced-off area large enough for a settlement and display ground to rival that of the Araim Kopia immediately to the north (which the Kabika did eventually establish, as can be seen on Map 3, which shows the disposition of land as of January 1986).

In the early stages of the dispute, senior Kabika men attempted to persuade the Araim Kopia that Silka should be allowed to build. But the Araim were adamant, and already in March 1982 some of them were urging a fight with sticks and clubs. Councillor Noma attempted to muster bureaucratic support: by April 1982 he was seeking to organize a visit by a land commission from Hagen, and to take Silka to court locally and at Tega. The land commissioners finally came to Kailge at the end of April, but remained only briefly. Once they had seen the area in question and held brief discussions, they announced that all their deliberations would take place in Mt Hagen! (No doubt a self-preserving decision.)

Later in 1982, the intensity of this dispute subsided considerably, from the time that Kopia-Kubuka became involved with others in the Marsupial Road War with Tea-Dena. Men from Kabika and Araim joined in side by side in the latter fight in September 1982. For all the time that there was talk of an imminent invasion of Kailge by the Tea-Dena, the talk of open warfare between the two Kopia factions completely disappeared. Perhaps emboldened by this, Silka began construction of his house in lower Kailge (see Map 3) and announced his intention to begin with the pig fence. There were arguments during this time which culminated in a major, very secretive night-time Araim Kopia meeting on January 2, 1983, at the house of our patron, Kopia\Kaja Yaya (who particularly wanted to fight, and whom Councillor Noma had trouble restraining).

During this time, there was also talk among the Araim Kopia of responding to the Kabika appropriation of lower Kailge not by fighting, but by moving to a block of land far to the east, in Melpa country; this had been offered to Kopia-Kubuka people by a Mt Hagen politician, who was just then running for national office.

The dispute dragged on until the end of our 1983 stay, by which time (November) there had been no resolution. Silka, voting with his feet (or higher parts), stayed on in his lower Kailge home. Councillor Noma remained equally determined to dislodge him, but by recourse to 'government law' rather than by fighting.

As the dispute settled down, Silka's son, widowed Michael, became interested in a young, then unmarried woman who was a dependant in the household of Kopia\Kaja Yaya's daughter. Yaya had been implacably opposed to Silka's land manoeuvres, but as a marriage was mooted between Michael and this woman, Yaya received pork from Silka's household and became on friendly or at least reasonable terms with him.

By the time of Alan Rumsey's return visit to Kailge in 1986, this dispute was said to have 'died'. Silka had built a second house for his family, next to the one the building of which had been contested in 1983, and six other Kabika men's houses had been built in the same area, which had been made into a *pena* ('display ground') within a stone's throw of the main Araim Kopia *pena* to the north (see Map 3). The area to the east and south-east of this *pena*, bounded by a fence on the south and the Ukulu River to the west (see map), was still used as a pig pasture, common to Araim Kopia and Kopia Kabika. This contravenes what is now said by the Araim Kopia to have been the plan of the Kabika in 1983 – to fence off this area on the north and plant sweet potatoes there. In that respect, the present disposition of the land is regarded by the Araim as a compromise, though this may be a post-hoc way of saving face, since we recorded no statement in 1983 to the effect that the Kabika intended to establish gardens in that area.

This incident seems consistent with standard anthropological wisdom concerning complementary opposition: unity of the *talapi* is a relative matter, and varies in inverse proportion to external pressure upon it (cf. Meggitt 1971). Thus whereas Araim Kopia had seemed to be moving towards inter-*talapi* warfare with Kabika in early 1982, after the external fighting with Tea-Dena in September, (and only then), Councillor Noma successfully persuaded other Araim to oppose the land appropriation by 'lawful' means, and people began seriously to consider the alternative of moving away.[14]

Where the received wisdom is here inadequate is that it does not tell us – apart from the facts of complementary opposition – what constitutes 'inside' versus 'outside', since we cannot assume the segmentary identities as given (by descent or anything else) in advance of the processes in which that opposition is manifest. Its difficulties in this respect will become clear in light of some further details concerning the relation between Kopia and a large, locally-resident population identified with a different *talapi*, Palimi.

3.2.4 Co-resident Palimi

As of 1986, there were 81 Palimi living in the greater Kailge area, who belong to four 'men's house' (*lku tapa*) groupings, as shown on Table 3–3.

Table 3–3: *Palimi segments resident at Kailge/Ibumuyl*

Palimi\Marapa	29
Palimi\Supub	10
Palimi\Kuluwu	35
Palimi\Yurupab	7
Total living	81

As their numbers might suggest, Palimi\Yurupab and \Supub are presently fairly insignificant in local territorial politics. The other two Palimi segments have up-and-coming young men and/or minor big-men; and were involved in land disputes with each other while we were at Kailge (see below).

Unlike Kopia, there is among the Kailge(/Ibumuyl)-area Palimi little correlation between the 'men's house' identities and patterns of residence or land use. Members of Palimi\Marapa and Palimi\Kuluwu live and work gardens interspersed with each other within a large pocket of land between the rivers Milya and Momola, in upper Ibumuyl (see Map 3), and at various other places within Kopia territory, on land identified with various Kopia segments, including Kupena, Tolab, Kaja, Kabika, and Galka. There is an interesting difference between the status of the Palimi claim on the land at Ibumuyl vs. the other areas: the latter are said to be Kopia land, on which Palimi people live and work on Kopia dispensation. This is true even of the holdings of Palimi Siki, a rising big-man, who is sometimes now said to be the *kolya pul* ('base man') of the area he occupies near Kailge. But this exception proves the rule, for, as we shall see, his claim is based on his status as a Kopia *abun-miyl* (matrifiliate). Indeed, his land is often spoken of specifically as Kopia*Kupena* land, in specific recognition of his maternal link to it.

By contrast, the upper Ibumuyl region is spoken of as Palimi land, pure and simple. A smaller region of lower Ibumuyl is occupied by Kopia\Kabika, but there is a well-established boundary between their land and the Palimi portion of Ibumuyl (see Map 3). Thus, a sizable group of recognized immigrants are now occupying a stretch of land on which the claim of the host *talapi* – Kopia and Kubuka – is said to have been permanently ceded, even though it is surrounded on all sides by Kopia and Kubuka land.[15] We know of no other case of this kind within the Ku Waru region (cf. section 3.1.5 above on the eventual segmentary assimilation of such immigrant pockets).

Palimi is a major exchange partner of Kubuka (see section 4.1). Individual Kopia and Kubuka view the co-resident Palimi as potential and actual exchange partners. In the most recent *makayl* payments of Kopia to Kubuka (ca. 1966, 1975), Palimi co-residents acted in concert with Araim Kopia. (See section 4.1.)

The Palimi trace their provenience to ancestral homelands (*por kolya,* 'arse place') within and beyond the Tambul range to the west of Kailge (including the named locales Takilya, Punya, Sijipai, Pokura, and Kulubi). Some Palimi say they came over to the Kopia side because of fighting, but not all explain the Palimi occupation of Kopia territory this way. Undoubtedly, better opportunties on the eastern side of the range have attracted them; but some men retain gardens and gardening rights in their home territories.

Palimi people seem to have got a foothold in Kopia territory from the time the Kopia returned to Kailge, following their rout by Tea-Dena and their valley-floor allies. Examples of particular Palimi links to Kopia land and people, on the basis of which they have rights in Kopia territory, follow.

Palimi\Kuluwu Noru says he moved to the Kailge area (he lives at Ibumuyl) at a time when there were already some Palimi established there. He married the sister of a Kopia\Tolab big-man. He says he still exercises land rights in his Palimi home area, making periodic trips there. He is emphatic that his children are Palimi, not Kopia. (One of his daughters is married to a Dena. As figures in section 4.2 show, there is little intermarriage between Kopia-Kubuka and Tea-Dena.)

While we were at Kailge, Kopia\Kaja Yaya had a Palimi *kedemadi yi* ('retainer') who helped him with garden work in return for lodging and shares in the returns. This man occasionally went off to paid plantation employment for weeks at a time. He also planted in his home area near Kulubi, returning there periodically. He generally came back from those visits home with Tambul-side specialties – cabbage, pandanus nuts – which he shared around our combined household compound. By 1986, he had returned to Kulubi: Yaya claimed that the two had 'grown tired' (*enebu turum*) of each other.

Kopia Yaya controlled a large amount of land in the lower Kailge area (along the Luip River) from the time of the Kopia return. It seems he came into control of all this partly because he is one of the few remaining Kopia\Kaja, who earlier claimed entitlements to lower Kailge, and partly because he was one of the first to return to the Kailge area after the Tea-Dena wars. He was a fierce fighter in his younger days, and is still a frequent advocate of fighting when others counsel different approaches to problems (see section 3.2.3). It is probably not surprising that much of his land is near the Kopia border, where even he thinks it would be somewhat risky to build a permanent house. Having large holdings and a small family (he married twice, but has no children of his own), he ceded use of a large area in lower Kailge to Palimi Yapo, partly in view of some promised *makayl* payments. Yapo died in 1981. His widow still lives in lower Kailge, his daughter having married a Kusika-Midipu man from near Palimung. During our stay at Kailge, Yapo's widow, a Sipaka woman from over the Tambul Range to the west, was engaged in a dispute over rights to coffee trees near her house. It is likely that encroachments upon her previously undisputed use rights arose because there was no longer a strong male in her household to ally himself fully with her interests. This is so partly because Palimi co-residents at Kailge, who had earlier supported her husband, were now beginning to think about the future disposition of Yapo's land.

Some of the land to which Yapo had gained rights was disputed between Palimi\Marapa and \Kuluwu. Besides Yapo, another now-deceased Palimi man, Ural, has sons (Aris, Winya) at Kailge who argued for their rights to the land. They are of the Palimi\Marapa segment. They were opposed by an aspiring or minor big-man of Palimi\Kuluwu, Lkuraya, who is a Kopia\Kupena *abu-n miyl* (i.e. 'woman-borne' or matrifiliate). His mother, Wakiyl, was a Kopia\Kupena woman, the sister of Old Nyiba, one of the Kopia who 'came up' and established early claims at Kailge (see section 3.2.1). Lkuraya gained rights to some of Nyiba's lands when the latter died in February 1982. But Nyiba has an adult son in Mt Hagen, who has recognized claims to a large share of it.

Overall, of the two Palimi factions, Lkuraya had greater sympathy from Araim Kopia people. He is considered by most people to have been more closely linked with Yapo during the latter's lifetime, working for him, contributing to his funeral, and later, it is said, looking after his widow.

Lkuraya has political aspirations (for example, he thought of running for Councillor while we were there), and wants to be seen to be judicious and equitable. After Palimi Yapo had died, he had extended an offer to Marapa that they and Kuluwu should jointly build a *tapa lku* ('men's house') on Yapo's land. At the end of a year, when no moves to act on this had come from Marapa, he said that he was withdrawing the offer. In a series of moots at Kailge in March 1982, it was decided that Yapo's holdings would go to Lkuraya, who, however, would pay an undetermined amount to Marapa. All decisions on particulars were complicated by the fact that during the period the moots were held, one of the Marapa men, Aris, got angry and kicked Lkuraya in the chest, creating even greater sympathy for him among Kopia and Kubuka participants. These advised Lkuraya to demand 300 kina compensation from Aris. Lkuraya (who did not appear badly hurt) had himself carried to the road and taken to the hospital at Mt Hagen. Upon his return he agreed to accept 50 kina from Aris.

What is especially relevant here is the way in which this intra-Palimi dispute got tied up with the intra-Kopia one (described in section 3.2.3) between \Kabika and Araim segments. In that dispute, Palimi\Marapa showed an initial inclination to side with Kopia\Kabika, and if the latter prevailed, expected to share in the division of lower Kailge with them. However, cooperation between Kabika and Palimi\Marapa was nipped in the bud by a fight between a Kabika principal, Silka, and a young Palimi(\Marapa) man. The young man, flush with coffee money and beer, approached Silka drunkenly at Kailge and began to joke and rough-house with him. Silka knocked him over, and in the fall the young Palimi\Marapa man lost two front teeth, and others were loosened. This initiated a period of confrontation and court action between the two men, unrelated to the land issue except in the sense that it put a stop to any cooperation between them.

Note the way in which different segments of Palimi initially became identified on opposite sides of the dispute between different sections of Kopia: Palimi\Kuluwu with Ariam Kopia and Palimi\Marapa with Kopia\Kabika. This would seem *not* to be predictable by the logic of complementary opposition, since we might thereby expect Palimi to relate to Kopia as a relative unity. What it shows is that the dimensions of sameness and difference which are relevant in the Nebilyer segmentary order are not entirely specified by the hierarchical structure of intra-*talapi* segmentation. Given the long history of association between Kopia-Kubuka and these particular Palimi segments, it is possible for them to become aligned in ways that cut across the boundaries of named *talapi*. It is under just such circumstances that the structuring of named segmentary categories may itself change so as to intercalate segments of a historically distinct *talapi* within another (cf. sections 3.1.5 and 3.2.1). This seems likely to happen here over the next generation or so, given what seems always to have happened in similar cases (ibid).

In any case, at a higher level, the logic of complementary opposition is still relevant for the present case. This is apparent from what became of *both* of these disputes in the face of external pressure from Tea-Dena. In the 1982 war, *all* Kopia segments and *all locally resident Palimi segments* opposed Tea-Dena (or sided with Kusika-Midipu-Epola-Alya-Lalka) as one, as same to different (see section 6.2.3). The fact that a relative difference within Palimi could become identified with a relative difference within Kopia, was entirely consistent with the identification of Palimi with Kopia *simpliciter* vis-à-vis other *talapi* (cf. Lederman 1986a on 'alignment').

3.3 CONCLUSION

In this chapter we have tried to provide some relevant details concerning segmentary-structural types (*talapi, lku tapa,* etc.), and particular tokens of them, which figure in the events to be examined in Chapters 6 and 7. Our viewpoint here (and in Chapter 4) has been largely of the traditional *post festum* variety, which, as we argued in section 1.1, provides a necessary, if provisional basis for the analysis of events. It is provisional in that it requires us to assume as a constant what we will later examine as a variable: the reproduction both of the types and of historically continuous tokens of them, in social action. Thus (in accord with Ku Waru people's ways of talking about these matters) we have freely indulged in formulations such as 'The Kopia-Kubuka fought against Tea-Dena', 'The Araim Kopia were adamant', 'Panguwu founded the Ukulupiyl segment of Kopia', etc. – formulations which beg as many questions as they answer. But, even while deferring most of those questions for later chapters, we hope to have established here that the segmentary identities invoked in formulations such as the above are not mere ideological obfuscations (as in

Sahlins 1965), or 'names' which 'simply outline a mode of creativity whose most serious aspect . . . is that of the exchange of wealth' (Wagner 1974:108). True, they are social creations rather than 'matters of fact' which could be specified on genealogical or on other *a priori* grounds (Sahlins 1965). And they do figure importantly in the exchange of wealth (itself a serious enough matter), as we shall see in the following chapter. But in the Nebilyer Valley[16] (as M. and A. Strathern have so fully and elegantly demonstrated for the neighboring Melpa), segmentary identities play a no less serious part in other aspects of social life, including warfare, residence, and the organization of economic production.

To say this is not merely to reassert the importance of 'the group' (or 'society') alongside the individual (cf. Gregory 1987), nor to revert to the assumption Feil attributes to Meggitt, that 'a person's behaviour and allegiance is [sic] . . . determined by his group membership and epiphenomenal of it' (Feil 1984:3). That would merely reproduce the same terms of debate which we rejected in section 1.2. Rather, our concern in this book is to open up the issue of social action in such a way as to reveal the problematical nature of actorhood in general. From this perspective, actors of whatever kind – person, group or what have you – cannot be taken for granted as 'empirically existing' units (Wagner 1974:106) or as theoretical primitives. They are hard won social constructions, which, if they are to exist at all, must exist at least in part as more or less contested 'representations'. That aspect of them will be explored at length in Chapters 5 to 9 below. For now it will suffice if we have established that *talapi*, even as semiotic constructions, are nonetheless of very real material consequence for Nebilyer social life.[17]

4. Ceremonial exchange and marriage in the western Nebilyer Valley

Having introduced the Ku Waru people and their ways of making segmentary social relationships, we turn now to some aspects of their social life which are partly consistent with that order of sociality and partly independent of it: ceremonial exchange and marriage. This will provide further necessary background for our analysis of events in Chapters 6 and 7, where we will explore some ways in which the significance of exchange transactions for these various dimensions of sociality is contested.

4.1 STRUCTURE AND HISTORY OF WESTERN NEBILYER CEREMONIAL EXCHANGE

New Guinea Highlanders are renowned for their elaborate systems of ceremonial exchange. The *moka* system of the Melpa people – eastern neighbors of the Nebilyer people – has been described in a monograph by Andrew Strathern (1971) and in many other publications by him and Marilyn Strathern. To the north-west, the *tee* system of the Enga has been described by Feil, Meggitt, and others (see section 1.2, references therein and below). In most respects, the ceremonial exchange practices of the Nebilyer, called *makayl*, resemble the Melpa *moka* more than the Enga *tee*. In the Nebilyer, all *makayl* (or *moka*) is claimed to have originated in claims for compensation arising out of warfare (cf. A. Strathern 1971:94ff. regarding the Melpa). Sometimes the parties between whom a *makayl* relation is established are ones who are said to have fought against each other. But in by far the majority of cases, they are parties who are said to have fought together as allies. Where the former is the case, the *makayl* transactions are talked about as a way of converting the relationship to an amiable one of wealth exchange. In either case, Nebilyer people, in common with the Melpa, see *makayl* as something which is transacted among people who are allies rather than enemies at the time of transaction. But this conversion (cf. M. Strathern 1985a) can go also in the other direction. That is, whether or not the transacting parties have been enemies in the past, Nebilyer people say that fighting is likely to result if *makayl* is not paid to whom it is owed: *naa tep molumul-kin olyo tongi* 'If we don't do it, they'll kill us'.

Furthermore, *makayl* is seen as being transacted among *talapi*, or among persons in their capacity as members of such groupings, just as are the acts of warfare from which it arises. We shall see in Chapters 6 and 7 that (as already suggested in section 1.2 above) in the practice of exchange, the question of who it is that is transacting is extremely complex and problematic, one which is hotly contested even at the moment of transaction. As we are here concerned with structural and historical description, we will begin by provisionally abstracting away these complexities, describing the transactions from that *post festum* viewpoint that allows us to say that a particular transaction took place between this or that *talapi*, or along this or that particular inter-personal 'road'. This is easiest to do when speaking of events in the remembered but distant past, as it is in close accord with the way in which the events are recounted by Ku Waru people themselves. That is, the battle of alternative constructions does have something like a determinant outcome in the way the past is made present in the political life of the people whose actions must presuppose it. The closer we get to the present in our attempts to tabulate exchange activities, the more patent the contestation becomes, and the more difficult it therefore becomes for the structural analyst to abstract away from it. Therefore, rather than just doing this, we also describe and exemplify some of the lived ambiguities that have to be suppressed in order to arrive at a synoptic, tabular account.

Once a *makayl* relationship is established, albeit arising out of warfare, the wealth exchanges themselves can continue indefinitely without further episodes of warfare. In theory (Nebilyer theory, that is), payments follow upon one another in orderly cycles, the phases of which are distinguished according to an imagery which harkens back to their putative origin in death compensation. These phases are as shown in Table 4–1, where unit A are those responsible for the death, and B is the unit of the slain.

Table 4-1: *Phases of a Nebilyer* makayl *exchange cycle*

Name of Payment	Direction
I. *kung pengi* 'pig's head' (sometimes also called *yi obil* 'man's bone' or *wanap ka* 'wanap vine'*)	B → A
II. *yi pengi* 'man's head'	A → B
III. *kung por* 'pig's hindquarter'	B → A

*Table note: In its strictest sense, the term *wanap ka* applies to an initial payment which is made in the same direction as the main payment (i.e., A → B), to placate the creditor(s) or aggrieved party in the interim (cf. A. Strathern 1971:95). In its more general sense it applies to any initiatory payment.

Phase I is an initiatory payment, which should be reciprocated with a much larger payment in Phase II, which is said to 'raise up the head' of those slain in battle (*Yi pengi apapa telymeli*). This is reciprocated by a much smaller payment in Phase III, typically of cooked pork.

This cycle of transactions resembles the Melpa *moka,* under comparable rubrics, as described by A. Strathern (1972), and the Enga *tee,* as in Feil (1984). In each of those exchange systems, there is a regular pattern whereby this entire cycle is later reciprocated in another two or three-phase cycle which reverses donor-recipient relations in each phase, i.e.

I. A → B
II. B → A
(III. A → B)

This may sometimes happen in the Ku Waru area as well, but the evidence for it was slight during the time of our fieldwork. For there at least, the connection between warfare and *makayl* was more than just a matter of 'dogma'. The only coordinated, inter-tribe payments in which the Kopia-Kubuka were involved during our fieldwork period in 1981–3 were actual warfare compensation payments, given for help in fighting rather than as returns of like for like. Both of the payments in question arose from the 1982 Marsupial Road War, and will be discussed extensively below (Chapters 6 and 7).

But those payments were not considered *makayl* (= Melpa *moka*). Why? Partly, it seems, because no one was killed. Hence the payments were quite small by *makayl* standards (only two or three thousand kina, or about US$2,500). Nor were they made as part of the usual three-phase cycle. We were told that if someone had been killed, the payments would have started immediately with a *wanap ka,* to be followed (presumably much later) by a *yi pengi* payment, much larger than the ones given.

But although these payments were not considered *makayl,* a striking fact about the Kopia-Kubuka in comparison to the usual Melpa and Enga pattern is that all of what they *do* consider to have been inter-*talapi makayl,* in which they have been involved within living memory, has arisen directly out of warfare. That is, the cycles of payments have not been made as returns in kind for an earlier payment cycle, but as compensation for deaths in warfare, incurred during the war between Kopia-Kubuka and Epola-Alya-Lalka-Kusika-Midipu-Tea-Dena-Jika-Kungunuka in about 1940 (as described in 3.2.2. section above). These will be discussed in the following section.

4.1.1 Kopia-Kubuka external exchange

All of the *makayl* in which Kopia has participated has involved only two pairs of *talapi*: Kopia-Kubuka, and Poika-Palimi[1], the latter having come to the aid of the former, and lost two men in the fighting (one from Palimi and one from Poika). As between Kopia and Kubuka, Kopia are identified as the *el pul* ('fight source/owner'), of that war. Accordingly, Kubuka made the first *yi pengi* payment to Palimi (after having received initiatory payments from them), and Kopia then made one to Kubuka. The first of these payments happened sometime in the late 1950s or early 60s, and the second sometime in the late 1960s. These payments both consisted almost entirely of pearl shells. Many years later, each of these payments was followed up by a payment of money and pigs. The Kopia-to-Kubuka follow-up payment was made in 1975, and the Kubuka-to-Palimi one in early 1981 (before our arrival at Kailge). The latter payment comprised about 25,000 kina (currently equal to about US$25,000), five pigs, and one cow. The Kopia payment to Kubuka included about 5,000 kina, and 160 pigs. The explanation we were given for these follow-up payments was that, in the interval between the first *yi pengi* payment (of kina shells) and this second one, the kina shell as a wealth item had become obsolete[2] and had been replaced by money. This meant that, in order to preserve the integrity of the *yi pengi* as a whole, money had to be given in addition to pigs or pearl shells or both.

The *yi pengi* payments by Kubuka were described to us as payments to Palimi rather than to the Poika-Palimi pair. In 1984, another *yi pengi* payment was made in that direction, this time by a single Kopia segment Kopia\Galka. This payment was also said to have arisen from the war of ca.1940. Unlike the previous payments, it was not said to have been made to the Palimi tribe, but to a segment of Poika – the Poika\Lopanuyl. They were given a total of approximately 100 pigs and 2,000 kina. One man from Palimi was also given approximately 100 kina.

After that, another Kopia segment – Kopia\Kabika – made a prestation to Palimi, totalling approximately 5,000 kina.

All of the *yi pengi* prestations described above are schematically summarized in Table 4–2.

Table 4–2: *Kopia-Kubuka external exchange transactions*

Direction of Payment		Items	Time
Kubuka	→ Palimi	mainly pearl shells	ca.1960
Kopia	→ Kubuka	mainly pearl shells	ca.1966
Kopia	→ Kubuka	pigs and money	1975
Kubuka	→ Palimi	mainly money	1981
Kopia\Galka	→ Poika\Lopanuyl	pigs and money	1984
Kopia\Kabika	→ Palimi	money	1985

A comparison between Table 4–2 and our discussion of the ca.1940 war in section 3.2.2. above, shows that the *makayl* payments take place in chain-like series of transactions which replicate, usually in reverse order, the series of acts of recruitment which brought all these tribes into the fighting on the same side. Of the three *talapi*, it was the Kopia who were identified as the original *el pul*, 'owners of the fight'. They then recruited the Kubuka, who recruited their (erstwhile) paired tribe, the Palimi (or Poika and Palimi, in some accounts). Accordingly, Palimi were first given shells by the Kubuka, and then Kubuka by Kopia. (The third and fourth transactions recapitulated the first and second in this respect, except in reverse temporal order.) A similar formal relation between acts of recruitment and chaining of compensation payments followed upon the 1982 war, as will be discussed below.

These enchained series of transactions are somewhat similar, albeit on a smaller scale, to what happens among the Melpa (A. Strathern 1971) and the Enga (Meggitt 1974, Feil 1984). Besides the difference in scale (Melpa chains have involved up to four links, Enga many more), the main difference is that these chains are all understood to arise directly out of chains of military recruitment.

In describing these exchanges so far, we have been treating them as 'inter-group' transactions. Unlike the Tombema Enga[3] that is one way in which *makayl* transactions are construed by Nebilyer people. But they are also simultaneously construed as transactions between persons or small cohorts, usually of close male kinsmen. That is, in *makayl* proper, the wealth items are not simply gathered together and given *en masse* by one group to another.[4] Rather, within the context of what is in principle a single, coordinated event, particular items are presented by particular individuals or small cohorts, to other individuals or small cohorts (usually of close male kinsmen in the recipient *talapi*).[5] For example, in the 1975 *makayl* payment by Kopia to Kubuka, the men of the Kopia\Tolab men's house gave to men in Kubuka, as shown in Table 4–3.

Table 4–3: *Kopia \Tolab contributions to the 1975* makayl *payment to Kubuka*

Nori, Kewa (F & S)	→ Laku	4 pigs,	K100
Noma	→ Ipupu & Unya (F & S)	9 pigs, cassowary	1
Kajipu, Don (F & S)	→ Kurupu & Tepra (F & S)	8 pigs	
Yapo	→ Ipupu	6 pigs,	K240
	→ Koimi	4 pigs,	K140
	→ Puku		K150
Pilya (Yapo's wife)	→ Kaulu		K140
	→ Wai	1 pig,	K40
Pangimi	→ Tamalu	5 pigs	
Owa, Esina (F & S)	→ Papa	1 tube of mambu oil	
	→ Ipupu	3 pigs	
Uwa, Mel (unrelated)	→ Tamalu	10 pigs	
	→ Tin	2 pigs	
	→ Karala	3 pigs	

As a part of this same prestation, a cow was purchased from funds contributed by all of the Tolab\Supub and given to Kubuka\Ping. It was then slaughtered and distributed by Unya, a leading Kubuka big-man.

Although they are useful for establishing that inter-*talapi* payments have an alternative identity as interpersonal payments, no single account such as that presented in Table 4–3 can be read as *the* authoritative account of which persons gave what to whom. What such accounts specify is the 'road' or 'way' (*kupulanum*) along which the goods moved. As to the precise identity of the givers and recipients, accounts often vary depending who is producing them and in what context. So as to hold context relatively constant, we have specified the transactions in Table 4–3 as in the account which was given to

Alan Rumsey on November 21, 1983, on a visit he made to the house of Nori, a frequent meeting place for men of the Kopia\Tolab segment. Besides Nori, those present included Owa, Kajipu, Yapo, Kewa, Nori, Uwa, Esina and Duni, all of whom are of Kopia\Tolab (and all but two of whom, it will be noted, are listed as donors on the table). But one of those not present, Pangimi, later gave a different account of his own transaction. He said that, yes, he had given six pigs, but only five of them to Tamalu. The sixth had gone to another Kubuka man, Dowa, (who, incidentally, has no known genealogical relation to Tamalu, and belongs to a different major segment of Kubuka). Another informant, Sirku, later said that Yapo had given ten pigs to Koimi. Sirku left Yapo's wife Pilya out of the list of donors.

What these examples seem to show (and they are in this respect typical of our interview data on exchange transactions) is that it is not only at the inter-*talapi* level of transactions that agency is problematic. It is also contested at the level of interpersonal transactions. The question of agency here is not one which could be settled simply by discovering the physical movement of goods on the day of the exchange event. For what from the outsider's viewpoint appear to be precisely the same movements may be construed in alternative ways, even under strictly 'interpersonal' descriptions. For instance, it may well be that Yapo handed over all ten of his pigs to Koimi, who then handed four to Ipupu. But whether he did that, or himself handed four to Koimi and six to Ipupu, the transaction could equally be 'represented' in either of the two ways attested above. The same goes for Pangimi's prestation to Tamalu and Dowa. Here again (as in the question of inter-*talapi* vs. interpersonal agency), the 'representation' is not something which can be considered apart from 'what's really going on' in the transaction (as in Meggitt and Feil in section 1.2): in large part, it *is* what is going on, and what makes the transaction one between particular persons as opposed to others.

It is here at the interpersonal level of transaction that women have at least a fighting chance (though against considerable odds) of being constructed as transactors. This is exemplified in Figure 4–3 by the separate place given to Pilya. This attribution was made by her own husband, Yapo, in the presence of his sub-clansmen, but in the absence of Pilya herself. Pilya is a woman who is highly regarded among the Kopia for her vigor, productivity and forceful *numan* ('will', 'consciousness'; cf. section 9.1). While all the while maintaining harmonious relations with the Kopia and with women who have married in from elsewhere, she has to a greater extent than most women, become identified as what we would call an independent operator. For instance, the extensive gardens which she works in lower Kailge are identified as *her* gardens rather than Yapo's, as is the house in which she lives (unlike most women's houses, regardless of how little time their husbands ever spend there). Pilya's is an exceptional case in that, though their major role in production is readily acknowledged, women do not *usually* achieve the status of acknowledged transactors, especially in inter-*talapi makayl* events, such as this one.[6]

Note that, even on this plane of interpersonal exchange, not all the transactors are individuals. In this case, only half of the donor parties were (four out of eight). The other four were pairs of people, three of them father-son pairs and one of unrelated men. Two of the fourteen recipients also comprised pairs of men (both of them father-son pairs), rather than individuals.

Unlike the relation between inter-*talapi* and interpersonal payments, these payments by pairs of people cannot be seen as consisting of discrete portions each identified with one of the individuals in the pair. It is not the case, for example, that Kajipu and Don's payment consisted of x number of pigs given by Kajipu and (8-x) by Don. Rather, both of them were equally identified with the entire payment of eight pigs. Similarly, the recipient pairs were identified as recipients-in-common rather than joint recipients; so that, for instance, Kurupu and Tepra were not seen as having been given x and (8–x) pigs respectively. It may well have been the case that, subsequent to the transaction in question, the two of them divided up the pigs in such a way. (More likely they were distributed to other people as well, each of whom had claims on them arising from other transactions.) But that division would not have been seen as a part of this *makayl* per se. As far as Kajipu and Don were concerned, they gave the pigs to Kurupu and Tepra.

Makayl transaction by 'consortia' is not at all uncommon among Nebilyer people.[7] In order to provide a sample of greater statistical significance than Table 4–3 (which concerns only one segment of the Kopia tribe), we have tabulated the proportion of donor consortia vs. individuals said to have participated in the 1981 payment to Kubuka to Palimi (cf. also Table 4–4 below). These are as follows: 25 individual donors, 6 two-member donor consortia, 2 three-member consortia. Of the 6 two-member consortia, we know three to be father-son pairs. (We are unable to say whether or how the other three are related to each other.) Of the three-member consortia, one consists of a father and his two sons, and the other consists of a father-son pair plus a man from the same *talapi* segment (Kubuka\Kuduyl), with no known genealogical link to either of them. (It is perhaps relevant to note that the latter is a man who has no siblings or children.)

The frequent presence of these consortia as *makayl* transactors shows once again that we should not think of the difference between inter-*talapi* transaction and interpersonal transaction as one between spheres of activity which involve *corporate groups* and *individuals* respectively. If there were any candidate here for 'corporate group' status, a better case could probably be made for the donor-consortium than for the *talapi*, since the former pools its resources into a common fund, whereas the latter does not (cf.fn.11, Chapter 1). But we find it unhelpful to think of either of these kinds of exchange agents as 'corporate', or to formulate the difference between them as essentially one of group vs. individual. For, in addition to the objection we have developed above (i.e., that neither kind of transaction involves *only* individual donors and recipients), we want to avoid the kind of reification to which the group/individual antinomy too easily leads: exchange agents do not enter into transactions in preconstituted form, as do biological organisms. Rather, as we hope to show below (Chapters 6 and 7), they are socially constructed in those very transactions.

As in the Melpa *moka*, many *makayl* transactions are between men who are closely related, either as affines or as matrilateral kinsmen. For instance, in the Kopia\Kabika-to-Palimi *yi pengi* prestation mentioned above, six of the ten interpersonal transactions which it comprised took place along roads defined in those ways. Four of these were between individuals, in (recipient-to-donor) relationships as follows: WB, BWB, ZH, FZD. Two more were along roads defined by classificatory matrilateral links which could not be genealogically specified, but were based upon the fact that the two recipients' mother was a Kopia\Kabika woman. (Both of these payments were by consortia, of five and eight people respectively.) The four other payments which made up this *yi pengi* (two of which were also by consortia) went to Palimi men to whom no matrilateral or affinal connections were claimed by any of the donors. Interestingly, the recipients of these payments were all among the Palimi people who live with the Kopia-Kubuka, at Ibumuyl or lower Kailge (cf. section 3.2.4.).[8]

The nature of relationships among donors and recipients is further illustrated by Table 4–4, which lists the individual transactions which went into the Kopia\Galka-to-Poika Lopanuyl payment listed above.

Table 4–4: *Kopia\Galka to Poika\Lopanuyl* Yi Pengi *payment, 1984*

Donor	Items	Recipient	Recipient's Relationship to Donor
Kupena	10 pigs, K200	Tidi, Puje (brothers)	½BDHB
Pigin	10 pigs, K100	Kudi	DH
Yaba	10 pigs, K200	Kudi	ZH
Sirku	10 pigs, K300	Kudi	'D'HZH
Sirku }	1 cow (purchase-jointly	Kudi	'D'HZH
Yaba }	at K250 each)		ZH
Yaba	3 pigs, K400	Ako ('F' of Tidi/Puje)	ZH'F'
Sirku	3 pigs, K500	Ako	'D'HZH'F'
Pigin	1 pig, K100	Ako	DHF
Kupena	K100	Ako	½BDHF
Kapu	10 pigs, K400	Nonongu	DH
Pangimi	10 pigs, K500	Nonongu	ZH
Ipsa }	K100	Nonongu	F½BDH
Kani }	10 pigs K100	Nonongu	F½BDH
Kiyl }	K100	Nonongu	?
Parlt	K50	Nonongu	H
Kapupu	1 pig, K100	Kudi	none
Pengakuyl	20 pigs	Kudi	none
Pengakuyl	10 pigs	Tidi	none
Kakuyl	4 pigs	Kudi	none

Table note: Yaba's wife is the daughter of a clan 'sister' of Sirku's wife, making her his classificatory daughter.

Several things about this prestation are worthy of note. First, the relationships involved are entirely affinal rather than matrilateral. Second, note that although the payment was described as one to the Poika\Lopanuyl men's house, only five men from that men's house were singled out as recipients. The links to all those men were established by the marriage of three of them to Kopia\Galka women, as shown on the genealogical fragments in Figure 4–1.

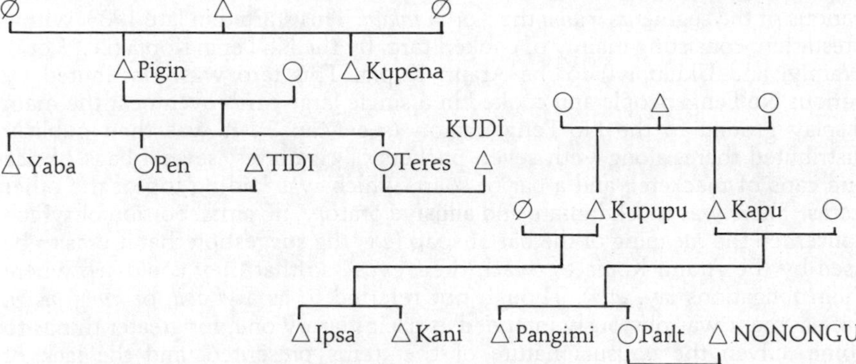

Figure note: Kopia names, lower case; Poika names, capitals

Figure 4–1: *Some marriages between Kopia \Galka and Poika \Lopanuyl*

These genealogies show the close affinal links between nine of the donors listed in Table 4–4 and four out of the five Poika recipients. Interestingly, the man who was credited with the major role in organizing and bringing off this *makayl* was not one of the eight donors with first-degree affinal relationships to Poika, but Kupena, whose connection to his Poika partners is through his half-brother's daughters. Notwithstanding the relative indirectness of this link, the entire prestation was in some contexts described as having been made by Kupena. As the leading big-man of the Kopia\Galka *lku tapa* ('men's house'), he was the one who was understood to have coordinated their exchange activities in such a way as to allow them *as a lku tapa* to take advantage of the road provided by the marriages of three of their women into a single Poika sub-clan.[9] This was no mean feat, given the fact that no segments of Poika as such had been involved in any of the inter-*talapi makayl* conducted by the Kopia and/or Kubuka within living memory.

As mentioned above, all of that *makayl* has been seen as arising out of the war of ca.1940, in which men from Poika and Palimi died when fighting on the side of the Kopia-Kubuka. For whatever reason, the previous *yi pengi* payments by Kubuka had been constructed as payments to Palimi alone.[10] Likewise, the *yi obil* initiatory payment which had bound the Kubuka to making those main payments was at first described to us as a payment by Palimi to Kubuka. But for purposes of this 1984 *yi pengi* payment by Kopia\Galka, that same *yi obil* had been re-interpreted as a payment by Palimi *and* Poika, to Kubuka *and* Kopia, thereby obligating the Kopia to follow up on Kubuka's earlier payments to Palimi. This is what the Kopia\Galka claimed to be doing, primarily by transacting with a Poika segment, but also by making, on the same day, a large cash payment to a Palimi man, Kalya, who lives with them at Kailge,[11] where he used the money to build and stock a trade store. Contributions were made to this payment by twelve men from Kopia\Galka.

4.1.2 Internal Kopia exchange

Perhaps the most significant new development in *makayl* exchange among the Kopia in the last few years has been the commencement of exchange among various of the segments *within* the Kopia *talapi*. This started in late 1983, with a prestation, consisting mainly of cooked taro, by the No Pengi Kopia (i.e., Kopil, Waipiyl and Ukulupiyl) to the Araim Kopia. This taro was contributed by various No Pengi people and cooked in a single large earth oven near the main display ground in the No Pengi region (see Map 3); it was then publicly distributed there, along with seven packets of cigarettes, several bags of rice and cans of mackerel, and a bar of soap, which was laid on top of the other items. There was much fanfare and allusive oratory, no small portion of which concerned the meaning of the bar of soap (e.g. the suggestion that it was to be used by the Araim Kopia to 'wash their eyes', so that they could see where their obligations lay, etc.). Though not referred to as a *yi obil*, or *kung pengi*, the payment was obviously intended as an initiatory one, for greater things to come. Given the unusual nature of the items presented, and the lack of precedent for internal Kopia exchange, there was even more excitement and speculation than usual about what the return might be, and when it would be given. In strictly confidential discussions among lower Kopia people, such unorthodox exchange items as winged beans or red pandanus were proposed as return gifts. In the event, money was given, in 1984, totalling approximately 1,500 kina. This money was contributed by nearly every adult Araim Kopia male (plus some of their wives and one man from Kubuka). It went mainly to eight men in the recipient segments, who then broke it down into smaller payments to others.

When Alan Rumsey revisited Kailge in January 1986, there was talk of two further prestations among Kopia segments. First, the gift of money by the Araim Kopia was to be followed up with another one from Kopia\Galka and \Kabika, also to the 'headwater' segments, \Kopil and \Ukulupiyl. Then the latter were to make a prestation of live pigs to the Araim Kopia. It was not clear whether this was to be seen as a direct reciprocation of the 1984 cash payment, or as the beginning of a second series of transactions in pigs. For, although both payments are explained as having arisen from the ca.1940 war, they are justified with reference to separate incidents in that war, one of which indebted the No Pengi to the Araim, and the other of which created a debt in the opposite direction.

4.1.3 Conclusions concerning Kopia exchange

To conclude this discussion of exchange structures and history, let us consider some possible inter-relationships among (post-1980) developments described above. Returning to Table 4–2, note first the fact that, after 1981, the *makayl* transactions became less and less related in form to the acts of military recruitment from which the entire sequence is said to have arisen. Instead of 'Kopia' transacting as a *talapi* with their immediate recruits, Kubuka, upper Kopia segments began transacting directly with *talapi* (or segments of them) which, having been at the other end of the chain of recruitment, had previously been at the other end of the chain of prestations. Then segments from upper and lower Kopia began exchanging with each other for the first time. The latter transactions were still said to have arisen out of the ca.1940 war, but many people were vague on exactly how. Noma, the leading big-man from Araim Kopia, justified them with reference to some very specific incidents in that war, but many others (including some men as old as he) were unaware of those incidents, or of any other specific ones as the basis of these exchanges. In general, for both the last phases of the Kopia-to-Poika-Palimi *makayl* and this new Kopia-internal exchange, the connection with particular acts of recruitment and deaths in warfare has grown increasingly tenuous, as memories fade and the number of people with direct experience of those incidents dwindles.

Under these circumstances, new possibilities arise for the construction of exchange relationships: for example, the one between Kopia\Galka and Poika \Lopanuyl, where the relationship could be seen to have been based more immediately upon intermarriage than military alliance. At a more inclusive level, the current prospects for *makayl* relationships involving Kopia *qua talapi* are based ever less directly upon the ca.1940 war, and more upon emergent marriage patterns which now align Kopia in a quite different direction, towards the Laulku to the west (as we shall see in section 4.2 below). Such are the new structural and historical grounds upon which some of the most remarkable performances of Chapters 6 and 7 will be played out.

4.2 NEBILYER MARRIAGE, EXCHANGE AND SEGMENTARY POLITICS IN COMPARATIVE PERSPECTIVE

Marriages create the *kupulanum* ('roads') which establish important connections with people socially more distant than one's own kin, and who belong to different *talapi* (at some level of inclusion) from one's own. In establishing links between sets of people who are *ipso facto* regarded as different from each other, Nebilyer marriage is a critical locus of the definition – and especially for women, partial transformation – of loyalties to kin and one's own segmentary affiliations, as in-laws and loyalties acquired through marriage take on importance.

Marilyn Strathern's (1972a) study of Hagen marriage established a benchmark, making explicit most of the terms within which the discussion of marriage in the western Highlands has subsequently proceeded. Her image of the Hagen woman – as 'in between', active intermediary between her natal group and that of her husband – simultaneously evokes most of the book's main themes: the contrasting nature of women's and men's roles and loyalties, both in respect to marriage as a central aspect of domestic organization and of wider inter-group organization at different levels; the basis for the differential evaluation of those roles, in the generic identification of women with production, men with transaction, in the cooperative orientation towards provisioning the household as well as creating the social and material basis for wider exchange; the implications of the significant extent to which women derive prestige from dimensions of their 'in betweenness' for their civil status in Hagen society, and the particular character, including modes of its contestation, of female autonomy here.

In the last ten years or so, the Highlands literature has participated in the rapid expansion of ethnography which takes women's life as a central focus (e.g. Feil 1978b, 1981, 1984, Josephides 1985, Lederman 1986). Feil (1984) argues for Tombema Enga (and implicitly, for other parts of the Highlands as well) that characterization of women's role as intermediary circumscribes it too narrowly. In his view of Tombema Enga, links through females (especially those directly established by marriage) are the structural basis of *tee* exchange, and this leads him to define women's position, in some senses at least, as 'pivotal' (Feil 1984:109). However – and leaving aside for the moment important differences between Enga and Hagen/Nebilyer social arrangements to which we return below – he moves, for our present purposes, too easily from description of some organizational aspects of exchange to characterization of women's position. The terms in which we might understand the relation between the structural arrangements of exchange partnerships, and their evaluation within the Tombema social configuration are little explored.

More recently, Josephides (1985) has taken a view of women's position among the Kewa of the Southern Highlands (see Map 1), an area which differs ethnographically from both Enga and Hagen. But her account makes less of such differences than might be expected. It seems likely that her theoretical stance lends itself to emphasis of similarities in social process, rather than differences, across these Highlands regions. For she argues that Kewa ceremonial transaction is a moment of social mystification, sufficiently grandiose in its realization to mask the fact of women's productive contribution. Ceremonial exchange, in other words, is a moment in which the exploitation of women is consummated, but in a way that remains unexposed or at least incompletely recognized because of the attribution to it of enormous social value. While one might take a similar view of Hagen *moka* ceremonial exchange, M. Strathern's depiction of the definition of women's loyalties and sense of interests within the larger social processes that shape their 'in betweenness' gives her Hagen study a subtlety concerning the social formation of female agency with which Josephides' flatter view of exploitation cannot compare.

Contrasting in some respects with all of these is Lederman's (1986a) study of exchange in Mendi (Southern Highlands: see Map 1). From her depiction of two contrasting and sometimes competing dimensions of exchange, group-centered *sem* vs. affinally-based *twem* transactions, we learn much about women's roles; in particular, we see how women as social persons are primarily constituted as sources or conduits of wealth in respect to the first dimension, but have a much broader role in the second, including a major part to play as transactors in networks linking kin and affines. These two dimensions, though they are not neatly distinguishable as two separate spheres of activity, nevertheless in Mendi seem to be fairly highly differentiated and institutionalized as ideal types. Lederman's account of women's different relation to them suggests the question of the extent to which women's participation in exchange may be explicitly recognized as such *in some contexts* elsewhere in the Highlands, but muted or suppressed on other occasions. We consider that such a distinction is applicable to the attribution of agency in Nebilyer exchange (section 4.1.1). Though Lederman overall ventures a less rounded interpretation of women's roles than does Strathern (1972a), here as in *Women in Between* we are presented with a broad portrayal of the conditions which shape them.

Our discussion of Nebilyer marriage is by no means a full ethnography of the subject, but is intended to illustrate important congruities between marriage and other aspects of wider political organization, especially inter-*talapi* alliance and large-scale exchange relations. It is important to the understanding of comparative Highlands marriage and gender relations to move descriptively and analytically back and forth between discussion of marriage as the central form of domestic organization, and its relation to other structural arrangements. In this vein, we find that a highly significant aspect of Nebilyer marriage is a particular, reproduced trend towards congruence with these other aspects of the socio-political order. The resulting configuration differs from neighboring areas of the Highlands, as we shall briefly illustrate by comparison with Enga. As a result, and even though each marriage generates its own relatively particular sets of linking ties, Nebilyer marriage is a significant index and aspect of higher-level socio-political relations. In attempting to piece together the history of *talapi*, tribes and tribe-pairs such as Kopia-Kubuka, as well as regional marriage patterns over time which involve many *talapi*, the patterning of marriage is an important dimension of political relationships and their re-alignment. For that reason, besides describing the place of marriage in the overall western Nebilyer inter-*talapi* configuration now, we will show in some detail the relation of changing marriage patterns to the consolidation over the last six or seven decades of Kopia as a *talapi*, and Kopia-Kubuka as a tribe pair in their present location.

The discussion will also point to an apparently emergent feature of regional marriage patterning: a developing difference between marriage patterns for men and women (i.e., the sources of spouses for each sex), those for men tending to coincide more strongly with established political alliances with people on the other side of the Tambul Range, and those for women showing increasing directionality downslope, away from the Tambul Range *talapi*, which are the focus of established Kopia-Kubuka political alliances, and towards the central Nebilyer Valley and Mt Hagen town, where seasonal access to cash from coffee sales, and development in general, tends to be greater than either on the western Nebilyer fringe or over the Tambul Range. This aspect of marriage patterning shows that it is subject to major involvement as a dimension of new socio-economic and political relations (see section 2.3). This is so particularly because traditional emphases on bridewealth and the valuation of women partly in terms of wealth transactions remain strong, seemingly not directly diminished by ongoing changes in the inventory of wealth items, including the increasing emphasis upon cash.

Though most of this section describes how marriage is a dimension of the broader socio-political order, we first give some brief discussion of its implications for domestic organization. (For much greater detail see M. Strathern 1972a.)

Wives in the Nebilyer, as in Hagen, usually go to their husband's place to live, but there is also a strong preference for virilocality on the part of men who, with respect to the local *talapi*, are *abu-n miyl* (matrifiliates, see section 3.1.5, also A. Strathern 1972:18). At Kailge, there were 26 *abu-n miyl* men and women (of 443 living Kopia, or 5.86%), and these were concentrated in particular sub-segments: 9 in Kopia\Galka; 12 in one particular sub-sub-segment of Kabika, Kopia\Kabika\Elpukub; and 5 in one sub-sub-segment of Kopil, Kopia\Kopil

\Teab. Men in this position are considered to have strong land rights on the basis of the maternal tie, and we saw no evidence that children of such unions were disadvantaged. This accords with the rapid 'conversion' of the status of co-resident matrifiliates into one equivalent to people whose affiliation is based upon a paternal tie (see section 3.1.5.), a situation widely reported for many parts of the central Highlands (see A. Strathern 1971:19–20 for an indigenous view of the sister's son's position).

At Kailge, such rapid conversion appeared to apply to Kopia matrifiliates, but less immediately or clearly to those few co-resident Palimi men (of whom there were 7, also 4 women) who had maternal links to Kopia. Discussion with a few of these men as well as other (Kailge-resident, but *yiyl-n miyl* 'patrifiliated') Palimi men, indicated that they strongly identified themselves and their children as Palimi (cf. section 3.2.4.).

Normative virilocality has for girls and women the consequence that, if the marriage endures, they will remain indefinitely in the husband's territory, though perhaps with frequent visits home. First residence for a young married woman is usually with her mother-in law, in the latter's house, under the arrangement that the girl be assigned garden plots to work by her husband's family. But the young groom continues to live for a time wherever he was accustomed to before the bride's arrival. (Often this means continuing to sleep and eat in several different locales as he may have done when a bachelor, for young men and boys are highly mobile in this respect; but some time after marriage a young man is expected to show signs of settling down.)

All these arrangements are coded in the terms in which people normally speak about marriage, differentiating male and female perspectives. A man is said to *lyi-* 'take' a wife (and this image applies over the duration of the marriage, so that a man is said to 'take' a wife of such-and-such *talapi*, or 'take' two wives, expressed with the habitual form of the verb, for which see Appendix B 3.2.3, and conveying the English sense 'has'). A woman, on the other hand, is said to 'go' in marriage, and indeed a usually observed feature of marriage negotiations – providing they get that far — is a question posed to the intended bride by one of the negotiators of her party, 'Will you go?' The image of going, as in the case of men's 'taking', rendered in the habitual verb-form, is used in a durative sense: 'she "goes" to a Kopia man', i.e., 'is married to' a Kopia. As M. Strathern (1972a:88) notes, people recognize that to force a girl into marriage may be useless, since by non-cooperation she may frustrate the arrangement. Thus a public declaration of her intention is sought, while the intended groom does not have a public role to play at the negotiations, but instead is expected to be embarrassed and perhaps not to appear at all. (However, as in one case we knew well, the groom did not wish to marry the girl chosen by his family and in the end, after some months during which he nevertheless sought her out for sex, succeeded in exhausting the patience of the girl and her family, and sabotaged the marriage.)

With the bride's relocation in her husband's home area, the groom is said to 'go' to the bride at night, and in the beginning this is expected to be furtive. After a few months or a year, and especially when she is expecting a child, the husband and his kin should build his wife a house considered to be her own. At Kailge there were very few married couples who cohabited openly. Generally, a woman and her young children live in her *abu lku* ('woman's house'), while her husband and perhaps older sons and other men are the regular occupants of his *tapa lku* ('men's house') (cf. section 3.1.2). Here as elsewhere in the Highlands, people consider it odd and remarkable for husbands and wives to spend too much leisure time in each other's exclusive company; and in our experience, both young and old married people tend to reproduce (at least, for public consumption) somewhat sex-specific notions of preference for companionship with members of one's own sex; e.g. 'women are bad, dirty, don't understand' etc., vs. 'we don't pay attention to what the men do, we women have our own affairs and stick together', and so forth.

Bridewealth is still ideally, and usually in fact, a condition of successful establishment of a lasting marriage. In 1981–83, when asked what bridewealth for a young girl ought to consist of, people gave remarkably similar notional amounts: ideally, at least twenty pigs or so, 1,000–2,000 kina, and at least one cassowary. But we found that, even for first marriages, actual transactions we observed or otherwise could document reliably rarely matched these expectations; and in the case of subsequent women's marriages, amounts negotiated were quite variable, and in some cases quite small.

Table 4–5 summarizes bridewealth offers and/or payments for which we were able to obtain reliable information. In relation to such figures, it is worth noting the following caveat: in any given marriage negotiation, the parties (especially the bride's) would like to establish what the payment will ultimately amount to (or at least a minimum), but usually not all of this is handed over initially. Hence in the table, figures listed as offers probably serve simply to give some indication of what people consider a possible opening position in particular marriage negotiations. Actual payments are what we saw being handed over, or what we established by interview to have been handed over (though it is sometimes difficult to consider this a hard datum since reports and attributions of particular contributions may vary).

Thus, in case 15, eight pigs were tethered and changed hands at a negotiating session held in the early weeks of the bride's residence at Kailge (with her mother-in-law, and intermittently also, with her husband's brother's wife). While a modest number, it was considered respectable. But only 260 kina of an anticipated much larger amount actually was handed over to her kin at this session on the Kailge display ground. As often occurs, the groom's negotiators made an undertaking that more would be given in the coffee season. Though girls do 'go' in marriage on a (partly) promissory basis of this kind (especially if they are keen on the prospective groom), it seems nevertheless to be an important parental consideration that some pigs and some money be handed over early on. This is a combined matter of appearances and of a strong sense of appropriate material return on the part of those who, over time, contributed to the bride's family on her behalf: they do not want to be seen to be sent away with little or nothing to show. But there is another consideration relating to the often promissory nature of cash payment. As people say in the hard-driving marriage negotiations: in coffee time we will all have money. The implication is, it would be desirable to have some now, during times of cash scarcity.

In case 11, at a late stage of negotiations the groom's people handed over only thirteen pigs, and no cash: an over-supply of pigs to feed was one of the reasons the groom's father, privately, had been strongly urging the marriage, as he saw an opportunity to make what he regarded as a favorable affinal

Table 4–5: *Bridewealth offers and payments*

Offer=O Payment=P	Reported=R Witnessed=W	Description of proposed marriage	Valuables offered/given Pigs	Kina	Cassowary	Other	Outcome
1.O	R	first marriage of young girl	16	600	2	—	girl refuses
2.P	R	second marriage of woman, no children	4	100	—	—	marriage entered into
3.O	R	second marriage of woman reporting, to coastal man	—	—	—	2 cows	bridewealth not given, woman leaves
4.O	R by mother of girl	first marriage of young woman	30	1000	2	—	girl refuses saying suitor is too old
5.P	R by mother of bride	first marriage of woman, about 1972/3	—	500	—	22 kina shells	marriage entered into, ongoing
6.O	R by intending groom	man wants to take second wife, not her first marriage	8	400	—	—	marriage not contracted
7.O	W	court case against man living with woman as second wife (not her first marriage), no bridewealth yet paid	—	500	—	—	parents sought 1000 kina, man offered 500, father eventually removes girl
8.P	W	first marriage of young woman	18	?	—	—	money expected; bride's relatives expected to return 6 pigs
9.P	W	young woman's third attempt at marriage; first two no bride-wealth changed hands	10	?	—	—	money expected later; bride's relatives return 4 pigs

10. P	R	young girl's first marriage	?	400	—	—	pigs and 600 kina expected; bride's relatives return 1 cassowary, 3 piglets
11. P	W	young girl's first marriage	13	—	—	—	2 cassowaries and up to 1000 kina promised. Bride's kin return 5 pigs, and her uncle gives groom's kin 200 kina and 1 cassowary
12. P	W	young woman's second attempt at marriage	—	750	—	—	pigs promised but number to be determined
13. P	W	former married woman, 2 children, reputed to be 'loose', goes to local widower	—	50	—	cooked pork	marriage lasts only a few months, woman returns to parental home
14. 0	R	first marriage of bride and groom	12	300	—	—	more money promised. Bride's relatives reject offer
15. P	W	first marriage of bride and groom	8	260	—	—	more money promised. Bride wishes to marry, refuses to leave intending groom's place
16. ?	W	first marriage for both	—	—	—	—	girl stays at man's place without bridewealth, her parents demand payment but no settlement reached

*Table note: W (witnessed) indicates that one or both of the authors observed transaction of valuables connection at a time he had a fair number of animals on his hands. The bride's uncle scored a competitive advantage at this session by being able to distribute as part of the return payment a total of 200 kina to the groom's party, of course in the hopes of establishing a sense of obligation for a large cash payment later. He also gave a cassowary, for which he had allegedly given cash. He was able to do this because he was employed in Port Moresby, and had more regular access to cash than his Nebilyer-dwelling relatives, who nonetheless were considered people of some means.

Thus, ready cash may confer certain kinds of tactical advantage in marriage arrangements. One mother who had received a very handsome notional offer from a reputedly well-to-do man for her daughter, who did not like the suitor, said she would not force matters unless the man appeared with cash in hand – in which case, she would try to get the girl to reconsider. But whether negotiations are brought to completion also depends very much on other factors besides the availability of cash, including the bride's stated intention. And a modest amount of cash, even if offered outside of coffee season, is often not sufficient to advance negotiations. For instance, in case 14 the groom's family offered 300 kina (and a number of pigs, although since this was simply notional, and the pigs were not tethered to be seen, it was difficult to establish a firm figure). The offer was refused out of hand.

An important aspect of the cash supply at present in the Nebilyer Valley is that it tends to be only seasonally available, and to nearly everyone at around the same time. Its valuation as a wealth object is thus also somewhat situational – its availability may confer greater advantage at certain times rather than others. It is evident that kin and perhaps the intended bride herself may be inclined to regard with favor prospective grooms with salaried employment, such as policemen or teachers, because of the promise this offers of a more affluent life-style. Such marriages, however, often entail a perceived disadvantage, that the couple will live away from close kin; and another that perhaps becomes clearer over time, that a salaried job often must be pursued under living conditions that actually require a cash income for subsistence, so that its expenditure cannot therefore be as discretionary as it may be in many households that are fully rurally-based.

The knowledge that a substantial bridewealth is being given for her is important to a young bride's self-esteem. M. Strathern (1972a:Preface) cites the case of a bride who refused to leave her husband despite pressure from her kin for her to do so in order that they might make higher demands. In that case, the bride was praised by her in-laws for having come 'inside', i.e., identified herself with them and their interests. As Strathern (ibid) notes, a woman is seen as 'having loyalties to distribute'. In a case which illustrates this general proposition, but differs from Strathern's particular example, we visited regularly with a family, of which an attractive, competent and desirable young woman refused several substantial marriage offers to go instead to a young man whom she preferred. His kin gave one cassowary, three piglets, and only 400 kina initially, but promised a total of at least 1,000 kina. After a time the bride became dissatisfied with the delay in additional cash payment, and encouraged by her eldest brother, who was then attempting to amass bridewealth for his own marriage, she returned home for a while, and a flurry of further negotiations rapidly followed. Here the bride was seen to show her loyalty to her own kin, especially as it was clear she liked her husband and wanted to stay with him.

High bridewealth payments create expectations of substantial future exchanges and material assistance among affines. But though the payment of *ab kuime* ('bridewealth') may be protracted, and may thus be difficult to reckon entirely separately from other, subsequent affinal exchanges, nevertheless in the western Nebilyer bridewealth is conceptually and transactionally quite distinct from large-scale *makayl*. Below we shall see that this differs considerably from the Enga situation, where the large *tee* cycles tend to subsume bridewealth and other wealth transactions.

Now let us turn to the intersection of marriage with two interrelated aspects of regional socio-politics, inter-*talapi* military-political relations, and the internal re-alignment and consolidation of segmentary identities over time.

Melpa marriage is summarized by M. Strathern (1972a) as a cross – and a partial contradiction – between the heavy constraints which enmity here places on marriage, and a fairly extensive set of prohibitions, most of which operate at lower and medium segmentary levels to disallow marriage with consanguines and even quite a large range of relatives by marriage.

Among other effects, these prohibitions bar direct woman-for-woman exchange, and probably also reduce the partial complementarity of marriage and cross-sex siblingship, such as is found e.g. in Kuma (Reay 1959), where a wife may in some respects be seen to replace a sister. Though it is a common enough Melpa and Nebilyer strategy to marry off a daughter with the intention of using her bridewealth to gain a wife for a son, nevertheless lower-level segmentary units cannot exchange women directly with other units of comparable order. Thus, although there is some preference for marrying where ties already exist, the notion of 'exchange marriage' (Strathern 1972a:72–7) is a notional generalization of this preference, summing up an existing situation of marriages between segmentary identities, generally stated at high segmentary levels, and limited by what we have referred to as marriage prohibitions.

These prohibitions do actually result in dispersal of marriages, within varying limits. Within larger northern Melpa 'tribes', M. Strathern found rates of intra-tribal marriages ranging up to 50% of unions. As discussed in section 3.1.3, the size of Hagen/Nebilyer 'tribes' is highly variable, and endogamy rates generally vary accordingly. But there are exceptions: in the Ku Waru area at least, some smaller tribes have higher endogamy rates than larger neighbors. Such variation comes about depending upon historico-political relations. If, for example, neighboring *talapi* are hostile, there is correspondingly little intermarriage with them, and endogamous marriage may then be more frequent than might be expected. Lower-level prohibitions are observed (e.g. that intermarriage between men's house units, *lku tapa*, should not be reduplicated); but in practice, particular formulations of segmentary identity and kin relations (e.g. the claim that two women come from 'different fathers' within a particular 'line', and therefore marriages may be contracted with both by different men) gives a limited degree of flexibility.

Upper and lower Kopia sub-divisions differ significantly as to where male members find wives. As Table 4–6 shows, Wiyal (upper) Kopia men currently sustain 31 marriages in the Tambul and westerly *talapi* over the range (in rank order): Laulku (11), Poika (8), Kanyiba (4), Mujika (4), and Palimi (4). Araim (lower) men likewise have married more Laulku wives than women of any other single tribal-level identity (5 marriages), as have also Kubuka men (13). But for Araim Kopia, the next three most frequently-married *talapi* are Kulka of the Nebilyer Valley floor, and Epola and Lalka, who are close neighbors on the Kopia (east) side of the Tambul range. Tambul orientation of Wiyal relates to other historical factors: the division includes Kopia segments (Kabika and Galka) – attributed earliest known residence in the Kailge area – and generally those who have matrilateral and other ties to Tambul such that, in times of trouble, they sought refuge there. The Araim division, on the other hand, includes sub-segments which most clearly trace their origins and specific forebears to the southern Nebilyer Valley.

The general Kubuka orientation towards the Tambul side is reflected in the rank ordering of men's marriages, a notable exception being a fairly large number of marriages (9) contracted with the Tilka (paired with Lalka), immediate neighbors of the Kubuka in their present location. (See also remarks further below concerning intermarriage with Kopia.)

Table 4–6: *Rank order of current Kopia, Kubuka and Palimi men's marriages*

KOPIA MEN			
Wiyal Kopia		Araim Kopia	
Laulku	11	Laulku	5
Poika	8	Kulka	4
Kanyiba, Mujika, Palimi	4 each		
		Epola, Lalka	3 each
Engal, Lalka, Kulka, Sipaka, Tilka	3 each		
Yurupa, Kunuka	2 each	Eltila, Engal, Jika, Kopilka, Kungunuka, Kusika, Moka, Mujika	2 each
Alya, Anamiyl, Epola, Jika, Kaika, Komoka, Kopilka, Kubuka, Kusib, 'Melpa'*, Moka, Mumiyl, Nega, Peraka, S. Highlands, Tea, Wanaka, Walu	1 each	Alya, Dena, Kopia, Kulyi-Koda, Kunuka, Memika, Nega, Palimi, Palka, Panyiba, Penabe, S. Highlands, Tea, Tilka, Tilka-Lalka, Ulka, Upuka, Wapaka, Waula, Yangipin	1 each
Total: 68 marriages		51 marriages	

ALL KOPIA MEN:	
Laulku	16
Poika	8
Kulka	7
Lalka, Mujika	6 each
Engal, Palimi	5 each
Epola, Tilka, Kanyiba	4 each
Jika, Kopilka, Kunuka, Moka, Sipaka	3 each
Alya, Eltila, Kungunuka, Kusika, Nega, S. Highlands, Tea, Yurupa	2 each
Total: 119 marriages (including single marriages shown above)	

KUBUKA MEN'S MARRIAGES	
Laulku	13
Poika	9
Tilka	9
Palimi	5
Sipaka	4
Kopia	3
Kusika	3
Tea	3
S. Highlands	3
Kulka	2
Kanyiba-Kudulka	2
Kaki-Sul	2
Anamiyl	2
Dena	2
Wanaka	2
Kungunuka	2
Jika, Kaika, Aika, Laima, Komoka, Yurupa, Kalapuka, Epola, Dalku, Upuka, Kunuka, Moka, Midipu, Peraka, Kubuka (by former Panyiba man whose descendents are now considered Kubuka\Kilib)	1 each
Total: 81 marriages	

KAILGE-RESIDENT PALIMI MEN'S MARRIAGES	
Madi (Mendi)	4
Laulku	3
Kopia	3
Kubuka	2
Mujika	2
Kaningab, Wanaka, Kalapuka, Mokui, Kopilka, Yurupa, Kulka, Tilka, Pirai, Sipulka, Kusika, Midipu, Sipaka	1 each
Total: 27 marriages	

*Melpa refers to the Mt Hagen region (see Map 1) and is not the name of a segmentary identity

At the earliest genealogical level for which we could collect detailed information, our genealogies reveal intermarriage among members of what are now sub-units of Kopia. (There is currently no intermarriage within Kopia: this would be regarded as incestuous.) Earlier marriages are those between: (1) a man of Kidi to a Kaja woman; (2) a man of Kaja to a Kupena woman; (3) a Kupena man, Pokia, to a Galka woman. This last is particularly interesting because Pokia was the son of Nyiba, whom we had sought out in the early part of our stay at Kailge because he had come 'up' (*wiji*) from Eraka, one of the Kupena\Tolab *mai pengi kolya* ('origin places'), when a young boy. Thus it appears that even by the time Nyiba's son was old enough to marry, there was no universal prohibition on Kupena-Galka intermarriage. In this upper generation level, there was also a marriage (4) of a Kabika man to a Kupena woman, and (5) of a Waipiyl man to a Kidi woman. Of these five marriages, three might be interpreted as between people who came 'up' to Kailge (Kidi, Kupena, Kaja), and members of men's houses then already present in the Kailge area: certainly Galka and Kabika, perhaps also Waipiyl, may be seen in this way. The other marriages – Kidi-Kaja and Kaja-Kupena – cannot, and so doubt is cast on their status as segments of a single, more inclusive Kopia grouping as such at the time of coming 'up'. An even stronger inference can be made that Kabika-Galka were not sub-identities of Kopia at the time. Clearly, Kopia as an inclusive identity encompassing the particular segments recognized within it today, was consolidated as such after the move to Kailge, in the context of regional military-political process (see section 3.2.2), including common orientation to alliance and marriage to the Tambul side.

Patterns of Kopia-Kubuka intermarriage are revealing of their consolidation as a tribe pair. There are six recorded marriages of Kubuka men with Kopia women, the three that are current into Kopia\Kabika, \Galka, and \Ukulupiyl, i.e., all Wiyal segments.

There are six recorded marriages of Kopia men to Kubuka women, five of these in the earliest generation levels, and only one current one. (One of the early marriages was to a Kubuka woman of a segment of Kubuka, Papai, not currently represented in the Kailge area.) There is no current repetition of marriage between segments of Kopia and Kubuka linked by an earlier marriage.

The sample of marriages between Kopia and Kubuka segments is small. But it suggests that Kopia segments are not all alike in their former, current, and potential marriage relations to Kubuka. All current marriages are of Wiyal Kopia to Kubuka. Here again there is evidence of internal difference between Wiyal and Araim, which is manifested in different external relations of each division, even though for some purposes there is a strong ideology of Kopia unity.

Overall, the evidence suggests that earlier on, Kopia men contracted marriages with Kubuka women (perhaps as the Kubuka were settling in larger numbers in the Kailge area from over the range), and that during this early period, few Kubuka men married Kopia women, though subsequently a few have done so. Overall, however, intermarriage has declined with their increasing consolidation as a tribe pair. Kopia and Kubuka men's marriages show similar strong orientation to Tambul, and Laulku in particular, but differ somewhat in their distributions of intermarriage with Nebilyer-side *talapi*.

Palimi men residing at Kailge likewise sustain more marriages with Laulku (four) than with any other single *talapi*. Kailge-resident Palimi men have married into two Kopia and two Kubuka sub-segments.

The patterning of Kopia, Kubuka and Palimi women's marriage is rather

Table 4–7: *Rank order of current Kopia, Kubuka and Palimi women's marriages*

KOPIA WOMEN

Wiyal Kopia		Araim Kopia	
Poika	10	Upuka	3
Tilka	5		
Upuka, Kulka, Kubuka	3		
Sepik, Laulku, Ipini, Jika	2	'Coastal', Eltila, Jika Komoka, Kanyiba, Kulka, Kunuka, Lalka, Laulku, Moka, Mujika, Opika, Palimi, Palka, Penabe, Poika, Waula, Walyi	1 each
Alya, Kulanika, Kunuka, Kusub, Melpa-Peki, Mujika, Murubu, Negka, Nokopa, Tola	1 each		
Total: 42 marriages		Total: 21 marriages	

ALL KOPIA WOMEN

Poika	11
Upuka	6
Tilka	5
Jika, Kulka, Laulku, Kubuka	3
Ipini, Kunuka, Mujika, Sepik	2
Alya, Coastal, Eltila, Kanyiba, Komoka, Kulanika, Kulka, Kusub, Lalka, Melpa-Peki, Moka, Murubu, Negka, Nokopa, Opika, Palimi, Palka, Penabe, Tola-Mur, Walima-Keri, Walyi	1 each
Total: 63 marriages	

KUBUKA WOMEN'S MARRIAGES

Kulka	6
Jika	4
Yurupa	4
Midipu	3
Laulku	3
Kungunuka	2
Palimi	2
Kusika	2
Walya	2
Dena, Yabuka, Sipaka-Puga, Kalapuka, Kipia, Poika, Wanaka, Ulka, Nega, Mujika, Kopia, Kubuka\Ping (husband is Kubuka\Papanguyl)	1 each
Total: 40 marriages	

KAILGE-RESIDENT PALIMI WOMEN'S MARRIAGES

Upuka	3
Kalapuka	2
Sipulka	2
Banz*	1
Alya, Kopia\Kabika, Wanaka, Dena, Jika	1 each
Total: 13 marriages	

*Banz refers to the locale in the Wahgi Valley (see Map 1), and is not the name of a segmentary identity different from that of men's (see Table 4–7). Wiyal Kopia women have gone in marriage to Tambul-side Poika more than to any other *talapi*, and this has been relatively recent. This must be seen in relation to the fact that Poika has been an acknowledged major *makayl* exchange partner of Kopia. But second in rank order are five marriages with men of neighboring Tilka, followed by three marriages each with Upuka and Kulka of the Nebilyer Valley floor. First in rank order for Araim Kopia women is Upuka; otherwise marriages of Araim women are scattered over Tambul, Nebilyer, Hagen-area and other *talapi*.

Kubuka women's marriages, likewise, show a scatter-distribution over Tambul and Nebilyer-side *talapi*, with no regional preponderance. As noted above, only one current marriage is recorded between a Kubuka woman and a Kopia (\Ukulupiyl).

Palimi (Kopia-dwelling) women's marriages show no particular geographical concentration, but are distributed over both Tambul and Nebilyer groups.

A comparison of the distributions shown in Tables 4–6 and 4–7 points to several generalizations.

First, for all of these *talapi*, men's marriages strongly reflect current, predominant socio-political orientations, which manifest aggregate individual links (of marriage and exchange) established over the past several decades. All Kubuka segments originated from Tambul; Kubuka sustains its most important exchanges with Palimi, its former paired ally, and correspondingly, currently has a preponderance of marriages with Palimi and other Tambul *talapi*. Wiyal Kopia likewise have a large percentage of Tambul-side matrifiliative ties (for those of Kopia\Galka the figure is 50%, for Kabika 55.7%, for Kopil 64.2%, for Ukulupiyl 77.4%, and Waipiyl 70%); and Kopia, as noted, overall sustains its most important exchange relation with Poika.

But a second generalization is that women's marriages for the three segmentary identities seem to be strategic from the perspective of individual households in that they are more evenly distributed over significant other (including neighboring), friendly-to-moderately-hostile *talapi*. In this area, women's marriages do not show the same degree of concentration or direct relation to established political alliance and major exchange, as men's marriages. Except for a significant number of marriages of Wiyal women into Poika, there is no clear preference for return of Kopia-Kubuka women to the Tambul side in marriage.

This leads to the third generalization, that many more Tambul women are marrying in to the Nebilyer *Ku Waru talapi* than are being returned to the Tambul side. The high rate of Tambul women's marriage into the Nebilyer must be understood partly in terms of the different socio-economic situations of the two areas. Tambul-side people tend to see the Nebilyer as a more favored area in that coffee provides a cash income for up to about half the year, while largely because of periodic frost and higher altitudes (and therefore greater inaccessibility), Tambul-side development of cash cropping is not as general, and has tended to take the form of larger business concerns which can afford initial capital outlays, rather than household small-holdings (section 2.1, 2.2).

Similarly, the Kopia-Kubuka and other people of the Nebilyer Valley fringe tend to see development on the valley floor, and prospects for it, as greater than is possible on the slopes which make up much of their territory. Clearly there is greater development on the valley floor in the form of roads, a larger school, police station, aid post, a regular regional market, a coffee processing plant, plantation development, larger trade stores, and beer clubs. Both between Tambul and Nebilyer, and the Nebilyer fringe and valley floor, then, we see a tendency for the greatest number of women to go in marriage towards areas in which there is felt to be greater prospect of development in a broad sense, and of cash-yielding activity, especially coffee holdings, in particular. This may be related to our earlier remarks on bridewealth suggesting that cash plays a part in the arrangement of marriages, both from the point of view of negotiators' estimate of its availability in the short term, as well as prospects for the longer term. From all of this we must probably conclude that there are new socio-economic influences on marriage patterning. Though the tendency to regard the central Nebilyer Valley floor as a favored location may be of long standing, perhaps even ante-dating the European advent, this is now heightened by people's feeling that development is desirable. Conversely, differences in directionality of marriage between men and women indicate that men as seekers in the marriage quest, requiring substantial wealth, are more likely to be able to gain brides from areas where they are perceived to have social connections with, and material advantage relative to, wife-givers. But a wife is perceived as desirable even if her kin have lesser material endowment and prospects than her husband's: she herself is a key valuable. Thus women's marriage appears to have the potential to be more innovative than men's, and to be more easily disconnected from dimensions of social life which are interwoven with the segmentary order including large-scale exchange and military-political alliance. We now turn to consider the relation of marriage to those dimensions.

In the Nebilyer and Hagen regions, as elsewhere in the Highlands, major exchange partnerships are largely built on matrilateral and affinal connections.[12] However, the fact that affinity in the Highlands is universally the backbone of exchange by no means results in identical exchange systems. In particular, recent ethnography points to a significant dimension of difference, the varying degree to which exchange construed as among networks of matrilateral relatives and affines (and sometimes including other kin) may be institutionalized and transacted separately from exchange in which segmentary identities are construed – at least at some levels – as major transactors. For example, as mentioned earlier, Lederman's (1986a) description of Mendi (Southern Highlands) reveals a high degree of institutionalization of two exchange dimensions – affinally-centered *twem* exchanges, and 'group'-centered *sem* exchanges.

We have noted that Mendi women have a considerable role as transactors in their own right in exchange viewed and organized as of the former kind, but a much more limited participation in the second, with respect to which they are most clearly conduits or sources of wealth channeled to their clan from outside. Despite their distinctness as ideal types, Lederman makes it clear that these two dimensions of transaction make conflicting demands, and to some extent are contradictory. Contrasting with their relative separateness in Mendi, we find that in Enga (see also further) the large *tee* exchange cycles have become an omnibus, 'totalizing' institution that subsumes matrilateral and affinal transactions, and apparently because of this, at least in some Enga sub-regions, are intimately bound up with the directionality of marriage.

It might be appropriate to say that, *if* Mendi and Enga were to be taken, respectively, as extremes of the relative independence of affinal network versus 'group'-centered dimensions of exchange, the Nebilyer would fall somewhere in the middle. As discussed earlier in this section, bridewealth is conceptually quite distinct from *makayl* major ceremonial exchange, though its transfer may be protracted in fact, and become enmeshed with considerations concerning other transactions. Certain other wealth transactions are important, especially mortuary payments to matri-kin of the deceased, and at this time also, varying with the nature of relationship to the deceased, commitment of one or several pigs to the funeral feast which takes place three weeks or a month after the death. Ideally, payments should also be made to matrilateral kin upon the birth of children, to mark certain episodes of their maturation (such as hair-cutting), and death (cf. A. Strathern 1971:13–4, 20–23). There are intermittent other demands on household resources which derive directly from affinal and kin relations, such as bridewealth contributions, which can be at least partly foreseen. Nowadays there are new kinds of demands too – contributions to clubs, church activity, school, motor vehicle purchase, and the like – which vary in terms of how funding is raised, but which tend to draw on kin and affinal connections in familiar ways. But in the western Nebilyer, such exchange transactions and other demands are not conceptualized and explicitly interlinked with each other to constitute a separate and dominant dimension of activity to the same extent that appears to be true of Mendi. Rather, each household is a semi-autonomous node in systems of networks, important among which are those constituted of the relatively exclusive ties generated by each marriage.

Contrasting with the relative systemic anonymity of these sets of affinally and matrilaterally-based mundane exchanges, is the salience of *makayl*, large-scale ceremonial exchange. As the account of its patterning in section 4.1 shows, it occurs infrequently and on a relatively large scale which requires coordination among donors as well as between them and recipients for the occasions to be adjudged successful. Very important in the western Nebilyer area is the notion of long-term major exchange partnerships construed as between high-level segmentary identities, and this also involves extensive intermarriage.

As far back as anyone can remember, it is said that Kopia and Poika have been major exchange partners and Kubuka exchange partner of Palimi and of Kopia, (cf. section 4.1). As noted in section 3.2, Kubuka and Palimi were formerly recognized as a Tambul-side tribe pair. Their earlier pairing has gradually been replaced by a pairing of Kubuka with Kopia, as the former became the immediate recruit of the latter in the ca.1940 war with Tea-Dena. Early on in the re-pairing process, there was considerable intermarriage between Kopia and Kubuka. Concomitant, however, with their growing consolidation as a tribe-pair, intermarriage between Kopia and Kubuka has decreased, and current marriages are only between Kubuka and some Wiyal segments of Kopia. As Table 4–2 and discussion have shown, the *makayl* exchange relation of Kopia and Kubuka continued at least into the 1970s, presumably for some time after sentiment had begun to arise that they were too close to intermarry. Such a lag between dimensions of marriage and *talapi*-level exchange appears to be common, judging by a comparable situation between Kopia-Kubuka and (Mujika-) Laulku. We have noted that the latter is now the source of a plurality of brides for men of Kopia and Kubuka, and as well, is second in rank-order for Palimi men residing at Kailge. In the compensation payment of 1983 (not regarded as *makayl*), Kopia and Kubuka organized their major exchange transactions jointly (see section 3.2.2 and Chapter 6), part of the process and outcome of their consolidation as a tribe pair. And it was only during that event that full-scale *makayl* of Kopia and Kubuka with some combination of the pair Mujika and Laulku was mooted (see section 6.2.6).

We have observed that major partnerships always involve high-level segmentary identities between which there is extensive intermarriage. But many members of each high-level unit will have affinal ties elsewhere that is, outside of units considered *makayl* partners; and these ties will, to some extent, both be channeled into transactions conducted with *talapi*-level partners; they also serve as a background to moves to re-define major exchange partnerships, in ways we briefly illustrated for Kopia-Kubuka in section 4.1.

In sum, in the western Nebilyer, mundane exchanges are neither subsumed within large-scale ceremonial exchange to the extent that is characteristic of the Enga *tee*; nor do they constitute as clearly defined a separate and competing dimension as they apparently do in Mendi. Instead, major *makayl* partnerships expressed at high segmentary levels stand out in high relief, and are importantly related to marriage density between the partners. But – and here we must take into consideration the size of these valley-fringe *talapi* – exchange partnerships do not emerge with all the *talapi* with which there is considerable intermarriage. Instead, the fact that this does not happen appears to constitute some of the basis for the occasional re-definition of major partnerships. This can be related to the way in which structures of military-political alliance intersect with those of marriage and exchange in this area, and it is to this we now turn.

In some parts of the Highlands, marriage patterning is not strongly tied to notions of alliance between or among segmentary identities; quite the contrary, for those parts of Enga for which studies are available, it is well documented that marriage is commonly contracted between bride and groom who are members of what are considered to be 'enemy' groupings (Bulmer 1960, Meggitt 1965:101, Feil 1984). The situation in Hagen/Nebilyer is quite different, as we have mentioned. Here marriage is common with people considered friendly, neutral, or possibly intermittently hostile ('minor enemies'), but rare with people accounted major enemies. People point out the disadvantages of attempting to carry on dealings with affines where relations are hostile, and particularly women are acutely aware of the fact that they may be accused of poisoning, or experience other difficulties in attempting to maintain relations with both husband's kin and their own.

Kopia-Kubuka are considered to have a joint *el parka yi* ('bird of paradise man'), or major enemy, the tribe pair Tea-Dena, who live not far to the south along the valley fringe, and whose densest settlement area is Kopola (see Map 2). According to our 1983 census, members of Kopia, Kubuka and Palimi are intermarried with members of Tea-Dena as shown in Table 4–8.

Table 4–8: *Marriages between Kopia-Kubuka and Tea-Dena*

	Tea		*Dena*	
Kubuka men	Tea\?	1*	Dena\Kunuka	1
	Tea\Purayib	2	Dena\Kaukulyib	1
Kubuka women		0	Dena\Kaskib	1
Kopia men	Tea	2	Dena	1
Kopia women		0		0
Palimi men		0		0
Palimi women			Dena	1

*Table note: Where only the highest-level name is given, this means that the secondary segment of the Tea or Dena marriage partner was not ascertained.

The main point to notice is how few marriages there are between people of these neighboring major enemy *talapi*, as compared with many other non-enemy tribes (see Tables 4–6 and 4–7). Secondly, although the sample size makes it of lesser statistical significance, there is a noticeable difference between Kopia and Kubuka in the greater intermarriage of members of the latter with Tea, perhaps to be explained partly by the existence of somewhat different relations due to greater proximity of some segments of Kubuka to Tea (especially perhaps Kubuka\Kuduyl, who have contracted the two marriages with Tea\Purayib, and the one with Dena\Kunuka). But it is striking for both Kopia and Kubuka that men appear more willing to take 'enemy' women in marriage – in which situation, as we have noted, they may be particularly disadvantaged – than are Kopia-Kubuka women to go in marriage to men of *talapi* considered 'major enemies'.[13]

Unlike Enga, then, western Nebilyer marriage frequencies must be seen as generally congruent with military-political alliance in that marriage with major enemies is infrequent and discouraged.[14]

This difference can be related to the fact that, unlike Enga *tee* exchange, Hagen *moka* and Nebilyer *makayl* are considered to derive from warfare (cf. section 4.1). Given that construction, however, it is not logically necessary that exchange be confined to allies and 'minor' as opposed to 'major' enemies; and in fact, other possibilities exist. A. Strathern's (1971:96) diagram of the directions in which warfare payments may flow distinguishes the possibility of *direct compensation* (i.e., payments between combatants) from *reparation* (given by a combatant to its allies). Though said to be possible, the organization of direct compensation payments appears to be much rarer than reparations, and it certainly played no part in the warfare events described in Chapters 6 and 7 below: there was never any talk of possible direct transaction between the 'major' enemies Kopia-Kubuka and Tea-Dena, for example. Rather, the common directionality of commitment and payment is shown by the fact that in those events, each combatant undertook payment to its recruits for wounds and damages. Thus, expressed at high segmentary levels, and ignoring indeterminacies which we discuss fully later on, payments were understood as by Kopia-Kubuka to Laulku, and by Kusika-Midipu-Epola-Alya-Lalka to Kopia-Kubuka on the one side; and by Tea-Dena to Tola-Wanaka on the other. However, recruits are not committed to paying for losses which they inflict on behalf of the major combatant for whom they fought. Thus, as in the 1982 events, the typical warfare payment situation is that in which major combatants are under pressure to compensate their recruits, who otherwise are not able to find a road along which to make a demand. These arrangements, then, may lead to tensions among allies almost as easily as they may consolidate good relations.

As everywhere, then, major exchange in the western Nebilyer is largely powered by relations of affinity and maternal connection. But major exchange is highly politicized, in the sense that the links between affinity and exchange are here mediated rather than direct ones. The mediating dimension is a distinctly military-political one which broadly relates to the construction of high-level segmentary identities as relevant agents in exchange.

We have now sketched the three sides of what we see as a characteristic Hagen/Nebilyer structural triangle. First, marriage is substantially subordinated to higher-level socio-political relations, so that it is rare with major enemies, and there is development over time of a significant marriage density with a few segmentary identities accounted friendly. Second, *makayl* is highly salient compared to mundane exchange, and from the perspective of each *talapi* is focused on another segmentary identity (or pair) with which there exists a high density of intermarriage. Thus, marriage density and major exchange are mutually reinforcing, up to a point limited by notions of marriage prohibition. And third, major exchange may be described as subordinated to military-political alliance in that it is said to arise from warfare, and even more specifically, transaction sequences and thus long-term *makayl* partnerships are developed among allies rather than enemies, despite the possibility of direct compensation. Thus, marriage, alliance and *makayl* are closely inter-related, in a systemic configuration which tends to limit the scope of *makayl*, containing (and perhaps intensifying) it within semi-stable military-political alliances.

A brief comparative sketch will show how greatly this differs from those areas of Enga where relevant observations have been made, by Bulmer (1960) on Kyaka (eastern) Enga, Meggitt (1964, 1965, 1974) on the Mae (central) Enga, and Feil (1980a, 1981, 1984a) on the fringe, easterly Tombema Enga. (For a more detailed comparison with Enga, and additionally with Mendi, see Merlan 1988.)

First, in none of these areas is marriage patterning significantly constrained by higher-level military-political relations. Of Kyaka, Bulmer (1960:308) notes that 'intermarrying clans are normally hostile'; in Mae, Meggitt (1965:101) found such a strong correlation between inter-group killings and marriage that he was inclined to see this as expressing a 'limited causal relationship between warfare and marriage'; and in Tombema, Feil (1984a:109) found of 569 marriages he recorded of members of his 'home', clan, two-thirds were contracted with just six territorially contiguous clans, of which four were regarded as major enemy groups; but with all of these there existed significant densities of affinally- and matrilaterally-based exchange partnerships, constituting the roads along which valuables moved in *tee* exchange. (See also Goodenough 1953.)

Second, *tee* exchange is an enormous, continuous regional system, though from the perspective of any given segmentary identity there is a concentration of exchange relations with a number of neighboring groups of comparable order. As noted, in Tombema Enga such concentrations clearly parallel highest marriage densities, contracting of which is not contained within military-political alliance, as is largely the case in Hagen/Nebilyer.

Tee exchange transactions move along extremely lengthy chains, the movement quite highly predetermined and regular, and conceived of as the *tee's* passage through particular groups (Feil 1984a:60). Meggitt (1974:172) also writes of the 'accepted order in which the clans should (and generally do) make their prestations'. These chains of transactions overall define very lengthy paths and connect many thousands of people. But goods are injected and removed from the sequence along the way so that at least in the past, there was differential concentration upon certain items of exchange along different segments of the *tee's* overall east-west configuration. Having moved in one direction, eventually the *tee* returns in the opposite direction, in a sequence which ideally consists of three, but more often two, phases.

The standardized directionality of *tee* contrasts very strongly with Nebilyer and Melpa, where both Strauss (1962:362–73) and A. Strathern (1971, Chapter 6) have described much more limited *moka* 'chains', and even these, Strathern speculates, may represent post-contact expansion of *moka* activities which followed upon the cessation or reduction of warfare (cf. section 4.1 re the western Nebilyer).

We have drawn from Enga and Melpa ethnography evidence that some of the structural dimensions of these two regions differ. We suggest that these differences may be related to differences in the structures and conduct of exchange at events such as those to be examined below.

This has also been suggested by A. Strathern (1979a). In an article mainly directed to the much-debated issue of who conducts exchange (then made topical by Feil's and Sillitoe's (1979) recent views of exchange as conducted by individuals rather than groups), he comments that '. . . The wider structure of the society would seem to hold the key to why the locus of competition and the relationship of individual men to their groups is different [in Wola] than the situation in Mt. Hagen' (1979a:108).

Among the Wola of the Southern Highlands (Sillitoe 1979:32–6),[15] parish (residential) arrangements are 'multicarpellary' (Hogbin and Wedgwood 1953), i.e., members of a number of different named groups may reside in one locale. Overall, this constitutes a significantly different emphasis upon local residential heterogeneity, and consequent named-group dispersion over locales, than is found in either Hagen or Enga. In such a situation, we might expect emphases upon formulation of participation in exchange events to be significantly different from either Melpa or Enga.

In relation to both the Tombema and the Wola, Strathern (ibid.) suggests that apparently 'the meaning of big-manship is subtly different' from Hagen. In Chapters 6 and 7, we provide comparative examples that may be useful as a basis for exploring such differences. In the Nebilyer (and Hagen), where the formulation of transactions partly depends upon marriage patterns and the building of partnerships on this basis, but also very heavily – seemingly more so than in Enga – upon the structures of past military alliance/hostility, it would appear that the exertions of big-men are strongly focused on meanings having to do with that level of inter-group, military-political alliance.

However, the structures of such alliance are inherently unstable. As

A. Strathern (1979a:106) notes, '. . . exchanging groups are often intermarrying ex-minor enemies with a history of feuding and killing as well as of cooperation against major enemies'. Part of the ideal outcome of Nebilyer exchange is the confirmation of good relations, but also, of equivalence between transactors. In such circumstances, relations between donors and recipients as formulated at the inter-*talapi* level are clearly not ones of amity in any simple sense. But given that the sources upon which transactors draw are largely affinal ties, which form ramifying networks extending outside particular groups, neither can relations among co-clansmen be seen as entirely solidary. As Strathern (1979a:107) has noted, for Melpa we must posit that cooperation and competition characterize both relations *between* donors and recipients, and within each set as well.

In a footnote in the same article, Strathern (1979a:111,fn.14) suggests that comparative analysis of speeches at *moka* and *tee* occasions might shed light on differences between the Enga and Melpa systems. That footnote could well be taken as an epigraph introducing the following three chapters of this book, which we hope will lay the groundwork, on the Nebilyer side, for just such comparisons.

5. Some linguistic structures of segmentary politics

In this chapter we will discuss some linguistic structures through which exchange events are constituted. The emphasis will be on the traditional forms of men's oratory – the structural patterns themselves. This will provide essential background for the following two chapters (6 and 7), where we will be concerned with situated uses of these forms, basing our analysis on transcripts of speeches made at three interrelated exchange events.

In trying to carry out the main task of this chapter – to describe a particular set of linguistic resources – there are at least two different ways in which we could proceed. One would be to start with given linguistic patterns or types, such as the indigenously recognized genre of *ung eke* 'bent' (i.e. figurative) speech, identify various instances of each type, and compare the uses of them across the range of contexts in which they are found to occur. This is the approach taken by Andrew Strathern in his (1975) study of the Melpa equivalent of Nebilyer *ung eke,* which he calls 'veiled speech'. An alternative approach, which we will follow here, is to start with full transcripts of what was said at particular speech events of the relevant sort – public exchange events – identify particular linguistic devices which are used at them, to look for possible interrelations among the various devices and between the devices and their contexts of use.

The three events which comprise the bulk of our sample are compensation events which took place in July and August 1983, arising from the Marsupial Road War of 1982 (sections 1.1 and 3.2.2).[1] As we shall see, there are a number of linguistic/paralinguistic devices, the use of which turns out to be limited almost entirely to public 'inter-*talapi*' events. The most obvious of these are the prosodic and choreographic devices which characterize the so-called *el ung* ('fight talk') style of oratory. These are described in section 5.3. Another, more subtle but no less powerful linguistic device which is almost entirely restricted to such inter-*talapi* events is the use of particular (singular and dual) grammatical categories to construct the relevant actors in exchange transactions as segmentary ones (section 5.2). This device is limited to events of this kind and tends to occur especially frequently just within speeches which are delivered in *el ung* style (which amount to about half the speeches at these events).

There are yet other linguistic devices which are used in a wide variety of contexts (i.e., not just public, inter-*talapi* ones), but which are also used especially often, or in characteristic ways, in *el ung* speeches. These include: lexical devices for referring to or constructing segmentary groupings (section 5.1), *ung eke* ('bent', figurative) speech (section 5.4); rhetorical questions (section 5.6); pairing (section 5.7); and interactional metalanguage, or 'talk about talk' (section 5.8). In talking about the latter, we open up questions (see also Chapter 9) on which we hope this and subsequent chapters of this book may shed new light: (1) why is there so *much* talk at Nebilyer exchange events, and (2) why is talk so highly valued among Nebilyer people as an aspect of social life?

5.1 FORMS OF REFERENCE AND ADDRESS AND THEIR RELEVANCE FOR SOCIAL ACTION

We begin exploration of the resources of Nebilyer speech in the public domain by considering the kinds of referring expressions typically used to formulate agents, or social actors. This seemingly simple task actually presupposes a number of fundamental assumptions on our part about what it means to use notions of agency and action in ethnographic description.

Our earlier discussion of Feil and Meggitt (section 1.2) will serve to illustrate the point that it has proven easier in the social sciences to construe notions of actor or agent in terms related (perhaps in an unexamined way) to Western commonsense notions of 'the individual', the singular person; and that when social 'groups' are invoked as agents, they too may have attributed to them just those qualities (motivation, intentionality, interests, etc.) that are assumed to make the singular person the quintessential actor type (cf. section 1.2). This assumption probably underlies classical social anthropological notions of the lineage (sib, gens, clan, horde, or what-have-you) as a single jural person (e.g. Fortes 1953), a notion based upon certain English common-law formulations of the 'corporation', which, along with Durkheimian sociology, exerted such a strong founding influence upon British social anthropology via the work of scholars such as McLennan, Maine, and Robertson Smith.

But notwithstanding the salutary distinction which theoreticians in that tradition have drawn in principle between social 'persons' and biological 'individuals' (Radcliffe-Brown 1965, Nadel 1957), those theorists did not provide a well-developed set of concepts for understanding agency or social action as such (nor did they intend to: the problem was considered by Radcliffe-Brown to be outside the scope of his 'natural science of society'). Thus it is not surprising that anthropologists who *have* tried to address that problem (e.g. Barth 1966, and in our ethnographic area, Sillitoe 1979) have in practice drawn more upon the rival functionalist tradition pioneered by Malinowski (1949), who *was* centrally concerned with human action, but who did *not* distinguish rigorously between the social person and the biological individual, and for whom 'bodily activities' were thus the paradigm case of human action. The inadequacies of such a framework for studying social action should be clear from section 1.2, where we showed that what might appear from the extra-semiotic viewpoint to comprise one and the same set of bodily movements could comprise different kinds of 'act', depending on the meaning with which it is locally invested. Accordingly, we are not prepared to accept any notion of social action formulated in pre-semiotic terms such that it is more 'naturally' attributed to individual organisms or actors than to other types of social agents.

For us, *social action* is constituted by the ways in which human agents typically give form to the various aspects, activities and experiences of their social life, and *agency* refers to the ways in which they formulate the possibilities of involvement and intervention in social action. Such typical ways of formulating action and agency shape, and are systematically prior to, the individual's sense of subjectivity, including his or her operative notions of the kind of agents that have transformative capacity. This is not to deny the importance of the realm of individual subjectivity – about which we have more to say in Chapter 9 – but simply to forestall the suggestion that, within any social system, 'the individual' is in some sense less problematic, more clear-cut, than any other kind of social actor. In our Nebilyer material, we take the social construction of actorhood as a problem for empirical investigation, including close analysis of linguistic and other semiotic resources typically used in this process.

When viewed from this perspective, the question of forms of address and reference becomes far more central than it otherwise would be. For, contra the dominant Western linguistic ideology (Silverstein 1979, Rumsey 1990), we cannot assume that social actors exist as language-independent *realia*, which language merely provides a convenient means of naming or directing attention to. Rather, specific forms of reference and address in each language provide essential means for the construction (always a more-or-less problematical one) of actors of this or that locally recognized type. This is true not just of the kind of actors/agents which anthropologists have identified as 'corporate groups', (the social constructed-ness of which we Westerners are perhaps more predisposed to accept), but also of those which we identify as 'individuals' or individual persons.

What is the nature of these linguistic means? While they are in some respects very different from language to language, there seems to be a central core of them which is common to all. These are just the means for constructing the parties to social action of one particular sort, namely, linguistic interaction. Every language has formal devices for indicating that the actor who is being referred to in a given stretch of discourse is the same one to whom the action of speaking is itself to be attributed (i.e., its speaker), or the one to whom it is addressed. These are the 'I' and 'you' of the discourse, which are represented not only by the singular personal pronouns (Ku Waru *na* and *nu*; see Appendix B.3.1) but also by the person-marking elsewhere in the grammar. In Ku Waru, as in many of the world languages (Benveniste 1971), the most important locus of person-marking is not the lexical pronouns (which are also less frequently used than in English) but the verb, which varies in form according to the person and grammatical number of its subject (see Appendix B.3.2). And every language has means for indicating that the referent is someone or something *other than* the speaker or addressee: the so-called third person which, again, in Ku Waru is marked mainly on the verb (ibid.).

Other aspects of the linguistic formulation of actors are far more specific to particular languages and forms of social life. One of these relates to the nature of possible incumbents of the 'speaker' role itself (cf. Rumsey 1989). Since the speaker is by nature a social *person* rather than biological organism or individual, the speaker role cannot be simply identified with a particular organism by whose vocal apparatus the utterance is being produced, any more than an exchange of transaction can be identified by naive observation of the physical movements of wealth objects (section 1.2). We shall see below that the 'I' of Nebilyer oratory is often a *segmentary* transactor which is by no means coterminous with the individual from whose mouth it comes. In order to understand how that may be so, it is best to turn first to the more explicit formulations of segmentary actorhood which are achieved by the use of segmentary names and other lexical expressions.

Our transcript data indicate that in speeches in the public arena, a significant distinction is to be made between expressions which achieve reference, and formulate agency, by overtly naming segmentary identities (at some level), and those which achieve reference without overt mention of segmentary identity names. The first, however, is not necessarily to be equated with the formulation of segmentary identities themselves as agents. Segmentary names can be used to identify groupings as agents, either as a collectivity (e.g. Kopia, see below), or in terms of its members (Kopia-*ma* 'the Kopia ones'); but also are used in collocation with personal names (Kopia Noma), or title plus name (Kopia *Kansil* Noma 'Kopia Councillor Noma') to designate single persons, thus, partly in terms of segmentary affiliation.

Other referring expressions – personal names, titles, what we call *place-titles* – designate singular agents without explicitly invoking their segmentary affiliation, though certain aspects of such expressions, such as place-name descriptors, also have segmentary resonances. Other designators such as regional names (like Ku Waru, Meam etc.), and directional terms (with meanings like 'down there' etc., see below) refer to even vaguer aggregates, and though these may not be definable as collections of particular *talapi*, nevertheless they too have segmentary resonances, reinforced by the nature of the events in which mention of them occurs, and sometimes also by their co-occurrence with *el ung* prosody (section 5.3).

5.1.1 Grammatical form

Segmentary identity names occur in various forms within the transcript. First, different levels of segmentation are represented by the difference among paired-tribe labels (Kopia-Kubuka), single tribal labels (Kopia), and lower-order segmentary names, which are sometimes preceded by the tribal name (Kopia\Galka) but sometimes occur by themselves (Galka). Segment labels sometimes are paired (Kupena-Tolab). In a few cases, larger groupings of tribes or tribe-pairs are designated within particular contexts as relevant, even higher-level social identities. For example, at line 205 of Appendix A, Kusika-Midipu-Epola-Alya are named as those to whom the amount given by Kopia-Kubuka must be conveyed, since together those *talapi* will later make a return payment.

Second, segmentary names may occur without any number- or set-marking (e.g. Kopia), with marker of plurality/collectivity *-ma* (see Appendix B.3.3.2.1), or with the pair-marking suffix, *-sil* (B.3.3.2.2). Such number- and set-marking is related to the kind of reference or contribution to reference the segmentary name makes in any particular context.

Segmentary names which have no number- or set-marking tend to be used in one of two ways: adjectivally, or in general, aggregate reference to the particular social identity (but not to its component membership). An example of the first kind occurs at line 306: *kopia lku tapa payl* . . . 'all the Kopia men's houses . . .'. There are numerous instances in which a segmentary name modifies such nouns as *kang* 'boy, fellow',[2] *ada* 'old man', e.g. *kopia kang-ma* 'the Kopia fellows', *kopia ada-ma* 'Kopia elders/old men'.

Segmentary names which are number-marked occur with the collective marker *-ma* (*kopia kubuka-ma*). Names with these endings designate (some of) the membership of the particular social identity (e.g. line 364, *kopia-kubuka-ma bung ti naa temula* 'We Kopia-Kubuka will not have a meeting', or line 1094, *el ung ya kopia-kubuka-ma para naa nyai-o* 'but don't you Kopia-Kubuka (pl) talk *el ung* back and forth'.). There is, notably, only one case in Appendix A of a single, tribal-level name marked with *-ma* (line 335, *kopia-ma,* where the reference is somewhat ambiguous but seems to be to Kopia money, 'Kopia ones [i.e. pieces of currency]', rather than to the membership of the Kopia *talapi*). In contrast, there are numerous instances in which a single tribal-level name modifies a noun phrase which is itself marked with *-ma* (e.g. *kopia kang-ma* 'Kopia boys'). This sort of construction is the single tribal-name equivalent of the plural-marked paired tribal names such as *kopia-kubuka-ma*. As is the case for tribal-level names, there are no instances either of plural-marked, lower-level segmentary names (such as *kopia kupena-ma*). That is, both tribal-level, and lower-level names are either used in aggregate reference to the social identity, or adjectivally, but are not marked with *-ma,* which makes reference to the segmentary identity in terms which appear to highlight its component members.

It is in fact the paired, tribal-level names which have the widest possibilities in terms of number- and set-marking postpositions: such pairs may have no postposition, may be marked with *-ma,* or may be explicitly marked as a pair with Dual marker *-sil.* (Examples of each of these possibilities are: 1, line 1759, *na kopia-kubuka ab mal-te kep mol-ko* 'I am not the son of a Kopia (or) Kubuka woman'; 2, the *-ma* example, in paragraph above; 3, line 1650, *nu kopia-kubuka-sil aki tekin* 'you (sg) Kopia and Kubuka pair do like that').

As some of the examples above have already illustrated, verbal agreement tends to vary systematically with number- and set-marking of segmentary group names (cf. Appendix B.3.2). Non-number-marked referring expressions at all segmentary levels tend to take singular verbal agreement (line 1707, *kopia-kubuka tepa ebab siba-lyi* 'Kopia-Kubuka will fight and win'; line 721, *galka tim-o* 'Galka gave'). Frequently, names of lower-level segmentary identities are followed by the noun *tapa* (or the nominal expression *lku tapa*) 'men's house' (see section 3.1.2), so that singularity of reference may be conceived of in terms of an understood ellipsis; e.g. *galka (–) tim* may be understood as *galka lku tapa (-n) tim* 'Galka men's house gave'. There is no such noun which typically follows a tribe-pair (such as Kopia-Kubuka); that is, there is no lexicalization of the abstract notion of group at this level (beyond the general use of *talapi* 'line', which is all-purpose in that it may be used in reference to any segmentary level). Nevertheless, from the fact that paired tribal-level terms are often marked with dual marker *-sil,* and that such phrases almost always take singular verbal agreement, one may conclude that such names precisely constitute a single set of two, a pair. (See e.g. line 788, *pe mudike-laulku-sil nyiba pelym-o* 'but so-called Mujika and Laulku live as a pair'.)

Contrasting with typically singular verbal agreement of non-number-marked and Dual-marked names is the typically plural verbal agreement of those paired names suffixed with *-ma*: line 1436, *mujika-laulku-ma . . . ok pangi-o* 'let the Mujika-Laulku assemble and come [to your aid]'. Plural agreement suggests that reference should be understood to be to the component members, rather than to the notion of inclusive segmentary identity.

Segmentary identity names may also be used in agreement with first person singular or plural verb forms. The tribal name Kopia is used in agreement with a first person singular verb in line 313, (*kopia . . . tekir* 'I, Kopia, am giving . . .'), and with a first person plural form in line 325 (*kopia . . . nosikumul* 'we Kopia . . . put . . .').

5.1.2 Context of use of segmentary names

We argue below that the use of *segmentary person* is more fundamental to the construction of segmentary categories than is the use of segmentary identity names. This is true partly because not every segmentary level which may be referred to by segmentary person has a monolexemic segmentary name – or indeed, any at all. As a basis of comparison, let us now examine more closely the contexts in which segmentary identity names are used. How that use contrasts with *segmentary person* is examined in section 5.2 and Chapters 6 and 7.

Examination of the transcript shows that single tribal-level names and/or lower-level segmentary names almost always occur in contexts having to do with the distribution of sums of money during the proceedings. Further, tribal-level names occur with great frequency in the transcript used attributively to identify persons (those wounded in battle, for example, to whom payment should be made, e.g. *poika kang* 'a Poika fellow').[3] Specific persons – such as the wounded – are never referred to by a paired-tribe label (e.g. as Mujika-Laulku), but always by the relevant tribe label.

This indicates that tribal- and lower-level segmentary names are relevant to the identification of specific persons (even if their identities remain unknown beyond the fact that they are e.g. 'Poika', or 'Poika\Akalyib'), and to the discussion of the allocation of specific sums of money. In what contexts are paired, tribal labels used, with or without the Dual postposition? Here a distinction must be drawn between instances marked with *-ma*, which make reference to (some sub-set of) the segment's component membership, and may therefore be used in relation to specific activities (e.g. 'we Kopia-Kubuka-*ma* will not meet', or 'you Kopia-Kubuka-*ma* do not answer in *el ung*'), versus non-number marked paired terms which refer to the aggregate social identity, and hence tend not to be used in contexts where what is being described are specific activities. Rather, such non-number-marked, paired names tend to be used in reference to general disposition, location, and history of political action of the social identity named.

While single and paired tribal names are used by a range of speakers within the transcript, it is noticeable that mention of lower-level segmentary identities tends to be predominantly by speakers who are members of the tribe or tribe-pair to which the sub-segments belong. The participants or big-men who belong to a particular segment are the most likely to assume the role of talking about the payments it (at various segmentary levels) is making. In the transcript we note that Kopia and Kubuka segments are *only* mentioned by speakers of those tribes. There are very few mentions of Mujika-Laulku sub-groupings as recipients of the payment, but here, rather than being mentioned by members of those tribes, we note they are mentioned by only two participants (one Kopia, one Kubuka) who have affinal links to them. The scarcity of mentions of Laulku sub-segments as recipients is probably somewhat atypical, and has to do with the fact that this payment is not construed as *makayl* but was (from the donors' perspective) repeatedly said to be made to Laulku (with a small extra payment to Mujika) as a whole, to be subsequently divided among themselves.

It is noticeable in the transcript that only a small number of men (or women) are mentioned (addressed or otherwise referred to) by personal name. Of these, only a minority of mentions are preceded by tribal name (Kubuka Unya, etc.). By far the majority are simply the name; and not only is the number of men mentioned small, but also the number of those who make these mentions is quite restricted: the majority of total mentions is made by only a handful of speakers.

Prominent men are also referred to by a small number of epithets including *kansil* 'councillor', *keap* 'kiap/magistrate', *tultul* (an older title formerly given under the Australian administration), and by a place-name title (e.g. Komapiyl, in reference to Kubuka Unya, whose homestead is at this place), or place-name plus noun ('man', 'boy') and personal name (e.g. *kubaliyl yi Kujilyi* 'Kubaliyl man Kujilyi'). In our end of the valley, a small number of prominent men were regularly referred to (but not addressed) by a term composed of place-name and *kang* 'fellow, boy' (e.g. Nukunuku *kang* in reference to Epola Koluwa, Kubaliyl *kang* in reference to Kujilyi). Such place-titles are not inherited, and a considerable majority of prominent men are not known by this kind of title. This suggests that residential stability is necessary for such a title to become a regularly-used identifier, but that this alone is not sufficient. We did not observe that two men ever shared a place-title of this sort (that is, for example, there is and apparently can be only one Nukunuku *kang*). These titles seem to be essentially markers of personal eminence, forming a system of 'men in the landscape' not strictly tied to the distribution of segmentary identities, but – as we have said – having resonances of segmentary affiliation. (In fact, not every tribe in our area had a man who was regularly known by place-title.)

In sum, in this event references to men by name usually were not preceded by tribal identifier. This is perhaps to be expected where all participants are well known to each other. Yet it is unlikely that use of tribal labels is often (or ever) simply a matter of clarifying reference. The examples in our transcripts would suggest that it is usually a way of underscoring relevant social difference (as we discuss extensively in Chapters 6 to 8 below). Men who hold any sort of governmental title are likely to be addressed and referred to by it, and those men so referred to turn out to be a sub-set of the otherwise most-mentioned men in this event.

5.1.3 Non-use of segmentary identity names

Where are segmentary identity names not used? Generally, they are not used when a speaker is attempting to point out and suggest the relevance of social difference while at the same time leaving the nature of that difference somewhat blurry or imprecise.

There are frequent mentions in the transcript of the notion of difference. Several speakers say that 'Meam fighting is different, Kaugel fighting is different', etc. For a range of assertions of difference, see Appendix A, lines 100, 108–9, 131, 336, 343, 424–5, 428, 1140, 1215, 1235, 1281–3, 1345–6, where some of these make use of regional labels (Meam, Lama as in line 100) as the basis of difference, others establish difference metonymically by reference to types of food and cultivation practices (e.g. line 428), and still others simply involve such expressions as 'a different (kind of) man'.

For instance, at lines 108–9 Kujilyi says, 'I stand here, a different man'. Earlier in his speech he had commented upon the absence of two prominent Epola men, Alya and Koluwa. He had identified himself as a Lama man, an Ulka-Upuka or Jika-Kungunuka (and thus distinct from Epola-Alya). By line 108, then, he has claimed that he is different from Alya and Koluwa, a difference that might be summarized by saying that he is Midipu, they are Epola. Yet he does not do this, for in past political history of this part of the valley, Kusika-Midipu and Epola-Alya have tended to be identified as friendly towards each other, even allied in common hostility towards other tribes (such as Kopia-Kubuka). For this reason, use of the tribal label 'Midipu' would not be adequate here to contextually establish the sense of difference that Kujilyi wishes to.

Unya's speech (line 413, ff.) is replete with allusive references to social identities to which he does not apply tribal labels. At line 442, referring to the forgetting of hostilities which was to occur under the rule of *gavman lo*, Unya refers to the Tea-Dena by the directional *mer-ayl* 'down there', and he simply addresses social identities which might be summed up as including Epola-Alya-Lalka-Kusika-Midipu as *nu* 'you (sg.)' (see section 5.2 on segmentary person). In lines 446 and 447 he again evokes approximately these social identities, in reverse order. His speech is remarkable for the fact that he does not use segmentary names, when they might seem to be handy ways of summing his intended references. Their non-use contributes to his speech a certain allusive or indirect quality, since the ways of referring he does use allude to his referents rather than naming them definitively (cf. Rumsey 1986:286–7).

5.2 THE GRAMMAR OF SEGMENTARY PERSON

Now that we have reviewed some of the most explicit, lexical means for referring to or instantiating segmentary actors/agents, we will introduce what we consider to be a more basic and more powerful way of doing the same thing, namely, the use of certain grammatical devices to implement what we call *segmentary person*. This is done via the intersection of the category of grammatical *person* per se (cf. section 5.1; Appendix B.3) and that of grammatical number. In common with many Papuan languages (and others throughout the world), Ku Waru makes grammatical distinctions not just between two number values (singular and plural), but among three: singular, plural and dual. But as in language generally, the choice of one or the other of these categories is not a simple reflection of the way things already were in the world before language was used to refer to them. Rather, reference to them within one category or another is part of what constructs them as *things* of one kind or another.

With respect to the kind of things with which we are dealing here – segmentary social identities or actors – there is no way an outside observer could predict which of the Ku Waru number categories will be used to refer to them. Insofar as we think of them as groups, each consisting of a plurality of individual members, we are perhaps inclined to expect each of them to be referred to with grammatically plural forms, as in English when we say such things as 'the Germans were fighting the Poles' (with grammatically plural subject and object). But even in English, we can also use the singular number and say, e.g. 'Germany was at war with Poland'. In Ku Waru, as it turns out, both kinds of formulation are possible, the latter (using the singular number for reference to each segmentary actor) is far more frequent, especially in public oratory. That this is so of third person references (i.e., reference to someone or something other than the speaker or addressee) should already have become clear in section 5.1, where we discussed the use of singular, dual, plural and 'collective' forms of segmentary names.

What is less expected from the Euro-centric viewpoint is that the use of singular number for segmentary actors is not limited to the third person categories, but is also common in the first and second. That is, words which we would otherwise translate as 'I' or 'you (sg)' (and verbs which are marked for 1sg or 2sg subject) are used to refer not to individual, physically present 'speaker' and 'addressee', but to whole segmentary units.[4] 'I' (*na*) in this context can be glossed as 'the segmentary unit with which the speaker is identified',[5] and 'you' (*nu*) as 'the segmentary actor to whom this utterance is addressed'. Similarly, the first person dual category is used in ways that can be glossed as 'two segmentary units, with one of which the speaker is identified', and the second person dual in ways that can be glossed as 'two segmentary actors, to one or both of which this utterance is addressed'. This does not necessarily imply that the physically present, speaking individual is included among the referents of his 'I', nor that the referents of his 'you' include individuals present at the speech event. For what is sometimes being referred to are activities which took place well before any of those people were born. For example, 'I fought with you' can mean 'My ancestors, *qua* segmentary unit, fought with yours'.[6] The third person singular and dual are also used in this way, for segmentary units, or pairs of them, which are neither speaking nor addressed. And the word *yi (-yl)* '(the) man' or *kang (-ayl)* '(the) boy' is used (without the collective postposition *-ma*) to mean '(the) segmentary unit' (e.g. Appendix A, lines 1566, 1786).

Strauss (1962:296) devised the term *Gruppen-Singular* for these usages, which was certainly on the right track. But given that the dual category is used in the same sorts of contexts with the same functional value, we will instead refer to this functional complex as implementing a contextually distinct, segmentary use of the person-number categories which we call *segmentary person* (SP).

With the partial exception of Strauss' (1962) seminal account, all previous discussions of segmentary structure and process in the New Guinea Highlands (and, as far as we know, in Africa as well) have drawn their linguistic evidence solely from the lexical realm – i.e., from the elaborate sets of taxonomically nested proper names for segmentary units ('lineages') at various levels (as in Chapters 2 and 3, and section 5.1 above). As the analysis in Chapters 6 and 7 will show, in Ku Waru, the grammatical device of *segmentary person* (realized mainly on the verb) is even more fundamental to the discursive construction of segmentary identities than are the lexical sets by which the *talapi* are named. We say so for at least three reasons.

The first is that, despite the frequency with which segmentary names occur in the transcripts, the occurrence of SP is even more frequent.

Second, while every named segmentary level can also be referred to by SP, not every level referred to by SP has a monolexemic name (for some examples of lexically covert segmentary categories, see sections 6.2.2 and 6.2.3 below). More important, some such levels *cannot* be referred to explicitly in any totalizing way due to their partial intractability to predominant indigenous modes of formulating such groupings via pairing (see section 3.1.3 re K-M-E-A-L).

The third reason why we see SP as such an important device for Nebilyer segmentary politics is that we agree with Whorf (1956) and Boas (1966) that a more powerful and ineluctable effect is produced on human conduct by covert (linguistic-) structural categories than by overt ones. As is probably true of all languages and speech communities, the discursive devices which are most accessible to the consciousnesses of acting subjects are lexical ones, those which put things into words. To *name* something is to call attention to it in such a way as to allow it to be called into question – to become an object of explicit contestation (cf. Irvine 1979). But within any social order, of the myriad structures which are reproduced in social action, it is only a small minority that are so explicitly accessible (cf. Bourdieu 1977 on Doxa versus Orthodoxy, Merlan and Rumsey 1986). Insofar as patterns of discourse figure in the reproduction of those structures that remain relatively *in*accessible to conscious reflection, it is mainly via aspects of *linguistic* structure which are also of that (largely inaccessible) kind, namely grammatical structures, such as those implementing abstract categories such as person and (grammatical) number.

There are other reasons for expecting that SP should remain beyond its users' limits of awareness. In an important comparative study of this general problem, Silverstein (1981) demonstrates the relevance of three different axes for distinguishing those linguistic indexes (in the sense of Peirce 1960 and Jakobson 1971) which are relatively transparent to awareness from those that are relatively opaque to it: 1) segmental/non-segmental; 2) referential/non-referential; 3) presupposing/performative.

The first of these (segmental/non-segmental) is a matter of whether or not the indexical meaning is expressed by a discrete, segmentable stretch of the utterance. We take this distinction to be a cline or continuum rather than categorical opposition, since: 1) a given meaning (e.g. first person singular) may be realized in multiple ways in a given language, some segmental and some not; 2) some segments simultaneously encode two or more meanings, and these so-called *portmanteau* morphemes are best regarded as intermediate in segmentability between simple ones and other non-segmental devices. In view of these two considerations, Ku Waru SP would seem to lie somewhere near the middle of the scale. It is implemented partly by free-standing pronouns, which are fully segmental, but far more often by person affixes on the verb, which are not only less segmental than free-standing words, but also less so than some bound morphemes, since they are portmanteau morphemes (see Appendix B.3.2).

As for the second of Silverstein's axes, he would presumably see SP as non-referential. The pronominals do of course have 'referents' but that is beside the point, for the SP value is itself implemented by the alternation between singular or dual vs. plural forms for a given 'referent'.[7] That is, what is signaled by the shift to SP is not a difference in 'referent' (this or that *talapi* or set of them), but a difference in degree of singularity or *solidarity* of segmentary identity as an attribute of the *same* referent.

With respect to the third of Silverstein's axes, we regard SP as a relatively 'performative' index rather than 'presupposing', since 'singularity of segmentary identity' is not given in the speech situation, but selectively invoked or created by the very act of using SP.

Thus, according to all of Silverstein's criteria, SP is the kind of linguistic device that is most likely to remain beyond the 'limits of awareness' of its users (speakers and addressees alike). Having now tried to bring it within those of our reader, we will be better able (in Chapters 6 and 7) to examine the situated uses of SP in the larger processes of social reproduction in which it plays a part.

5.3 *EL UNG* ('FIGHT TALK')

Throughout the greater Hagen-Nebilyer-Kaugel area, there is a special, prosodically and paralinguistically marked oratorical style known in Melpa as *el ik* and in the Nebilyer dialect by the cognate term *el ung,* the most literal gloss for which is 'bow and arrow talk', 'fight talk', or 'war talk'.

This style is regularly used at all kinds of exchange events involving transactions between segmentary units: warfare compensation, *makayl* ceremonial exchange, homicide compensation. In keeping with the highly gender-specific nature of these spheres of transaction, it is used only by adult males (but cf. sections 7.2, 7.3.2 for an account of a partial appropriation by women).

At first we were uncertain why *el ung,* 'fight talk', is so named, but the matter was clarified on a return fieldtrip of 1986, when Alan Rumsey, observing an episode of tribal warfare, heard the prosodic patterns of *el ung* being used from behind the battle line. (A re-enacted version of this speech was recorded, and is transcribed as Appendix C; cf. section 7.4.2 below and M. Strathern 1985a, regarding the relationship between warfare and ceremonial exchange.)

The distinctive prosodic features of *el ung* are as follows. The extent of pitch variation from syllable to syllable is much less than in the everyday language (for which, see Appendix B.2.1): in *el ung,* sequences of anywhere from one or two to a couple of dozen syllables are pronounced on a single, nearly level pitch contour, which terminates with an abrupt fall to an overlong [a::] or [o::].[8] One or the other of these vowels is added to the last word of the line as a 'line-terminating *el ung* marker' (henceforth, for greater simplicity, '*el ung* vowel'). That is, they make no lexico-grammatical contribution to the line, but serve only to mark it as *el ung,* and to bound each line as a prosodic unit. If the last word of the line happens to end with the same vowel as the *el ung*-marking one, that vowel is lengthened without adding an extra syllable (see e.g. lines 420–3). There are no pauses within a line of *el ung*, but there are often pauses between lines.[9]

The length of the pause, and a change of *el ung* vowel (from a:: to o:: or vice versa) can be significant in marking shifts of subject matter within an *el ung* speech, or in otherwise bounding off one section of a speech from another (for examples, see section 6.2.6 below).

In its use at exchange events,[10] *el ung* is also characterized by the following paralinguistic features. As each orator begins an *el ung* speech, he starts striding briskly, in a more-or-less straight path as he speaks, usually brandishing an ax in one hand, and sometimes a spear in the other. After covering a distance of approximately ten metres, he pivots around abruptly and returns over the same course. He continues this, back and forth for the duration of his speech.[11]

In practice, the distinction between *el ung* and non-*el ung* is not a categorical one. There are some passages in the transcript in Appendix A where the intonation contours are intermediate between the fully levelled-out *el ung* style and the normal rises and falls of non-*el ung* prosody. These occur at lines 500–15, 740–93, 871–85, 893–8, 1063–5, 1169–70, 1212–39, 1255–1304, 1612–33, 1646–55, and 1674–87[12] (total: 180 lines). Some of the above lines are also missing the final *el ung* vowel. But this seems less indispensable as a mark of *el ung* than does its distinctive prosody. For example, the speech by Ipupu at lines 1515–80 is in clear *el ung* prosody throughout, but lacks the final vowel on lines 1560–80. Nonetheless, he is interrupted at that point by another speaker who tries (unsuccessfully) to cut him off, saying 'we have talked enough *el ung*'.

Passages which are in (phonetically) 'full' *el ung* occur at lines 413–89, 515–44, 800, 807–26, 864–8, 910–1060, 1065–82, 1481–1582, 1714–36 and 1792–1817 (total: 452 lines). Close examination of these sections of the transcript will reveal that they are marked, not only by the use of the *el ung* vowel at the end of each line (the only one of the above-discussed features which is indicated in the transcript), but also by certain lexico-grammatical and semantic features.

First and most obviously, many of the speeches start with two or more repetitions of the vocative *(i) yi-ma-o:* or *(i) yi-ma:*, '(you) men (here)', calling attention to the speaker's claim on the floor and making clear the nature of his addressed audience (i.e. adult males).[13]

While this form of opening is one which occurs *only* in *el ung* speeches, those speeches are also characterized by the especially frequent use of certain other rhetorical devices which also occur in other contexts.

One of these is parallelism: repetition with variation inside an established syntactic frame (cf. Fox 1974, 1988). A simple example occurs in lines 1036–7:

> *kaspis*-kiyl tekir-o
> *I'm just giving [money] for potatoes*
>
> po pubu-kiyl tekir-o
> *I'm just giving it for sugar cane*

The frame is established by the first line, which is repeated in the second, with *kaspis* ('potatoes') in place of *po pubu* ('sugar cane'). A somewhat more elaborate example of parallelism occurs in lines 1031–4 of the same speech, where the first half of the parallel pair comprises two lines of *el ung* (lines 1031–2), and the second half comprises two more lines (1033–4), the second of which is identical to the second line in the first half (1032). Another four-line parallel set occurs in lines 1042–5, this time with the first and third lines identical and the variation between the second and fourth. Within *el ung* speeches, each half of such a parallel pair is always made up of one or more whole lines of *el ung*. It is this use of prosodically well-bounded lines as constituents that gives a distinctive cast to the parallel structures used in *el ung*. While parallelism is used in a wide variety of other contexts in the Nebilyer,[14] within oratorical contexts, it is much more frequent within *el ung* speeches than within non-*el ung* ones.

One of the standard uses of parallelism within *el ung* speeches is in a set of more-or-less fixed expressions which occur (optionally but quite frequently) at the end of an entire *el ung* speech, or distinct section of one,[15] and present some pairs of alternative possibilities, usually concerning the disposition of the wealth objects being presented on the occasion of the speech. Examples in the transcript include:

If you want to 'carve it up' and take it then go ahead and do so/
If you want to cradle it in your arms and take it, then go ahead and do so

(lines 825–6)

If you want to take this and sacrifice to Kilkai
then go ahead and sacrifice to Kilkai
if you want to take it and sacrifice to Maip
then go ahead and sacrifice to Maip
(where Maip and Kilkai are local spirit cults, for
which other names could be substituted in other areas)

(lines 1049–52)

Perhaps the most frequently used of all such expressions (which happens not to occur in this transcript) is:

koyik nun-lum, koyik nui-o
If you want to bake and eat it, then bake and eat it

kalk nun-lum, kalk nui-o
If you want to roast and eat it, then roast and eat it

There is further discussion of parallelism in section 5.4 on the use of tropes and in section 5.6 on the use of rhetorical questions.

Another feature which is correlated with *el ung* is the use of the linguistic category of 'segmentary person', as discussed in section 5.2 above. Informants' exegeses (which are often incorporated into the transcript in square brackets) showed that almost all grammatically singular or dual person references within *el ung* passages (whether by (mainly pronominal) noun phrases or by person marking on the verb) are construed as references, or potential references, not to individuals alone, but to segmentary units with which they are identified. In other words, the person references within *el ung* speeches are, to a much greater extent than elsewhere, *segmentary* person references. Exactly how much greater? In order to establish that statistically, the most useful method turned out to be an indirect one, whereby what we tabulated was not the use of SP per se, but the relative incidence of person references of a kind which were clearly *not* in SP, viz. those which were grammatically plural.

Why calculate incidence in this way, i.e. by determining which forms, because they are plural, *cannot* be interpreted as SP? The answer has to do with differences in the possible referential ambiguity of grammatically singular, dual, and plural number categories. In their exegeses, informants frequently judged singular and dual person references to be ambiguous between SP and non-SP values. Where singular and dual forms occur, it is sometimes very clear in context which instances *must* be taken as SP. But we are still left with some instances where it is difficult to clearly decide between SP and non-SP readings. This underscores the overall rhetorical force of SP: to blur the distinction between the singular transactor in the speech situation, and the political identity (however precisely definable in context) with which, by use of SP, he may be understood to be identified. But given this potential for ambiguity, a count of grammatically singular and dual forms is, paradoxically, not as definitive a measure of SP as a negative count of what *cannot* be taken as SP, i.e., grammatically plural forms.[16]

To quantify this kind of indirect evidence for SP within *el ung,* we counted grammatically plural references within two 250-line samples of the transcript, one in *el ung* (lines 910–1059, 1481–1579) and the other not (lines 1–249).[17] The results are shown in Table 5–1.

Table 5–1: *Plural references in* El Ung *vs. elsewhere*

		In *El Ung*	Elsewhere
1pl	Verbs (or verb sequences)	4	28
2/3pl	Verbs (or verb sequences)	21	52
1pl	Pronouns	1	6
2/3pl	Pronouns	1	3
Total Plural References		27	89

What the table shows is that the incidence of person references with a grammatical category that is clearly *not* SP is less than one third as great within *el ung* than elsewhere in Appendix A, even though the entire transcript concerns segmentary politics and contains many instances of SP even outside of the *el ung.*[18]

Moreover, a fair portion of the instances of plural forms that do occur in the *el ung* sample are largely irrelevant to the question of SP, because they occur as indefinite or 'impersonal' subjects (e.g. lines 1488, 1491, 1494, 1527, 1577) or in reported speech (lines 1535, 1557). Others are exceptions that prove the rule. For instance, three of the plural references occur in lines 1483–5, where the behavior of the addressee(s) is being contrasted explicitly with that of the 'ancestor' (i.e. ancestors), in comparison with whom the addressees are accused of talking as if they had their 'minds in the menstrual hut' – the antithesis of concerted male action in the public sphere. This negative characterization is coincident with a shift out of SP, after the same people had been referred to in 2sg SP in line 1482.

In conclusion, the above data lend further empirical support to the claim made in Rumsey (1986:289) that 'oratory always serves to index something about its context of use, i.e., that segmentary groups are involved as significant interactional entities'. In particular, the use of *el ung* prosody and paralinguistic features serves to mark increased likelihood of a shift from the normal person values of the singular and dual categories to their specifically oratorical 'segmentary person' values. Though the latter are also implemented in non-*el ung* oratory, the SP interpretation is more strongly 'forced' by occurrence within *el ung*.

5.4 *UNG EKE* ('BENT SPEECH')

Another feature which tends to co-occur with *el ung* is *ung eke* 'bent speech'. The nature and uses of the equivalent speech style among the Melpa – called by the cognate term *ik ek* – have been well described and exemplified in A. Strathern (1975), to which we refer the reader for supplementary discussion (see also Rumsey 1986).

A necessary characteristic of bent speech – what makes it 'bent' — is the use of tropes.[19] All instances of it which we will discuss below would probably be identified (in translation) by most of our readers as figurative. But the converse does not hold: not everything in Ku Waru speech which we might regard as figurative is considered by Ku Waru people to be *ung eke*. Accordingly, in order to identify instances of it within our transcripts, we relied entirely on our Ku Waru informants' judgments about the matter. As we worked with them on the draft transcripts of men's speeches, our linguistic assistants identified many *ung eke* passages, from which we selected a sample of twenty to discuss with a wide range of other informants. We did so partly in response to the recommendations by our language assistants, mostly young men, who, while readily identifying instances of *ung eke*, would often say they didn't understand its meaning or import (*ung mong, ung lapa*: see Appendix D). We conducted interviews with twenty people, of all descriptions (male/female, young/old, high/low status, etc), most of whom had been present at the events represented in the transcripts.[20] Where possible, the speakers themselves were included among those from whom comments were sought. Except for some of the latter, each of the interviewees was questioned about most or all of the same twenty passages in our sample. Questions asked at the interviews included the following: Who is speaking? Who is he speaking to? 'Is what he is saying *ung eke*? What does it mean? Why did he say it? Why did he say it in that way?[21]

One thing that became clear from these interviews is that there is a large stock of more-or-less standard figures which we could call *ung eke* commonplaces. In the case of most of these expressions, what is fixed about them is not their precise wording, but the image conveyed. Consider, for example, lines 940–44 in Appendix A (*sirku nokum, kamaya nokum,* etc.). The image here is of stiff, sharp grasses which pierce the feet when one has to walk through them. It is widely used in *el ung* tropes referring to the dangers and hardships of battle. What is fixed and commonplace here is not a locution as such, but an idea or image, which may be evoked by reference to a number of different objects, the relevant experience of which is similar in some respect.[22]

Let us examine some of the *ung eke* images found in Appendix A, and some additional ones drawn from speeches we recorded at the later payments at

Palimung and Kopola. These are tropes which were agreed by all of the people we consulted to be *ung eke*. Further below, we shall examine variability in their responses concerning the interpretation of these tropes.

Speakers make frequent use of images of slippery things: logs, vegetation, and ground (mud). These are usually said to be or understood to be located in the forest. Slipperiness stands for precariousness, so the force of such images is to suggest a need for caution, and to cause the audience to consider what the speaker has in mind as requiring caution.

Vegetation described as slippery typically includes mushrooms and fallen trees. In Kopia Noma's second *el ung* speech (transcript, line 1029 ff.) a nothofagus beech tree is said to be at the spirit cult places of Kilkai and Maip, sunk into the ground, on which the unwary may slip. The tree is *puruyl* 'rotten', which suggests not only slipperiness but long-term decomposition and rot (but cf. Noma's own comment in section 6.2.6. for an interesting qualification of this). The tree image is understood as an allusion to a grievance, and involves a further conventional association of tree with 'man', connoting an unavenged wounding or death. Explicit imagery of man as tree usually makes use of tree types which are especially sturdy or tall, such as *karaip* ('nothofagus beech') in the above example, or *waima* (a very large conifer species) in the following excerpt from an *el ung* speech at Kopola by Wanaka Parka:

ang ekepu nu nyikin-lum-a
Brother, what you are saying now

kunumang waima lu pulurum-kin-a
at Kunumang an ax chopped down a waima *tree*

yab tilupu te-ne
One person

turum-kily-i
felled it

The imagery is related to and supported by the practice of giving male names which are those of certain trees: one of the Kailge magistrates is named Waima.

The image of man as tree, and the sturdiness of the person, is also supported and echoed in rhetorical formulation of persons as of enduring value. A frequent rhetorical assertion is that the value of a man is not fully substitutable by that of any valuable or payment (cf. Wagner 1975:92). In the Palimung event (which is discussed in Chapter 7); a speaker, Midipu Mai, referring to Kopia Uwa's having been injured while riding on the Midipu car, says to the Kopia: I am giving you only a poor thing [money], a small thing. The notion that money is not commensurable with the value of a person, though it may be made to stand for a person in compensation payments, is made even more explicit by Midipu Kujilyi, who having accepted responsibility for the trouble, says, 'If a man had died, oh money, could you replace a man?' (line 46). Similar sentiments were expressed in all the major payment events we attended. Hence also the minimization of the significance of these payments (compared to those made for a death) in the statements of several speakers in the transcript: We are not buying/paying for a man, we are simply compensating for the wounded ('buying new blood', e.g. line 1088).

The identification of man with tree expresses the value and irreplaceability of the (male) person, the person as a *todul* 'strong' thing. There is also constant concern with *talapi* size and strength which finds expression in a number of typical images. Inadequacy in *talapi* strength may be expressed by an image of small or dwarfed body size, or by shortness or inadequate size in other objects. Kujilyi, talking of small *talapi* size in a way that (rather unusually) places it in a positive light, on one occasion said:

> po makupiya kolumayl lu naa tolym
> *the ax does not cut short sugar cane*

His meaning (according to his own exegesis) was that a small *talapi* may not be the object of hostility as easily as a large one. A nearly identical expression – *po makupiya langulyuyl* 'broken-off piece of sugar-cane' – was used by Unya to describe 'himself' (Kubuka) at line 983. Expression of small body size (see line 473) contrasts with substantial body size, the latter a common metaphor for considerable *talapi* strength (see line 901 when Tamalu speaks of *yi kap-ayl* 'fat' or 'large man').

There is a standard imagery of 'ally' represented as dependent female. A transparent metaphor is that of ally as wife, as for example in a speech by Lalka Kewa from the Palimung payment (see Chapter 7):

> They stopped it like that and now that man down there (Tea-Dena) (is) thinking that (Epola-Alya-Kusika-Midipu) is my wife, now that man (Kopia-Kubuka) is taking her back, he is thinking this . . .

Here Kewa imputes to Tea-Dena the thought that Kusika-Midipu-Epola-Alya-Lalka used to be *his* wife, but now Kopia-Kubuka is taking her. He uses the verb (*mang-*) ordinarily employed to mean 'return bridewealth payment' (and thus effect the return of a woman).

A related turn of phrase is that of 'taking a wife', meaning 'to gain as ally'. The speaker-orientation in the use of such dependent female images is generally male. That is, speakers talk of 'taking a wife'. 'getting her back', etc. and their implicit identification is with the male role. From this perspective, the ally is female, bargainable as is a wife concerning whom one makes and debates a bridewealth offer.

But orators do not *always* assume the male perspective. A noticeable exception in Appendix A is the way in which the role of Kujilyi is constructed through female imagery. At line 743 Kopia Kupena cites Kujilyi's (alleged) self-characterization as a prostitute who solicited the help of other people. Kujilyi, having chosen to mediate for the Epola-Alya, was in need of help, and had to ask others for assistance. Kujilyi himself, rather than take up the image of himself as prostitute, chooses when he speaks to substitute (line 802) a perhaps slightly blander one of himself as unmarried woman concerned about whether anyone would marry, i.e., help, her.

Another (somewhat cryptically) female image is the rendering of the notion of living in accord with or getting along with someone as 'sleeping in the netbag'. The basic image is probably that of the child sleeping in the netbag/womb (*wal*). In the Palimung payment, Kopia Noma says to Kujilyi and Koluwa:

kopola yi peam-nga
in Kopola Peam's

ala-wal-na pebu nyikin pilyin kanapa
underarm netbag I will sleep, seeing you said that

aku-na nunu pi-o
you sleep there

In other words, you two managed your affairs in such a way as to be associated with Dena Peam. Particularly small underarm netbags may connote carrying of poisons or secreted objects. Noma also says of Peam that he brought a snake in a netbag into the area near Kailge. But the most neutral sense of 'sleep in the netbag' seems to be 'to live tranquilly, peaceably with'.

In the Palimung event Kopia Ladikang employed an image of a netbag splitting at the bottom or front, suggesting trouble or disruption of regional harmony:

sipi kudanga *bruk* nyim-lum i nyib kanab-a
if it breaks at the bottom I shall be aware

kere-kid *bruk* nyim-lum i nyib kanab-a
if it breaks in front I shall be aware

'Bottom' and 'front' were meant to be interpreted as geographical references. The common understanding of 'bottom' was as reference to the Tea-Dena and/or Tola-Wanaka who live 'down' in the lower Nebilyer Valley. 'Front' was understood as a reference to Poika-Palimi on the other side of the Tambul range.

While slipperiness connotes possible accident and the need for caution, various images of trouble are common. Kujilyi once spoke of trouble as chips flying:

mara karel-ayl-kiyl-o bur naa nyipiyl nyib
saying 'let mara chips not fly'

kongun teamiyl nyibu tekir-o
let us work [together] I mean to say

Images of *kupulanum* 'road', *ka* 'rope' and *pol* 'bridge' expressing 'relation to, connection with' are very common, and not always regarded as *ung eke*. (For example, someone asked why she does not visit in a certain place may say: *ka naa lelym* 'there is no rope', i.e., 'I have no links there'.) But such basic images can be elaborated in ways that are regarded as *ung eke*. Numje (at the Kopola payment) used the image of a wire bridge snapping to suggest possible future trouble and/or the breaking off of a relationship:

kunutapiya-te lyirin nyib naa nyib-a
I will not say you took up the shield

waya polayl kuluni-yl tungu nyiba molo leba-ja?
when you tread the wire bridge will it snap, or remain?

That is, I will not reproach you now; but in future will there be trouble between us, will our (formerly amicable) relationship endure or not?

Imagery of 'looking after' or 'watching over' is common in big-men's speeches, as they attempt to depict themselves as having mediatory roles in regional relations. In the Palimung event, Kulka Pokea, emphasizing his advantageous position as mediator in the western Nebilyer troubles (see Chapter 7), said that people should look upon him as 'father', and ask him for help when necessary. He also expressed his guardianship of the region through an analogy of parts of the valley to parts of his own body. Kailge, he said, was his head (that is, important and essential to him). In a different analogy (but similar in that it constructs the big-man as physically present over a part of the region larger than his own's *talapi's* territory) Kulka Kanuba said that he was a snake. By this he meant nothing negative. Rather, he elaborated the image by saying that his head is at Tabuga and his tail at Kailge, and that if anything happened throughout the valley, he would sense it. In the Palimung event, Poika Nori spoke of himself (or the Poika-Palimi more broadly) as *kera dowa* 'eagle', who can watch over relations on either side of the Tambul Range.

Several sets of common images, often constructed in parallel form, derive their suggestiveness from belonging to the range of events or signs that are commonly understood as *temal* 'omens'. The importance of omens is that they underscore and express the notion that the future is unclear, holds options, may be either this way or that way. A common omen is the weather on the day of a public event: the weather is treated as suggestive of the state of social relations. Thus, at Kopola (see section 7.3), Wanaka Parka said of the rain to Dena Numje:

> ang-a, pudi kare kuyurubul-kin
> *Brother, when we roasted winged beans*
>
> kolya ena purum kanilyi
> *it was sunny then*
>
> ekepu lo-te tokum-ayl, pilyikin-i?
> *now rain is falling, do you understand?*

One speaker in the Palimung compensation, Kulka Kakuyl, varied the suggestiveness of the rain image by formulating a notion of 'rain in the mind':

> kolya lo tokum ilyi-a
> *it is raining here*
>
> nu-nga numana-kid tokum-kilya
> *(and) it is raining in your mind*
>
> numan-ayl pilyikir-iyl
> *I intuit this [sense this in my mind]*

Another omen involves contrasting 'light and dark' (or 'red and black'), whether the referents be human skin-color or, as is frequently the case, the color of pools of water. At the end of a speech in the Palimung compensation, Lalka Kewa said: 'As you return home, you will come to the confluence of the Luip and Ukulu Rivers; and if you see there a red lake, we will take notice of this; or if you see there a black lake, we will take notice of this'. Most people asked interpreted the image in general as the option between war and peace. 'Black' connotes peace, tranquil living; and 'red', turbulence and hostility. Similarly, we were told that as different sides approach a battlefield, people will discuss which set of combatants looks 'lighter' ('redder'), and those will be victorious. Regardless of the specific value of each term, the general significance of such parallel figures is to suggest that the course of future events is not settled or clear, that there are various possibilities.

Making light of the portentous nature of the omen is the source of humor in a remark made by an unidentified bystander about Kopia Kupena's apron threatening to fall off: 'His loincloth is falling down, so something is going to happen', he says to audience laughter. In other words, something untoward is happening, what can it mean? Kupena picks up the joke: 'My front loincloth is falling, I thought it was for nothing', he joins in, where the force is understood as: it is not for nothing, it is indeed portentous. 'As I talk about this money it is falling down', Kupena adds (Appendix A lines 730–732), suggesting that the significance lies in this.

Making use of another fairly standard parallel image, Councillor Noma says in reference to Kujilyi: 'If he tells me to go to the forest, I will take notice of that; or if he tells me to go to the cultivated area, I will take notice of that'. Most people interpreted this as: I will be watching you for indications of what you will do. The choice is understood to be generally between keeping the peace or engaging in further fighting. Perhaps contrary to our expectations, people understand the 'forest' option to mean 'live peaceably', the 'cultivated area' to signify trouble. The contrast is thus similar to one established between the cool and shade of Palimung as a more suitable locale for that payment to take place, versus the hot, open area of Sibeka, where both of the latter attributes are associated with what Sibeka actually was during the fighting, a battlefield (cf. section 7.2.2).

Other standard tropes include that of the place 'burning' to describe or suggest warfare and trouble (e.g. line 56), 'shelling one's betel nut' to signify making a payment or distribution (line 65), and analogy of former fights with contests between two animals or insects (e.g. line 445, when Unya speaks of the tussle between frog and grasshopper). We may note also the everyday use of the pair marsupial/dog to connote irreconcilable difference, inextinguishable hostility and the like (cf. section 5.7 and Lancy and Strathern 1981:782). But all of these expressions have a certain transparency, and do not necessarily raise the question whether the speaker has a particular incident in mind to which he wishes to allude, or a particular message which he wishes his audience to relate to those happenings which are the ostensible raison d'être of the public event. Let us examine several tropes of a contrasting kind, all identified as *ung eke*, about which there was the least concurrence in the exegeses.

At lines 143–4 of Appendix A, Kujilyi says: 'Well, when you're about to cut up a pig, they put something which we're going to eat underneath and cut, not right on the ground'. Some of those we asked for their understanding of this trope interpreted it as follows: when he says we carve having put something underneath he means, let us not simply give money, let us also give pigs, let us do things properly. Given the importance of a prestation of pigs (usually arising from an episode of warfare, and requiring future return), to interpret the trope in this way is to attribute to it not only this general significance, but to entertain the possibility that Kujilyi is covertly suggesting some more specific and immediate actualization of this conversion to higher-level exchange.

One woman consulted had a quite different view: If I were not here, you would not make a payment, you would not have sufficient determination (she used the Tok Pisin word *pawa*); but since I am here, the distribution(s) will be made. On this interpretation, Kujilyi intends that which goes underneath to be understood as himself, who makes the payment possible. The interpretation of one rising young man, the adult (twice-married) son of a local big-man, was basically the same: if I were not here to tell you what to do, you would not make this payment. But I am here, and that is good and proper, like putting vegetables under the pig when you carve it.

Kujilyi himself said his intended meaning was as follows: 'pig' is to be understood as 'fight', and *manya mel nomolu* 'the thing underneath that we will eat' as compensatory payment. Thus, whether or not anyone dies in the fighting, we will still pay compensation. When presented with the second interpretation cited above (whereby vegetables=Kujilyi and pig=compensation payment), he said that, too, was a possible meaning, and in fact was much the same as what he had intended. Thus, the second interpretation supposed the image to enlarge the person and role of Kujilyi beyond what he apparently intended, but this is in keeping with what people understand to be a pragmatic implication of the use of *ung eke* by male speakers in the public arena.

At lines 211–12 Kujilyi uses another trope which was universally identified as *ung eke*: 'When it rains they say it's sunny: When it's dark they say it's getting light'. Apparently following this up he says, at line 213, 'Thinking it's night, I myself am sleeping'. Interpretations of this, too, were variable. The rising young man would not interpret the trope as recorded (he had been present at the event, too). He said that Kujilyi had made a mistake and should have said: *Lo topa-kin kunungu pakap obu, Subulu molum-lum kiya kadap obu* 'When it rains I will come wearing a tarp/covering, if it is dark I will come with lighted torch'; i.e., I will stand by you and help you, rain or shine. An older woman informant gave an interpretation similar in some respects: When it rains you provide me with shelter, when it is sunny, I shall walk around without; i.e., you help me when I need it. Both of these informants were apparently thinking of another standard trope, which however is slightly different from what Kujilyi actually said. Because of some similarities with what he actually said, they assumed he had meant the other. In a discussion of this speech with Kujilyi, he said his intended meaning was that plans (for compensation events), once set, should not be changed. The intent of what he actually said was to criticize those who, seeing one situation in force, then assert that something else is the case. Interestingly, the wife of Kopia Councillor Noma, Ab Nulya, understood Kujilyi's trope in a way similar to what he intended: '. . . We set a day, let us do it on that day. Let it not drag out; if it drags out, you, drinking beer and doing other things, will use up the money, let us give shortly'. In other words, she understood not only his intended *general* meaning (that set plans should not be changed), but here explains how she thought that general meaning was to be taken in these circumstances. Though most women we consulted concerning *ung eke* claimed not to be able to understand it ('that is how men talk, we women do not understand', some said), when presented with specific quotations from this event at which all had been present, most had an interpretation. It was noticeable that certain women more prominent in public life (like Ab Nulya) tended more often to give at least the general sense that the speaker himself claimed to have intended.

For a further example of an *ung eke* trope which the speaker, Councillor Noma, intended to have a specific reference, see section 6.2.6. In that instance, nobody understood the particular reference, but all understood in general what he intended to say: that he had a grievance, and that he was exploring whether the Laulku would be willing to take up his gambit to develop further exchange relations.

All of the examples we have given illustrate that *ung eke* tropes are typically known to the audience, who are familiar with the general significance of each. Despite this seeming standardization, use of *ung eke* in speech-making is regarded as difficult. As one woman said, speakers use *ung eke* when 'their minds are illumined' (*numan-ayl pa tolym-kin*). Mastery seems therefore to consist not so much in the coining of tropes (though no doubt some usages are innovatory), as in the usage of a stock of known images in ways that are considered meaningful and suggestive in context (cf. Merlan 1989).

An example is the cited trope employed by Kujilyi, where his intended meaning was that set plans should not be altered. The period before a major prestation is always fraught with suspense about whether the intending donors will be able to amass their resources, or whether some disruption will intervene, hence whether the event will be realized as planned. Part of the effectiveness of such a trope is that it alludes to the uncertainty which is palpable to all participants in the planning of such events. Kujilyi's other trope ('carve pig with something beneath, not directly on the ground') seemed to be regarded as even more highly suggestive. At the same time that it was taken as bearing on immediate, important events, the relation of the parts of the trope to each other, and the whole to current circumstances, seemed subject to even more variable interpretation.

In short, the allusiveness so highly valued in *ung eke* inheres in the employment of tropes[23] in ways that can be seen as portentous, particularly for inter-*talapi* relations. In the most successful uses of tropes there is always an element of uncertainty concerning how they may be related to circumstances. Orators work at introducing images into events, and thus – whether the tropes are interpreted exactly as they intended or not – contributing to the sense of outcome of those events, rather than at coining new tropes.

5.5 SPEECH GENRES, TROPES AND REMARKS ON INTERPRETATION

We have now given examples of *el ung*, a specifically oratorical speech genre, and *ung eke*, indigenously recognized tropes, which often occur in *el ung* speeches, but also are used in many other contexts, oratorical and otherwise. Because there has been some confusion about this in the secondary literature which has drawn upon A. Strathern (1975), we want to emphasize that *el ung* and *ung eke* are not mutually exclusive codes.[24] Rather, they are indigenously distinguished along separate axes of contrast: *el ung* is distinguished from other prosodically marked genres, such as *tom yaya kange* (a kind of chanted epic tale) and *ab kunana* 'courting songs', and from *ung urip* 'casual conversation'; while *ung eke* is defined (contra Bloch 1975:26) in *binary* opposition to *ung kuni* 'straight/direct speech'. (See section 5.8 below and Appendix D.) The latter dimension of contrast is one that cross-cuts the former, so that given stretches of *el ung, tom yaya kange, ab kunana*, or *ung urip* are independently classifiable as either 'bent' or 'straight' (i.e., figurative or non-figurative) speech. Thus, as we have seen, within the context of men's oratory at an inter-*talapi* exchange event (Bloch's (1975:26) 'situation of confrontation from status'), some of the *ung eke* figures occur within *el ung* speeches[25] and some in non-*el ung* speeches. There is even a positive correlation between the two, as discussed in section 5.3.

For the figures whose meaning we have discussed, we have mentioned various alternative interpretations given to us by informants who were present at the events where they were used. The variability among exegeses concerns both what philosophers would call the *sense* of the tropes and their *reference*. In other words, there is sometimes disagreement about what the 'literal' or 'straight' (*ung kuni*) version of the same passage would have been (or even about whether it is appropriate to look for one), and sometimes disagreement about which particular people and incidents are being talked about, even in the 'straight' version. Sometimes there is more agreement about one than the other: as in the case of Councillor Noma's figure of the rotting trunk of a nothofagus beech tree (line 1047), there was agreement upon the general sense, but no agreement about what *was* the grievance he alluded to (cf. section 6.2.6). The latter sort of disagreement – about *reference* – is one which in our work with informants was not confined to discussions of *ung eke*. It was also frequently encountered among exegeses of passages which everyone agreed were *ung kuni*, especially when they occurred in speeches which were delivered in the *el ung* style. For example, in discussions of Unya's speech in lines 413–25, there was disagreement concerning the meaning of his *ung eke* in line 415, but also concerning the reference of all instances of the 3sg ('he', 'him') in lines 418–420 and 422–3, none of which contains any *el ung*.

These are examples of what A. Strathern presumably means when he describes *el ik* as 'allusive':[26] references within it are relatively indirect and potentially multiplex. This is in fact one of the more basic semantic attributes of *el ung* (and of Nebilyer oratory in general), of which the use of *ung eke* can be taken as a specific instance. In bent speech, the fact that the sense is indirectly conveyed entails that the reference is also indirect. But while indirectness of sense is a sufficient condition of indirectness of reference, it is not a necessary condition. This is also achieved through what A. Strathern (1975:203) calls 'compressed' language, by which we take him to be referring, at least in part, to the sorts of ellipses found in the examples from Unya's speech, discussed above, where new third person participants are introduced into the discourse without the use of any explicit referring expressions (proper names, definite descriptions, demonstratives, etc).

The use of segmentary person – a ubiquitous feature of *el ung* speeches, as we have seen – leads to ambiguities of reference within the 1sg and 2sg categories of a kind which are not otherwise possible. In other contexts, the reference of these categories follows directly from the most basic feature of their context of use: the obvious presence of a speaker and addressee, to whom all non-quoted instances of 1sg and 2sg respectively may be taken to refer. In *el ung*, where these formal categories are used with their SP values, their reference becomes much less patent. In those contexts, it is no longer directly calculable from obvious features of the speech situation, and becomes potentially highly variable in scope. The SP use of *na* 'I', recall, was glossed as 'the segmentary unit with which the speaker is identified' and *nu* 'you' as 'the segmentary actor to whom this utterance is addressed'. Even assuming that every one present when such a form is used has a thorough knowledge of the segmentary identities of all the participants (and for the most part they do), there remains the problem that people belong to segmentary categories at many different levels on the segmentary hierarchy. As we shall see in Chapter 6, SP reference is made on a sliding scale over various of those levels, and is regularly extended so as to include within a single referent segmentary units for which there is no common name, but who are 'paired tribes', or who are military or political allies. This applies not only to the personal pronouns *na* and *nu*, but to all verbs inflected for 1sg, 2sg, and 3sg in SP contexts, and to all 3sg anaphoric elements, and to certain singular nouns which are regularly used as SP forms (*yi*, etc., as discussed in section 5.2).

5.6 RHETORICAL QUESTIONS

A typical feature of ordinary Nebilyer speaking, as well as speech-making, is the posing of rhetorical questions. These are formally of two types: information questions, that is ones that, if answered, would require a substantive response; and those that have the usual form of yes-no questions, in which the clitic *-i* is suffixed to the last word of the question.

We are calling 'rhetorical' questions which, rather than being directed to any interlocutor for an answer, instead appear to be posed as a way for the speaker to construct his own continuing speech. Within Nebilyer speech-making, rhetorical questions have a particular value in that they provide a means for the speaker to make appeal to his audience while at the same time furthering his speech uninterrupted. That is, the speaker poses a question but intends to retain the option of answering it himself, and in fact, in most cases he would seek to override anyone else who attempted to interpose an answer. Further, most such questions are not taken up or answered directly by the speaker, either, but are used as a resource for the self-contained advancement of the speech.

The question is an important speech resource because its form suggests engagement with an audience. But the *rhetorical* use of questions must be described as ironic in that, while such questions are *apparently* intended to engage, the speaker's *actual* intention is to continue on uninterrupted. This contradiction between form and intended function perhaps accounts for the often somewhat aggressive-seeming manner or feeling-tone of rhetorical questions.

Rhetorical information questions are exemplified at lines 1–4, 6, 15, 426, 774 of Appendix A. In lines 1–4, Kubuka Tamalu poses a number of questions which he clearly does not intend to be answered, but to set the stage for what he sees as the determinations that must be made regarding the money to be presented. Thus he asks: 'How many . . . were wounded in the fighting?'[27] and 'How much tobacco do you smoke? How much betel . . . and cabbage do you (sg) eat?' The implicit suggestion is that the recipients of money will be able to spend it on these things.

At line 6 Tamalu asks another stage-setting rhetorical question: 'What about this little problem – this thing that happened to us?' (i.e., the fighting and obligations resulting from it). In a sense Tamalu takes up his own gambit here, developing his speech by saying, 'That's what I want to straighten out', and starting to talk about the money raised.

At line 15 he poses another question: 'I'm taking this thousand, and how much will be left over?' This again might be said to be a question to which an answer is expected, but Tamalu clearly does not expect it now. Taking up this question he adds, 'When I see [how much], I will say, When I have found out, you shall listen and I will tell you' – anticipating that he will eventually supply an answer to this question.

Kopia Kupena's question, at line 426, illustrates the very common use of (both kinds of) rhetorical question to ridicule, but is immediately directed to problems of trying to control his audience. As the crowd becomes unruly, he asks, 'Where do you come from?', implying (as we also might understand it), you have no sense of propriety.

At lines 774–5 Kopia Noma, having said in *el ung* that 'he' gave three hundred kina, poses the question: 'Why did I do it?' He gives a somewhat cryptic response: 'A man who lives near the riverside always takes people's hands' (to help them). Only in the next few lines does it become clear that he is suggesting an analogy between a man's proximity to the riverside, and the proximity of Kopia to Epola, whom he is therefore inclined to help.

The second kind of rhetorical question is signalled by the clitic *-i*, which marks ordinary yes-no questions. Although ordinarily the yes-no question does not presuppose a particular answer, rhetorical uses of this question form are often to be understood as sarcastic or accusatory, and to presuppose a particular answer: either 'yes' or 'no' according to how the question is phrased.

For example, at line 39 Kubuka Tepra, who is trying to make people sit down, uses a strong command form (the Perfective – see Appendix B.3.2.2). Then at line 40 he poses the yes-no question: *Kung mabola kalung-i*? 'Have you put on pig grease?' To do so is to decorate oneself and make oneself ready for public display. When he asks this in this context in which he is trying to effect crowd control, the self-evident answer is 'no'. Those addressed are being further told that they are not qualified to get up to speak, and should therefore sit and be quiet.

Other yes-no rhetorical questions occur at lines 46, 118–20, 149–50, 274, 524, 581, 671, 1777. We will briefly examine the first three and the last of these.

At line 46 Kujilyi asks rhetorically: 'If a man had died, oh money, could you replace a man?' Obviously he does not expect the money to answer. The force of his question is to suggest, no, money cannot replace a man.

At lines 118–20, Kujilyi uses a rhetorical question to make the point that one cannot act alone, one requires allies: 'Will you put on a forehead plate by yourself, or put on feather headdresses by yourself?'.

At lines 149–50 Kujilyi says, 'You have eyes but think I don't? You have a mind and I don't?' Kujilyi is clearly attributing to his audience (or selected persons in the audience) the thought that he, Kujilyi, does not have these senses. The presupposed answer to these questions is, 'Yes, I do have these senses, despite what you may think'. The circumstances here are that Epola-Alya, who will contribute to the future return payment to Kopia-Kubuka, are not represented; only Kujilyi is present from the cluster of allies who will sponsor the return payment. He wants to make it clear that he will carefully observe the Kopia-Kubuka outlay and make a sufficient and appropriate return. So, the considerations underlying his questions run, do you think your senses are finer than mine, such that you will think of all of those who are deserving, and you think I will not act appropriately when the time comes?

At line 1777, alluding to the future repayment, Kubuka Tepra asks with reference to Kujilyi: 'Is he like a [European] company?', i.e., are his resources so large and limitless? The inference is clearly 'No', our expectations of Kujilyi must be reasonable.

In these questions it is noticeable that there is a kind of standardized relation between question form and suggested inference: the presupposed answer or inference to be drawn is the opposite in positive-negative polarity of the question form. That is, if the question is phrased positively (as in line 40, 'Have you put on pig grease?') the presupposed answer is negative; if the question is phrased negatively ('. . . I do not have eyes?') the presupposed answer is positive. Whereas in ordinary usage there is no such firm expectation (*Nu kanun-i*? 'Did you see (it)?' *might*, other things being equal, be expected to be answered either 'Yes' or 'No', i.e., is not *necessarily* taken to be ironic), in these contexts of understood rhetorical usage, questions of this form are generally taken to be so, and to be answerable by the opposite polarity to the way in which they are posed.

The frequent use of rhetorical questions is of special interest for the way in which it focuses attention on the *activity of speaking* as it is being realized. It does this by making patent a tension between form (which suggests an answer is being elicited) and intended effect (which is not to elicit an answer, or at least not from anyone besides the speaker). This use of a speech resource to focus on the activity of speaking is something the rhetorical question has in common with 'talk about talk', another important resource to which we turn in section 5.8.

5.7 PAIRING

Already at several points in the discussion so far, we have pointed to the centrality of *pairing* in various aspects of Nebilyer social life. In Chapter 3, we showed that Ku Waru segmentary structures tend to be binary ones, so that their elaboration, both by internal division and by external combination, tends to result in multiply ramified hierarchical structures with just two branches at every node. In assessing (and dismissing) the relevance of descent for the indigenous representation of such segmentary structures, we pointed out that, insofar as particular *talapi* have origin myths, these generally refer not to a single apical ancestor or progenitor, but to an ancestral pair of brothers. From the examples of rhetorical parallelism in this chapter, one can see that it is almost always a 'parallelism of pairs', and that the linguistic and paralinguistic structure of *el ung* in particular involves several other kinds of pairing as well (cf. section 8.1 below).

Within the New Guinea Highlands, this emphasis upon pairing is by no means limited to the Nebilyer Valley, nor are we the first to have noticed it. As in so many other matters, Hermann Strauss pointed the way. Listing the names of seventy tribe-pairs in the 'Mbowamb' (Hagen/Nebilyer/Kaugel) area (which, incidentally, include Kopia-Kubuka, Mujika-Laulku, Epola-Alya, Poika-Palimi, and Tea-Dena, attesting that these pairings were current at least as early as 1956), Strauss asks:

> Why do the Mbowamb never count up their groups one by one, but always combine them into pairs, each treated as unity? They speak of each such pair using the dual number, as for two individuals.
>
> This pairing of groups can be explained in terms of the Mbowamb mentality. Pairing of this kind is used for many other things as well. One speaks for example of *mugl moi ragl* 'both heaven (and) earth'; *ants kadlimp ragl* 'both sun and moon'; *rumbul röngmö ragl* 'both night and day'; *tepam mam ragl* 'both father and mother', etc. The months are reckoned in twos, each pair related as elder and younger brother. Animals, birds, objects, foods, wealth items, etc. are always combined into pairs. Counting itself is done in pairs. People feel uneven numbers to be in need of completion. One cannot really properly reckon with a single thing; it is not complete, but only like the half of a whole . . . This way of thinking, 'completion', is to be found in language and so also in the entire perception of reality. In my opinion it is not a matter of a 'principle', and also not of a 'male and female principle' – but of the living experience of a need for completeness, the dependence of all beings and things on others, upon a completion or 'fullfilment', without which a single being or thing is 'out of line' or 'out of place', standing off by itself and unrealized.
>
> (1962:15–16, our translation)

The Stratherns' Melpa ethnography contains many additional, valuable details and insights concerning pairing and related matters. In an interesting comparative study on the subject, Lancy and Strathern (1981) argue that pairing among the Melpa (as opposed to the coastal Ponam people, who are presumably more 'typical' in this respect) is an 'alternative to the taxonomic mode of representation'. The Melpa language provides relatively few levels of lexicalized superclass-subclass distinctions (of the type animal-mammal-marsupial, etc.), but *instead* provides pairings of the type 'marsupial-dog', and 'marsupial-bird', 'pig-dog' (see also Strauss's examples, above), which designate classes for which there are no monolexemic (i.e. semantically indivisible) labels, and which do not fit into consistent taxonomic hierarchies, since they typically show overlapping or disjunctive membership rather than subclass-superclass relations.

While we do not fully concur with Lancy and Strathern's view of pairing as an *alternative* to 'taxonomy', this is not the place to take up the matter in detail. Suffice it to say that: 1) Ku Waru is virtually identical to Melpa with respect to the patterns they discuss; 2) while this pairing *tends* not to precipitate in elaborate sets of superclass-subclass relations, their absence or paucity cannot be an essential concomitant of it, since, as Lancy and Strathern themselves point out, relations of that kind are quite extensively developed in one of the areas of vocabulary where pairing is also most in evidence, i.e., segmentary names (as in Chapter 3 above; see Lancy and Strathern 1981:784–6).

What is for our present purposes most important to notice about Hagen/ Nebilyer pairing as opposed to classical 'cognitivist' understandings of 'ethnotaxonomy' (as per, e.g. Tyler 1969) is its *productivity* – what Lancy and Strathern call its 'flexibility'. Consider, for example, the following three Ku Waru pairings (precisely parallel to the Melpa ones we have cited from Lancy and Strathern above):

1 *lopa-kera (-sil)* (the pair of) 'marsupial and bird'
2 *owa-lopa (-sil)* (the pair of) 'dog and marsupial'
3 *kung-owa (-sil)* (the pair of) 'dog and pig'

There can be no fixed, hierarchical relationships among the three classes associated with each of these pairings, not only because a single term may enter into more than one pairing, but because the relevant semantic features of a single such term can vary freely from one pairing to another, this or that feature becoming relevant by association with the other term. Thus, what is relevant about 'marsupial' in example 1 above, is what it has in common with 'bird', i.e., that it is a creature of the forest, for which one goes hunting. This pairing is in fact used not just for marsupials and birds, but as a cover term (in the absence of any monolexemic one) for *all* hunted creatures of the forest, of which these are the salient exemplars or 'prototypes' (cf. Lakoff 1987). By contrast, the arboreal habitat of the marsupial is irrelevant in example 2, where what counts is the chronic antagonism between marsupials and dogs. *Owa-lopa* is, again, used not just in reference to these two but for any chronic antagonists – those who, as we say, 'fight like cats and dogs'.[28] Even a single pairing of terms may pick out different common semantic features according to the context of discourse. This is illustrated by example 3, which is sometimes used as a (non-pejorative) expression for 'domestic animals' (i.e., which sleep in the house), and sometimes as a pejorative expression for people who are uncouth in ways common to those two animals (greedy, incestuous, etc.).

The various semantic characteristics that become relevant for such pairings are usually not what Western theorists would consider *definitional* or *denotative* features, but rather, contingent, or 'connotative' ones. They are not fixed specifications within some abstract, formal structure that we can call *the* Ku Waru (or Melpa) *language*. Rather, they are aspects of people's myriad common experiences of the two sorts of things which are paired – common, that is, to people who share in a particular form of life – one in which, for example, pigs and dogs sleep indoors, birds and marsupials live mainly in uncultivated areas, where they are hunted by men, etc. Given a particular set of lexical forms (linguistic 'types') and a shared range of experiences of particular applications of them (contextualized 'tokens'), almost any aspect of that shared experience can become relevant, according to what is common to both of the paired types. In this respect, such pairings work in a similar way to metaphor, which, in Black's (1962:40) felicitous phrase, juxtaposes two distinct 'systems of associated commonplaces'.

Thus, unlike the lexical categories themselves (and the grammatical structures of compounding which they employ), these pairings are not necessarily elements of linguistic structure per se. They range from fully standard 'lexicalized' ones, such as */yi-ab/*, 'man-woman' for 'person' (widespread in Papuan languages; cf. Tok Pisin *man-meri*), to highly innovative ones arising from particular historical circumstances, or even made up for particular occasions.

Examples of pairings of the latter sorts have already been given above in our discussion of expressions referring to segmentary units (section 5.1). They are one of the several ways in which orators at exchange events work at constructing relations of sameness and difference, a process which we examine in detail below (Chapters 6 to 8). The productivity of this mode of pairing – which is what we have tried to bring out here – is fully consonant with what Sahlins (1981, 1985) would characterize as the 'performative' (as opposed to 'prescriptive') cast of Ku Waru sociality (see further section 7.4.1, Chapter 9).

5.8 TALK ABOUT TALK

A constant feature of public talk in Ku Waru is self-reflexivity: what is talked about is – in large part – the talk itself (cf. Rosaldo 1973, Goldman 1983, ch. 5). In the next two chapters (e.g. in sections 6.2.7., 7.2.3), we will be exploring some of the situated uses of this 'talk about talk' at two exchange events. Here we will limit the discussion to some of the general features of such talk, including the lexico-grammatical resources available for it in Ku Waru (see Appendix D), and their typical uses. However, we also indicate and briefly discuss the extent to which the formulation of social action as *interaction*, particularly through 'talk about talk', is a constant feature not only of public talk, but of Nebilyer speech generally.

As shown in Appendix B.4.3, the Ku Waru verb *nyi-* is used to frame reported speech. In most such contexts, it can be glossed as 'say'. It is also noted in Appendix B that not all reported speech is explicitly framed by any verb. Sometimes the framing 'clause' consists solely of a ergative-marked noun (phrase) or pronoun, referring to the speaker. In other passages which were understood by our exegetes to be reported speech, there was no explicit lexical or morphosyntactic mark of this whatsoever. Examples from Appendix A (expanded with word-by-word interlinear glosses) are as follows:

Example 1
659 pe na-nga kung koyip nob telka-ja pe
and I-Gen pig roast-NF-1 eat-NF-1 do-Sjv-1sg-if then
if I had roasted and eaten a pig

660 i nabitini kung obil-ayl koyipa noba
this what do-Fut-2sg pig bone-Def roast-NF-3sg eat-Fut-3sg
siba nyikim
give-Fut-3sg say-PPr-3sg
[my ally would say] . . . 'what are you going to do; he says he's going to roast and give me a pig bone'

661 na-nga kupulanum wi pukur-na-d nyikir
I-Gen way up go-PPr-Loc-Dat talk-PPr-1sg
I'm talking about what I do up there

Example 2
1527 wily-ola kubuka epu turung-kin-aa
up there kill-RP-2/3pl-Com
when they killed Kubuka Epu up there

1528 kung pengi sai kibolu paie-ni
pig head give-Imp-pl club-Ins
[I said] 'give a kung pengi *('pigs head' payment) [and when they refused], with a club'*

1529 epola koluwa turud-a
hit-RP-1sg
I struck Epola Koluwa

In each of these examples, in order to make sense of what is said, one must be able somehow to infer that the speaker is attributing the words to another speaker or speech situation – to his ally in the first example, and to himself at an earlier occasion in the second example. Further, one must be able to infer at a certain point – with the words *na-nga kupulanum* in example 1 and with the words *kibolu paie-ni* in example 2 – that the reported speech has ended and that the speaker's words belong to the current speech situation alone.

What is especially interesting from our sociolinguistic viewpoint is that the threshold between reported speech and speaker assertion is sometimes indeterminate. Consider the following example from an *el ung* speech:

467 nu ya na-kin-a
you (sg) here I-Com
you and I

468 modalu wal-na pebu-o
netbag-Loc sleep-Fut-1sg
[say] 'I will lie in the netbag' [i.e. we will fight as allies]

469 modalu wal-na peab-o
netbag-Loc sleep-Opt-1sg
'I want to lie in the netbag'

470 mawa mel tin kanapa-o
request sort of do-Prf-2sg if
if you ask me to

471 na ku *wan kina* i nyib *takis* top
I money this say-NF-1 levy do-NF-1
ku *tausen* nyibu tep-o
money thousand say-Imt-1sg do-NF-1
I levying 'one kina', giving one thousand

472 i tep telka-kiyl-o
thus do-NF-1 do-Sjv-1sg and
that's what I could do

473 pe na yi mel-weyl-na
but I man very small-Loc
but I am a very small man [i.e., we are not many]

474 nunu kep-a i bo naa lyirin kani-yl-a
you and this cutting not take-RP-2sg this
and you [K-M-E-A-L] did not take our planting [i.e., did not encourage us to stay here]

Lines 468-9 are clearly being attributed to another speech situation (or situations) in which these words were/are said not only by the present SP 'speaker' ('Kopia-Kubuka') but also by the present 'addressee' ('K-M-E-A-L').[29] The idea is that each of these segmentary 'persons' has pledged its support for the other in times of war. By line 473, the Kopia-Kubuka speaker has clearly moved out of this reported speech and is asserting in the here and now that his *talapi* (Kopia-Kubuka, or Kubuka alone) is only a small one. In the following line (474), he reverts to the fact that the presence of his own *talapi* was in the past *opposed* by the K-M-E-A-L, who were their major enemies. This theme contrasts strongly with the reported speech in lines 467–8, wherein statements of current goodwill are attributed to both the former sides. But what about the intervening lines, 470–2? Do they belong to the reported speech or to the here and now? As far as we can tell, the answer is impossible in principle to establish. These lines can be construed as being attributed to both sides in the present alliance, as commonplace understandings concerning the state of play between them – i.e., that each side is willing to pay ample compensation to the other when the circumstances arise. In this reading, they belong not to the present situation, but to the same generalized set of speech situations to which lines 468–9 belong. But lines 470–2 can also be construed as attributable to the present speaker. According to this reading, he is contrasting what his *talapi could* do with what they *are* doing in view of the fact that the *talapi* is small, and not a long-standing ally of the K-M-E-A-L (as referred to in lines 473–4).

Such threshold-indeterminacy between reported speech and current assertion is by no means infrequent in Nebilyer public discourse (nor elsewhere, but that is another matter). Other passages which can be construed either way may be found in Appendix A, lines 167–9, 341–2, 421–2, 424–5, 1619–20. We need not assume that ambiguity of this kind is due to 'performance error' (Chomsky 1965), i.e., to unintentional failure to make full use of the grammatical means available in Ku Waru for the formal marking of reported speech as such. Rather, ambiguity in general is an inherent, ineluctable feature of the discourse of segmentary politics.[30]

Ambiguity of this particular sort (i.e., that which results from suppression of overt lexico-grammatical boundaries between reported speech and the utterance within which it as embedded) is an instance of what Bakhtin (or his translators) called 'heteroglossia', the intermingling of distinct social 'voices' within a single utterance (Bakhtin 1981, 1986). Heteroglossia is a more general phenomenon because it may also be found in utterances which are, as far as the grammar is concerned, clearly marked as reported or non-reported speech. We will be arguing below that Ku Waru oratory is at least sometimes also heteroglossic in the latter way (see section 7.3.2).

One of the most frequent uses of oratory at public events is in continuing efforts to ensure orderliness of the proceedings – a directive function. Such usage will be amply illustrated in our discussion of events in Chapters 6 and 7. Here we simply note that, in addition to giving instructions, advice and warnings concerning dress and decoration, comportment and group presentation, handling of money, and other matters, speakers constantly attempt to introduce order into speech-making itself. In hopes of resolving competition for the floor, and limiting the extent of speech-making, functionaries at public events sometimes attempt to roster speakers (see section 7.2.1); but such efforts are usually defeated for, though it may be possible initially to establish such a roster, the move from one appointed speaker to the next frequently fails to occur in orderly fashion, and in events we observed, the roster is generally abandoned. Even more commonly, speakers may direct comments to unruly bystanders in efforts to command audience attention.

Besides the use of reported speech, and the directive function of speech, there is much talk about talk in Ku Waru which comments upon what speech act theorists would call its illocutionary force and perlocutionary effect. The lexico-grammatical means for this are mainly of two sorts: 1) head-attribute noun phrases with the word *ung* (or dialect variant *ing*) 'word(s)', 'language', 'speech', 'topic' as head noun; 2) compositional expressions, most of which contain the root *nyi-* 'say'. We illustrate both kinds of resources in Appendix D. Here we will only summarize what we consider some significant aspects of each.

Note the wide variety of glosses given for *ung*. It is used across the entire scale from what linguists analyze as 'minimal free forms' (roughly, words) to the longest texts. Nor does it refer specifically to elements of linguistic *form*, as opposed to *content* or *meaning*. Thus it is best glossed in some contexts as 'topic', 'subject', or 'issue', and commonly, in the even more specific sense of 'troubled issue, problem'. Nor do Ku Waru people distinguish between what linguists (following Saussure) call *langue* ('language') and *parole* ('speech').[31] Thus *ung* refers not only to features of the linguistic code, and topics as general categories, but also to what is done with the code – what is said about those topics – at particular occasions. The wide range of types of talk as social action which *ung* encompasses perhaps is paralleled by the broad extent to which talk about talk is a highly typical way of formulating social interaction: speech has an important place both in the characterization of action types, and processes of interaction. This is eloquently evinced in Appendix A by the fact that the verb *nyi-*, 'to speak', is the most frequently occurring in the entire transcript: it is used 638 times.

The list of expressions in Appendix D – expressions used to characterize speech, and the other general act-descriptors which also apply to speech – is by no means exhaustive, but rather provides an indication of the suppleness of the lexico-grammatical means available in Ku Waru which can be productively used for all sorts of more-or-less innovative forms of commentary on what is said. Note that, in keeping with the compositional nature of Ku Waru verbs in general (see Appendix B.3.2), most of the meaning-making power of this metalinguistic system resides in the grammar – in patterns of combination, e.g. the multiple pairings of *nyi-* 'say' with other verb roots – rather than at the level of lexicon per se. This is worth stressing in view of Goldman's (1983) remarks about the 'economy [read: scarcity] of speech act descriptors' in Huli, where 'Only the act of "saying" is lexically realized' (Goldman 1983:29). If 'lexically realized' means 'realized by a single mono-lexemic element', then Ku Waru is also very economical in this respect. The only monolexemic verbs of 'saying' are *nyi-* 'say', and *walsi-* 'ask'. But see what a wealth of things can be said about talk by combining these and other elements within a few basic grammatical construction types!

Appendix D does include most of the more frequently occurring metalinguistic expressions in Ku Waru, with a bias toward those which tend to occur in public speech of the type found in the transcript Appendix A. But not all conceivable forms of commentary about speech are equally likely to be made. On the contrary, a look at the lists will show that the commentary is particularly elaborate with respect to what Halliday (1985) calls the 'interpersonal' aspects of speech rather than its 'experiential' (logical-cum-ideational) or 'textual'ones. Though there is some commentary on the latter two (e.g. on what one may justifiably say about the ripening time of coffee at Palimung vs. Kailge: Appendix A, lines 165–70), there is far more commentary on talk as a form of interaction among social personae. The majority of expressions in the lists are of this kind. Specifically, it would appear as though public speech here, as among the Huli (Goldman 1983) is construed as a form of ceremonial exchange. This is particularly evident from the expressions which are attested in Appendix A (i.e., the items in Appendix D with no M preceding their line numbers). The talk about talk at such events serves primarily to construct the interaction as one of a particular kind, following norms of reciprocity, and allowing for the individual display of each verbal 'prestation' (cf. Goldman 1983). We shall see in the following three chapters that this is a special case of the more general function of speech as the ultimate medium for the 'discursive redemption' (Habermas 1984) of acts of exchange.

At public events of the kind we examine in the next two chapters – warfare compensation payments where wider political relations are very much in focus – there is a continuous flow of talk. Speakers take up aspects of events that have led up to the payment, but usually not in a neat narrative format. What they say is less an orderly, sequential representation of 'what happened', than a complex weaving together of remarks about the nature of previous relations among those they formulate (at various levels) as the social actors involved; their participation in events deemed relevant to the present one; notions of what is being compensated for – injury? deaths? of whom?; the nature (including amounts) of the payment being made; and the identity of donors and recipients at various levels, with many people in each category taking opportunities to express their particular perspectives regarding all of the above; and foreshadowings of implications of present transactions for future political relations (generally, with much emphasis on the restoration of a tranquil way of life) and possibly, for future exchanges which may be seen as linked to the present one.

The overall effect may be unsettling from any Western perspective which might take as primary within such events the orderly establishing of issues of 'fact', who did what, and a clear sense of the relationship between such facts and the present payment. (See for example the discussion of *el pul*, the 'cause' of the fight, in section 6.2.1). What is produced seems rather to be a collage of somewhat divergent perspectives on political relations, the participants having sufficient familiarity with the bases for those different perspectives – understandings about previous events and the nature of involvement of social actors in them – which provide a somewhat variable set of grounds for their participation in the present transactions.

At these events, talk relating to all of the above matters is interwoven with the material transaction – counting, distribution – of the compensation payment itself (though this only tends to emerge as a clear focus of activity after considerable initial speech-making). Invariably, it adds to the complexity and confusion of the scene. As the material transfers become imminent, a great deal more of the talk also tends to focus on this, and on such matters as appointing reputable guardians and counters of valuables, malfeasance or confusion on previous occasions (see section 7.1), and so forth. Frequently, much of the audience loses track of what is happening with the transfers. (This may be increasingly true today, since many transactions involve money, which can be closely managed by only a few people. However, money, like other valuables, is generally put on display, see sections 6.1, 6.2.5.)

In this chapter we have described kinds of speech resources, many of them restricted to or especially frequent in the public arena, and it is important to adumbrate the relation between them and the general nature of the talk of these public events.

We have described valuable means of formulating actor types through use of segmentary names and other referring expressions, and observed that one of the uses to which orators put *el ung* is to give (their) summaries of the present transaction, employment of *el ung* also 'keying' their summary as having significance for inter-*talapi* relations. We have noted the strong coincidence of use of 'segmentary person' with *el ung,* and pointed to this intersection as a critical moment in the multi-leveled formulation of agency as partaking of individual and segmentary dimensions simultaneously. We have introduced the resource of tropes identified as *ung eke,* noting that their valuation as such increases to the extent they can be interpreted to relate suggestively to aspects of context, and to speaker views and intentions. Many of these resources, then, are significantly constitutive of aspects of the event in other than strictly 'textual' ways, as we observed above.

A number of these resources, perhaps even more than those already mentioned, particularly highlight the salience of speech as social action. They do so by focusing on and being themselves instances of interactional modes of constituting events. The rhetorical question, and the constant re-evocation of earlier events in speech and as speech through talk about talk, renders the sense of the flow of events as one which is formulated and continually monitored by means of speech. That is, much of actors' practical consciousness – their sense of what is going on, and how to carry on (cf. Giddens 1984:7) – is constituted as discursive consciousness; and this is also *re*cursive in that the social past is also very significantly evoked as speech transaction. The extent of this speech-oriented reflexive monitoring produces and sustains a dialogic sense of ongoing social life, in which it is difficult for events, and the issues of how they came about and who took part in them, to be reduced to a single-dimensional or monologic, 'factual account'.

6. Warfare compensation payment to Laulku: an analysis

The event to be examined in this chapter is the public payment presented on July 24, 1983 by Kopia and Kubuka – the first in the series of compensation payments arising from the Marsupial Road War of 1982 (see section 1.1 for summary of those events, and section 3.2.2 for details). Our general aim in this chapter is to exemplify and elucidate the discursive construction of segmentary social identities, and of transactions among them in the public sphere of inter-*talapi* relations. In addition to the background material presented in Chapters 1 to 5 above, essential data for this analysis have included: (1) notes on our attendance at this (and other linked) events, in which we were generally spatially separated and in different company, hence viewing the proceedings from differing perspectives; (2) sound recordings of the speeches made at this event; (3) the full transcript of those recordings which is reproduced in Appendix A; and (4) extensive commentary about the speeches by participants and other observers at the event, much of it on the basis of (2) and (3).[1]

Though it is based upon careful consideration of extensive evidence of all of these kinds, the analysis presented here does not purport to be a final or definitive one. To claim as much would be the height of arrogance, since the meaning of exchange transactions is chronically contested among the transactors themselves (as we hope to show). It should go without saying that the same is true among would-be analysts of those transactions. One of the main reasons why we have thought it appropriate to reproduce the full transcript here, and such full detail concerning the background to this event, is to enable others to have access to some of the principal material upon which our analysis is based, and thus to have at their disposal the means for independently formulating queries about that analysis and perhaps trying to improve upon it (cf. Goldman 1983, Merlan and Rumsey 1986). We realize that our close recourse to the sometimes minutely reproduced detail of actual events may at times place difficult demands upon the reader, but we hope it will help to open up the ethnographic record in such a way as to contribute to a more fully accountable anthropology of situated action.

One of the problems one faces immediately in trying to analyze what goes on in an exchange event of the present kind is that the oratory tends to comprise multiple topical strands, each of which gets taken up and put aside many times during the course of the event (cf. Goldman 1983:14 on Huli disputes as 'multiple claim affairs'). Accordingly, rather than moving sequentially through the transcript, the main body of our analysis (section 6.2) will be organized by topics, each of which will be separately followed through the course of its development (as is done in Merlan and Rumsey 1986). There are, however, identifiable phases in the development as a whole, and the topical analysis will therefore be preceded by a synopsis of the overall event, including some discussion of how it got started and what happened after it finished (section 6.1).

6.1 IMMEDIATE BACKGROUND AND SYNOPSIS OF THE EVENT

In order to understand many aspects of this event, it is important to bear in mind the following indigenously recognized ground rules. When segmentary units are recruited as allies in Nebilyer warfare, compensation is paid in a sequence of transactions which reverses the original order of recruitment. Thus, for instance, if *talapi* A recruits B and B then recruits C, B must first pay C, and A then pays B (cf. section 4.1). Part of the rationale for this ordering is that the amount which A should pay B depends upon the amount B has paid C. Ideally, the amount paid by A to B should be at least twice as much as B has paid to C, so that B fully recovers the amount it has paid out, and gains an increment at least equal to that amount. In these terms, the players in the present game are, A–Kusika-Midipu-Epola-Alya-Lalka, or K-M-E-A-L; B–Kopia-Kubuka, (the present donors); and C–(Mujika)-Laulku.[2]

Compensation payments of this kind are always staged in public, usually at one of the main *makayl pena* 'prestation grounds' of the donor *talapi*. Normally, adult members of the donor and recipient *talapi* at such an event appear in the full regalia of ceremonial exchange: plumes, face paint, oiled skin, etc. (see A. and M. Strathern 1971). The payment is laid out by the donors, and there is sometimes a mock charge by the recipients, who run in a circle around the outer edge of the *pena*, brandishing spears and axes and shouting 'eee eee eee' ([i: i: i:]) (cf. section 7.1; Appendix C).

Such a display was deemed inappropriate at this event, because of the then-recent death of Wangi, a prominent big-man of the Poika tribe, long time allies and affines of the Kopia-Kubuka (section 3.2.4). Public mourning for Wangi had already started at his home in Owamul, and if arrangements had not already been made with the (Mujika)-Laulku for the compensation event to be held on this day (July 24, 1983) many Kopia-Kubuka would already have left for the funeral. Even for people of allied *talapi* who stay behind on such occasions, it is considered improper to be seen working or behaving in a light-hearted way, lest one be suspected of secretly rejoicing in the death, or even of having plotted to bring it about. Given their prior commitment to pay on this day, men from Kopia-Kubuka quickly arrived at a compromise with the (Mujika)-Laulku whereby the event would go ahead as planned, but without the usual festive apparel. There was also an understanding that the proceedings would be kept brief, so as to allow people to leave for the funeral on the same day; see, e.g. lines 33–35, and also references to Wangi's death as a reason for expediting the present event at lines 164, 180, 359, 631, 828, 1159, 1593, and the transition in the transcript to discussion of arrangements to go to the funeral from line 1816 to the end. At line 1612 it looks as if the event may be nearing an end and people are on the verge of shifting their attention to the funeral when Tilka Rabi seizes the floor. There follows a long stretch (amounting to about 200 transcript lines) in which men from Tilka talk about their role in relation to the fight interspersed among speeches of Mujika and Laulku big-men, addressed to quite different concerns from those of the Tilka speakers.

In view of Wangi's death, some speakers feel that the use of *el ung* oratorical style (cf. Rumsey 1986) should be strictly limited.[3]

Given that death, why were the proceedings held at all, rather than being postponed, as often happens in such cases? No doubt part of the reason was that the local coffee crop was at its peak, which meant that the amount of cash on hand was now sizable, but would be rapidly diminishing over the next few months. Kujilyi (lines 180–5) urges people to come back directly from the funeral and not to scatter, as he is concerned that the coffee money on hand will be dissipated, making it harder to raise the return payment.

Also relevant for the timing of this event – and for understanding portions of the transcript – were two other incidents (besides the death of Poika Wangi) which had occurred shortly before, and which were much on people's minds (and of special concern to people of Kopia-Kubuka and K-M-E-A-L).

The first incident was a road accident in June 1983, in which a PMV (Public Motor Vehicle) operated by Midipu Lkirim (see section 2.3) went off the road, throwing several of the passengers off the open back of the truck. One man, Kopia Uwa, was knocked out by a blow to the head (see line 225). He was taken to the Mt Hagen hospital, where he lay in a coma for several weeks. Especially given the ancient enmity between Kopia-Kubuka and K-M-E-A-L (section 3.2.2), the liability which this accident created against the latter became a source of considerable tension, and intense speculation. There was talk of renewed warfare between the two if adequate compensation were not forthcoming. If Uwa died, something on the order of 20,000 kina and/or many live pigs would have to be presented. If he survived, the amount owed would depend on the extent of his recovery (though *some* compensation would still be owed even if he recovered completely). Under these circumstances, knowledge of his condition became a highly valued form of capital, and reports of it even more difficult to interpret than usual (cf. section 9.1). By June 20, there were (highly confidential) reports of his having been able to speak clearly enough to have requested sweet potato, some of which he was then able to eat. By June 30, he had recovered sufficiently to be released from the hospital, and been secretly brought back (under cover of darkness) to Kailge, where he was sequestered day and night in one of the Kopia men's houses. As of July 24 (the time of this compensation event), all of us at Kailge were under strict orders not to reveal his presence, but instead to encourage the K-M-E-A-L to believe that he was still in the hospital, his whole body already 'dead' except for the heart and lungs. Given the number of affines and other visitors that come and go between Kailge and Palimung-Kubaliyl, it seems highly unlikely that anyone could still have been unaware of the true situation by then, but Uwa's presence at Kailge was not yet being openly acknowledged by either side (part of the scarce epistemic capital consisting, as usual, in knowledge about whether 'they know that we know'; whether 'they know that we know that they know', etc.).

The second important incident comprising essential background to this event was the fighting which had broken out in May/June 1983 between the Kulka, eastern neighbors of the Kopia-Kubuka, and the Kilipuka to the south, the tribe of Nabuka Mara, who was then the premier of the Western Highlands Province. If Uwa's accident was perceived as a potential source of conflict between Kopia-Kubuka and K-M-E-A-L, the prospect of all-out warfare between Kulka and Kilipuka was seen as a reason why the former schism should not be allowed to develop (see lines 418–25 and Rumsey 1986:285–290). For in the latter conflict, both of the parties to the former one were implicated on the same side, as allies of the Kulka. Given the almost magical powers attributed to Mara, the need for a united front was keenly felt among the tribes who in the course of events had been thrust together as allies on the opposing side.

Having reviewed some of the background to this event, we will now provide a brief overall account of its sequential development.

By Saturday, July 23, a large contingent of Laulku (and a smaller one of Mujika) had already arrived at Kailge for the prestation. On the morning of the 24th, men of various Kopia-Kubuka sub-groupings met in their local men's houses to count up their respective contributions. The payment consisted entirely of cash, mostly in two-kina notes, which were tacked in piles of five to large display boards. The boards were decorated with flowers (see Plate 6), and most were labelled with a putative total amount and name of donor or donor men's house.[4] At about noon, these boards were brought out on to the main *pena* at Kailge. Before the event could get started, it was important to have men present from the Kusika-Midipu-Epola-Alya-Lalka alliance (Unit A in terms of the above discussion) to see exactly how much was given, so as to know how much would be expected of them later on. By noon, only one such representative had turned up – Midipu Kujilyi, the leading big-man of the K-M-E-A-L alliance. There had been a strong feeling that at least one Epola-Alya man should turn up as well, since the Epola in particular had been identified as the main *el pul* 'fight source' (for reasons discussed in section 3.2.2). But by early afternoon, the speech-making started anyway (partly on the very subject of the non-appearance of the Epola-Alya (lines 36, 95–114)). The only Alya representative to attend came later, and only made one speech just before the gathering was about to disperse so that people could proceed to Owamul (lines 1792 ff.).

As with most public oratorical events in the Nebilyer, there is no obvious formal indication of the transition from preliminary talk to focused speech event. Some largely unfocused (i.e. mainly dyadic) talk had already gone on by the time we switched on the tape recorder for Tamalu's speech, with which the transcript begins. By that time, the spatial configuration of people on the Kailge *makayl pena* 'prestation ground' had already become established in the typical pattern for such events, i.e., with the male audience sitting in the *pena*, facing inward and the women sitting in small groups on the sidelines, chatting among themselves and apparently paying little attention to the men's speeches (though actually keeping their ears cocked; they can often report afterwards in considerable detail on what was said). Among the men, competition for the floor is generally quite strenuous. Within the limits of certain global constraints (to be discussed below), turn taking among the speakers is 'locally managed' (Sacks, Schegloff and Jefferson 1974), i.e., there is no pre-arranged order in which they should speak. Generally, the audience sits while the speaker stands, until he closes his speech by sitting down. At that point, there is usually a rush of men trying to gain the floor by standing up and beginning to speak. Usually one of them soon manages to win out, and after that he is almost always allowed to speak until he yields the floor by sitting down.

At inter-*talapi* events such as this one, speakers seem to limit their individual attempts to gain the floor according to certain tacit conventions[5] or expectations concerning the order in which each segmentary unit should be heard from.[6] In warfare compensation events of this kind, it seems that the ordering of speakers by segmentary unit is expected to replicate the order of recruitment to the fighting. Thus, in this compensation event, the ordering of individual speaker-turns is largely consistent with the overall order: 1. Epola-Alya-Lalka-Kusika-Midipu; 2. Kopia-Kubuka; 3.(Mujika-)Laulku. The main speeches of the latter come towards the end of the focused event (lines 1612 ff.), and are interspersed, as noted above, by speeches of Tilka (who are rewarded for their friendly neutrality via specific kin ties linking Kopia and Tilka). One surmises that if a representative from Epola-Alya-Lalka had been present, he would have spoken first.[7] This was one reason why the non-appearance of any such representative made it difficult to get started. Since Kujilyi ended up being taken as a representative of the K-M-E-A-L alliance as a whole, it was with his first speech that the event really got under way. (The previous speech, by Tamalu, was largely prospective talk about how the event should proceed, and was followed by more of the sort of unfocused talk which had preceded it.) But Kujilyi's acting as representative of the entire K-M-E-A-L bloc is mentioned several times as problematic: various speakers raised the question of whether he can be seen as such. This issue is important because the Epola-Alya-Lalka are expected to contribute to the return payment later, so they must be seen to participate in these present events which will shape later ones.

Interestingly, perhaps because he was still hoping an Epola or Alya speaker would turn up, Kujilyi first spoke in such a way as not to unambiguously command the floor for himself. Several other men were still on their feet and Kujilyi had not yet stood up. Most of his remarks were not clearly audible on the tape, nor to most of those present, if we are to judge from the directives in lines 39–43. By line 45, Kujilyi has stood up, most of the audience is seated, and the exchange event is definitely under way. His first speech (lines 44–190) is a long one, in which he discusses some of the background to this exchange, and tries to position himself with respect to it. In essence, his position is that he and his closest constituents (the Midipu and their paired tribe, the Kusika) were not directly responsible for the fighting, and have an identity quite distinct from the Epola-Alya, but that he approves of the compensation which is being paid to Mujika-Laulku and that the Kopia-Kubuka can rest assured that he as the leading big-man of the alliance, and as a 'Lama' man (lines 100–108) will take it upon himself to see that they are handsomely rewarded for their efforts, and fully compensated for their own contribution to the fight.

Following Kujilyi's first speech, there is fairly brief interchange between him and Kubuka Tamalu, after which the floor is generally held by Kopia-Kubuka speakers for a continuous stretch, until about line 1169. After that, there are speeches by Mujika and Laulku men, interspersed among further contributions by Kopia-Kubuka, Midipu (Kujilyi), Alya[8], and Tilka. The Mujika-Laulku segment of the proceedings is clearly distinct from the earlier segments, not in containing *only* speeches by Mujika-Laulku, but because it is only after line 1169 that there *any* speeches by men from those tribes. Furthermore, most of the other men who speak during that time are men who have already spoken earlier in the proceedings.

During the Kopia-Kubuka segment (approx. lines 215–1168), there are two interruptions to the proceedings, which define major transitions in the overall staging of the event. The first comes after line 412, when a fight breaks out between two Kopia (teenage) boys. This led to a rapid breakdown in audience attention to the main business of the day, and chaos reigned for several minutes, during which we switched off our tape recorder to save tape. What finally got people's attention back upon the speechmaking was a speech by Kubuka Unya in the *el ung* style – the first *el ung* speech of the day, Kubuka Tamalu having declared at the outset that no *el ung* was to be spoken. Within a few seconds after Unya began, there was a dramatic drop in the level of crosstalk and background noise. Thereafter, *el ung* was used many times during the course of the afternoon, often at other times when audience attention to the speech making had begun to wane (see e.g. lines 910, 1169).

The second obvious hiatus in the proceedings happened after line 837, when the setting changed as the money display boards were carried from the Kailge display ground to the Kailge Community School ground, some 300 meters to the north (see Map 3). The significance of this shift may be understood in terms of the following considerations.

Relative to the Kailge display ground, the school ground lies further up along one of the main 'roads' (i.e., mountain tracks) to Mujika-Laulku territory. Thus, taking the money there could be read as a metaphorical way of taking it to the (Mujika-)Laulku. Several aspects of the spatial configuration of participants in the event, and of the speaker-addressee relations in the oratory, independently attest to the homology: Kailge display ground is to Kailge school ground as Kopia-Kubuka is to (Mujika-)Laulku. First, not all the visiting Mujika-Laulku even appeared at the display ground during the portion of the event which took place there. Some waited up at or near the school ground. Second, those Mujika-Laulku who did appear there did not stand together in an identifiable bloc, as did men from each of the various Kopia-Kubuka men's houses, and as the Mujika-Laulku themselves did after the proceedings had shifted to the school ground. Third, most of the speeches made by Kopia and Kubuka orators at the display ground were addressed to Midipu Kujilyi and/or to other Kopia-Kubuka, while most of the speeches they made on the school ground were addressed to (Mujika)-Laulku. It could be argued that, though people of the Mujika and Laulku *talapi* had been present on the display ground, Mujika and Laulku as segmentary identities were not present, or represented as such, until after the move to the school ground.[9]

The shift to the school ground is also significant in another way, in view of the following. Unlike warfare, the paying of compensation is understood by Nebilyer people to be in keeping with the rule of 'government law' – part of what they see as the New Order, to which they are generally quite favorably disposed (section 2.3). Since the Community School system is also a part of that order, it is appropriate that the climax of the compensation event – the handing over of the money – take place on the school ground.[10] (See section 2.3 on the concept of *gavman lo* and section 6.2.7 below, concerning this theme as addressed at the present event.)

The shift to the school ground was followed by the turning over of the display boards to men from Laulku. One reason why there are relatively more stretches of crosstalk and inaudible speech after line 837 is that after the boards are turned over to them, men from (Mujika-)Laulku start to remove the money, count it, and divide it up for distribution. This is always an activity which is closely scrutinized by interested clansmen to make sure they are not short-changed.

The third major bloc of speeches – the '(Mujika-)Laulku (and Tilka) segment' of the proceedings, which begins at line 1169, has the highest proportion of *el ung* speeches (though there are also many during lines 731–1168). It runs until line 1815, after which the Mujika-Laulku and Kopia-Kubuka are no longer addressing each other as such. The topical focus at that point shifts abruptly away from the exchange matters at hand to the death of the big-man, Poika Wangi[11], to how he should be mourned, and to the arrangements for getting people to the funeral.

What we have said so far concerning the overall contour of this event is summarized in Table 6–1.

Table 6–1: *Phases of speech-making at the Kailge compensation event*

Approximate Line Numbers	Predominant Segmentary Speaker/ Addressee Relations	General Topical Focus	Setting
1–43	none; no use of segmentary person categories	Preliminary remarks concerning background to the event and how it should proceed	Kailge Display Ground
44–214	K-M(-E-A-L) → Kopia-Kubuka	Role of K-M and Kujilyi in the fighting; nature and significance of the present payment to Mujika-Laulku	" "
215–807	Kopia-Kubuka → K-M-(-E-A-L)	" "	" "
807–1168	Kopia-Kubuka → (Mujika-)Laulku	Role of (Mujika-) Laulku in the fighting; nature and significance of the present payment	Kailge Community School Ground
1169–1815	(Mujika-)Laulku ⟷ Kopia-Kubuka (interspersed by Tilka)	" "	" "
1816-end	none	The death and funeral of Poika Wangi	" "

6.2 TOPICAL ANALYSIS

Before we can begin this analysis, some introductory remarks are in order concerning the general notion of 'topic', and our choice of particular topics to address. Quite simply, a topic is what a given stretch of talk is *about*. In given instances, this is of course difficult or impossible to determine in a categorical and exclusive way. This we can tolerate as analysts, just as all of us (barring major psychoses) do in everyday life.[12] It simply means that all such determinations must be treated as provisional and relative to point of view. (We will say something about our own below.)

The notion of topics as significant units of talk is by no means foreign to Ku Waru people. As shown in section 5.8 and Appendix D, the word *ung* in various context glosses as 'language' or 'speech', *and* as 'topic', or 'subject matter' (see also Appendix B.3.3.1 concerning the use of the genitive postposition for *about*). Examples where the latter glosses are appropriate occur in Appendix A at lines 79, 1083, 1255–6, all of which refer to 'talk about (the) fighting' (*el(-ayl)-nga ung*), line 1287 'talk about pig', and line 225 'talk about the boy' (*kang-ayl-nga ung*). As these examples show, speakers do explicitly label various topics as such, especially when they are trying to *exclude* them from discussion, as is true in all the examples we have just cited. Another word which can often be glossed as 'topic' is *ul*, which also glosses as 'affair', 'business', or 'project' (cf. A. Strathern 1982:293). Examples where the former gloss is appropriate occur in Appendix A at lines 169, 190, 208, 214, 220, 313, 394, 617, 803, 1166, 1185, 1196, 1432, 1479. The majority of these explicit references to topics also occur in contexts where the speaker is trying to exclude the topic from the present forum, often unsuccessfully (exceptions will be noted below).

Therefore, although the participants at this event are clearly operating with a meta-linguistic notion of 'topic', their *explicit* uses of it in the transcript do not provide much direct evidence for a revealing analysis of what it is 'about'. For this, we relied more upon discussions with informants (some of whom were also participants), both about this particular event as represented in the transcript, and about the historical background to it, as treated in Chapter 3. We do not claim that the catalog of topics treated below comprises *the* subject matter of the event in question, or that our exposition of any of them is exhaustive. Rather, the topics were selected as potentially interesting ones to analyze as a basis for addressing the larger questions of structure and event, action and representation which were posed in Chapter 1. For all of them show with particular clarity that what is 'really going on' at the event is not something essentially non-discursive which merely gets 'talked about' in the more-or-less empty rhetoric of tedious 'harangue-utans' (Sahlins 1963:290). Rather, the talk figures crucially in constituting the exchange transaction as of one kind or another, from a range of always contestable alternatives.

One of the features that makes these topics interesting from this point of view is that they are all ones which were taken up and developed by more than one speaker. This allows us to study the way in which the topics first get raised, and then worked upon by successive speakers from various structurally and historically divergent positions. We can observe the ways and extent to which given speakers do or do not get identified with particular topics, either as the interactional 'source' of the topic within this particular event, or as its (full or partial) content (i.e., the extent to which participants at the event themselves become topics, or come to figure in the topics). We can observe the sequential distribution of the topics at the event, to determine the extent to which they are treated in compact stretches of contiguous speeches vs. widely scattered ones. As we proceed with this analysis, one may compare it with the results of the sequential one in section 6.1 above. This will show that although the two are in principle distinct, there are some interesting interrelationships between them (a matter to which we return in Chapter 8).

6.2.1 Constructions of a big-man: Midipu Kujilyi

Most of the main speakers in the Kailge compensation event – Midipu Kujilyi, Kubuka Tamalu, Kopia Waria, Kubuka Unya, Kopia Noma, Tilka Dop and others – are locally considered prominent men, and often (if not always) counted as *yi nuim* 'big-men'.[13] Yet of all of them, only Kujilyi, and his past and future actions, are elaborated as a topic within the event. Let us consider why this is so, how his persona is constructed through talk by himself and by others, and what these constructions show about evaluations of men in public affairs.

Kujilyi, considered both as participant and constructed persona, emerges as the central figure of the day's event. He is in fact the single person most often referred to and spoken to within the transcript (though clearly his own participant role is greater during the Kailge section of the event than after the shift of scene to the school ground).

Everyone understands the immediate reason for Kujilyi's presence at Kailge: he has come to observe how much money is given and to whom, so that, based on this, he can organize an appropriate return payment to Kopia-Kubuka at some (relatively near) future date. Kujilyi is expected to make this return because he recruited Kopia-Kubuka to the fight on behalf of Epola-Alya who, Kujilyi says at line 1133, were not doing very well on their own against Tea-Dena. The Kopia-Kubuka, in turn, recruited (Mujika-)Laulku, so that in the chain-like structure of alliance and resulting obligations, Kujilyi is not directly beholden to the latter, who of course are being compensated on the present occasion. Because Kujilyi recruited Kopia-Kubuka, he is the pivot between the present event and the expected return payment to Kopia-Kubuka (which took place the following month, and is the subject of Chapter 7).

Kujilyi's actions in these recent hostilities were of considerable interest locally because they contravened hitherto standard relations of alliance and hostility in this end of the valley (section 3.2.2). The set of small tribes, Kusika-Midipu and Epola-Alya-Lalka, are considered allies, and indeed Kujilyi had acted as ally to Epola-Alya-Lalka by recruiting Kopia-Kubuka to their aid in the fight. (But in acting as ally, Kujilyi also seeks to distinguish himself from Epola-Alya-Lalka,[14] as we shall examine in detail below.)

Beyond this, however, Kujilyi's actions in recruiting Kopia-Kubuka to aid Epola-Alya-Lalka were a departure from understood existing patterns of traditional alliance and hostility because relations between these *talapi* are typified as having been hostile, apparently, since shortly after the consolidation of the Kopia at Kailge earlier in the century (see section 3.2.1). In fact, recent relations of Kopia-Kubuka with Epola-Alya-Lalka, and certainly with *their* allies Kusika-

Midipu, had lately not been as bitter as formerly. But until recently, Epola-Alya-Lalka had still been considered allies of Kopia-Kubuka's major enemy, Tea-Dena. Kujilyi's recruitment of Kopia-Kubuka in aid of Epola-Alya-Lalka against Tea-Dena overtly signalled an alteration of the previous typification of relations between the former two as that of hostility. Because of his having acted in this way, Kujilyi becomes the subject of variable characterizations in the talk at Kailge, each of which shapes different views of his role in these events.

There is one possible view of himself that Kujilyi wishes to forestall, that of himself as the *pul* 'source', or close to the source, of recent trouble. Despite the fact that Kubuka Unya refers once to Kujilyi as the *pul yi-yl* 'source/cause man' (line 991) of events leading to the Kailge payment, and though Kujilyi accepts the burden of having recruited Kopia-Kubuka on behalf of Epola-Alya ('the trouble was certainly mine', he says at line 45), quite clearly he does not wish to be seen as the ultimate *el pul* 'fight source', as this is locally understood. For this characterization carries a negative judgment of impetuous, injudicious behavior and trouble-making. Kujilyi would rather be seen as a negotiator, mediator or facilitator who interceded on behalf of Epola-Alya, and succeeded in recruiting former enemies to help them. It is in this sense that he accepts responsibility for recruiting Kopia-Kubuka, as his version of his involvement (lines 116–68) clearly shows. In his efforts at recruitment, Kujilyi could expect Kopia-Kubuka to be fairly positively disposed to take on a joint confrontation with their long-term major enemy, Tea-Dena.

Kujilyi identifies Tea-Dena as the *el pul* (line 1117) because of the earlier troubles involving Dena Peam, and Epola as those who took up the fight (line 1118) once Dena Peam had come into Epola (line 1124). He speaks of himself as having been drawn into the fight because he is neighbor and ally of Epola (line 1132). But at the same time Kujilyi makes it clear that he is different from Epola-Alya, and in doing so he seeks to distance himself one step from the 'fight source'.

Kujilyi uses broad regional categorizations to establish that his origins and affiliations are different from those of Epola-Alya. Having commented on the fact that neither (Epola) Alya[15] nor (Epola) Koluwa has yet appeared at Kailge, at lines 100–1 he says, 'you see *me* here, a Lama man, acting the part of [in the guise of] a Jika-Kungunuka, and Ulka-Upuka'. Lama, as we noted in section 2.1, is the broad designation applied to people on the northern rim of the Nebilyer Valley towards Mt Hagen town. Kailge-area people apply this term to Jika-Kungunuka, whom Kujilyi mentions, and to Yamka further towards the town. As a regional term it contrasts with Meam, in which general category most of the people of the Nebilyer Valley floor, among them Epola-Alya-Lalka, are usually included (section 2.1).

Usually Kusika-Midipu would also be considered Meam, but Kujilyi has announced himself as Lama. At lines 102–4 he says that his father was active in (*moka*) transactions. (It is likely the case that the volume of *moka* exchange was greater, and stimulated to a greater extent by European contact, among the Melpa closer to Mt Hagen town than among at least the valley-fringe Nebilyer *talapi*.) At lines 105–7 Kujilyi elaborates his claim to difference, referring in a rather detailed way to his father's house site in Jika territory. His identifying himself as Lama connotes a background of active transaction in a way that is understood to contrast with the Meam identity and more marginal transactional reputation of the Nebilyer fringe *talapi* Epola-Alya-Lalka. He summarizes this differentiation of himself from Epola-Alya-Lalka: 'I stand here, a different man', i.e. not to be identified with at least the two Epola big-men he had previously named. At line 109 he repeats: 'Both those two didn't come' (but he still seems to expect that they will shortly).

In the early part of the event Kujilyi is concerned to differentiate himself from Epola-Alya but at the same time to ward off any fears that, because of the Epola-Alya absence, those who are to make the eventual return are not adequately represented.

Kujilyi's self-characterization notwithstanding, none of the subsequent speakers stresses or even refers to his purported 'difference' from Epola-Alya. Implicitly or explicitly, the Kopia-Kubuka speakers all lump the Kusika-Midipu (Kujilyi included) together with the Epola-Alya-Lalka as an alliance with which they must deal as a bloc. Especially after the interruption to the proceedings (line 399) they stress the fact that those allies were formerly major enemies. (See sections 3.2 and 6.2.2 below.)

Kopia-Kubuka thus emerges from this talk as reluctant new ally of Epola-Alya-Lalka and Kusika-Midipu in the fighting. Against this background, Kupena develops an image of Kujilyi as suppliant which is taken up by other speakers.

Kupena represents Kujilyi (at lines 743–6) as originally having spoken of himself as 'prostitute' (cf. section 5.4): 'I am like a prostitute, I go down the Puyl grade [between Epola-Alya territory and Kopia-Kubuka], I went around from man to man [soliciting], but now I'm getting old, if a man sees me, will he marry me?', i.e. will anyone come to my aid? Kupena further develops the image at line 754: Kujilyi, he says, copulated with us all (brought us all into the fight through his solicitations).

Kupena develops a different female image of Kujilyi at lines 761–7. He likens Kujilyi to a girl, but to make another point. At this time in the day's event there were no major spokesmen from Epola-Alya present. (Only one Alya man appeared late in the day, see line 1792 ff.) In terms of the logic by which those closest to the fight source should be heard first (cf. section 6.1), there is a feeling that Epola-Alya should be represented and precede Kujilyi in speech-making. For in the return payment, Kujilyi will partly rely on Epola-Alya to contribute, and their absence is felt to detract from his capacity to speak authoritatively about the return event.

The proverb to which Kupena briefly alludes is of a girl who was asked to bring a pig, and brought only the lead rope. Later, her mother came actually bringing the pig. Kupena likens Kujilyi to the girl: he brought only the rope. Kupena does not complete the likeness, but his implication is that the mother (Epola-Alya) will actually bring the pig. The inference he leaves everyone to draw is that Kujilyi cannot effectively dispose of matters without Epola-Alya. Kujilyi had anticipated this complaint at lines 158–60, and again takes up the point at lines 802–806, saying that the Epola will respond to complaints about their absence when they do arrive.

Another allusion to Kujilyi as prostitute is developed at line 1065 by another speaker. Kubuka Pus says, 'Kujilyi got a small piece of soap', creating an image which our exegetes understood as that of Kujilyi washing and prettying himself as a prostitute would do before seeking to attract customers.

These images of Kujilyi as prostitute and as young girl are seemingly not flattering, in that they focus on aspects of his dependence on others in this affair. Both depict him as supplicant on the one hand, and not in full control of resources on the other. Kujilyi does not take up either of these images of himself, and we do not know whether he originally spoke of himself as prostitute as Kupena suggests at line 743. Note that the construction of Kujilyi here is 'heteroglossic' (see section 5.8) in that we cannot unravel the original authorship of the image of Kujilyi as prostitute, nor attribute it to the voice of any single speaker at the present event.

At line 802 Kujilyi speaks of himself in terms of a seemingly somewhat more euphemistic female image: 'At first I was like a young unmarried woman' (i.e., without allies), he says, referring to his position before he recruited Kopia-Kubuka to the fight. This might be taken as a slightly milder (self-) portrayal, to the extent that it may connote his desirability as ally, and hence his having some options in contracting alliances, as a young and attractive prospective bride might have. (However, this suggestion is ours, not that of our interpreters.)

Kujilyi's role in these events gives rise to two different aspects of constructions of him. As pivotal negotiator and one who will be a key director of the later return payment, he participates as a central figure in the present event (see lines 300, 347, 382 at which Kopia Waria, who takes a major part in the talk about money, emphasizes that Kujilyi must know the amounts and how they are distributed). But also, as negotiator of aid by Kopia-Kubuka to their traditional enemies Epola-Alya-Lalka, he is open to constructions of himself as suppliant female. Notably, these images are mainly taken up by Kopia and Kubuka speakers; Kujilyi apparently only takes up this female imagery in line 802, where he scales down the depiction of himself from that of 'prostitute' to 'unmarried woman' (*wenepu*).

Though the image of him as prostitute may seem unflattering, the construction of himself which he most wishes to deflect through his talk in this event is that of himself as part of the source of the trouble. In order to do this, as we have discussed above, he distances himself from Epola in particular, his nominal traditional ally, who are one step closer to the recent revival of hostility with Tea-Dena. The view of himself as director, negotiator and transactor is the one which he wishes to promulgate.

In terms of self-presentation, it is notable that Kujilyi never (in this and other events we attended) uses *el ung*. He prefers a more 'government-like' mode of talk in which he usually seeks to explicitly develop an internal structure (as at lines 125–6, where he says he has concluded his first point, and will now proceed to another). In private conversation Kujilyi observed to us (regarding the use of *el ung* and *ung eke*) that, today, some men understand the *bo kupulanum* 'the indigenous/native road' (including speech styles), and some can deal with the *gavman kupulanum* 'government road' (those matters of administration and government considered to arise from introduced models), but few are good at both. However, he counted himself an example of a man who is adept at both. In the use of *ung eke* 'bent speech', he considered himself preeminent in the area, and interestingly, said that he considered Dena Numje good at it too, second only to himself. In his preferred role as mediator, Kujilyi strongly advocates a return to regional harmony, including common use of roads, school and court area (lines 1165–8 of Appendix A).

It is important to note that different emphases are given to the etiology of hostilities in particular events. In the Kailge payment, Kujilyi refers only briefly to Dena Peam (line 1124) as an issue in the earlier fight (though he clearly identifies Tea-Dena as the 'fight source', line 1117). This aspect of past events having to do with Peam is not as relevant or highly contested here as are constructions of Kujilyi's own role on behalf of Epola-Alya-Lalka. This is so partly because it is Kujilyi who will take a major part in organizing the return payment. Thus constructions of him as suppliant with respect to Kopia-Kubuka, and as transactor of payments, are relevant to that future event.

In the later Palimung event, however, the details of Dena Peam are mentioned many times by a number of speakers (see Chapter 7). Just as Kujilyi wishes to distance himself from Epola-Alya-Lalka at Kailge, so later, at Palimung, the Epola-Alya wish to distance themselves one step from the 'fight source', with which they had become closely associated on account of and in the person of Dena Peam. Hence in that event the Epola-Alya refer many times to Dena Peam as the precipitating factor, but more specifically identify the 'fight source' as internal Tea-Dena difficulties which resulted in Dena Peam's moving to Epola territory.

Mediation, direction and negotiation of public affairs are valued and may entail the highly valued activities of wealth transaction. But this payment event illustrates that no public transactor wishes to be flatly identified as the *pul* 'source' of trouble, since this connotes injudicious behavior, and confers no special opportunity for entering into balanced wealth transactions. Big-men like Kujilyi are willing to publicly assume some aspects of what we might consider responsibility (or liability at least) for the troubles, but only to the extent that their involvement can be positively interpreted as the result of their active participation in the mediation of public affairs.

Here we have summarized aspects of Kujilyi's 'presentation of self', and the (somewhat different) construction of his persona by other participants. These processes exemplify our statements (section 5.1) to the effect that the construction of the individual social actor, here a recognized big-man, must be taken as problematic to the same extent as the constitution of any social actor type; but they also illustrate more clearly why that is so. The example of Kujilyi shows how 'big-man' and 'segmentary' aspects of actorhood are only formulated in relation to each other and to events in which they are discursively mobilized.

'Kujilyi' as 'individual actor' is identified throughout as the one who recruited Kopia-Kubuka, and in this, right from the start of this event, he is preeminent in ways that are continuous with his local standing as Councillor, Magistrate, owner of a local trade-store, influential big-man – all very widely and commonly seen as dimensions of his person which rest partly upon his standing within the pair Kusika-Midipu. But he apparently felt moved to act in relation to the local troubles not simply on the basis of his position within that tribe pair, but within the wider alliance unit K-M-E-A-L. That is, the grounds of his earlier action in recruiting Kopia-Kubuka were ostensibly a gesture of concern for Epola-Alya in their renewed difficulties with Tea-Dena. Though there exist some differences between Epola-Alya and Tea-Dena which are known to all (going back to Dena Peam, and also the recent hostilities), these two pairs have nevertheless been considered traditional allies, and Kujilyi plainly felt it important to sustain good relations with both – but could he, under the circumstances? Because hostilities had broken out between them, he appears reluctantly to have abandoned the attempt to mediate directly between them – though we know he had initially offered to do so. Aspects of Kujilyi's style – his avoidance of *el ung* (despite his pre-eminence as speaker in this and other events), his tendency to organize his speeches into 'points', his emphasis upon regional harmony and obvious desire for reasonable relations with the Dena big-man Numje – all point to certain personal preferences which, however, Kujilyi is obviously not entirely free to realize in these circumstances.

The course of action he eventually took was to intercede for Epola-Alya, and to try to gain help for them from Kopia-Kubuka. We have already observed how, in explaining his mediatory role between these (former, now perhaps best characterized as 'minor') enemies, he deploys an aspect of his personal background – his father's links to Jika and Lama more broadly – which seems to distinguish him from both Kopia-Kubuka and Epola-Alya. Apparently, such a construction of himself as different from both (and, by implication, and perhaps especially important within the present event, also from Tea-Dena) can have force against the background of a general understanding within the region that there are graduated degrees of hostility, that between Kopia-Kubuka and Epola widely felt to have been greater – and closely related to specific episodes of warfare – than that between Kopia-Kubuka and Kusika-Midipu. Thus, aspects of Kujilyi's identity are variably mobilized and take on significance in relation to each other in specific events, but cannot be neatly separated into pre-existing individual and segmentary dimensions. What is clear is that here he must mobilize some aspects of his background to claim individual distinctiveness, and to de-emphasize for his Kopia-Kubuka audience those aspects of his eminence which are strongly tied to his position within K-M-E-A-L.

Having placed himself in the mediator's role, Kujilyi is constrained by the logic of chain-like, pair-wise constitution of social relations to acknowledge that he solicited Kopia-Kubuka on the one hand, and on the other is also dependent upon Epola-Alya to complete his capacity as return-maker in a subsequent payment, though he seems to constantly work to reduce claims by others concerning the extent to which this is really to be read as dependence upon them, rather than their equivalence in this matter – when they come, they will speak for themselves, he says. (Especially the subsequent payment event, described in Chapter 7, made clearer certain aspects of Kujilyi's support network within his own locale which appear to underpin some of his capacity to promise to finance the return.)

There have tended to be two styles in studies of politics and the position of the big-man in the western Highlands. One is seen in clearest form in the work of Meggitt (1971) who argues that, as occasion arises, the segmentary system 'defines' leadership:

> . . . with the system in action or in compression, that is, with situations in which units of the same order are in overt or covert opposition or competition. On these occasions the segmentary system defines, in an unequivocal idiom of agnatic descent, the identity of the actors as followers, which in turn specifies the Big Man who should now lead.
> (1971:200)

This is consistent with Meggitt's view that, under such circumstances, the 'group acts as a monolithic unit in opposition to other, like groups . . .' (ibid.).

The other, more tempered position places less emphasis on the segmentary order as automatically there to be mobilized, and determinant. It may be exemplified by A. Strathern's (1971:28) statements to the effect that 'big men and the ceremonial exchange system are important in establishing segments and maintaining their inter-relations'; that big-men 'create new sub-clan and sub-sub-clan names'; and that the 'activities of big-men complicate processes of group segmentation and fission'.

While Meggitt's position is based on the notion that structural properties of the segmentary order have a constraining influence over individuals, Strathern's is nearly its inverse in depicting big-men as architects of the segmentary system (at least at certain levels). However, what both views have in common is the clarity with which they envision personal and segmentary dimensions as structurally pre-given and separable.

We would argue instead that there is no distinctive category of social description or explanation that may begin from a premise of two such clearly separate dimensions of structure/agency. There are rather reflexively monitored activities of situated actors, constituted within specific events of certain types according to understandings of the dimensions of those events in terms of which meaning potentials are taken up and shaped. There is considerable indigenous consciousness of what those potentials are, and it is one of the defining and necessary characteristics of 'big-manship' as locally conceived that one's contribution to events be such that one becomes crucially associated with the identification of those events as ones of particular kinds. Within such a context, the Kujilyi that emerges as a relevant actor – Kujilyi as 'woman-in-between' – is just as much a *social* creation as are the segmentary identities in the name of which he acts.

6.2.2 Epola-Alya(-Lalka) and Kopia-Kubuka

Some speakers evoked former hostilities between Epola-Alya(-Lalka) and Kopia-Kubuka, a background Kujilyi had clearly in mind when he undertook the mediatory role described in the previous section. Some of these evocations were so direct that some participants sought to suppress them. The most contentious of them (see below) seemed to be those in which particular Epola big-men were cited as former opponents of Kopia-Kubuka. On the other hand, especially some allusions to difference and opposition formulated in SP, though suggestive, were not so received during the event, and later were judged irresolvably ambiguous by our informants, a contrast which provides some insight into strategic differences in the situated uses of the resources for formulating agency discussed in section 5.1.

As noted earlier, a major interruption in the event occurs at line 399 with the fight between two boys. This absorbs many onlookers' attention for a few minutes. Kubuka Unya succeeds in refocusing attention with the first *el ung* speech of the day (lines 413 ff.). It is only from this point that there begins to be developed in the talk considerable reference to former hostilities within the region.

For example, at line 415 Unya uses the image of grasshopper and frog fighting. At lines 419–22 he brings up briefly the recent injury of Kopia Uwa on the Midipu car (see section 6.1). The next speaker, Kopia Kupena, continues to develop such references, as at line 445 where he reintroduces Unya's image of forebears fighting like 'grasshoppers and frogs', and observes that Kusika-Midipu-Epola-Alya-Lalka (addressed as *nu* 'you', singular) and Kopia-Kubuka (*na* 'I') are not traditionally allied (line 446), and neither are Tea-Dena (*mer-ayl* '(the one) down there') and Kopia-Kubuka. But, he points out over the next few lines, we have now fought together; however, my 'uncle-cousin people' (maternal kin), my supporters (those 'at my back', line 456) are over the Tambul Range. He seems to compare the recent cooperation between Kopia-Kubuka and other valley fringe *talapi* with the long-standing, kin-supported connections Kopia-Kubuka has to the Tambul side.[16]

At lines 734–5 Kopia Kupena makes the most direct reference to former relations with Epola-Alya: 'The Epola-Alya fellows swore upon the river Ukulu, the Kopia fellows upon the river Nebilyer' after an allegedly bloody battle between them (see section 3.2.2.). (For this reason, today, neither tribe-set is supposed to drink from that river upon which their oath was taken.) So, Kupena says, he first thought that Tea-Dena and Epola-Alya-Lalka should fight each other: 'let them burn each other's houses, I thought' (line 740). That is, in view of former enmity his first reaction was to not aid Epola. However, he was persuaded by Kujilyi's supplications. This is an indication of the kind of attitude Kujilyi no doubt realized he would have to mediate (see section 6.2.1).

Kubuka Unya's first *el ung* speech, which makes many allusions to former hostilities and alliances, is notable for doing so by means of segmentary person, rather than by the use of segmentary names. This is no doubt because segmentary person provides a way of alluding rather than referring directly to the identities involved in former hostilities, and requires that the audience themselves do much of the work of interpreting the pronominal categories. Closer analysis of Unya's speech enables us to illustrate some of the points made in section 5.2 concerning the way in which segmentary person can make reference, or at least be understood to allude, to *talapi* groupings for which there is no monolexemic label.

Unya's first lines of *el ung*, in which he alludes to the Midipu car incident (lines 419–22) are broken off by talking and surging of the crowd watching the fight. Following up on that allusion at line 424 he says, seemingly in reference to Kusika-Midipu, or perhaps to the combined Kusika-Midipu-Epola-Alya-Lalka, 'You are not my agnatic kinsman'. But then he begins to develop the point that Kaugel-side people, too, are 'different'. He resumes this point at line 427 by talking of the grubs (different foods) the Kaugel-siders eat, and the sweet potato mounds (different cultivation methods) they use. When 'I' went there (to the Kaugel side), he says at line 430, 'I did these things'. Here he refers to Kubuka taking refuge with Kaugel-side kin during earlier bouts of fighting in the Nebilyer.

At line 435 Unya mentions the advent of *gavman lo*, its effect being such that Kopia-Kubuka could return (many from the Kaugel side of the range) and re-occupy the Kailge area (*meba sukud um*, line 437). An achievement of the peace was the building of main roads (line 439). (This is often referred to, and in the Kailge area road-building is something which tends to be credited to Councillor Noma, since he was Councillor then and is seen to have political connections with Mt Hagen.) During the peace, Unya says, 'even the one down there (*mer-ayl*) is mine (line 442), and you (sg) too, I said, were mine' (line 443). The expression *mer-ayl* is a reference to Tea-Dena, the second to the K-M-E-A-L. (The only big-man present from the latter *talapi* is Kujilyi, but in view of Unya's extensive use of segmentary person in this speech, *nu* cannot be taken to be addressed only to Kujilyi.) In other words, the advent of *gavman lo* meant that former hostilities should be forgotten.

At line 446 Unya continues: *nu na-kin* 'You (K-M-E-A-L, as in line 443) and I are not allies', and further *mer-ayl* 'down there' (the Tea-Dena) are not our allies either. *Eltili* 'you two' – that is, K-M-E-A-L and Tea-Dena – 'yourselves ['company'] are allies of each other' (line 448). The 2/3du pronoun here (*eltili*, the emphatic/reflexive/reciprocal form of *elti*) provides a good example of the encoding in segmentary person of non-lexicalized or 'covert' segmentary identities, such as the K-M-E-A-L and Tea-Dena alliance, as does singular *nu* for K-M-E-A-L (line 446). Unya goes on to address remarks to Kaugel-siders in the audience regarding the money payment (454–73), and to say the payment will be modest because 'I am a very small man' (line 473), i.e., the Kubuka are not numerous.

At line 474 Unya resumes reference to K-M-E-A-L: 'you (sg) did not take our planting', but 'hearing that government law has come, now you think I am your ally'. He then develops an immediate practical consideration: that Kusika Au had paid for the coffin and other funeral necessities of a Kubuka man (to whom Unya refers as 'my eldest son', line 483), and for this is to be repaid 54 kina (line 488), comprising his original outlay of about 30 kina, and an added 24. (This constitutes a sort of 'side-debt', that everyone will now be aware of, and to which some response will be expected in the forthcoming return payment by K-M-E-A-L to Kopia-Kubuka.)

In another speech, again without mentioning a *talapi* name, Unya speaks of K-M-E-A-L as 'my neighbor' (line 533), seemingly suggesting that proximity is grounds for transformation of formerly hostile relations between them and Kopia-Kubuka.

At lines 1529–30 Kubuka Ipupu (Unya's father, a renowned man but at this time past his prime, well into old age as locally reckoned, and with diminished participation in public affairs) insists on dwelling upon (Kubuka's part in) former hostilities with the small valley floor *talapi*: 'I struck Epola Koluwa, I struck Epola Tuse', he says. At lines 1548–51 he seems to blame the Epola collectively for causing him to dissipate the wealth he should be expending on acquiring wives for his (Kubuka's) sons. His having named Epola Koluwa and Tuse makes it likely that some of his later third person references (as at lines 1552–3) may be understood as to Epola, whom he accuses of not cooperating by not having appeared for this event at Kailge. Ipupu's speech touches on enough contentious issues, so that his *el ung* is interrupted by Kubuka Tepra (lines 1581–2), and his efforts to resume speaking are quashed by another Kubuka speaker. There is some tendency for younger participants to regard such remarks as inflammatory resurrectionism on the part of old men.

As we remarked (section 5.2), some SP references in these speeches are sufficiently allusive so that those who worked through the transcript with us were either unsure of how to interpret them, and/or differed in their understandings. An example of unresolved ambiguity occurs at line 450, where Unya has just said that K-M-E-A-L and Tea-Dena are *kampani* 'allies'. 'You two fought', he says and 'he saw you, you were weak' (lines 449–51). The 'he' here was usually taken to refer to Tea-Dena, but the context provides few clues, and these references and accordingly the sense of these lines remain ambiguous. Such ambiguity ought not to be regarded as a deficiency of the SP resource, but rather as one of its inherent qualities which makes it consistently suggestive and less available to overt contestation than the use of segmentary identity and personal names.

6.2.3 The role of the Poika and Palimi

As has been widely noted in Highlands ethnography (e.g. Berndt 1964, Sillitoe 1979, Feil 1984), when a segmentary unit is nominally involved in warfare, it is seldom if ever the case that every adult male of that unit joins in the fighting. For the Nebilyer area, we can say that, in general, the further out a segmentary unit is from the 'fight source' along the chain of allies, the lower the proportion of men who participate. Furthermore, some men invariably join in from units which are not, *qua* segmentary identity, recruited as allies. In general, if these men are recruited at all, it is along roads of close matrilateral kinship or affinity. But there is always room for disagreement about the basis of their participation. One such disagreement in the present case concerns the role of the Poika and Palimi tribes. In the past, these two tribes have been the main allies (and sole *makayl* inter-clan exchange partners) of the Kopia-Kubuka (section 4.1). In the fighting for which compensation is here being paid, several men from these tribes did participate, and at least two of the Poika were wounded. On the day of compensation, many people from those tribes turned up. Would they be included among those compensated? If so, which of them? Or would there be a payment to 'Poika' as such?

Though these questions were no doubt on many people's minds, they were not mooted until well into the proceedings. This first occurs after line 584, in a fleeting interjection by another (unidentified) speaker in the midst of a speech by Midipu Kujilyi. The latter had been giving an account of who all had been injured in the fighting, and what *talapi* they came from. He had mentioned just one man from Laulku and two from Kusika. The effect of this is to downplay the combined contribution of Kopia-Kubuka and Laulku in comparison to his paired tribe, the Kusika. Not surprisingly, a speaker representing the former bloc, Kubuka Tamalu, later breaks in (line 593) and emphatically 'corrects' this to *three* Laulku. But before he does this, there is the interjection (after line 584) to the effect that there was also a Poika who got wounded. Whereas the later correction regarding Laulku is not taken up by Kujilyi (who refers again to a single Laulku in line 603), the remark about the Poika *is* taken up and incorporated into his account (in lines 585, 594). Speaking as a big-man from Kusika-Midipu (who must later organize a payment to Kopia-Kubuka), Kujilyi advises that the Poika be paid compensation from the amount of money which is 'left over' (*ku lep*) after the appropriately 'rounded' sum of 2,200 kina (see section 5.7 on pairing) has been paid to Laulku (lines 587–9).

As soon as Kujilyi finishes the speech in question, Kubuka Tamalu immediately seizes the floor. Now that the issue of Poika has been publicly raised (and recognized by a big-man representing the alliance to whom the Kopia-Kubuka are accountable for the day's proceedings), Tamalu makes haste to set forth a position. His speech, (lines 633–53) is in part an attempt to justify the Poika not being paid compensation (at least not *qua* Poika) at this time.

In lines 633–4, Tamalu picks up Kujilyi's remark about the Poika man's having been wounded, and claims that the matter is 'finished' (*pora nyikim*), i.e., a non-issue. In support of this claim, Tamalu makes subtle use of segmentary person, so as to group the Poika together with the Kopia-Kubuka as relative 'insiders' vis-à-vis the Laulku. In line 635, he uses the first person dual pronoun *olto* to mean 'we Kopia-Kubuka and (Mujika-?)Laulku'. *Olto-nga ung* 'These words of us two' means 'the things we Kopia-Kubuka and (Mujika-?)Laulku are talking about between us today'. The implication is that these are matters which have already been thoroughly canvassed between Poika and Kopia-Kubuka before the payment was given in this form. In line 636, the reference of the first person dual category then shifts to another segmentary pair: the pair of Kopia-Kubuka and Poika-Palimi – just those tribes among whom the matter has purportedly already been discussed. These are people who fight on the same side as a matter of course. The first person singular pronoun (*na*) in line 637 can be construed as referring to Tamalu himself, to the Kubuka tribe, or to the pair of Kopia and Kubuka. (Notice incidentally, that SP, here as elsewhere, not only 'personifies' the *talapi*, it also amplifies the person of Tamalu.) In any case, the effect is to point to bonds of co-residence which identify Kopia-Kubuka and Poika-Palimi together in a way that Laulku is not identified with any of them.

How and why, you may ask, did the *Palimi* get into this account of Tamalu's? The wounding at issue had happened to a Poika man, yet in line 636, we understand Tamalu's dual SP form to refer to Kopia-Kubuka and Poika-*Palimi*. This is dictated partly by the local logic of segmentary pairing: while tribes are paired, a pair is appropriately paired only with another pair (cf. section 3.1.3). And since the pair of Kopia and Kubuka is in this case the relevant reference point for insider status, the segmentary identity to be paired with it would have to be the pair of Poika and Palimi. In case we might have had any doubt about the applicability of the segmentary logic to this particular case, Tamalu makes it explicit in the following line (637), when he says 'I myself stay with Poika and Palimi'.

Tamalu's following out of the segmentary logic in this case was not motivated solely by its being 'good to think'. Rather, it is only by virtue of that logic that he is able to make his claim about close co-residence. For, of the pair of Poika and Palimi, it is only the latter who co-reside in large numbers with the Kopia-Kubuka (see section 3.2.4). At least some of those present at this event will also be aware of the fact that the Kubuka are said to have formerly been paired with the Palimi rather than Kopia. But by virtue of the present pairing between Poika and Palimi, the former are also included within the paired pair of coresident insiders.

Having made this identification, Tamalu then goes on to explain (in line 638) that there is one outstanding *makayl* debt (metaphorically referred to as a 'rotten vegetable') that remains to be paid within this alliance. That is a *yi pengi* payment, which is owed for the death of a Poika man in war of ca.1940, referred to above. It was explained to us privately that this outstanding debt was one reason why the Poika were not recruited *as a talapi* to assist the Kopia-

Kubuka in the 1982 war. That was presumably one reason for Tamalu's mentioning it in this context – as an explanation ostensibly addressed to the Laulku for why the Poika were not being compensated. But our experience of these matters, and remarks from our exegetes suggest that the 'private agreement' with Poika on this score was probably not as secure as Tamalu avers, and that his remark was also covertly aimed at the Poika, to preempt any claim they might be thinking about pressing at this time. He is presumably also trying to reassure them by suggesting that the Kopia-Kubuka will later use the compensation they get from Epola *et al.* to make *makayl* to Poika, and that he will press for this compensation to be paid soon.

Later on these proceedings, some of the money was in fact presented to some men from Poika. But Tamalu's speech (lines 633–53) helped to assure that it could not be construed as having been given to 'Poika' as such. What happened instead was that 120 kina was given to particular men from Poika for the role they played in the fighting. This is described by Kopia Waria in lines 1363–70. He specifically identifies the Poika man who got shot as *abu-n miyl kang-ayl* 'the woman-borne boy', i.e., an honorary Kopia-Kubuka via matrifiliation (see section 3.1). This helps further to undercut any possible inference that his wounding ought to result in compensation to Poika as such. So also does the complete absence of any SP references to Poika or Poika-Palimi in the speech in which Waria formulates the role of these Poika men in the fighting.[17]

It can be seen from this example that the question of whether the Poika participated as a *talapi* in the fighting – and therefore in the compensation event – is not one which can be addressed independently of how the matter was discursively constructed by those concerned. Particular men identified with a particular *talapi* are agreed to have taken part, and to have incurred injury for which compensation would ordinarily be paid. But from this the conclusions to be drawn for segmentary politics are not self-evident. The men's actions are subjected to various competing constructions using both explicit appeals to a relationship of close identification or 'sameness' among the relevant *talapi*, and the more subtle device of SP to *presuppose* such a relationship.

6.2.4 Kubuka and Kopia

Although Kopia and Kubuka are currently harmoniously paired tribes, there are several ways in which their separate identities are taken up and underscored by both Kopia and Kubuka participants in this event. The fact that this distinctness is important must make us wary of interpreting some uses of segmentary person as references to Kopia-Kubuka as a pair.

At two places in the transcript speakers assert that there is a special commitment on the part of Kubuka to maintaining a relationship with Laulku, greater than and distinct from the Kopia commitment to them.

The first such statement is made by Kopia Waria. At line 313 he says: 'I Kopia, am giving 700' ('pounds', i.e. 1400 kina) to Laulku to secure commitments (Tok Pisin *plan*). Later, at line 324, having indicated that Kubuka functionaries (Tepra and/or Tamalu) will hold and then pass on Kopia's money to Laulku, he explains the reason for this by saying that Laulku is on Kubuka's road. This is literally true, since the road over the Tambul Range by which people travel to and from Laulku territory comes into Kubuka country. At lines

334–7 Waria makes his own perspective clearer, saying that he has no in-laws among the Laulku, and is throwing away his money on them. Clearly, importance is given to distinguishing the separate contributions of Kubuka from those of Kopia (see lines 9–10, 227–57 where mainly Kubuka Tamalu tallies the Kubuka monies).

Why does Waria, certainly the main Kopia functionary handling money on this day, work to organize it so that the money will first be 'held' (*abolupa*) by the main Kubuka functionary, Tamalu, and *then* transferred to Laulku?

The answer seems to lie in a special concern of Kopia Waria's, that of attempting to ensure that some of the *ku lep*, or 'extra' money, will be presented to the Tilka, to Tilka Dop in particular. (This aspect of the event is discussed in section 6.2.5.)

At line 677 there is a second claim of special relationship of Kubuka to Laulku by Kubuka Tamalu. He speaks of having several concerns, but of his thumb[18] as his 'big road', i.e. his major concern in this payment (and perhaps at other times too).[19]

Other expressions of separate Kubuka identity are found in the speeches of Kubuka Unya and his father, Ipupu. At line 430 Unya refers to how 'I' went to the Kaugel side and followed their customs (during bouts of fighting in the western Nebilyer). In line 431 he distinguishes Kopia from Kubuka in this respect, saying 'he' (Kopia) went to the lower (*meri*) Nebilyer. In fact, this would be true of only a small minority of Kopia, many of whom fled to the Kaugel side, others closer to Mt Hagen town, and elsewhere (section 3.2.2.). But Unya's remarks do reflect the greater diversity within Kopia than Kubuka, such that especially some of the lower Kopia have significant links to areas other than the Kaugel side. His remarks may also allude to the putative origin of the Kopia tribe in the southern Nebilyer.

At line 437 Unya speaks of the return to Kailge area, 'He (our forefather) brought us back'. Despite the seeming specificity of this reference (to a single forefather, in line 436), our exegetes took Unya to be speaking of both Kopia and Kubuka here, especially as he then goes on to talk of the accomplishments of road-building, usually attributed mainly to the efforts of Kopia Councillor Noma.

At line 473, when Unya, speaking of the money being given, says 'I am a very small man' , he is understood to be talking of Kubuka as a small tribe, as distinct from Kopia. The Kopia are nowhere referred to as a 'small' tribe, though of course compared to the large valley floor *talapi*, *all* of the valley fringe *talapi* are small. The immediately relevant contrast is with the larger Kopia *talapi*.

At line 1527 Kubuka Ipupu talks of the death of Kopia Epu, responsibility for which seems to be attributed to Epola. He continues at lines 1529–30, 'I struck Epola Koluwa, I struck Epola Tuse', which is aptly and ambiguously both a statement of participation by himself and by Kubuka as a *talapi*. That many of Ipupu's first person references are to be taken as encompassing both these references, but not reference to Kopia, is indicated by line 1571, where he says, 'I fought along with the Kopia old men'. Just as Kubuka here is distinguished from Kopia, so there is reason to think (because of lines 1529–30), that certain other third person singular pronominal references (as at line 1552–3, 1558) are specifically to Epola, as distinct from the pair Epola-Alya.

To return to an earlier point in this section, a special relation to Laulku is attributed to Kubuka. One small detail of the links between the two emerges elsewhere in the transcript. At line 1247 Kubuka Koropa speaks of 'covering' (paying for) the shield of a man named Bai. This man is usually considered a Laulku, but lives with the Kubuka, having a connection there because his father's mother was Kubuka. Koropa says (line 1253) that Bai is being given *ku lep*, 'left over money', but that this will not happen again. Should further trouble arise, Bai will be considered a Kubuka for all intents and purposes relating to the payment of compensation. This is an attempt to make Bai's 'difference' (non-Kubuka *talapi* affiliation) non-transactable in future.

Schematically, the set of reciprocal relationships of recruitment and compensation at stake in the day's event can be represented in two alternative ways, shown in Table 6–2.

Table 6–2: *Alternative constructions of some enchained inter-*talapi *relationships*

(A) K-M-E-A-L	⟷	KOPIA KUBUKA	⟷	LAULKU (+MUJIKA?)		
(B) K-M-E-A-L	⟷	KOPIA	⟷	KUBUKA	⟷	LAULKU

The top row (A) shows the recruitment to the recent fighting of Kopia-Kubuka by K-M-E-A-L as a bloc and further recruitment of Laulku by Kopia-Kubuka. (Both diagrams ignore complex issues of internal differentiation within K-M-E-A-L and the intermediary status of Midipu Kujilyi – questions which are not relevant to the topic at hand, but are addressed in sections 6.2.1 and 6.2.2 above.) We will describe in section 6.2.6 how a special initiative is taken by Kopia Councillor Noma to fully realize the usual pair-logic in the case of Mujika-Laulku, by making a small presentation to a transactor that can, at least for some purpose, be seen as the Mujika *talapi*.

The second row (B) shows how the suggestions of the main money-handlers, Kopia Waria and Kubuka Tamalu, would construe their tribes' relations to Laulku: they speak of Waria (representing Kopia) handing money to Tamalu ('Kubuka') to hand on to Laulku. This would make Kubuka an intermediary in this transaction similar to the way in which Kubuka is (historically at least) an intermediary between Kopia and Kopia-Kubuka's main exchange partners, Poika-Palimi (see section 4.1). This latter construing of the relationships is incompatible with Noma's attempt to address the Mujika directly, because Kubuka's special links are only to Laulku.

This section has provided examples of how the external relations on the part of the two members of a tribe-pair are constantly differentiated in certain small but significant ways. To some extent this process continues existing differences between them which result from their past cumulative development as *talapi*. Though their structure is reproduced in segmentary terms, the continuity of these social identities over time is understandable only as the outcome of a constant dialectical interaction between historical particularities (including events such as the Marsupial Road War of 1982) and the logic of segmentation, not as unproblematic transmission of unambiguous, fully elaborated segmentary$_2$ structures (cf. section 3.1).

Note here, in particular, the indeterminacy over whether Kopia and Kubuka are, for present purposes, the 'same' segmentary transactor, an issue which is similar to the one involving the Poika-Palimi in section 6.2.3 above. Here, the alternative possibility is that there is a difference between the two – Kopia and Kubuka – such that the latter should be interposed *between* Kopia and (Mujika-) Laulku as a third actor which is of the same order as Kopia, but whose relevant relation to it is one of exchange-mediated difference rather than consubstantiality. These two different sorts of relationships will figure importantly in conclusions to our analysis below (Chapter 8) under the rubrics *serial parity* versus *compositional parity*.

6.2.5 Payment to the Tilka

The Tilka, just south of Kopia-Kubuka (see Maps 2 and 3), are a small tribe,[20] nominally allied with the large central valley floor Kulka. Their territory lies in a long, narrow strip along the Tambul slopes between that of Kopia-Kubuka and Tea-Dena, a critical intermediate position between major enemies. Key Tilka representatives who were present at Kailge for the payment were Tilka Councillor Dop, Rabi (a magistrate), and Tilka Alko.

In section 6.2.4 we noted that Kopia Waria suggests (lines 320–1, 329) that the Kopia seven hundred ('pounds') be handed to Kubuka Tamalu or Unya to be passed to Laulku. This suggestion seems contrary to our expectations concerning the importance of being seen to be an active transactor. Why does Waria make it?

The answer seems to lie in a special project that Waria works to realize throughout the event, and in which he eventually succeeds: agreement that some of the *ku lep* 'extra money' should be given to Tilka, in particular to Tilka Dop, who is Waria's maternal first cousin.

The intention to make a prestation to Tilka is mooted early in the day by Waria. He says that from his perspective, giving to Laulku is 'burning' his money (line 337), since he has no in-laws or maternal kin there. At lines 340–44 Waria says that people might (correctly, he implies) attribute to him a feeling of grievance: You have no relatives there (on the Kaugel side), and so you might feel bad about throwing your money away. You are a Meam woman's son (line 343). So saying, Waria goes on, they may give me back some money. Everyone understands that if this happens, Waria would like it to be given to Tilka Dop. This is also the sense of an earlier remark, at line 315, where Waria says that he is handing money to Tamalu; but perhaps Tamalu will return some to him?

The name 'Tilka' is not mentioned by Waria throughout these passages. But everyone present knows that when Waria (line 343) imputes to others the remark about himself, 'You are a Meam woman's son', he is referring to the fact that his mother is a Tilka woman. Thus Waria makes a bid for a return of *ku lep* to Tilka.

What constitutes 'extra money'? The participants in this event clearly have in mind the notion that a nice round (preferably even) sum should be presented to Laulku (cf. Strauss as quoted in section 5.7), and anything above this will be considered 'extra', the small change, and distributed to other transactors. Waria suggests at line 301 that the round figure might be one thousand ('pounds'), or two thousand kina). At line 1311 Kubuka Tepra still holds to this as the amount that should ideally go to Laulku. Eventually (as at line 1334), the rounded amount given to Laulku is 'one thousand one hundred' (that is, two thousand two hundred kina). Discussion of the disposition of the 'extra' (*lep*, from English 'left') occurs at various places in the transcript, but Waria's purpose is realized at around line 1349 when he definitively announces that he is setting aside money 'for my cousin',[21] and further at lines 1737 ff when Kubuka Tepra follows suit by announcing a smaller prestation to Dop.

Waria's purpose in suggesting the transfer of money to Kubuka (on the grounds, as noted in section 6.2.4, that Kubuka is on Laulku's road), and a return of 'extra' money to himself (acting both as Dop's relative and as Kopia functionary), seems to be simply to gain wider support and acceptance of his project of giving to Tilka. For him to give to his cousin as such would not confer on the transaction the wider significance of recognizing Dop's role in relation to the fighting, nor could Waria hope to use general funds to give to his cousin as such. (Cf. Strathern's 1971:164, 193 account, relevant here, that the 'bigger' men are, the less is the proportion of their transactions with close kin.)

Thus, by sharing some of the *functionary* role during the event with Tamalu, Waria is better able to play something of a *transactor* role, anticipating and directly influencing the allocation of the *ku lep*.[22]

Though the prestation to Tilka is channeled through a specific kin link, late in the event Tilka speakers develop the *talapi*-level implications of the payment to themselves. They are at pains to clarify their role in the fighting, and to stress that their help to Kopia-Kubuka took the form of non-combatant aid. This is important because of their geographical position between the major enemies Kopia-Kubuka and Tea-Dena (see Map 2).

The Tilka speeches form a kind of appendix to the main event. Just as people are on the verge of leaving for Owamul, Rabi seizes the floor: 'I want to say just a little bit'. The Tilka speeches are interspersed by those of Mujika and Laulku, the latter elaborating their attitude to the presentation just made (e.g. Mujika Kasipa, lines 1637–58) and taking up Kopia Noma's remarks concerning a grievance he harbors towards them, see below, section 6.2.6. The Tilka and Laulku speakers have quite different concerns, so that in this segment, at some places there is little topical continuity from speech to speech, as where Laulku Nui's speech from 1714 to 1736 follows that of Tilka Alko and precedes that of Kubuka Tepra, who have some shared concerns.

Tilka Rabi begins by identifying himself as a Meam man (line 1612). In terms of this general label, he is the 'same' as both combatants in the recent fighting, K-M-E-A-L and Tea-Dena. Rabi represents himself as having been well disposed towards both sides: 'Let the Kulka stand guard on the other side of the Puyl' (line 1618) – in other words, let them guard the peace by virtue of their large numbers and central position. (The Kulka have traditionally adopted a position of neutrality in respect to western Nebilyer hostilities.)

Rabi dwells on the prerogatives of a non-combatant who remains friendly towards both sides: we will collect compensation both from Tea-Dena and from you, he says (lines 1619–20), because we said of both of you 'may you (sg) remain alive' (*kona pani*) (line 1616). But he also suggests that a non-combatant role is necessary when one's numbers are small (lines 1622–3). In the last part of his speech he seems to suggest that fighting may recur, and that he will still be there to buffer it. At line 1631 he says 'It's here at the Sibeka road that you will be fighting', and adds that it is right that he should get money (line 1633). Such direct formulation of this is found objectionable, and there are silencing shouts from onlookers.

Remarks by Kopia Kajipu at lines 1661–72 are partly addressed to Rabi. Kajipu asks whether the Tea-Dena (to whom he refers by those names) have paid the Tilka, as Kopia-Kubuka have done. This seems to be a self-congratulatory remark on the proper behavior of Kopia-Kubuka, but also somewhat premature in that the Tea-Dena had not yet staged their presentation to allies and friends, but were to do so shortly. Kajipu makes somewhat acerbic remarks concerning the payment to Laulku: I could give you more, he suggests (line 1663), but instead will spend my money on acquiring wives for my sons and on giving to Poika-Palimi (lines 1664–5) (the *makayl* partner of Kopia-Kubuka). Kajipu returns to invidious comparison of Kopia-Kubuka with Tea-Dena: the Tea-Dena (again referred to by name) do not 'have the eyes of a flea or cockroach' (line 1667), i.e., lack a close appreciation of how people feel (the same image which has just been used by Mujika Kasipa about Noma: see section 6.2.6). If they had such, he implies, they would 'do the right thing' (i.e., give to Tilka, though he does not mention the tribe name). He adds, I am just giving to Mujika-Laulku (referred to by name) 'for nothing' (line 1669), just to sustain good relations. He could be taken to mean either that he is not paying for a death, or that he is not seeking to secure war commitments. He appears to mean the latter, as he continues, 'I, the patrol officer's law-abiding man, give' (line 1670), equating the institution of European law with recompense to allies.

Tilka Alko's speech is rather different from Rabi's. His intended audience are apparently the Mujika-Laulku. We ('our forefathers',[23] Alko says, stressing continuity) previously helped Kopia-Kubuka (against Epola-Alya and Tea-Dena (lines 1680, 1689). None of these *talapi* is mentioned by segmentary name, but Alko speaks, e.g. of the rivers Kukapu and Aluwu, the borders of Tilka and Tea-Dena territory (line 1677). If they (Kopia-Kubuka, not referred to by name) had asked me to help, you wouldn't get any money (line 1692). You came and are getting money (line 1695). I carried off the corpses (there were actually none, here Alko simply means that Tilka had a non-combatant role). It is fitting that I receive money (line 1696). Do you (sg) (Laulku, not referred to by name) want to take up the fight (of Kopia-Kubuka)? If you want to help instead of me, I'll leave my place (implying, Tilka territory) to you (line 1703). But this suggestion seems to be made purely rhetorically, for at 1708 Alko asks 'Why will you (pl) come?' I will hold (restrain, keep in check) the fight. But, he concludes, I think your (implying, Laulku) minds are turned to fighting – so you may come and fight for them.

Kubuka Tepra (lines 1737–53) initially addresses himself to Tilka (Councillor) Dop. At 1737 he asks him, 'Do you hear, Shorty?' (Dop being indeed of rather short stature). Tepra announces a small Kubuka prestation to Tilka (line 1747), having said (line 1741), 'I saw that you were the only one who came behind [and supported] me'; i.e., the Kulka, nominal allies and paired tribe of Tilka, did not. Further (lines 1750, 1752) if other Tilka had helped I would give to them too. But they did not, so you use up the 'pound' by yourself (line 1753).

The definitive (and last) Tilka speech is made by Councillor Dop (lines 1754–68). He underlines that his contribution was not to fight, but to 'hold' or 'contain' the fight through his influence. At line 1754 he says, 'Don't think they will give this money (because) I fought'. Certainly some of the men saw their faces, some of (my) boys fought down there (aiding Tea-Dena). But only myself, being 'in the middle', 'I' said not to (line 1757). This first person reference is apparently *not* to be understood as segmentary person, since many speakers refer to the fact that Dop was the only (or main) Tilka man who took a stand. And he continues, '[Though] I'm not the son of a Kopia-Kubuka woman, nor of Epola-Alya or Kusika-Midipu woman', but of a Kungunuka woman, 'there were many sons of Dena women' (among the Tilka). Thus Dop suggests he was able to contain the fight, saying 'no' to those who might have become involved. At line 1766, Dop says, 'you may think that I fought, but do not think so'.[24] At line 1768 he starts to say, 'The men down there (i.e., the Tea-Dena) hearing (this) . . .', but unfortunately his final words are not audible on the tape. He was presumably about to say: The Tea-Dena may suspect that I fought for you, but I did not, and I will later disabuse them of this idea (at their own compensation event, where Dop probably expects to receive payment).

Kubuka Tepra makes concluding remarks (lines 1769–91) concerning the prestation to Tilka. At lines 1770–2 he says to Kujilyi that the money given to Dop 'is the affair of the two of us', meaning that the matter is not one he expects Kujilyi (*et al.*) to take into account as such when he makes the return payment. The first person dual reference here was variously interpreted as Kopia-Kubuka and Tilka, and even Kubuka and Tilka; but its overall force is clearly to exclude Kujilyi. This is amplified by Tepra's further remark to Kujilyi, 'I won't blame everything on [you]' (line 1773), but he adds (line 1783) that he will go to Kujilyi for a return of his money. A remark at 1782 is addressed to Tilka representatives: 'Don't feel angry . . .'. Tepra tells Tilka not to be angry with Laulku for receiving more money than they. To Kujilyi he says, 'They are sending you back', i.e., matters with Laulku have been concluded, and that is the part that concerns you, so you may go; if there is any left, I give to him (Tilka, see lines 1787–8).

This sequence is interesting because it evinces Kopia-Kubuka concerns with satisfying two allied *talapi* who played rather different roles in relation to the fighting. Of the Tilka, Kopia and Kubuka spokesmen want to recognize chiefly the role of Dop. Yet Dop (and other Tilka) were not active participants in the fight. The Kopia-Kubuka presentation to them recognizes their important buffering role. For their part, the Tilka prod the (Mujika-)Laulku, suggesting they are outsiders who need not have intervened. But the latter sided with Kopia-Kubuka in a way the Tilka did not. The Mujika-Laulka receive a larger payment, and their reaction to wider exchange relations is also tested (see section 6.2.6).

6.2.6 The role of the Mujika

One of the more interesting matters at stake in this event concerns the role of Laulku's paired tribe, the Mujika. As we have seen above, some Mujika men fought alongside the Laulku. Should they be compensated along with the latter? This was a question on which men of Kopia-Kubuka apparently did not agree among themselves. When the money was placed up on the display boards, none was specially allotted to Mujika. It was to be left up to the Laulku to distribute it. Before this was done, one of the Laulku speakers suggested that the Kopia would perhaps increase the amount to be given in light of the fact that there were two Mujika men whom they themselves would have to reimburse because those men – both from the Mujika\Pujilyib segment – were married to Kopia women (lines 1453–4).

This remark cut two ways. Insofar as it was addressed to the Kopia-Kubuka, it could be heard as an attempt to get them to increase the compensation payment. But it could also have been heard by the Mujika as an announcement that the Laulku did not consider it necessary to compensate the Mujika as a *talapi*. Rather, compensation was owed to men from Mujika who had aided the Kopia because of specific affinal obligations. Or, if this was going to be made into an affair of *talapi*, the transaction would at most be to the Pujilyib segment rather than to Mujika in general.

But this construction was contravened by men of one of the Kopia segments, who presented 200 kina to Kasipa, a big-man from one of the other Mujika segments. When accepting it he said 'You are giving to Mujika' (line 1656), and praised them for being more sensitive to his position than the other Kopia-Kubuka had been: 'You look with the eyes of a flea' (line 1649) (i.e., You can see the condition of my skin as if from that close up; see M. Strathern 1979 on the skin as an indicator of psycho-bodily states). He also contrasted the Laulku invidiously with these fine flea-eyed friends, saying 'I thought *they* would give' [us something] (line 1657).

What difference would it have made if that 200 kina had been given to only one of the Mujika men's houses, or only to Laulku? In one sense, less difference than one might think. For the money would probably have been quickly divided up along lines of kinship, affinity, and indebtedness, such that a fair share of it would probably have ended up in various Mujika households anyway. But in another way, the difference is extremely important. For compensation events of this kind always have the potential for developing into *makayl* (see section 4.1). We have said that this overall transaction was not generally considered a *makayl* event at the time, but during the course of it, there were attempts to develop a *makayl* sequence out of it. One of these was made by Noma, a leading Kopia big-man, in the *el ung* speech in lines 1029–1060.

This speech is one of the most remarkable in the transcript: a dazzling display which makes it clear why Noma is widely regarded as the foremost orator in the Kailge area.

One thing the speech illustrates is that skill in this genre does not depend upon the use of original tropes (cf. section 5.4). Indeed, Noma's speech repeats several figures which had already been used by his Kubuka rival, Unya, only a few minutes before. Compare, for example, Noma's opening parallel figure involving a shield and the Princess Stephanie's bird of paradise (lines 1031–4) with Unya's similar figure in lines 931–4. Compare also Unya's parallel figure concerning the Kilkai and Maip spirits (lines 963–6) with Noma's in lines 1042–5, and 1049–53. See also the way in which Unya's reference to nothofagus beech logs in line 971 is echoed by Noma (line 1047).

But note the subtle transformation which Noma has wrought upon Unya's image. Whereas Unya has spoken of *sunga kare* 'some logs' of nothofagus, which merely mark the location of the spirit-cult place where the money is to be 'roasted', Noma has spoken of *karaip puruyl-te* 'a rotting trunk' of nothofagus, on which the Laulku are in danger of slipping.

This is a standard way of alluding to an unrequited grievance or debt (see section 5.4). By locating the rotting tree in the dense forest between Kopia and Laulku (see Map 3), he has metaphorically located the debt as one between Kopia and Laulku. In his later exegetical remarks to us concerning his own speech, Noma said that nothofagus beech tree is one that takes a very long time to decompose, remaining firm and slippery on the inside long after it appears rotten on the outside. He said that what this figure had therefore been meant to suggest was that his grievance is a very old one, which the Laulku might have thought to have 'died'. Various features of Noma's speech suggest what his grievance is about. In order to understand these, and the point of the speech as a whole, one must first note a few things about its overall structure. On purely prosodic grounds, the speech may be divided into three discrete segments.

The first section begins with the standard, floor-preempting lines (1029–30) which formulate and index its addressee: 'Men/Men!' This is followed by seven more lines in 'full' *el ung* intonation (as described in section 5.3). Six of these lines are in parallel structures, and the other line (1035) is in thematic antithesis to the first parallel set. The two themes of these 7 lines are (1) that the fighting was not very intense and (2) what if being given is not much. One presumes that (2) follows from (1). (Though, given the thematic shift in the second section, we have reason to doubt that (1) is the *only* reason for (2).)

The break between the first and second major sections of the speech (after line 1137) is prosodically marked in at least four ways: (1) by a fall in pitch over the duration of the last word of line 1137 (instead of the usual level pitch followed by abrupt fall to the line-terminating vowel); (2) by an extra long pause after line 1137 (2.1 seconds as opposed to inter-line breaks of under .5 seconds in the previous seven lines: see transcript for details; (3) by a shift after line 1137 from *-o* to *-a* as the line-terminating, *el ung* vowel (cf. section 5.3); and (4) by a change in tempo, the lines becoming shorter, with most of them no longer bounded off by pauses, but only by pitch drops and *el ung* vowels, which themselves are much shorter than those in the first segment.

The end of the second section of the speech is marked by the fairly long pause after line 1052 (the first in six lines), and, perhaps more clearly, by a gradual trailing off of the *el ung* intonation and omission of the *el ung* vowel on the last four lines (1049–52). In addition to these prosodic markers, the section ends with a parallel figure just as does the first (cf. section 5.3). The explicit theme throughout is the homeward journey of the (Mujika-?)Laulku; the implicit one (conveyed by *ung eke* 'bent speech') is Noma's grievance.

It is interesting that the line *na-nga yiyl-a* 'my man' comes at the beginning of this section, for it operates in conjunction with the later rotten tree trunk image in reference to his grievance. We have noted above that one way in which the latter image differed from Unya's previous version was in its grammatically singular (rather than collective) number. Recall also the commonplace metaphorical equation in Ku Waru between 'tree' and 'man' (section 5.4). In view of the former, grammatical relationship (singular number concord), the latter, thematic relationship, and of their imputed co-presence at *Tikiyl* (lines 1040–7), we may infer that Noma's grievance is both a 'tree' *and* a 'man', i.e., that it concerns the death of a man. If so, the most likely inference would be that the man was a Kopia-Kubuka ancestor, for whose death the (Mujika-?)Laulku are being held responsible and for which they have never paid compensation. Such are the standard grounds for starting a *makayl* exchange.

Our later conversations with Noma revealed that 'a man' did indeed lie behind his image, but not in just the expected way. He said his grievance concerned a mission his father had performed as an assassin for the Mujika-Laulku, during a war which they had fought at least fifty years ago. His father's sister had been married to a Mujika man, and his father been given to understand by them that he would be amply rewarded for his services. In the event, they cheered him for his bravery, but gave him nothing.

We questioned many of our other exegetes concerning this speech of Noma's, and no one was aware of these details concerning Noma's grievance. But nearly everyone realized that he was expressing a grievance, and understood him to be making a bid to have this compensation payment interpreted as an initiatory payment for a main payment to follow from Mujika and/or Laulku to Kopia. If Noma succeeds in this, it will have been a major coup, given the fact that no *makayl* has ever been transacted between Kopia-Kubuka and Mujika-Laulku. But as Noma no doubt perceives, the time is right for it, given the fact that the last of Kopia's other *makayl* obligations are about to be discharged (as per section 4.1) and Laulku now has far more affinal links to Kopia than does any other *talapi* (section 4.2).

After Noma's speech, nearly every Laulku and Mujika speaker took up his remark.

The first Laulku speaker after Noma's *el ung* is Yako, who takes up the issue of Noma's grievance head-on. He says (lines 1177, 1195) that the matter raised by Noma of *uj pol* (tree trunks) lying on the road (lines 1176, 1180, 1194) was concluded long ago (even though it would seem, line 1196, that he is not absolutely sure what grievance Noma is referring to). Yako says his conscience is clear (line 1178), but if there is a matter of some previous Kopia death as he surmises (line 1198), then the man responsible must have left sons and appeal should be made to them (line 1207). In any event, nobody was killed in the fighting (at line 1205 Yako says he did not 'fight' for the money he is receiving, thus qualifying the hostilities as minor) and Kopia-Kubuka is therefore giving this money not to pay for any dead but rather to enhance its own reputation (lines 1187, 1206). Yako says it is therefore right that he should take it, saying 'thanks' and going (line 1208) – and by implication, not thereby incurring any return indebtedness. At lines 1209–10 he repeats, 'I don't understand/hear what you are saying about your ancestor, those trivial words we've been saying, I don't hear them'.

By denying that there is any such debt outstanding, Yako is clearly fending off Noma's suggestion that this event might be viewed as part of a larger exchange sequence based (retrospectively) on Noma's grievance.

There appears to be a veiled reference to Noma's grievance in Laulku Nui's speech (starting from line 1255). After saying he does not 'understand fight talk' (1255), he nevertheless says that he often helps people out and incurs injury (lines 1266, 1269, 1270, 1275) but is not sufficiently recompensed (line 1276). However, now that he is receiving compensation from Kopia-Kubuka he is glad of it (line 1278) and it will make him feel good; he will have no bad thoughts about the present events (line 1280). He will return home and not think about fight talk (lines 1285–6). But as for talk about pig (line 1287), sometime he will think about this.

Some people took the last remarks to refer to what Noma had said, and to imply that Nui would eventually take up the matter of Noma's grievance.

Nui appears to revert to the possibility of future exchange (line 1296). 'You haven't given any cooked pork', he says, 'that is a sort of mistake' (line 1298). By this he presumably means that if Kopia-Kubuka expect to initiate an exchange sequence on the basis of Noma's grievance, they should make appropriate prestations. Today you are (only) giving money, I will not reproach you, he says (line 1302), for you are (only) compensating us for those who were wounded (there were no deaths). This seems to suggest that money is adequate for lesser compensation, but only pork would do if this were a matter of a death on which long-term exchange might be based.

Laulku Simji assures Kopia-Kubuka of continuing support in case of trouble (lines 1429–30). As to this slippery tree trunk (Noma's complaint), this has already been dealt with (lines 1432–3). At the end of his speech, however, he suggests (line 1462) 'You are now making a *yi obil* payment' for 'that man'. To refer to the latter he uses the demonstrative *adi*, which designates something not visible to either speaker or addressee, i.e. the 'tree trunk'-cum-'man' out in the forest at Tikiyl.

Every speaker who takes up Noma's image understands it as a reference to a death: the 'tree trunk' which blocks the path is a man for whom compensation was not made and should be made. If it were, this would remove the tree and unblock the path. Many speakers take up the tree image as such, e.g. claiming that it has already been cleared away. The general nature of the Laulku response is to claim that the grievance has already been dealt with. But the Laulku (e.g. Nui, line 1287 ff.) show some inclination to leave open the possibility of future exchanges, to which the present payment will very likely be seen as relevant. Noma's gambit is taken up, yet his complaint that a past score has not been settled is warded off. At line 1297, the defense is clinched by Nui's saying that no pork has been given, and further, he asserts that the Kopia-Kubuka are just paying now for the blood of the wounded, not for any graver matter (line 1303). Thus, the state of play as he represents it is that there is no uncompensated death on either side, that the present payment cannot by itself be seen as the initiation of *makayl* exchange, but that the possibility of beginning such exchange is of interest. By saying that the Laulku are justified in taking compensation money, Nui tosses the ball into the Kopia-Kubuka court: he has indicated an interest in future exchange, but not conceded any basis of indebtedness on the part of Laulku towards Kopia-Kubuka.

These interventions by Laulku speakers show how they operate with a general *sense* of Noma's rotting log/man trope without exploring its precise reference (cf. section 5.5). It is sufficient that they understand him to be making a bid to establish exchange relations, and that he is suggesting their indebtedness.

So far in this exegesis, we have said little about the role of the tribe who are the announced topic of this section: the Mujika. This is because the first three speakers to respond to Noma's speech – those discussed above – are all Laulku. But recall that Noma's own explanation of his tree/man image had referred specifically to an unrequited service performed for the *Mujika*. This is consonant with the shift in both theme and addressee that takes place in the third part of his speech (beginning at line 1053). There, after telling the Laulku to take the money and go, he says 'Mujika will feel badly about it' (line 1056). Then the addressee shifts to a specific Mujika man, Kasipa, whom Noma invites to come and take the 200 kina which have been set aside for Mujika.

After all the Laulku speakers have spoken, each trying to deflect Noma's challenge, Mujika Kasipa gives two speeches. The second of these is the one already cited above, in which he praises Noma for his sensitivity to his (Kasipa's) skin condition (as above) and formulates the transaction as a payment 'to Mujika' (lines 1637–58). In the first of his speeches (lines 1464–1514), Kasipa goes further than any of the Laulku toward openly accepting Noma's challenge (lines 1505–6), suggesting that he had in fact been advocating a *yi pengi* payment to Kopia for a long time, but that others had delayed it (line 1507). Unfortunately, sizable portions of this speech were inaudible (after line 1479) or missed during a tape change (line 1496), which makes some of the recorded portions more than usually difficult to construe, but it is clear that it is foreshadowing future *makayl* exchange (e.g. lines 1502, 1508). This is a cause in which – whether or not he is aware of the specifically-Mujika source of Noma's grievance – Kasipa alone among the Mujika-Laulku has openly declared himself as Noma's ally. This makes it clear why it was important for Noma to work towards constructing this present payment as one to the Laulku *and Mujika*, and what kind of difference that could make for the future course of events.

Here again, the kinds of alternative constructions which are being discursively contested can by no means be dismissed as mere 'commentary', 'harangue', or 'display', however brilliant some of it may be even in purely aesthetic terms. For the successful conversion of this compensation payment to a *makayl* initiatory transaction would be a matter of very real material consequence, given what it would imply for the future course of Kopia exchange relations (cf. section 4.1).[25]

6.2.7 *El plan* or *gavman lo*?

Is the day's event to be viewed as securing allies for future fighting, or as a compensatory payment to allies which is in keeping with both local custom and *gavman lo,* the new, centralized, European-introduced political order? Various speakers raise and address this question. The latter is unqualifiedly deemed praiseworthy, while the former is a shadowy business, fraught with danger and spoken of indirectly. Hardly anyone will admit to making *el plan* 'fight plans', while a number of speakers declare their adherence to paying allies, and thus 'making law'. Many (but not all) of the latter also decry the use of *el ung* because it is thought of as a medium of aggressive display and one in which suggestive formulations of inter-*talapi* relations are cast (cf. A. Strathern 1975).

Kujilyi, early in the day, is the most explicit in his assertion that the payment being made is to secure allies for future fighting, rather than to make recompense for injury. At lines 50–3 he says, 'Now if a distant man dies' – he apparently had in mind a certain Laulku Wama, wounded in the fight – 'you will make a first [interim] payment'. Later, he adds, you will make major compensation, or if he lives, you'll pay for 'new blood'. But 'you are not giving as they do when they pay for "new blood", you are giving as they do when they make plans to fight'. In a standard image (section 5.4), he adds that Sibeka was 'burning', and he urged Kopia-Kubuka 'let us two go' (to fight together). Now appropriate payments are being made to allies and Kujilyi expresses his thanks (line 60). At line 91 he reiterates that fight plans are being made. But at line 74 he advises his audience against future involvement in trouble: fighting is no good, he says (something often said in these events, but which does not necessarily translate into unwillingness to fight in particular circumstances).

In his declaration that fight plans are being made, Kujilyi seems to want to confirm the new relationship of alliance with Kopia-Kubuka. But he also wishes to avoid a definitive break with Tea-Dena, and says in several places that normal relations should be restored – people should walk the roads, use the courts, and send their children to school.

At line 313 Kopia Waria also speaks of the payment as securing war commitments with Laulku. Later on, however, he vigorously denies this (lines 1388–9, 1408). The latter goes along with his statement that the amount of money being given is not great (line 1394). He minimizes the effort that was required to amass it (lines 1391–3), disparaging the idea that war commitments could be secured with this amount. The money is not a great amount, he implies, because we are not planning to fight again.

In a statement that diminishes his (Kopia's) degree of involvement Waria says (line 1395) that he simply took on Kujilyi's fight and now is paying for the wounded. The remainder of his speech is intended to discourage the Laulku from becoming involved in Kopia-Kubuka affairs and expecting payment for it. Even if there is future fighting, he says, do not come; I will come to you in Wembil (over the Tambul Range) if Kailge is destroyed. 'I won't see (your) face here again' (line 1404); come and help only in extreme circumstances (line 1405). But, he implies, war is unlikely: I've made no war plans, I only assisted Kujilyi.

Kubuka Tamalu denies that he is preparing war. Preferring to see himself as taking a wider political role, he says he is 'building cooperation' (or 'federation, alliance', *yabu pipilyika tekir*). 'I'm compensating my man', he also says (line 904), using the expression *yi mekir*, which is ordinarily applied to making a major compensation payment (for a death). But, Tamalu continues, by doing this, I am making *lo*.

Kubuka Unya, though he employs *el ung* style at a number of points, warns the Laulku that he considers the present payment to be full recompense for their involvement; they should not come back, he advises (lines 999–1000). You may think, he says (line 1002), that I'm making fight plans, but you are wrong: 'I don't want to see people getting splinters from the *mara* tree' (i.e., getting in trouble).

Many speakers say they reject fighting and do not wish to hear talk of it: Kupena at lines 1216, 1225 (where he terms *el ung* 'thick', or fraught with dangerous and unpleasant meanings); Laulku Nui at lines 1255 and 1715 (where he says that *gavman lo* constrains such talk); and Kajipu at lines 1083 and 1085, who also says that he won't listen to *el ung* (line 1089), citing in this context the fact that he has joined the church. His apparent linking of *el-nga ung* 'talk about fighting' with *el ung* 'fight talk' is also implicit in many other speakers' injunctions not to talk *el ung*, e.g. in lines 830, 893, 1085, 1105, 1338, and 1581.

There is thus general denial that war plans are being made, and that there is any intention to fight again. Most speakers stress what they see as the positive activity of 'doing' or 'creating' *lo* by paying their allies.

Lo as a meaningful local category cannot be taken as the equivalent of English 'law'. It is not an abstract structure in terms of which order is maintained and judgment passed on the rights and wrongs of political interaction; not 'social order' or the absence of hostility (cf. M. Strathern 1985a). But *lo* does take up one of the negative valuations of a part of the indigenous political system also implied by 'law', namely the patently destructive exchange of blows itself as opposed to the mediated transactions to which it is inextricably related. Opposed to this negative valuation is a strongly positive estimation of the sustaining and creating of social relations by appropriate mediation, by paying reparations for persons wounded (or killed). The two kinds of transactions may indeed be inter-convertible, but saying this itself implies a difference between them (see section 8.1), which in our experience is a genuine difference in the higher moral valuation of the positive side of these cycles.

Speakers talk of 'doing' (or 'transacting') *lo*, of 'making' or 'creating' (*mim te-*) it. It is thus a social creation or accomplishment, not an abstract system which exists outside the activities which shape it (cf. Strathern 1985a). Transcript passages which illustrate the concept of *lo* follow.

At lines 903–4 Kubuka Tamalu says, 'With this talk I am building cooperation' [*pipilyika*], 'I am compensating my man [the wounded], I am thereby creating law'.

At line 1083 Kopia Kajipu tells everyone not to talk abut fighting (see also lines 1089 and 1094 where he speaks against the use of *el ung* and at line 1090 says it is incompatible with the church). At lines 1087–8 he puts forward his view of the nature of the day's event: 'I've come for my lad who got wounded, I'm paying compensation for the new blood of this man who got injured'.

At line 1183 Laulku Yako, in responding to Kopia Noma's remarks about the 'fallen tree' (section 6.2.6) in the road between Laulku and Kopia says that he already made or established *lo* in relation to that matter (he refers to having given some cassowaries).

At lines 1277–8 Laulku Nui, having said that his aid and support are usually insufficiently recompensed, says, 'I always think I am [being treated as] something different but now that you are turning the law right side up, I am happy'. In other words, you take me seriously by recognizing me in your payment.

At lines 1669–70 Kopia Kajipu says that though he believes he is giving 'for nothing' (nobody has died), still, he gives as the *kiap*'s law-abiding man. Here he explicitly relates the indigenous concept of mediation (through prestation) with *lo* as he understands the *kiap*'s efforts to establish order.

At line 1696 Tilka Alko's use of the concept of *lo* shows that it resides not simply in giving, but also in accepting prestations which sustain and mediate social relations. He says, 'Making *lo* I'll take it [the money]; it is right that I do so' (line 1696).

To conclude this section, one of the injunctions against the use of *el ung* in the transcript is especially telling. This comes late in the proceedings, during the long speech by former big-man Kubuka Ipupu (see section 6.2.2). Another Kubuka transactor breaks in at line 1581 and tries to cut him off by saying *el ung mada nyikimul* 'we have talked enough *el ung*'. But of course, under these circumstances, ordinary talk is unlikely to command the floor. So Tamalu delivers this injunction itself in *el ung*!

This is perhaps related to a general paradox which lies in the way of attempts by many speakers to equate traditional style compensation transactions with 'government law': compensation is an integral part of the larger system of alliance and hostility, and to pay allies helps to sustain it. So also do expressions of support for particular people and *talapi* (as Tamalu's for Kujilyi at line 1230). While not of exactly the same order (see section 8.1), nor equally valued (see above), wealth exchanges on the *pena* and military ones on the battlefield are partially mutually 'convertible' within the traditional socio-political order: 'the more disputes are "settled" then the more they will erupt' (M. Strathern 1985a:123). This conclusion of Strathern's is not without its indigenous advocates: Midipu Kujilyi seems to be expressing a similar understanding in the speech in which he says 'when sky and earth come to an end, that's when the fight will die . . . now [i.e., at the moment of wealth transaction] we say no but it will go on being that way' (lines 81–5).

In accord with Kujilyi's remarks, we may note in concluding this chapter that, despite attempts to assimilate the day's proceedings to *gavman lo,* and despite the fact that the wealth objects presented are two-kina notes rather than pigs or shells, the terms of reference on which the event proceeds belong almost entirely to the order of segmentary business as usual. All of the major political relations at stake are relations of balanced reciprocity, complementary opposition, sameness or difference within a single segmentary order. There are disagreements about particular cases, as we have discussed in detail: about whether the Poika and Mujika lines figure as transactors (sections 6.2.3 and 6.2.6); about whether Bai participated in the fighting as a Laulku or as the grandson of a Kubuka; about whether specific plans to fight are being sealed by this payment to Laulku. But there is no challenge to the implicit premises that an allied but different line must be paid by that which recruited it; that people of the same segmentary identity do not exchange either blows or wealth objects; or that transactions of both those kinds are at least partly interconvertible. Nor is there a challenge to the premise that the public political arena in which those conversions take place is an exclusively male one. For a woman to speak at this event would be unthinkable.

Or would it? We shall see in the next chapter that matters do not always proceed so smoothly: with *gavman lo* have come new activities, in some of which women participate, which in effect challenge the segmentary order. Accordingly, the event to be examined there, though arising from the same historical incident as this one, does not proceed according to similarly unproblematic segmentary terms of reference.

7. Compensation at Palimung and the Kulka women's club

On August 14, 1983, a large gathering came together at Palimung, on the Kailge-Tega road, for the staging of the return compensation payment by the allied tribes Kusika-Midipu-Epola-Alya-Lalka (K-M-E-A-L)[1] to Kopia-Kubuka. This was the second and final phase (on the K-M-E-A-L side) of a cycle of compensation payments resulting from the Marsupial Road War of September 1982 (see section 3.2.2 for details). The first phase, described in the previous chapter, had taken place three weeks before, on July 24.

An unusual feature of the Marsupial Road War, and of this second compensation event, was the part played by a local women's club, called the Kulka women's group. We briefly describe the formation and activities of these clubs in the western Nebilyer below, in section 7.1.

In an unprecedented initiative, members of the club marched out between the opposing sides on the battlefield, bearing the Papua New Guinea flag. With some support from provincial offices (which they had contacted), they made gifts of soft drink, cigarettes and 100 kina (from the club's accumulated money) to either side. They planted the flag and told the combatants to go home, which they eventually did.[2]

This remarkable intervention at the battle resulted in some equally remarkable features of the compensation event, including public speaking by women. The way in which the club members represent their interests and themselves presents in some ways a startling contrast to other aspects of the event, which is otherwise dominated by segmentary, male-centered representations of social life.

Recall that the Marsupial Road War is said to have arisen from a series of events involving Dena Peam (see section 3.2.2) who, having quarreled with members of his own paired tribes, moved into Epola territory to live with his affines. While he was there, he and some Epola stole foodstuffs from his Dena tribesmen, leading to further conflict. Because of this, Dena Peam had long since left this part of the Nebilyer Valley by the time of the events of 1982–3, and was said to be living in the southern Nebilyer, at Alyimp. But ill-feeling between Dena and Epola remained, and the hostility of 1982 was triggered by yet another theft of store-bought foods, generally agreed to have been perpetrated by Epola against Dena. In the event to be described, Dena Peam was repeatedly identified by some participants as the *el pul* 'source of the fight', though he was no longer in the area. Speeches at this event reveal the rhetorical importance of the *el pul* as those past events in terms of which the current situation is presented. But a basic organizational question remains: how is it that such accounts of the past are 'made present' (cf. Bloch 1977, Barthes 1982), as the discursive ground on which the exchange event proceeds? In what does their importance consist?

Unlike Chapter 6, this chapter will not be based upon a full transcript of what was said at the exchange event.[3] This chapter must therefore be organized somewhat differently. We begin in section 7.1 with a brief account of the formation of women's clubs in this part of the Nebilyer Valley in the early 1980s, mainly to give the reader a sense of their activities and orientation towards the 'new order' of *gavman lo* and *bisnis* (see section 6.2.7, also section 7.4 and Chapter 8 below). Then in section 7.2 we describe the unfolding of the Palimung payment event, in which the Kulka women's club played a prominent part. Rather than presenting extracts of speech transcript as a separate appendix, the ones to be addressed are included in the chapter itself. And rather than separating the synoptic, sequential account of the proceedings from the topical analysis, both are combined into a single section (section 7.2), which takes the form of a running precis of what was said and (otherwise) done, which *includes* a partial topical analysis. The latter is not as extensive or multi-stranded as the one in Chapter 6, but concentrates on those topics which can be interestingly compared with, or linked up to, the ones treated in Chapter 6, and the theoretical concerns of the book as a whole. In section 7.4, we analyze in more detail the one aspect of the proceedings in which it *differs* most interestingly from the Kailge event (or any other public exchange event we attended), namely the participation by the Kulka women's group. Between these two sections, there is an interlude (section 7.3), in which we describe the participation of the same women's group at a subsequent event at which compensation was paid to them by the opposing, Tea-Dena tribe pair.

In our discussion of both of the payment events (at Palimung and Kopola) in which the women's group took part, we seek to understand the women's participation in the earlier battlefield events, and also the constitution of them and/or their club as transactors in the payment events we describe here. Of especial interest is the women's formulation of the grounds from which they act and speak, how they locate themselves and, also, are located by others in relation to the reproduction of the segmentary political order. We argue that the relation is complex: through their actions on battlefield and prestation ground the women do not fully reproduce the order of segmentary politics-as-usual; in fact, in some ways they overtly seek to repudiate its rationale. But their position is in many respects novel and contestable, and there are recurrent openings in the action for the women's position to be at least partly appropriated by and assimilated to the grounds and inextricably linked conduct of segmentary-politics-as-usual. It is not *simply* that other, male transactors attempt to effect this appropriation, though that is partly the case; but also that, over the course of these events, in finding voices with which to speak the women themselves increasingly move towards emulation and appropriation of male modes of political conduct.

Because of the way in which this chapter is organized, with all transcript material included within it, most of the analysis in which we attempt to demonstrate that overall movement will not come until all the transcript-cum-précis of the events has been presented in sections 7.2 and 7.3. Meantime, given the oratorical norms described in Chapter 5 and exemplified so far, we urge the reader to pay close attention to what each of the speakers says at this event, and, in particular to similarities and differences among the women's speeches, and between theirs and the men's. But first, some relevant background details about the platform from which the women will speak.

7.1 WESTERN NEBILYER WOMEN'S CLUBS

From early 1982 onward, women's clubs (*ab klap*) began to form and gained popularity in many parts of the Nebilyer Valley. One such club at Kailge really only gained momentum from early 1983. However, another had formed somewhat earlier in Kulka territory at Kumaku, about a half-hour's walk away from Kailge, with which our Kailge women's club had a great deal to do. The most prominent women members and leaders of the Kulka club were daughters of a Kulka big-man and Councillor, Pokea, who lived at Kumaku.

These clubs, from the members' point of view, were to promote money-making by engaging in (*bisnis*) activities in which women were primary participants. But from the early meetings of both Kailge and Kumaku groups, men were never excluded, and there was never any suggestion that they should be, though the number of participant men was generally small. In both groups, the officiant role was exercised by a male *kuskus* or *kilak* 'clerk'. For the Kailge group, this was a young, recently-married literate man, son of a big-man of Kopia\Tolab; for the Kulka group, it was the husband of a club leader, one of the daughters of Kulka Councillor Pokea. The Councillors and a few other local prominent men were seen to support the clubs, frequently came to meetings, and were asked for their help in a variety of ways. Women's associations had existed prior to independence, under the 'Welfare section'. Ms S. Bonnell, sometime provincial planner in the Western Highlands government and with long experience in women's affairs, speculated (in an interview of 1986) that the earliest precedent for women's associations may have been *kiaps'* wives' work with local women in meetings specially convened for the purpose of advising them on nutrition, sanitation, handicrafts and so forth. During the last year of the Chan government (1982), a nation-wide survey was made of the activities of women's associations, and on that basis, a national government grant of 335,000 kina was made to those showing the greatest promise. Sexton (1982, 1984) and Warry (1985) discuss women's groups elsewhere in the Highlands. In the Nebilyer, a grant of 900 kina had been made to Kumaku. Undoubtedly, the formation of the Kailge club was greatly stimulated by seeing this example of involvement in government-supported, hopefully lucrative activities. It was clear that women were attracted, too, by the possibility for wider involvement in provincial political affairs, for in many of the meetings they avidly discussed women's council activities in Mt Hagen. But the primary political activities of the Kailge club were with the Kumaku group.

After a few months, the Kailge group divided. There was an active club which met in Kubuka territory and tended to include women married into the Kopia\Kabika segment, and a club which met at Kailge and included those married into all the other Kopia segments in the Kailge (and upper *no ukulu*) area. We briefly describe here the typical Kailge club meeting; occasional visits to Kumaku showed that the conduct of meetings there was similar. We intend this account to give the reader a sense of the ritual attitude, the excitement and high expectations which people brought to club activities – a sense which should prevent any false, complete identification on the reader's part of *bisnis* as locally understood with the ideal, instrumentally-rational model of European 'business'.

Though the *kilak* usually made an effort to enforce a starting-time on these night-time club meetings, (and people would ask the time of anyone present who had a watch, which was usually either a man, or Francesca Merlan), a start was never made by the clock. Women would come (with younger children) when they felt the time was about right. Mystique attaches to the night-time meeting, and generally these gatherings would not get under way before 9pm. Frequently they lasted into early morning. The emphasis on punctuality, and on holding meetings at night, is an indication of the ritual attitude with which people approached the activities of the club and the values it represented, in particular, the promise of engaging in cash-producing work.

When people had gathered in one house or another (usually on the Kailge *pena*, in what was then ostensibly the Kopia\Tolab 'men's house'), the clerk would call roll. Sometimes small fines were levied on members who had failed to come, and entered against their names in a roll-book. Then money was collected. People were expected to contribute regularly to the club, and the contributions were also entered in a notebook and receipts issued. The money was kept locally for a time, but eventually banked in Mt Hagen. People were supposed to contribute a basic amount (around 6 kina) to participate in the club's activities, and this was to go into its coffers; but there was much deferring and defaulting. Altogether the handling of sums of money usually took up a great part of every meeting, and people saw this as perfectly in line with the club's ostensible main purpose of engaging in *bisnis* and gaining access to the market economy. In general much more time was spent on these internal collection activities than on developing ways of bringing in money from outside.

Money collection was followed by an activity called *eksenda* (presumably from English 'agenda'). This was supposed to consist mainly in proposals for club activities, but seemed often instead to have a largely group-therapeutic character: people complained about what they saw as wrong with the club, and made proposals about what should be done. For instance, for a long time the women thought they should have a separate club house (so they did not have to meet in a men's house). But this could only be done with men's cooperation, and, it was felt, the men were not responding to the need. Many *eksenda* were held on this subject, the need for land discussed and eventually the Councillor said the house could be built on some of his land. Men promised to participate in the building. But when ground-clearing and digging for the house began, the Councillor protested that it was far too close to his *abu lku*, 'woman's house' (where his wife lived, although she had approved the site). This caused another round of delays, and the house had not been completed by the time we left at the end of 1983. Among major projects the club undertook were planting of peanuts and other cash crops, and many *eksenda* revolved around complaints that women were not contributing work-time equally, and so forth. (Work-days were set at club meetings, and though no specific promises to help were extracted, it was expected that women who agreed to the proposed work-day would come for some period of time at least.)

The *eksenda* was frequently delayed or taken over by the clerk, who often made club grievances his own, leveling them against the club participants: people were *bikhet* ('big head') and not contributing money, not working properly, not building the club house, not attending meetings, and if they did not try harder, he would quit, and so on. The directive and accusatory role of the clerk had something in common with that of young men who were the leading functionaries of locally-organized religion-oriented, night-time 'fellowship' meetings (see section 2.5) which had been extremely popular until the women's club meetings began to supplant them in the local round of activities. In both kinds of meetings, it was younger men placed in the position (because of literacy, numeracy, maleness) of trying to organize, using the best European-style tactics they knew (roll-call, establishing turn-taking in speaking, though this usually fell quickly into disarray etc.), but still, in the end, contributing less momentum to the whole venture than might have appeared. The Kailge women's club's successful projects, such as decorating themselves and appearing in the large Hagen Show, came to fruition largely because the women who wanted to participate were strongly motivated by a feeling of competitiveness (e.g. between Kailge and Kumaku, and later, of both with other women's groups), and were able to draw upon networks available to them to collect decorations, arrange transportation, provision themselves, get men to participate, make contacts in Mt Hagen, and so on.

The Kulka club at Kumaku acted somewhat more expeditiously than the Kailge one in building, not only a club house, but a large compound of several buildings, which they subsequently enclosed with a fence, and in which they sponsored a large, regional fete at which the main attraction was competitive decoration and dancing involving several local women's clubs.[4]

7.2 UNFOLDING OF THE EVENT

On the morning of August 14, before the Kopia-Kubuka started for Palimung, people gathered at the Kailge *pena*. A few men from other *talapi* were present, and they made some speeches attempting to suggest (in view of what was about to take place) a particular interpretation of the relations of their *talapi* to Kopia-Kubuka. It was most apt that they make these speeches at this time and at Kailge, when they could get the floor and expand upon their basis for claims upon Kopia-Kubuka before the latter went to meet the donor *talapi*.

7.2.1 Preliminary speeches at Kailge

An attending Palimi man spoke saying that while the Kopia-Kubuka alliance with Mujika-Laulku was only recent, that with Palimi was of long standing (cf. sections 6.2.3, 6.2.6). Two men of Poika spoke, the first reiterating that 'our' (i.e., Poika-Palimi and Kopia-Kubuka) alliance with Mujika-Laulku is only recent; and the second introducing here the image of Kujilyi as a woman whom 'we are going to take in marriage', so let us dress up.

Another speech was made by a Kulka man from Tabuga (see Map 2), a man who had friendly relations with the Kopia Councillor Noma (whose mother had been a Kulka), but who otherwise rarely came to Kailge. In an image of 'looking after' (see section 5.4), he described himself as a snake whose head was in Tabuga and his tail in Kailge, so that he immediately sensed anything happening in the western Nebilyer: one always looks after one's cousins, he concluded.

The main preparatory speech at Kailge, however, was made by Councillor Noma. It had at least two clearly identifiable themes: attempts to impose organization and orderliness upon the group that would go from Kailge; and representation of himself as a man who had been drawn into the 1982 fighting reluctantly, and who otherwise was in favor of amicable inter-*talapi* relations and conciliation. The latter parallels Kujilyi's similar reluctance, described in section 6.2.1, to be seen in any way as an *el pul* 'source of the fight'. Since both themes seem to be important in all events of this kind, it is worth examining each more closely.

Noma was concerned that the Kopia and Kubuka make a good impression: that the internal composition and the strength of each unit be clearly demonstrated. There is thus here a concern with segmentary representation of the social world. Let the Kubuka bunch together, and the various Kopia men's houses, he said; no dancing ahead, and no straggling. But those who were dressed in European fashion he deemed unfit to walk in the main parade: let them walk behind (closer to the women and children). Since, however, Poika Wangi's death had occurred less than a month ago, he proclaimed (in keeping with what the majority had already done) modified decoration, without face paint.

Like some other participants (notably Kujilyi) throughout the day, he urged orderly participation in the speech-making:

na nyibu, na nyibu i naa nyai
'I will talk, I will talk', do not say this

aku na nyid-kin aku yi *sekan* yi nai nyiba ola moluba
when I have spoken whoever will speak next will stand up

yi aki-yl nyim-kin
and when that man has spoken

sekan yi nai molupa oba nyiba yi aki-yl
whoever is after him will talk

This instruction, and numerous others like it, are attempts to establish an orderly state of affairs which, in our experience, is never realized in these events. It certainly was not realized here, even though later at Palimung representatives of K-M-E-A-L with the encouragement of Midipu Kujilyi, wrote down a roster of speakers.[5] Some of those on it actually spoke, but so did many who were not. People are conscious enough of the fact that efforts are made to organize turn-taking at these events, and of the frequent lack of success, so that one of the magistrates who was on the list opened by poking fun at the whole notion of attempting to regulate competitive speaking: they just wrote my name down because they thought it was a good idea, he said; otherwise, I wouldn't be talking.

In the same way that Noma began the struggle to organize speech turn-taking, he also began to try to organize who would eventually count the money that would be given. He pointed out that some money had gone astray in the Laulku payment in July; and Magistrate Unya suggested who might count the money for each men's house. It was generally agreed that it would be much better if the money were given to each men's house separately, rather than as a lump sum to Kopia and Kubuka, because everyone realized the potential in the latter method for a general scramble. In the end, at Palimung, the counting turned into a crowd scene of considerable confusion, and there were rumors and accusations of unfairness and theft.

Noma's second theme was that he had not been eager for the fight. As we have said (section 2.3), he is generally thought of as a man of *gavman lo,* one who had early contact with the European patrol officers and encouraged the building of the Nebilyer Bridge, the Kailge-Tega road, and other projects which people associated with either *gavman lo* or *bisnis* (such as his son's ultimately unsuccessful efforts to establish a large trade-store at Kailge). He had made a strong alliance with the Tilka across the river Luip (*no luip pol lyirid-ilyi-o, uj watipa pol lyirid-ilyi-o* 'I took up the Luip bridge, I made a bridge of *watipa* tree' [strong]), so presumably feared no attack from that direction (in which the Tea-Dena also live, see section 6.2.5). I did not take up the fight, he said; the *kang* raskol-*ma* 'rascals' (young, irresponsible boys) did so. Later, he said, I roasted pig – in fact, before the battle in 1982 men had sacrificed a pig in Engal-suku, a forest above Kailge dedicated to Kur [spirit] Engal (Map 3). In a series of (partial) *el ung* remarks partly directed to the Kulka man mentioned above, Noma added:

ekepu *gavman* okum ilyi-o
now government is coming/here

ekepu *gavman* okum ilyi-o
now government is here

na-nga pel, ekepu kung ilyi kuyud ilyi
my cousin, I roasted this pig

nu obil kare akap tab nyib mola
I (am) saying, shall I give you some bones

ku moni kang-ma eni-nga ku pudu-ma lying-ayl pukumul-o
we are going so the fellows will get their due/what is owed

nu perik okun na-nga lapa lku-na pin-o
why have you come, you slept in my father's house

el-kin aji tip tebu nyib tirid-ilyi
I said I would hand on the fight

ekepu *lo* lekim-kin ilyi-o
now lo *is instituted*

medi-nsipu mere Tapula lku *kapa* kanakur
looking down to Tabuga I see a 'haus kapa'[6]

mere wiji-tikin kanakun ilyi
and you look up and see

ya kalyke lku *kapa* kánakun
a haus kapa *here at Kailge*

ui ada-ma moluring ilyi
before the old men lived

i teku moluring mel mui-topa
they made something like a border [of a mat]

wal-mel kolu-topa
like edging on a netbag

i tek tiring-iyl
this is what they did

ekepu nunu *pren* nyilyn *pren* nyilto-kin nunu molto
now you call them friend

mere tola-wanaka-sil tea-dena-sil
the Tola-Wanaka and Tea-Dena down there

elti-ti mere ga punya-na nosil na kuduringl yi-yl
those two, destroying the sweet potato garden 'pulled' me in

na naa pubu nyirid-ilyi
I will not go, I said

na kulka ab mal-ayl molyo na naa pubu mol
I am a Kulka woman's son, I shall not go, no

This is the extracted middle section of Noma's speech, which was delivered in partial *el ung* prosody (with few line-terminating *el ung* vowels, as above). Here Noma suggests that those going to the compensation will only retrieve what is coming to them for helping (*ku pudu-ma*, where *pudu* expresses the notion of a balanced return), possibly with nothing left over for redistribution. Noma compares the preparation for war of the *ui ada-ma* 'old men of before' (edging of a netbag or mat)[7] with present, better times in which law is instituted, and people at Tabuga and Kailge can see each other's *haus kapa* (metal-roofed buildings, i.e., their respective churches). He stresses that he was pulled into the fight by the destruction at Sibeka, though he had been determined not to go (and, he later says, had threatened to jail trouble-makers). But now that the compensation is taking place, he adds, will they receive *mabola tuwal* 'pig grease' (a large payment)? However much is given, it does not amount to 'buying a man' but rather, he says, will be used by women and children (which suggests a small amount). He seems inclined to play down the extent of fighting, and especially to stress his own reluctant participation in it, and continuing peaceable intentions. He says he has no idea how much may be given (*ku naba naa pilyip pukur-o* 'not knowing the amount I go') but that in any event his disposition is serene (*kupa lyapi mel moly-ayl* 'I am like a white [puffy, cumulus] cloud').

7.2.2 The march to Palimung

With that, the crowd set off for Palimung. Its movement was by no means casual or haphazard (see Plate 5). Once over the log bridge at the River Ukulu, we marched along the main road in dense formation, as a single large column, four to six abreast, men in front, women behind. The children were more randomly distributed: older boys generally went with the men, girls and younger boys went with the women, or scampered around outside the main column. We followed the established road (Map 2), past Sibeka Garden and over the River Puyl towards Palimung.

By the time we got to the outskirts of Palimung, our dense column had inevitably become long and thin. There we stopped to mass again and prepare for a single concerted entry.[8] The final entry into Palimung was a dramatic one. As often happens at such events, it took the form of a mock charge by the visiting male cohort, i.e. the Kopia-Kubuka, who ran in brandishing spears and axes and shouting battle cries (see Plate 7). When they got to the clearing where the payment was to be presented, they continued their charge, running in a large circle around the edge. At this point, there were only a few men present from the K-M-E-A-L alliance. Most were gathered down the road in the opposite direction from which we had come, preparing for their own dramatic entry.

After the mock charge had died down and most of the Kopia-Kubuka had sat down, there was a series of short speeches concerning an issue which had already been mooted during the march and the wait at the outskirts: whether the Kopia-Kubuka should have waited at Sibeka for the K-M-E-A-L to arrive from Palimung and present their compensation there.

The standard practice when making *makayl* or compensation payments is for donors to present them in one of their own prestation grounds. Why should anyone now have suggested otherwise? In order to understand what their reasons may have been, one must bear in mind the meaningful uses of space and movement which were exemplified in section 6.1. There we saw that the overall movement of the event proceeded as if according to the homology: Kailge *pena* is to Kailge School ground as Kopia-Kubuka is to Mujika-Laulku, so that the movement from the *pena* to the school ground represented (among other things) a movement from Kopia-Kubuka to Mujika-Laulku – a movement of wealth in the opposite direction to that of the earlier recruitment event, as per standard requirements. From the Mujika-Laulku point of view, the terminus of the first movement and the origin of the second was Kailge, and by going there they identified themselves with Kopia-Kubuka vis-à-vis Tea-Dena and K-M-E-A-L. They had not previously been enemies of any of those *talapi*, and had now become so only by way of their identification with Kopia-Kubuka. That identification was sealed by their return trip to Kailge to accept compensation.

Similarly, at the Palimung compensation event, the movement of Kopia-Kubuka towards Palimung reenacts their earlier recruitment to fight on the side of the K-M-E-A-L. But in this case their enmity with Tea-Dena was *not* only a result of that recruitment: they had formerly been major enemies of both the Tea-Dena and the K-M-E-A-L. We shall see that later on at these proceedings (unlike at the Kailge event), a real ambivalence is expressed on the donor side about whether they wish to identify themselves with the recruits (in this case the Kopia-Kubuka) as opposed to the Tea-Dena. In other words, there is doubt as to whether the new set of alignments should be accepted as a basis for future action – a doubt which was also expressed by some Kopia-Kubuka speakers (vis-à-vis the K-M-E-A-L) at the Kailge event (see section 6.2.7.).

It is against this background that we can understand the preference expressed by some Kopia-Kubuka for Sibeka over Palimung as the setting for the present payment.In this case (unlike in the recruitment of the Mujika-Laulku by Kopia-Kubuka), the original mobilization had not entailed a movement by the recruits to the recruiters' home territory for massing against the enemy tribes. Rather, the contingent of Kopia-Kubuka (and their recruits, the Mujika-Laulku) had met the K-M-E-A-L halfway, at Sibeka, a large sweet potato garden which is a kind of no-man's-land, between the borders of Kopia-Kubuka, Epola-Alya, Tea-Dena, and the neutral *talapi* Tilka and Kulka (see Map 2). That this meeting was spatially 'halfway' – though determined in part by geography and tactics – was consonant with other aspects of its meaning as a segmentary-political event, since the only historical basis for an alliance between Kopia-Kubuka and K-M-E-A-L was their common enmity with the Tea-Dena (section 3.2.2).

Given that the original socio-spatial movement went only halfway, only as far as Sibeka, should the return for compensation require a further movement, right into the K-M-E-A-L heartland? That seems to have been at least one of the questions Kopia-Kubuka men had in mind as some of them began to grumble on the march to Palimung, and as they continued to debate about the locale after they had finished their mock charge.

Given that at least some of the K-M-E-A-L were present during the latter discussion, the terms in which this delicate question could be raised were necessarily muted, but some of the remarks are telling. The first speaker, Kopia Mel (the brother of Councillor Noma) was understood by our exegetes to be making the point that, if the event were staged at Sibeka, this would be taken by the Tea-Dena and others as a sign that plans were being made to fight again, i.e., that an alliance was being sealed against the Tea-Dena in particular (who, recall, are the K-M-E-A-L's former allies). Mel instead announced that

ya ilyi-nga mada pora nyiba-o
it will conclude here

What will conclude there? Presumably their concerted fighting with Tea-Dena, and the resulting compensation cycle which it had started at Kailge.

His next lines were:

yi-te lelka-ja-o
had a man died

ilyi koluwa nyim kep-o
this is what Koluwa said:

sibeka ga punya neked-o
'sibeka sweet potato garden down there'

yi-te naa lirim-o
[but] no man did die

That is, Koluwa, a leading Epola big-man, had agreed that the event should have been staged at Sibeka if a man had been killed in the fighting, but since no one had been, it should not be. What is the implied connection between whether someone had died and the proper locale of the compensation event?

In light of Mel's remark in the previous line (and the foregoing discussion), we can understand him to be implying that, if a man had been killed, this would have firmly committed those present to an alliance against the Tea-

Dena. Under those circumstancees, it would have been proper to stage the event at Sibeka, thereby addressing the Tea-Dena (from whose territory Sibeka is clearly visible). But since no one was killed, such a pointed demonstration is neither necessary not desirable.

Mel concludes his speech by adding a positive reason for holding the event there at Palimung instead:

> ya kolya koma koma lim-o
> *this place is cool and moist*
>
> pangiya pangiya lepa
> *it is shady and serene*
>
> ilyi-nga tian nyib tekir ilyi-ko
> *so you should do it here, that's what I say*

Several subsequent Kopia speakers pick up and endorse Mel's argument that Palimung is preferable because it is a cool, moist, shady place as opposed to the sunburnt garden space at Sibeka. In view of the commonplace Nebilyer/Melpa imagery of hostility, aggressive intent as 'heat' (cf. section 5.4 above and A. Strathern 1975), we may understand these remarks both literally and as metaphorical reformulations of the position vis-à-vis Tea-Dena. They may also allude to the relationship between Kopia-Kubuka and K-M-E-A-L, given the doubts expressed at the Kailge event about how 'cool' that might really be (section 6.2.7). If so, then to stress the coolness of Palimung is to argue in justification of having come all the way into the heartland of the K-M-E-A-L instead of only meeting them halfway. It is probably no accident that the latter alternative (which presumes the relationship to be still 'hot') was not openly endorsed in any of the six speeches on the subject (all but one by Kopia men) at Palimung. What was said on the road has become unspeakable in the *pena*.

The other speaker on this topic was Midipu Mai, the man in whose *pena* the crowd has assembled. Speaking in *el ung* (in the Meam dialect also used by many other speakers at this event), he says:

> tibeka ga punya nyikimil aku-na naa pilyikir-o
> *they say Sibeka garden, I won't listen to that*

But for Mai, the question of where to hold the event is significant at a lower spatio-segmentary level than for the Kopia-Kubuka. As far as the latter are concerned, the place where they are is Palimung, a 'big name' whose most specific reference is to the main *pena* of the Epola-Alya (see Map 2), but which is also used (especially by outsiders) to denote a more-or-less extensive region around it (just as the 'big name' Kailge is used in relation to Kopia-Kubuka territory). But while the Kopia-Kubuka speeches all refer to the place where they are as Palimung (which they identify with K-M-E-A-L), Mai refers to it as Tapulku. For him, the difference is crucial. For even though the place is only a few hundred feet from Palimung proper, it is over the boundary into Midipu territory, rather than Epola. In his view the Epola are the real trouble-makers, not 'himself' (the Kusika-Midipu). Hence he wishes to make the distribution within his own borders:

> ya na-nga makayl pena-na tekir-kiyl-o
> *here I am giving in my own display ground*

tapulku mai-ma tuku tekir-ayl, mere epola mere lyip welti mudukur
I give at Tapulku, 'inside' (my own territory), and by-pass the Epola down there

alya makayl pena med mudup
and also by-pass the Alya display ground

na-nga ya makayl pena kutika-midipu-na ya kolya oi-na tuku tekir-kiyl-o
in my own display ground within Kusika-Midipu borders I make my presentation

This identification is consistent with the fact that the man who was seen (at Kailge anyway) as having recruited the Kopia-Kubuka (however reluctantly) was also a Midipu, Kujilyi, the leading big-man of the K-M-E-A-L alliance. We shall see below that Midipu Mai has reasons of his own for wanting the event to be staged at a place which is identified, not just with Kusika-Midipu in general, but with him in particular.

Even as Mai speaks, Kujilyi has already arrived, and audible in the distance are the war cries of the main cohort of K-M-E-A-L men, who are about to make their own mock charge upon Mai's *pena*. As they come running down the road, most of the assembled crowd gets up and hurries to the road to view the oncoming charge. Just as the Kopia-Kubuka men had done before, the K-M-E-A-L surge onto the *pena* and run in circles around it, brandishing spears and axes. They are joined by the Kopia-Kubuka men who run among them in the same direction, re-enacting the entry of Kopia-Kubuka into the Marsupial Road War as allies of K-M-E-A-L, and at the same time reproducing their participation in it as *distinct* from that of K-M-E-A-L, but involving Kopia and Kubuka in common (i.e., as 'the same' segmentary actor vis-à-vis K-M-E-A-L).

Eventually most sit down, and the speech-making begins again. With this, Palimung (Tapulku in particular) is firmly established as the setting and there is no further discussion of locale and dress, both dimensions which shape such events as communications of a particular kind. But the effort to establish order in the two most significant forms of exchange transacted – speech-making and giving of money – goes on throughout the day, and is especially unsuccessful in respect to the latter. Midipu Pana was evidently charged with attempting to get speakers to follow the pre-established roster, but he appears to intervene only twice in the proceedings with any success.

7.2.3. Men's and women's speeches at Palimung

Shortly after the Kailge crowd was installed at Palimung, and Kusika-Midipu had appeared with the money-laden display boards, two significant speeches were made which focused on implications of the day's events for inter-*talapi* relations. In a brief *el ung* speech, an Epola big-man, Tuse, made two points: since nobody died in the fighting the compensation will not be large; and though this event may mark a change in the relations of Kopia-Kubuka and Epola-Alya, relations could be precarious and let us therefore not dwell on past problems. Instead, he says, I am paying for your troubles and injuries. On the precariousness of the changed relations he says in an *el ung* speech (from which the following is extracted):

ekepu kang te-ne temani tok nyin-lum-a
now if any fellow of you gives an account

ung lupu mare temani tok mekin pui-a
take away with you a different story [do not emphasize the earlier ones]

kopia-kubuka kang-te-ne temani naa tui-a
Kopia-Kubuka fellow, do not tell tales

pe epola-alya kang-te-ne temani naa tupiyl-a
and let Epola-Alya not tell tales

tilpapi top toba nyiba
this will cause us to slip

Tuse uses the standard concept of things wet and slippery to connote the precarious, uncertain, or possibility of trouble (see section 5.4).

A few seconds after Tuse, Midipu Mai introduced a quite different topic. Owner of the display ground where the event is being staged, he is also the father of Lkerim, on whose truck Kopia Uwa had recently been injured (section 6.1). Though compensation had been discussed and some had been paid separately for this, Mai tries to relate today's compensation to that for Uwa, to demonstrate his concern for the maintenance of good relations. He does this by suggesting that although he is giving money to Kopia-Kubuka, money is not as important as men. He starts his *el ung* speech with a brief allusion to the Epola as the source of trouble:

yi-maaa
men

nukunuku yi tara-n-a
the forefather of the Nukunuku fellow [Epola Koluwa]

kera turum-lum-a
killed a bird [started the trouble]

ala-wal-na pebu nyirim-lum-a
and said, I will sleep in the netbag

aku nukunuku yi tara-n tirim-lum
that is what the Epola forefather did

na molup pilyip-a
(this is what) I understand . . .

Shortly shifting to speak of Uwa, he continues:

turum-lum topa kibu langapa
he was hit and his leg broken [not the precise injury]

topa puku puku topa tirim-aaa
in his getting hit, it broke

puyl pula top a-aa
across the river Puyl

na pukur-aaa
I go

wayl yi apa-aa
my uncle at Walyo

nu mel na-nga-te molurun-lum-aaa
you were mine

ekepu lepa nyim-lum-aaa
now if he lies there

ku *mon*-ayl-lum-aaa
the money

mel nyiringa tikir-kiyl-aaa
I give you an unimportant thing

yi-te naa tibu, mel koropa we-yl
I am not giving a man, but a poor thing

yi mel todul-ayl-o
a man is a 'strong' [valued, significant] thing

komapu nyilymolu ilyi-nga-aa
we live in harmony

wangintai nyib
saying, may you feel better

wan kina tekir kalya-aa
I thus give (you) one kina

nok pani nyib
saying, take it and use it

komakoma lentikir-kilyi
I bring it for you

pangpang nyikin pui-a
take it calmly and go

Then, still early in the day, the Kulka women's club appeared. They came in on parade, to scattered applause, carrying a flag. They were dressed in identical T-shirts (kept spotlessly clean for official occasions of this kind), each bearing the national bird of paradise emblem on the chest, and most had bright yellow sunflowers in their hair. Midipu Kujilyi cleared a 'space' for them in the proceedings by saying that they would pray. This is unusual at exchange events, and is an indication of the connection between Christian and new *gavman* values which the Kulka women's club represents and was attempting to enact.

Kulka Pokea announced again that the women's club would pray, and one of the club women did so – but at such low volume that she could not be heard at any distance. After this, Kulka Pokea took the floor and made a long speech recounting the alliances involved in the fight (he referred to Tea-Dena and Tola-Wanaka, of whom none were present, by tribal name; but to Epola as 'Koluwa', Kusika-Midipu as 'Kujilyi', and Kopia-Kubuka as 'Noma', all of whom were present). Pokea also focused on the role of the women's club in stopping the fight and posting the flag. Assimilating his segmentary position (that of neutral Kulka) to that of *gavman lo*, he pointed out that he intended to receive money from both sides. When they have their presentation 'down there' (at Tea-Dena), *plak-iyl-ko meb pubu* 'I shall again go carrying this flag'. Here his first person pronominal usage encompasses himself (as Kulka Councillor), but also the Kulka club. Through these usages he assimilates them to his position; but some of his pronominal references are first person plural, 'we' (generally in contexts to be understood as 'we club members'). Later he reaffirms:

mere kudanga meb pumulu ultuku, tali-nga
we will carry it down there tomorrow or the next day

wanya *plak*-iyl meb pumulu ilyi-nga
we shall carry it (there) and so

eni-nga pudumong ul ime-nga te kanak lying-lum
and if you get into any (further) trouble

eni yabu kanu-ka ob kanu naa kanakumul-o
we do not (will not) see you

In his speech, Pokea also stressed the innovative aspects of the club's action:

ui *mak* tenga molurumul
before we were living in different conditions

ekepu *mak* tenga lupu kodi tenga tuku molkumul
now we are living in changed conditions

mak kodi tenga tuku molkumul ilyi
in new and different conditions

ekepu *lo* kani-yl *senis* tep ul mare kodi-nga tekimil ilyi
now we are changing the law, they are doing things differently

ab kupari-kil ul-te lupu eni-kin ya ui kani wanya *plak*-te kani monturumul
'mad women', along with you before we did something different and put the flag up ['mad women' a thought attributed to others]

ekepu olyo yabu-kil eni-nga *mak* tenga lupu
and now we people, according to your different way of proceeding

wanya *plak*-ayl meb tuku okumul
we are coming in bringing the flag

The bringing in and raising of the flag here re-enacts the battlefield scene in the same way that the men's mock charges are a re-enactment.

Pokea then introduced his daughter, Kodu, by saying that in the Nebilyer area some women do *kongun mel-we koltal* 'a little bit of work', and that Kodu *onunga kolti eni-kin nyiba tekim*, 'will say a little word to you'. Kodu's complete speech (later referred to as [speech] K in the analysis at section 7.4), was as follows:

(1) na-nga bi-lyi kodu pokea
my name is Kodu Pokea

na ya napilya kudanga *distrik kansil*-nga
here in the Nebilyer side District Council

kansil mak turing-iyl ab *naba wan*-iyl
they voted me number one woman [women's leader]

ya ab-ma-kin kongun telyo, kongun telyo ilyi nabolka ul tim-na
I work with these women, I work with them and what happened

(5) ui ya *kansil* molo *woman kansil* ul ilyi-nga
before, this council, or about this women's council

ya abu-l ab mel-we-kil kongun tiring ilyi-kin tek molkuk-kin
only a few women were working, and while they were doing so

ya kopia-kubuka-kin tea-dena-kin el mel tiring-iyl
the Kopia-Kubuka and Tea-Dena sort of fought

na-nga abu el ul kayi-te mol nyik el-ayl *brukim* tek
and my women, saying war is not a good thing, they stopped the fight

ku *na* mel mare tiring ilyi-nga
and they gave money and things

eni-n *bekim* tek tik tengi ime-nga
you are about to make a return (payment), and for these

lyingi-me-nga wanya *plak*-ayl mentipun
things which they will get, (we) bring the flag

ya yabu mel-we i koltal eni-n kongun telymeli-ke
and these few people who work [do club work]

ku *amamas* telymeli ilyi-nga, i tek ung-iyl molymeli
are proud of [getting] the money, they did this [and so] are here talking

yabu kalya-ma tek ung mel nar
what in the world did these people do

plaua kuku au nyik tek ung mat molymeli-me
these people who've come decorated with flowers are here

no nung molo tek ung mel nar i nyik pilyik tengi
have they been drinking or what? this is what you will think

ilyi-nga *toksave* tekir
and so I am informing you

[audience applauds]

Pokea's other daughter, Mijiyl, introduced by Pokea by name, spoke immediately after Kodu, and her complete speech (speech M) was as follows:

na ing mare awuntipa nyi naa nyibu
I will not speak at length

pilis matres na *kansil* na . . .
the village magistrates and councillors and . . .

pilis matres yabu lupu lupu ing ilyi-nga na-ni age nyikir
for the village magistrates' and others' invitation I say thanks

Kansil-ayl-nge ul ilyi tepa kodupa lyim
the Councillor [Kujilyi] invited us

ilyi-nga na age anum-uyl nyikir
and for that, I say, thank you very much

ya noi el tiring ilyi-nga ya ab anum mel koltal
they fought down there and so, just a few older women

kongun kubilek tiring
were working at first

tek molku-kin ilyi-nga puk noi kubu tiring
they were (working), and going down they worked at Kubu [in Tilka territory]

noi kalyke ya med palimung kolya-ma-nga tiring ilyi-nga
down at Kailge and here at Palimung they were working

ya kolya-ma-nga el-ma naa tiang
'let them not have any fights around here'

ab-ayl kongun-ayl todul pupiyl nyik pamul
saying, 'let the women's work grow strong, let's go'

wany-ayl mek ok eni-n *brukim* tiring
bringing the flag they stopped it

pe teku-kin pe pipilyi kolkumul nyik-kin ku *wan*-kina tiring
and giving, saying, we are ashamed/embarrassed, they gave 'one' [i.e. a few] kina

mere-kid *wan*-kina tik, ya-kid *wan* kina tik tiring
one kina down that way, and one kina this way

(15) ilyi-nga yab moluyl-ne ing awuntip naa nyibu
here in public I won't talk much

ul ting-iyl age anum-uyl nyikir, mada nyikir
for what you did [inviting us], I say thanks very much, I've said enough

Mijiyl's consternation at talking in public is even more palpable than Kodu's. The remarks at beginning and end – 'I will not talk much' – are fairly standard for men, too, but by them are usually more honored in the breach than the observance. Here, however, the speaker makes good her promise. It is likely that a woman who spoke at length would be criticized by men and women alike for behaving inappropriately. (For example, during the walk up to Palimung, when some Kopia wives walked quickly and got ahead of some of the men (cf. above), a wife of the Kubuka magistrate scolded loudly: 'Such women the Kopia have married!' As it was, a few men in the crowd around us grumbled when the women were invited to speak.) Mijiyl even claims that the feeling the women had as they came onto the battlefield was one of embarrassment at their own (unusual) behavior.

Like Kodu, Mijiyl speaks of the club work rather modestly, but says that it was important to break up the fight so that work could 'grow strong' – in other words, fighting is at variance with aspects of the desired, modern order which the club represents. Her speech makes it clear, too, that the way of stopping the fight was not by the autocratic methods of the former European *kiaps*, of simply marching in with a .303 rifle, ordering everyone to go home or be jailed. The club women accomplished their aim through instituting a mediatory exchange: they gave equal amounts of their club money to either side, and also prevailed on Hagen authorities to bring soft drinks and other items to give. Hence the situation of the women's club at this event, and that which followed several days later at Kopola, is most comparable to the situation of the Tilka (paired tribe of the Kulka): they adopted a mediatory, non-combatant role and return was made to them by both combatant sides.

The women's leaders were obviously proud of their accomplishment, but this was perhaps touted more by several of the male speakers than by themselves. Immediately after Mijiyl, Midipu Councillor Kujilyi, having mentioned some of the different tribes represented in the crowd, continued as follows (this speech is referred to in section 7.4 as KUJ, and . . . indicates brief segments omitted, some muffled or otherwise unclear as indicated):

(1) ya napilya el kolya-te lelym, pe napilya *skul* kolya lelym-ko
here in the Nebilyer there is a police station, and a Nebilyer school

ed pos lelym-ko, pe napilya *didiman opis* lelym-ko
and an aid post, and a Nebilyer agricultural extension office

lelym aki-yl-nga mel pora
there is everything

ya napilya kudanga noku-te naa nokuring, mol
and they did not watch out for the Nebilyer area, no

ab-kil-n ya molupa ya *polis*-kil kep wate-ko
(only) these women, and even the police (did not)

patrol kiap kep wate-ko, nyiba ya . . .
and also the patrol officer, now

olyo-nga ya napilya kuduyl *kiap*-ayl um molym ilyi-nga
our Nebilyer 'European' kiap *has come and is present*

ya ung nyikir ilyi-nga te *tanim tok* tengi
as I talk will someone translate (for him)

mol kuduyl *kiap*-ayl pilyaga, pe ya molupa tirim kuduyl-iyl
let the kiap *hear, he was here (at the time)*

pe pipilyi kolti koluba molo
will he be a bit embarrassed or

ilyi-nga te *tanim tok* tengi molo mol? . . . [waits for response]
is anyone going to translate or not?

ilyi-nga ya mel kil-in naa nokuring
all these agencies didn't watch out

olyo aima te naa nokurum mol
not one looked after us, no

ilyi-ka abu-l medipulu oba molupa-kin
just the women came and stayed

nela tibeka kalya-na el top pepa-kin
down there at Sibeka when the fight was on

plak-ayl meba oba aku-na montirum
brought the flag and raised the flag

montipa-kin ul-iyl *brukim* tirim akin
and in raising it stopped the fight

pe kulka yab mare-n nyik oi tentik ya yab kuberi pupa
and some Kulka people laughed (at them) and said

plak me-pupa el *lo* pantipa tekim mel kana
some people are taking the flag, just like they're laying down the law

kolya we-kuba-nga nyik lyingi mel molo
they won't be able to

yabu turil yabu-ma nyik yabu-ma lyik ung-kiyl tik tiring
they're 'flea' [insignificant] people

ilyi eni ya pudumong lyik telymeli
you are trouble-makers

yabu kalya-ka yabu koeli kapola-kuba el *brukim lo* tepa tekim-ayl
(but) they stopped the fight

yabu-ma-nga *oda* mat *oda*-te li naa lelym
as for a court order, they don't have one

yabu-ma-nga *opis*-te naa lelym . . . [unclear word or two]
and they don't have an office [are not acting for a government agency]

nyiring aku-na yabu-ka gol tok nyiring
they said this, but what they said was wrong

aku-na pe pupa *lo* pim ya wily-ola . . . [short segment unclear]
and they went and established law

topa mudupa ku 200 kina notuk, *skelim* tek 100 kina mere dena-ka tik
they put down two hundred kina, they counted it out and gave 100 down there to the Dena

100 kina olyo tik, olyo no *kola katan tupela* mola *wan* . . .
and 100 kina to us, and to us two cartons of Cola, or one? . . .

te tik tok *kembrij paket* te tik, kim *kapis* te tik,
and a packet [carton] of Cambridge cigarettes, and some cabbage

anian-pul kare tik tiring
and a bundle of onion

mer kumaku tiring aku-ne ekepu yabu-kil ung nyang nyirid mel
this they did at Kumaku [in Kulka], and I said those people should talk

ekepu ung nyikimil, i yabu-l-nga ung ilyi
now they are talking, those people who've come

ekepu ya ku ilyi
and now this money

eni tea-dena yab kanu-ma-nga mare
and some of you people

ka-li-yl yabu awuntipa-ko ok molymeli
a great number of you who've come are friendly with the Tea-Dena

ya eni abolku-l ya-kid *nambawan* ok, pe
now first you've come here and then

mere-kid puk ku kina tingi-kin, pe ya mek ongi-ko
you'll go down there and they'll give money, and you'll bring it

ongi aku-na ya yabu-te-ne el molupa
you'll come, (when) one person was injured

nabolka ul-te *brukim* tek tiring
they stopped the fight

ul aku-na mong lyik ting kanapa-lum
and if they get in trouble for that

ya neka *witnis* ul-iyl nyiring
they said that Neka [Kujilyi's daughter] will be witness

pe mere yabu-ka mong-te lyik ul te ting kanakun
and if they [Tea-Dena] start anything down there

ya mere dena ab kopil *witnis* upiyl nyiring
let Dena Kopil [a woman] down there come and bear witness, they said

i nyib maku top tirimul ilyi-nga ekepu ya ku ilyi-nga tep
we chose them [to keep an eye on things], and now we're giving this money

ung nyib timul akin yabu-ka pupa mere yi kani-yl tepa tipa tim
and having talked of it, somebody [from Tea-Dena] will carry the word

i nyib timul kani-yl-nga, i kupulanum ilyi
we said like this, and so in regard to that

yabu-kul-nga i nyib montikir-kiyl
about these people, I'll stop talking of it

ekepu olyo yi-kil el-ayl tiring-iyl tea-dena-l kanapa lyirim ya
now they fought, the Tea-Dena took it up

Plate 1. The Kailge school ground, showing in background the *ku waru* 'cliffs' on the eastern slopes of the Tambul Range, for which the nearby area is named. Note Catholic *haus lotu* (church) under construction at right

Plate 2. View from Kopia territory across the River Milya (see Map 3) to Kubuka territory. Sweet potato garden in foreground; behind are *kunai* thatched houses and kiosk-style trade store. Further back note area of grassland indicating extensive cultivation on the lower slopes

Plate 3. Bridewealth negotiation in progress on the Kailge display ground. Standing speaker is acting on behalf of a visiting delegation for the intending groom, making a marriage offer for a Kopia girl. Foreground, two prominent Kopia/Tolab men listen

Plate 4. Kopia Councillor Noma in our house, helping us interpret recordings of his public speeches

Plate 5. Kopia-Kubuka march to Palimung, August 14, 1983; here are pictured mainly women and children, the men having gone ahead

na-ni ya *raisbek* kil-nga, *raisbek* tal tipu
I gave some ricebags, two of them

oma *katan*-ke tipu na-nga lku-na lelym mek pai nyib
and a carton of fish, it's at my house, take it, I said

el-ayl mol, nyirid, nyib tirid ilyi
no fighting, I said, I talked like that

ya pilyipa kelipa yi-yl-nga el *brukim* tepa oba molupa
I said this many times and

ya mong kani-yl lyirim-o, el kani-yl tirimul ilyi-nga
the trouble started, we fought over this

ekepu yi-te lipiyl nyik, nu kopia-kubuka-te lin kep
now saying a man may've died, if a Kopia-Kubuka had

ya epola-alya kutika-midipu-te leba-ja kor-ko lelka
if an Epola-Alya or Kusika-Midipu was going to, they would've already died

yi kani naa lirim-o . . . yi lupu lupu ok molymeli
nobody died . . . various people have come and are here

olyo-nga ung-iyl pilyipa molym, ya yab kit kit pilyik med puk
and are listening to our talk and will hear it and go down there

ilyi-nga mare nyib modamiyl, ekepu eni nyai, ilyi mada nyikir
so let's send a message about this, now you all talk, I've said enough

At lines 49–62 Kujilyi recounts some of the earlier events in the history of hostilities and other relevant episodes in a rather terse way that is hard to follow. His main points are: Epola-Alya first gave *moka* to Jika-Kungunuka, and later demanded compensation from Tea-Dena for helping them against the Kopia-Kubuka. But Tea-Dena, instead of paying, got into a brawl in the old court area at Sibeka and killed a Kusika man, Peng. Kusika-Midipu initially gave Tea-Dena a pig and some money. Following upon hostilities within Tea-Dena (the 'Marsupial Road War', see section 3.2.2), Dena Peam stole rice bags from Dena Tani. Kujilyi attempted to avert hostilities by acting as mediator, offering his own rice bags and other goods (from his trade store) to replace those that had been taken.

It is notable that the mediation by the Kulka women's club seems to be similar to that attempted by Kujilyi (lines 73–5) between Epola and Tea-Dena: the offering of a conciliatory payment, on the part of someone who is not identified as the source of trouble.

Kujilyi's speech evinces concern for what will be reported elsewhere (especially to the Tea-Dena) of this event (lines 80–2). Like many speakers from Epola-Alya-(Lalka), he emphasizes that the Tea-Dena trouble was initially an internal problem which Dena Peam brought to Palimung, thus deflecting any possible identification with the *pul* 'source' from themselves. But even more than this, the Kopia-Kubuka and Kusika-Midipu points of view coincide in their attempts to isolate Epola as the more specific source of trouble within the alliance. Throughout this event, the Epola speakers Alya, Tuse and Koluwa seek to reject this identification by constantly returning to the point that the trouble originated from Tea-Dena.

Kujilyi's speech was followed immediately by one from Kopia Councillor Noma, who said that his father had fought with the Tea-Dena, but that he had

Plate 6. Display boards with kina notes being brought into Palimung by Kusika-Midipu et al, August 14, 1983

Plate 7. Kopia-Kubuka mock charge into Palimung to accept compensation payment, August 14, 1983

Plate 8. Kulka Councillor Pokea (mid-photo, white shirt and tie) introduces his daughter, Mijiyl, at Palimung, August 14, 1983. Left of centre are seated members of the Kulka women's club wearing identical T-shirts; note Papua New Guinea flag planted to their left.

Plate 9. Warfare in the lower Nebilyer Valley, 1986 (see Appendix C). In foreground would-be combatants approach battle line; enemy line is visible along the middle ridge, spectators on the distant one.

epola-alya-ka kanapa lyirim, el turing akin
and the Epola-Alya, they fought and then

pe kutika-midipu-til pupa bulumingi-na apu turum
the Kusika-Midipu helped them ['carried them on their backs']

pupa wi jika-kungunika-ka oba kanglurum
and the Jika-Kungunuka up there embraced [the fight]

el-ayl i tek pentik ne kopia-kubuka-tal-kin tiring
they kept going and the Kopia-Kubuka fought

tiring kupulanum aki-yl ya ui ya ul tiring aki-yl tepa
they fought, that's the way things happened

yi pengi tepa, pe ya kung-owa-te naa tirim lelym
giving compensation, not a pig or dog was giving, it remains [to be sorted out]

yi penguwa talko-nga tirim, tepa pora ntirim kupulanum aku-na
compensation was given and then

pe yadu-kin molupa-kin ya kung-owa-ma yadu tipa modupa-kin
a return was given

ekepu mere na kung pulu-na lyibu nyirim
now I want to get pigs, he [Epola Koluwa] said

ting aku-na ya kutika peng kani mek adak
they went around with Kusika Peng and killed him in the court area

ya ne-d *kot eria*-kin notuk kutika peng kani turing
they killed Kusika Peng down there in the court area

pe olyo ya kung mere-wiji koyipa teyl
we gave to them and they returned ['roasted']

kani-kin altepa ya med koyipa tipa yi-kin tipu
and we gave to them again

i tepu ul tirimul aki-yl-o
that's what we did

tirimul aku-na pe yi-kul *kot eria*-kin
we did this, and the court area

ya tilupu-na molup takurumul pe oba ya palimung kani lirim
we built it and used it together, it was at Palimung

kang-abola *skul* kang-abola kani-tip el kani-yl top kintipu
we sent our children to school and fighting was bad

i tep molumul kani-yl ya lopa kalyeb-eyl eni-ni montiring-i
we stopped, and then they were hunting marsupials at night

oba mere ui kona turung ilyi mere aj-ko tiring
and then they killed a man back in their [i.e., Tea-Dena] place

oba *belhat* tiring aki-yl mere aj-ko tiring
they had an argument, they fought back home

ya kolya ilyi-nga naa tiring, pe ya dena peam kani wik-id olka
not around here, and then Dena Peam came here

oba molurum kani-kin pe *raisbek* kani-yl lyiring
he came and stayed and then they took the rice bags

raisbek kani-ke ya pudumong peba tekim naa nya
those ricebags, (I saying) don't say trouble will start

stopped. Using what is said to be a familiar image, he spoke of himself as waiting and watching to see what others would do: what you do, I will consider, he said (see section 5.4). Then, in *el ung* and as if addressing Dena Peam, he said: you brought a snake here in a net bag, you brought it into my home Warap (up the mountain from Kailge, i.e. into my territory), you thought to let it bite people, you said let fire burn people, but now I take it to my place, Kailge, and put it under my mat. In the conclusion to his speech, he addresses Kujilyi and Koluwa in *el ung*:

kubaliyl kang-ayl-a
Kubaliyl fellow [Kujilyi]

nukunuku kang-ayl-a
Nukunuku fellow [Epola Koluwa]

kopola yi peam-nga
in Kopola Peam's

ala-wal-na pebu nyikin pilyin kanapa
small netbag I will sleep, since you thought this

aku-na nunu pi-a
you sleep there

ala-wal-na pebu nyikin pilyin kanapa
since you thought, I will sleep in the small netbag

aku-na pi-a
you sleep there

na punya uj-iyl langap notup pukur-kilyi
I'm going to chop my garden trees

tengelti ob-ayl noda kudu wamie-ma
one day I'll come and those mushrooms

noly-ayl nobu-kiyl-a
that I always eat I will eat

kim kud kibilyi
and the greens

noly-ayl nobu-kiyl-i
that I eat I will eat

na *lo* tipiyl
let him (them) make recompense [lo] *to me*

Noma identifies Peam as the trouble-source, and Kujilyi and Koluwa as those who made an accommodation, however troublesome, with him. And so, he says, you said 'I will sleep in his netbag', now you must rest content with what has come of it. All along he emphasizes that he is getting this money on account of Peam. If there is any more to be given, he will come and get it – he will 'eat' those things to which he is accustomed. (Some of the people we asked about this took Noma to be offering help again, should it be needed in future.)

Epola Alya spoke immediately following, stressing again that Dena Peam and not the Epola are the trouble-makers: *Epola-nga ul-te naa pirim, Dena Peam-nga ul pirim* 'the Epola did nothing wrong, it was Dena Peam's fault'. He refers to having fought *raisbek el* 'rice bag war'. Now law is coming up (*ola okum*), and we shall follow the good road. I'm not harboring thoughts of fighting (*el-nga numan naa pantip molkur, mol*). There is no outstanding trouble between us and Tola-Wanaka (*Tola-Wanaka-til-kin na-kin pudu-te kep mol*): they simply helped the Tea-Dena. You Kopia-Kubuka are usually on good terms with us (you chew betel and drink beer with us). He concludes with an *el ung* speech that sounds slightly more equivocal: if government law had not come up, were not so strong, I would do as my fathers did (i.e., fight). But it constrains me. (None of the people we asked, however, took this speech as signalling a desire to fight, but rather as a conventional remark about the strength of government law.)

Many of these speakers focused on the background of inter-*talapi* relations. But Kopia Mel (Councillor Noma's brother) refocused attention on the Kulka women's achievement:

> wanya *plak*-ayl puk mek ok moduring ilyi-o
> *they went and placed the flag there*
>
> *gavman*-nga el *masket* kare mek pu naa puring, mol!
> *they were not carrying government 'muskets'*
>
> *gavman*-nga *yunifom*-te pi naa pirim mol ilyi-o
> *they were not wearing government uniforms, no!*
>
> ilyi ab mel pangi-te nyi-pilyik[9] ab-nga *pawa* pirim.
> *you may think women are a weak reed but they had determination*

Epola Koluwa, like all the Epola speakers, places the blame on Dena Peam: I, an old man, may say something wrong. Don't think I'm fighting my own fight, I'm fighting Dena Numje's fight. He got help before from Ulka Kudulka and Kob and Akalyib. The fight goes on and on. I want to put a stop to it, Numje should use the court area and school. Thus Koluwa indicates that he holds no grudge, and wants to reinstate amicable social relations along with joint participation in those activities which are part of the order of *gavman lo*.

A first Alya speaker, Uyl, puts the blame on Peam, and not on the Epola (-Alya).

The second speech of Epola Tuse is equivocal. He emphasizes he is compensating Kopia-Kubuka so they will not feel bad (*eni boni lying nyib-kin-o/ ku kina ilyi tikir-kiyl-o* 'saying that you took on a burden/ I give this kina'). But he refers to Tea-Dena as *na-nga ab min* 'my wife' (and is in fact married to a Dena woman). He refers to spending his youth with the Kopola 'boy' (Dena Numje), and says he is not paying for a man, but rather for 'new blood' (is just making a minor compensation). He implies that he wants to return to his wife, but wishes all to be amicable. He concludes with a familiar image of slipperiness: there is a slippery tree at Sibeka, which will remain there. The implication seems to be that this payment, while intended to ensure good relations with Kopia-Kubuka, should not be taken as a definitive statement of alliance with them against the Tea-Dena. Matters are less clear-cut, and will remain so.

Other Kopia speakers (e.g. Ladikang) simply say they will take the money and attempt to be vigilant about any future trouble. Kopia Kupena (from upper Kopia) opens a speech in a way that interestingly reiterates the standard sense of the potential divisiveness of *el ung* (see sections 5.3, 6.2.7): though I am considered a big-man, he says, *el ung naa nyib-o* 'I will not talk *el ung*'. But then, in a brief speech he makes use of *el ung* prosody, largely to say, 'bring your children to school (at Kailge)'; Kupena is a member of the school board. He also remarks on the amount of money earlier received for Uwa's accident.

Kujilyi (KUJ, line 7) had referred to the fact that the *kuduyl kiap* – the government officer stationed at Tega – was present in the crowd. Though *kiaps* had largely been Europeans during the Australian Administration, many, like the one referred to, are now New Guineans. *Kiap* Beni was invited to speak. Not being a local, he spoke in Tok Pisin, and his message was rendered fairly freely by Kulka Wani in the local language. The following is an abridged but otherwise verbatim version of what he said:

plenti wok bilong yumi insait long westen hailans
there is plenty of work for us in the Western Highlands

i gat bikpela bikpela traibel pait, na mipela tupela birua
there is a great big tribal fight, and you and I are enemies

kompensesen i wanpela samting i savi bringim mipela klostu
compensation is something that is able to bring us together

i no ken wokim wanpela samting
nothing could be done

dispela taim dispela pait i kirap na epola-alya
when this fight began, the Epola-Alya

na mindipu na dena, ah?
and Midipu and Dena, huh?

bikpela pait i kamap long gaten, i no kamaut kaikai nogat
a big fight started in the (Sibeka) garden, no food was collected

em i pasim rot bilong bisnis
and it closes the road to business

na pasim rot ol man i stap insait bilong wokim bisnis
it closes the road and keeps all those inside from working at business

o painim kaikai, kain olsem, em i no gutpela pasin
or getting food, that sort of thing, it is not good

olsem na nau em wanpela samting yupela wokim na mipela amamas
and now you are doing something about which we are proud

nau sepen o eit tausen pela man i stap yumi lukim
now seven or eight thousand people are here[10]*, we see (them)*

bai yumi witnisim dispela kompensesen
soon you and I will see this compensation

lain bilong kansil kunsili, noma i stap
the tribes of Councillor Kujilyi and Noma are here

bai husat man i bagarapim, bai yumi go na witnisim nau
and whoever will 'bugger it up' later, later you and I will witness it

sapos yumi kirapim pait, yu lukim haumas tausen mani nau bai gon
if we start a fight, you see how many thousands will be consumed

sapos nogat pait em dispela kain samting bai no inap kamap
but if there is no fight then this sort of thing can't happen

pasin bilong yumi em olsem, baim kompensesen
this is how we do things, paying compensation

na mekim yumi go sindaun long wanpela lain, em i gutpela
and making it so that we live together, this is good

yupela baim na mipela amamas, bai mande mi putim long redio
you are paying (compensation) and we are pleased, later Monday I'll put this on the radio

mi putim toksave long redio
I'll put an announcement on the radio

olsem na las tok mi autim
and now this is the last thing I'm going to say:

yupela olgeta i stap bai amamas long ol dispela meri
all of you here will praise these women

ai ting ol i no stap dispela pait bai no inap stap pait go mo yet
I think if they had not been there the fight still would be going on

olsem dispela gavman grup i wokim olsem na pait i go stap
now this government group made the fight stop

olsem na yumi paitim han long ol na tok pinis nau
so you and I shall clap for them, now (my) talk is finished

The *kiap* is obviously not fully aware of the structure of local alliances and hostilities, and seemingly commands only the names of a few *talapi* and their representatives. His view of fighting is a typical governmental one (some aspects of which are also expressed on occasion by local people as well), namely: it interferes with normal daily life, and with conduct and development of *bisnis*. Beni also says it represents a 'waste' of money: *haumas tausan mani nau bai gon*? (a view we did *not* hear expressed by local people). His view of compensation payment is that it creates harmony (*yumi go sindaun long wanpela lain*). Hence, he stresses that the provincial government is pleased with this payment, and he will have it announced on the radio.

From his speech, it seems Beni is not aware that it is only allies on one side who are making compensation payments on this day, and that the payment therefore has a simultaneous harmony-creating but also divisive potential. It is certainly true, however, that most speakers up to this point have advocated the resumption of normal social relations in the Palimung area, urging Numje to use the courts, walk the roads, and bring his children to school.

Following a number of speeches from male speakers less closely linked to Palimung (e.g. by Tambul-siders), Councillor Kujilyi's daughter Neka came forward to accept money being given to the club (not much money had been allocated at this point). A sign indicated that 220 kina were being given to the club, representing a 'profit' of 20 kina to them; and that, separately, 400 kina were later to be given to Kulka. Neka is married to Kulka Dumu, the club's *kuskus* (secretary), who generally took a very active part in club affairs.[11] Neka (speech N) spoke as follows:

ya eni ab lupu lupu ok molymeli i-me kep
you various women (i.e. from various talapi*) who have come and are present*

pe eni yi lupu lupu ok molymeli i-me kep
and even you various men (i.e. from various talapi*) who have come and are here*

wi *haken* el yi kalya-ma-n kep el *brukim* naa tiring mol
and also the Hagen police, you didn't stop the fight, no

pe ya yi awilyi molkumil nela tela
and the important men/officials down in Tega

yi kalya-ma-n te-ne el *brukim* naa tirim mol
none of them stopped the fight, no

mere kudanga ab dena ab kopil ya kudanga na el *brukim* tirid-iyl
(but) down there, Dena (woman) Kopil, and here I stopped it

mere-kid kep wi-kid kep na ab kayi-te kep mol
even down there and up there, [they say?] I am not a good woman

na pudumong lyip molyo, ku-te kanap lyip-kin el-ayl *brukim* tirid
I always am getting into trouble, (but) I got some money together and stopped the fight

el *brukim* tirimul ilyi, ekepu ya ku *wan* kina tipa tekim
we stopped it, and now they are giving 'one' kina [i.e. small amount]

pe ya yi awilyi kare kep wai ya ul tiring adiyl-nga kep wi *haken* . . .
and even those officials from up in Hagen whom they told to come

wi *haken* yi awilyi kalya-ma-nga te ui nyirimul *adam tokum* nyikimil
of the officials in Hagen we told one called Adam Tokum to come

kalya-yl urum-kin, yi nabuka mara nyiyl kalya-yl ui nyirimul
that one came, (but) the one they call Nabuka Mara we told to come before

yi-yl naa urum, ekepu ya ku moni awilyi-yl tik tekimil
that man didn't come, now you are giving big money

mong tapu tekimul, ekepu ya med ul mare mong pepa tim-lum-o
and we're watching out, now if there are some problems down there [at Tea-Dena]

olyo-nga ya tep pora-nsikimul, ekepu-nga mere-kudanga kep
giving things here we are finishing it off, and now down there

ya kudanga kep pepa pora-nsikim ilyi-ko
and here, too, the trouble is over with

eni-nga ku *wan* kina-ke tikimil kep wanya *plak*
they are giving 'one' kina and the flag [is here?]

ekepu ilyi mada
now that's enough

Neka adds briefly: Now there are two beer houses in the vicinity (at Yubika and Tega), axes are taboo. A male voice from the crowd seconds: *Aku tika nyikim* 'That's for sure!' – beer houses are widely regarded as potential sources of trouble.

Like the other speakers on this subject, Neka emphasizes that nobody who might have been expected to intervene actually did so, only the women. The potential for women to operate across segmentary boundaries is stressed by her saying that Dena *ab* Kopil in Tea-Dena, and she herself in Palimung area cooperate in watching out for trouble. Kujilyi, too (KUJ, lines 42–5) referred to the fact that a decision had been taken: Neka should keep an eye on things from Kumaku, and Kopil from Tea-Dena, and they would be able to report if any trouble was brewing in either place. Here one aspect of the 'in-betweenness' (Strathern 1972a) of women is drawn upon: they are presumed to be able to act in ways that are not bounded by segmentary affiliations. In case of any trouble they would, as Kujilyi says, 'witness' against the trouble-makers, i.e., report to authorities suspicious activities in the *talapi* into which they are married.

Neka reports that only one provincial official who was invited, Adam Tokum, came. The failure of Nabuka Mara to come is not surprising, in view of the fact that he had quarreled with his Kulka in-laws, and that there had been fighting between his *talapi*, Kilipuka, and Kulka at the time (cf. section 6.1). Neka asserts that the trouble in which the women intervened is over with, but her addition regarding the beer houses recognizes the continuing potential for trouble.

As the afternoon wore on, the action became increasingly focused on the distribution of money. A payment of 170 kina was made to Tilka Councillor Dop by Kujilyi. Here again, as at Kailge (section 6.2.5.) Tilka Dop was given money for 'sitting on the side'. Kujilyi reports:

> wi olyo-nga, mere olyo-nga-ko, kuni adakumul nyiba adurum
> *up there they are ours, and down there too, we go straight, he went around saying [i.e., both Tea-Dena and Kopia-Kubuka are 'our own']*
>
> aki-yl-nga mere yi-ma-n ing mura tiring, eni tok nang nyib tekimul
> *for that they [Tea-Dena] were cross with him, may you have a smoke, we say [i.e., we are giving money for that]*
>
> el-ayl-nga tapu top i ul-te mol *tambu* mi, ya ki ilyi ola modukur
> *we did not fight together, truly I swear not and raise my hand [here Kujilyi raised his finger to the bridge of his nose]*
>
> ok lyai-a . . .
> *come and get it*

The last remarks again reflect Kujilyi's concern with what will be reported of this event to the Tea-Dena. Whatever they may think, he says publicly, Dop maintained a non-combatant role. In a brief acceptance speech, Dop also dwelled on this point, as he had at Kailge (section 6.2.5.).

At least two speeches just slightly later in the proceedings (and just before the money distribution and counting broke up into mass confusion) exemplify the gradual absorption by some speakers of the Kulka women's club action into the discourse of segmentary, inter-*talapi* relations. A Kulka, Koika, refers to the two Kopia ancestors, Tebun and Watinga, and says they used to make speeches. But they are gone, and now Councillor Noma and Midipu Kujilyi have instituted *gavman lo*:

> . . . ilyi pepa pupa ekepu *lo tru*-yl wed okum
> *there was trouble, now real law is being instituted*
>
> *lo tru* wed okum ilyi-o
> *real law is coming*
>
> ekepu eni kang-ma pipilyika yabu tekimil
> *now you fellows, people are joining together*
>
> kalya-mel pipilyika tekimil-o
> *like that they are joining together*
>
> *no bia* nok-kin eni pilyik nai-o . . .
> *when you drink beer be careful*

ya yi anum-uyl *kansil*-ayl-n ekepu
the old Councillor [Pokea]

lo pentipa pora-ntikim-ilyi
has brought about the establishment of law

ilyi pilyik molai-o, ya mel *plak* ilyi *plak*-iyl kanakur-ayl
understand this, this flag, this flag I see

ya kulka abu-l mek ok talko-nga ne tibeka ga punya monturing-o
the Kulka women brought it and raised it in Sibeka

ekepu ya *plak*-iyl oba *nambawan* tepa
now in the first place, about this flag

plak-iyl ku tikimul-iyl, *plak*-iyl, pe te tikimul
we are paying for the flag, we are giving on account of it

ya upuka mentai nyikim ilyi-o, ekepu nu ya kara puni mel molo
the Upuka say to bring it (for them), now you'll not be rambunctious

nu wanya *plak*-kin nu-nga lku keripul-na molupiyl nyim-o
they said for you to let the flag be on your doorstep

This Kulka speaker later made reference to having voted for Thomas Nakinch (National Parliamentary Member, and an Ulka). This is significant because there had been intense fighting between Kulka and Ulka in the early 1970s. He says (in an *el ung* section of his speech) that in this case, *on-te naa lirim-kiyl-o* 'nobody has died', but before (in the Ulka-Kulka war), *yi on lirim, papua niu gini pilyirim pilyikin-i-o* 'men died, and Papua New Guinea heard of it, do you understand?', and so he urges the combatants to take the money and not to fight ('look after the flag').

In his final long speech of the afternoon, Kulka Pokea, in a much more extensive use of segmentary person, refers to himself as having put up the flag: *wanya plak-ayl monsip molurud kolya pani anum* 'I put up the flag on a very fine day'. He repeats that he will also go to Kopola:

tali-nga kongun *tunde*-kin mere kopola pukur
in two days' time on Tuesday I'll go to Kopola

tola-wanaka ku mong-te tiba nyikimil
they say they'll give money to Tola-Wanaka

ilyi-nga wanya *plak*-ayl meb pukur
for this I'll go bearing the flag

ku *wan handet* kina ya wij urum kani-yl
just as one hundred kina came up

wan handet kina med purum kani-yl-nga pukur-kiyl-o
and a hundred went down, for that I go

Pokea sees himself as mediator: because money was given each way he will go. He also says he will carry word of today's activities to Kopola: *elti-nga ung-iyl meb kopola pukur-kiyl-o* 'I will carry the words of you two to Kopola'. He refers to himself as the 'father' of the combatants, and tells them to ask him for assistance. He also refers to Kopia-Kubuka as his 'head' in the forest (cf. section 5.4), thus suggesting the image of the factions as parts of this body.

In the distribution of money, recall that while club money was given to the women, a separate 'Kulka' allocation was made to Pokea. Thus, he is able to be identified with the women's club action and on occasion speaks of himself as the arbiter. In this way the club action is susceptible to representation as 'Kulka'; but Kulka segmentary identity, and the importance of the Kulka in the local mosaic of the inter-acting *talapi* identities, is not submerged in that of the club.

A Poika, Nori, makes a speech in which he says that Tambul-side people might wonder what the fight was about; but he will go and report now that it was only a stick-fight, a thing of small account. He will praise Pokea:

kulka pokea na-n kaip nyib
Kulka Pokea, I praise you

wanya *plak* mekin okun ul-ma tekin kaip nyib pab
you bring the flag and do good things, I will carry your praise

mel lupu we-yl-kiyl-o
the rest is of little account

lo pensikin elti *kansil*-sil-in ul kayi-yl tekibil-o . . .
you are establishing law and you two councillors [Noma and Kujilyi] are doing the right thing

olyo okumul ya aku-ma nunu lyik polabi-na nosipu
we come and I take you and put you on my lap

yi lupu-ma nyik nyib akin
I'll say what the others have said

yi kewa yab urum kani-kin yi ekepu molkur-o
the Europeans came and (now) I am that kind of man

Poika Nori concludes (as had Pokea) with an image of watching over: that he is like an eagle up in the mountain who watches over Mujika-Laulku, Engal-Kanyiba, Kopia-Kubuka, Kusika-Midipu, as well as Poika-Palimi affairs.

From this point the talk at this gathering increasingly turned to the distribution and counting of money, and the crowd's attention was no longer focused on a single orator.

This concludes our running précis of what was said and otherwise done at Kailge and Palimung on August 14, 1983. Most of what we ourselves want to say in general about this event comes later on. Part of it concerns segmentary-business-as-usual, in this case a chain of compensation payments among allies. In that respect, this event can best be analyzed in relation to the previous one at Kailge (as described in Chapter 6). This we will do in Chapter 8. Given our focus in this chapter – the actions of the Kulka women's club – the Palimung event can best be considered in relation, not to the Kailge one, but to another one which took place a few days later, in which they also participated, again as recipients of compensation, this time from those against whom the Palimung tribes had fought – the Tea-Dena. After presenting a brief summary of what happened at that event, and transcript of the club representative's speech there, we will be able to turn, in section 7.4, to a general consideration of the women's actions, in which we analyze their speeches at both these events as a connected series.

7.3 INTERLUDE ON A SUBSEQUENT EVENT AT KOPOLA

On August 17, 1983, another compensation payment was held at Kopola, in Tea-Dena territory. The purpose of that gathering was compensation by the Tea-Dena of their allies (chief among them Tola-Wanaka, and Nokopa-Anamiyl) who had assisted them in the same round of fighting of September 1982. Though there are many continuities between the events of August 14 and 17, the second event revealed many background political issues of central importance to this alliance which had not figured in the Palimung compensation. By the same token, the issue of Dena Peam as 'fight-source' hardly figured in the Kopola event. Brief mention was made of him in connection with the claim that Peam's Epola supporters had wounded a Laime man, an ally of Tea-Dena; but there was no extended account of the allegedly internal Tea-Dena problems.

If anything, the event of August 17 was dominated by a more immediate problem: the Wanaka complained that they were being given insufficient compensation for the injury of one of their men, and towards afternoon there seemed to be a serious possibility of fighting on the display ground, within the alliance itself.[12]

Here, we will not recount the additional complexities of the Kopola compensation, but will just summarize the role played by the Kulka and the women's club, who again made their appearance early in the day.

The day of August 17 was rainy, and as we and many others were gathering at a central display ground, Dena Councillor Numje focused the crowd's attention by wondering, in *el ung,* whether this might be a *temal* 'omen' of unresolved problems and future fighting (see section 9.1). Kulka Pokea and the women's club members appeared to applause, Pokea carrying the flag, and Numje quipped: Is the rain falling because the flag is coming? But he quickly added, *plak-iyl yadu lyikir* 'I take/accept the flag': *ung lupu mare nying-lum naa pilyikir-o* 'I will hear/understand nothing but that'. As he took the flag he threw down a spear he had been carrying.

Chief speakers for the club were again Pokea, and Dena *ab* Kopil (who had been identified by Kujilyi's daughter Neka as her counterpart in stopping the fight). Kopil (speech KOP) spoke briefly as follows:

yabu pikuyl anum-uyl egl-in kolung-lum-o
a lot of people were suffering from hunger

aya, ilyi papu tekin-o
'sister, you are doing the right thing'

yabu pikuyl anum-uyl aima *bagarap* teba tirim-iyl pilyip molup-o
people were really going to be in dire straits, I understood

el kani-yl yi-te-n naa konsirim mol
no man stopped the fight

na-n kani pilyipu konsipu yab pikuyl kani *bagarap* tirim-kin
I heard about it and stopped it, when people were 'buggered up'

kulka-ma tiring-kin-o
when the Kulka fought,

gai koyip-o
I roasted sweet potato

mere-kid yi-ma-nga gai koyip-o
roasting sweet potato for the men down there

mudulya mudulya tep ul kayi-me tekimul nyib
I did this all the time, saying, we are doing right

ab gai kuyai wai nyirid naa uring-o
I told the women to roast sweet potato and come, they didn't come

ab ung mura tip-o, ul i mel tirid-iyl-o
I scolded the women, this is the sort of thing I did

ya molup kanarud ilyi-o,
I, being there, saw this

gavman ga punya para-na-o
on the flat government sweet potato area [Sibeka, former site of a village court building]

elti tiringl-kiyl-o kanilka-o
you two fought, and I, seeing it

kapola naa mel tirim kanap-o
seeing it was not a good thing

el kani-yl yi-te-n molo
that fight, no man

na-ni gai punya-na konturid-o . . .
I stopped it in the sweet potato garden

[one line unclear] . . .

ilyi aima papu tekin-o
you are doing the right thing

The last remark was addressed to Numje, who had just taken and was holding the flag.

Kopil, too, emphasizes that the fighting was not stopped by any man, but by novel or unexpected people – herself. People praised her for her action. She refers back to the time of the Kulka-Ulka war (of the early seventies) and says that she did what she could, helped to feed the fighting men, and thought all the time that she was doing the right thing. But, she suggests, other women did not think so – they did not respond to her command to come and help. The quasi-confessional character of these statements mitigates any self-aggrandizement one might be tempted to read into Kopil's speech. She implies that this time, she could see that fighting was the wrong thing – and so she intervened. Now she praises Numje for his declaration that he will accept and hold the flag.

Much of Kopil's speech is made in short contours ending with -o but the vowel not drawn out. Is this the prosody of *el ung*? Usually, *el ung* is characterized by a very clearly intoned style of the entire contour and lengthened final vowels (section 5.3). Kopil's lines are not drawn out in this way, rather the whole style is rather more clipped. However, it partakes of the *el ung* style in its structure of short lines and final vowel. It has a measured quality and is doubtless tailored for the public arena in which Kopil was here required to speak. We must also note Kopil's use of the first person singular pronoun: is it related to uses we have called 'segmentary person' (section 5.2)? These and other issues concerning the women's speeches are more closely examined in section 7.4.

The Kulka women's club as such did not figure further in the proceedings after the presentation of the flag and return of money to them. Later in the afternoon, during the general presentation of money, Kulka Pokea was given one hundred kina for the combined Kulka\Kunukub-Midipub (segments); and the Kulka segments Teab-Milyakab were separately presented with 100 kina. There was presentation to entire segments as well as to individuals (the wounded); and even one presentation of thirty kina to a Kubuka whose mother had been Tea. Unpleasantness developed, as mentioned above, over presentations to the Wanaka.

7.4 THE ACCOMPLISHMENT OF THE KULKA WOMEN'S CLUB

7.4.1 Theoretical background

Lévi-Strauss' (1966) distinction between 'hot' and 'cold' societies has, it would seem never been viewed as particularly persuasive or apt for comparing many parts of Melanesia with the West. Rather more noticeable has been the tendency to find seemingly strong similarities between New Guineans and Western bourgeois (e.g. Sahlins 1963) in certain ways at least. For example, however mistaken it may be (cf. Wagner 1975), many observers have characterized New Guineans as 'materialists' or 'primitive capitalists' (Finney 1973), because of their great concern with exchange of material objects and interest in becoming involved in European-style *bisnis*. Such characterizations, however, are based on all-too-superficial parallels between aspects of 'their' and 'our' practices, and contrast with the vast Melanesianist literature on such subjects as 'cargo cultism' (e.g. Lawrence 1964), which tends to stress what appear to us more unfamiliar aspects of the New Guinean fascination with the European advent and material culture.

There is also a relatively recent strand of literature (Wagner 1975, M. Strathern in press) which points to and seeks to illuminate 'the notorious Melanesian readiness to accommodate change and the unexpected'. This literature does not assume similarity between aspects of 'their' reality and 'ours', but attempts to develop terms in which we may talk about the distinctive Melanesian orientation towards change and the unexpected, partly in relation to the European advent.

We want to locate our discussion of the matters raised by the Kulka women's club in relation to this recent literature. We want to ask *why*, perhaps paradoxically, the women's action was both regarded as noteworthy accomplishment, and at the same time able to be readily incorporated into the structure of events and social relations as described in this chapter. This perhaps comes down to the issue of what was new and what was conventional in what the women did, from at least two perspectives: as recognized by those involved, and as seen by us observers (of course, the two perspectives need not entirely coincide). Before we explore this, however, let us turn briefly to consideration of some of these recent ideas about the ready accommodation of New Guineans to change. This will provide some of the groundwork for our conclusions concerning the relation between 'tradition' and 'transformation' in these proceedings.

Wagner (1975), who writes against a background of field experience among the Daribi of Chimbu Province, may be read partly as an objection to limiting the 'social' to the conventional, or convention-observing. For Wagner is concerned with the relation between convention and 'invention', the creativity of social reproduction.

Wagner also uses 'invention' in a second sense, that of the construction of culture by the anthropologist. The two senses relate to each other in that 'Anthropology will not come to terms with its mediative basis and its professed aims until our invention of other cultures can reproduce, at least in principle, the way in which those cultures invent themselves. We must be able to experience our subject matter directly, as alternative meaning, rather than indirectly, through literalization or reduction to the terms of our ideologies' (1975:30–1).

In his interest in the creativity of social reproduction Wagner shares some concerns with those who recently have sought to explore and re-define long-standing action-structure (e.g. Giddens 1979) and history-structure (Sahlins 1985) antinomies in anthropology.

Sahlins (1985:153) sees the distinction between 'structure and event' as pernicious, for the relation between them rests on a paradox: structure is only virtual until used to engage the world in action. Further, in praxis cultural categories are 'risked', and may undergo functional re-evaluation. This is because cultural categories do not follow from the world directly but from particular symbolic schemes (and the two need not be isomorphic). Thus, for Sahlins, an 'event' is a relation between a happening in the world and a particular cultural scheme, a 'happening interpreted' (ibid.) – and every such relation, as noted, entails a risk of the cultural categories themselves. Sahlins' formulation privileges the conceptual, insofar as he maintains that 'praxis always begins in concepts of the actors and of the objects of their existence, the cultural segmentations and values of an *a priori* system' (p.154).

Perhaps most pertinent here, Sahlins (1985:xii–xiv) makes a distinction between 'performative' and 'prescriptive' structures (both are ideal types), differentially 'open' to history (xii): 'The performative orders tend to assimilate themselves to contingent circumstances; whereas the prescriptive rather assimilate the circumstances to themselves – by a kind of denial of their contingent or evenemential character'. Though both can be found in different areas of one and the same global social order, nevertheless in Sahlins' performative type, in which events are frequently valued for their departures from existing arrangements, we encounter and recognize some of the New Guinean 'problematic', the 'readiness to accommodate change' cited from M. Strathern (in press), above.

Following Wagner (1975), M. Strathern (in press) seems to urge us towards the consideration of how cultures 'invent themselves'. In exploring why the study of material culture became so thoroughly divorced from social anthropology, she argues that material culture, from a social anthropological perspective, is largely regarded as 'background' or 'illustration' of the social system from which it comes; we (re-)contextualize it, and our understanding of it (insofar as we have any) lies at the level of this (verbalized) re-analysis. Such referentiality – the construction of the social frame around the artefact – detracts from its original, *in situ* capacity to stand for 'whole perception' (see also Wagner 1986a). Phrased positively, her argument suggests the importance of understanding how our 're-contextualizations' differ from indigenous ways of understanding and acting in the world; phrased negatively, it leads towards the conclusion that the indigenous ways of understanding and acting are all that there is for us to report, since any analysis falls into the trap of 'constructing' frames.

Melanesians, Strathern argues, are concerned with 'images' and the effects these create: 'It was not the ground rules of sociality that people were concerned to represent to themselves, but the ability of persons to act in relation to these. This ability to act was captured in a performance or an artefact, improvisations which created events as achievements. In this sense, all events were innovatory' (M. Strathern, in press).

This passage evinces a Durkheimianism perhaps not fully intended by Strathern, in its assumption that self-*representation* is the principal cultural 'concern'. Be that as it may, Strathern argues that the European advent was, like an artefact, taken by New Guineans as a kind of image or perhaps performance, which could be grasped for itself, for the effect it had. Europeans may have thought their advent unique, but New Guineans already lived in a world in which images did not exist until composed (in performance, etc.). Hence, the 'surprising' advent, she suggests, was one surprise among others. Further, the New Guineans may have been most surprised because of a sense that they created the effect, authored the European advent (as reflected, perhaps, in the fact that Europeans were widely seen as 'ancestors', not completely foreign beings). Strathern also observes that there seems to be a widespread assumption on the part of New Guineans that European attributes are transferable to themselves (and do not reflect a vast, unbridgeable gulf between two different 'kinds' of social beings). Hence, the European advent provoked self-knowledge, it made New Guineans think about what they might be – one may say, what they may have been all along – with their new-found awareness of other possibilities. This provides some interesting insight into the ways in which Highlanders were able to deal with the European advent without experiencing a sense of radical discontinuity.

Sahlins (1985) and Strathern (in press) are at odds. Sahlins posits the fundamental importance of an indigenous symbolic scheme which will, it seems, invariably be engaged to interpret the contingency of events, very likely reordering the structure to some extent in the process (cf. similarity with Giddens' 1979 'duality of structure', or the notion that structural properties are both medium and outcome of social action). The performative/prescriptive distinction is proposed as a major contrast in the way in which events may have significance with respect to a cultural scheme – i.e., whether the scheme is relatively 'open' to re-evaluation, or 'closed'. If the latter, events are not evaluated as 'new' but identified in some way with the received order of structure. But all praxis is related to a symbolic scheme. Sahlins does not, however, explore why particular parts of a social order should be relatively susceptible to re-evaluation, others not. We are left with the (nonetheless interesting) observation that there exist major differences in this respect.

Strathern, on the other hand, is seeking an insider's position, within the Melanesian 'invention' of self. Their cultural convention, she argues, lies not at the level of contextualization within a framework, but at the level of image. The European advent was a self-contained image: New Guineans did not have to evoke the wider milieu from which Europeans came.

But here Strathern seems to assume that for New Guineans not to attempt to construct the European frame is equivalent to their not having any framework within which the coming of Europeans had and continues to have significance. Quite the opposite, the case of the Kulka women's club (and others like it) suggest to us Highlanders' constant concern with the redefinition of the political-economic order. This concern is a blend of the conservative and the forward-looking: conservative in that aspects of what is seen as 'traditional' are regarded – 'misrecognized' – as fully compatible with the envisioned new order; and forward-looking in that people evince a will to identify with the new order, without much wasted nostalgia for the old. In other words, the sense of profound loss that might accompany a perception of radical discontinuity between the new and old, the indigenous and foreign, is not found here.

The question then becomes: how may we understand the absence of a sense of radical discontinuity? Following our analysis of the innovatory and the conventional in the actions of the Kulka women's club, we take up discussion of this question in the final chapter (Chapter 9).

7.4.2 The accomplishment

There are numerous reports of Australian *kiaps'* surprise at frequently being able to intervene in Highlands tribal warfare and, with minimal manpower, successfully order the combatants to disperse (see e.g. Sorenson 1972:362, regarding the Fore of the eastern Highlands). This no doubt varies with the intensity of warfare; as exemplified in Appendix C, some battles are conducted at low intensity over a fairly long period of time.

However, as Meggitt (1977) and M. Strathern (1985a) have clarified, such interventions often do not ultimately resolve conflict, which is likely to erupt again. Strathern (ibid.) has emphasized that the indigenous social system does not assume a model of 'law and order' as a normal state, and conflict as abnormal; but rather operates with notions of the commutability of states of affairs through the mediation of social relations by exchange, warfare and other means: 'the more disputes are "settled" then the more they will erupt' (loc.cit., 123; cf. section 6.2.7 above).

Just as the *kiaps* were surprised at their 'successes' in dealing with fights, so we may find it surprising that the unarmed Kulka women's club was able to march onto the Sibeka battlefield and persuade everyone to go home. In certain ways, their ability to do this derives from the same background condition, identified by Strathern, which made possible the *kiaps'* 'success': underlying notions of the potential for mediated commutability of states of affairs. Superficially it looks as if the Kulka women were drawing upon the same source of authority as the *kiaps*, in that they wore 'uniforms' and brought the Papua New Guinea flag. Indeed, there is constant reference to the flag, holding it and looking after it etc., in the speeches reported above. Many people, like Poika Nori, speak of the European presence as having made a definitive difference in the ways things are, and the way people are: the Europeans have come, he says, and I am now that sort of man. (Cf. also the first speech by Councillor Pokea.)

But in certain ways, though the Kulka women made use of government symbols, what they did was grounded in quite different principles from the typical *kiap*'s actions; and examining the difference may also give greater insight into the symbolism of *gavman lo*.

The *kiaps* acted on the assumption that, if met with resistance, they would act forcefully and authoritatively. They carried guns and were prepared to use them if crossed, secure in the knowledge that none was available to the local people. The extent to which their methods were coercive was made plain, for example, when people failed to report for corvée labor: they were rounded up and jailed. Following warfare between Tea-Dena and Kopia-Kubuka in the 1950s, many combatants were jailed. Nebilyer people seem to have had a considerable degree of admiration for the resoluteness of such European behavior. This is reflected in their views of European legal proceedings[13], as well as in the announced admiration of people like Councillor Noma, who worked closely with a European *kiap* in the Hagen area, for their decisive actions (even if violent).

The women's club, however, had no such authoritative backing. This seems to be recognized by many speakers, in a way: they say the women were laughed at by some who said they had no office, no uniforms (T-shirts notwithstanding, apparently), no muskets etc. Underlying this is a fairly realistic appraisal that, if it came to it, the provincial government – which (recall from section 7.1) maintains official administrative links with these women's clubs, and also provided the Kulka club with some of the goods to placate the combatant sides in 1982 – would find it difficult to impose itself in an area like Kailge. Government clearly commands some respect, but people have plenty of evidence that it is not effectively coercive and does not operate on the same lines as the Australian Administration did. Just at this time, the Western Highlands Premier's *talapi* was engaged in tribal warfare, said to have been incited by him, just to the south of Kailge.

The women's action is clearly regarded as an achievement – the more so for the ultimate absence of any ultimate forceful sanctions to act upon. The mere fact that *women* intervened is considered remarkable: many speakers comment on the fact that no men, even officials, did so. But the flag appears to be less a symbol of government *authority* than of a new order with which people wish to identify, and to which the women's clubs are seen to belong. The clubs are a new avenue for self-discovery concerning the possibilities of identification with the cash economy, and involvement in provincial politics. The ostensible purpose of these clubs is to engage in *bisnis* – they provide an unusual opportunity for women to do so. The Kulka club had 200 kina on hand with which to make prestation to both sides. Thus, the effective action of the Kulka women was to mediate through exchange the relation of the combatants. It was not within their conception to try to stop the fighting *except* through such mediation.

In doing this, they were acting as big-men and mediators may often act –

seemingly not for their own benefit, but offering options of resolution (see Strathern 1972b, Read 1959, Goldman 1983). They and everyone else seem to recognize the possibility that the 'solution' they mediated may not be permanent – as Kulka Pokea says, if there is any more trouble, we will not see you. Thus, they do not (completely) share the *kiaps'* optimism concerning the permanence of their problem-solving.

We do not know what was said on the Sibeka battlefield about returns to the Kulka club. But it seems that everyone expected that their money would be returned, with some increment. This is in keeping with the fact that, within the clubs, careful track is kept of monetary contributions, receipts are issued to individuals who put money into the common bank account, and so forth. (At least at Kailge, this fund was not really communal, and visits to the Kulka club suggested that it worked in much the same way.)

Therefore, a natural expectation might have been that the money would be returned in just such a public compensation payment as later actually took place. But to whom would it be returned? That question is more difficult than it sounds. By accepting the club's gifts on the battlefield, both sides complied in recognizing the club as a transactor in the public sphere of warfare and warfare compensation (which is, as we have seen in section 4.1, the prototypical sort of exchange among Ku Waru *talapi*). But that is a sphere in which there is no precedent for women to be recognized as transactors, either singly or in concert. That was presumably why, in his brief introduction before the first female speaker of the day, Councillor Pokea emphasized the 'changed' nature of current circumstances and people's joint capacity for acting in new and different ways. Speaking 'heteroglossically' (Bakhtin 1981, cf. section 5.8), he even characterized the women (and presumably himself for cooperating with them) as *kupari* 'mad, insane'. Though not explicitly marked as reported speech, this characterization echoes or anticipates other voices besides that of Pokea the Councillor — presumably those of other onlookers. The woman who was introduced, his daughter Kodu, concludes her speech with a more explicitly *attributed* characterization of her club's behavior as that of people who have been drinking too much. *That,* she says (i.e., that probable misconception) is the reason for her appearing in order to explain their motives (K17).

Clearly the social identity in question – the Kulka woman's group – albeit acknowledged as a transactor, is not one of a type for which there is an established place at these proceedings. This is further borne out in comparison with Chapter 6, where all transactions followed one or both of the two sorts of 'roads' discussed in section 4.1, i.e., between segmentary units or within interpersonal networks (in that case exclusively matrilateral or affinal ones).

Accordingly, the established ways of speaking at exchange events do not provide a ready-made position ('subject position' 'voice', call it what you will) from which this 'mad' sort of transactor may speak for itself. For any of these women to attempt an outright appropriation of the 'language of segmentary politics' (as described in Chapter 5) would no doubt have been a disaster: all were keenly aware (and there was recurrent grumbling from the audience to remind them) of the risk they ran of being shouted down even by appearing to say 'a few words' under the announced patronage of two prominent big-men (see Kujilyi's remark at KUJ 32).

Nonetheless, we would argue that a distinctive new voice or 'transactor position' did emerge for the Kulka women's club even over the course of the four short speeches by women transcribed above. To establish this, we will now make some further observations concerning the form and content of each of the four women's speeches in succession.

Consider how the first of them opens: 'My name is Kodu Pokea'. By comparison, in all the many speeches transcribed in Appendix A, there is not a single one which opens with a self-nomination, or self-description of any kind. There is however, one point in that transcript where a speaker is told that he *ought* to have opened with a self-description. It comes after a speech about proper conduct on the school ground, by Komi, who is the elected chairman of the school's board of management. He is told 'You should have said "I, the man who looks after it, am talking"' (line 862). This is a partial exception that proves the rule. The rule, which belongs to the new order of 'government law', is that self-descriptions are relevant or obligatory just when a person is speaking from a position of elected or appointed office.

Hence Kodu's next three lines (K2-4), describing her qualification as elected head of the Nebilyer Women's Council (a valley-wide federation of women's groups). The closing line of her speech (K17) is also telling, in that in it she attempts to explicitly classify the speech, as *toksave,* which is Tok Pisin for 'announcement', 'informative message'. Like the opening, this closing is in sharp contrast to traditional genres such as *el ung,* in which the speeches never conclude with any such explicit self-characterization. Concerning the body of her speech, it will suffice here to note the following two points. First, note her use in lines 12 and 14 of the word *yabu* 'people' (lit.: 'man-woman'. cf. section 5.7) to refer to the relevant actors in her story (cf. also Pokea's use of *olyo yabu-kil* 'we people' in his speech introducing the women, above). In the men's speeches at Kailge, the actors referred to are almost always *yi, yi-ma*: 'man', 'men'.

Second, note that there are no person references in her speech which are construable as 'segmentary person' (as in section 5.2), even where she is referring to, e.g. the participants in the fighting (or, as she refers to it in line 7, that 'sort of a fight'). Given all these features, Kodu's assumed 'voice' seems clearly antithetical to those of the male segmentary arena. It is not a distinctively female voice, opposing the latter as female to male. Rather, it is, above all, the voice of 'government law' as opposed to those aspects of *bo ul* 'indigenous practice/custom' which are negatively valued (at least in certain contexts) by men and women alike (albeit more often by the latter).

The next speech, by Mijiyl, elaborates somewhat on the immediately preceding one by her sister Kodu (their names, by the way, mean 'suffering' and 'compassion'), but is very similar in form and content: no use of SP, careful justification for speaking (lines 2–4), repeated assurances the speech will be short (lines 1, 15) and similar accounts of how and why the women stopped the fight. The account stresses the trans-segmentary character of the initiative (lines 7–9), and adds to Kodu's account the more dramatic gesture of planting the flag on the battlefield.

The third and last speech by a woman at Palimung, by Councillor Kujilyi's daughter Neka, is quite different from the first two. In both form and content, it is much more like many speeches by males (as represented, e.g. in Appendix A). In the former respect, note the rhetorical use of parallelism in lines 1–2, and the repetition from line 3 to 5 and 6 to 8. As for content, note that Neka gives no justification for speaking, never says her speech is going to be short, or expresses any reservations or embarrassment about speaking. Perhaps emboldened by similar remarks which have been made by men (notably her father Kujilyi) since the first two women's speeches, Neka glorifies the action of the women's group by comparison with all the other people or agencies who were not able or willing to stop the fight. No such invidious comparison was made by either Kodu or Mijiyl. And whereas the latter two (especially Mijiyl) have referred to a widespread opposition to fighting by women from various places, Neka has included women from other tribes (which would include, e.g. women present from the Kailge women's groups) among those disparaged by her invidious comparison.

The fourth speech by a woman, three days later at Kopola, resembles male oratory in yet other respects. As described above, in its prosody and line-terminating vowel, it is in partial *el ung* style. It too contains no justification for speaking, no assurances of brevity or expressions of reservation about speaking. Furthermore, it contains a clear instance of 2du 'segmentary person' (line 14) and instances of the first person singular which, while not unequivocal, can also be understood as SP-like. But what is interesting about these is that one of the actors they can be construed as referring to is not a segmentary category or group per se, but the Kulka women's group (most of whom are not 'Kulka' except by marriage). In this sense, while borrowing the traditional rhetorico-grammatical category of segmentary person, Kopil has put it to a new use which is potentially *anti*-segmentary. Rather than opposing the system from without (e.g. by assuming the voice of 'government law'), this would be like subverting it from within. The same goes for the way she constructs *her* invidious comparison, which is not to outsiders in general but to *man* in particular (KOP 4,16), while all the while intoning in quasi-*el ung*!

Though Kopil adopts some of the resources of men's oratory, and some of its magnifying tone, her speech and that of the other women is notably unlike that of men such as Kujilyi in that the women do not detail the complex histories of inter-*talapi* hostilities and other relations. By this silence, the women's speech underscores the fact that they do not entirely share men's commitment to the reproduction of the segmentary order. Their lack of commitment to its rationale is partly to be traced to the generality of the female experience as wife among other wives, 'woman-in-between', whose immediate loyalties are perforce distributed widely and who often, as women's talk about their attitudes reveals, have occasion to lament and oppose male inclination to pursue political action, especially warfare, on a segmentary basis.

Some aspects of women's position inherently provide a basis for the emergence of centralizing relations and disposition towards neutrality within a segmentary political system, something which men evidently (if ambivalently) admire as a political possibility, but one difficult to subscribe to consistently and difficult to achieve. Thus, note that the battlefield accomplishment of the Kulka club was to intervene between two directly opposed sides, a thing that Kujilyi had aspired to do in attempting to mediate directly between Tea-Dena and Epola-Alya, but could not (see section 6.2.1.).[14] Unlike the Kulka club, who converted battlefield hostilities into exchanges involving words and things mediated by themselves, Kujilyi had to resign himself to the conversion of his words into a mediated arrangement for further hostilities, in his recruitment of Kopia-Kubuka to aid Epola-Alya against Tea-Dena. The inherent female basis for commitment to centralizing relations thus strongly predetermines the women speakers' 'failure' to evoke and recreate the complexities of segmentary opposition in their speech-making, despite their appropriation of some aspects of male rhetorical models. And though neutrality is a disposition arising from aspects of women's life within this social order, nevertheless the club's ability to mediate directly between the two opposing sides was probably only possible in this case because of the broader history of regional segmentary politics; 'Kulka'(-Tilka) has historically maintained a position of neutrality as between these particular combatant sides (see also below). Thus, in this respect the historically particular relation of the Kulka (-Tilka) as a *talapi* is analogous to that of women in general as actors who are 'in-between' other segmentary identities.

We hope to have established by the above comparison that over the three days between Kodu's speech and Kopil's, the women (each of whom presumably heard the other's speeches) moved successively away from the established voice of 'government law' and experimented with ever more radical forms of 'mixed' voice which positioned them somewhere outside of both that realm and the traditional segmentary one.

But their position there was by no means secure or stable. For many forces were in operation which tended to force the club's operations ever more into the segmentary realm. This tendency is evident above in the discursive constructions of the club's big-man patrons such as Kujilyi and Pokea, e.g. in the latter's use of quasi-SP 'I' to mean 'I = Kulka = Kulka women's club', and, for that matter, in Mijiyl's implicit, invidious comparison between the Kulka women's club and other chapters.[15]

As we mentioned above, the Kulka women's adopting the mediator's role was probably made possible by the long-standing Kulka neutrality with respect to the warring western Nebilyer factions. It seems doubtful the club could have intervened in a fight involving, for example, Nabuka Mara's Kilipuka tribe, with whom the Kulka were just then on terms of enmity.

The novel elements involved in the Kulka club action thus include: the initiative seen to be largely (but perhaps not entirely) taken by women, who are not usually directly involved in mediating combat; the trans-segmentary nature of (some) women's club activity (though ultimately the clubs are to an extent encapsulated within the local segmentary framework); and a new use of a familiar form of mediation, exchange (i.e., prestation clearly involving expectation of return). The exchange was new in that it was carried out in the name of symbols of the 'new' order, which people associated with the post-European period: *bisnis* development (the involvement of the clubs in what are usually fairly minor money-making activities), and acknowledgment of central government, as represented by the flag. But, as mentioned, it would appear that the government is (now) less clearly seen as a source of authority and coercion (as it was during the Australian Administration) than as a form of organization which offers possibilities for identification with it, and utilization of it, which people may seek to take advantage of. People typically say of *gavman lo: wed okum* 'it is coming out/developing', defining it as something which offers a new perspective on the conduct of political relations, and efforts to constrain conflict. Its salience seems to be that it offers the possibility for redefinition of the *molupa kujuyl kupulanum* 'common weal/tranquility', rather than that it constitutes an effective authority. Aspects of the common weal include the shared use of main roads, schools and courts; and this shades into the expression of good (inter-*talapi*) social relations through drinking beer and playing cards together, as men often say in their speeches.

People can see, by the frequent breaches of it, that *gavman lo* is *not* a fully effective authority. For example, on a return trip in January 1986, Alan Rumsey found that further bouts of warfare had occurred in this general area during our two-year absence. A man we knew quite well had become a Councillor, was quite involved in the fighting, and when wounded, refused to seek outside medical help because he might lose his *'namba'* (Councillor's badge). But people evinced no serious concern that the government could intervene effectively in that case.

We would not wish to leave the reader with the impression that *gavman lo* is locally meaningful *only* as a conceptual 'image' with aspects of which people wish to identify, but without seeing the government as having any capacity to intervene in or constrain aspects of their lives. Clearly, branches of *gavman* do intervene locally – as when, around this time, the Western Highlands Premier had been stood down for allegedly inciting tribal fighting, and the government blockaded roads and took other action. Undoubtedly, many new constraints and possibilities for action are introduced into their lives by the development of the cash economy, government institutions such as roads, schools, police, and their growing reliance on Mt Hagen as a center from which, increasingly, even their sense of political direction and social change emanates. But, in keeping with the general point of M. Strathern (1972b), we emphasize that local people do not see all aspects of this as discontinuous with their custom, nor as simply imposed from without. And especially since the departure of the Australian Administration, they appear to correctly perceive, with mixed regret and relief, that there is much less possibility of straightforward coercion, and much more leeway for their direct involvement in the workings of locally-sited government agencies (such as land courts) that often have something to do with the conduct of politics at the levels we have described in this book.

There are aspects of *bo ul* 'indigenous practice/custom' which people see as continuous with *gavman lo,* not opposed to it. One of these is in fact the practice of giving compensation, paying for woundings and killings. In many speeches at the Palimung payment, men repeated that it is good to make such payments, to give *kopong* 'grease'. Any such payment of reparation may be referred to by the phrase *lo te-* 'to make/do law'. The use of the Tok Pisin term emphasizes that people see this aspect of their indigenous practice as continuous with *gavman lo,* not in conflict with the new order. But this, like the Kulka women's distribution of goods and money to create a mediating structure to stop the fight, is more clearly a reassertion of a traditional theme, 'misrecognized' as compatible with European governmental ideas and values. The simple fact is that the 'new order' is modeled on special indigenous readings of European values, while at the same time there is some recognition that European ways of constructing events (such as court cases) are different.

Kiap Beni praised people for making peace, but was evidently under the false impression that peace was being made directly between the major combatants.

In any event, he also expressed the view that such payments are a waste and a deflection of money from such worthwhile, progressive matters as *bisnis*. This reflects more closely the attitude of the former Australian Administration.

By imposing on the combatants the obligation of future exchange, the Kulka women's club adumbrated the new use of an old form of mediation. Though this new use is ostensibly trans-segmentary and emphasizes the symbols of central *gavman*, it constantly runs the risk of being drawn back into the system of segmentary relations in which the clubs after all are embedded.

Finally, the Highlands have provided some of the classic anthropological case material on male-female gender dichotomies. How are we to read here the reception of the fact that it was women who put a stop to the fight? Again, there are indications that the women's role here may be partly a reassertion of an old theme in a new form. Women often represent themselves as more strongly opposed to fighting than men, less interested in the historical-political issues that give rise to it. Yet, individual women are sometimes seen as capable of fierce group loyalty and physical bravery (see e.g. Kopil's statement above regarding her role in the Ulka-Kulka fighting). The Kulka women's club action participates to some extent in the constant dialectic of gender differentiation in that the women emphasize their peace-maker, non-segmentary aspect, and win from the assembly repeated recognition of the strong moral position this places them in, *as opposed to* men who might have been expected to do something about the fighting, but did not. Whatever their differences, all of the women's speeches above differ strongly from those of most of the men, in their unequivocal denunciation of warfare, and in their lack of concern for tracing the etiology of this bout of it in particular. The recounting of particular past episodes (such as those relating to Dena Peam) is divisive and, as such, foreign to the message the women convey.

8. The events in perspective

In Chapters 5, 6 and 7 we have discussed some of the linguistic structures of segmentary politics, and what was done with them at three separate exchange events (in considerably more detail for the first two events than for the third), In this chapter we shall be attempting to draw out some implications of that analysis for the general questions raised in Chapter 1 about wealth exchange transactions. Before we can do that, we must first resume the discussion of segmentary structures and exchange which was opened in Chapter 3. Having now looked in some detail at two exchange events, we are in a position to elaborate upon that discussion in ways that may clarify the relationship between the two spheres (i.e., segmentary structure and exchange). This we will attempt to do in section 8.1, where we will argue that segmentation, exchange, and warfare are alternative moments within a single integrated order of practical/conceptual activity. That 'traditional' (*bo*) order is one which, as the events make clear, is in at least some contexts treated by Ku Waru people as incompatible with the highly valued, newer order of *gavman lo* and *bisnis*. In section 8.2., we consider the question of how these two orders are or are not brought into conflict with each other, an issue about which there is more to say in light of the general model developed in section 8.1.

In section 8.3, we return to the more general questions of structure and event to which this book is ultimately addressed. In particular, we re-open the question raised about ceremonial exchange in section 1.2: Who transacts with whom? We argue for the crucial relevance of linguistic evidence for addressing that question, and for understanding those aspects of Ku Waru sociality which are modeled in section 8.1.

8.1 STRUCTURES AND PROCESSES OF SEGMENTATION AND EXCHANGE

As a starting point for this discussion, let us consider the relationship between the Kailge event discussed in Chapter 6 and the Palimung one in Chapter 7. Having both arisen from the Marsupial Road War of 1982, the two events are phases of a single compensation cycle. The first of them is of central relevance as context for the second, and the prospect of the second context for the first. Taken in combination, the two events can be understood as stages of a single movement within the sphere of segmentary group politics. More particularly, the Palimung event can be seen to follow on from the three phases of the Kailge event in such a way as to manifest an overall movement from the most distant recruit back to the 'fight source' of the Marsupial Road War. At each stage of that movement, a different order of differences among segmentary identities becomes relevant, as represented in Table 8–1 (cf. Table 6–1 above).

Table 8–1: *Orders of relevant segmentary difference at the Kailge and Palimung exchange events*

Stage in the Proceedings	Relevant Difference(s)
Kailge School Ground (lines 807–1816)	Kopia-Kubuka (cum K-M-E-A-L) vs. (Mujika-)-Laulku
Kailge Display Ground (lines 215–806)	Kopia-Kubuka (cum Mujika-Laulku) vs. K-M-E-A-L and Kopia-Kubuka vs. (Mujika-)Laulku
Kailge Display Ground (lines 44–214) and Palimung	Kusika-Midipu (especially Kujilyi) vs. Epola-Alya and Dena Peam
Palimung only	Dena Peam vs. K-M-E-A-L and Kopia-Kubuka (cum Mujika-Laulku) vs. K-M-E-A-L

This table provides only a first approximation of the orders of difference which are relevant at the stages indicated. No such listing could be definitive, for, as we have seen in Chapters 6 and 7, one issue which is frequently contested is the matter of just how far down in the segmentary hierarchy the relevant differentiae lie. Thus, for example at Kailge there was some conflict as to whether Kopia and Kubuka should be treated as a single unit or as two differentiated ones (section 6.2.4), and whether the segmentary transactor being addressed was Laulku alone or the pair of Mujika and Laulku (section 6.2.6). Similarly at Palimung, there was conflict over whether and to what extent the Epola(-Alya?) were transactionally distinct from the Kusika-Midipu.

Both at the low level of analytical delicacy indicated by Table 8–1 and from the more complicated picture developed in Chapters 6 and 7, certain generalizations can be drawn concerning the nature of the movement at these events through the chain of recruits back to the fight source.

First, the differences among the segmentary units which are relevant at each stage are in close accord with Evans-Pritchard's famous principle of 'structural relativity', i.e., that 'groups' [read social identities] are relational entities in which the hierarchical level of relevant internal subdivision varies directly with the degree of 'structural distance' between the groups in question (Evans-Pritchard 1940:135–7, 195–8).[1]

At the events in Chapters 6 and 7, this principle holds for the differentiation both of social space and of *talapi*. As for the former, recall the way in which the distinction between the (otherwise) inclusive space 'Palimung' and the 'small-name' place Tapulku become relevant only within the K-M-E-A-L heartland, and even there probably only for the K-M-E-A-L, not for Kopia-Kubuka (section 7.2.2).

As for the structural relativity of *talapi* distinctions, it is, for example, only in speeches by Midipu Kujilyi and other K-M-E-A-L that distinctions within that cluster become relevant (constructions of Epola alone as 'fight source', etc.), and only in speeches by Kopia-Kubuka (particularly the latter) that the difference between those two becomes relevant (section 6.2.4). Furthermore it is only in speeches by Kopia men that the difference among various Kopia men's houses become relevant, and likewise for Kubuka.

Moreover, it is only in speeches made *on the Kailge display ground* that the Kopia vs. Kubuka distinction and lower level ones become relevant. This shows the way in which the structural relativity of space intergrades with that of *talapi*. Another example is provided by the way in which the role of the Mujika is first raised on the Kailge school ground, a space which, we have argued, was metaphorically associated with Mujika-Laulku (section 6.1).

Structural relativity, in Evans-Pritchard's sense, is a very general fact about human social life, which, while probably universal in segmentary lineage systems, is by no means limited to them.[2] Having shown that it is a feature of the Ku Waru segmentary order as manifest at these two events, let us now explore in somewhat more detail the nature of the Ku Waru social relationships in which it is evident. This will reveal more of what is *specific* to the Ku Waru segmentary order, including ways in which it differs from the systems of classical African lineage theory.

All of the social relationships among *talapi* which are implicated in transactions at the Palimung and Kailge events – both at the overall level indicated by Table 8–1 and at the level of greater delicacy reached in Chapters 6 and 7 – belong in principle (Ku Waru principle, that is) to one of two fundamental, mutually exclusive types:[3]

- relationships of difference which are mediated by exchange
- relationships of sameness which preclude internal exchange but conjoin parts of a single transacting unit.

Relationships of the first kind at these events include, above all, the one between Kopia-Kubuka and Mujika-Laulku and that between K-M-E-A-L and Kopia-Kubuka, the main pairs of transacting units at the Kailge and Palimung events respectively. In many contexts at the events, each of these units is treated as an internally undifferentiated bloc, which is of the same order of structure as the others, but different from them in some important respect(s). Some of the more prominent differentiae which are appealed to at these events include: foods eaten, cash crops grown, swearing on the River Ukulu vs. the River Nebilyer, methods of sweet potato gardening (mounded vs. checkerboard), and such broad regional designations as Meam, Kaugel, Lama, and Awa (sections 5.1, 6.2, 7.1).

As for the other kind of relationship, that of sameness which precludes internal exchange, clear examples at the Kailge event include the relationships among the Kopia men's houses, and among the Kubuka ones; and, at the

Palimung event, the relation between Kusika and Midipu. At the events discussed, the relationships of the latter sort are discursively reproduced, partly through explicit appeals to coresidence (e.g. line 637) or 'sameness'/'oneness' (e.g. line 984), but far more often through the use of person forms which *presuppose* it – i.e., the segmentary person forms.[4] Of course there is, *a priori*, no reason why these forms could not be used for the other sort of relationship as well: a Midipu speaker could, for example use the first person dual category (or even first singular) to refer to 'We K-M-E-A-L and Kopia-Kubuka', or a Laulku to refer to 'We Mujika-Laulku and Kopia-Kubuka'. But no such uses are attested anywhere in the transcripts. Segmentary person, if used at all, is always used to refer to segmentary identities who are represented as acting together as a unitary transactor (whether on the battlefield or on the *pena*), never for those represented as transacting with each other.[5]

So far in our exemplification of the two types of relationships, we have cited some which at the events in question were treated as clear cases of one type or the other. This is of course not always the case. Much of the analysis of Chapters 6 and 7 showed that the work of representation was concerned with alternative constructions of relationships as of either one kind or the other. This was true, e.g. of the role of the Kubuka, who were alternatively positioned as part-to-whole within the Kopia-Kubuka pair, or as transactor between Kopia and Laulku (sections 6.2.4, 6.2.5). Likewise, (Kusika-)Midipu was alternatively positioned as part of K-M-E-A-L or as transactor between Epola-(Alya) and Kopia-Kubuka (sections 6.2.1, 6.2.2, 7.1).

Up to this point in the summary of relationship types, we have been concerned only with the alternative possibilities for relationships among *talapi*. The distinction which we have claimed to be centrally relevant is between relationships among like units which cooperate in exchange but do not exchange with each other, and those among 'different' units mediated via exchange. This same two-way distinction applies not only to inter-*talapi* relationships, but also to interpersonal ones. The relevant dimension of 'sameness' on the latter axis is that of same-sex siblingship (or, more generally, consubstantiality) vs. relationships mediated by a cross-sex link, i.e., matrilateral relationships for males, patrilateral ones for females, or affinal ones for either. The two cross-cutting dimensions of sameness-difference and *talapi*-level vs. interpersonal relationships yield four relationship types, all of which are among the ones being posed as relevant alternatives for some of the transactions at the events in Chapters 6 and 7.

Thus in addition to the contested cases we have just cited, involving same vs. different at the *talapi* level, there are other cases where the contested alternatives were inter-*talapi* vs. interpersonal, where the fact of difference (and therefore the possibility or necessity of exchange) is assumed, but the relevant dimension of difference (e.g. Meam-to-Kakuyl or affine-to-affine) is contested. An example of this kind is the case of the two men from Mujika\Pujilyip who are married to Kopia women (section 6.2.6). Did they participate in the fight as Mujika-Laulku or as the brothers-in-law of specific Kopia men?

As for the other kind of relationship within the inter-personal category – the one of sameness based on consubstantiality (of which same-sex siblingship is the prototype) – this becomes relevant, for example, in the case of the man called Bai, who, recall, is nominally a Laulku (through his father's father), but who has grown up with the Kubuka, where his own father, on the basis of maternal connection, had lived as a young man (section 6.2.4). At this event these details of Bai's life history are allowed to be overridden by his inherited 'difference' from the Kubuka (i.e., he receives compensation along with the Laulku), but it is announced that hereafter he will be treated as a Kubuka, i.e., as 'same' on the basis of his shared substance, via the usual Highlands route for the famous 'absorption of non-agnates'.

To recapitulate, the four-cell matrix of relationship types is shown in Table 8–2, with examples in each cell. The examples with question marks are those cases which were contested.

Table 8–2: *Types of transactional relationship at issue in the Kailge and Palimung exchange events*

	Same: should transact jointly	Different: should transact with each other
Talapi	All Kopia men's houses All Kubuka men's houses Kopia and Kubuka? Mujika and Laulku? Kusika and Midipu Kusika-Midipu and Epola(-Alya-Lalka)?	Kopia and Kubuka? Kopia-Kubuka and K-M-E-A-L Kusika-Midipu and Epola(-Alya-Laulka)? Kopia-Kubuka and (Mujika-)Laulku
Interpersonal	Bai and his Kubuka 'brothers'	Two men from Mujika\Pujilyib and their Kopia brothers-in-law

Table note: ? indicates that the relationship was contested.

It should not be concluded from the paucity of examples in the bottom row of Table 8–2 that interpersonal relationships are less important or less frequently contested than inter-*talapi* ones in Nebilyer social life generally. This is rather an artefact of the fact that the events from which the data are taken were instances of the inter-*talapi* transaction *par excellence*, i.e., transactions arising out of warfare. Had the events been e.g. bridewealth transactions (which are conducted in public as per M. Strathern 1972a), most of the relationships being discursively reproduced or contested would have been of the interpersonal sort rather than the inter-*talapi*.

Note the number of actual cases listed in the table which did not belong unambiguously to one or the other of these two types, but whose nature was contested or variably constructed at the events. This fact does not invalidate the categories in question: their effect is not to allow a full specification of 'how things are', even for some hypostasized moment in Ku Waru history (much less for 'the system' generally). Rather, they are part of the *a priori* ground of Nebilyer social life, specifying not what is actual but what is possible – what can conceivably count as a transaction at all. Given the degree of evident indeterminacy as to what *is* actual, these four relationship types should not be reified as separate domains of Ku Waru social life, but thought of rather as alternative modes of sociality – alternative ways of doing – as a result of which the 'units' of Nebilyer social life – *talapi*, affines, agnates, etc. are more-or-less problematically achieved or reproduced (cf. Maclean 1985, M. Strathern 1988).

The modes in both the left and right columns of Table 8–2 are capable of providing the basis for a more-or-less indefinitely extended polity.[6] But the way in which units aggregate is radically different as between the two. In the exchange mode, the relations among units are chain-like and non-hierarchical: Mujika-Laulku exchanges with Kopia-Kubuka (combatants' blood for compensation), and Kopia-Kubuka with K-M-E-A-L, but this establishes no direct relationship between Mujika-Laulku and K-M-E-A-L, and no more inclusive, bounded unit including all and only those three blocs as constituents. In the other relational mode – that which links same-to-same in unmediated consubstantiality – units aggregate (or differentiate) as hierarchically-ordered parts of a well-bounded whole. Kopia-Kubuka, for example, is a bounded unit comprising Kopia and Kubuka, each of which is further sub-divided at lower segmentary levels, as shown in Figure 3–1.

What we have said so far concerning these four relationship types is in fairly close accord with at least some of the results of other Highland ethnographers. The distinction on the horizontal axis of Table 8–2 closely follows the one made by Wagner (1967) for the Daribi between *be bidi* and *pagebidi*, which was developed into a more generally applicable model by J. Weiner (1982). Our vertical axis would apparently be of less relevance for the Daribi (Wagner 1974). However, closer to the Hagen area, Lederman 1986a has argued that among the Mendi people (some 60 kms southwest of Kailge: see Map 1), there is a thoroughly institutionalized distinction of just that sort, i.e. that between *twem* and *sem* as discussed in section 1.2. Our four-cell matrix also bears some relation to a typology recently proposed by M. Strathern for a much wider area (all of Melanesia), based upon a distinction between two types of sociality: 1) 'substitution', i.e., 'the replication of like units'; and 2) 'reproduction', which adds without replicating. She adds:

> The two types of sociality are gendered. Replication and substitution can be conceived as same-sex relations, reproduction and increment as mobilising cross-sex relations. In social terms, the same-sex association may be all-male (the encompassment of initiates in a men's house) or all female (the identity between a woman and the plants she tends); and the association takes a collective (a men's house group) or a unitary (a 'mother') form. Where persons are involved in a collectivity of this kind, the presumption is of parity between them. Cross-sex relations, however, turn on asymmetry and interdependence (the division of labour in work, debts owed to a patrilateral or matrilateral kinsman, the inequality of affines). (M. Strathern 1986 MS-B: 21)

Though this formulation is suggestive, it is not adequate for our purposes because, although it allows for the construction of 'collectivities' (via the aggregation of same-sex ties among persons), it is not concerned with relations among the collectivities themselves.[7] Within our interpersonal category, the relevant dimension of difference *is* essentially a matter of cross-sex vs. same-sex ties, as appreciated by Strathern, Wagner and Weiner. But this will not do for the inter-*talapi* relations, where, as we have seen in Chapters 6 and 7, other kinds of difference become more salient. And the distinction between interpersonal and inter-*talapi* relations itself would not seem to be easily accommodated within Strathern's scheme. For that, the best model seems to be Lederman's.

What we do find especially valuable in Strathern's account (which agrees with Maclean 1985, Lederman 1986a and others in this respect) is her emphasis on the *interdependence* between alternative modes of sociality. For example, in Maring:

> The brother's specific relationship with his sister is juxtaposed to his general relationship with other males of his own clan. Each anticipates the other in the sense that the brother cannot dispose of his sister without mobilising clan relations, and clan relations have their source in the specificity of the domestic tie which gies [sic] them an object to dispose.
> (M. Strathern, 1986 MS-B: 20)

In view of the material presented above in Chapters 3, 6, and 7, and our four-cell analysis in place of Strathern's binary one, we would elaborate upon the above by adding that inter-*talapi* relations of exchange-mediated difference presuppose inter-*talapi* relations of sameness and vice versa; and that inter-*talapi* and interpersonal relations (or even relations among 'parts of a person') generally are also mutually presupposing (as Lederman 1986a also shows for the Mendi).

But there is more to it than that. For the Ku Waru area at least, we can add that not only does each kind of relationship presuppose the others, all share a basic structural feature in common: pairing.

Consider first the relations of exchange-mediated difference. Though these may in effect bring many transactors into a single set of relationships, they are always pair-wise relationships of direct exchange. Each of the two partners in such a relationship transacts directly only with the other partner, and contracts obligations of reciprocity to him (or it) alone.[8] In Chapters 6 and 7, we saw that this was true of the recruitment-compensation process involving K-M-E-A-L, Kopia-Kubuka, Mujika-Laulku. Transactions among them were strictly pair-wise, involving the former two in one phase and the latter two in another. Accordingly, note that the relations of difference which are a necessary condition of such transactions are binary, non-transitive relations (cf. Weiner 1985). Thus, it is not directly relevant whether each of the parties to the alliance is 'different' from *both* of the other two. All that is relevant is that Kopia-Kubuka is different from K-M-E-A-L and Mujika-Laulku is different from Kopia-Kubuka. Thus, it was unnecessary at these events to invoke two *different* sets of differences: the key diacritic opposition between *Meam* and *Kakuyl* sufficed for both the relevant relationships: relative to the Kopia-Kubuka, the K-M-E-A-L were *Meam*, but relative to the Mujika-Laulku, the Kopia-Kubuka were *Meam*. Or, in proportional terms: Meam is to Kakuyl as K-M-E-A-L is to Kopia-Kubuka as Kopia-Kubuka is to Mujika-Laulku.

Similarly, at the interpersonal level, if A is an affine of B and B is an affine of C, that is a sufficient condition for A to exchange (or continue to exchange) with B and B with C even if A and C are brothers (and therefore may not themselves exchange).

Another, related feature of all kinds of exchange relationships in Ku Waru (and apparently a widespread one in the Highlands generally) is that they presume an ultimate *equivalence* (in Read's 1959 sense) between the two parties. As opposed to systems of indirect exchange as modeled by Lévi-Strauss (1969), or hierarchical ones as in Dumont (1970), exchange here is always direct, and does not permit of 'encompassment' of one term in the relationship by another. And unlike some other systems of direct exchange, this one is not underpinned by a dualism of yin and yang – of chronically and essentially opposed orders of being, between which there *must* be exchange because each is incomplete without the other. Rather, this is a system in which it is not only permitted, but for many kinds of transaction positively required that the return prestation be one of *exactly the same* order as what was given. True, the *amount* which is returned may differ from (exceed) that given, creating an imbalance (it could even be called hierarchy) between the parties; but a basic premise of the system is that this imbalance will be reversed in the next phase of the exchange. In other words, the situation in the long run is one of what A. Strathern (1971:11) calls 'alternating disequilibrium', or what we prefer to call *serial parity* (notwithstanding Strathern's valid claim that a synchronic *state* of parity is seldom, if ever, achieved).

This terminological innovation is not merely a matter of half-full glasses as opposed to half-empty ones. We intend the term *serial* to apply not only to a temporally extended series of transactions, but also to a laterally extended chain of linked transactors as exemplified in Chapters 6 and 7 and A. Strathern 1971 (Ch.6).

As for the term parity, we use it in order to bring out what is common to exchange relations and segmentary ones. Recall the distinction we made above between the ways in which the different kinds of relationships proliferate: different-to-different (i.e. exchange) relations in chain-like, non-hierarchical series and same-to-same ones within well-bounded, internally subdivided hierarchical structures. The latter have certain formal features in common with segmentary lineage systems of the classical African variety, and some important differences, as many Highlands ethnographers have stressed since Barnes (1962) (cf. Chapter 3 above). However, among the non-African features, there is one in Ku Waru of a kind which has not been widely appreciated (but see Lancy and Strathern 1981). That is the pre-eminence of *pairing* as the preferred mode of segmentation (including both fission and fusion). We have already shown in Chapter 3 that the Kopia *talapi* is more-or-less stably segmented in an almost entirely binary way at three lower levels of named divisions. Given the analysis developed in Chapters 6 and 7, one can now see just how pervasive is pairing as a way of linking 'tribes' (i.e., named *talapi* of the most inclusive order, such as Kopia and Kubuka) into higher-level social identities which are constructed (however problematically) as unitary transactors. This is true even where the possibility of doing so would seem to be flatly denied by the exigencies of history, such as in the case of what we have called the K-M-E-A-L alliance, which from our outsiders' viewpoint appears to comprise five units, but which Ku Waru people nonetheless invariably manage to construe as a pair of pairs (see section 3.1, also Lancy and Strathern 1981:184–6).

This relentless reshaping of history into bipartite structures (also exemplified in section 3.2.1), and the reciprocity which holds between partners in *serial parity*, will no doubt put many anthropologically informed readers in mind of Lévi-Strauss' structuralist model of 'dual organization' as a ubiquitous form of 'primitive' social organization – the more so if these readers are familiar with Rubel and Rosman's (1978) attempt to model a wide range of New Guinea social systems (including the Melpa one) as instances of dual organization, or transformations of it. We consider this quite inappropriate for the Hagen/

Nebilyer area. Before we can show why, we need to introduce some other forms of parity besides the serial one discussed above.

First, consider the type of pairing exemplified most immediately above – pairing as a form of subdivision of *talapi*, or aggregation of them, into hierarchically ordered clusters such as K-M-E-A-L. These are instances of what we will call *compositional parity*, as distinct from the serial parity of partners in exchange. It differs from serial parity in that it holds between parts of a well-bounded whole, which whole may itself be paired with another unit of the same order. Some other, related differences between the two kinds of parity are as follows. Compositional parity is exclusive: each unit enters into only *one* such relationship with another unit of the same order. Serial parity is non-exclusive: each unit may in principle enter into any number of such relationships with other units of the same order. Compositional parity is outward-looking, insofar as it presupposes joint opposition to some other unit(s) of the same order. Serial parity is inward-looking and holds between the two members of any exchange dyad, who are not thereby jointly opposed to any other unit.[9]

The latter difference is one which has important implications for the question of the relationship between warfare and exchange, a topic which has been adumbrated in our discussion several times so far (e.g. in sections 6.2.7., 7.4.2) but not fully developed.

Following in part upon Fitzpatrick 1980, Marilyn Strathern has recently mounted an effective challenge to the notion that warfare and exchange are somehow inherently opposed to each other. True enough, indigenous 'orators (mediators, dispute settlers) comment that to exchange wealth is better than to fight' (Strathern 1985a:124). But we cannot infer from this that exchange either operates or is understood to operate as a form of 'social control', since:

> an underlying premise [of such comments] is that the two activities [i.e. exchange of wealth and fighting] are convertible. It is not simply that the exchange of gifts enables people to settle their differences peaceably, but that either exchange or warfare can turn into its alternative. (ibid.)

The latter is true partly because wealth exchanges not only settle differences but also 'afford a facility for the mobilization of allies in warfare' (loc. cit: 123; cf. sections 6.2.7., 7.4.2 above). The examples we have discussed above amply bear out Strathern's claim that warfare and exchange are largely inter-convertible. But one can turn that claim on *its* head and point out that, for one activity to be convertible to another, the two must have been *different* activities (cf. section 7.4.2.).

This we take to have been implicit in several orators' (e.g. Mai's) remarks to the effect that money can not really pay for the life of a man. Accordingly one cannot say for the Ku Waru area that the 'exchange of blows' is an exchange of the same order as exchange of any kind of 'thing' (*mel*) (as D. Brown 1980 does for the Polopa). It is similar in that it presupposes a relation of difference among the combatants, but of another order in that the *talapi* who oppose each other in warfare are not normally the *same* ones who then exchange objects. True, *talapi* that have fought in the past can thereafter come to exchange objects (as in the case of K-M-E-A-L and Kopia-Kubuka in the events of Chapters 6 and 7).

But to the best of our knowledge, this has never occurred in the Ku Waru area except when, as in the present case, both the erstwhile protagonists have been joined in opposition to a common enemy (according to the famous principle of complementary opposition). That is, in terms of A. Strathern's (1971:94) distinction between 'reparation' (payments to allies for injuries and deaths inflicted in fighting for which one is liable) and 'direct compensation' (payments to those on whom one has inflicted death or injury), the latter only takes place between relatively minor enemies.[10]

In other words, though warfare and wealth exchange are organized by the same principle of reciprocity, they are nonetheless distinct and partially opposing spheres of activity. Fighting among *talapi* presupposes wealth exchange among them as a means of securing allies. The latter also presupposes the former, because without it allies would be unnecessary. But for the same reason, the range of inter-*talapi* relationships within which blows are directly convertible into things[11] (minor enemy relationships) also presupposes other relationships ('major' enmities) in which no such conversion is possible. And of course, both spheres of activity presuppose relations of sameness on the basis of which unitary transactors within them are constructed. While parties within relations of exchange-mediated difference are expected sometimes to fight, parties who are 'same' should not fight, especially with lethal weapons.

To summarize the above, the range of relationship types we have discussed can be represented as in Figure 8–1.

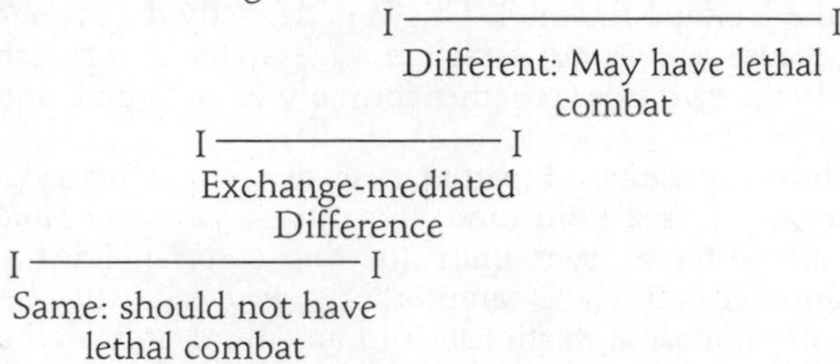

Figure 8–1: *Some overlapping types of relationships among* talapi

The top two lines show the types of inter-*talapi* relationship based on difference, i.e., warfare and wealth exchange. They overlap in that a given pair of *talapi* may both fight (as minor enemies) and pay each other compensation (both direct compensation and reparations). At the top right is a range of relationships in which there is fighting but no compensation. The relationships of exchange-mediated difference overlap with those of sameness in that a given pair of *talapi* (or segments thereof) may in some contexts exchange with each other and in others transact jointly with a third segmentary actor, relative to which they are 'same' to each other, sharing a common difference to it (e.g. Kopia and Kubuka, which transacted jointly with their erstwhile enemy, K-M-E-A-L, but have also carried on exchange between themselves (section 4.1)). The top and bottom lines do *not* overlap, because relations of sameness at least in theory preclude engaging in lethal combat with each other.

We have said above that relations of sameness aggregate via compositional parity and relations of exchange-mediated difference via serial parity. What about those relations of difference which are *not* mediated via exchange, i.e., warfare between major enemies (as shown at the top right corner of Figure 8–1)? Those present a more complex case. At least in the Ku Waru area, where the largest compositional units are small in comparison to such valley-floor tribes as Kulka and Ulka, or Hagen-area ones such as Moke and Jika, warfare between major enemy *talapi* seems always to entail the mobilization of the most inclusive compositional units of which those *talapi* are a part (Kopia-Kubuka, Tea-Dena etc.).[12] But beyond that, other segmentary units are usually brought in chain-like *serial* formations such as those discussed in Chapters 4, 6 and 7 above. Insofar as the damages inflicted in battle become 'converted' to payments of wealth, these payments too take place in lateral series which follow (in reverse order) the individual acts of recruitment which are understood to determine the composition of each side in the fight. Any of the pairwise links in this chain can also develop into a temporal series of reciprocal *makayl* payments between those two *talapi*. But unlike in those subsequent exchanges of wealth for wealth, the acts of recruitment and warfare themselves cannot be understood as matters of serial parity alone. For although the recruitment to each side is serial, the extent of both series is determined by something more like our principle of compositional parity: each tends to be of about the same length (of the same order) as the other. Thus, in the Marsupial Road War, just as the K-M-E-A-L recruited the Kopia-Kubuka who then recruited the Mujika-Laulku, so the Tea-Dena recruited the Tola-Wanaka who then recruited the Nokopa-Anamiyl. This is not exactly the same as compositional parity, because it does not establish a hierarchy of successive bipartite divisions. Nor do the two sides together form a well-bounded, unitary whole. But almost.

What they do comprise is a bipartite field of combatants which displays what is best regarded as a third kind of parity: *oppositional parity*. Whereas *compositional parity* conjoins two units (in this case, military alliances) in opposition to another unit of the same order, *oppositional parity* between two units does not presuppose a relationship to any third unit. Rather it merely juxtaposes two units, or parallel series of units, in balanced opposition to each other. Each of those units may itself be compositional in its internal structure (i.e. an internally ramified *talapi* or cluster such as K-M-E-A-L), but that is irrelevant to the relation of oppositional parity, which obtains between the opposing sides, not among the units on each.[13]

Although it is important to note these differences, what we want to emphasize here is that they are differences within a unity. Serial, compositional, and oppositional parity are all variants of a single way of making relationships which is pre-eminent in Ku Waru: pairing.

Having introduced all three of these varieties of pairing, we may now return to the question of dual organization raised above. Hagen/Nebilyer pairing is quite distinct from Lévi-Straussian dual organization. It is at once more specific and more powerful.

Lévi-Strauss (1969) argued that reciprocity was more basic than dual organization, which latter was its outcome. For Ku Waru, we would argue to the contrary that relationships of reciprocity are but one instance of a more general phenomenon of pairing, of which compositional binarism is another instance. The latter is not dual organization in Lévi-Strauss' sense, because the segmentary halves do not ordinarily exchange with each other, nor can serial pairing provide the basis for any consistent, over-arching dual organization, given the non-exclusive, non-transitive nature of these relations (see above discussion on *Meam* vs. *Kakuyl*). But to exclude compositional binarism or serial pairing as aspects of Ku Waru 'dualism' would be to force the system into a procrustean bed. Serial, compositional, and oppositional parity are alternative moments within a single processual order, and are (in principle and in practice) interconvertible. This was amply demonstrated at the events discussed in Chapters 6 and 7, where, for instance, the relation between Kopia and Kubuka, and that between Kusika-Midipu and Epola-Alya-Lalka were variously constructed as ones of serial vs. compositional parity, and where the erstwhile relation of oppositional parity between K-M-E-A-L and Kopia-Kubuka was, at least for now, converted to one of serial parity.

Whereas reciprocity is the elementary principle in dual organizations of the Lévi-Straussian sort, for Ku Waru, *pairing* is the elementary principle, of which (positive and negative) reciprocity and contextually restricted dual organization are just some manifestations among others.

Our examination of the structures and uses of talk in Chapters 5 to 7 has shown some of its other manifestations, and how these might be related to the kinds of parity just discussed.

Consider the several kinds of binarism which are basic to the form of *el ung* oratory. First, there is the striding of the orator, who always follows a two-way, back and forth trajectory across the display ground, often carrying a spear in one hand and an ax in the other. Second, there is the elaborate use of parallelism, whereby the prosodic lines are organized as matching pairs, and even four-line pairs of two-line pairs (a kind of compositional parity). Third, the pitch contour of each prosodic line in 'full' *el ung* comprises two level steps, an abruptly lower one for the *el ung* vowel at the end of the line, and a higher one for rest of the line, so that the prosody of the speech as a whole comprises a series of step-wise alternations between two pitch levels. Fourth, there is the alternation between the *el ung* vowels *-a*:: and *-o*::, which is used to mark off one section of a speech in thematic juxtaposition to another (section 6.2.6.).

Closely related to these binaristic formal features of *el ung* are the linguistic and paralinguistic means by which segmentary social identities and relationships are reproduced or contested. Whether the social relationships be serial or compositional, the parallel structures of *el ung* and other Ku Waru oratory provide a strikingly iconic means for rendering them. For one thing, in many cases the thematic content of parallel lines is a literal realization of the parity of segmentary 'lines'. This is true for example of lines 734–5: 'The Epola-Alya swore on the river Ukulu / The Kopia swore on the river Nebilyer'; line 1215: 'Meam fighting is one thing / Kaugel fighting is another thing'; lines 1345–6: 'I am not the son of a Mujika-Laulku woman / I am the son of a Meam woman'; cf. also lines 1235, 1281–3.

In addition to these cases of literal parity between rhetorical parallelism and social pairing, there is, we submit, a more general way in which each of the two is reinforced by the other. For what is reproduced at occasions such as those discussed in Chapters 6 and 7 is not just a specific set of social pairings or segmentary structures. (Indeed, we have seen that *their* reproduction is often problematic.) What is also reproduced or inculcated (and perhaps more effectively and importantly so) is a general set towards the world – a habitus (in the sense of Bourdieu 1977) – the habitus of *pairing*, the manifestations of which are also evident, not just in segmentation/exchange/warfare, but in many other forms of Ku Waru practical-conceptual activity as well (cf. section 5.7 and Lancy and Strathern 1981).

A characteristic, common feature of *all* the uses of pairing among Ku Waru people is that, unlike many forms of dualism and dual organization elsewhere, the pairings here tend not to be regarded as absolute, immutable facts about the universe (as already appreciated by Strauss, quoted in section 5.7), but as contingent and potentially transitory products of human agency: pairings are *made* rather than given (section 5.7). Accordingly, the making of them is a performance which has the potential for revealing that which is new and surprising, rather than conforming to what is prescribed (cf. section 9.1).

In section 8.3 below, we will return to the question of the role of language in the construction of specific pairings. Before doing so, we will first return to the question of the relation between the *bo* order and the brave new world of 'government law', and re-examine this relationship in light of the distinctions we have just made among various kinds of parity.

8.2 THE SEGMENTARY ORDER AND THE KULKA WOMEN'S CLUB

In section 8.1, we considered some relationships among the three events discussed in Chapters 6 and 7, and drew from them some generalizations concerning the nature of the traditional Ku Waru segmentary order. Much of what went on at those events can be understood as the construction and contestation of inter-*talapi* (and, to a lesser extent, interpersonal) relations of sameness and difference – relations which aggregate into polities or oppositional fields according to three kinds of parity, all of which are essentially a parity of pairs. At the Kailge event, the reproduction of that way of making relationships (if not any particular set of them) proceeded more-or-less unopposed. This was not true of the Palimung and Kopola events. There, as we have seen in Chapter 7, the Kulka women's club, following up on their decisive intervention on the battlefield in 1982, appeared as an unprecedented new kind of transactor in the sphere of exchange among *talapi*.

In light of the more general model of that sphere which has been made possible by a consideration of all three events, we now return to the question: what kind of transactor was it?

As we described in Chapter 7, club spokeswomen, and other speakers such as Kopia Mel and Kulka Pokea, represent the club as espousing the order of *gavman lo*. The club had in fact been partially sponsored by the provincial government, which at the women's request had provided some of the goods which were presented on the battlefield. The club also asked at least two government officials to appear at the Palimung event. In her speech, Neka said that one of the thoughts she had had in putting a stop to the fighting was that club work should grow strong. Each woman speaker emphasizes that only a few women had initially done club work, but that it had been gathering momentum. The women had cash on hand to offer the combatants. In all these ways, members of the club work to demonstrate that what they had to offer was a more powerful option than engaging in warfare, an activity from which nobody would derive benefit. They derived an identity, on the basis of which they intervened, from an association of the club with *gavman lo*. But what kind of entity is *gavman*, and what is its perceived relation to segmentary business-as-usual?

Since the earliest days of the Australian Administration, the government has sought to present itself as powerful but beneficent, *disinterested* and even-handed with all who come under it. But its subjects have often found this claim difficult to accept, or even incomprehensible (see e.g. Hallpike 1977:5). For in the indigenous segmentary order there is nothing equivalent to this; mediation by big-men was probably most similar, but it was not possible for big-men to be seen as completely disinterested parties. While the Nebilyer people certainly understood that the government was attempting to put a stop to warfare, the very terms in which they represent their own relation to this effort seem to be shot through with the partisanship of the segmentary order. Unya, in his speech at Kailge (Appendix A, line 442), says that when *gavman* came in, he had to regard even former major enemies like Tea-Dena (*mer-ayl*) as 'mine'. In other words, he does not speak of the complete levelling henceforth of segmentary difference and interest, but he talks from a position within the segmentary order of taking on identifications with people and *talapi* who were formerly in opposition. The language is still that of segmentary person.

Thus, however explicit or inexplicit Nebilyer people's understanding of governmental claims to disinterestedness may have been, or be presently, in their own reaction to such governmental aims as stopping warfare they do not assume that segmentary difference no longer counts. What they do espouse explicitly is the notion that inter-*talapi* relations are to be made compatible with the governmental ideal of cessation of hostilities. But this is accomplished by segmentary-type identifications, or reversal of relations, with former enemies. Also, the fact that people talk of paying warfare indemnity for injury and death as 'making *lo*' is consistent with an interpretation of 'law' as the maintenance of the peace, but achieved on a segmentary basis. There is no clear concept of a global political order within which segmentary relations will be irrelevant.

There are however, some contexts in which the segmentary order is seen to be in conflict with the proper functioning of *gavman*. There are, for instance, frequent complaints about the *wantok sistem*, the favoring of those people who in any given context may be identified as one's own (relative, segment, or larger grouping): that is not allowable and should not be done. Magistrates, for example, in their training are impressed with the idea that they should deal fairly with everyone, not hear cases if they cannot be even-handed, not allow their decisions to be determined by money or gifts, and so on. The extent to which magistrates, councillors and other people talk about and inveigh against the *wantok sistem* indicates that it strikes a chord of recognition. And, in fact, people try to build networks of this kind within which they can pursue their own interests. For example, a tribunal from Hagen was supposed to adjudicate an internal Kopia land dispute (see section 3.2.3). The principal spokesman for one side had some connections to members of the tribunal and made gifts to them to dispose them favorably to his case. Hearing of this, and not to be put at a disadvantage, the principal spokesman for the other side did the same. Was the situation then completely balanced, and nothing accomplished? Something seems to have been accomplished in any event, because the tribunal was thus obliged to consider the interests of both sides. The possibility of *wantok*ism, that *gavman* may not be disinterested, but can be dealt with in the terms of the segmentary order, is never far below the surface.

And it is in respect of these matters that the action of the women's club is most striking and experimental. For the image of *gavman* that they project is much more explicitly non-segmentary, and points to the possibility of a global order within which not only would warfare be disallowed as disruptive, but the segmentary order itself, of which warfare is a part, would be set aside as incompatible with the desired aims of keeping the peace and establishing *bisnis*, steadily expanding cash-yielding relations with the modern market economy. This is evident in at least two ways (cf. Gordon and Meggitt 1985).

Consider first the nature of the club's intervention in the fighting. It came between two combatant sides already arrayed on the battlefield (Tea-Dena and allies on one side, Epola-Alya-Lalka-Kusika-Midipu and allies on the other) and persuaded them to desist by offering an equal payment of cash and (store-bought) items to each. How and to what extent does this transaction jibe with the traditional notions of compositional, serial and oppositional parity?

The women seek to establish a position for themselves (under the patronage of two prominent big-men) by claiming to speak in the name of *gavman lo*. But they do not represent the essence of this relation as any capacity on their (or the *gavman's*) part to act coercively. Their message is that the acceptance and legitimacy of centralized government is closely bound up with the development of *bisnis,* relations with the modern market economy. For this to take priority, warfare must cease. The way in which they achieve the cessation of hostilities is to offer prestations to each combatant side. The mechanism for assuaging feelings is still prestation, as in *bo* fashion. The payment is more significant for the novelty of the message it conveys in this context, than for the amount. (It would not have been considered sufficient for an indemnity payment such as is usually made for injury, for instance.) It comprises largely items which must be bought with cash, not the most valued items of the traditional economy. And, if accepted, it compels reciprocity of *both* sides with the same third transactor, acting in the name of *gavman lo*.

What this expresses is clear enough: conflict is to be neutralized by and in favor of acceptance of the values of *gavman,* and this is most keenly perceived as the association of a centralized political system with development of *bisnis*. Relations with this new transactor disrupt the opposition between combatant sides, and establish, not a serial pairing, but a new kind of three-way relation in which each side owes reciprocity to the club. This is suggestive at least of a condition that we might contrast with the segmentary order by terming it 'universal parity', in which formerly distinct segmentary *talapi* establish common relations with the central political system-cum-market economy,[14] and the political relevance of segmentary difference is thereby undermined, in at least two ways. First, the building of pair-wise serial relations laterally with allies becomes less relevant as efforts are directed towards *bisnis* and wealth accumulation, rather than redistribution; and second, the expectation of temporal, serial relations (of prestation and return prestation) is dissolved into generalized reciprocity between *gavman* and those who espouse its values. These notions are not expressed in so many words by any of the participants at this event. But the women's club action was revelatory in that it dramatized that *these* are the values in the name of which warfare is to be put aside. Many of the male speakers urged a return to the spheres of social life most closely associated with the ideals of *gavman*, namely courts, schools and the highroads. And the *kiap*, Beni, most nearly represented the close relation that everyone responds to between centralized government and *bisnis* when he asked the crowd to think of the amounts of money that are consumed in making warfare indemnity payments.

Speaking only in the name of *gavman* values, the women differ strikingly from the men in what they say. They do not recount the history of hostilities, nor do they refer to the other payments taking place at these same events. They (along with Kulka Pokea) focus upon the fact that they will receive a return payment at *all* of these events, thus emphasizing the superior position of the transactor who is not limited to serial pair-wise relationships, but is in between and mediates conflict. As we pointed out in section 7.4, the club is similar to the Tilka in its in-betweenness, but has a more commanding relation to events in that it originally made prestations to break up the fight on the basis of values everyone holds to be important, and does not merely receive them for having stayed out of it, as Tilka does.

The first way in which the club's action suggests the setting aside of the segmentary order, then, is by dramatizing that the possibility of universal parity resides in the linkage between *gavman* and *bisnis*, a powerful suggestion since many aspects of both resonate with practices (roll-calling, time-keeping, turn-taking) and values (orderliness, and the very discovery and exploration of new values) that people wish to embrace.

The second way in which the club's action undermines the segmentary order is by adopting a peace-keeping strategy in which women will keep watch on events within the *talapi* with which they live, and carry reports of any trouble to the club and government authorities (see Kujilyi's speech, lines 42–5). The fact that this is a *women's* club is directly relevant to their adopting this strategy.

The outstanding ethnography of M. Strathern (1972a) develops the key image of Melpa women's 'in-betweenness', their position as 'participant intermediaries' (loc.cit. p. 280) between their *talapi* of origin and those into which they marry. Women's shared experience of in-betweenness does not, however, by itself provide the basis for the formation of any kind of solidary female associations. In the main, Hagen and Nebilyer women are seen (and see themselves) as having value insofar as they abundantly fulfill expectations of them as producers and mothers, committed to the interests of husbands' people and (partly through this) their own kin. As women in between, wives' commitment and dependability towards husbands and affines can be brought into question. A negative side of their in-betweenness is the stereotype of the female poisoner (cf. M. Strathern 1972a:99, 268–9), or the woman who undermines her husband's interests more subtly by non-cooperation.

But in the club's suggestion that women keep watch over the *talapi* where they live their in-betweenness is treated as having an additional positive value.

Women almost invariably represented themselves to us as having been opposed to warfare in the past on the grounds that they feared its destructiveness; as an aspect of inter-*talapi* relations, it is quintessentially a male activity. For a man to report on the activities within his *talapi* is unthinkable, and can only be interpreted as subversive of *talapi* solidarity. For a woman to do the same is not only thinkable, but attributed a positive value when it is in the interests of keeping the peace. Women opposed warfare in piecemeal fashion in the past (cf. Neka's speech in section 7.2.3), but the club provides them a position from which they can consolidate and legitimate their opposition to it: it stands in the way of the realization of what should be a collectively-held value, the development of *bisnis*.

As we pointed out in section 7.4.2, however, there is some contradiction between the message dramatized by the women's club, and the larger event in which they find themselves, where pair-wise payments between *talapi* which acted as allies are to be transacted. In this context, to the extent that they insist that no man, no woman, no government official stopped the fight, but only themselves, they tout their own achievement as big-men typically do, and construct for the club an identity which is *talapi*-like in opposing itself to other transactors. Insofar as they could be seen merely as women intervening in men's activities, they run the risk of being dismissed, and indeed as we noted in Chapter 7, there was some murmuring in the crowd against their being allowed to speak. But because they represent values which everyone is eager to explore, the club's achievement is referred to by a number of male speakers, who succeed partially in putting into words the club's opposition to the segmentary order and the potential it offers for self-discovery in their observation that 'no man stopped the fight'.

However compromised they may have been, the action of the women's club posed a radical new alternative to the traditional segmentary order insofar as it foreshadowed the supersession of serial, compositional, and oppositional parity by a new condition of universal parity between *gavman* and the governed. But within the payment event itself, club members progressively made for themselves a position from which to speak by constructing the club's relations to other agents as ever more *talapi*-like.

8.3 ACTION AND REPRESENTATION, STRUCTURE AND EVENT

To return now to the question we posed in section 1.2, who transacts with whom in Highlands exchange systems? Our analysis in Chapters 6 to 7, and Lederman's (1980, 1986a) partly comparable material from Mendi, should have made it clear by now that that question is one which is hotly contested, not only in the anthropological accounts of exchange systems (as in section 1.2), but in the systems themselves. But the alternative possibilities in the exchange systems are not the same as those entertained in the descriptions (section 1.2). That is, in actual practice, it is never a case of Meggitt's solidary 'corporate group' confronting other groups nor of individual, concrete human organisms whose exchange activities can be traced without regard for how they are indigenously represented. Rather, the terms among which the exchange relationships obtain are social identities which are constructed in the actual practice of exchange.

This was abundantly evident at all three of the events we have considered. In each case, the transactions were of a kind for which the main relevant transactors were understood to be *talapi* or various combinations of them. But close analysis of what went on at those events revealed that in no case could the internal unity or external boundaries of those units be taken for granted. Nor was the boundary always clear between inter-*talapi* relations and the various inter-personal relations which partially cross-cut and partially compose them (e.g. sections 6.2.1, 6.2.3, 6.2.5, 6.2.6, 7.2). Nor was the nature or meaning of the transactions themselves (sections 6.2.6, 6.2.7). All of these were matters which had to be worked upon, contested, more-or-less successfully hammered out in the public arena. This much was true even at Kailge, where the nature of the contest itself was relatively clear and unproblematic. Even the latter was thrown open for contestation in the other two events, as discussed in Chapter 7 and section 8.2 above.

In claiming that social identities and relations are constructed in the actual practice of exchange, we do not mean to suggest that they are constructed *ex nihilo* at each new exchange event. Rather, there is an ongoing dialectic between structure and event such that structure figures as 'both medium and outcome in the reproduction of practices' (Giddens 1979:5).

What is the nature of the relevant structures in this case, and to what extent are they firmly 'in place' as available 'medium' at any given event?

Still under the sway of the African descent model, most accounts of central Highlands social organization until the early seventies posited an elaborate set of functionally specified segmentary 'levels' as in, e.g., Meggitt (1965). (See sections 1.2, 3.1.3; cf. A. Strathern 1971:31–53 for the Melpa area.) As this has proved unsustainable, some more recent investigators have downplayed or denied the importance of segmentary 'groups' altogether (as in section 1.2). The analysis we have presented here certainly supports the more recent position insofar as it shows that nothing like a full and fixed set of social functions or relationship types can be assigned to any particular level in the segmentary hierarchy. Indeed, there would seem to be *no* clear criteria for drawing any useful distinctions among fixed segmentary 'levels' ('clan', 'subclan', 'lineage', etc.) in the Ku Waru area at least (cf. section 3.2). But, as opposed to Feil and Sillitoe, we cannot conclude from this that segmentary structures are not of major importance in Ku Waru social life. Rather, we would argue on the basis of examples treated here that they play a crucial role, not in the form of fully-elaborated structures 'in place', but as what Bourdieu (1977:72) calls 'structuring structures', i.e., in this case, as *ways of making relationships*. Specifically, we would argue for the centrality in Ku Waru of the habitus of pairing and parity described in section 8.1, which generates not only structures and processes of segmentation, but also of exchange, in a single order of mutually-presupposing relationship types.

In the medium of these few basic 'structuring structures' and a wealth of more-or-less untidy historical detail of the kind described in section 3.2, events are played out in ways that establish momentarily more-or-less stable configurations of social identities such as Kopia-Kubuka, K-M-E-A-L, Mujika-Laulku,

Tea-Dena, Tola-Wanaka, and the relations of hostility, alliance, or exchange which variously obtain among them. At a more fundamental level, and over a much longer and broader run of events, what gets reproduced at them are, as we have already said, the practices of pairing and parity themselves. Even this is not unproblematic, as we saw in section 7.4. Nor is it only under the recent radically changed circumstances that the 'structuring structures' themselves have come to be only variably reproduced. To judge by other Highland ethnographies, the strictly 'traditional' Ku Waru structures of parity described above seem not to have been present in just that form even among such relatively close peoples as the Enga. We can only conclude that these structures, though more stable than any particular set of inter-*talapi* relationships themselves, are a relatively evanescent historical product, in comparison with, e.g. specific tuber-gardening practices which we know from the archeological record to have been in the area for at least 7000 years.

The practices of pairing and parity are necessarily, at least in part, practices of 'representation' or signification. We agree with Giddens (1979:39) that there are no 'signifying practices' as such: 'signification should rather be understood as an integral element of social practices in general' (ibid). In light of examples from Lederman (1980), we argued in general terms (in section 1.2) that the nature of Highland exchange transactions is underdetermined by the strictly non-'representational' criteria which seemed to be decisive for Feil and Meggitt, hence the wide latitude for their diametrically opposed conclusions about the role of groups and individuals in a single exchange system. In light of the extended examples developed herein, we hope to have provided a new and more openly accessible kind of evidence to substantiate that argument, and to have opened the way for comparative studies of the kind intimated by A. Strathern (1979a) when he pointed to the importance of close attention to what is *said* at exchange events in any attempt to understand the differences among exchange systems (cf. A. Strathern (1978:79f) regarding the importance of what is *not* said).

Though the main form of signification which we have treated has been linguistic, we hope to have provided enough evidence to demonstrate the important role of some of its non-linguistic forms as well.[15] The examples we have treated in most detail have concerned meaningful uses of *space* at the Kailge and Palimung events (sections 6.1, 7.2.2). Our discussion of the paralinguistic features of *el ung* oratory (sections 5.3, 6.2.6, 8.1) should also have demonstrated their general relevance in this respect.

To focus upon the 'representational' aspects of exchange is by no means to dissolve the material aspects of the transactions into some ethereal realm of disembodied significations. Whether a transaction gets constructed as one between *talapi*, between this or that combination of *talapi*, or as an interpersonal one, is a matter that has very real material consequences, as Mujika Kasipa, Kopia Noma, and their wives well know, and as Lederman also makes clear for the Mendi. And the 'representations' themselves are always both 'material' (i.e., realized in concrete 'signifiers') *and* 'ideational'.

Nor do we mean to suggest that the battle of alternative constructions is waged in the same way in all Highland exchange systems. Indeed, we suspect, in light of Feil's account, that the role of the segmentary identities is quite different as between the Enga *tee* and the Melpa *moka* – more different than is suggested by Meggitt's account. For at least in areas along the main *tee* roads, where the order of public prestations is rigidly fixed on a clan-by-clan (and sub-clan by sub-clan) basis, the inter-clan aspect must be taken for granted – backgrounded – to a far greater extent that among the Melpa (much less the Ku Waru people), where it is explicitly constructed as the transitory and problematic achievement of big-men such as Noma and Kasipa (as in section 6.2.6). What we *would* argue is that these differences can be better specified by paying careful attention to the ways in which the transactions are indigenously represented, both at the moment of transaction and in other contexts.

Close attention to these matters in the Ku Waru area has lead us to emphasize the importance of *pairing* as the fundamental form of social relationships, which are variously constructed or converted along the twin axes of sameness/difference and inter-*talapi*/interpersonal relations, with corresponding variation in the kinds of parity entailed by each.

How and to what extent does an understanding of these relationships depend upon close analysis of language use? One of our aims in this book has been to develop an account of language use that was not merely ancillary to a social-anthropological account of exchange, but integral to it: an account which overcomes the antinomy of 'language and society' to encompass social action, treating speech as one of its several forms or moments. The model we have now developed of Ku Waru exchange, as summarized in the last paragraph, is, we maintain, just such an account. It is a general model of Ku Waru segmentary structure and exchange, rather than of language use in particular. But while it is supported by many other kinds of evidence as well as the linguistic (e.g. by census data and tabulations of exchange transactions, such as those in section 4.1), linguistic evidence is also crucial, for the following reasons.

First, it is indispensable for understanding the social construction of sameness and difference. At the level of interpersonal relations, this might seem difficult to credit, since the main dimension of sameness/difference is linkage via same-sex vs. cross-sex siblingship, surely matters which are not essentially linguistic. But of course, no purely biological specification of these matters could independently reproduce the relevant distinctions (for reasons discussed in section 3.1). There would, for instance, be no way to predict from his genealogy alone that Laulku Bai would end up being treated as a same-sex sibling by the Kubuka. It is by now a commonplace of Highland ethnography to note that 'siblings' are *made* as well as born (the famous 'conversion of non-agnates').[16] The process by which they are made is a matter of social action, of which signification is again an integral aspect. If this particular process was not especially prominent at the events treated here, that was only because they happened to be inter-*talapi* events rather than interpersonal ones.

Analysis of language use is perhaps even more essential for understanding the construction of sameness/difference at the inter-*talapi* level. This is partly because the bases on which those relations are constructed are far more variable. Whereas at the interpersonal level, it is essentially a matter of siblingship or consubstantiality, at the inter-*talapi* level, almost any contextually available differentiae can be drawn upon, including, in the present case, ways of making gardens, crops grown, rivers sworn upon, and shared regional identities. The relations are therefore not amenable to an *a priori* structural model of the kind which anthropologists have developed on the basis of abstractly specified kinship relations. Rather, close attention must be given to how the relations are constructed/represented in the actual contexts of transaction. This is partly a matter of non-linguistic representation, as we have seen, for example, in the social differentiation of space at Kailge (section 6.1) and Palimung (section 7.2.2). Language also figures crucially, both via explicit invocation of such differences as those mentioned above, and, perhaps even more important, via the use of segmentary person.

Without close attention to the latter, one would remain largely oblivious of the construction of 'sameness' between and within *talapi* at inter-*talapi* exchange events. For although 'difference' is often lexically invoked, the main way in which social identities are linguistically marked as 'same' is by grouping them together within a single category of segmentary person. This can be either singular or dual. *Talapi* or combinations of *talapi* referred to in either way are thereby marked as 'same' relative to each other and as 'different' from others referred to in opposing person categories. Recall for example, how by referring to the combination of K-M-E-A-L and Tea-Dena in the second person dual, Unya pointedly identified them as same (i.e., as former allies) as opposed to Kubuka or Kopia-Kubuka, to whom he refers in the first person singular (section 6.2.2). And when he comes to a point where he has to refer to the combination of Kopia-Kubuka and K-M-E-A-L (line 443), he pointedly avoids using the first person dual pronoun, instead constructing a conjoint noun phrase comprising *two* SP pronouns, a second person singular (for K-M-E-A-L) and first singular for (Kopia-)Kubuka (section 6.2.2).

Given the ubiquity of such usages at inter-*talapi* exchange events, and their pre-eminence among the means for constructing/contesting inter-*talapi* relations, it is apparent that some of the essential evidence one needs for understanding what goes on at these events is *linguistic* evidence. It is highly unlikely that even a running translation of the speeches would be sufficient for this. For the grammar of segmentary person is not carried into English or Tok Pisin. What is required is close study of the actual linguistic form of the speeches as they are delivered in the original language.

What makes the values and uses of segmentary person opaque to translation is precisely what makes it so powerful as a form of social action, i.e., the fact that it is implemented with linguistic structures of a kind that are, as shown by Silverstein (1981), largely beyond the limits of awareness of speaker and addressee alike: viz., bound (verbal) morphemes rather than words, performative, non-referential indices rather than presupposing, referential ones (cf. section 5.2). Explicit *assertions* of sameness or difference, for the same reason that they are easier to translate, are also more easily contested in an explicit way (cf. Bloch 1975).

The second reason why language use is especially crucial for an understanding of these exchange systems concerns the nature of its relationship to other dimensions of social action. Language of course is not the only form of communication. Wealth items, too, can be used to 'say' things. Are the two media potentially equivalent alternatives, or how do they compare? In the Western common sense view which *opposes* 'talk' and 'action', actions are sometimes said to speak louder than words. And insofar as things may take the place of words, they would seem to speak more *clearly* than words. Thus it is not surprising that many anthropologists in their accounts of exchange systems would seem at least implicitly to agree with Gewertz's claim that:

> [Exchange items] have the advantage of tangibility. Unlike words, they cannot be easily qualified, contradicted, or disavowed. Relationships established and maintained through conversations are open-ended. They can develop in a number of ways, many often threatening to the status quo. Exchanges on the other hand, can only be accepted or refused. If accepted, the terms of the relationship remain substantially the same. If rejected, the relationship as presently defined is terminated. (Gewertz 1984:211)

But if anything at all has been established by the analysis in Chapters 6 and 7 above, it is surely that *wealth exchanges* are 'open ended' and 'can develop in a number of ways, many often threatening to the status quo'. We saw this in Noma's attempt to use the present payment as a means of shifting the major *makayl* relationship of Kopia-Kubuka from Poika-Palimi to Mujika-Laulku (section 6.2.6); in the frequently-remarked indeterminacy about whether the payments were a means of ensuring the peace or preparing for war (section 6.2.7.); and in the potentially radical challenge to the status quo which was posed by the battlefield prestation of the Kulka women's club, to cite but a few of the many examples. In none of these cases does the acceptance of payment imply that 'the relationship will remain the same'. It could not, for it is not clear in any of these cases what *is* the current state of the relationship (e.g. do the Mujika-Laulku have a continuing compensation debt to the Kopia or do they not? Are the Kopia-Kubuka really the allies of the K-M-E-A-L, or their enemies?) In the case of the Kulka women's club, there was *no* established relationship between them and the *talapi* to whom they made a payment on the battlefield. Not only that, but there was at the time not even an established *type* of relationship that it could be: no *conceivable* 'relationship as presently defined'. At the time, the action could only be construed as 'mad', 'insane' or 'drunken' (section 7.2.3).

Nor is it really the case that exchanges 'can only be accepted or refused'. True, the objects themselves can only be left in place or taken away. There are no other logical possibilities. But *exchanges* in their full specificity as social constructions are by no means so limited. For the movement of objects, though it plays a part, can never by itself constitute the transaction as such. Thus we have seen time and time again, both here and in Lederman (1980), how precisely the *same* movement of material objects is *alternatively* constructed as this or that exchange transaction.

Thus, commonplace as it is in the literature on exchange, we cannot accept the terms of Gewertz's contrast between the meaning of words and the meaning of objects.[17]

This is not to say that there is no difference. On the contrary, while rejecting the terms of Gewertz's distinction, we think there is an important one to be drawn, and that her formulation does touch upon some essential features of talk which are relevant for such a distinction. While our analysis, as opposed to Gewertz, suggests that exchange items do not differ from words in the extent to which they may be 'qualified, contradicted, or disavowed', there is a fundamental asymmetry there in that, while the main means for qualifying the meaning of speech is more speech, the meaning of objects is not generally qualified with more objects, but with speech. This is true not only of wealth objects, but of the other non-linguistic media as well. Consider, for example, the use of space and movement at these events. Not only was it used meaningfully, but there was in each case explicit verbal *commentary* about its uses (sections 6.1., 7.2.2). The same goes for combined linguistic and paralinguistic features which mark off *el ung* oratory (sections 6.1, 6.2.7.), the *temal* 'omens' which were discerned at Kailge and Kopola (section 5.4), and the Kulka women's use of the Papua New Guinea national flag (section 7.2.3) And of course there was extensive metalinguistic commentary throughout, concerning the meaning and import of what had been, was being, or would be literally 'said' (i.e. with speech) at these events (section 5.7 *et passim*). All of this meta-level commentary – whether it concerned speech or other media – was done with speech. This would seem to provide ample support for Benveniste's claim (cf. Silverstein 1976:16, Habermas 1984) that:

> language is the interpreting system (interpretant) of all other semiotic systems. No other system has at its disposal a 'language' by which it can categorize and interpret itself according to its semiotic distinctions, while language can, in principle, categorize and interpret everything, including itself. (Benveniste 1969:131 [our translation]).

In the final chapter we refer to and argue against predominant tendencies in Western thought which would separate language from action and consider it mere representation of a reality (social or otherwise) which is given independently of it. In light of the examples discussed in the preceding chapters, we must insist even more strongly upon the claim that language use too is a form of action. But we can begin to see that there is a sense in which certain unique powers of language as 'representation' (i.e. its (meta-)semanticity) do sharply set off some of its uses, not from 'action', but from other *forms* of action.

Particularly in light of the massive indeterminacy as to the meaning of wealth transactions, both at the level of tokens (Chapter 6) and at the level of types (Chapter 7), it is evident that exchange transactions in this area can seldom if ever be constituted as such without what Gewertz calls 'qualification', here as elsewhere an open ended process in which *the* final, definitive meaning of the exchange is never established. The fact that language plays a uniquely important role in that process is another reason why close attention to what is done with it can provide essential evidence for understanding what is happening, both at particular exchange events on the *makayl pena*, and in the larger social order which is reproduced and transformed at them.

Of course, not all of Nebilyer social life consists of such events, nor does speech figure just the same way in others.[18] Our focus upon ceremonial exchange events has been a more-or-less contingent one, motivated in part by ethical considerations,[19] and in part by strategic ones, in that we thought we could best demonstrate the sociological value of attending to talk by aiming our investigation at a single, well defined ethnographic quandary, such as that of section 1.2. But at least some of the understanding we have developed by examining events of that kind can be deepened by relating them to other aspects of Nebilyer social life, which they in turn help to elucidate. This we will do in the following, final chapter.

9. Perspectives on 'event'

In this chapter we develop conclusions in quite a different way than we did in Chapter 8 – by attempting to characterize some of the constitutive dimensions of Nebilyer social action more broadly, widening the scope of our consideration from the public events we have examined to some aspects of everyday Nebilyer social life. One of our aims in doing this is to illuminate the concept of 'event' itself, a term which we have so far been using as though its meaning were self-evident.

In order to broaden the inquiry into other kinds of social action, and the role of speech, we must ask how and on what bases speech itself is constituted as a form of social action, alongside and in relation to others. The main issue we will be exploring in this chapter, then, is: how may we characterize the bases of Nebilyer social action? This leads us to examine the significance indigenously attributed to 'events' as occurrences which stand out from the ordinary flow of life-as-usual. We will show that there is something like a Nebilyer concept of event, which is strongly oriented towards the discovery or disclosure of new significance, both in large-scale public transactions, such as those we have analyzed in the previous chapters, as well as in everyday life, and that speech is crucial as medium and activity within the indigenously valued forms of social action in both spheres.

Part of what we seek to do by plumbing indigenous notions of event can be related to the concerns of Wagner (1975) and Strathern (in press), which we discussed in section 7.4. There we mentioned Wagner's (1975) injunction that anthropology take as one of its aims to render the creativity of social reproduction, how cultures 'invent themselves'. In the phenomenological tradition, he places upon this aim the even more stringent requirement that fulfillment of it enable us to experience our subject matter 'directly', as 'alternative meaning', rather than through reduction to our terms. In attempting to define the bases of Nebilyer notions of event, part of what we are indeed aiming to do is to characterize *their* concepts of significance and novelty. Whether or not this can ever allow us to achieve Wagner's second aim, we do think it desirable that we at least attempt to make our ethnographic analyses more accountable, by showing that they enable us to understand how people invent themselves. This we think we can do by pointing to important dimensions and processes which are common to the constitution of public transactions such as those we have already discussed, and the constitution of everyday social action, some aspects of which we are about to discuss.

The matters we have raised here also relate to ways in which we would like to contribute to a greater unification of anthropology with language studies. Underlying our discussion of event within the flow of social life is our interest in contributing to the development of a unified approach to the bases of social action which includes its linguistic and other aspects. Unless we can begin to develop an approach which can take these into consideration jointly, we will remain caught in one or the other of the current impasses which afflict both anthropology and language studies – in which, on the one hand, our claims that attention to language use should occupy a central place in ethnography are skeptically received because social action involving speech is seen as of lesser materiality (hence of lesser consequence) than other forms of action such as the transfer of wealth objects; or, on the other, that language-focused ethnography is commended but its relation to other aspects of ethnography remains unclear, or lodged within a framework inadequate to deal with social action in broad terms.[1]

This view of language is not peculiar to anthropology and linguistics, but deeply rooted in Western philosophical tradition. Without rehearsing here the diverse currents of thought in language philosophy, we will simply allude to the difference between the Lockeian-cum-Saussurean notion of language as conventional – with no intrinsic relation to 'things' but to ideas only (cf. Aarsleff 1983:63) – and the (Leibnizian) view of language as 'natural' – exhibiting regular correspondences to what it represents and thus providing insight into the operations of understanding. Though different and opposed in certain respects, these have in common the presupposition of separate realities, whether things or thoughts, concerning which it is language's function to enable communication. Neither view envisages that langage may have both creative and pragmatic dimensions of its own aside from its presumed *communicative* function, i.e. that 'reality' is not something entirely apart from its social transaction in speech. On certain bases related to these, which we will not attempt to draw out in any detail here, structural linguistics from Saussure onwards has largely gained its successes by abstracting from the pragmatic properties of language, treating events and action as peripheral to the definition and replication of linguistic structures.[2]

The student of social life who most clearly stands out for having advocated the treatment of language as *action* is Malinowski (see e.g. 1949). But his approach unfortunately falls short in its pervasive organicism: his tendency to take as the prototypic action the 'bodily act', a direct expression of the needs of the human organism as such (cf. section 5.1).

The marginalization of language vis-à-vis other forms of action stands in sharp contrast to the Hagen/Nebilyer view of the matter, as already suggested by the early patrol reports and other ethnographic observations (including our own) in section 2.5, where we described the striking volume of talk which characterizes proceedings at public events in the Hagen/Nebilyer area (cf. Merlan and Rumsey 1986:69). Also introduced there were observations showing that Ku Waru people themselves highly value speech as a mode of social action. Men compete for the opportunity to speak, and known competence in speech-making is one of the defining abilities of prominent men. Talk, and the activity of talking, is not indigenously considered mere verbiage, but a form of social action which, in some contexts at least, is perceived as the most salient and socially-valued form of *doing*, efficacious action.

The same is true elsewhere in the Highlands. Goldman says of the Huli (Southern Highlands):

> In this culture, actions do not speak louder than words, and words are not said to be 'translated' into actions. For Huli, saying and thinking . . . are not quiescent states but modes of 'doing'; speech is not 'insubstantial' in comparison with actions. (1983:36)

The competitiveness of social situations in which people seek to seize the speaker's role exemplifies the importance Huli place on talk as a chief medium of social activity: not merely as commentary on the action, but a key part of it.

Goldman (1983:8) further argues that there is a 'structural homology' among Huli behavioral domains predicated on 'pigs, paint, and parlance' – i.e., exchange transactions, the public display of self-decoration, and talk. These three domains are 'interchangeable modes of self-presentation' (ibid.), all modalities which men use in 'coming outside' to present themselves through display (op. cit., p.102). In subsequent clarification of this notion of homology, Goldman (pers. comm.) has emphasized that the correspondence is not posited by himself as analyst, but rather reflects a prevalent Huli view of the matter. We might note comparatively that we characterized a great deal of the 'talk about talk' at Nebilyer public events as focusing upon its interpersonal rather than experiential or textual aspects (section 5.8), and in the Nebilyer as in Huli, we find well-developed means for formulating speech as a kind of exchange (see e.g. some of the metalinguistic expressions in Appendix D). But in the Nebilyer, at any rate, the existence of these means is not the basis for elaboration of an encompassing ideology of speech as exchange; these means remain available to social actors as partial, not exhaustive, characterization of speech activity in context.

Also relevant here is M. Strathern's (1985a) argument – already cited in sections 7.4.2 and 8.1 – concerning the convertibility of Hagen institutions of disputing, warfare and exchange. This argument resonates with (and indeed draws upon) Goldman's account of Huli insofar as Strathern emphasizes that talk is regarded as continuous with other dimensions of social action, rather than constituting a privileged domain of commentary on them. Rather than being directed towards maintenance of law and order as a desired social condition, wealth exchange, dispute and display are all types of exchanges directed towards the assertion of equivalence (1985 MS, p.5, cf. also Read 1959). In overt political and judicial confrontations any of these types of exchanges (and also the exchanges of blows in warfare) are converted into others. Like the other media, talk does not transform social relations as such. Rather, it serves to explore their possible (re-)definition. Each act of conversion – e.g. from warfare to wealth exchange – sustains the convertibility of the media.

This argument of Strathern's about 'Hagen', which is meant to apply, *inter alia,* to the Nebilyer Valley[3] may in some ways seem to contradict our conclusion in Chapter 8 (in line with Benveniste 1969), that speech occupies a special place vis-à-vis other forms of action in that it is the only semiotic medium that can serve as interpretant of all the others. Not so, for at least two reasons. First, our own argument on that score was about language in general, and draws its evidence from our own analysis of what went on at the events in question, whereas Strathern's argument, like Goldman's, is basically an attempt to explicate the indigenous perspectives on the matter, and to show how it differs from our own Western ideology. Second, even from this point of view, Strathern is not claiming that speech is taken as totally equivalent to other forms of social action, nor is she denying that it functions as the interpretant of other forms of social action. What she is denying is that the moment of interpretation ('commentary') is regarded as separate from and posterior to the action which it serves to interpret '. . . talk cannot be abstracted as a commentary on acts already completed as it were – that is, as not part of the acts themselves' (1985a:128). In this respect our own findings are in complete agreement with the Hagen view being characterized by Strathern. That view may not include anything corresponding explicitly to our notion of language as the ultimate metalanguage, but it certainly does valorize speech as a form of social action, and as integral to other forms of it.

So we now proceed to ask: what kind of social order is this, in which speech is one of the most highly valued forms of action? How does speech, as one of them, relate to others? What dimensions underlie indigenous notions of action and event here? How are these dimensions noticeable in the routine activities of everyday life? And, finally, are they observable in the activities we have analyzed in the context of large scale public events?

We will approach some of these questions by examining several concepts which we think are constitutive dimensions of social action. One is a contrast between notions of concealment and revelation; another, a concern with what we call 'contingent' or 'novel juxtaposition' of elements of meaning, related to the pervasive supposition that new significance may be revealed; and a third, the kind of active, urgent disposition that characterizes much of people's social involvement. These dimensions must, in part, be seen as often observable aspects of Nebilyer subjectivity, internalized by social actors as dispositions on the basis of which they 'improvise' in characteristic ways; in part, as well, they are observable features of institutions, standardized or typical modes of acting, which we will cite as examples of the everyday.

Partly for practical and ethical reasons we have already mentioned (see Chapter 8, n.19), our exemplification of these dimensions in everyday life is not based on transcript material, but on the more usual sort of ethnographic participant observation of social life which occupied much of our time in the Nebilyer.

9.1 THE CONCEALED AND THE REVEALED IN PERSONS AND EVENTS

Important among Nebilyer concepts which can be discerned in the formulation of social action is a tension between concealed aspects of events – talk as well as other kinds of events – and a concern with discovery or revelation of that assumed hidden dimension (cf. Barth 1975, Jorgensen 1981, Wagner 1986a:133–5).

Several central Highlands ethnographers have reported indigenous views of motivations as unknowable, imperceptible and intangible. D'Arcy Ryan reported from Mendi, for example, the image of invisibility of intent:

> Certainly, there was a consistent refusal to speculate on the motivation of others, and queries in this field were invariably met with the reply: 'Do I see inside his mind?" (1961:iii)

A. Strathern (1981:229, n.4) reports an identical Hagen comment. He remarks that the unverifiability of intention invites caution, since one never knows what another person may actually be thinking. In the Nebilyer Valley, we frequently noted people's impatience with being asked to speculate about what anyone might do, on the same grounds, that one cannot know. Or, if not with impatience, people would respond with a 'Who knows?' kind of attitude, often expressed as a balanced pair of options, of the sort 'Will they give me something [e.g. for damages done to my garden by pigs], or will they not give me something?'

Yet none of this can be taken as lack of concern with what is on people's minds. Nebilyer people bring to social interaction the pervasive assumption that the actions (including talk) of others do not truly reflect their intentions, but may be intended to deceive. This assumption appears to reflect and reinforce notions of both the unverifiability and importance of what others' intentions and motives really are. The notion of intent constituted in relation to and through interaction is thus not one of its unavailability to the acting subject ('unconscious' motivation), but rather its opacity and possible concealment in relation to others. The ever-present possibility of deceit within such opacity intensifies the search for revelation of real motives, as Strathern (1972b) has reported of the conduct of disputes, and this can be a critical element in conflict resolution. A judicious and strong-minded mediator is able to direct ('dig out') the 'talk' (*ung*) in such a way that people's real motives will come out.

The pervasive assumption of possible deceit is manifested in attitudes towards theft. It occurs often enough so that people are constantly on their guard and seek to protect themselves against it. We were told that in the days before locks, strands of banana leaves were hung in house doorways. The occupants, in order to ascertain whether people had been there in their absence, would carefully suspend a difficult-to-detect article (such as a hair) on it, and look for this upon returning. Naturally everyone was familiar with the practice, so it would have had some deterrent effect.

Common among daily frustrations is the gardener's discovery that someone has stealthily dug up her sweet potatoes, or plucked ripe pandanus fruit from his tree, or picked ripe coffee from trees where it was abundant. On account of such discoveries people often set up *tambu* (Tok Pisin),[4] obstructions built across paths or around trees, which are intended to keep people out and warn would-be trespassers of the owner's displeasure at some theft or other occurrence.

People are annoyed by petty theft but do not seem to think of it as having formerly been less common. But though petty theft arouses ire, demands for damages, etc. suspicion of it does not damn the suspect and is not made an issue of abstract morality. Rather, theft is seen as something that anyone might think of and commit, given the right circumstances (except that it seems to be regarded as undignified, especially for adults, to be detected in petty delicts). Even where there exists suspicion among familiars (perhaps family members), those involved often continue on apparently amiable terms at the same time as moots etc. are held over the matter.

Equally pervasive is the suspicion that others are practising other forms of 'deception, lying' (*gol tokum, gep nokum*). The usual Tok Pisin equivalent of these indigenous phrases is *trik*, and the indigenous phrases have in common with it the fact that they may (unlike English 'lie') be applied both to deception perpetrated by saying or by other forms of doing (cf. M. Strathern 1972b:21).

Casual observation of interaction between mothers and children suggested that preparedness for the possibility of deceit may be instilled early by common and perhaps generally accepted use of it in attempts to secure children's cooperation. We have numerous diary entries of the following kind: a woman, wanting to get her reluctant child to follow, tells it: come along, we are going to eat (when the child would have very much liked this, but this was not at all the immediate purpose). Or a woman tells her child, whom she wants to persuade to go down to the Kailge display ground: People are going to give out money there!

Deceit in the collective interest can be positively valued and collectively managed. In Chapter 6 we recounted an incident in which reports by Kailge people on the condition of a Kopia man who had been injured while riding on the PMV (Public Motor Vehicle) of the neighboring Midipu were collectively managed so as to make those people believe for some weeks that he was at death's door. During that time he improved rapidly.

In the same way, we found it was extremely difficult to establish the extent of warfare injury unless we saw the wounded ourselves, because ways of talking about it tend to be dramatic, partly to protect perceived collective interests.

A. Strathern reports the salience of the Hagen concept of *noman* – which has among its senses 'will' and 'mind' – and relates this to the kinds of typical social enterprises in which people engage:

> We may expect that in a society within which individual choice, uncertainty, and strategy are overtly recognised as important, and in which an important part of social relationships consists of networks of individually created and maintained exchange ties, the idea of individually chosen action will itself be strongly conceptualised . . . (1981:282)

Strathern emphasizes, however, that *noman* cannot be adequately understood as just *individual* will, intention, desire, motivation, understanding. Proper *noman* is oriented towards maintaining relationships with others (1981:283). Indeed, an inference to be drawn from his discussion is that while *noman* is, in one sense, an aspect of the person, it can only develop through social interaction; another of the senses Strathern attributes to it is 'social consciousness'; we could also suggest 'mutuality'. Of a person who acts with due regard for public sensibility Nebilyer people may say: *numan pelym* ('she or he has mind/social consciousness').[5]

Thus, *noman* spans a range of senses from 'individual will' to 'social consciousness' (Strathern 1981:283). We think that the various uses of this concept point to an indigenous feeling for motivation as the key issue in social action.

The concept provides the main and standard way in which people can and do talk about the 'real' reasons for their actions (cf. also Strathern, ibid.). For instance, a woman of whom we asked why she had made some contributions to a *makayl* prestation, replied that the idea had formed in her mind. In saying this she was emphasizing her own authorship of the idea: it had been what she wanted to do, and was to be distinguished from her contribution to her husband's effort, for which he received direct public acknowledgment. (Cf. also Lederman 1986a:128 for an anecdote illustrating the frustration produced when a person in Mendi is denied the possibility of receiving recognition for her authorship of an action.)

Autonomous motivation is regarded as the most highly valued reason for action. Engagement of the *numan* renders action achievement or accomplishment (though, as noted, this is not to be read simply as asocial self-interest). This concept is not accompanied by a great fixity of judgment about types of action.[6] Nor is there an indigenous theory of *personality* as we know it – an elaborated notion of persons exhibiting traits continuously over time, ideally somewhat impervious to change – except insofar as the concept of *numan* bears some limited resemblance to this. A person who repeatedly succeeds in bringing difficult projects to fruition (such as arranging large and complex exchange transactions) is recognized for this. But the use of the term *numan* usually focuses on the relation between a person and a particular project which he or she has in mind (as in the case of the woman, cited above, who made *makayl* contributions), and is not especially reserved for description of persons as agents constant in their characteristics through time. Whenever a person shows himself or herself to be particularly determined, it may be said that he or she has a 'single *numan*', is single-minded; but of a person who is not able to plan or bring off a project it may be said that he or she has 'many *numan*', or is diverse-minded. The latter condition is stereotypically that of women, as Strathern (1981:283) observes, and the former that of men, but any individual, male or female, may be credited with single-mindedness for accomplishing a particular project.

Thus focusing on disposition to act in relation to particular projects or events, *numan* is not part of discourses about character or personality in general. As we suggested above, this interpretation of *numan* is consonant with, and perhaps even unites from a different perspective, the various senses of the term as discussed by Strathern (1981). Projects can be undertaken and carried out by a determined, single social actor; but some projects require the participation of many people. The same term is used to characterize dispositions to act in relation to personal and *talapi*-oriented projects.

The observer of Nebilyer social life is bound to be struck by another form of explanation of action, besides that of the project or determination formed in the mind. That is the frequency with which people say of some action or event: *we tekir* 'I am doing it for no reason'. (See e.g. Appendix A, line 406.) The adverbial *we* conveys the sense that no determination is involved, no project or end envisioned.[7] This can sometimes be a way of deflecting inquiry, but the salience of this form of explanation highlights the importance of the contrast between doing something in a determined way (in which case a person can be said to have *numan* with regard to it) and doing something that is not part of any conceived project. The fact that this is a basic contrast leads on to the important point that *numan*, though sometimes appropriately glossed as 'mind' or 'consciousness', is not to be equated in any way with concepts of self-knowledge or introspection. Simply, it focuses on the dispositions people form and engage in relation to actions and events.

Though Nebilyer/Hagen people say the disposition to act, the *numan* cannot be seen or verified,[8] it is crucially important to the undertaking and possible outcomes of action. Under these conditons of simultaneous unverifiability and importance of *numan*, the ability to reveal or draw out the concealed (as capable dispute mediators are thought able to do), to suggest interpretations of social action, is an accomplishment, the movement from the hidden to the revealed locally perceived as an *ul* 'action, event' accomplished through talk.

Is there any equivalent in events themselves to the unfathomability of the *numan*? Are other matters besides human disposition significant but unknowable? That they are, is suggested by the salience of the concept of *temal*, perhaps best translated 'omen'. Something striking or unusual, possibly counter to hope or expectation, is often taken as perhaps a bearer of meaning for the course of events – a *temal*. In Chapter 5 we mentioned two *temal* images which are somewhat standard in these public events, that of weather as an indicator of the condition of inter-*talapi* relations, and, similarly, color imagery (dark versus light, or 'black' versus 'red') as a portent of peace or hostility (section 5.4; cf. section 7.3). We noted too, that at one point in the proceedings the fact that the speaker's loincloth threatened to fall down was jokingly treated as *temal*, but here fun was made of what this rather ludicrous omen might portend; the speaker himself made a facetious suggestion that it might have something to do with the distribution of the money. In public events of this kind the possibilities of interpretation are so limited as to constitute a conventional framework of opposing options. But the possible interpretations in other contexts are not so limited, so that even what a *temal* might portend is in a sense concealed, or at least is not strictly bounded by an interpretive frame. We return in section 9.4 to find this a fundamental attitude towards the significance of events, related to actors' experimentation in various modalities with novel juxtapositions of potentially meaning-yielding resources.

There thus seems to be a common dimension in orientation both to persons and events: the possibility of concealed significance. The attentiveness to a dimension of the concealed gives to the local conception of the noteworthy event a particular inflection, as that which may be construed as having a covert dimension, something yet to be revealed. We will briefly illustrate this in respect to practices and attitudes by which things of value, aspects of persons, and food are constituted as possibly having a covert dimension capable of being explored and unpacked to reveal new significance.

9.1.1 The revelatory quality of things

The force and frequency with which Highlanders in particular, among New Guineans, have been characterized as 'primitive capitalists' (e.g. Finney 1973) does not adequately prepare one for the extent to which 'things'[9] are invested with the expectation of potential revelation.[10] In our view, this quality is sustained precisely because their significance *is* never unequivocal: valuables are used to articulate social relationships but are never a self-sufficient representation of those relationships. Hence any exchange transaction is accompanied by continuous interpretive effort in the form of talk – in the public arena, as we have seen, rhetorical torrents in which orators attempt to suggest interpretations of the present transactions and their relation to future ones.

Lederman (1986a:84) likewise has pointed out the inadequacy of a simple economistic view of exchange relations, description of them in terms of 'debt', 'credit' and the like. She characterizes Mendi exchange as consisting in contextually-differentiated gift types, each phase of transaction entailing different social obligations between giver and receiver. She too argues the irreducibility of social relations to expression by the material objects per se, and the importance of the concomitant semiotic ambiguity of objects of wealth and display:[11]

> The various kinds of wealth . . . are not clearly differentiated contextually; they are not distinguishable as mediators of different types of social relationships, nor do they circulate in separate spheres of exchange, nor is each associated with a different type of social actor. Wealth objects themselves are therefore symbolically ambiguous. Indeed, each particular item stands primarily for its own history of social linkages, and only occasionally for a transcendent social meaning. (ibid.)

It is probably in terms of indigenous efforts to explore the effects of wealth objects, and to cause them to produce social effects more clearly, that we may understand historical shifts in the valuation and currency of particular items. People in our part of the Nebilyer Valley indicate that they gave up using pearl shells in major transactions in the early 1970s. This was just around the time that some trees planted in the 1960s began to return coffee profits (see section 2.2). Formerly, shells had been curated and admired as objects of value and beauty in typical Highlands fashion.

The demise of the pearl shell as exchange item came in the wake of long-term mass importation of them into the Hagen area by Europeans (see e.g. A. Strathern 1971:108, Hughes 1978, Connolly and Anderson 1987). But the local view of the shift in valuation of the pearl shell does not invoke the European-induced increase in supply in the way we might expect. Although people realize that Europeans brought shells in large numbers, and also that typical requirements for them became much greater (by the early 1970s a bridewealth payment in this area which included fewer than about 20 pearl shells was regarded as somewhat mean, but cf. Vicedom and Tischner's 1943–48:206–7 records of Hagen-area bridewealths which typically included far fewer than seven pearl-lipped shells among other items), they never cite any of this in explanation of why the pearl shell 'went down' (*manya purum*) as a wealth object. They attribute its demise rather to their own recognition of the greater suitability and flexibility of other valuables: pearl shells were just put by in storage, and just 'lay there', they say, while money circulates. Thus the demise of the pearl shell is portrayed as the result of their recognition of superior properties of other items and their having chosen to adopt them. That this is their view, and that no nostalgia attended the shift to exchange of money, is illustrated by the fact that Nebilyer transactors say that they heaped together and burned their shells.[12] They did not passively sit by as the pearl shell 'went down', but actively declared a new era in the matter of wealth exchange by this dramatic act (see section 9.3).

We saw that careful attention was paid to choice of objects during the establishment of internal Kopia exchange relations in 1982 (section 4.1). As Lederman says for Mendi (see above), no particular kind of valuable was unequivocally considered appropriate for this kind of exchange. But, partly related to that indeterminacy, great thought was given to what it might be – what might most dramatically produce the desired effects of surprise, pleasure and estimation of worth by the recipients. We were privy to some of the discussions, as the Kopia Councillor, who was much involved in the matter, often visited us at night. So determined were the donors to create a dramatic effect by surprising the recipients with the choice of the gift item that parts of these discussions were carried on in whispers, for fear that people coming to our house or passing by might overhear. Thus we heard the relative merits of special foods such as red pandanus, taro, winged beans, combined with varying amounts of money, argued out.[13] Because these are special foods they could be used to articulate these 'new' social relations; and conversely, it was because importance was attributed to the whole scheme of establishing these relations that men vied with each other in alternatively suggesting taro, or winged beans in what sometimes seemed semi-comical whispered conversations.

There is ready acceptance of some, particular new items of self-decoration, and some of these, too, are valued – at least in part – for their possibly revelatory qualities, including their incompletely determined linkage to the unfamiliar European social order. In the Nebilyer (but also apparently in the Highlands and New Guinea very widely) wrist-watches are highly sought-after as items of adornment (where we were, people wanted Seikos with hand-action, not digital watches). These are desired as much by those who cannot tell time as by those who can; their 'utilitarian' value is certainly not of primary importance. A man to whom Francesca Merlan once remarked upon the avidity for watches made the interesting comment that they were valued because, like kina shells, they come from far away, and 'we don't know about them'.

9.1.2 Persons (especially anthropologists) as events

The film *First Contact* (Connolly and Anderson 1984), includes footage originally taken by Mick Leahy during the original Wahgi Valley expedition of 1933 (see section 2.2). Leahy succeeded in capturing on film the manner of the first reactions of central Highlanders (among them people in the vicinity of present Mt Hagen town) to the European explorers. The latter were surrounded by large crowds marveling at them and their things, so that they resorted to cordoning off their camp-sites. Their journals record how even their faeces were carefully scrutinized by Highlanders attempting to decide what kind of being they might be.

Although Hagen and Nebilyer people are now much more familiar with Europeans, we found that first reactions to us, the first Europeans to live for an extended period in the western Nebilyer Valley, were strikingly similar to scenes of nearly fifty years earlier shown in the Leahy footage (which we were able to view in Mt Hagen in 1982, after we had spent some time in the area).

Anthropology has recently confronted more seriously than ever before the question of the conditions under which ethnographic representations are produced, and the extent to which they are made possible by continually shoring up and defending certain ways of thinking about difference. Given the timeliness of these issues, it is startling – perhaps a salutary shock – to experience oneself as the 'other' battered by the onslaught of Highlanders' curiosity and numerical superiority.[14]

We described in section 9.1 the concept of *temal* 'omen' among other indications that for people of this area, a fundamental aspect of orientation to events is that they may be meaningful and portentous – there is a persistent inclination to approach them in this way – but there is not a clearly defined calculus for pre-figuring what that significance may be. The relative open-endedness of possible meaningfulness leaves ever more to be experienced and discovered, possibly even the terms in which new kinds of meanings might make sense. Related to this, we found the attitude which people evince when confronted with something novel (like us as accessible Europeans) is not aptly described as one of simple, satisfiable curiosity. It is a more rapacious desire to experience and explore the novelty for what this might make manifest about possible differences. Because people bring this disposition to encounters, what they discover can be experienced as informative about possibilities which may lie untapped within themselves.[15]

Since difference can be experienced as the uncovering of new, heretofore covert possibilities (something we explore further in sections 9.2 and 9.4), ultimately it need not produce a radical sense of disjunction between 'the way we were' and 'the way we are'. Rather, some aspects of existing practices can be seen as compatible with the new (a point we elaborated section 7.4 and also return to in section 9.4; cf. also Sahlins 1985: xii, who writes of performative social orders that value 'departures from existing arrangements, as people may then act upon them to reconstruct their social conditions'). And though the already-existing arrangements can be brought into contact with the new in an altered order, aspects of the new may become familiar without undermining the expectation that there are other aspects of an indeterminately vast 'other' yet to be discovered.

In the Nebilyer, the appearance of Europeans was (and continues to be) an event. But insofar as the European advent can be objectified as a circumstantial happening valued for the differences it may reveal, Europeans themselves can be at least partly assimilated to the already-in-existence order of those who were beyond the pre-European horizon of known peoples. From the Nebilyer perspective, foreign and unknown peoples to the south (in the Southern Highlands) are called *kewa*, a term which designated these unknown peoples in a broad way (its reference not limited to the people in the Southern Highlands who are called Kewa). These were mysterious and frightening cannibals – in fact, the Nebilyer phrase for anthropophage is *kewa nui*, the '*kewa* eater'. One way of referring to Europeans is by this term, *kewa yab*, '*kewa* people'.

9.1.3 The meanings of food

In section 9.1.1 we discussed the revelatory potential of things, especially those deemed to be particularly valuable. We mentioned food only briefly there, in relation to deliberations Kopia men made about items to be given in intra-*talapi* exchange. As that example illustrated, foods, like other things, are differentially valued depending partly on kind, and the context in which they figure. There is a relation between these two such that some foods (in our area, pandanus nuts which only grow at higher altitudes, and taro, which is also uncommon – to say nothing of pork, meats in general, and store-bought foodstuffs, for example) are considered special and are appropriately given or consumed as part of what constitutes some exchange transactions and other events as more special than others. But enormous social importance attaches to the allocation and consumption of ordinary foods in everyday life. And in everyday contexts the consumption of foods is understood to have certain social implications regular enough so that they might be called 'effects'. This stands in contrast to the potentially indeterminate and innovatory quality of foods as primarily wealth objects and display items in contexts like the Kopia intra-*talapi* distribution, where – as the planners of that occasion clearly sensed – the significance that might be attached to one item or another was more indeterminate.

In section 3.1.5 we sketched the importance of food (Ku Waru *langi*) to Nebilyer concepts of personal identity and relatedness. We observed there that Nebilyer ideas of consubstantiality are not based on genealogy but rather on the assimilation of nutritive substances (*kopong*, Tok Pisin *gris*) which ultimately derive from the ground and are absorbed through eating of foods. Related to indigenous notions of substance as derived from foods is intense interest in what people eat. This is a subject of fascination beyond anything an outsider might imagine. People are perpetually interested in what others eat and in gifts of food, even more so if the foods are delicacies and thus tokens of special recognition. People may feel a keen sense of deprivation and frustration (*popolu*, cf. M. Strathern 1968) if they think they are being slighted, or an equally keen sense of satisfaction upon being recognized by gifts of food. This satisfaction is epitomized for us in our recollection of a chance meeting with a man returning to Kailge from a feast in another locality, who happily greeted us by announcing as we passed on the path: *na kung nokur* 'I am eating pork'.

There is general great interest in what other local people eat, but the fascination in this matter is also intense in regard to the relatively unfamiliar; and accessible as we were, we had to answer many questions about European diet, and endure much speculation about our own. When asked (which was frequently), we had to list and describe European foods. Given that the European diet is known to be very different to the local one, the logic of substance urges the supposition that some other differences from local people – skin color, hair color and length, etc. – may be accounted for by the difference in the foods Europeans eat.

An aspect of the general social significance of food that comes as something of a surprise is the considerable anxiety that can surround its discretionary allocation. Inclusion in this is an important part of feeling welcome in any household. Complaints that people have outstayed their welcome are commonly expressed in terms of their 'eating up' one's food. Some of our neighbors, for instance, had living with them a long-term guest, a woman whose Enga husband evidently had no intention of returning for her from the coast where he had gone to work. As time wore on she received offers of marriage from local men, and her hosts said she should marry: she had eaten up their *langi mong*, the pick of their food, and should think of them and the fact they would receive some return in the form of bridewealth if she married.

It is a sign of good household management to be able to feed people unconcernedly, and people speak highly of those who are friendly, good managers. But feeding people can be fraught with tension if – on special occasions, or on a daily basis – the providers of food feel that they are losing discretion over it. Then, presumption upon one's food becomes a prime source of complaint and resentment against others. This has a quality akin to the sense of risk people feel about the uncertainty of exchange and the indeterminacy of future return.

Women are the chief suppliers of the daily diet, and householders are pleased if they can convey the impression of providing for visitors. They are concerned to provide special foods for special occasions; often store-bought rice, tinned fish, with hot drink and sugar, as well as salt, available. People also like to be seen to be able to unconcernedly serve ordinary foods, too, such as sweet potato and greens, to whoever is around when a meal is prepared. (Special invitations to ordinary meals are not issued.) But people still like the decision to serve a meal to be discretionary, and the unexpected appearance of guests in a household can cause annoyance and sometimes a scramble to put preparations out of sight. The other side of the coin is that proper etiquette demands that anyone approaching a homestead (who has not been summoned, or is not a household familiar) and observes eating in progress should make a point of going past as if headed elsewhere, rather than entering inopportunely. Doing the latter regularly may leave one open to the criticisms of not eating at home, coming around to scrounge, and the like. (The more eminent one is, however, the more easily one can get away with presuming on any meal or festive event, even though this may still arouse criticism and resentment.)

One woman commented that native custom is to give food to those whom one likes, and purposely withhold it otherwise. Then, she remarked, when people come and are not fed they have to think to themselves: we sat there and sat there and we were hungry. One of our close neighbors remarked several times that she never served food to her husband's parents, towards whom she felt considerable ill-will. She thought they had made insufficient effort to gather bridewealth for her. She showed Francesca Merlan a small stone she had hung in a dark corner of the house signifying the strength of her displeasure and determination not be be reconciled with her in-laws; but her main way of making her displeasure overt to them was to not serve them food.

We have indicated that the significance of foods, like that of other things of value, can be unclear and potentially revelatory, the more so in contexts in which the nature of the social relation that food transaction partly constitutes is in some sense out of the ordinary and not clearly formulable. In day-to-day domestic contexts people have a clear sense of some of the regular and multiple meanings of the allocation and consumption of foods.

9.1.4 The body as event

While *numan* is unfathomable, the condition of the body may provide direct evidence of internal dispositions and states. M. and A. Strathern (1971) discuss at length the manifestation of the quality of dispositions in bodily appearance, and good appearance as consisting importantly in shiny, taut skin, and body tone. O'Hanlon (1983) has emphasized for the Middle Wahgi the extent to which attention to appearance is focused primarily on group contexts, and good appearance is taken as indicative of the satisfactory quality of intra-segment relations.

Likewise, in the Nebilyer, bodily appearance is taken as indicative of attitude, disposition, and is even an important indication of social worth. Shining skin and generally youthful-to-mature appearance are valued, as is tall stature. People pay attention to and lament greying hair, loss of teeth, and bodily weakness in general. Women usually take pride in fecundity; childlessness is remarked upon, and regarded as a flaw. There is a version of a widely-found concept (see e.g. Meigs 1984 on the Hua of the eastern Highlands) that the supply of vital substance (*kopong* 'grease') is finite. Women who have had a number of children will say that their grease is exhausted, they have used up what they had in child-bearing and nursing, and hence now are slack-skinned, and unable to bear further.

Certain kinds of bodily abundance are taken as significant. For example, women complain that their hair is *surub* 'short', and will not grow. But that their own hair *may* be said to grow long and this unusual feature be taken as exterior manifestation of special qualities is shown by the following anecdote. The daughter of Kopia Kera saw a Tea enemy near her Sibeka garden plot during a period of intensifying hostility between Kopia-Kubuka and Tea-Dena, about twenty-five years ago. Loading her netbag with stones, she got close enough to surprise him, hurl them at him and fell him; then she ran off. The Tea were so impressed by her, this manly woman, that they importuned the Kopia to let the whole matter be settled by their taking her in marriage. She did not want to go in marriage to enemy territory, however, and refused. She later married a Poika man, thus of a *talapi* with which there were long-standing amicable relations. Her hair, it is said, grew much longer than usual from the time of the Sibeka incident.

There are no people living the rural Nebilyer life-style who grow fat; the life is physically too demanding. People tend rather to be well-muscled and strong unless afflicted by disease or weakened by age. But they do occasionally see fat townspeople, New Guineans as well as Europeans. Bodily abundance tends rather to be admired unless truly excessive, in which case it seems to be found frightening. The basis of this fright once again seems to be the concept that bodily substance is to be accounted for by what one eats. What could people eat to achieve this size? And what kind of creature could be the result? When our valley was visited by two collectors from the Museum of Brussels, one of whom was very tall and fat, people wondered to us: 'What does he eat?'. To our horror and dismay, he innocently and jokingly managed to convey through gesture and in broken Tok Pisin to the crowds of children who followed him around that he ate children. The report spread quickly up and down the valley, and we were questioned about him for weeks after his departure. Their darkest suspicions were confirmed: a self-confessed *kewa nui*!

One is scarcely prepared for the close scrutiny of one's body (by members of one's own sex) that one is subject to. People seize one's hands, arms and legs, examine for bruises or new marks, run hands through one's hair (and also, may seek to inquire about or examine whatever one is carrying unless discouraged from doing so). The most uninhibited in all this are the children, but it is noticeable that adults are also very aware of such things, especially changes in bodily condition. Here again, it is not that there is a definite calculus for determining the significance of all of these aspects of bodily condition, but rather that they are taken as indications of possible significance.

As in the Hagen area, much effort goes into the creation of effect through body decoration in public display. Sporadic bouts of warfare occurring in the western Nebilyer also provided the chance for us to learn that many people dress carefully when going out to the battle lines (though not as elaborately as for other public display). They will get new leaves to cover the buttocks and borrow new, bright-colored *wanya* (caps) in order to create a good appearance. During one battle, a man of a neighboring *talapi* (who shortly after became Councillor there) scored something of a coup by managing to borrow and wear a chain-mail vest belonging to his father-in-law, who had traded it for his hair-wig to the Museum of Brussels collectors when they passed through our end of the Nebilyer Valley.

As we have described, people's general disposition towards events is to anticipate that which may upset complacency, causing a ripple or stir. But though this may be an interesting, and in some ways sought-after experience, there is a concept that such an experience also disequilibrates. When attributable to a particular source, the disequilibrium should be mediated by a gift which compensates the person whose condition has been altered.

A common way of expressing fright and surprise, shock, or disequilibrium is by the expression: *na miniwal pukum* (lit.) 'my spirit goes' (*mini-wal* 'soul-bag'). There are certain non-linguistic concomitants of such disequilibrium. For example, older people who unexpectedly saw us, unknown Europeans, walking around in areas remote from town would often continue to approach us, shaking their heads in amazement and whistling intermittently on a single pitch. (This fashion seems not to be reproduced among younger people.) Generally, when they got close they would shake hands and continue expressing amazement, either by exclamations such as a! a! a!, or more elaborately to any local person with us (since they generally assumed we would not understand). As this description suggests, the manifestation of such disequilibration is itself something of a conventionalized display, a performance of amazement. People did not generally make any requests in these circumstances.

But sometimes people will demand compensation from the one who produces this effect on them. One day a Kailge woman who had always seen Francesca Merlan with her hair pinned up came into our house compound for a chat, and found her walking around with her longer-than-shoulder length hair down. She made a few exclamations and seemed, for a moment, to be genuinely discomfited. She then demanded some money (not a specified amount). This was the first example of compensation-for-disequilibrium which began to make clear to us what was involved. People are disposed to appreciate the novel, unexpected or unfamiliar, but finding it, may register a shock. The rapid transition from one condition to another is ideally compensated by a gift (cf. Schwimmer 1974, Schieffelin 1976, Hallpike 1977:234 on claiming compensation for upset of the emotions).

9.2 CONTINGENT JUXTAPOSITION

In the previous section we exemplified extensively the pervasive assumption of covert significance, showing in the process that there are some kinds of events – signally including persons, and many kinds of social encounters and transactions which are dialogic by nature – which are inherently filled with revelatory potential, others (like conditions of the body, less immediately transacted and transactable among social actors) which are thought to index the unknown in ways that appear to be indigenously viewed and commented upon as more standardized registers of 'effects'.

A second, constitutive dimension of Nebilyer social action is what we call *contingent juxtaposition*. To illustrate what we mean by this, we will here cite just one institutional practice of everyday life, a certain aspect of Nebilyer naming; but we will return in section 9.4 to develop the point that many important meaning-making resources we discussed in the context of our analysis of public exchange transactions also exemplify this dimension, and that indigenous notions of 'event' and the particular nature of novelty are importantly related to it.

To make clear the significance of the example, it is necessary first to briefly outline certain (other) structural bases of Nebilyer naming practices. As in Mt. Hagen (A. and M. Strathern 1968), a pervasive gender dichotomy underlies certain fairly structured areas of male-female differentiated names. Many boys' names are after birds of the air (e.g. *dowa* 'eagle'), some of which are birds particularly recognized for their beauty and sought-after plumage (*kuruwi, parka, suba,* birds of paradise). Girls are less frequently given the names of birds, and these are limited to the less spectacular birds of the ground (*porltap* 'chicken'). There is thus a metonymic relation between 'boys/male' and 'upper/air', and between 'girls/female' and 'below/ground', which is based upon and in each case restates the proportion male:sky::female:ground.

While girls are frequently given the names of exchangeable wealth objects (*sumuyl* 'gold-lipped pearl shell', *moni* from Tok Pisin 'money', *toya* from Tok Pisin 'toea', and so on), males are only rarely given such names (but we know of both men and women named after the bailer shell, *tami* or *taim*). A few male names are those of particularly sturdy forest trees which evoke an image of solidity and *immobility* (see the discussion in section 5.4 of the person, especially the male person, as a 'strong' thing). These parts of the naming system assume a gender dichotomy as a basis of signification. The association of female with below/ground resonates with aspects of female demeanor in the public domain where men are also present: women sit in groups on the margins of display grounds while men sit, but may also stand and speak, in the center; if women must cross a public space during a public gathering they bend their heads down and move rapidly in a semi-crouching posture.

To turn now to what appears to be a different basis of naming more inclusive than the foregoing, names which fall within the semantic fields mentioned above, as well as names which have other semantic bases, are frequently given in commemoration of a particular event at or around the time of birth, a 'natal event'. About 1960, men from Kopia killed a Dena man. A European patrol officer came into the Kailge area and jailed those who were considered trouble-makers. A Kailge woman who bore a male child just at that time named him Wai, and this is said to be in commemoration of the *banis waia* (Tok Pisin 'wire fence') in which the men were held in captivity.

Another boy born about the same time was called 'Ambak', from Tok Pisin 'humbug', a name which again commemorates the troubles of that period.

The name of another boy, Pai, has a somewhat more complicated mode of relation to historical associations. The word *pai* means 'pet', as in the term *owa pai* 'pet dog'. At the time of the boy's birth, his father was away for a time on the other side of the Tambul range. A Kailge clan-brother of the boy's father helped the mother with chores, chopping wood for her, and helped look after the boy. This man named the boy, calling him 'Pai' because, as he explained to us, his own name is Owa 'dog'. The sense of this is not self-evident, because *owa pai* means 'pet dog', not 'dog's (own) pet'. Yet the latter seems to be the sense he intended in giving this playful name. He remarked that had the child been a girl, he would have received something from her bridewealth payment by now.[16]

This man, Owa, was himself named during a period of fighting in the western Nebilyer. He said his name alludes to the fact that dogs are aggressive and bite people, and it was given to commemorate this particular period of unrest. So, too, was a contemporary of his named Opa 'fight' during this time.

A woman, Pilya 'mushroom', was so named by her mother because she was picking mushrooms on the day of the birth.

A woman we regularly visited with gave birth to a daughter on a day when we joined other people of her hamlet in roofing a house. Hearing that the child had been born, Alan Rumsey suggested to her husband the name *kolu* 'wild sugar cane grass', which we were cutting as thatch. He liked the idea, but then later gave the child the name *kiya* 'torch', which is one of the other uses to which the grass is put. He attributed main authorship of the idea to Alan, nevertheless, despite having modified it somewhat.

An increasing number of people are given forms of European names, and it appears that now these do not necessarily commemorate a knowledge of or relationship with any particular European (though they are certainly an important manifestation of the intensified relation to introduced institutions in general). But earlier, some babies who were given European names were named after particular people, such as storemen at the Kuta (Ku Waru Kusa) store established by the Leahy brothers (see section 2.2). In these cases the Europeans themselves, or a particular meeting with them, were special events commemorated by naming, so that these names were given on the same basis of contingent relation of the birth to another event as the others described above.

This kind of naming is based on a relation of contiguity between some event and the birth, the latter commemorated by a name which alludes to the former. We have seen that there are some structural bases, such as the opposition male:female, which bound what may typically count as names. Thus it is not the complete absence of structure that is striking about these onomastic practices. But rather, even where such patterning is patent, it is the contingent association of natal event with another which is the most salient factor in the selection of a particular name, and determines that *it* be given rather than some other which would be equally acceptable on structural grounds.

In Nebilyer naming practices, certain elements of pattern are uncontested and backgrounded typifications (the most obvious example, which we have illustrated above, is that of gender difference); but beyond this, those elements do not provide the rationale for the selection of a particular name. The main structural pattern in terms of which these forms are considered names is precisely that they commemorate contingencies contemporaneous with the birth, rather than conform to some predictable pattern.[17] Nor is there a clearly defined framework for interpreting the possible significance of the relation between natal event and the life course of the individual whose name alludes to it. The name seems to abide as a possible but unexplored source of meaning, its main effect residing in its evocation of specific circumstances. Such names have in common with 'food names' (see A. Strathern 1977a) the fact that they are based upon and evoke a historically particular event or circumstance (in the latter case a specific act of commensality).

9.3 ACTIVE DISPOSITION

The emphasis upon disposition to act (section 9.1) is manifested in the generality and high valuation of a particular actional style. People are usually not content to simply let events unfold or happen. More prevalent is a style according to which people seek to actively grasp events, make plans, make things happen. This emphasis was obvious at Kailge in such matters as the course of women's club activities, the plans of the Councillor's wife to start a store, a young man's seizing upon his in-laws' suggestion that he go work for his wife's uncle in Port Moresby, secretive planning concerning what items might be given in the developing internal Kopia exchange prestations, and in many other matters. The energetic planning and intention to grasp situations is consonant with a sense of urgency which people express, reflected in conventional remarks which they often make and which contribute to the setting of interactional tone: *ena pora nyikim* 'the sun/time is finishing' (i.e., time is passing, we must get on with things), *ena pukum* 'the time/sun is going', *lo oba tekim* 'it's about to start raining' (the implication again being, let's get on with things), and so forth. Sometimes remarks such as these are made early in the day, an indication that they may not be understood simply as references to the actual time of day, but are part of the construction of events. They convey a sense of urgency and open-endedness about what may be done to move events along and discover what they hold in store.

The concomitant – and opposite – of the sense of urgency in relation to events and the desire to discover their potential is a sense of surfeit, malaise or boredom to which people frequently give expression. When people become exasperated with humdrum, feel a lack of things happening, they say: *(na) enebu tokum* '(I'm) bored, fed up' and the like. Though we may find it difficult to imagine acceptable use of the expression 'I'm bored' to excuse ourselves from a situation, Nebilyer people may say this as a way of taking their departure. If a person has sat playing cards for a long time in public, he or she may easily say, *Na enebu tokum, pukur* 'I'm fed up, I'm going'. The apparently greater acceptability of this over its English 'equivalent' seems to be due to the fact that it is taken as an expression of one's own experience of disengagement, and need not be taken as a comment on the quality of other people's sociality. At any rate, the inverse of the disposition to actively grapple with events is this clear formulation of a concept that nothing worthwhile is happening.[18]

The urgent personal style that people often bring to events is manifested in the near-impatience to get things moving, and in the close, ebullient and sometimes invasive scrutiny or inquiry of persons and objects that we discussed above in relation to the expectation of the revelatory quality of events. However, it must also be pointed out that people are often critical of this prevalent style, and oppose it by their disparagement of headlong action and high valuation of calm consideration and the ability to persuasively influence and shape the interpretation of events. For instance, in the Nebilyer, as in Hagen (A. Strathern 1971:79–80) men who advocate a headlong plunge into warfare are considered hotheaded and are generally less influential overall than those who are considered capable of intensive discussion and sorting out of affairs.

In section 9.1.1, we cited an example of shift in valuation of the kina shell which was ratified around the time that Nebilyer people began to realize monetary returns from their coffee plantings. We pointed out that people did not passively watch the 'fall' of the kina shell, but organized collective burning of much of their pearl shell wealth, dramatizing to themselves their active participation in a new era of wealth objects. Related to this, we suggested, is the fact that they do not (in our area, at least) relate European importation of shell to its devaluation, though they are well aware of the great numbers of them introduced, for example, by the Leahy brothers across the valley. Instead, people talk of their own realization of the superiority of money as wealth object.

Similarly, Connolly and Anderson (1987:267) recount collective burning of shields and weapons in the eastern Nebilyer Valley (close to the Leahy brothers' Kuta store); here, once again, people collectively declared their sense of, and desire for, active participation in new aspects of the socio-political order they perceived the European advent to inaugurate, rather than merely construing their role as to passively accept an order imposed upon them from without.

9.4 CONCLUDING REMARKS: ACTION AND MEANING

In section 9.1.3 above, we have suggested that a particular indigenous emphasis on the emergent and performative (rather than prescribed) nature of events can be related to assumptions concerning the importance as well as the ultimately unknowable nature of motivation and disposition to act, and further, of general potential for disparity between the apparent and the concealed. The first of these relates to a premium on action taken to be the result of engagement of the *numan*. The second, the potential for disparity, is part of a tendency to place emphasis not upon a notion of the replication of existing patterns or action types through particular tokens of them, but upon 'event' as that which is suggestive of further, unexplored significance. In other words, indigenous emphasis and interest is *not* focused upon the conformity of action to structural 'types', but upon 'event' as that which may offer the possibility for revelation of meaningfulness and exploration of the difference this makes. This is consistent with the fact that in Ku Waru, as in Melpa, a single term *ul* is used in ways that could be alternatively glossed in English as either 'structural type' *or* 'event' (or, more colloquially, 'matter', 'affair', 'concern', 'activity', cf. A. Strathern 1982:293). And, in reference to language, the single term *ung* covers the senses of the linguist's *langue*, language as a set of types, and *parole*, speech, utterance in context, situated speech *event* (cf. section 5.8).

Returning, then, to our question at the start of this chapter about what kind of social order this is, we may ask: in what sense is this an emphasis upon 'novelty'? What kind of 'invention' (Wagner 1975) is this, and what modes of social action does it involve? In order to be able to address these questions in a more general way, we will first consider what there is in common as between the everyday practices we have been discussing so far in this chapter, and those discussed in the preceding eight.

In section 5.4 we described the place within political rhetoric of the highly valued resource of *ung eke* 'bent speech'. Though our examination was limited to its use in that context, A. Strathern (1975:190) notes and illustrates Melpa use of allusive speech across a range of activity types including children's games, songs, and disputes, and *moka* prestations. We noted that in public speech *ung eke* is considered a difficult accomplishment, evincing illumination of the mind – but not primarily because the images orators deploy are perceived as novel ones. Rather, the achievement is evaluated as the strategic deployment of by-and-large familiar images of known general sense, within political contexts such that possibilities for future political action are suggestively foreshadowed. Certainly not the effect of such public rhetoric, nor probably even speaker intention, could be aptly described as overt shaping of a single public interpretation of events. Rather the use of *ung eke* is a form of persuasive action that presupposes the importance of disposition, engagement of the *numan*, as that which shapes cooperation (cf. Lederman 1986a:30). Actors in the public arena suggest political possibilities in relation to what are seen (perhaps from a number of diverse perspectives) as the circumstances and relevant background of the present event, and are acknowledged according to the suggestiveness of that refraction.

We note the similarity of the basic form of action involved here to that which we found in naming practices (section 9.2). There, we observed that it is not that typical structures of naming are lacking, but rather that these alone cannot account for the selection of one name rather than another in particular instances. And further, indigenous emphasis is placed on what *can* account for this, namely, the giving of a name which commemorates some contingency contemporaneous with the birth. In just the same way, the indigenous appreciation of *ung eke* does not focus on the issue of the absolute novelty, or otherwise, of the tropes, which as we have seen (section 5.4) are generally, like names, tokens of a number of well-known types. Here again, indigenous evaluation of their poignancy focuses on the suggestiveness of their use in relation to specific circumstances.

Another speech resource we showed to be pervasive is rhetorical parallelism – usually of paired,[19] successive lines so that the binarism of options being presented is iconically mapped onto the formal structure. Consider some of the standard tropes exhibiting such rhetorical parallelism: 'if you want to carve/cradle it' (the payment); 'if you want to bake-consume/cook-consume it';[20] 'if you see a red/black lake'; 'if you go to the forest/cultivated area', etc. These are paired options of familiar general sense; but note that the conclusion, the apodosis, is generally a single one, not paired: 'do so', 'consider it', or the like. No particular outcome or course of action which varies with each option is overtly prescribed. Rather, appeal is made to the perceptiveness and capacity for engagement of the hearers; and this is consonant with modes of (political) action in which disposition and autonomy are both recognized as important, and in which contingency in both assumed and reproduced.[21]

So far we have returned to mention specifically linguistic resources of the public domain; but each can be seen as encompassed within a broader mode of binary juxtaposition of elements as meaningful action, where outcome/significance is not clearly prefigured, but in which *the* signal outcome is reproduction of the possibility of option, the relevance of that which is not yet certain, and of engagement of actors in taking up the possibilities for future action.

Not only is binary juxtaposition the salient mode of action in use of (*ung eke* and parallel) speech resources in general, but we have already indicated (Chapter 8) how it underlies the constitution and revaluation of relationships within the political order: exchange-mediated relations of difference, and conjunctive relations of sameness. While in the literature (e.g. A. Strathern 1975) emphasis has been placed upon large scale inter-group events and the kinds of action that go on there as validatory, we have emphasized that generally pairwise political relations of all the kinds we have described are known not to be, and are not taken as immutable social facts; and that contexts of activity such as warfare payments cannot be seen just as confirmations of existing relations, but equally are contexts in which relations of sameness and difference can be subjected to risk and revaluation by the same modes of action which at other times may confirm them. Again, a signal outcome of such events is that political relations are seen as mutable products of human agency. This mutability precludes the building up of encompassing, dualistic frameworks which replicate and magnify pairwise difference.

We argued in section 8.3 that Nebilyer segmentary relationships cannot be regarded as a form of dual organization in the Lévi-Straussian sense, but that they are instances of a more general Nebilyer habitus of pairing. In light of the discussion in section 5.7, and in sections 9.1 to 9.3, we can now also distinguish that habitus from systems of dual *classification* (of which dual social organization is sometimes taken as a special instance, or sociological infrastructure, as in Durkheim and Mauss 1963).

In section 8.1 we said that Nebilyer serial pairing could not provide the basis for any single over-arching dual organization, because such pairings were non-transitive and non-exclusive. This is consistent with what we showed in section 5.7 about the nature of Ku Waru pairing as a form of classification: each term can enter into any number of different pairings with other terms, each of which draws upon a different aspect of its meaning. Accordingly, these too are non-transitive relations: e.g. 'dog' is paired with both 'pig' and 'marsupial', but this implies nothing about the relationship between 'pig' and 'marsupial'.[22] But in light of our discussion in sections 9.1–3, we can now see more clearly that different pairings, in drawing upon different aspects of meaning, do not merely bring out something that was already known to have been there.

Rather, the activity of pairing (or 'making twos', as it is called) in segmentary relations and elsewhere in Nebilyer social life, is a form of juxtaposition by which people work to reveal and act upon new or previously latent aspects of what is.

Consider also juxtapositions effected by the Kulka women's club. They drew on practices that have precedents in the realm of segmentary politics, such as the acceptance of political relations of enmity construed at the level of segmentary actors, and the possibility of conversion or mediation of those relations. But they brought such practices into relation with others that they see as belonging to the new action/meaning order of *gavman lo*, including the notion of a new kind of equivalence and acquiescence of all segmentary actors in relation to it. It would appear that what people most appreciate in such juxtapositions is the sense, not simply of the 'novel' as an absolute value – that never seen or known before – but of how they highlight new relational possibilities for the exploration and constitution of action without forcing a radical sense of separation between what was and what is. Thus, as we observed in section 2.3, contrasts such as that between *bo* and *kewa* styles of action need not be uniformly antithetical, but can be placed in relation to each other to highlight new possibilities for constituting action – not amounting to assimilation of the social order to 'contingent circumstances' (Sahlins 1985: xii) which can be objectively defined as such, but reproducing the potential for revaluation of experience. To illustrate by means of another previously given example, the collective action of burning kina shells might seem like a complete break with the past in the face of the 'contingency' of European advent – but was it? In the indigenous view, when confronted with other possibilities the kina gave way to revaluation, and while people might sometimes wonder at their previous simplicity in having curated shells that 'only lay there', nevertheless they credit to themselves as their own 'invention', in Wagner's (1975) terms, the appreciation of superior values.[23]

Part of what we have shown by relating modes of action of the public domain to those of everyday life is that these continuities lie not in indigenous conceptualization of action considered as separate from it, but in ways of acting/meaning where these must be taken as simultaneous. As to the more specific question concerning the nature of Nebilyer social order, we have shown that ways of acting/meaning both assume and reproduce a specific notion of contingency – that which is possible but not certain – as fundamental medium and outcome, but that this amounts to a continual possibility of revaluation by juxtaposition of partly-known terms, rather than to a notion of frame-breaking novelty.

The Nebilyer emphasis on simultaneity of action and meaning brings us back to the way we opened the main argument of this book (in section 1.2). As a way of setting up the question of who conducts exchange, we began with a close critical reading of opposing answers to it in two accounts of Enga *tee* exchange, trying to tease out some fundamental difficulties with the way the question was being asked. We sought thereby to motivate an alternative approach in which we would pay close attention to the 'representational' or semiotic dimensions of exchange transactions. Having begun by thus opposing our approach to that of Feil and Meggitt, we would like to close by highlighting what it has in common with theirs, in opposition to most semiotic ones.

What we share with them is a central concern with just such questions as 'Who conducts exchange?' – questions of agency and social action, which our analysis is not intended to supplant, but to help answer. This proposed alliance runs counter to a tendency in anthropology for questions of 'meaning', 'symbolism' or 'culture' to be separated from those of intentional, interested *action* in the social world where those symbols are used.[24]

Against the approach of Feil and Meggitt, which eschews questions of meaning, we have argued that action cannot be understood without including meaning in the picture. Having now tried to develop an analysis which does so, we want to close by pleading the converse: for students of 'meaning' to pay close attention to how the meaningful forms ('types') are *used* in situated social action.

There are at least two good reasons for doing so.

First, it is only by attending to the pragmatic dimensions of semiosis – the relation of signs to their contexts of use – that semiologists (including linguists) and cultural anthropologists can develop a productive working relationship with other investigators of a more materialist bent, such as demographers, archeologists, political economists, and many social anthropologists. In our case, we hope our close examination of the situated discourse of Nebilyer segmentary politics has shed light upon processes of social reproduction, contestation and transformation which are by no means purely discursive, but in which speech plays an essential part along with (and more-or-less integral to) other practices such as specific forms of warfare, marriage, animal husbandry, gardening, etc. We, the authors, are more expert in recording and analyzing speech than gardening or pig-rearing practices, and this probably influences our point of view on Nebilyer social reproduction generally, but there is no doubt that we are talking (e.g. in Chapter 8) about what is broadly the same social order as that described and analyzed from various viewpoints in the massive literature by A. and M. Strathern and others mentioned in section 2.4., many of whose findings have further illuminated ours, and, we hope, vice versa. Such mutual illumination is only possible on condition that cultural or semiotic analysis not lose touch with what Geertz (1973:30) calls the 'hard surfaces of life . . . within which [people] are everywhere contained'. The best way to meet this condition is, we suggest, to train the analysis on concretely situated social action.

The other reason for our plea for an action-oriented semiology follows from Wagner's injunction that anthropologists respect the 'inventiveness of their "subject peoples", so as not preempt their creativity within our own invention' (Wagner 1975:159; cf. introduction to this chapter). For wherein lies that inventiveness if not in situated action? Recall, for example, what is common to the creative, relevatory quality of Ku Waru personal names and of the best *ung eke* oratory: it is not seen to reside in the name itself, or in the oratorical trope *qua* trope, but in the way they are deployed in relationship to some specific context. This is consistent with the Ku Waru use of the word *ung* cited above, which subsumes both *langue* (language system) and *parole* (situated speech event), a usage for which there is an exact parallel in the Daribi language studied by Wagner (1978:55). It is impossible to begin to do justice to the brilliance of Nebilyer oratory as *langue*, much less to its most accomplished practitioners, such as Noma, without full verbatim transcripts of particular instances of it, and background such as we have provided in relation to the Marsupial Road War payment. An added advantage of verbatim transcripts in a work such as this is that they allow us to study the meaning of action, not as something 'purely subjective and personal' (Wagner 1988:xi), but as a public, social creation. Such transcripts cannot take the place of more strictly anthropological forms of invention, but can in turn provide a highly useful context for them, as we hope to have shown in the later chapters of this book. Moreover they allow us to develop those inventions in close counterpoint with those of the actors themselves.

Appendices

Appendix A: Transcript of proceedings at compensation payment to Laulku by Kopia-Kubuka at Kailge, July 24, 1983

For details concerning the staging of this event, and analysis of many of the speeches, see Chapters Five and Six. Most of the placards on which the money was displayed had inscriptions, which read as in the first two columns below. The third column shows the *talapi* segments with which the respective contributions were later identified. (The spellings used in the first column are not necessarily the ones used on the signs, which were read out by Alan Rumsey for the tape, but not written down at the time).

1. *Lain bilong Dama*	200 K	(Kubuka\Ping\Komolab)
2. *Lain bilong Lkuraya*	250 K	(Palimi\Kuluwa)
3. *Lain bilong Kupena*	220 K	(Kopia\Galka)
4. (no name posted)	600 K	(Kopia\Kupena-Tolab)
5. (no name posted)	200 K	(Kopia\Ukulupiyl)
6. *Lain bilong Unya*	200 K	(Kubuka\Alyimula)
7. *Lain bilong Waria*	25000K*	(Kopia\Kabika)
8. *Lain bilong Tamalu*	200 K	(Kubuka\Ping\Kilib)
9. Kubuka Kudul	250 K	(Kubuka\Kuduyl)
10.(no name or amount posted)		

* Given the total amount which was later added up, this should apparently have said 250 K.

Transcription conventions followed below are: speakers' (*talapi* + personal) names in capital letters, each in a full line preceding the speaker's first words; plain type face for Ku Waru (or Meam) words, italics for interlinear glosses and English or Tok Pisin words used in the speeches; background information, interpretive comments, or other interpolations enclosed in square brackets. To facilitate the identification of segmentary person values (as in section 5.2), English glosses which would not otherwise carry over the relevant information about number (e.g. the pronoun 'you', and imperative verbs) are further specified as either singular (*sg*), dual (*du*), or plural (*pl*) (cf. Appendix B.3).

KUBUKA TAMALU

1 wiyl-ala yi el mulurum aki-yl nabisiyl
how many people from up there [over the Tambul Range] were wounded in the fighting?

ya mongu mel-we kolsi pirim
there was a bit of trouble here

yi akul wiyl-ala nabisiyl toku nokun
man from up there, how much tobacco do you (sg) smoke?

buai mong nokun, *kapis* nokun
how much betel nut do you (sg) chew? How much cabbage do you (sg) eat?

ilyi-nga i tekin nyikir
this is what you (sg) do, I say [i.e., you can take the money and buy those things with it]

ekepu ul aki-yl-nga nabitiyl ya ul layiri-layiri olyo ya tirim
but what about this little problem --- this thing that happened to us?

ilyi lyip kuni teab-a
that's what I want to straighten out

aki-yl ya lyip kuni tep-ne
and in order to straighten this out

na nanu tep ku awilyi-yl na nanu sing-iyl
I myself have raised a lot of money

bonunga Kopia-ka-kin sukud muduk sing
yesterday the Kopia (pl) contributed

ekepu na-nga ku-yl midi lelym-o
now I alone have the money

meb i pu-bu tekir
I want to take it

oba ku *sikis handet* tepa na nanu sukud mudupa sim
'he' (sg) [i.e., the Kopia] gave me six hundred ['pounds']

na nanu *foa handet* tid
I myself [i.e., Kubuka] gave four hundred

tausen-ilyi lyikir ekepu-nga ku *lep* nabisipa kolsi peba
I'm taking this thousand, and how much will be left over?

aki-yl-nga kanap-lyanga nyibu
when I see, I will say

ya yi ku ilyi-nga korup nu pilyani nyib nyikir
when I have found out, you (sg) listen and I will tell you [Laulku]

yabu bo kanu-ma-nga naa pukur-o
I'm not 'going to' specific relatives and trading partners [i.e., this is a block payment to Laulku]

ne tiluri waka-na nabisilya i nyib-ayl-nga
how much will be left over up there? [on the display boards], is what I'm asking

aki-yl lyip kuni tep-lyanga pamilyi
having straightened this out, let's go [to Poika Wangi's funeral]

aki-yl midi lyip kuni teab-o i nyikir
I just want to straighten this out, that's what I say

ya kang yi-ka eneni ilyi-nga na kani ne-ala ilyi-nga pely-ayl ku anum-uyl ang singilyi
since I myself live over there [where it's hard to grow coffee] brother! [addressed to Laulku], these fellows have given me lots of money

ne ulu mel-we
this is just a trifle

ne manya kang-kil eneni nabitiyl-a
you (pl)[Kubuka] fellows down there, how much do you have?

ne kopia waria nunu telyti aku-mel tekin yad pui i nyaba
you (sg) [the other Kubuka] should do as Kopia Waria does; go join him, is what I want to say

ku *handet* aku-ma tep-kin ne ku mong *lep* kolsi pim-lum
when we count how many hundred there are, if there's some left [over and above the one thousand 'pound' mark]

ya lyik eneni kopia-ka terilek
you (pl) Kopia take it and put it together

nabolka yabu-ma-nga ul mong mare kaningi
what people will help see [you] through [your] troubles [i.e., fight with you as allies]

ilyi-nga lyik kuni teang ilyi-nga nyimulu tekumul, ilyi nyikir
that's what you (pl) should straighten out; that's what we want to talk about, I say

30 ya we ung-ma ekepu nu midi bonunga talko-ma naa un-iyl
yesterday and the day before we made speeches for nothing; you (sg) didn't come

kolsi nyibu nyikin pilyin-lum aki-yl nyani
now if you (sg) want to say a little, go ahead and speak

wiyl-ala-ma kep ya manya-ma kep olyo wiyl-ala bonunga talko-ma
the people from up there and we from down here, those who were here yesterday and the day before

mujika-laulku-ma langi supingi tungi tungi el ung nyik nuimka-yl palum
the Mujika-Laulku, feasted and talked el ung *until their throats were sore*

ung kalya-yl-nga ekepu ya kor oba pirim
speeches of that kind have already been made

35 ekepu ya kola lku-na wiji lyikim mel-ayl samiyl
now the mourning house is beckoning [i.e. we must go to Poika Wangi's funeral], so let us give these things quickly

adi yabu kaningi yabu mare naa okumil-na tep molumulu, yi-ma sukud naa okumil
the people who were to come and watch are not coming; men are not coming

i nyikir
that's what I say

[These are Tamalu's last words. They are followed by 13 seconds of inaudible unfocussed talk. Kujilyi's first audible words are as follows]

MIDIPU KUJILYI

yi kudulyi-yl ung nyilkuna ilyi aima age anum-uyl nyikir
for what you (sg) say, 'red' man, I say thank you very much

KUBUKA TEPRA

eni manya molung-ko
you (pl) remain seated

40 kung mabola kalung-i
have you (pl) put on pig grease? [i.e., you haven't, so you can't speak]

ung pilyik takan molung-ko
listen and be quiet [strong command form meaning literally: 'you (pl) have been quiet']

KUBUKA UNYA

kang-kiyl perepera tokun ola-ko modukun
boy! stand up and wave your hands [to silence the crowd]

ya med okun nyin
come (sg) out here and talk

MIDIPU KUJILYI

aima ku-yl ya, ku-yl tekin kakana monsum ilyi aima age anum-uyl nyikir
here you (sg) are giving a lot of money, I say thank you very much

45 ya ul na-nga-yl mong kani-yl sika
the trouble was certainly mine

ekepu yi-te lelka-ja pe ku-ma-n ekepu yi tansini
if a man had died, oh money, could you (sg) replace a man?

mel keri kuku lepa marai kara lepa medin kola topa telym nyilymeli
the thing which is said to have the effect of contorting the mouth, wasting the shins, yellowing the moustache

mel kani-yl ekepu adi lyid ekepu idi kor lyikin-ilyi
that's the thing I took on over there, and now you (sg) (Kopia) are also taking it [i.e., the fight] on

pe ekepu tep tebu mel nar
and I don't know what I'll do

50 ekepu antipe yi-yl kolupa nyim-lum
now if a distant man [Laulku Wama] dies

adi wanap ka tokun modukun-ayl
you (sg) will make a first [interim] payment [wanap ka: see section 4.1]

penga yi mini tekin
and later you (sg) make a big compensation payment

mola yi molupa nyim-lum memi kona-yl pe tekin
or if he lives, you (sg) will pay for 'new blood'

memi kona pe telymeli mel naa tekin
you (sg) are not giving as they do when they pay for 'new blood'

ya el telymeli *plan* nyilymeli mel tekin
you (sg) are giving as they do when making plans to fight

ya meri kolya-ma topa kalapa tim ul-ma pabiyl nyid
the place was on fire down there [at Sibeka], so I said 'let us two go'

kupulanum ilyi pe
this is the sort of procedure

aki-tikin uj pul moluba, kopu leba, polu tekin ama tokun
you (sg) do like that, and if there's a rocky hill [between you] you (sg) can break it and build a bridge [i.e., establish good relations]

gai puku tani i nyib notip tekimul
'may you (sg) divide the sweet potato', we're doing that

ime-nga na *amamas* tekir, aima age anum-uyl nyikir
and I'm happy about it, thank you very much, I say

ilyi *namba wan poin*
that's the first point

namba tu, ul pulu-yl ilyi na pilyip tudukur-kiyl el-ayl
secondly, as for the source of the trouble, I know about this fight

ilyi pilyip tudukur pe timul-kin tep-kin ekepu ne nanga kangi-na leba
I don't understand it, we fought, and it will be 'on my skin' [my liability] over there

na pe tep nyibu mel nar ilyi na pilyip tudukur-o
having done it, what can I say? this I do not know

ya ekepu nu-nga yalamuyl ekepu pilka tokun tekin-ayl
now you (sg) are shelling your betel nut

na-nga kangi pol-na notidani
and putting it on my palm [i.e. passing the responsibility on to me]

ilyi-nga ekepu nu ung-te *skelim* tep naa nyibu molkur-kiyl
so I'm just going to stay here without making a speech

na nanu yalamuyl pilka tum akin nyidu-mel nu molku pilyani
when my betel is shelled, you (sg) can stay and listen

pe yi lupu-ma molku pilyik teangi
and let other men stay and listen

idi el-ayl kang-te ya molku-lyanga kung-te tongi
in the fighting, some fellows will kill a pig

ab-te tongi ya, ul nabolka ul-te tim akin
they'll rape women, or whatever

ab paka naa tui ya, pe kung paka naa tui
don't you (sg) help in the matter of the woman or the pig

pe lku *brukim* tekin ku *tausen*-te lyini-ko
or if you (sg) break into a store and steal a thousand [kina?]

paka naa tui nyilym kalya-yl, el ul-iyl ul kit-iyl
don't help; fighting is a bad thing

ekepu el kupada-kil olyo yi kuluyl-ka epola kung mako tepa
now because of arrows and spears the few Epola giving pigs of European breed

pe obo kung tepa tepa notipa pe
and giving and putting native pigs

kung pulu-na nobu nyiba tirim kani-kin
saying, I'll take them back and then

ekepu *bagarap* tekim-ayl ya na kolubu-ko
now things are really buggered up [This presumably refers to a makayl *payment which the Tea-Dena were about to present to K-M-E-A-L before the fighting broke out], and even if I die*

ya na-nga kari mid kalya-ma el-ayl-nga ung nyingi-ko
my offspring will still talk about the fight

pe akilyi-nga meba lim-te pe el-ayl-nga-ko nyingi
and if they have any [children], they'll still talk of it

ilyi-nga kulu naa kolym, mulu-ma-sil pora nyim-kin
this fight will not die, when sky and earth come to an end

ya el-ayl koluba-kiyl-o
that's when the fight will die

ilyi kolya olyo-nga-na kawu mol
this is not only so in our area

ya kolya-ma-nga payl payl i tepa pelym peba ilyi-nga
it's that way all around here, and will be so

ekepu ya mol mol nyikimul kalya-yl i tepa pelym peba-nga
now we say no but it will go on being that way, concerning which

mol nyik telymeli pe
they say no, but

ekepu eni kang-ma-n molkuk kanak-lyanga abu tun kep pe
now you (pl) fellows sitting (around) and watching, if you (sg) rape a woman, or

kung-te tun kep pe mel aki-yl-nga-te
if you (sg) kill a pig, or some such thing

nu-nga yadu ok lying kep pe paka tun kep
they'll come back and take yours (sg), or if you (sg) go to someone's aid

olyo ilyi ekepu el-ayl temulu tekimul, ekepu el tekimul
we will fight about it, now we are fighting

ekepu ya kuduyl keap okum-ayl pe
now the European patrol officer is coming, well

naa olkada el-nga *plan* nyilymeli ul ilyi-nga *plan* tekimul-ayl kanikin-i
if he were not to come, as they make plans for fighting, we're making that sort of plan, you (sg) see

i tep tekimul ul-iyl
that's what we're doing

ekepu olyo ya lyip tilipu mudup naa nyib molkumul-o
we are doing so, now as we receive (money) we're not going to stay together and speak

ya uyl wed naa um-lum-o ing-iyl na ya gu suduyl-na lyipa
Uyl hasn't come, so I'm speaking first

gu kalang-ku-yl silym-ayl
he is going last

meri ya alya wed naa um-o
over there [Epola] did not come

koluwa wed naa um-o tek ting mel nar
[Epola] Koluwa didn't come, what happened to them?

ya ilyi-nga ok molku-kin ya ku-yl tekin ul-iyl ku-yl-ti tekin nyikin telkuna-yl
you (sg) have come here and are giving money

na yi-yl-ya lama yi-yl kanakimeli-ya
you (pl) see me here, a Lama man

jika kungunuka talapu, ulka-upuka talapu
acting the part of a Jika-Kungunuka, an Ulka-Upuka

na-nga lapa-yl-nga tumuyl awilyi lyipa ab por piyl lyipa
my father got big kina shells, and women with greasy bottom

mel aku-ma lyib-ayl lyirim
he wanted to get such things

mel aku-ma yu-nga lyiba pilyirim
he knew how to get such things

aki-yl-ne nunu-nga lku kolu ne aku-na lelym kalya-yl
his house site is still there [in Jika territory]

neka uj-kin lku abu-lku kol-kin pe minyiba uj-kin
with pandanus tree, and woman's house site, and bread fruit tree

uj kalyipa tor-kin ne molym
the casuarina trunk is still there

nanu kanap tep molyo, ya ilyi yi-te lupu-yl molyo
I always see it, I stand here, a different man [a Kusika-Midipu, as opposed to Epola-Alya-Lalka, who should be here, as the Epola are responsible for the fight]

ya yi tal wed naa ungl-lum
but those two didn't come

ol nyingl mel pilyamiyl
when they come and talk later, we'll hear

aki nyingl-ayl pe nyingl-ayl wiyl-ala kolya-na pup nyimulu
the two will speak and we'll speak with them when we go up there

nu-nga ekepu ya ku lyini tekin olyo ekepu ing-te nyi naa nyimulu
now you (sg) are about to get money, now we won't say a word

olyo-nga ing mare nyimulu-lum ekepu ilyi-nga nyib tada lemulu
we might say something later on; for now we'll conclude

i ilyi ya ilyi nyib tikir-kiyl
that's what I say

ekepu ya ku-yl, ya kepa, pelipa, bilyipa kolipa
now the money, uncles, cousins, brothers- and fathers-in-law

yabu kanu-ma aujipa wed urum-iyl
such people, many of them, have come out [to Kailge to watch]

aprui-o, ya uj marlti tekin-kin ya
so go (sg) ahead and distribute, and dance marlti *here*

mai dumu-iyl nunu kanakun nyini molo
will you (sg) put on a forehead plate by yourself, or

kera nunu kanakun nyini manya mudun
put on feather headdresses by yourself (sg)?

molo ulyi wapi nunu tini
or will you (sg) do your own paint?[i.e., no you won't]

yabu pul tin kalya molupa lyipa kuni telym
the way a friend standing by straightens it for you (sg)

pi olto tongi ting kayl-na ya nyiba mong todul kanapa
if they're about to kill us two, [a friend] will give you a meaningful look

pi yabu pul tin-ko
if a friend of yours

[The next three lines are an aside to Pus]

kang pus manya ung naa nyi
Pus, don't mumble

ui kalya *namba wan* te-ko nyib mudud
that was the first point I made

ekepu ing medepa te nyikir-kiyl
now I'm speaking on the next point

aku-na kalya yabu pul te-n mong ekeda kubulupa maka lyipa
like that, a friend acting as ally, winking

nabolka ul telymolu kalya-yl ul todul todul we-yl-kiyl
the sorts of things we do, those are very strong things

kalya-yl olto-nga yab-ayl pul-iyl aki-yl molym-kiyl
a person who does things like that is our (du) true friend

yabu te-n kanapa-kin oba pukum, pa! pa! nyilym
but a person who passes by and seeing, says Go! Go! [and fight]

kub alkala lyipa yabu kalya-yl yabu olto-nga yabu-te mol, yab lupu-yl-nga
shouting a war cry, a person like that is not one of ours, but different

ekepu olyo-nga ya yabu kepa pelipa yabu
now our uncles and cousins

yabu autiyl wed uring
a lot of people came out

nu ya i tep tekir bi tokun tani
as I'm doing this, you (sg) write their names down

pilyip ilyi yabu-kil adi-yl lyipa *aut* tekim-lum
hearing these people [mentioned]

nyib na pilyip pubu, i kupulanum ilyi
we'll say it and having heard it I'll go, this way

ya ilyi-nga nyib pora-nsimulu ung-iyl nyikir
we'll finish talking with that, our speeches, I mean

wiyl-ala pup-kin i we-namu nopopa nyim
and go up there, he spoke in public [for nothing?]

na kep ing-te nyi naa nyib
and I too won't say a thing

poj mare molum-lum pilyip nyibu
if there's any mistake I'll speak up when I hear it

mol-lum we kanapa na nyibu olyo-nga ing aki-yl ya ilyi-nga nyimulu
or if not, I'll just talk, or rather, we'll just talk about it here

i kupulanum ilyi i tepa lekim
that's the way it is

pe kung kuptini tekin-kin
well when you (sg) are about to cut up a pig

manya mel nomolu kare-nga-ko notuk koptilymeli mai midi-na naa koptilymeli
they put something which we're going to eat underneath and cut, not right on the ground

ya ul ilyi ekepu tek tek pe ne na molkur-ko
now (you are) doing this, and I am down there [at Palimung]

nyik pilyik tekemil
you (pl) think this way

aku-na, pe nu yabu bi naa lin aku-na
well you (sg) haven't called a person's name

pe molym-ko nyiba pilyipa purum *pablik* kolya-na nu molto-ko
but he's there, he thought of it and went, you (sg) are in a public place too

nu-nga mong angalyilym na naa angalyilym-i
you (sg) have eyes but [you think] I don't?

nu-nga numan pelym na numan naa pelym-i, ya aku mol medipul-ayl-nga
you (sg) have a mind, and I don't? that's not how it is at all

ilyi-nga nu yabu kil lyikir kil lyikir kil lyikir nyikin
as to that, you (sg) say you (sg) keep calling out people's names

morujana pilyip o yabu kil lyipa pora-nsikim pilyikir-ayl
I listen in public, yes, he's finished calling out names, I see

pe medepa molup nabolka ul temulu kil
and later, what shall we do

yunu-nga yabu-kil yabu *hap* waku tobu nyikin
if you (sg) say I'll leave out some of his people

yabu na-nga kare nyib pilyip pubu
I'll be reminded of my people

kupulanum ilyi ing pengi-te nyib tikir ilyi nu pilyikin
that's my main point ['head word'] I'm making, do you (sg) understand?

ing mong-te, te ya nyirid-iyl kani-yl nyikin nekeda muntani
this message, I said it, so you (sg) transmit it [to Palimung]

nyib nyirid-iyl pe Alya-n nyiba mudulka-da ing tika nyib pilyilka-yl
I said, and if Alya sent it I would think it true

pe ulyi-n nyiba mudulka-da ing tika nyib pilyilka-yl pe
and if Uyl sent it I would think it true

kujilyi nyikim ilyi ung gol-mel tum-lum waria kalya nar
Kujilyi says this and he might be lying, where is Waria? [i.e Waria might think this]

ya kupulanum wed oba molupa ung pengi pengi tilupu-te nyik yakudu mudai
if someone comes right here, you (pl) tell me the main point only

na pilyab
I want to hear it

i nyirid, kani-yl ekepu *wik* autiyl oba pukum-ayl
that's what I said, now many weeks have come and gone

ekepu wilyala yi-yl kulum-iyl abulkum-ayl
now the man up there [Poika Wangi] has died, and is holding us [back]

165 yi-yl naa kolka-da pe *kopi* nu-nga kolya kubilepa polu tolym pe
if the man hadn't died, well, 'the coffee ripens first at your place

na-nga kolya aili lepa polu turum i nyibu ya
and then ripens later at my place', saying this

kapola kapola-ko polu turum, nekedanga kubilepa polu turum
'it ripened at the same time, eh, over there it ripened first

ya kudanga mai koma lelym kani-yl pe
here the ground is wet, as we know, well

aili lepa polu tolym kolya-na oba kubi lekim ul aku-na
so it ripens later, and as for its ripening sooner

170 ing mong ilyi lawa tiring, nabolka ul-te tiring-da aku pilyip tudukur
you (pl) were mistaken --- I don't know what you (pl) did [i.e. how you managed to go ahead and pay compensation first]

pe *moni* mel, *moni* mel te tilupu-yl
well as to money, it is the same thing [as what we get]

medi *moni* mel ul-te kalya telymeli i-kin ul-te kalya naa telymeli kalya-kin pe
it is the same thing as the money they give down there, but they don't give it with this one [sense unclear]

te kalya we kalalu nyilym
in that case it will be delayed a long time

ekepu eni ul ilyi tek tek pora-nsing-kin
and now when you (pl) have finished this

175 altepa ul-te tek nying kanapa
and if you (pl) do something else again

i yi-ma eni-nga *kopi bek* kare lawa tek *kopi* lyik kawa-nsik
men, you (pl) wrongly take some of your coffee bags and save them

telymeli, nyib pilyilyo, ilyi nyirid kani-yl
you (pl) do so, I believe, I said this

ya nekeda naa pukum-kiyl ilyi ing *promis* tekin pijilydu kanapa
since he doesn't go over there, if you (sg) tell me what you have in mind

ekepu-ko nyikin si ilyi-nga ya na pilyip-ko nekeda pubu
tell me now to give to you (sg), hearing this I'll go over there [to Palimung]

180 pe pup wiyl-ala kola lku-na pukur-ayl
and then I go up there [next day] to the mourning house

pe aku-na pebu ya kelip madu obu pukur
I'll sleep there, I'll go and come right back down

kusika kang-kil medipulu wiyl-ala molungi
only the Kusika will stay up there [i.e., not we Midipu]

aku-na ki mong nabisipa wiyl-ala molungi
how long will they stay up there?

ilyi gai kuyung i-kin wawan wiyl-ala naa molang
when they've roasted sweet potato, let them not remain after that

185 madu wai i nyibu medipulu wiyl-ala-ko nyib tibu i nyirid
come down, I'll say, I'll send a message, I said like this

ilyi pelym ilyi
this is what remains to be done

ing ilyi midi na pilyikir na boni tekim
it's all I can think about, it weighs heavy upon me

boni tekim-na molkur i-kin ya ing nyib tadu mudurud kani-yl
I remain concerned, I sent a message back here

eni tobulkuk nyiring mola mol
did you (pl) discuss it or not?

190 ekepu aku-na kamukamu nyik ting ul na pilyab i nyikir
now give (pl) me the final word, I want to hear about the matter, I say

KUBUKA TAMALU (overlap with last line above)

kujilyi-nga ung nyikim ilyi pilyik molai nyangi
consider (pl) what Kujilyi says and speak

MIDIPU KUJILYI
ilyi
this

KOPIA KUPENA
na pilyip molyo
I know

[10 seconds of inaudible remarks by Kupena and someone else, to whom Kujilyi responds in the following]

MIDIPU KUJILYI
te ya eni ku-yl tenga tek-lyanga ku *namba* tok tengi
here's one lot [of money], count (pl) it and give it
mong *lep lep* kare tingi
you (pl) will give some more
ilyi-nga *namba* tok pora-dai pe mel buk-na tok monsuk-kin
finish counting, and when you (pl) have written it down on paper
namba lyik tilupu muduk tai
put (pl) it all in one place
ilyi-nga tai
do (pl) this
ya *skelim* tek nabolk-ul tek moki tek tingi
count it and doing whatever you (pl) have to, you (pl) will distribute it
ul aki-yl ilyi-nga tek pora-dai
finish up (pl) with this matter
i teang olyo yabu-ma ob topa
you (pl) do this and we folks, getting ready...

[Kujilyi is cut off by the following speaker]

KUBUKA TAMALU
o, aki-yl ku mon-ayl *lep lep* nyikin
yes, you (sg) are talking about that extra money
ku aki-yl abolup molymolu
we're holding that money
oba, ku, ku ya tin
well, the money, give (sg) it here
kang-yi kopia tim ku-yl ya kusika-midipu epola-alya-ma nyib sab, ya
I'll tell the Kusika-Midipu and Epola-Alya how much the Kopia have given them

MIDIPU KUJILYI
o, ing-te kalya ya [1 sec. inaudible]
yes, about that
ya ing peng-ayl-nga kalya ya ul nawu ya kung *na* ab *na* tenga naa nyikir-o
about the main matter, I'm not talking about anything else, such as woman trouble or pig trouble
dina i tepa ul tin-ja nabolka ul ime-nga ung tin-ja
if you (sg) have a debt or talk (sg) about something like this

[interrupted here by some cross-talk, on which he comments in the next line]

yi-til eltili ol nyingli ung-iyl lelym
you two men [Waria and Tamalu] still have some words to say
ya nu nyikin ung kalya-yl yabu ansipe yabu molkumil
while you (sg) are talking there are people far away
lo tum-kin ena tekim nyikimil
when it rains they say it's sunny
subulu tokum-kin wi tagum nyikimil
when it's dark they say it's getting light
subulu tokum nyib nanu uru pep-ko molkur
thinking it's night, I myself am sleeping

i ul ilyi waria-kin
this matter rests with Waria

KUBUKA TAMALU [slight overlap with the above]
o ilyi waria yuyu abolupa molym
yes, that's something that Waria himself is holding [i.e., the answer to your question]

i ung nyibu tekir ilyi
that's what I am going to say

waria nunu-ko abolupa molym-kiyl
since Waria himself is holding it

na-nga nanu ku *paun* singi-yl-nga nosip molkur-kiyl
as for me, I'm just holding the money which you (pl) [Kopia] have given

tausen ilyi-nga nosip molkur nyib pilyikir
I'm just holding the thousand pounds

ya i ul ilyi-nga ya yi ilyi abolupa molym
but as for that information, this man is the one who is holding it

ne nunga ung-ti nyikin aki-yl waria abolupa molym
Waria is holding to himself the answer to the question which you (sg) asked over there [at Palimung]

waria-ko kanakun nyirin-iyl
which you (sg) asked Waria when you saw him

unya abolu mola waria abolkum-ja
perhaps Unya or Waria is holding it

ilyi opayl pudu tangl
tomorrow those two can reply to it

ekepu ya ung kalya-yl ya tep kuni tep molup ya kang-ayl-nga ung nyamiyl
today, let's stay and talk, straightening out the talk about the boy [Uwa, who was injured in a motor accident for which Midipu were held responsible]

ya ul ilyi ya ui lyip kubi samiyl
let's settle this affair first

ku *handet* telsip pup-lyanga
going and giving a hundred ['pounds', i.e. two hundred kina] each

ne ku *lep* aki-yl-nga na kubuka ping
the left-over money there [pointing the display boards] is from me, Kubuka\Ping [men's house]

mel aki-yl-nga parka olto-nga tapa-na
this one is from Parka and my men's house

unya-nga tapa kelipa pupa
Unya's men's house, and

mera-la tapa wanmuyl-nga tapa
that men's house over there, Wanmuyl's [another name for Parka] men's house...

[gap of five seconds, during which Tamulu loses the floor and Yaya shouts to regain it for him]

o, ya ping tapa ing nyikir-kiyl
yes, this is the Ping men's house, as I was saying

kuduyl kalyanga-sil tapa ilyi aki-yl-nga
this one is from the Kuduyl and Kalyanga men's houses

na kubuka ping mel aki-yl-nga parka olto-nga tapa
I'm like a Kubuka\Ping, this is Parka's and my men's house

kelipa pupa mer-la tapa wanmuyl-nga tapa
leaving that, Parka's men's house up there

oo, ya ping tapa ing nyikir-kiyl kuduyl kalyanga-sil tapa ilyi
yes, the Ping men's house here, as I say, Kuduyl and Kalyanga here

aki-yl-nga ne ku *handet*-te nyik telymeli kani-yl-nga
as to that, they say one hundred

ne ku *foa handet* nanu mada tid aku-mel
that four hundred over there I myself [i.e. my men's house] gave

ya ku *lep lep* tal waria nabiyl nyik
the two piles of extra money [from Kuduyl and Ping], they say to Waria let's

take it

ne na kubuka ping ku *handet* pe ku kum *faipela* ilyi-nga molym nyikir-kiyl
Kubuka Ping's one hundred, and five 'fists' are left, I say

altepa kum *tripela* na ku kum *eitpela* tid ilyi-nga
and again three 'fists', I gave eight fists

pepa ne-d molym, kum taltika
it's down on paper, three 'fists'

KUBUKA UNYA (slight overlap with above)

kum *faipela*-ko nyin
you (sg) should say [lit.: said] five fists

KUBUKA TAMALU

pe mol, kum *faipela* [coughs] ya yadu ok ilyi kalya nying-kiyl
no, five fists they told me coming back here

na ku kum na ping medipulu ku kum *eitpela* tid
I gave, I myself, Ping, gave eight fists

ku *handet tri handet* tid aki-yl
I gave three hundred

aki-yl-nga ya *lep* ku kum *eitpela* tid
for that there were eight extra 'fists' which I gave

KUBUKA TEPRA

lep-ti mol, *wan handet* kina
nothing extra, one hundred kina

KUBUKA TAMALU

ku *handet* kina tid aki-yl-nga ekepu-nga *faiv*-iyl tolab-ayl sid-iyl
I gave one hundred, and now I gave five to Tolab

UNIDENTIFIED SPEAKER

faipela
five

KUBUKA TAMALU

faipela tolab-ayl sid-iyl, ekepu-nga kum aki-sipa molym
I gave five to Tolab, now there are that many left

kuduyl yunu kuduyl tapa aku-na kum tal nyab-e
Kuduyl is left, shall I talk about the two fists?

KUBUKA TEPRA

kapola
o.k.

KUBUKA TAMALU

yi-te pelym-i
one man remains, eh?

kum tal kuduyl tapa-nga
two fists of Kuduyl men's houses

kum tal oba suku pelym-ilyi
two fists remain in the middle

lep tim naa nosud-iyl
I didn't keep the extra

ekepu waria-n na-n ne-la pep tangalyim-nga urudu
now Waria and I came in the day having slept up there

nabitiyl yabu lyiba nyirim-lum
how many people might he have told

[lots of interjections during the next six lines]

ku *plasta* naa turum-luyl
he didn't paste the money up [on the board]

mola koluwa naa um-lum, kujilyi
now if Epola Koluwa doesn't come, Kujilyi

kujilyi-nga tomulu tuju naa tujamiyl-kin
let us not blame Kujilyi

waria nunu-n lku pelto aku-mel kopia berlto-kin berlto-kin berlto-kin
Waria, you (sg) live at home, you count and count your money

olyo-n ekepu ku anum-mel te te-n berlto-kin
now you (sg) are counting your fortunes

ekepu ne *pasim* tekin nu-nga lalyikin tekin
now you (sg) put it up, you (sg) put it in your netbag

kayi teani eni-nga ku *moni* ku kum *faipela* o *sikispela* lelym
do (sg) it nicely, your (pl) fifty or sixty kina are there

eni-nga kum *faipela* meri-kid kum *sepen-pela*
your (pl) fifty kina down there, or seventy

[short inaudible exchanges with others regarding the amounts]

oba, ekepu ilyi-nga waria nunu sip sukud modukur
and now I give you (sg), Waria, all the money

mel-ma tekin aki-yl nunu sikir nyikir-o
you (sg) give things, so I give to you (sg), I say

ne na pep tangalyim kani urud
I slept and came at daybreak

eni-nga suku yab te-nga ul-te tirim-uyl na naa kanarud
one of your (pl) 'inside people' did something, I didn't see [because he slept in and came late]

na-nga ku awilyi-yl ya wiyl-ala nangi mek pai
you (pl) take and 'eat' my large amount of money

KOPIA WARIA

olyo i ya yi kudulyi-yl ku kum *faipela* ilyi ya yadu sipa nyikim-kiyl
the 'red' man is giving us back fifty kina and talking

pe olyo yabu-r tomulu-i
are we going to kill anybody? [i.e., we're not]

adi ku *namba*-yl tai, *namba* top kujilyi ya yadu-ko simul-ayl
you (pl) count up, we'll write and tell Kujilyi how much

wiyl-ala aku-na *paul* ting naa pilyimulu ku *namba* toku
up there they'll foul it up when writing the number, we won't hear

ku *wan tausen paun*-ilyi ku *wan tausen paun*-iyl ya
this is one thousand pounds, here's one thousand pounds

wiyl-ala ilyi-nga kolupa pora-nsikim-kiyl ...
it [our debt] is getting finished off up there...

[interjection from floor, ya *wan tausen* 'here's one thousand...]

i ya wi ku *namba* tangi
you (pl) write the amount

pe ya lyip kuni tep nyamiyl, ku *wan tausen* ilyi ya
let's say it correctly, here one thousand

wiyl-ala pora nyikim-iyl pe ekepu ku *lep* nabisiyl molkum
it's finished up there, how much is left?

ya na yadu sikim-iyl ku-yl kep wiyl-ala aku-na *hap lep* mare pukum molo
here now he's giving to me, and the extra amount is going up there is it?

ilyi pilyip-kin ku *namba* top pe wi kang-ma *notis* tok monsaing pe
when we've heard the amount, let the fellows write it up on the board

wi ku *namba*-yl pilyini pe ku nab-ayl top nu sip i teamiyl
up there you (sg) will know how much, writing it up there we'll tell you (sg), let's do so

ku *wan tausen tu handet* pekim molo pe *wan tausen tri handet* pekim molo
if there's one thousand two hundred, or one thousand three hundred

pe *wan tausen faiv handet* kina pekim molo
or one thousand five hundred kina

nabisiyl ilyi aima nab-ayl nu pilyan-a pe yi lupu-ma pilyangi-na
how much it is, you (sg) just listen and let the others hear

pe olyo pilyip teamiyl ing nyikir, ya yi lupu lupu-ma pilyik pangi
let us listen, I say, and let the others hear it and go

ilyi yadu tekir ilyi
as for this I give it back

PALIMI SURU

kang yi-sil ung many-iyl mada tek nying
people, stop (pl) mumbling!

[interjections]

KUBUKA WAIMA

mad kuduyl mare kanakur-ma
down there are some 'red' people, I see

kang-ma ung naing, takan molai
boys, let (pl) them speak, be quiet!

KOPIA WARIA

ilyi yi-ko ku *wan tausen paun*-iyl tep pora-nsimulu
with this we'll have given one thousand pounds

ekepu ku *lep* nabisipa pekim
now how much is left?

eni kang *namba* tok aku-na nosik tai i nyikir-kiyl
you (pl) fellows write down how much, I say

eni ku kabu tokumil yi-ka
you (pl) are counting the money

ya ku ilyi *namba* ??kaya kang kuduyl ilyi-nga ku ilyi *namba* topa oba sikim-iyl
here the amount the 'red man' is writing down and handing over

pe na ya ku *paun lep*-te ya pensip moly-ayl aku-na *joinim* tep-kin
here I'm holding on to an extra pound, adding that in

wi aku-na ku *lep lep* nabisiyl lekim-ja
how much is left over up there

aku-na *namba* top-kin, ya *kansil* pilyipiyl pe
writing the amount, let the councillor [Kujilyi] hear.

olyo pilyip-kin ku *tausen*-ayl tepa oba
we'll hear when a thousand is reached

ya na ku-yl yadu nobu tirid
I wanted to keep the money back

puba ku-yl kep *namba*-yl midi top *kansil*-ayl samiyl
let's just write the amount and give it to the councillor

pe ne yuyu meba pupa pe yi lupu lupu okumil-ma pilyik teang
and he'll take it, and let the other people hear

ilyi aki-yl-nga nyikir aku *namba*-yl-nga nyikir
that's what I say about that, about the amount, I say

ya ku ilyi ku-yl ang ya kopia lku tapa payl kanu-ma pe pupa-kin
brother, this money was given by all the Kopia men's houses

sikis handet tim, *sikis handet* nyab-a molo
they gave six hundred, shall I say six hundred or

kang kalya-ka ku *lep* kare tengi?
are those fellows going to give any extra?

KOPIA ABUNMIYL WARIA

seven handet
seven hundred

UNIDENTIFIED SPEAKER

o, kopia ku *seven handet*
yes, the Kopia, seven hundred

[ten seconds of inaudible remarks, shouting]

KUBUKA UNYA

kang yi-me kur-n tekim-i, bali mapi talu-yl mar
are those fellows sweating, with those rubbish loincloths on?

KOPIA WARIA

kopia ku *seven handet-o*, **kopia ku** *seven handet* **tekim ilyi ya**
Kopia seven hundred, Kopia is (sg) giving seven hundred

kopia ku *seven handet* **tekir-o, tep ya el-ayl-nga ul aki-yl** *plan* **tep**
I Kopia am giving seven hundred, in doing so we're making war commitments [i.e., securing our alliance with the Laulku]

kang ya kubuka kang kel-ayl yadu sikir-o
and I'm handing it over to the little Kubuka boy [Tamalu]

ekepu nu-ni aji tin-lum te, i nyib na-ni ung-te mol
now if you (sg) might give one back, but I'm not suggesting anything

yunu-nga kupulanum ilyi nosipa pelym mel
he's making his own road [to Laulku]

ilyi-nga-ja na nanu telka-yl
that's just what I would do

ne kang-ayl oba bulu-apu mola
is that [Kubuka] fellow over there the 'back borne' [i.e., the recruit (of the Laulku)? (the obvious answer being 'no, he was the one who recruited them')]

ekepu ilyi-nga ne yuyu nokupa pelym-ayl
now he himself is watching out

ne kopia ku *seven handet* **teri lep tep**
we Kopia giving seven hundred altogether

kang-ayl abolupa sipiyl nyib
saying let the fellow hold it and give it

ya kang kudulyi-yl *keap*-**ayl-kin abolkuk saing nyib-kin**
saying let the 'red' fellow [Tamalu] and the kiap [Unya] hold and give it

kubuka tepra-kin ilyi-nga nela nosikumul-o
we put it over there with Kubuka Tepra's

eni-nga kupulanum-na aki nyikir
it's your (pl) road, I say [i.e., the alliance with Laulku is for the Kubuka to maintain, since the road to Laulku [literally] comes through Kubuka territory rather than Kopia]

kopia ku *seven handet* **tekimul, tep nela aku-na nosikumul**
we Kopia are giving seven hundred, giving it we put it over there

nosikir aku-na kubuka yuyu ku *foa handet* **tekim**
I put it there, Kubuka is giving (sg) four hundred

ku *foa handet* **tekim akilyi pe**
'he' is giving (sg) four hundred and

olyo ku *seven handet* **tekimul, ku** *eleven handet paun*, **ku** *eleven handet paun* **tekimul akilyi**
we are giving seven hundred, eleven hundred pounds, here we're giving eleven hundred pounds

yunu abolupa tekim nyikir-o, ilyi kubuka-yl yunu tipiyl
Kubuka is (sg) holding it, I say let Kubuka give it

nyib sukud mudukumul-o, i ku ilyi
we say, and put it in, this money

yunu abolupa nela yuyu kupulanum nosipa pelym-mel
holding it over there 'he' [Kubuka] is building a road [to Laulku]

i pekim, ya ku *paun* **ilyi midi**
it's like that, only that pound here [the fifty kina previously mentioned]

ilyi ya ne kubuka-yl nu nunu ku tin-iyl, altekin ne boni kuluni
down there, Kubuka, you (sg) gave it yourself, don't (sg) feel angry [with us]

ku ilyi altepa ne ku *ten*-**ka kelipa mad sikim**
he's giving ten ['pounds', i.e., twenty kina] down there [i.e., to Kopia, to give to Tilka, for their help]

mad sikim akilyi pe ya na ya na-nga ku-yl tid ilyi ya kopia-ma
he's giving it, I say I've given mine, these here are the Kopia ones

na ya bilyipa-kolipa kepa-pelipa aima torupalyi-te ilyi-nga naa molym
I don't have brothers-in-law, fathers-in-law, uncles or cousins there [among the Laulku]

na-nga ku-yl ilyi-nga tepi kalkur
doing this I'm burning my money [i.e., I won't get it back]

kang kapiyl monsurung ekepu ang nu-n pukun te-pui nyib
the fellows got hurt, now I say, 'brother, you (sg) go'

yunu tep sikir aku-na na boni kolubu nyib
I give to him, saying I'll suffer a feeling of grievance

nu-nga kena pelipa bilyipa-kolipa-te naa molymeli adi-lum nu kis pilyikin
'since you (sg) have no uncle, cousin, brother- or father-in-law there you (sg) might feel bad'

adi-yl nu *ten*-ka terilek tek na yadu sikimil-kiyl
you (sg) give ten, they give it back to me

nu pilyibu nyikin kalya-yl-nga nyikir
you (sg) say 'I'll understand' that's what I'm talking about

ten-ka tekin-kin nu meam ab mal-ri-lum, i nyik-lyanga
'you (sg) give ten, you're a Meam woman's son', saying this

na *ten*-ka tek yadu sikimil ilyi, nanu yadu lyikir-kiyl
they give me back my ten, I take it back

yu-nga ku anum-uyl ya i tep modubu tekir, pupa pora nyikim
I chuck in his large share, that finishes it

ekepu ya i ku ilyi *namba* top samiyl
now let's reckon the amount

ya *kansil*-ayl kep pilyipa tipiyl
let the councillor know [how much]

olyo pilyip ya yi keli-ma pilyik kapola tensangi
we know it, so let the ordinary men know it

ku *wan tausen*-ayl pora nyikim, *handet lep* nabisiyl pekim
it's already reached one thousand; how many hundreds are left

ilyi-nga wi pup *notis* top monsup
let's put a notice up

namba top teamul i nyikir
let's reckon the amount, I say

aki-yl wi lyip kuni teamul
let's get that straight

[here someone else is trying to get the floor. His cross-talk is inaudible]

aaa, ung-ti, ung ti kalya ya kamkam nyab-a, na nyibu nyikir
um, I want to say one final thing about that, I'm about to say

na ya wilyi ung-te nyikim kalya-yl
like what he's saying up there

kalya-lyi, olyo ang ku ilyi-nga midi temulu nyib tirimul tirimul tirimul
like that, brother, we kept on saying we were going to give this money

ya ung kani midi aima nosup kilirimul we lelym-kiyl, pilyi pilyirimul-kiyl
there's still some talk which we've put away, some remains, we've known it for a long time

nosip kilirimul-ilyi we lelym-kiyl
we put it by and it's still there [i.e., we haven't finished our speeches yet]

ya ku-yl-nga temulu tep tep adap ya ung kani-yl we nosip kilimul
we've been so busy giving money that we've forgotten to say certain things

we lekim-kiyl-o, olyo ya ultuku kola lku-na pukumul-kiyl
it's there, tomorrow we go to the mourning house

pup mad omulu, akin nu pukun mad-ko oni
we'll go and come back, you (sg) too will go and return

ung aki-yl ang olyolyo, olyolyo ung-iyl *miting* tep
as for that word [that still remains], brother, we'll have a meeting

olyolyo maku top kanap-lyanga nyimulu-kiyl-o
we ourselves will get together and talk about it

nu ui puku li naa li olyo maku top kanap nyimulu-kiyl
don't you (sg) get jumpy, we'll meet and talk about it

[lots of inaudible remarks from the audience during the next 5 lines]

ya ung-te kopia-kubuka-ma *bung* ti naa temulu, mol
as for this one word, we Kopia-Kubuka will not have a meeting

ung-iyl lekim-kiyl
that talk is pending

ung nu pilyibu nyikin kalya-yl
that talk that you (sg) say 'I want to hear it'

nu-nga ung *kwesten* kalya-yl pudu tokur, ul ilyi we lelym ilyi
I'm answering your (sg) question: the matter is still pending

ku kalya-yl-nga ku *handet*-te kalya top manya modung-kiyl
when we were counting you (pl) left out that money, that hundred

ku ola ku *eit handet*...
the money which is up [i.e., the true amount of 'left over' money on the display board] is eight hundred...

KOPIA WARIA

na pilyid-i
did I hear it?

na eni-nga ul aki teng aki-yl na pilyab-a...
I want to hear about what you (pl) will do

UNIDENTIFIED SPEAKER

kang meri kili nyikimul...ul aku-na nar-ayl...
hey fellow down there, stop (sg) we say...what's the matter?

KOPIA SIRKU

manya molai, kang ku-yl kanangi, eni nabim-ya
sit down, boy, let them see the money, what are you (pl) doing that for?

KUBUKA WAIMA

eni aku-ma-ka eni ned aku-ma-ko kopia-kubuka mare nyib kanakur-iyl
you (pl) all down there, I'm talking about some (of you) Kopia-Kubuka that I see

eni aku-ma nabina pipisikimil-o
you (pl) all, why do you block the way?

sowa pai
Sowa, go (pl) away!

[several seconds of unfocussed cross-talk]

MIDIPU KUJILYI

nela kudanga yi-te lyangi, ya kudanga yi-te lyangi
you (pl) should get a man from that side, and one from this side

ya waria nyikim yi-yl yi *foapela* lyik aku-na manya molai
as Waria says, you (pl) should get four men [one from each men's house group] and sit down [to look after the money]

nyik kayi tek ku i tepa i tepa ku *namba*-yl nyik ama tok
talking in an organized way, like this and this, saying and keeping in mind the amount

[long stretch of unfocussed cross-talk]

eni yi *foa-pela* maku top sikir aku-na manya molkuk ol tai
I choose you (pl) four, sit down and whisper

manya molkuk nyai, ya ung-te nyikir, ilyi kum liai
sit (pl) down and talk, I'm saying something else, listen (pl)!

KOPIA WARIA

kansil-ayl ung nyikim-kin na kul tep tep tep kayi tid-kin eni pungi-kiyl
while the councillor is talking, I'll straighten out the money and then you (pl) can go

taburup kalya pungi nyik pilyini...
you (sg) think you (pl) are going to go soon? [i.e., you're not]

ya ku-ka altepa ya ilyi-nga *joinim* tep *plasta* tobu tekir
adding all the money in, I want to write another sign [i.e., a revised one]

eni takan molai
you (pl) be quiet!

MIDIPU KUJILYI

mada nyai
stop talking!

kang yi-ka olyo-nga kolyana ya yi kuburi, waria
there aren't enough men in our place, Waria

yi kuburi aji-aj mare naa molymeli
there are not enough men left behind

ada ku-ma sik mudai, sik mudung-kin penga morinsiba tekim
old man, contribute the money, when you (pl) have given it, the place will become empty [i.e., the crowd will leave]

KOPIA WARIA

kansil nyan ku kalya-yl-kiyl-o, ilyi ya nela kang-kin ya tek ok sikimil-kiyl-o
Councillor, before you (sg) speak, the fellows over there [i.e. the Kubuka] are coming and giving it

i ku ilyi-o i ku ilyi ya i kang-kin nela ok na tek ok madu sikimil...
this money, these fellows are coming and handing it down to me...

[shouts]

KUBUKA TEPRA

olyo ku *seventi* kina sikimul
we are giving seventy kina

KOPIA WARIA

i ku ilyi ya na ya yi-yl-n miyl abu-n-miyl ku-yl na nanu tidu ku-yl...
this money is [what was given by] me, the man-borne [i.e.Kopia-Kabika] and woman-borne [i.e., Palimi]; 'I' myself gave it [shouts]

KOPIA PAIK

eni el-ayl-nga ul ilyi-ko tiring-kiyl
you (pl) did the same as this when you fought! [i.e., all talked at once; i.e., shut up and listen]

KOPIA WARIA

i ku kum *seven-pela*...i ku kum *seven-pela*
this one hundred forty kina...this one hundred forty kina

ilyi na-nga tapa-n yi-n miyl abu-n miyl nanu lyid nyikir
this is [from] my men's house - [those] borne [into it] by men and women - 'I' myself raised it

ilyi ya kang yi-kin tek ok sing ku-yl tek ok sukud mudukumil...
the fellows came and gave it, they're contributing it...

KUBUKA TEPRA

kang nu adi owa-ri
boy, are you (sg) a dog

[proceedings interrupted by a fight between two boys; cross-talk for about thirty seconds, then the following]

KUBUKA UNYA

kang, aku-ma nabina perikimil-o, kang-o...
boy, what's that for, what are you (pl) doing it for, boys...

UNIDENTIFIED SPEAKER, PROBABLY KOPIA SUBA

abolkuk lakuk aki-yl to-lensi-o...
hold (sg) them and (sg) kick them...

KOPIA WARIA
gabrien adi aki-yl tupiyl kelai aki tupiyl kelai
let him hit Gabriel, leave (pl) them alone, let (pl) him hit him

KUBUKA TEPRA
kang eni nabolka lyingi, aku-na suku pukumil elti-li teangl kelai-a...
boys, what do you (pl) want, they're going in, let the two of them go at it, leave (pl) them...

PALIMI SURU
tupiyl naa pai-a...
let him hit him, don't (pl) go...

KOPIA WARIA
kera-doa-ma-i mola yi-ma?
are (you) animals or men?

ALAN (aside to another spectator)
ku *moni* wa lyikim mola
is he stealing money, or

LAULKU PILYIP
we tekibil-o
they're doing it for nothing

ALAN
a
oh

KUBUKA DOKI
aku elti-li teangl, suku naa pung-ko, kang-yi-sil...
let the two go on, don't (pl) get in the middle, those two young men...
uri adi midi kanaim
we see the shame of it!

KUBUKA WAI
kang ul aku-ma-ka eni adi kanangi
fellow(s), look (pl) at that over there!

KOPIA KUPENA
apa
for goodness' sake!

PALIMI SURU
kang ul aku-wa-ka uri
the shame of it!

[Tape off for a few minutes as the crowd's attention shifts to the fight between the two boys. Switched on again as the following speaker gains audience focus by making the first *el ung* speech of the day. There is a dramatic drop in the level of audience noise during the first few lines of his speech.]

KUBUKA UNYA (*el ung*, in medias res)
yi-lupu-te oba naa tim-o
no stranger came and got involved
ui-nga ya kupulanum ilyi-nga-o
before (on) this 'road' [i.e. this way of fighting]
upiya-tok-sil pula topa abolurum ilyi-o
a grasshopper and frog fought [cf. line 430 below]
ekepu-nga *sande*-ilyi-lum-ayl
perhaps today is Sunday

na-ni kinya-nga *de* ilyi-nga-o
what shall I say today?

ekepu-nga yu-nga yi-dukuna mel-ir lyiba ilyi-o
now he will recruit many allies

turum adi-yl-a
he struck once

altepa toba kanapaa kelipa-a
now he wants to strike again

ekepu ola madu pa-a
now you (sg) are putting one thing on top of another

ka-n topa-a
a car striking him

ul ilyi tekim nyiba pilyiba-a
'he is doing this' he will think

nu na-nga yi-tara-wawa-te mol-ayl-o
you (sg) are not my agnatic kinsman

ya kakuyl yi lupu-yl-o
this Kaugel man is different

[here the crowd's attention shifts back to the fight, and there is unfocussed cross-talk for about 20 sec. The first audible words are the following]

KOPIA KUPENA

tema-nga nyik adalymeli-ma, kang kik piyl mare kanakur-ayl
where do you (pl) come from? [your] skins have no grease, I see [i.e., you are poor people]

KUBUKA UNYA (in *el ung*, picking up from where he left off above)

wi kakuyl yi lupu-yl-o
the Kaugel man up there is 'different'

topipupu le top-o
squeezing the excreta out of topipupu *grubs [and eating them: this sort of grub is found in the higher, Kaugel area but not in the Meam area]*

ga mudu tep-o
making sweet potato mounds [a high-altitude method of cultivation, not generally used on the Meam side]

purud-iyl pup aki tirid-o
when 'I' [i.e.Kubuka] went there [as a refugee from earlier fighting with Tea-Dena] I did these things

meri kolya-ma-nga purum-uyl-o
while 'he' [Kopia] went to that lower area [Suruk; see section 3.2.1]

ku polup-o
we are [like] stones [in the ground, which can't be moved]

ul aku-a tirim-o
these are the things he [the ancestor(s)] did

pe tilyipu topa tirim-iyl-o
he 'married many wives' [i.e., made many enemies]

gavman lo olka-o
the government law having come

ada-n tilu-n-o
our one forefather

meba sukud um kani-yl-o
he brought [Kopia-Kubuka] us back here

molup pilyip-o
staying here and hearing [about the government law]

kupula *baret* kanuwa opimi top lyipul pansibul-o
we built these roads

molup pilyip-o
staying and hearing

gavman lo tilupu-yl abolupul mebul adabiyl nyibul tibul kani-yl-o
we two said to each other 'let us uphold the one government law'

mer-ayl kep na-nga-ko
even down there is mine [i.e., at Tea-Dena]

nu kep na-nga nyib molud kani-yl-o
you (sg) too [i.e., K-M-E-A-L] I said, were mine

elti-li kani tingl-lum-o
you two yourselves [Tea-Dena and K-M-E-A-L] did like that

tara-ma-n ui upiya tok-ma puku-topa abolurum-o
our ancestors fought like the jumping grasshoppers and frogs

nu na-kin *kampani*-te mol-o
you (sg) [K-M-E-A-L] and I are not allies

pe mer-ayl *kampani* mol-ko-a
and the one down there [Tea-Dena] is not an ally [of ours] either

eltili *kampani* kanisil-o
you two yourselves are allies of each other

tel ol-a
when you two fought together and came

nu kani kani-yl-ka-o
and he [the Tea-Dena] saw you (sg)

erim-arim turum-o
(you) were weak

pe na naa tid nyib ya
well, I won't say I didn't do it [fight]

el tobulu kapola
we two fought together

adi na-nga apa-pel-yab-a
over there, unseen, are my maternal uncles and cousins

torupalyi yab-a
my ancestors

yab kanuwa bulumingi-na molupa
those people, seen, being 'at my back' [i.e., helping me in the fight]

molum kanuwa
he stayed, seen

kapiyl kona-wa-nga
as for those who got injured

pe tolka-ja
if they had gotten killed

ul-te lupu-te telka-ya nyib-lyanga
would I have done differently?

pe ya ku kina mel-te ilyi-a
as to this money

i nyib pilyip-lyanga
this is what I think

na yi-r moly-ayl-nga-a
I am 'one man' [i.e., we are few]

pas modud-kilyi
I've given all I have

na yi-r molka-ja-a
if I were many

ku pengi ilyi-ka-a
[I would have given] 'head money' [i.e., a larger payment]

nu ya na-kin-a
you (sg) and I

modalu wal-na pebu-o
[say] 'I will lie in the netbag' [i.e. we will fight as allies]

modalu wal-na peab-o
'I want to lie in the netbag'

mawa mel tin kanapa-o
if you (sg) ask me to

na ku *wan kina* i nyib *takis* top, ku *tausen* nyibu tep-o
I, levying 'one kina', giving one thousand

i tep telka-kiyl-o
that's what I could do

pe na yi mel-weyl-na
but I am a very small man [i.e., we are not many]

nunu kep-a i bo naa lyirin kani-yl-a
and you (sg) [K-M-E-A-L] did not take our planting [i.e., did not encourage us to stay here]

ekepu-nga *gavman lo* okum pilyik-lyanga
and now, you having heard that government law has come

pe nu na-nga dukuna nyikin pilyikin-ayl-a
now you (sg) [K-M-E-A-L] think I am your ally

mel-ir adi-yl lyipiyl nyib-lyanga
I saying [to Kusika Au] 'let him get that coffin' [for a Kubuka man who had died]

i tekir kalya
I do like that

ne abu-n kep-a
it's like what the woman said [when she had sex with a man]

i ku *moni* ilyi-a
this money here

abu-n yi tokur nyiba pilyilyim
the woman thinks 'I'm doing it to him'

yi-n ab tokur pilyilyim
and the man thinks 'I'm doing it to her'

[the point of this parable is presumably that Kusika Au shouldn't think *he* was buying the coffin; the Kubuka will take ultimate responsibility for it]

na-nga kang kumulaya kani-yl-a
my eldest 'son' [the Kubuka boy for whom Au bought the coffin]

lirim-kin-a
was lying dead

wilyi kang-ma-n-a
those fellows up there

uj *kes baim* tiring kani-yl-a
bought (pl) the coffin

ku *lep*-ayl kusika au-nga
the extra money is for Kusika Au

uj *kes baim* tirim ilyi-nga ku *fifti foa kina* sikir
he bought the coffin, for this I give 54 kina

oba lyipiyl
let him come and get it

KUBUKA PARKA

yadu sirim-mel ku isipe sirim
how much money did he give us?

KUBUKA UNYA

yadu ku *teti* kina mel sirim ilyi pe kum tal *foa kina*-kin sukud mudup sikir
he gave [us] about thirty kina, and I am giving adding on twenty four

ilyi ya ku *fifti foa* sikir oba lyipiyl
I am giving fifty four kina, let him come and get it

ya ku *namba*-yl-nga ya lku tapa-ma-nga
the amount of money from this men's house

na yi pepa kanuyl yi-ma-n *toksave* tiai
those who know how to read and write give the information

pikim tep ya lupu lupu ya *tu handet kina, tu handet kina...*
picking them, these various two-hundred-kina parcels...

oltoto lyip teripul *namba* topul naa tibul
we two didn't add them together

aki-yl ui naa tibul
we two didn't do that first

ku *tausen* medipulu ya *namba* awilyi aki-yl-nga medipulu nyikimul
we are talking about a thousand kina, a large sum

ekepu *bung* tep tep ya
collecting it

ne na-n nyib-ob ya mong *lep*-r ya kopia kang-ma sibu
after what I say, if there's any left I'll give it to the Kopia fellows

kopia kang-ma-n na topa mensikim mekir i nyikir
the Kopia 'boys' gave (sg) to me and I make a return

ilyi olto-nga ul-iyl isipul tekubul
that is how we two do

oba ya alya-yl naa um-lum-o, epola-yl naa um-lum-o
and if Alya does not come (sg) and if Epola does not come (sg)

i tibul-iyl sika nyikin
we'll certainly do that, you (sg) say

nu yi bulumingi-na yi-yl nu-kin na-kin isipulu lku lkeripulu kup-na pepul nyib-ja papu
'you (sg) [Epola and Alya] and I are allies and we are at each other's doorstep' --- if I said that, that would be o.k.

pe na uj kalyipa we talabu ya *namba kansil*-wa na nosikir-wa
shall I plant casuarina tree for nothing? I wear the badge of an elected councillor

nu nuyl nyikin pilyiyl-wa akuwa nu pom-ko mekin wa
you (sg) think you will 'eat' it, but you (sg) are supporting me instead

ekepu na akisil nyibu tekir ilyi-a
now I want to speak

na kapola naa tekim-a
but I'm unable [i.e., the money given by Kubuka is insufficient]

yi subu uj marlti tepa pansikir-iyl
in giving it I'm like a 'dwarf' dancing

kilkuwa-malkuwa tekim
he does it out of step

nu-kin na-kin tiabiyl, i nyikir-a
let us you (sg) [Kopia] and I [Kubuka] give it, I say

pe nu na-kin teabiyl i nyibu tekir-o, oba
let us you (sg) and I give things [to K-M-E-A-L] I want to say

[here the addressee presumably shifts from Kopia to Mujika-Laulku]

isili-a nu kep wi ansipe yi-yl-a
the two, even if you (sg) [Mujika-Laulku] are a distant man

elti ui piringl-a
you two lived (together) before

pe piringl kopong tirim-ni
when you two did so, were you prosperous [lit., did you put on grease]

pe piringl kik(u) turum-ni
or were you two poor [lit.: or did you put on ashes?]

pe na naa kanakur-a
I (did) not see

pe na-kin ya tara-ma-n-a
well, I and (my) ancestors [K-M-E-A-L]

molupa ime-nga
remaining

nyibu-ko nyirim-lum-a
he [K-M-E-A-L] said he wanted to speak [fight with me]

aki tirim aki-na
he did thus

ui ul i-ma tel moluringl-kilyi
they two lived doing like that

pe naa tiringl-ri-nga tekir nyikin pilyini ...
you (sg) think we two didn't do that? [i.e., we did]...

pe nyirim aki-na
he spoke like this

pe isipe tekim nyik nyi-a
say (sg) that that's how it is [if anyone asks you when you get back home]

kulsik lyil aboluringl tiringl akin
they didn't heed any attempts to make peace

mel-ma bulibali nyirim-kilyi
things were destroyed

opimi turingl aki-kin-a
when those two fought

por-pedek-ma pula tol kalkul aboluringl
people [lit.: hindquarters and shoulders] were fighting (du) and dying (du)

kupulanum aki lekim ilyi
it is thus

ekepu-nga yununu
and now he himself [K-M-E-A-L]

na-nga yi kup adilyi
my neighbor

kiditapa-sil sidu-lum ilyi
I [Kopia-Kubuka] gave a bad thing [fight] [to Mujika-Laulku]

pe *gavman lo* okum-kin
the government law is coming

kolya-ma-nga pilke tol abolkun kalya-lyi
but those two are still fighting, you (sg) restrain them thus

teamiyl nyiba ul-uri kep naa um-lum
saying 'let us do it', even if something does not happen

ya na kang-ayl-ni we tebu nyiba *tausen* ilyi modulka kik pan tokum-o
saying 'I'm just a kid just doing it for nothing', it's all gone

ekepu-nga yunu oba
now he [Mujika-Laulku] is coming

ne nunu pukun temani tun-kin pilyipilyi
now when you yourself (sg) [K-M-E-A-L] go there and tell the story, let him hear [how the compensation was given]

abu-ma temani tung-kin pilyipilyi i nyikir-o
I say let the women (pl) go and tell him [K-M-E-A-L] about it

ku ilyi ya sikir ilyi
I am giving this money

kang-ayl oba lyipiyl nyikir-o
let the fellow come and get it, I say

ilyi mada nyikir
I've said enough

[about a minute and a half of relative confusion]

KUBUKA NAYA

na ung-te kanakur-ilyi...olyo wiyl-ala Kulubi kung kani-kin uj *bokis baim* tirim-uyl...
I want to raise one matter...when we went up there to Kulubi for a pig roast [by the Poika] he bought a coffin

[fifteen seconds of inaudible cross-talk]

KUBUKA PARKA

kang-ayl pe yuyu naa um-i
so the fellow didn't come himself?

KUBUKA UNYA

ku *teti kina* waku turud i nyikim
he [Kusika Au] says he spent thirty kina

kang mel *sutkes*-na *pauda* uj *bokis*-na mel-ka payl lyirim
the fellow got everything, the talcum powder, coffin and all

lyirim akin pe lyik oba tolulu-talulu nyiring
he [Au] did that and they wasted it [i.e., the boy who was given the money to buy the coffin spent it on something else]

ned *kar na* mel-ma lekim kalya-yl ya ul ilyi tek
down there [at Palimung] there is a car and things
pe ok ik-d ik-d tekemil ilyi-nga
and coming to here they do this and that, for this
pudu-yl top mudab-a ilyi *bekim* pudu-yl tokur, *profit*-te naa sikir
I want to give it back, I'm returning it, I'm not giving any extra

MIDIPU KUJILYI
o, *teti kina* waku turum nyib pilyikir
yes, he spent thirty kina
ekepu aku-na ku pe nabisipa pekim, pekim aku-mel-ilyi...
now how much money is left, is left like...

KUBUKA UNYA
ku *fifti foa kina* pekim, eee, *twenti foa kina* mel simul pe ne yu-nga *profit twenti foa kina*
there are fifty four, aaa, we gave about twenty four kina for his 'profit'
akin lyipa terilepa *fifti foa kina* mel
adding up about fifty four

MIDIPU KUJILYI
fifti foa kina, ee, ilyi kapola midi pe
fifty four kina, that's all right
wi olyo-nga yabu-te kalya-na lim-kin
if one of our people is hurt and lying up there
i-kin obilka leba-kin
or if there are old people
pe yabu-ma ya nosik midi naa molung aku-na
and people were not looking after them
wi lyik suku muduk mek ongi-yl pe ongi
you (pl) [Kopia-Kubuka] will take up a collection and bring it up there
ilyi pe kubi-lek mek ongi aki-yl-nga pe
they'll bring it [the coffin] first, so
kapola-ko tek mek uring
they did right to bring it
pe ya ekepu ya *paun*-te pensik sin aki-yl kapola-ko tin ilyi
well now, you (sg) had a pound and you (sg) did right to give it
kupulanum-te lupu-ko lelym-kiyl
that's our special way of doing things
ya eni yabu kis-ma wilyi *Hagen haus-sik*-na pekimil-ayl
the ordinary people stay at Hagen hospital
pe wilyi kolungi akin pe yabu-te-n jika-n teba-ko moka-n teba-ko
when they die up there then someone, a Jika or Moka, can help
ya yi mare ulka-upuka-na pung kanakun mel kanak lyik suku muduk
or here some Ulka-Upuka go up and take up a collection
uj *ket*-te lyamul teamul suku mudup teamul nyik tengi
'let's get a coffin, let's take a collection', they'll say
ul ilyi-nga lekim i nyikim-ayl kang-yi-yl yunu
that's how things are done, he's saying, that fellow [Unya]

[brief inaudible interjection here by another speaker; then Kujilyi continues:
kolum ul ilyi ya i tepa ya ekepu ya el ilyi ya el lyirim kupulanum aki-yl
to make it short, this is how we do things when fighting
wiyl-ala yi-yl ya laulku-yl el monsipa...laulku-yl el monsipa pe...
that man up there, the Laulku who has an arrow wound...
[during Kujilyi's last few words there are cries of 'Waria, Waria...']

PALIMI LKURAYA (in a low voice)
ya *kansil*-ayl ung nyiba tekim-kin yi-ka *lain* tek tek
here when the Councillor is about to talk, you men make a line

eni aku-na kuni tek molai meri *kansil*-ayl ung nyiba tekim
you (pl) remain in good order, down there the councillor is about to speak

pilyi-kayi tek wi aku-na manya molai
stay in order and listen, and sit down (pl) down there

KOPIA NOMA
[bids to be audible, raises voice]

eni kang mare el ung nyik tekimil, mare naa nyik tekimil-ayl
some of you fellows are talking el ung *and some are not*

yi tenga ung nyiba tekim, e! mel-ayl manya pum-na nyib pilyikir
another wants to talk, hey! did something fall down there!?

ya ung nyiba pelym-o, ung naa nyai-o, mol nyikir-o
he wants to talk, there's more to say, don't talk (pl), I say no!
[regains floor]

MIDIPU KUJILYI

el kani tirimul ilyi-nga yi bilyipa kolipa kepa pelipa ok molku-kin pe
when we (pl) fought that fight, and a man was mortally wounded, his uncle and cousin coming and staying

meri tekimil ul i-yl kanamiyl pamiyl nyik wed purung
'down there they are doing [something], let's go see', they said and went

kanakun pe lo-mong el-mong kabu toni
can you (sg) count the raindrops and arrows [i.e., no you can't, because latter are as numerous as the former]

wi laulku kang-ayl el molurum nyikir-ilyi
up there a Laulku boy was wounded by an arrow, I say

KOPIA PIPIRU (aside)

abola nai okum ilyi, nai okum
who's that girl coming, who's that?

MIDIPU KUJILYI

ya nela kusika kang tal, e?
and over there Kusika, two fellows [got injured], eh?

[another speaker interjects: there was a Poika]

ilyi poika kang-ayl el molurum-o, pe...
a Poika was wounded, and then

laulku kang-ayl el molurum, poika kang-ayl el molurum
a Laulku fellow, and a Poika, were wounded

[a minute or so of multiplex cross-talk]

ekepu yunu nosipa-kin ke *lep* tim ilyi tok mudai
now when he [Kubuka] puts it, whatever's left, contribute (pl) it [to him]

i tepa oba i tepa ilyi-nga i tep nyib mudukur
that's what I advise

na pe ob kanub-ayl ya ung nyikir ilyi
and I'll come and have a look, what I'm saying here,

***pilai* tep ung-iyl nyikir nyik pilyikimil**
you (pl) think I'm just joking around here?

lyik ung-kiyl sikimil nyib pilyikir-ayl
you (pl) people aren't afraid, I see

[some words inaudible]

kang laulku kang-ayl el mujirim ilyi nyikir ilyi *namba wan*
the Laulku fellow was wounded, I say, that's the first thing

KUBUKA TAMALU

kang, laulku kang yupuk
fellow! three Laulku

MIDIPU KUJILYI

e, el munsirim-o, pupa wi poika kang-ayl el munsirum
huh? he was wounded, and up there a Poika was wounded

pupa oba wi kusika kang-ayl el munsirum-o
and again up there a Kusika was wounded

pupa wi kang kunuka kang-ayl el munsirum-o, ne upuka kang-ayl el munsirum
and up there a Kunuka was wounded, and down there an Upuka

ilyi ya meri olyo ku-yl tiring kani-yl
they gave us money for that

i tepa, ilyi olyo ya yi molkumul kupulanum aki-yl-nga-te
like that, and we're here, if we fight again

ya olyo-nga kudanga yi on lyipa te kupulanum i tepa i tepa
one of ours will get the body, like that

ne bi naa lekir-kiyl ilyi oba suku pukum-kiyl...
I'm not mentioning the name, this too goes in [to consideration, apropos their later compensation payment]

ul *sevenpela* mel ilyi-nga nemnum-nemnum nyiba
seven matters, thinking only of this

laulku kang-ayl kanakun, nananu kanabu tekir-iyl
you (sg) are taking care of the Laulku fellow, so I'll take care of you

i ul tal oba we-d pukum ul-kil-nga apurukun lyini-telya
these two go out of consideration, about that if you (sg) count up

lim-te kanap ilyi nosikimul-lum-o
if one is left we (pl) might contribute jointly

pe mel nuyl mel-ayl ya lyi-sip pup kanab-a
I'll go look at and get some edibles

KOPIA WARIA (overlapping with the previous speaker)

naa pilyip molymulu, eni aku-na manya pilyai-a
we don't understand, you people sit down and listen (pl)

MIDIPU KUJILYI

ya *namba* apurukun lyini-te kanakun lyikin pora-nsikin
you (sg) count the amount and finish (sg) reckoning it

ilyi na lyikir-kil midi notikir-ayl
I'm getting that, I'm just putting that [word in my mind]

pe ilyi nai lyiba nyai, pilyip na lkudu pab i nyikir
say (pl) who'll get what, having heard this I'll go home! I say

ilyi kalya nyab-a pilyikin-kin pe
I want to say this, you (sg) listen, well

eni kang *fopela* wiyl-ala no pengi kang-te molupiyl
you four fellows, and let one man stay who's from up at No Pengi [Ukulu headwaters]

ya manya kang-te molupiyl, ya ola ilyi-nga kang tal molangl
and one man from below, let two men stay up here

ya ilyi-nga eni kang tal molangl ing nyikir
and let two of your (pl) men stay here, I say

molku-kin pe ol tai, ol tok lyik pe
and you (pl) whisper [among yourselves], having done so then

nyik na tangi nyikir kalya-yl ilyi-nga nyid
and then tell (pl) me, I say, I was talking about this

ekepu adi pilyik nyai nyikir, i ul poj i nyib sikir-kiyl
now I say you (pl) talk there; this is the main matter I'm talking about

ya ing mong-te nyikin montukun ilyi, pe wilyala kep nyimulu-ko
as for this other matter you (sg) are raising [Poika Wangi's funeral]; we can speak of it up there

pe ne kep nyimulu-ko pe ung ilyi pudu naa tokur nyikin naa pilyi
we can talk about it over there [at Palimung]; don't think (sg) I'm not responding to that

pudu tokun ya pudu tangi-na pe olyolyo nyib meb pumulu ung-iyl
you (sg) respond, let them respond and we'll keep those words in mind what you've said when we go [i.e., we'll have private discussions about it among ourselves at Palimung]

ilyi nu-nga ung nyikin montikin kalya-yl
this matter you (sg) are raising, that is

ya ung nyikir ilyi ya aki-yl adi pilyik kuni tek
these words I'm saying now, you think about it and clear it up

molkuk ol tok tok i tek i nying Waria ing nyikin kalya-yl
talking low, talk (pl) about this, like what you (sg) say, Waria

i tepa laye ing-te kongu lyiba-kiyl
doing this he'll 'bite' this matter [ref. to Waria's remarks about Poika Wangi's funeral]

siba-kiyl welkudu-alkudu ul-ilyi naa tiai
when they give it, don't go (pl) back and forth

kopi pora nyiba kelkim-kiyl
the coffee is nearly gone

pilai kas tepa no *bia* num yi-yl tepa pora-ntikim
fellows who play cards and drink beer are finishing up

ekepu ya ul ilyi sulipialipi tokum, nu kang no nun kang-ayl
now here the money is insufficient, you fellow (sg) who drank beer

kang-ayl-ni pilyik kongun-ntukun nui
(let that) fellow consider and drink (think about what he's doing)

ekepu-nga kornga lyikimil-ilyi
now they've already gotten it

mad ung akin ok-kin lupu lupu naa pai
and when you come back down [from Poika funeral] don't (pl) scatter

tilupu tenga molku ol tok pora-ntik-kin pe kelku-pangi
stay in one place and finish discussing it and then go (pl)

[i.e., As soon as you come back from Wangi's funeral, come straight to me and talk about our payment to you. Don't waste time going 'back and forth', or my people will have spent all their coffee money on cards and beer before I can organize the payment to you]

KUBUKA TAMALU

poika kang nyikim, eee! laulku kang nyikim
he says 'a Poika fellow' or 'a Laulku fellow'

ilyi nyikin pel pora nyikim, poika kang-te el munsurum aki-yl
what you (sg) are talking about, cousin, that's finished, a Poika was wounded

olto-nga ung-iyl kornga pilyipa lyilym
as for these words of us two he [the Poika] already understands about that

el ya naa telybolu i kupulanum ilyi, ime-nga pansip tep ime-nga pansip tep
we two do not fight on this 'road' [i.e., within the Kopia-Kubuka-Poika-Palimi alliance]; we do it together over and over

na nanu poika-palimi-sil-kin molup telyo
I myself stay with Poika and Palimi

ya yu-nga ul-uyl malsip malsip modup te midi kim imi tuyl-te pirim
we've got all of his matters cleaned up except for one old 'rotten vegetable' that still remains

ilyi naa pelka-ja i wiyl-ola ilyi-nga pubu na mokabu naa lyibu nyilka
if it hadn't been for that, I wouldn't be demanding compensation [from the Epola, et al] so soon

ya luip ukulu kep-ma-nga um-lum mokabu naa lyibu nyily-alyi
here by the banks of the Rivers Luip and Ukulu I wouldn't be demanding it

ekepu ya kim imi tuyl-te ilyi ya pelym midi
but there is this one 'rotten vegetable' remaining

kang akul midi nabitiyl-te
that boy, which boy is it?

poika kang-ayl-kin
with the Poika fellow

bulu-yl pupul pobera polubulu nyibul tekibul-ayl, kapola naa tekim
we two turn our backs and daub them black [expressing our shame because we are unable to pay them]; this is not right [this remark was said to have been addressed to Kujilyi]

poika kang-ayl yadu pukum-kiyl, laulku kang-ayl yadu pukum-kiyl
the Poika fellow is going back home, the Laulku fellow is going home [the Poika referred to here is presumably a man who came to fight without being asked]

memba ya oba tep tiribul yabu kare suku nokuk yi kare olto i tek tiring
we two voted in members [of Parliament], looking after our people, some men did like this to us two

ku pelybul-ayl-nga
we two are stumped

kung-na mel-te koyik nok telymeli kani-yl-nga ne we bi tokur-kiyl
since one generally roasts pork and gives it, I'm not going to mention names

mel-te si naa sikir, yabu tilke dop-n nyiyl kalya-yl ya molum
I am not giving anything, people; Tilka Dop is here [i.e., if we gave pork to others, we'd have to give to him]

pe poika kang-sil ilu midi bi naa lekir-kiyl, bi na naa lekir
so I'm not mentioning the names of the two Poika, I am not mentioning their names

nu-n lian nyib pilyikir, ya laku makupilyi na-ni bi naa lekir
I'd rather let you (sg) name them, I am not mentioning the names of the two sons of Laku

yabu-ma bi naa lekir nyikir, nu-d manya nyibu pilyini, i ul sika tekir, ee
I'm not naming people, I will tell you (sg) secretly, that's what I'm really doing

ike manya pukum, ya-kin pabu-lyi eneni...
this [money] is already gone to you five... [the 'five' are possibly Mujika, Laulku, Tilka, Poika, and Palimi]

PALIMI LKURAYA

faiv nyikin-i
you (sg) are saying five?

KUBUKA TAMALU

laulku-yl pabu-yl
Laulku is the fifth [lit., 'thumb']

PALIMI LKURAYA

yadu *faipela* nyikir
I say five

ilyi pelym nyikir-o
this remains, I say

KUBUKA TAMALU

ku *ten* aku-ma ku le top tep tekimul kalya-ma pe
the money they're giving is not really money

pe na-nga kung koyip nob telka-ja pe
if I had roasted and eaten a pig

i nabitini kung obil-ayl koyipa noba siba nyikim
[my ally would say] 'what are you (sg) going to do; he says he's going to roast and give me a pig bone'

na-nga kupulanum wi pukur-na-d nyikir
I'm talking about what I do up there

pe kung-ur naa kuyud-iyl, mel kalya-ma ya keripudu-na pulym
I didn't roast a pig, such things all go in the mouth [i.e., there are none left to give]

mel sipitaka tuyl-te ya nosip molymulu
we're holding the fight

sipitaka tokur
I'm holding the fight [lit.: I'm pulling out cordyline]

nanu ekepu bulkud nabitep-ja
what shall I do now at the back [i.e. as an ally in the fight]

eni laulku kunsiliyl-winjangiyl bali sur tolymeli yabu
you (pl) Laulku\Kunsiliyl and \Winjangiyl are people who wear your loincloths short [when fighting]

wi aku-na akisipa pelym
up there it's like that

ya manya oba tauwu sulu boni-ma alym-kel gaima-ma noba pulym
down here people go around eating different kinds of bananas, beans

na ya moly-ayl
I live here

anum pulu-yl sikir-ayl, mel-te kung no-ma imi koyip noly-ayl
I give a lot to my mother['s people], I roast and eat pig fat

pe nabisiyl bulkud yabu-te molung-na nyibu-i
but can I say anyone stays and helps me?

ilyi naa nyikir
I'm not saying so [i.e., I'd like to give to Tilka Dop, but no-one helps me]

ilyi naa nyikir-kilyi, idu ung kolsi nyikir kalya-yl
this I'm not saying; what I say now

ung lupu mel-te nyidi-kiyl, ilu bi naa lekir nyikir
I said something different before, I'm not naming him [Dop]

yabu *fopela* abolu-yl-ka ee!
let us 'hold' four [talapi], *hey!*

nyab-a kela, a!
I want to talk, stop (sg) it!

[cross-talk]

wi na-nga kupulanum awilyi-yl pabu-yl
up there my 'big road' is the fifth one [i.e. the one to Laulku]

fopela abolup yadu modukur, na-nga kupulanum awilyi-na pabu-yl lekim
I send back four, my main road is my thumb [i.e., Laulku]

ya na nabisiyl ya ul-iyl walsikal tiabiyl nyikin pilyikuna-ja
how shall we two give to them right now, if you (sg) thought so

ya ul-te yadapa nyib sab
I can relay something to you

ekepu ilyi-nga gasinami polupa telka-ja kapola
now if the grass had grown (over the battlefield) [i.e., if it had been a long time since we fought] that would be o.k.

olto-nga mare pilyikir ilyi-ka
I'm thinking of our (du) affairs

nu nabitelta-yl adi ime-nga ob i nyib telkubula-lyi pe
what are you (sg) [Kujilyi]? why don't you come and tell us two to talk about it here?

na ok naa nyilkuna-lyi-nga anginansikim
because you (sg) didn't come and tell me, a lot of time has been wasted

ya ok yadu tekir-ilyi aku mare telkuna-ja
if you (sg) [Kujilyi] had come before

olto isip tilu-na molupul yabu-luma ok isik kanak molkuk
we two would stay together and people would come and see and stay

ekepu na yabu-ka naa abolulyo nyikin kalya-yl
now you (sg) say I'm not holding people [with some allies]

yab *fopela* abolup yadu modukur
I'm holding and sending four back [i.e., all but Laulku]

kupulanum awilyi-yl-na *faipela* abolup modukur
the main road is the fifth one

isipe pekim
that's how it is

[fifteen seconds of unfocussed cross-talk by various men including Kopia Noma - remarks such as *takan molai* 'be quiet']

KOPIA KAJIPU

ya, ya, yab ung naa nyai-o ya
here, here, people, don't talk (pl) !

[eight seconds of unfocussed remarks such as *manya molai, manya molamiyl*, 'sit down, let's sit down']

KUBUKA TAMALU

eni yab ororapi ororapi eni yab e
you (pl) people shut up! hey you people!

mel kari molymeli-ka koyik nongi-kiyl
what do you (pl) want to do, roast something [i.e. women's private parts] and eat it?

eni yab orora naa nyik ti ul-ri-ni
you (pl) shut up and let this thing happen

manya molai i nyik maku tok
sit (pl) down, talking thus and staying in one place

[six seconds of cross-talk]

ya ku *handet* ilyi tamalu-kin parka-kin tingl ku *handet*-yl-o
this hundred ['pounds', i.e. two hundred kina] here is the hundred that Tamalu and Parka gave

i ku *handet* ilyi unya tepra-sil-n tingl ku-yl-o
this hundred is what Unya and Tepra gave

i *handet* ilyi kiliyl dama-sil tingl-o
this hundred Kiliyl and Dama gave

ping lku tapa waku maka-nsipa *tri handet* pora nyim
altogether, the [Kubuka] Ping men's house has given three hundred

i ku *handet* ilyi kuduyl-kalyanga-sil tim o
this hundred here was given by [Kubuka] Kuduyl and Kalyanga [men's houses]

[whispered onto the tape by Alan Rumsey: 'two hundred and fifty kina, according to the sign']

i ku *foa handet*
this four hundred

[whispered by Alan Rumsey: 'five hundred sixty, Mr. Noma' [as on the sign]]

i ku *handet* ilyi
this one hundred

ku *tu handet* na kupena tolab-sil tid-o
two hundred, I, the Kupena-Tolab have given

handet tal
two hundred

tep ob-kin na tolab mansipa ku *handet* i tid
I, Tolab, alone have come and given this one hundred

UNIDENTIFIED SPEAKER

e
oh?

KOPIA KAJIPU

tep ob-kin na tolab mansipa ku *handet* i tid
I, Tolab, alone have come and given this one hundred

i sil kupena tolab-sil lyip *joinim* tep ku *handet* tal
these two, Kupena and Tolab joining together, two hundred

ku *tri handet* na tid
three hundred, I gave

KUBUKA TEPRA

buk-na ku *handet* tal pelym
there's still two hundred on the display board

KOPIA KAJIPU

o
yes

ku *tri handet*
three hundred

[whispered by Alan Rumsey: 'ku three hundred, no sign']

ku *handet* ilyi no pengi tim
this hundred No Pengi ['headwater' people] gave (sg)

KUBUKA TEPRA

ku luburu naa luburui-a emina nani-kin
don't shake (sg) the money, eat (sg) your wife!

KOPIA KAJIPU

kopil tapa-n tim-uyl-o
Kopil men's house gave (sg)

i *handet* ilyi ukulupiyl tapa-n tim-o
this hundred Ukulupiyl gave (sg)

i ku *foa handet* tim-o
this four hundred it gave

[shouts of 'seven handet' in the background]

KOPIA SILKA

aku mol-o, ya
not that, hey!

KOPIA SIRKU

aku-ma olyo penga nyib simulu
we'll tell this later

KUBUKA TEPRA

akisik nyi-lyik pa
go on (sg) telling them!

KOPIA KAJIPU

ku *handet* ilyi galka tim-o, kewa galka
Galka gave (sg) this hundred, Kewa Galka [full name Galka-Kewangiyl]

KOPIA OWA

kum tal, kang-yi
[and] two fists, hey!

KOPIA KAJIPU

i *handet* ilyi kabika tim-o
this hundred Kabika gave (sg)

[Alan Rumsey aside for tape: 'two hundred fifty toea'].

KOPIA KAJIPU

i *handet* ilyi palimi abun-miyl tim-o
this hundred Palimi Abu-n Miyl (matrifiliate) gave (sg)

lku tapa-ma-nga lupu lupu i tep timul
thus each of us (pl) various men's houses gave

ekepu lyik *joinim* tek-kin
now they take that and add it up

KUBUKA TEPRA

aki-yl olyolyo nyimulu
we [Kubuka] will discuss that ourselves

[Alan Rumsey aside for tape: 'Palimi two hundred fifty']

KOPIA KAJIPU

pe eneni nyai-a
well you (pl) talk

KOPIA KUPENA

ne ku *handet*-ma-o ku *handet* ilyi-nga lyip taku mudukur aku-ni ku *wan tausen*
taking those hundreds and adding this hundred, I am giving one thousand

UNIDENTIFIED SPEAKER

bal-ayl kulsikim-alyi, ulu-ri teba-kiyl
his loincloth is falling down, so something is going to happen [i.e. it is an omen (temal)]

KOPIA KUPENA

ya, ku, olu-bal kulsikim-alyi ya we tekim nyib pilyid ya
here, money, (my) front loin cloth is falling, I thought it was for nothing [i.e., don't think so; one exegete proposed that it was because of Poika Wangi's death]

ku ilyi-nga nyib molka kulsikim
as I talk about this money it's falling down

ya, ku *tausen* na naa tebu nyirid-o...na naa tebu nyirid-ilyi nabimna-o
here, I won't give a thousand, I said...I won't, I said, what for?

ya epola-alya kang-ma no ukulu mi nyiring-o
the Epola-Alya fellows (pl) swore upon the river Ukulu

ya kopia kang-ma no napilya mi nyiring pilyip-lyanga
the Kopia fellows (pl) swore upon the river Nebilyer --- we knowing this

eltila eltili kapu el-ayl tiringl-ayl tiringl nyib pilyipu
thinking about the fact that those two fought over things [i.e., because compensation was not paid]

ne-d lku kalya-sil noba sungunsipiyl nyibu na mol nyirid-o
let them over towards there [Tea-Dena] burn down their houses, I said no

akilyi nabina-o, eltila lopa ayl pala puduru-nga molo
what for? those two didn't give a marsupial tail [allusion to the Dena Peam's argument over his 'marsupial road' (see section 3.2.2 for details)]

lu kubamung puduru-nga elti tekibil i nyib pilyirid-o
or the two were doing it over a stone ax, I thought

elti-nga lku-yl ui nupiyl nyib pilyirid kanilyilyi
let them burn each other's houses, I thought

na-nga ku *tausen*-ayl nanu oma-*rais* nobu nob molubu
I'll spend my thousand on eating fish and rice

nyib pilyirid-o
so I thought

ya midipu kujilyi nu nyik-lyanga ab *pasindia*-yl molkur-alyi
Midipu Kujilyi you (sg) said 'I'm like a prostitute'

puyl waru manya pukur-ayl-ka ilyi ui yi-ma pup adurud adurud
'I go down the Puyl grade', he said, 'I went around from man to man'

kinya-nga pingje purum-ilyi
'now I'm getting old'

yi-te-n kanapa lyiba ya nyirin-kiyl-o
'if a man sees (me), will he marry me?' you (sg) said

pe na-nga ku *tausen* ilyi we leba-i-o
'will my thousand just be for nothing?

kujilyi nunu tokun tepi kaluni nyib pilyirid-o
Kujilyi, I thought you (sg) would burn the money

lku-suku pup tapaba nyib tirid-kin
when I went home and got all the weapons

lku pi-te naa kalurud-o
I didn't burn an old house [in the fighting]

kapiyl-ku-r kep naa turud-o
I didn't wound anyone

kani-yl pora nyirim-o
that is finished

olto-nga yad el-ayl-o
that fight of ours (du)

nu-nga kapu el tiringl kani-yl-nga na payl topa meba purum-iyl
when you two had your fight 'over things', she [Kujilyi as prostitute] copulated with us all [lit.: me-all] and took us [into the fight]

pe na yi-r naa turum-o
but not a man of mine was killed

nu kepi te naa turum-lum-o
nor was any of yours killed

adi tepul kulu turubul kani-yl-ko
we two fought without injury

ya ku *tausen* ilyi-o
as for this thousand

epola-alya-sil kubi-na ol molkubela-na
if Epola and Alya had come (du) first

kabu top silka-yl-ko
I would have told them the amount

kangabola talsini
you (sg) will act like the child [in the following proverb]

kung kare nyirim-kin
when he had asked her to bring a pig

abola nu kub ilyi nu mek un ya nyirim-o
he said 'girl, you (sg) brought only the leash'

anum nu mek okun ya i nyirim kanumel
'mother, you (sg) are bringing it', he said like that

na nanu epola-alya-sil-kin isip nyilka-lyi
I would have spoken to Epola and Alya like that

kujilyi nu abola kom-ayl molurun
Kujilyi, you (sg) were the eldest girl

nu kung ka-yl mekin nu kubi lirin kani-yl-o
you (sg) came first holding the pig lead

kinya-nga na-nga ku *tausen* ilyi nu-nga kangi-na nosinsikir-o
now I give this thousand of mine for you (sg)

mada nyikir-o pe altepa ung-uri nyibe
I've said enough, now he'll talk again

KOPIA NOMA (starting immediately after the previous speaker)

ya ku-yl-o
this money

ya ku *tri handet* tid-iyl
this is the three hundred that I gave

na-n tid-o
I gave it

na-n tid-iyl-o
it's what I gave

tid-iyl i nabitim-na
why did I do it

no kep pepa yab-ayl-ni yabu ki abolulym-o
a man who lives near the river-side always takes people's hands [to help them across]

yabu ki abolulym ilyi
he always takes people by the hand

olto tapu-topul
we two stay together

ya kang koluwa-kin olto tapu-topul pelybul-ayl ilyi
this fellow [Epola] Koluwa and I live together

pe na-ni mel-te naa tid-iyl, i nyib pilyip tid
well I haven't given anything, thinking thus I gave

i nyib pilyip tid-ilyi
I thought this

kang-ma ku-yl lepa nyim kanapa
if the fellows are talking about money

ya yi-ma uj pol tebu-kin tensi-pai nyid i ku-yl tekimil-o
here I want to make a bridge [to Epola-Alya et al]; I said go and make it for me, so they are giving this money

ku tekimil ilyi-o
they are giving money

ekepu wiyl-ola yi-yl-n na-kin kapu naa teb-o
so now the man from up there [Mujika-Laulku] and I won't fight over things

ya ku tep nusid-iyl-o
I gave the money

kang laulku kang-ayl-o
a Laulku fellow

laulku kang-ayl el munsirim-o
a Laulku fellow was wounded by an arrow

pe mudike-laulku-sil nyiba pelym-o
but so-called Mujika and Laulku live as a pair

laulku tid kanapa mudike naa sikir-o
I gave to Laulku but I'm not giving to Mujika

pe sibu-ilyi-nga-o
I want to do so

na siwalayl naa lim-o
but there's no way for me to do it

ilyi na naa tekir molo-o
I am not doing so, no

ku pimu payl-te tep nusid lelym-o
I put down the money 'with no orifices' [i.e., without having heard from Epola about how much they will give us]

UNIDENTIFIED LAULKU MAN

ya ya ya *kansil*-ayl-nga ung nyikim-ayl...ya ya...
here the Councillor is talking...

***kansil* olyo pilyikimul...ya...**
we are listening to the Councillor...here...

[some lines lost during tape change]

UNIDENTIFIED SPEAKER, PROBABLY A LAULKU

kelip pamiyl nyib pilyikir-o...
I think we should leave ...

UNIDENTIFIED KOPIA SPEAKER

pamul eni ya ing-ilyi...
let's go, this talk here...

KOPIA NOMA

ya ul-ilyi ui-o ya kang-kil-n, e e
first this here, fellows, hey!

ui takan molui
first be (sg) quiet

[starts *el ung* style in the next line]

ku-yl-ooooo
this money

[interrupted by cross-talk, of which only the following line, by unidentified speaker, is audible]

walsimolu
we'll ask

MIDIPU KUJILYI

ya yi yabu tongi-te kep nanu ab wenep-ayl kubi-na molup molup tirid-o
a man they will kill, at first I was like a young unmarried woman

na ul penga kalya-nga naa nyibu-kiyl *kot*-te teba-yl
I won't talk about that, there'll be court (over it)

penga nu-nga *kot*-te tentibu ya
later I will take you (sg) to court

ya epola-alya-ma ok molung-kin
when the Epola and Alya come (pl)

ing kalya-ma wed-lyik pudu tang-ayl
let them respond to those words [ref. to earlier complaints by Noma and Kupena about the Epola not coming]

[inaudible cross-talk; Noma gets the floor by resuming his *el ung* speech, as follows]

KOPIA NOMA

ya ku-yl-o
this money

ku-yl-o
the money

ku-yl el kupulanum ya lelym-o
this is fight-road money

ku el kupulanum ya lekim-o
it's fight fight-road money

na-nga pel-o
my cousin

na-nga pel-o
my cousin

na-nga apa-o
my uncle

el kupulanum ya lekim-o
the fight-road is here

kupulanum kil-nyiyl-na nu pirin-lum-o
you (sg) live near the road

kanga tolkuka-ja-o
if a fellow had been killed

i tep nyilkubola-o
we two would have spoken like this

i tep melkula-o
I would have paid compensation like this

ku-yl kanap-o
looking at the money

na gai koni-ma nobu naa kaniyl-o
I don't eat konima *sweet potatoes*

kim *kapis* nob naa kaniyl-o
I don't eat cabbage

kaspis nobu naa kaniyl-o
I don't eat potatoes

mel-ma nu-ko nolto-lum-o
these are the things you *(sg) eat*

moni wa tep nu-nga kangi-na nosinsikir-o
I am giving you (sg) lots of money [lit.: putting money on your skin]

kop-sikin mekin kuda puni-lum kuda pui-o
if you (sg) want to 'carve it up' [like pork] and take it, then go ahead and do so

kanglku mekin kuda puni-lum kuda pui-o
if you (sg) want to cradle it in your arms and take it, then go ahead and do so

[20 seconds of unfocussed cross-talk]

UNIDENTIFIED SPEAKER

yi on we lelym-o
the man's corpse is there

ada wangi wilyi lelym-o
old man Wangi is lying up there

manya modup pubu tekir-o
I want to go there and bury him

nabina tek okumeli, el ung-iyl...
what are you (pl) doing this for? el ung... [i.e., don't talk el ung]

KOPIA PIGIN

ku *namba* awilyi-yl ya ilyi-nga wai nyimul-ayl
come (pl) here and we'll tell you the total

[*several minutes of cross-talk, during which Noma tries to get the floor by speaking* el ung. *The following are his first audible words*]

KOPIA NOMA

eni yabu kit-ma koni tiai-o
you (pl) rubbish people, straighten up!

[Tape off, on again after a few minutes, when audience again becomes focussed]

KOPIA WARIA (who tries to line up the various men's houses, so that each can make its donation in sequence)

aku-na kubuka kuduyl pipiyl-o, kuduyl-kalyanga-sil
let Kubuka Kuduyl be there, the pair of Kuduyl and Kalyanga

kuduyl kalyanga pek modum aku-na ya kang na-nga-ka piai-o
Kuduyl and Kalyanga stay there, and my fellows [Kopia Galka] you (pl) stay there too

835 aku-na pepa mudum akin aku-na ya galka pi-o
when that's done, Galka you (sg) join them there

galka pepa aku-na kupena-tolab-sil
Galka, and then the pair of Kupena-Tolab

kupena-tolab ya pipiyl-o
let Kupena-Tolab be there

[several minutes of cross-talk and then silence as people examine the display boards, then tape off for a few minutes as the boards are moved from the Kailge display ground to the school ground, and the crowd reassembles there]

KUBUKA KOMI (who is treasurer of the school board)

pena-na yabu meri pena-na ya kolya *skul* kolya-na ne
on the display ground [we should give the compensation] instead of at the school ground

kolya kalya-ma-nga wedu pup telkumola-yl ya *skul* kolya
we should go to such a place, but the school ground

840 ul ilyi-nga ya ul-ilyi ya kolya kanap molymolu kapola naa tim-na
to transact this business here [on the school ground] is not right

skul kolya-na meba sukudu obu kongun tepu ku simulu tekimul
having brought it into the school ground, we are going to give money

ku-ka simulu tekimul ya *skul* kolya-na
we are about to give money here on the school ground

ku *ten* kina mel *baim* timul
we paid ten kina for [permission to do] this

ya ola molym ku *ten* kina mel *baim* tep timul
it is up there, we paid ten kina

845 ilyi yabu-te naa kanak molku kang-abola le kare-ka weli weli ting
the thing is, when nobody was around watching, children defecated and made a mess

kang-abola le kare-ka weli-weli tengi
children will defecate and mess it up

pe ya pea po-elki *na buai* nok weli weli tengi
and also sugar cane husks, and chewing betel nut they will mess it up

naa teai-o
don't do (pl) it

yabu ya yi mare nokai nyimul
we've delegated some men to look after it

850 eni kanak molymeli, eni ku *ten kina baim* tengi
they are watching you (pl) and [if you do any of these things] you'll have to a pay ten kina fine

ya *skul* kolya ilyi, kang-abola ya weli-weli tengi
the children will mess up the school ground

pe ya langi *na* po *na* mel kare-ka *makis* tekimil kalya-yl
so, as for the way they are selling food, cane and different things

ya *insait* ilyi-nga naa tiai, kor nyib pora-nsikumul kalya-yl
don't (pl) do it here inside [the ground], we've already finished saying this

naa kanak ya wiyl-ola po na anginsikumul kanakur
I see over there they're ignoring this and selling sugar cane

i-kil lyiku-nok ting-akin
they're taking it and eating it

pilyi-kongunsuk lalyik mek wedu pai-o
you (pl) think about this and take it away in your netbags

nosungi yabu kare-ka ya wiyl-ola ku *ten kina* molym
the ten kina which has been paid for this place is already up on the board

ilyi-nga *ten kina mo sukurim* ten-kiyl-o
you'll have to give more than that [if you litter the place]

ilyi eni *skul* kolya-na *toksave* tep nyikir-kiyl-o
I'm just informing you (pl) about the school ground

ten kina ya *skul* kolya *baim* tep
we paid ten kina for the school ground

plak-kiyl *baim* tep timul-kiyl-o
and we paid for the flag

KUBUKA PUS

na nokulyo yiyl-n nyikir nyin-ka
'I, the man who looks after it, am talking' is what you (sg) should have said

KUBUKA TAMALU

ya ana-o ilyi mada, ilyi mada eni-nga *skul* kolya
here brother, that's enough now about your (pl) school ground

ilyi mada-o ung-ma-kin kanu-ma bonunga-talko-nga-o pora nyim-o
that's enough, enough talk, yesterday and the day before; that's all

kor-nga pilyirimul kanum-o
we heard that before

ekepu ku sibu tekir na ung-ur naa nyib-o
now I'm about to give money, and won't say a word [i.e., won't say much]

eni kep ti naa nyang-o
don't you (pl) say one [i.e., much] either

ya ku-yl ekepu sip pora-nsibu tekir
now I want to finish giving the money

[about thirty seconds of inaudible cross-talk]

UNIDENTIFIED SPEAKER

ku kabu kubilek tolymeli mola
you (pl) count the money first or

akiyl ku-yl ya pansip molymolu, ilyi eni pilyik nyikimil-i?
we have the money, do you (pl) understand this as you talk

KUBUKA TAMALU

kanga ya, kang-yi yupuk el molurum kaniyl-o
fellow, there were three men wounded

ob ob *pasim* tep-o
I/we stopped coming

lku uji *pasim* tep-o
I/we stopped collecting firewood

punya kongun *pasim* tep-o
I/we stopped our garden work

kubi kelsik naa turum-o
his feet weren't sore

ul lupu-ri naa tirim-o
he [i.e we] didn't do anything else [but fight]

lku ponga naa turum-o
he didn't make house-posts

mara naa nurum-o
our calves weren't sore

ku *handet* kina kang-yi el monsurung ilyi-nga nosikir-o
I'm giving one hundred for the fellow who was wounded

foa handet-o
four hundred

tultul-nga koma lensikir-o
I'm carrying on my shoulder for Tultul [also known as Laulku Nui]

foa handet-o
four hundred

[the following line is unclear]

ya mongayl mal sikir
I'm giving to Mongayl's son ?

[in background: 'faiv handet']

ku *foa handet*-o yapu koma lensikir-o
four hundred I give to Yapo mentioning his name

[some inaudible exchanges]

ku *nain handet* mel-ayl-nga *wan handet* ilyi kang-sil-nga mel sikir-o
about nine hundred, one hundred I give to the two boys

kabu top sukud lyikir
I count it and take it inside

kang taltike el molurum akilyi-nga kang-kil-nga nenem-ayl
the three boys who were wounded, it's for them alone

eni kep abolku kanung kep eni nyik singirang
but if you (pl) [Kopia] hold the money [and count it] they won't disturb you

tultul ilyi-nga *foa handet* molkum, yako-nga *foa handet* molkum
there's four hundred for Tultul, and four hundred for Yako

idi yako-nga, idi *tultul* ilyi-nga
over there is Yako's, and there Tultul's

ti ku nabitepa ku *wan tausen* tep
another lot is how much? I give one thousand

wan handet, pe *wan tausen* pe ku *handet* tep
one hundred, one thousand and then one hundred

pi *wan tausen foa handet seventi kina* tep, akiyl-nga tep monsikur
so one thousand four hundred seventy kina, that's how much I'm putting up

akisipa mel tekir, el ung mare na ekepu naa nyib-o
that's how much I'm giving, I will not talk el ung

ul-iyl ya kang-sil kapiyl mokabu tokur-o
I'm compensating for the wounded boys

na yadupa yabu pipilyike [or pikuyl tekir?] telyo kalya-yl-o
I'm working for future cooperation

ya yi mare-kin el mong lyayl-waip tep el langinsibu nyib
showing off our arrows with some of these men, saying 'I'll take the fight'

ku-te kumu top meb, ku suruyl-te ka kopa-top meb sibu
making up some money, tying up some money with a hole in it and bringing and giving it

meb naa adakur-kiyl-o
I don't go around doing this [i.e., this is the first time]

yabu pipilyike [or pikuyl-nga??] mim tekir-o
I'm building cooperation,

pe el tobu nyilka-ja
so that if he [the enemy] should say 'I'll fight'

isipe tolka, nu yi kap-ayl isipe lyik ugiyl sip melka-yl
if I should fight, I would scare even you (sg), a large man into fighting

isipe melka mel tekir
I would compensate you thus

pe i ul ilyi yabu pipilyika [or pikuyl-ma] mim tekir
with this talk I am building cooperation

na na-nga yi mekir *lo* mim tekir akilyi
I'm fathering/compensating my man, I am thereby creating law

ui yi-ma-n ul ilyi te-kinsiring, ekepu *lo* mim tekir
people before made a bad job of this [i.e., didn't pay compensation]; now I'm building law

ya meri manya kolya pekim kalya-yl kabilyip saba nyib tekir-ayl ...
down there where I tread the ground [pointing to an area adjacent to the school ground that was formerly used as a social club]

eni ku *tausen*-ayl sip poransikir ekepu mada nyikir
I am handing over this thousand, and that's all I have to say

ya pilyin yi talsi nyibu nyikin pilyin-lum ku moki tiai
hear (sg) me you few men, and though you (sg) may want to speak, just give (sg) the money instead

[here Kujilyi says something inaudible, to the effect that the Laulku shouldn't worry about how much the Kopia-Kubuka are going to get in the later payment from him]

KOPIA SUBA

ku ilyi ting kis lim-kiyl, komapiyl nyi
they gave this money and it turned out bad [i.e., the amounts don't add up] Komapiyl [place name for Kubuka Unya] you (sg) talk

[inaudible cross-talk for about fifteen seconds]

KUBUKA UNYA

ku-o
money

i ku-o oladu-madu tim-o
this money has gone up and down

yi *pilai kas* adum-kiyl-o
the man [i.e., men] are coming around playing cards

lku tapa tenga topa pimi nyik pilyin-o
you (sg) [Laulku] may think some [Kopia] men's house groups are not giving enough [because they wasted their money playing cards]

ku *namba*-yl tim-iyl-o
this is the amount he gave

eni *skelim* tek sikimil-ilyi-o
they are counting it and giving it out to you (pl)

na nanu moki tep sab-o
I myself will divide and give it

kang ku *handet*-te topa manya-nsim
the fellow has lowered the amount by one hundred

ya ku talapi ilyi-nga-o
this line-up of money

ku molkum ilyi-nga ku *lep*-ayl-o
the money that's here is the left-over money

ku *tu tausen kina tu handet*
the two thousand two hundred kina

aku nu mudike-laulku-sil
that's for you (sg) Mujika-Laulku

molkum akiyl-o
it is there

pe na-nga na nanu ku *namba* lupulupu tid-iyl-ko-o
'I' myself contributed the money [so I know the amount]

lyipa terilepa-o
adding it together

ku *tu tausen*-o
two thousand

foa handet-o
four hundred

***seventi kina* isipe tekir ilyi-o**
and seventy kina; that's how much I'm giving

ku *namba* anum-uyl tekir-o
I am giving a lot of money

nu-o
you (sg)

nu na-nga tara-o
you (sg) are my father

kunutapiya mini ilyi-nga telka-ja papu-o
if I fight, you (sg) too will bear a shield; that's good

nu na-nga tara-o
you (sg) are my father

kera-bonungu menir-nga telka-ja papu-o
if I [told you to] bring the plume of a Princess Stephanie's bird of paradise (Astraphia Stephaniae) or a ribbon-tailed bird of paradise (Astraphia mayeri), that would be good

nu na-nga tara-o
you (sg) are my father

nu na-nga pela
you (sg) are my cousin

nu na-nga apa
you (sg) are my uncle

ul akisipa-ri mola-o
this is not that sort of affair [i.e., we Kopia-Kubuka are not the 'owners' of the fight, so I haven't asked you bring those plumes, as I would have done if we had been]

lu nokum-o
the ax bites/cuts

lu nokum-o
the ax bites

sirku nokum-a
sirku grass bites [the feet]

lu-n nokum-a
the ax bites

sirku-n nokum-a
sirku grass bites

kamaya-n nokum-a
wild sugar cane grass bites

ilyi-nga tekir ilyi kanakun-ya
that's why I'm compensating [you], you (sg) see

nu nunu-n pilyikin-a
you (sg) are thinking about it

numan-ayl boni pilyikin-o
your (sg) mind is heavy (aggrieved)

na nyirim adiyl-a
he [the Kusika-Midipu] told me so

na wena tokum nyikin pilyin-a
you (sg) thought I was off the mark

na nanu numan-ayl-din-a
I thought to myself

nu na-kin-a
you (sg) with me

boni awiyl-te pilyini-a
will feel very aggrieved [for not giving you enough]

na kolya-ma-nga pilyip telyo-kin-a
I feel this

isip tid-kin-a
when I have done this

yi mare-kin-a
and some men

mel isipe kanak bi naa lelymeli-a
don't call out (pl) my name like this [i.e., praise me]

mel isipa-ri-r molup kolubu nyik pilyilymeli-yl-a
they think 'I will remain like this until I die'

pe tokumil kang-ma
but as for the boys who get shot

ul lupu mare tek melkomela nyik pilyin-a
don't think (sg) they would do something different [if I /we had got shot]

ya mekir i mel melkomela
they would pay compensation the way I'm doing here

pe olyo isip mep akiyl-o
well we are compensating thus

ku sikir ilyi-a
I am giving this money

nu mekin pukun pukun-a
you (sg) take it away

kilkai-ri-nga kuyini kanapa
if you (sg) are going to sacrifice to the Kilkai spirit

i-ka nyib pilyip molkur-kiyl-a
as I suspect is the case

maip-ri-nga kuyini kanapa
if you (sg) are going to sacrifice to the Maip spirit

i nyib pilyibu molkur-kiyl-a
as I suspect is the case

mekin pukun pukun-a
you (sg) take it

abilya eked okum-o
the Abilya River comes from that way

wijaka eked okum-a
the Wijaka River comes from that way

mekin pukun-a
you (sg) take it

karaip sunga kare pelym-kiyl-a
there are some nothofagus beech logs lying there [between those rivers]

aku-na mek pukun koyikin kanui-a
so you (sg) take it [the money, metaphorically equated to a pig] and try to roast it

kim pupa nyim kanapa
if the grease goes on the vegetables

sika nyib tara kanab-a
I want to see this, father

pe kim naa pupa nyim kanapa
but if it does not

isip nyib kanubu-kilya
I say that's the way it is

ya na-nga nosikir-ayl tekir nyi-pilyin-a
do you (sg) think I'm putting my own money? [i.e., don't think so]

ya wiyali ang-a
my Wiyal [upper Kopia] brother

kim *kapis* noba naa kanalym-a
is not accustomed to eating cabbage

[some cross-talk, making a few lines of Unya's speech inaudible]

ya wiyali ang-a
my Wiyali brother

kaspis kalya-ma-nga-te noba naa kanalym-a
doesn't eat potatoes like that

i nyibu tekir-ilyi-a
this is what I want to say

na po makupiya langulyu-yl-a
*I am the broken off piece of sugar cane [i.e.my 'line' (*talapi*) is short; we Kubuka are not numerous]*

olto kuniming yi tilupu kani-sil-a
we two from Kuniming [the Kubuka and Laulku talapi*] are 'one man'*

nu mek ilyi-nga
you (sg) taking the money

nu boni peba nyib-lyanga
I'm thinking you (sg) might remain aggrieved

nu na-kin kubi kulyiwu tin nyib-lyanga
I'm thinking you (sg) might get long-faced with me

nu numan-a pensikir-kilya
so now I'm easing your (sg) mind

na-kin ung mare nyibu nyik pilyin kanapa
if you (sg) want to say anything to me

ekepu ilyi-nga yadu modukun nyi
send (sg) it this way now

ne pul yiyl-kep pilyipilyi
let the 'owner' of the fight over there [i.e., Kujilyi] hear

mola naa nyibu nyikin pilyin kanapa
but if you (sg) think you don't want to say anything

koma-yl-kin pipi top modukur-a
I'll stop it up with koma *grass [i.e., money]*

nu nunu ang aji molui
as for yourself, brother, stay (sg) back [if you don't want to say anything]

pe na-kin *pe* tekim *pe* tekim nyin kanapa
if you (sg.) say 'he's paying me'

pipi tum top modukur
I've already stopped it up

gavman-nga *lo*-nga nyiba
there is government law [so we can't fight]

na ku ilyi sip pora-nsikir-a
in giving this money I have concluded (the matter).

pilyi-kelk un-lum-a
if you (sg) forget about it and keep on coming

nu mong lyip-sib-a
I'll make trouble for you (sg) [i.e., get you jailed]

lupu ung-te tekim nyikin pilyin-a
if you (sg) think 'he's talking differently' [or strangely]

el-nga *plan*-te tekim nyik-pilyin-a
if you (sg) think 'he's making plans for future fighting'

na olk mara lyikimil ime-nga ti naa isip naa kanubu nyib tekir
I don't want to see people getting splinters from the mara tree [i.e., I'm not looking for trouble]

i wi tekir, i nyikir
I will not do so, I say

tausen-wa tekir-o
I'm giving a thousand

tausen foa handet tep
one thousand four hundred

KOPIA LADIKANG

yi-ma-aa
men

yi-ma-aa
men

kuniming yi yako
Yako, man of Kuniming

kuniming yi nui-o
Nui, man of Kuniming

na-nga ku *handet*
my money there

[cross-talk, making some lines inaudible]

nu-nga tobiyl kirip-a
your (sg) [place called] Tobiyl Kirip

na-nga ku *tausen* wal
my one thousand

mara gom-na nosain tekir-a
I'm giving you so you (sg) can put it on a bed of mara leaves

molo nu-ni aku mada lipilyi
or if you (sg) say 'let it stay like that'

lyik kadi teku nyin-lum-o
or if you (sg) want to put it in your house

pe olto-nga pea-yl pe moludu kepi
it belongs to the two of us together

pi molud kepi na ung ti naa nyibu
even later I won't say anything

aku-ma aji sikir-kilya
these people to whom I am giving now

kojiliyl *na*
Kojiliyl [Laulku men's house group] and

wijangilyi pilyipilyi
Wijangiyl [another Laulku men's house group], let him hear

[inaudible cross-talk]

pe nu-nga kadi lanya-nga
your (sg) real father

yi lu-n num
an ax cut the man

yi kamaya-n num
wild sugarcane grass cut the man

na-nga ku *wan tausen* lepa nyim-lum nu sikir
I am giving my one thousand to you (sg)

[some lines inaudible]

...mulu akiyl sikir, mai-pola sikir-o
I give to the mountain, and to the ground

maikali sikin-o madi kola sikin-o
you (sg) will give me a bad skin and make me neglect my normal work [because of fighting]

i tek ti-a
you (sg) should do like this

KOPIA NOMA [pause lengths in seconds shown after each line]

i yi-ma-oooo [last two syllables 3.5 seconds long; pause 2.17]
men!

i-yi-ma-oooo [.37]
men!

kunutapiya peng kera pelka-ja-o [.43]
if there were a feather on the shield

el adi-yl tekir nyib pilyilyka-o [.40]
I would really think I'm fighting

kera mek bulumingi-na telka-ja-o [.44]
if I fought on the back of the Princess Stephanie's bird of paradise

el adi-yl tekir nyib pilyilyka-o [.37]
I would really think I'm fighting

yunu laimkangi lyip tekir-o [.37]
as it is I'm just going around quietly

kaspis-kiyl tekir-o [.35]
I'm just giving [money] for potatoes

po pubu-kiyl tekir-o [2.1; falling pitch over the last three syllables]
I'm just giving it for sugar cane

na-nga yiyl-a [0.00]
my 'man'

mensik pukun pukun-a [1.23]
you (sg) take it for him

tikiyl kang-ayl-a [0.00]
the Tikiyl man

tikiyl sokudu pukun-a [0.00]
you (sg) go into to Tikiyl

idi kani-na-a [0.00]
there, where, as you know

kilkai lelym-kiyl-a [0.00]
there is a Kilkai spirit-cult place

idi kani-na-a [0.00]
there, where, as you know

maip lelym-kiyl-a [1.47]
there is a Maip spirit-cult place

idi manya suku kalya-na-a [.30]
and there, half sunk into the ground

karaip puruyl-te pelym-kiyl-a [0.00]
there's the rotting trunk of a nothofagus beech tree

siyl-topa toba kanakun-a [0.00]
watch out, lest you (sg) slip and fall on it

mekin pukun kilkai-ne kuyini kanapa [0.00]
if you (sg) want to take this [payment] and sacrifice to Kilkai

kilkai-na kuyui [0.00]
then go ahead and sacrifice (sg) to Kilkai

maip-ne kuyini kanapa [0.00]
if you (sg) want to take it and sacrifice to Maip

maip-ne kuyui [1.30]
then go ahead and sacrifice (sg) to Maip

moni ilyi lepa nyim kanap-o [.97]
this money which is here

nu lyin kanapa-a [.96]
you (sg) take it

nu tid kanapa [0.00]
I gave it to you (sg)

mudika kit pilyiba [2.20]
the Mujika (sg) will feel badly about it

mudika kasipa [0.00]
Mujika Kasipa [man's name]

okun ilyi-nga ena lyirin kanarud kanilyi [0.00]
I saw you (sg) come here and stay in the sun [on the battlefield]

handet ilyi koma lensikir-o [0.00]
I'm carrying this hundred ['pounds', i.e., two hundred kina] for [you]

ilyi-nga ok-lyi
come and get (sg) it

KUBUKA TAMALU

handet-tal ui kolya tilu-na suku okum-kiyl nyib pilyikir
two hundred are coming to the same place [i.e. to Kasipa] I think

adi-nga ekeda-nga lyip ku *sikis handet* mudud ilyi-ko tekir kalya-yl
when I gave that [to Mujika], I put six hundred to one side, I am giving that [to Laulku]

KUBUKA PUS

[first few lines inaudible]

ekepu ku *moni* ilyi-o
now this money here

el na-nga-te naa tirid-o
I did not fight

midipu yi kujilyi-ooo *sop* kolum-ayl lyirim-a
the Midupu man Kujilyi got a small piece of soap

kubaliyl ola angalyirim-a
he was standing at Kubaliyl [his home]

tea-dena kang-ma aku ung-ma kapola nyirim-aaa
the Tea-Dena fellows said 'very well'

ilkili-ilkili tirim kanapa
the [Tea-Dena] (sg) pushed

ma palimung nyiba nyiba lyirim pilyipa
and thinking [they] had destroyed Palimung [in Epola territory, where Dena Peam was living as a refugee (see section 3.2.2)]

kunu karipi tirim pupa
taking a karipi *shield*

sibeka pup kunu pulurud-a
I took a shield to Sibeka [battlefield, see map 2]

aki tirid aku-wa
I did thus

na el-na adupu tely-wa ya
do I generally go around fighting? [i.e., I don't]

na-nga bi mare naa molym-a
I do not have any big names

kubaliyl yi kujilyi
the man Kujilyi of Kubaliyl

teman-wa ya pilyip nyikir-e
I have heard a story and am telling it

yadu *tausen*-wa kingpan tonsikir-o
I dust off my one thousand

laulku yi nui-a
Laulku Nui

laulku yi yako
Laulku Yako

mekin pukun pukun wi koyilymeli kolya aku-ma-nga kojiliyl kanai-o
you (sg) take it, they 'roast' it there at Kojiliyl, go ahead (pl) and do so

laulku yi nui aku nyib kanab kiki tum nyib kanab
Laulku man Nui, I see that you are ashen [instead of greasy; i.e., that are not prosperous, so I'm giving you money]

mada nyikir
I've said enough

KOPIA KAJIPU

el-ayl-nga ung ausipe naa nyai, nyab-e
don't you (pl) talk so much about the fighting

yi tabu mela mudin kidipidi-na pepa kerikali noba telym nyikir-o
in-laws, when you eat, things stay in the moustache and beard, is what I am saying

naa nyai
don't say (pl) it!

eni ya ku *moni*-yl sikimil nyik kalupulaku nyik
instead of giving money, you (pl) talk until you're short-winded

[some lines inaudible]

na-nga kang kapiyl mokab-ayl okur
I've come for my lad who got wounded

kapiyl mokab-ayl ya memi weningi *baim* tekir
I'm paying compensation for the 'new blood' of this man who got injured

ya eni-nga el ung mare nyikimil aku-ma na naa pilyibu
as for this el ung *that you (pl) are talking, I won't listen to it*

na-nga lku lotu-na ob sukud purud-iyl
I have joined the church

i ku *mon*-ayl naa pilyibu...
I don't want to hear about this money

mola yi *tabu* nu-n molkuk pilyin-na ung mare nyik nying-lum
but if you (sg), in-law, hear (sg) and want to speak (pl), then go ahead

naa sik nying kanapa
if you (pl) don't give money

[several lines inaudible]

el ung ya kopia kubuka-ma para naa nyai-o
but don't you Kopia-Kubuka talk (pl) el ung *back and forth*

ya ilyi...ya...kolya-yl na pilyip molup-kin
here...when I look at the place

[cross-talk]

suril lkurina mong angalilym-ayl
I have the eyes of a flea or a cockroach [i.e. I, the lower Kopia have eyes that can see the condition of your 'skin' in microscopic detail, so I realize that the Mujika feel slighted not to have been paid compensation]

kubuka tamalu-kin na meri wijuyl na *handet* lensikir
together with Kubuka Tamalu I, the lower Kopia, bring one hundred for you

ilyi pora nyikim-o
this is finished

ya ku *tri handet kina* na meri wijuyl-n tid
I, the lower Kopia gave three hundred kina

ilyi pora nyikim-o
that is all

na meri wijuyl-o
I the lower Kopia

ya ku *tri handet* tid-ilyi-o
I gave this three hundred

tepu *handet* tal tep laulku kupulanum tep mudup
I gave two hundred to Laulku, put it in their 'road'

handet ti tep mudika kupulanum modukur tekir ilyi pora nyikim
I give one hundred to Mujika, that is over with

eni-nga el ung tumja mare nyikimil ilyi na naa pilyibu
I won't listen to any of your (pl) thick el ung

naa pilyibu-kin
since I won't listen

el ung naa nyai
don't talk (pl) el ung

KUBUKA KOROPA

aku-ma tata kapola nyikim
what father [Kajipu] is saying about them is right [i.e. they shouldn't talk el ung*]*

[some lines inaudible]

KUBUKA PUS

ku lyip ora-nsip ku sibu tekir
having shown the money, I want to give it

MIDIPU KUJILYI

[some lines inaudible]

ya mel, eni ung nyangi, ung kupulanum lyip talsinsab...
you (pl) speak, I'll prepare the way for you...

pilyikimil el turum-uyl topa-kin epola-alya-sil lyirim-a
you (pl) know that when there was fighting, Epola-Alya took (sg) it

pi tepa oba na-nga kangi-na nosinsirum
then 'he' came and put it on my skin

jika kungunuka sirid
I gave it to Jika-Kungunuka

[shouts from others]

KOPIA NOMA

yi-te ung nyilym ilyi-kin kolumu midi ko telym-kiyl
here a man is talking and he keeps getting interrupted

pensingi lyingi nyikimili
do you (pl) want to pocket it [the money] and take it away?

MIDIPU KUJILYI (gets floor)

el ilyi i tepa turum nyikir-o
this war was fought, I say

tea-dena-sil-nga el pul ilyi
the Tea-Dena pair were the source of the fight

el-ayl epola-n kanapa lyirim...
the Epola took up that fight...

jika-kungunuka-sil silym kani-yl na naa sirim
'he' [Epola-Alya] did not give the fight to Jika-Kungunika as 'he' usually does

el aki-yl-nga mel-ma-n nomulu nyiring aki-na purumul-o
in this fight, they said we'll 'eat' some things, so we went [i.e., we fought in order to get compensation]

purumul akin meri *hankap* tok ab nunu-nga mangapa
we went, and then, putting on handcuffs, getting their women back

yi topa altep medu kung maku top yi meri tirid nurum
wounding men, killing European pigs, I gave them to the man down there and he ate them

noba pensipa-kin ekepu
and now, having eaten them

el-ayl tep, dena peam nyiyl-te mek wiji uring
we having fought, they brought up a fellow named Dena Peam

mek ok montulkumela
they brought him and established him

na-nga nanu ung nyib aki-lyi ya
and what I myself said about that

ing suku *bamp* moluba nyikim-na nyib pilyip tekir-o
there will be an argument here, I think

lo lekim-kin aki tek monsuring
when law was established they brought him in

akin pe tek ola-manya tek *rais bek* kare-ka torulku lyiring
and then, going like mad, they seized some rice bags

el-ayl tirimulul-ayl
and then indeed, we fought

el-ayl tirimul aki-na pi
we fought [together], for

olyo kang-yi *pilai kat* tep kolya tilupu-na molymolu molurumul akin
we fellows all play cards and live in the same place

adilyi ne kang-yi-ka weningi tintirim kani-yl tirim
and those fellows over there [Epola-Alya] didn't do very well [at fighting]

el-ayl lyip tapurumul
we took the fight and helped out

ij lyip kangi-na nosintuyl-mel tirid akin
I sort of took it and put it on my own skin

ya kang-yi-yl ya
this fellow here [Laulku Anis]

ab-yi-yl kanilyi ya oba molurum
the husband [of a Kubuka woman] came and stayed here

kang yi-ka-kin tapu tok adak el kani-yl montulka
going around with our fellows, he got wounded in that fight

el kani-yl montulka el-ayl-nga *kompensesen* tekir ilyi
it's for that wound he received in the fight that I'm paying compensation

kang-yi kakuyl el lupu, meam el lupu
Kaugel fighting is one thing, Meam is another [i.e., Kaugel people have not usually gotten involved in Meam people's fights, as they did in this one]
pe ing nyik ilyi-kin pilyik pilyik konguntuk kang-yi el monturum
talking about and considering the fellow who was wounded
kupulanum ilyi-nga *kompensesen* ilyi ya pilyik *tu handet kina* nosik-kin
for this, thinking about compensation, they put two hundred kina
kang pi eni yi payl ung-iyl nabina
but why have all of you men come?
ya *kopi de*-kin nyik iji meri
saying it's coffee season
ku *handet lep* tek nosik pe i tek mel tingi pilyikir aki-yl
contributing one hundred or more, they will do like this, I think
ilyi-nga ing mong ilyi nyai-o
you (pl) [Laulku] tell me this
eni yi-ma ya
you (pl) men here
ekepu kuduyl *keap* okum-na nyimulu-ro
now the European patrol officer is coming, we said
pi kuduyl naa olka-da pi mel kintiyl pilyikin-i
if he hadn't come, it would be bad, you (sg) know?
kintiyl mekin adalkuna-yl
you (sg) would have kept carrying around something bad
pe ekepu el tebulu, el *plan* nyilybolu
now we two will fight, we two talk about fighting
kani-yl-nga ekepu tekir
it's for that that I'm doing this now
pe ekepu [*lo*?] el tekimul aku-na
and now we (pl) are fighting
na-nga meri yi kuluyl-iyl kapu el-wa tep
my allies down there, we had a fight over things
mel-nga kapu tepul-kin naa tirimul lelym ilyi-nga
we hadn't given each other things
el ung-iyl naa nyai, mol, i nyikir
*don't make (pl) fight talk (*el ung*), no, I say*
olto-nga kapu el tiribul kani-yl-nga mel-ma ti naa tirim ekepu
we two fought over things - he hadn't given things
eni ya ku *mon*-ayl kang-ayl el muntirum memi aki-yl-nga pantikim
about the money, the fellow was wounded, and smeared with blood
olyo kola lku pumulu akilyi nyamul
we're going to the mourning house, let's talk of that
ya eni ya yi molkimil aku-ma molku-kin nu-nga nunu parka el kani-yl
you men here, while you (pl) stay here, he [Tea-Dena] is your (sg) major enemy
adi na tuku-na maku turud kanakur
I see I am in the middle, I joined up
ola pul yi-yl-n kanapa, i tek telkuna-r-ko, i-tek telkuna-r-ko
as God above watching, you (sg) should do this but you (sg) will do that
nyiba kanapa mulurum, adi kuduly-iyl naa olka-da i tep nyilkumola
He was watching, if Europeans had not come we would have talked thus
ekepu kuduyl *keap* okum ilyi-kin
but now the European patrol officer is here
meri kang yi-ka *skul* kang-abola mek wangi nyib
we fellows down there say you (pl) bring your kids to school
kot eria-iyl tukudu lyip tebu-d pilyip-kin
I'll listen [to your cases] in the court
ya ul ilyi-nga meri yi-ka mawa tep
and so asking the men down there [Tea-Dena]
meri yi-ka *lo* pantip tebu nyikir-o
I want to make peace with the fellows down there, I say [i.e., restore the earlier

situation, whereby the Tea-Dena could send their children to Kailge school, and use the Palimung village court]

[inaudible cross-talk]

LAULKU YAKO

ku *moni* ilyi-o
this money

ku *moni* ilyi ya, ya *pilai kas*-o
this money, playing cards

no bia nok ya olad-mad tekimil kalya-ma
drinking beer, the young fellows really go at it

yabu midi tok molkumil, kang-ma meri el-na ok suku puring
they're always fighting, they went down there into the fight

kapiyl munsiring ilyi-nga ya ku *moni*-yl sikimil nyib pilyikir-o
they were wounded, and it's for this, I think, that you (pl) are giving money

pilyikir-ilyi
I understand

tek
they giving [compensation]

ya wiyl-ala, uj pol mare pelym nyikimil aima
well up there they say there are some tree trunks remaining [a reference to Noma's grievance]

na ya sumuyl kung kanu-ma-ni tep-lyanga pipi top *lo* tep pora-nsirid yi-yl-o
I am the man who sealed up that matter and brought law by giving kina shells and pigs

kalya-ma tep pora-nsirid-ilyi ekepu na-nga nanu walu ob
having finished that, I have come with a clear conscience

no koma-liyl nobu, uru kona pep, ekepu nanu walu-sip nanu ob molyo
drinking cold water, sleeping soundly, I have come with a clear conscience

ekepu na-nga ui, kera laime uj pol mare pepa tirim-kin
now before, my, [sic] that is, maybe those tree trunks were there for cassowaries

yi mare na-nga lku kiripul-na ok tiring i-me isip sirid
some people [Kopia] came to my house and I gave them [cassowaries]

pe kera ya madu mek ok tiring-lum pe mek olad puring-ma
they brought the birds down here, they took them up

nanu *lo* tep pora-nsirid-kiyl-o
I gave and concluded the matter

uj pol mare nyikimil
they talk about some logs

kalya-ma ekepu ya ul ilyi ul ilyi na el tebu nyib olka-ja
as to those, if I had come wanting to fight

namo-na ob meri suku pulka-kin tara, tokum-lum nyikin telkuna-o
if I had come down there 'in public' [i.e., if the Mujika-Laulku had come to fight en masse], you (sg) would have given, saying 'ancestor! how fiercely he fights! [i.e., you would be giving out of gratitude]

pe nu-nga bi molupiyl nyikin-kin ku *mon*-ayl wed lyikin sikin
but actually you (sg) are giving this money just to enhance your (sg) own reputation

i nyib pilyip na molkur-kiyl-o
that's what I am thinking [the implication being that the Mujika-Laulku did not come en masse. A further implication which one of our transcription assistants read into this was the claim that the only men who had come en masse were two of the Laulku men's house groups: Kujiliyl and Wijangiyl, who should therefore get the lion's share of the compensation]

kelku nunu numan-na ung-kul mare pilyikin tekin nyin-lum
if you (sg) have something else on your (sg) mind [i.e., Noma's grievance]

nu-nga numan-na sukud tekin
that's a product of your (sg) own imagination

na nanu we midi ob ku *mon*-ayl lyip meb pukur-kiyl-o
I am just coming to get the money, and will take it

eni lupu lupu yi mare-n molkuk pilyik-lyanga
you (pl) various people, here listening

yi kalya-yl olu kalya-na pobera tolym molo nabitelym nyik pilyingi
you (pl) might think [i.e., don't think] 'that man's belly is black or something' [i.e., that I have a grievance or will make trouble]

mi mol-kiyl-o, uj pol mare nyik tekin
honestly not! those tree trunks you (sg) are talking about

kalya-ma i kalya-yl ulsi mudup nyib pora-nsid-kiyl-o
I already got rid of those

kalya-yl ya ul mare ya yi mare toring ulu mare tek nyiring-lum
that business about some men getting killed or whatever happened over there [in Laulku country]

kanu-ma kuluyl naa pelym-kiyl-o
those things are not 'covered'

kani yi-ri topa nyirim-lum, yi-yl-nga mala-ri meba monsipa purum-kiyl-o
if a [Kopia] man is said to have been killed, he left sons

eneni kanga-n kalya lku kiripul kanilymeli kalya-yl naa kanilymeli-lum
did you (pl) fellows see them [the sons] at your doorsteps or did you not?

eneni lku kiripul-na kanak kanak kalya-yl
you (pl) yourselves saw them at your doorstep

eneni no-yl kulkuk pipi tok monsilymeli-kiyl mola
you (pl) fetched the water, covered it up and put it away [said by one exegete to be bent speech for 'reached a private settlement']

puk nyiring-lum kanapa ul kanu-ma tep pora-nsirimul
when you (pl) went [to Laulku territory] we finished that business

kung por lyip kanap kelip aima sumuyl adum kanu-ma-kin
getting pig hindquarters, looking and leaving them, when the kina was still around

aima tep kanap kelip aima kani-yl tep on tirid-iyl ekepu
doing a lot of that, I have finished it off now

ku *moni* nu-nga kona-nga-yl i kona-nga-yl-nga el naa tirid-iyl
your (sg) new money [that you're giving now], I didn't fight for it

pe nu-nga bi molupiyl nyib ya wilyi ada palyi nyikim
so I say let your name be enhanced, as old brother-in-law [Kajipu] says

i mel nunu pukun mel lyid kola pukun tini nyib pilyip
if you (sg) want something [for that grievance] you (sg) will go and cry [to those sons] I think

na age nyib aki-yl-nga pukur-kiyl-o
I say 'thanks' and go

nu-nga tara nyikin ung aku-ma naa pilyikir-o
as for what you (sg) are saying about your ancestor, I don't hear it

ya i ung laie mare nyikimul kalya-ma naa pilyikir-o
these trivial words we've been saying, I don't hear them

KOPIA KUPENA

na ung-ur pilyip nyikir, eni kang-kin nyab-e
I want to say one thing, I want to talk with you (pl) fellows

[cross-talk for about ten seconds before Kupena again regains the floor]

el ung nyik eni yi kangwa-kin mokunabi mel-ir tekimil
you (pl) talking el ung *and just concentrating on that*

yabu lupu lupu molymeli-o
various different sorts of people are here

olyo el-ir tep ya ku *mon*-iyl
we had a fight, and as for this money

meam el lupu-te-yl, kakuyl el lupu-te-yl
Meam fighting is one thing, Kaugel fighting is another

el-ayl-nga bi naa liai-o
so don't even mention (pl) the name of fighting

ku *mon*-ayl olyo el yi yadayl lyik angansik tiring
this money is for the fighting which you (pl) started

akilyi midipu kujilyi-nga punya kongun tirim
this Midipu Kujilyi did his 'garden work' [i.e., fighting]

akilyi-nga na tapor-alyi-o nyiba *rais* nobu nyib
he said I was his spade, and I saying 'I want to eat rice' [a meal of rice and tinned fish being the usual gratuity given in return for help in garden work]

kujilyi-nga punya ulki-nga purud-o
I went to work in Kujilyi's garden

meri dena numje-nga tapor-ayl lyirim akin
down there 'he' took up Dena Numje's spade

tola-wanaka-sil suku *rais* nobu nyiba suku urum-o
the Tola-Wanaka, saying 'I want to eat rice', came (sg) in

aj-aji yi aku-ma-nga nokopa-anamiyl mare uring-kep
some distant men came (pl) in from Nokopa and Anamiyl

mujika moropang-daku mare uring kepi aku-ma yu-nga lyiba aku-ma-nga uring
some Mujika\Moropang-Daku even came (pl), he got them, they came

olyo ung ausiyl naa nyimulu-o, el ung, ung tumje aki-yl
we won't talk a lot [about that], fight talk, that is thick [i.e. we'd have too much to say about that subject if we got into it]

el ya tea-dena-sil yunu sibu nyirim-lum
the Tea-Dena pair said 'I want to give the fight to him [Tola-Wanaka]

tola-wanaka-sil meri luip-ukulu kepu-ma-nga el aboluyl yi
the Tola-Wanaka man who is a holder of the bow and arrows down at the Luip and Ukulu grade

aki-yl ne abolingi-o
will bear them [i.e. will attack us again] over there [at Palimung]

ya eni el-ir tek nying-lum, na midipu kujilyi-kin
if you (pl) say we shall fight again, I, with Midipu Kujilyi,

apulu tapor-nga el nyib el aki-sipa abolubu
saying 'it's a fight of digging stick [i.e. Kujilyi] and spade [me]' we two will take up the bow and arrows thus

yadupa ung ilyi-nga eni kapiyl mokab-ayl-nga
this present talk is about injury and compensation

kang ya manya-te silkumela-yl
my boy, they could give it down here

pe mili lep meb adumul kani-yl-nga
we carried the trap around [i.e., spread the news] concerning that

nyib ya pena-obil-na ob sikimul-kilyo
having said so, we are giving the money in public [lit.: 'on the bone of the display ground']

eni kakuyl yi lupu, olyo meam yi lupu-kiyl, pilyik-lyanga nyingi, nedu
you (pl) Kaugel men are one thing, we Meam another, think of this as you (pl) talk, over there [at Palimung]

na nyib pora-nsab, kinye-nga eni medipalyi-nga
I want to finish speaking, now you later on

ung-te medepa medepa kang-te-n wedu lyik naa nyai-o
later on don't one of you blab (pl) our affairs [to the Laulku]

el olyo-nga ya kuruyl el-ayl-o, el-ayl olyolyo ya nyib molymulu
the fight is our local fight, we're talking about our fight here

eni-nga ku mokab-ayl-nga nyib kinye-nga ku *namba*-yl sai-o
we're talking of your (pl) wounded, now say (pl) the amount for them

PALIMI LKURAYA

ya ku-ma sik kikapu tek ung-iyl nyai nyikimul ilyi
give (pl) and finish giving the money, talk (pl) of that, is what we're saying

[cross-talk for about five seconds]

KUBUKA KOROPA

na ung-ur naa nyib-o, palka-n kunutapiya lyirim akin
I won't say anything, when Palka took up the shield [Transcription assistant: 'Palka' was probably a mistake. He meant to say 'Laulku']

ya kang-ka kani el monsuk ul aki-yl tiring
and the fellows got wounded

pe ne kang-ayl kunu lyikim-kin i nyik
and saying the fellow over there was taking up the shield

kang-ka el teamul nyik teku-kin
the fellows said 'let's fight', and when fighting,

kang-ka el monsuk aki tiring-na ekepu ku-ka lyip kuni tekimul
the fellows got wounded, since that's what happened, now we're straightening matters out (by giving compensation)

ekepu meri kang-ka ku *tu handet* **kina mel nosikimul aku-na**
now we're giving about two hundred kina for that boy down there

ekepu kunutapiya-yl aku-na kulkuk, bai-nga kunu-kuyl
now we're 'covering' [i.e., paying for the use of] the shield over there, Bai's shield [Bai brought a shield to use in the fight; see section 6.2.4]

wawa nyani-o
father you (sg) talk...

[some lines inaudible]

ya ekepu-nga ya ku tekimul ilyi-o
now we are giving this money

nu ekepu *pas taim* **ekepu kulup pora-nsikir-kiyl-o**
now, for the first time, I am completely 'covering' you (sg) [i.e., giving full compensation]

penga ul ya nabolka ul pudumong-ur peba molo akin
whatever trouble may arise later on, or whatever

ekepu olto kubuka yi todul-we-yl-kiyl
we are two are strong Kubuka men [Ping and Kuduyl]

altepa nu ku-te *lep*-**te naa lyini makuna**
you (sg) will not get money again, that is right [i.e., henceforth Bai will be treated as a Kubuka, and expected to fight in their cause without requiring compensation]

aki ya yi ung-ma payl pilyangi nyib ya *toksave* **tekir**
I am making this speech so that all the men can hear

LAULKU NUI (following immediately upon the previous speaker)

el-nga ung naa pilyikir-o
I don't understand fight talk

el-nga ung naa pilyikir-o
I don't understand fight talk

na ya kalyka-o
I, here at Kailge

aji-aji wali-o
[meaning unclear: could be glossed 'I'm like an young aji-aji *tree']*

el ung aku-ma pel naa pilyip pekir-o
those fight words, I do not understand, cousin

kung-pupu waim molkum ilyi
here stands a greased pig-stake

kolku ling-kin ku *mon*-**ayl isip lyibu nyib pilyikir-o**
when they [Kopia and Kubuka] die, I will get money like this, I think [as maternal death payment]

mel-ayl-ko lyip nobu pubu-ko
and I will get things

el-nga numan naa pilyip pekir-o
I not remaining with fighting on my mind

nu-nga nunu nyikin ya manya molkun-o
you yourself (sg) keep talking of it down here

na-nga aji-aji walu lekim-o
[meaning unclear: could be glossed 'I'm like an young aji-aji *tree']*

na yi we-ma-nga ob isip sukusuku pup isip keangayn nyib adalyo mel-o
I'm always going around among other men and helping them [fight]

adap pu-pu-pup nanu kakuyl uru pep
wandering around all over the place, I myself live in Kaugel

pelyo aku-ma-nga
I live there

pengi purunsilymeli-o
they always shave my head [and jail him for fighting]

mel-ma agike agike pulyo-ko
I always get injured

yi-te-ni kanapa bi naa-nsilym
nobody notices and calls out my name [to give me compensation]

makayl pol-pek aku-ma pansilyo-kin kolupa au nyiba molym-kin lyilyo
when I make loans to finance other people's exchanges, after he [the borrower] has used them and had his ceremonial exchange, I collect on them

aku lyiyl ul adu-mel tin-lum-o
now you (sg) are doing as I do

pengi purunsilymeli-kin
when they shave my head

[some cross-talk, but Nui keeps the floor]

monsup agike-agike puly-alyi
I always get injured

mel te-n kanapa bi naa-nsilym-ayl
nobody notices, calls out my name and gives me something

mel lupu-te nyib pilyilya-lyi kinye nu-ni *lo* topeli tokun telkuna
I always think I am [being treated as] something different [not human, sub-human] but now that you (sg) are turning the law rightside up

na *amamas* tekir
I am happy

ilyi midi ama tekin pilyip pukur-a
you (sg) do this, I will remember you

ung mel kis-we nyib naa pilyip pukur-a
I'll go home not remembering any hard words [that we've had between us]

meam tauwu gom, tauwu gom-a
Meam banana leaves, banana leaves

kalyipa gom kalyipa gom
casuarina leaves, casuarina leaves

oladu mara gom mara gom-ayl
up there [on the Kaugel side], mara leaves, mara leaves

akisipa lelym-kilyi
that is how it is [i.e. Meam and Kaugel are different, and shouldn't get involved in each other's fights]

el ung-ma
fight talk

naa pilyip pely-ayl pebu pukur-kilyi
I don't think of them, I will go sleep

pe kung ung-a
and as for 'pig-words' [i.e. plans for a return payment of pigs]

walsi tep pilyily-ayl pilyibu pukur-a
I will go, realizing that I'm eventually going to think of them [This was said by one of our exegetes to imply that Laulku will eventually take up the matter of Noma's grievance]

walsi tep pilyilyi aki-lyi
thinking of you sometime

nob pilyip molup-kin
when I 'eat' this [money] and taste it

akisip pilyip tirid ilyi-a
that is what I will have thought

na ada mel kis lidi-lum-o
and if I get to be an old man

kang-ka nyiba lepa lim-lum
what am I going to do with my boys?

kompensesen ilyi adi tekin-lum-a
now you (sg) are giving compensation

penga tapu kawa-nsiba-ja
later on will our paths diverge?

pe mel nabolka sini
what will you (sg) give then?

kung kanul-ma-nga te koyik naa sirin
you (sg) haven't given any cooked pork

lawa mel pekim-alyi
that is sort of a mistake

mosbi lewa
'Port Moresby liver' [i.e. money]

adi kinye sikin-lum-alyi
you (sg) are giving that today

nob pukur-kini
I 'eat' it and go

pe na-ni ung-ur naa nyibu pukur-kilyi
I will go and not talk [say no word of reproach]

kang-ayl-nga memi-wa *baim* tekin-kiyl-a
you (sg) are buying the boy's blood [i.e., paying compensation for wounds]

nob poransip pukur-a
I consume it and go

KOPIA SIRKU

wilyi ku *namba* toba tekim ilyi pilyikin-i?
he is about to give the amount, you (sg) hear? [i.e., be quiet and listen]

nu yi pim-i
are you (sg) deaf?

KUBUKA TEPRA

olyo-nga ung lawa-yl-nga ku *namba* kalya-yl ku *handet*-te waku tumul
due to our mistake, we have have lost one hundred kina

ku *handet*-te waku tum-o
one hundred was stolen

akilyi-nga nyab-a
I'll talk of that

pi ekepu ya ena pora nyikim ya ku-yl eneni lyik nok pangi
it's getting late, you (pl) distribute the money and go

ku, ku *wan tausen paun* ku *namba* kel-ma-nga pe nyimulu-o
one thousand 'pounds', the small amounts we will talk of later

mama nu-ni nyani
uncle, you (sg) talk

yi-te naa nyai, ku *namba* keli ilyi ya nyiba pora-nsipiyl-o
none of the rest of you (pl) talk, let him finish giving the small amounts

ku abolupa molkum-ayl nyipiyl
he is holding the money, let him talk

ya wiyl-ola oladu ku *wan tausen paun* ilyi pora nyim-uyl
up there one thousand pounds is finished (has been given)

ku-yl kang-ka-nga kalya pora nyim
the money for the boys has been given

ku *nain handet paun* i-ke ilyi kalya naa nyim nyikir-kiyl
this nine hundred pounds, he did not speak about it, I say

ilyi suku-na kolum tep eni-nga *kadis*-na nosikumul-kiyl-o
these (amounts) we'll 'break' (divide up) and put in the middle

ya ku *foa handet*-o yako, *foa handet* mama nu-nga ku *handet* tilupu-yl
this four hundred kina is for Yako, uncle [Nui], your (sg) four hundred, your one hundred

suku-na kolum tensikimul, kalya-yl naa nyimul-uyl
we'll cut it in the middle [i.e., divide evenly between Yako and Nui] - he did not say that

naa nyim-na nyikir-o
since he didn't say it, I am saying it

ya ku lelym-ka ilyi kolum tensikir-o
this money here I am dividing and giving

ya ku *buk*-ilyi ilyi-nga ku *handet*-tal pekim
on this board there are two hundred kina

olad *handet*-te pepa, manya-d *handet*-te pepa
towards the top there is one hundred, and below one hundred

kalya-yl kanapa lawa tepa tilupu-yl nyiba pilyipa nyim
looking at that he made a mistake and thought there was only one (hundred)

ekepu ilyi-nga *handet*-tal pelym, ya ku ilyi-nga
here there are two hundred, of this

suku-na kolum tensip-o
so I divide it

nu ku *foa handet tenpela pius* pe wikid lapang
you (sg) four hundred and ten fists up above, father

foa handet tenpela pius pora nyikim-o
four hundred and ten fists is finished (has been reckoned)

[some inaudible interjections here re Kubuka]

ya i ku ilyi wi mujika-yl-nga ku lyipa terilepa *tu tausen tu handet...*
with the Mujika's up above, taking it all together it's two thousand two hundred...
[Exegetes: this is a mistake. He should have said two thousand four hundred]

KOPIA KUPENA

wijangiyl ku *faiv handet ten-pela pius* nya
say (sg) there's five hundred [pounds] plus one hundred kina for the Wijangiyl [men's house group]

KUBUKA TEPRA

wijangiyl-nga kelep nyikir, mujika-laulku ku lyip terilep nyikir
I've finished Wijangiyl, I'm reckoning up Mujika-Laulku [i.e. I'm not talking only about the Wijangayl men's house, but about all the Mijika-Laulku]

mujika-laulku ku kakuyl mulu-yl oladu ilyi-nga
Mujika-Laulku's Kakuyl-mountain money, there is one thousand pounds

ku *tausen paun*-ayl pepa *handet* tilupu-yl
there's one thousand pounds and one hundred pounds [=2,200 Kina]

aku-na pora nyikim-o, ekepu ku nu-nga abolun
that is finished, you (sg) hold your money

ku *namba* aki-yl tok sukudu modukun pi ku *namba* pora-nsikin
you (sg) contribute that amount, a large amount

ekepu nunu-n ku *namba* tokun pora-nsi
now you (sg) finish counting

KUBUKA TAMALU

i ku mi moki tep samiyl, el ung naa nyi
let's divide up this money and give it, don't (sg) talk el ung

KOPIA WARIA

olyo ya kolya ena pora nyiba tekim pamiyl
the time's passing so let's go

ya wilyi yi-ma le mong nokum-na melymeli-ko
for these men are getting restless [lit.: anuses are itching]

olyo kep aku tekim
and the same goes for us

olyo aki tekim ilyi ya ku ilyi-o, ilyi ya na ya ku ti nyim-o
so are we, so, as for this money, he [the Kopia Kubuka] told me to give it

na mujika-laulku ab mali-r molo-kiyl-o
but I am not the son of a Mujika-Laulku woman

ya ku ting ilyi-nga na *handet* tid-ko lelym-ayl pe
they gave money, and I gave one hundred

na mujika-laulku ab mal-ir naa molkur-ilyi-o
I am not the son of a Mujika-Laulku woman
na meam ab mal-ayl molkur meam ab mal-ayl
I am the son of a Meam woman, a Meam woman
na kang-yi el monsuring ilyi-nga-o
about the boys who were wounded
kang na-nga kang keli-ka el monsuring
my [Kopia\Kabika] young fellows were wounded too
ilyi-nga ya na-nga kang pelipa-yl yi-yl-nga ya ku kina-ke nosinsikir
and so I am putting money for my cousin [Tilka Dop, who is Waria's mother's brother's son]
el tenga lyipa i naa tirim, mol-o ya
he did not take up the fight
na-nga kang-ma kapiyl monsiring akin
when my fellows who were wounded
kang yu-nga pelipalyi-ma lyip oba yaduyadu tirim aki-yl-nga
for the fact that he came and carried his [wounded] cousins back
ya ku *paun* ilyi
and so this pound here
ku kina ilyi ya na-nga pelipa yi-yl sibu-d tekir nyikir-o
this money, I came to give it to my cousin
ya ku tid-iyl tep ob eni-kin
I'm giving the remainder to you (pl) [Laulku]
sukud sukud tid-iyl
I gave it 'inside'
ya ku ilyi na-nga pelipa yi-yl ya yi ya sibu tekir
this money here [an extra two hundred kina] I want to give to my cousin here
ne eni molung-ayl-ko tepi-tapuyl ya moluba-yl-ko
and to you (pl) [Tilka] over there who look after me during the fire-time [i.e., by night as well as day. This is in comparison to the Laulku, who live too far away to do so]
ya ku kina ilyi ya na-nga pelipa yi-lyi bilyipa-kolipa kepa pelipar-n-ko silymeli
this money, here my cousins, brothers- and fathers-in-law, uncles and cousins are giving
kani-yl ya i ku kina-kil nosud-ka ilyi lekim
for this I put the money and it is here
i ku ilyi
this money here
[some inaudible cross-talk about the amounts]
ilyi ya ilyi-nga kelip nyikir, ya ku ilyi-o
as for this, this I've already talked about, this money here
ilyi ya ne poika kang-ayl el monsurum ilyi poika abu-n miyl kang-ayl
a Poika boy was wounded, a Poika woman-borne [matrifiliated] boy
el monsirum aki-yl-nga ne angin poika kob kang-ayl oba molurum
he was wounded, and his Poika/Kob brother came along
akilyib kang-te ne altepa angin topa lu-n tum kanakur-iyl
an Akilyib boy was there too, and his brother was hit him with an ax, I see
altepa aju lyirim
and he [the Kob] pulled him [out of the battle]
kudikudi aj lyipa memi kalapa tirim aki-yl-nga
he dragged him out and his blood ran
poika kob kang-ayl-kin oba abu-n miyl kang el molurum aki-yl-kin
and a Poika Kob fellow came, and a woman-borne who got shot
akilyib kang-ayl-kin
and an Akilyib fellow
ilyi-nga ku *handet* kina lepa kum tal, *wan handet twenti kina*
for this there are one hundred kina and ten pounds, that is, one hundred twenty kina

KOPIA PENGAKUYL

pe meri-kin-d akilyi akisipa-ko nya
and say (sg) how much is down there also

KOPIA WARIA

wan handet twenti kina-ko ilyi-nga *wan handet twenti kina*
one hundred twenty kina, that is, one hundred twenty kina

ekepu ku *namba* lyipa terilepa kujilyi-o ku *salim* tekir
and now adding up the amount I give it to Kujilyi

ilyi ku *tu tausen foa handet kina* waku tokur-o
I am giving (up) two thousand four hundred kina

ya ku ilyi, i meri ku ilyi kep
this money, and even this down over here

pe keli ilyi kep, ku *tu tausen kina*-o pe, *tu tausen kina*
and even this small amount, two thousand kina, so, two thousand four hundred kina

pe bo ung lepa kina-kin *wan tausen tu handet, handet* tal
or as they say in local usage, one thousand two hundred

KOPIA SIRKU

kapola nyikim-a
what he's saying is right

KOPIA WARIA

na tara pilyip nyikir
I understand, 'father'

nu naa pilyikin nyikin
you (sg) talk without understanding

ya isipe mel waku tokur-o
I am giving this amount

ilyi-nga waku tokur ilyi, ekepu-nga ya eni kang-ma ya na ya kolya-yl-nga
I am giving this amount, you fellows

eni el-ayl-nga *plan* tep nyikir nyik pilyingi-o, mol
don't think (pl) that I am making war plans

ui ya tara midi molupa ya kolya-ma-nga tirim, kujilyi
my ancestor lived here and fought, Kujilyi

nu-nga lanalyi-ma turum-ko, jika-kungunuku-ma turum-ko
and fought your (sg) fathers, and the Jika-Kungunuka

ya kusika-midipu turum-ko, tea-dena-ma turum-ko
he fought these Kusika-Midipu, and the Tea-Dena

yi tal-n midi molupa turum kani-yl
only 'two' [i.e., a few] men were here and fought

ekepu ya ku i-we ya el *plan* tepa tim nyik, mol
now you think that I am planning war with this money, but no

el *plan*-te tim nyik pilyingi mol-kiyl
don't think (pl) I am making war plans

KUBUKA TEPRA (aside)

ya ku ilyi-nga ku kum tal naa lim
twenty kina is missing from this money

KOPIA WARIA (ct'd)

ya tidu-wa yi-te-wa midiyl nob ku ti naa tid
I did not work hard for this money, I did not

ku *takis* top ku *wan-wan*-ayl-nga ku *wan tausen* tekir-ilyi
I 'taxed' people, and [collecting] one-by-one [a little at a time] I am giving this thousand

ten kina nyib *takis* tokur ilyi ku sibu tekir ilyi ya
having levied a tax of ten kina each I am about to give this money

nu yi *plan* tep yi lyibu tekir pilyin-o, mol
do not think (sg) 'I will get these men' [as future allies, by means of this

money], no [i.e., it is not alot, because we're not planning to fight again]

kujilyi-nga el lyinsid ilyi-ka ekepu ya yad kangalyi kapiyl mokabu tokur
I took on Kujilyi's fight, and now I am giving (back) compensation

na ya el na nanu tebu nyid el nemnem-nsip tebu ilyi
if I myself say I want to fight [i.e., if I were the 'owner' of the fight] I'll do it by myself, and really concentrate on it

pe na-nga ya kalyka mai lyiba, ya *lotu* **lyiba nela siping mai lyiba**
if he [the enemy] wants to take Kailge, the church ground, and Siping

i-kin tep te-pup wiyl-ola webuyl molud akin
then I will have gone up to Wembil [in Laulku territory] to stay

webuyl lyim akin na kanini-yl akin kanini-yl
when he takes Wembil you (sg) will see me, that's when you'll see me

na ya el *plan* **tid nyik ya yi-ma-n aku nyik tengi**
as for your saying I've made war plans, men, don't think (pl) that

ui tara midi molurum-iyl ekepu na midi molkur-i
before only my ancestor lived here, but now, is it only I that lives here? [i.e., no, there are plenty of us]

molup pilyip ya kujilyi-nga el lyinsip molyo-kiyl
staying here and hearing about it, I am just taking on Kujilyi's fight for him

nu takan ku ilyi-a kapiyl mokabu top sikir-kiyl, mekin pui
and now I am giving you (sg) this compensation, so take it and go (sg)

altep kubikulyuwa ilyi-nga naa kanubu-o
I won't see (your) face here again

na okun lyin-ilyi ya kolya-ma noba noba pora-nsim-kin
you come (sg) and help me [only] if they come and completely destroy everything

webuyl wiyl-ola noba pora-nsim akin na kaniyl ya ilyi-nga num ilyi-nga lekir-kilyo
and likewise, if they come and destroy Wembil I will be there

i nyib-ayl akin nyibu-o
as I speak now I will speak then

eni penga kaningi-kilyo, na-nga el ti *plan* **ti naa tid-o**
you (pl) will see later, but as for now I've made no plan to fight

nu-nga el *plan* **tinsid ilyi**
I made a war-plan for you (sg) [Kujilyi]

tinsid ilyi-nga ya kang kapiyl mokab-ayl top modukur
having done so I am paying off the wounded fellows

medi ung mare lawa tengi, naa nyai
if you (pl) speak later, you'll make mistakes, so don't speak (pl)

UNIDENTIFIED SPEAKER

kang-a, engl kuduyl-kin-o
fellows, during the [recent] famine

engl kuduyl-kin yako el kupsirim kaniyl-o
during the famine Yako cut the arrows [out of people's flesh]

yako kang mare el kupsirum molo engl kuduyl-kin kolya aima engl anum-uyl-kin
Yako cut out some fellows' arrows during the famine when there was great hunger

kung aima memi aboluyl-ma kani-yl olyo memi abolupa purum
we are used to getting pig's blood on our hands, but he went around handling our blood

na-nga el kupsirum ilyi-nga ku *paun*-**tal ya ilyi-nga ola nosikir**
he cut out my arrow and so for this I give him four kina

kang mare el kupsirum-lum ya oku yako el kopsirim ilyi-nga
and for Yako's having also cut out arrows from some other fellows who came here

PALIMI LKURAYA

eni yako bi monsikimil ilyi el kupsirum ilyi-nga bi monsikimil molo...
you (pl) mention Yako's name because he cut out your arrows, you mention it for this or...

KUBUKA PARKA
ku ilyi ola nai-nga-yl monsinsung
for whom did they put this money up here?

KOPIA SIRKU
aku-na meri mudunsa
put it over there [for them]

KOPIA SILKA
aku-ma meri nok pungi pangi, olto ang pengi kapola-lyi
they will consume that and go, let them, we think the same

nu aki-yl nokun pui, ilyi nunu nyiba pansipa aki-yl
'you (sg) consume it and go', is what he told you (sg)

nunu pukun ui abolkun mola
when you (sg) go, first you (sg) hold it [i.e., keep it to yourself]

pe olto yi kapola-lyi altep...
and we two similar men again...

KOPIA KUPENA (amidst much inaudible cross-talk)
kang molymeli ilyi-nga el kupsum-lum yi kupena-n tongi-lum
since he cut the arrows out of those fellows who are here, they [the enemy] might poison him [i.e., so don't identify him by calling his name]

LAULKU SIMIJI
ya olyo-kin ku anum ti sikim-o
they're giving us a lot of money

olyo mujika-laulku-sil ya
we Mujika-Laulku

nu-nga ya ilyi-nga pek molkuk-kin kapu el-te pim-lum-o
you (sg) stayed here and there was a fight over things

ya kang ya pilyimul oba ya apa *winim* tekim-o nying-lum
if we hear uncle they are coming here and destroying the place

kang-te oba-kilyo
a fellow will come

ya...ya apa-kin tekim nying-lum, kang-te ya oba-kilyo
uncle, if you say he is doing this [destroying Kailge], a fellow will come, I

ya ul ilyi ya uj ulyi tok-pansik uji pol-te pansuyl-te tok lyik modungi
as to this affair, this slippery tree trunk which has been placed there [Noma's grievance], you (pl) can pick it up and throw it aside

ya wiyl-ala adalyn me-pupa kakuyl sirim molo pui nyiba modurum
you (sg) go around up there, he took it [the grievance] to Kaugel, or has already resolved it

ya luip kalipa kep-ma-nga aku-na ok pang-kilyo, mujika-laulku-sil
if it [the fight] comes to the banks of the Luip and Kalipa [I'll say to] Mujika and Laulku 'come, let's go'

kinye alte-kelingi-o, altek kuru-muru tongi
then you (pl) will quit, will you (pl) hide again? [i.e., no you won't]

mujika-laulku-ma aku-na ok pangi-o
let the Mujika-Laulku assemble and go [to your aid]

kang molym ilyi ya ya na yi-yl
there's a lad there, and I, a man

tea-dena-nga yi-yl na-nga tara-n nyirim pilyily-ayl-o
my father told me I'm a Tea-Dena and I believe this

eni-nga yi-te mol-o, aku-na ok pungi-kilyo
I'm not your man, but they [Laulku] will come

ya ab kang moluyl-na ne ya
some of [your] women have married us

ab talsi ya wiyl-ala molkubil kalya-yl mel wangl-o
two of them are up there, so let those two come

ya ku-yl mep pup ya yi-ke kinya ya, uj pol kalya-ma lapsipe kalurum
I will take this money and the fellow who put the tree trunk across the road can cut it and burn it

akin ya mujika-laulku-ma apa-pel-ma-n ok pangi-kiyl-o
so that [having settled that matter], the Mujika-Laulku uncles and cousins can get together and come

kinye ya nu ku-yl tekin kamkam kakuna modun ilyi-n nyab-i-o
today you (sg) give a large amount of money, I'll speak of this

meri yi-yl-kin el tel aduring-kiyl
you (pl) went around fighting with those men down there [Tea-Dena]

midipu kujilyi nu-n yi kare aki-yl-nga suku tekin turun-kiyl
Midipu Kujilyi, you (sg) have killed some of the men within [this talapi*]*

yi aki-yl-nga ya pansik tekin-ayl-ya
here you (sg) are forgetting about those men

ku yi-yl ku-na *namba* tum kalya-mel pilyikin yumel-mel kabu tokun
the man gave the amount, you (sg) get it and distribute it [i.e., count it out separately within each men's house]

ola modukun manya modukun tengli aki-yl elti-nga ul-iyl ya manya tiayl-o
whether you (sg) count high or low, that's your business; you two do it here amongst yourselves

aki-yl elti-li nyil mel pangl-kin-i
you two take that and go

kinye ya ya yi mujika-laulku yi-te ya
now a Mujika-Laulku man, here

mujika-laulku pujilyib-ilyi-nga ku kinye te tensikin ilyi
Mujika-Laulku\Pujilyib is the one for whom you (sg) are giving money today

kopia abu tal kom-aki-yl-sil ya ilyi-nga
it's on account of the two Kopia women, elder and younger sisters [who are both married to Pujilyib men]

ya ilyi-nga manya yi kare-kin molkuk tingi tapu-na tekimil-kiyl-o
sitting down here [in private confab] with some of the other men, they will give us more money

pe nuimil ya wilyi aku-wa punya punya tekir
later when we spend the money [?? sense unclear]

kubuka-nga kubuka-palimi-sil ya kubuka ab-te mirim-uyl
a Kubuka-Palimi [married] couple had a Kubuka daughter [who married a Laulku man]

kurali obayl mirim kolup pulyayl-kiyl-o
she brought a kurali *flower [a flower used for body decoration, which grows in the Nebilyer Valley, but not in the Kaugel. This is a reference to a fight which started over this incident. Details obscure]*

altekin el *plan* tin-lum na yi-r kuludu-lum, paka tobu-kiyl-o
if you (sg) plan to fight again, or if one of my men dies, I'll make the funeral platform

laulku-kujiliyl-wijangiyl-sil-ni nu-kin pansipa kola lku ongi-kiyl-o
you (sg) are going to come to the funeral with Laulku/Kujiliyl and /Wijangiyl

ya nyikir i mel ilyi-nga molungi-ma oba i pupiyl-kiyl-o
after I have finished saying this, those who will be there can go

mujika-laulku yi oba pe nabolka ul-ma tengi
what will the Mujika-Laulku men do?

adi yi obil-ma sukudu modukun sikin-lum-ayl
you (sg) are now making a yi obil *payment for what happened way back when [a reference to Noma's grievance]*

wily-ola yi-ke midi meri el-ayl top kalab pupiyl-kiyl-o
regarding that 'man' up there [Noma's grievance], I will fight to the finish down there [with Tea-Dena], so let him go

MUJIKA KASIPA

el-alyi el-ayl pe ya ne epola-alya-sil-kin-i el-ayl tengi-d
as for fighting, well in order to be able to fight with the Epola-Alya

olyo ya nela siping kalya-na olad siring-kin
they gave to us at Siping [in Kubuka territory]

eni-nga kapu el-ir ya kubuka tamalu-nga pena kalya-na
in Tamalu's display ground, when you (pl) had fought over things

nela dena-kin epola-alya-kin el-ayl kor-nga te-lyik aduring
the Dena and Epola-Alya fought [with Kopia-Kubuka] long ago

aduring-kin adak adak pe kinye kamu
they did so, and they fight now too

el-ayl ting ilyi-nga olyo kanap pilyip telymola kanilyi oba...
we saw them fighting, and we already know about it, and...

ekepu olyo mare ya kopia-kubuka-te pupa
now some of us and these Kopia-Kubuka

ne epola-alya-sil-kin langi koyiba pe
are going to roast [pig] with the Epola-Alya over there [in preparation for future fighting]

epola-alya-sil kusika-midipu-kin pelym kani-yl ab aprali tepa
the Epola-Alya live with Kusika-Midipu, grabbing [i.e., marrying] each other's women

yi kuli topa pelym
the men live in separate places

ga koyipa oba naa sirimul, ul ilyi tekim-ayl
we did not roast and give potato, but that's what they did

nanu ab-kid ul ilyi numan moluyl-kid ul ilyi tekim nanu numan tekim
when they did this, I was really grateful to the women, it really pleased me

olyo pipilyi mel tekim nyib pilyikir
now we are sort of ashamed, I think [because the Kopia-Kubuka have given them so much compensation]

aki tekim ilyi-nga pe
that's how it is, and

meri ung kalya-ma sike nyilymeli, pe mare kalya-ma gol tolymeli..
most of what they [the Kopia Kubuka?] been saying down there is true but what some of them have said is a lie

ul ya ime-nga nyib molubu tekir
these are the things I want to talk about

[35 seconds inaudible]

aki-yl mada nyikir
that's all I have to say

[short pause, then the same speaker resumes, with *el ung* intonation, as follows]

kang yi-ma, ung nyi naa nyi
fellows, don't (sg) talk

tara-n kep ung mare akisik mare nani nyirim-uyl, na-d kep
my ancestors talking as you (sg) are, to me

ung mare akisik naa nyikimil-o
you (pl) are not not saying the same thing they did

numan-ayl ab kiye-lku-na pansilymel-alyi
you (pl) are putting your minds in the menstrual hut

pe sike ung mare nyikimil nyib pilyily-ayl
I think some of what you (pl) are saying is true

pe waip-ung mare nyilym-kilyi
but some of what he is saying is lies

kum yi-lyi
a greedy man

nyilymeli aki-ne
they say

ku *wan tausen*-ir kep
one thousand even

adap naa lyilyo
I do not go around and get [cf. Laulku Nui's speech (line 1255-1304) where he said he never gets compensation, but gets jailed]

yama yi-r nyilymela-lyi
they say 'a greedy man'

nyik puk puk-o
they keep on saying

ka kopsilkuk-o
untying the rope

numu kulumul nyik naa silymeli
they do not glorify my name [??]

we leba ung-ma
the words will be for nothing [i.e., not understood]

[some lines missed during tape change]

aji-aji pupa-oo
going back

ung mare nyim-lum-oo
if he says something

we leba ung-ma nyim
those words that he said will be for nothing

aku ung lku kirip-na
as for those words, in the corners of men's houses

olto-lu pebulu molo
shall we two sleep or

olto-nga lku kirip-na
in our house-corner [i.e. no, we will discuss the matter there]

nu ok pini-a
will you (sg) [Noma] come and sleep?

kakuyl yi nyiring-ir nyiba pukum nyik pilyingi
you (pl) think I'm just a poor Kaugel man who goes around saying this?

mel aku-ma-nga
in regard to those things

kewa malye toly-ayl tobu-kilyi
I dance the kewa malye *[a fast dance] and I will do so [i.e., I will reciprocate the payment quickly]*

uj kerltip tely-ayl tebu-kin
I will do a kerltip*-tree dance [another fast dance]*

apa lku ping nolym-aa
the men's house is getting sooty [a stock expression, meaning that he 'built a house' (i.e., prepared to make makayl*) to the Kopia-Kubuka long ago, but the other Mujika-Laulku have held it up]*

aku-ma ok pengi-ko
you (pl) [Kopia-Kubuka] will come and sleep

langi nyikimil kalya-ma-nga
the food you (pl) are talking about [i.e., the food given by Kopia-Kubuka to allies during the fighting]

mare lim-lum nobu pubu, naa lim-lum
if there is some I'll eat it and go, and if not

aki kelip naa nob peab pe pubu
I'll sleep and go without eating it

ya kolya misi-man kolya-ma nyikimil-alyi kep
you're talking here at the mission ground

ultuku kung por moluba-kilyi
tomorrow the pig will be sick

ku *moni* **lyip pak sab-o**
so getting the money, I'll share it

[applause, but hardly any pause before the following line]

KUBUKA IPUPU (in *el ung* intonation, some lines without the additional final vowel)

kang yi-ma
men

[much cross-talk]

kang yi-ma
men

meri palya kang-ayl-kin-a
a fellow from Palya

sumuyl sirimul-a
we gave kina shells

we lyirim-ulyi-a
he got them for nothing

tep meb ob ob-a
I/we doing, bringing, coming

kang kalya-ma-nga te naa moluring
there weren't any young fellows such as there are now

mepa ob-oba nyirim-a
he brought it [the compensation] back to his place and said

tada-ada lepa nosipa kelipa
leaving it alone

naa lekim nyirim-kin
when he said it is not there

abu-n miyl simiji sibu nyirim-kin
then he said 'I'll give it to [Laulku] woman-borne [i.e. matrifiliate] Simiji'

mepa oba
bringing (them)

wily-ola kubuka epu turung-kin-aa
when they killed Kubuka Epu up there

kung pengi sai kibolu paie-ni
[I said] 'give a kung pengi *['pig's head; see section 4.1] payment' [and when they refused], with a club*

epola koluwa turud-u
I struck Epola Koluwa

epola tuse turud-a
I struck Epola Tuse

kibolu monsipa pipkau nyirim-a
getting a stick, he was rebellious

top naa konsirud-o
I did not kill them altogether

lu sipi-n pea turud-o
I also hit them with the ax

kibolu-ma-ni kep pea turud-u
I also hit them with sticks

we tekimil-lum nyiba
saying, 'they're just doing it for no reason'

kung pengi pansipa
putting the pig's head

makayl kani-yl u lyip ob
I got that makayl *payment already [from the Kopia, who were the 'owners' of the fight]*

temaltiyl pena suku ung-lum nyibu
I say if they had come to Temaltiyl [i.e., Kubuka Tamalu's] display ground

sumuyl sangi nyibu
I wanted them to give kina shells

ui sirid kanuwa
I gave before

akuwa nokun pansikin-a
you (sg) have 'consumed' and are keeping those

altekin sumuyl sikin-o
and you (sg) again had given kina shells

sumuyl pilyingi kanuwa
those pilyingi *kina shells [a certain type, very large]*

we lekim nyib pilyimul-alyi
we thought it was just for nothing

aku-wa-nga meri manya
down there

numika-na pansikin pansikin-a
you (sg) put it on your neck [i.e., poor quality kina shells, worn on the neck instead of mounted]

el altekin para-nsilkuna-a
you (sg) start the fight again

na-nga ku *moni* kang-ma-nga ab lyinsibu nyib tidu
I said I'd get wives for my sons [with the money; i.e., but now I can't, because you've gotten us into a fight again]

na nanu kupulanum kalya-na tepu
I, doing thus

yi welwel telyo-na
I have men all over the place [i.e., many sons]

lyibu nyib tely-alyi
I keep telling them I'll get [wives for them]

ung pipkau nyiba adalym-lum-a
he [the Epola] goes around not cooperating

pe ya naa um-lum-o
he does not come here

ekepu eni pukumil-lum-kin
so now you (pl) will probably go

ui telymeli kalya-ma
the way they did before [when the Epola did not give compensation for the Kubuka man who was killed in the fighting referred to above]

nanu molup *pas* tep teyl-kilyi
I was the first to pay

temulu-ko nyik telkumela telkumela
they keep on saying we will do it

yi kalkuk naa lyikimil-ilyi
there are not enough of them [Epola??]

pulye kalye-a
a helpful person

wily-ola aku-na akisipu
up there like that

maduadu madu sipu
looking down

kanap molyo-kin
I look

mek puk puk
taking it

noku ung para-ma naa nyai
getting it, do not speak (pl) in public

isip sikimul-kin
we give thus

yi tal tebu nyibu telka
I want to give to two men [i.e., Laulku and Mujika]

kung adu
wild pig

korupa molum-kin
he was looking for

kang-ma-nga kung tukapu ada-ma sirim kanilyi
the fellows gave twenty-four pigs

pi aku-na yi...
then that man...

[some words inaudible]

kopia ada-ma pe el tirid-kin
I fought along with the Kopia old men

yi nuim-na pansipu
killing all the big-men

kinye molupa
now living

yi kalapa
procreating men

pepa pukumul-kilyi
we live, and populate the place

meri lku nurum-kilyi
down there [at Kopola, in Tea-Dena territory] the house burnt

na monsik kelkik puring
they left me

na nanu wily-ola paparali molupu
and I, living up there at Paparali [where he was taken as a boy by his mother]

mad ob ya kalap lyipu
coming down and breeding

na nanu aki tepu tidu
I do thus

KUBUKA TEPRA (in *el ung*, breaks in)

el ung mada nyikimul-o
we have talked enough el ung

ekepu eneni ku-yl eni-ni ok lyai-o
now you (pl) come and get the money

[10 seconds of inaudible cross-talk]

KUBUKA IPUPU

ku mel payl-o
you two take the money and go

yi we-ma-n isik naa telymeli-o
other men don't do as we [Kopia-Kubuka] are doing [i.e., give money like this]

UNIDENTIFIED SPEAKER, PROBABLY KUBUKA TAMALU

ada-yl mada nyin-ka, ada-o, ung kapola nyikin-o, ekepu kela
father, you (sg) have said enough, old fellow, enough, now stop

[inaudible cross-talk for 20 seconds]

KUBUKA TEPRA

kolya ena-yl pora nyikim...
the time is going by...

olyo ena pora nyikim yi nuim nyai nyib nyikir
the time is going, big-men you (pl) speak, I say

ku-yl elti pilyik lawa modungli
if you two [Mujika and Laulku, or Laulku/Kujiliyl and Wijangiyl?] count the money you'll make a mistake

ne ku kolum maku-na molkum
that money has been shared equally

wijangiyl kang-ma ok lyai-o
Wijangiyl fellows come and get (pl) it

i wi ku okum aji pa
the amount is being given over there; you (sg) go!

kujiliyl aji molkuk ok lyai ekepu olyo wedu pukumul nu nyikin pora nsi
Kujiliyl [Laulku men's house group] come and get (pl) it, we are leaving

[37 seconds of inaudible cross-talk]

MIDIPU KUJILYI

ya no pengi kang yi-kil wi aji pukumil-kiyl
the 'headwaters' men are going back that way [via the mountain track, to Poika Wangi's funeral (the others to go by car on the main road)]

UNIDENTIFIED SPEAKER
ultuku apa
tomorrow, uncle

MIDIPU KUJILYI (amidst much cross-talk)
pengi kang-ka aji pukum ekepu pukum-kiyl
the head-of-the-river fellows are going home
olyo ya lupu lupu pukumul
we are dispersing
ilyi-nga puk yabu wi karaipiemul puk manya tiang
going, let them drop us up at Karaipiemul [in Poika territory]
nu uj punya kupula naa ui, ya *bares*-na midi pumulu-kiyl
don't (sg) come through the forest, we will only travel on the road
ya kupulanum ilyi-nga pumul-ayl pe olyo yabu pumulalyi gu languba-kilyo
we'll go on the road, the whole lot of us people [lit: 'the teeth will break' (idiom for 'whole lot')] will go
ung ilyi-nga nyikir-kiyl
that's what I'm talking about
eni yi mare oladu pung-lum
if some of you (pl) men go up
yi paka-yl wi kapul pena suku tum-lum
if they are having the funeral up at Kapul display ground
ilyi kola lku lyipu naa sikim-kiyl
that's not a good place for the mourning
ya meri piadi midi tum-lum-o
if they're just having it down at Piadi
[inaudible cross-talk]
ya yi olyo-nga yi molkimil-iyl *bares*-na midi pubu-kiyl
as for our men who are here, I'll just go on the highway
pe yi-te naa kanakun ilyi-nga nyab nyiba nyikir
some of you don't pay attention; that's why I'm talking

KOPIA KUPENA
olyo kar-na lyibe-ja...
will a car take us up...

KOPIA KAJIPU
na ung laie kolsi nyab-o
I want to say a word
aki-lyi na nyab, kili nyib nyilymulu kani-lyi
I want to talk, we say stop [talking]
nu nyab-ko nyikin-ayl
you (sg) too say you (sg) want to talk
nu-nga *rum*-te aku-na suku lelym-i
is there any room there for you (sg) inside [the car] [i.e., no, there isn't, so more people will have to go on foot, via the mountain track]

TILKA RABI
[first 15 secs. inaudible, except for the line 'laie kolsi nyab', '*I want to say just a little bit*']
na ya meam yi-yl-o
I'm a Meam man
nu kusika midipu aku-ma kep-o
whereas even you (sg) Kusika-Midipu
epola-alya kep-o
and Epola-Alya
ya ukulu kepu yad ui nyirid-iyl
I told you to come to the Ukulu River

nu kona pani nyib nyirid-o
I said 'may you (sg) remain alive' [i.e., I rescued you]

tea-dena-ri yad um-lum aki-yl kona pupiyl nyib nyirid-o
'and if a Tea-Dena comes, let him live too'

ne-d puyl nek-d nyim kulka-ne nukupiyl nyirid-o
I said 'let the Kulka stand guard on the other side of the Puyl [River]

na opalyi tea-dena tim-kin na *ap*-ti isip lyibu-kiyl-o
if the Tea-Dena give compensation, I'll get half

ya nunu ya ilyi-nga *ap*-ti isip lyibu-ko-kiyl-o
I'll get half from yours (sg) too

na yabu kona yi-yl nyirid-kiyl
I, the one who rescued each side from the other, said this

na yi-ti lupu meri *neka* kibu-na ilyi-nga abolup, ilyi-nga abolup top
if I [i.e., the Tilka] were as numerous as the seeds of a red pandanus fruit

sukusuku tep adurud ilyi
I went around getting involved in fights

nu yi kapiyl kona-yl nyib nyirid-iyl-o
I talked about you (sg) people who got wounded but didn't die

el monsikin opayl opayl kolya sibeka lelym-kiyl-o
because you (sg) might later get shot at Sibeka

pi ya nu mudika laulku nu molkun aku-ma-o
you (sg) Mujika-Laulku are here

poika palimi nu molkun aki-yl kep
and Poika-Palimi, you (sg) are here

[here three lines of Rabi's *el ung* are inaudible, as Kajipu, standing closer to the microphone, said the following to the person standing next to him]

KOPIA KAJIPU

ya olyo-n ku *wan tausen*-iyl we sikimul
we're giving this one thousand for nothing [because no one was killed]

i nyab nyib nyikir
that's what I want to say

we ung-ti mol
not any empty verbiage

TILKA RABI (ct'd)

lelym ilyi ya sibeka *haiwe* ilyi-nga elti-li el tel molungli-o
it's here at the Sibeka road that you two will be fighting

ya we i-kid kang-ti um-lum kona puni un-i
if a lad from here comes you (sg) will be o.k.

na mel-ma nobu nyib aki-yl kapola-kiyl-o
so it's appropriate that I'm getting these things to 'eat'

[15 sec. of cross-talk, including shouts of *kela, kela* 'stop it!' by Kajipu and others]

KUBUKA TAMALU

tauwu aku-na ola angilya tauwu
Banana [Tamalu's food name for Kajipu (cf. section 3.1.5; A. Strathern 1977)] *you (sg) stand up [and speak]!*

tauwu aku-na ola angilya tauwu angilya, yi ti lupuwu angalyiba
Banana, get up, Banana get up (sg) or somebody else will get up

[5 sec. inaudible]

UNIDENTIFIED SPEAKER

tepra ya
Tepra, here

[38 sec. of multiple overlapping speech, during which Mujika Kasipa starts speaking. His first audible words are the following]

MUJIKA KASIPA

ya ku *moni* tekir ilyi
here is the money that I'm transacting [lit: 'doing']

ku *moni* tekir ilyi ya
this is the money that I'm transacting here

kopia kajipu, kopia luburuyl eni tekimil ku *moni*-alyi
Kopia Kajipu and Kopia Luburuyl, this is the money you (pl) are transacting

ya kubuka-yl sikimil-ayl ku *mon*-ayl tekim-ayl
and this is money that Kubuka (sg) is giving

nu yi aima mong angalyilym-ayl aima kanakun tekin
you (sg) [Kajipu] are a man who has eyes, you (sg) are looking

tep tep tep no kep kayi mare-nga el i-mi elki tolyo-ko
at the good place for fighting [near the river] I break their bows and arrows [when people from my talapi *want to fight]*

kalabus kep telymeli-ko
and they put me in jail

i yi-ma-n ku *moni* aima naa telymeli
these men just do not give money [like this]

pe ku *moni* ya kilyuwa-kid lelym-ayl tengi
there is money up towards Mt. Giluwe, but will they give it?

kelkupa kung sumuyl-ma kep naa telymeli-o
no way! nor do they give pigs or kinas

kung sumuyl-ma, kung sumuyl-ma naa telymeli-o
they do not give pigs or shells, pigs or shells

ekepu ku *moni* ilyi ya, suril-nga mong-ayl-o
now this money here, flea-eyes!

suril-nga mon-pel-nga mong-oyl-ni kanakun bi nsikin tekin-o
you (sg) look with the eyes of a flea and recognize

nu kopia-kubuka-sil aki tekin
you (sg) Kopia and Kubuka pair do (sg) like that

ekepu ku *moni*, ku *moni* sikin-alyi
now here you (sg) are giving money

yi kis-ma-ni lyik mek pung-ayl
the 'bad' (ordinary) men [i.e., the Laulku] will take it and go

nu kelipa no ukulu tum-ur-nga ola pani
may you (sg) get across the River Ukulu even when it is in flood

kelipa no napilya topa pim-ur-nga
and the Napilya even when it is in flood

ola pani nyib-ayl pe na yi-yur-ni nyibu
may you (sg) get across, I shall say, I, a mere man [a kind of proverbial blessing, like 'may the road always rise to meet you']

ya mudike-nga ku *mon*-ayl sikin-ayl
here you (sg) are giving to Mujika

laulku sim-ayl pakisipa siba
they already gave to Laulku, I thought they *would give [i.e. pass on some of the money to Mujika, but now you're giving directly to us instead]*

yi-yl oba pirim-ulyi
the man who came and slept here himself

[inaudible cross-talk]

KOPIA YAYA

kelai...
you (pl) stop...

kung makayl tingi-ma el ung nyikimil molo...
are you (pl) who are speaking el ung *going to give away pigs or...[i.e., you're not going to do so]*

KOPIA KAJIPU

kang ya
hey, boy!

eni tea-dena-ma-n-o ku *tausen*-te nosinsung-o
did the Tea-Dena put down one thousand kina for [you]? [addressed to the Tilka, apropos of Rabi's speech]

wi *handet* tal eni silka-yl, na-n ya ku-yl naa sibu
I could give you [Laulku] two hundred [kina], (but) I will not give the money

ya nanu ab lyipu pe manya lelka-ri na nu poika-palimi-sil ku-yl tepu
when I have obtained wives [for my sons], if any money remains, giving money to Poika and Palimi

pe altep poika-palimi-sil sip telka-lyi
I would give to Poika-Palimi

na ku *mon*-ayl eni wa lyikimil
you (pl) [Laulku] are stealing my money

ya eni tea-dena-kil-ni suril lkurulkuna mong kolupa
you (pl) Tea-Dena, you do not have the eyes of a flea or cockroach [i.e., you do not see the condition of the Tilka's 'skin']

kanak kuni naa tekemil
you (pl) do not see and do the right thing [i.e., pay the Tilka, as we are doing]

na-nga mujika-laulku-sil...na-nga ku-yl we namu sikir
my Mujika-Laulku...I am just giving my money for nothing

na keap-nga *lo* yi-yl-ni molup sikir
I, the patrol officer's law-abiding man, give

ku *tausen* ilyi sikir nok pai i nyikir
I am giving this thousand, take (pl) it and go, I say

TILKA ALKO

eni yi ung nyik nyik ung kayi we-ma midi nyikimil
you (pl) men, talking and talking, are only saying nice things

ung nyik nyik ung *namba ten*-ma midi nyikimil-ayl
speaking, you (pl) are only speaking the very best words

[goes into *el ung*]

ung *namba ten*-ma midi nyikimil-o
you (pl) are speaking only the very best words

ya wanultu-n nyikin ung ilyi-o
Wanultu here, you (sg) are speaking

ya luip-kalipa kep-ma lirim-a lekim-o
these Luip and Kalipa embankments have long been here and still remain [i.e., things don't change]

ya kukapu aluwu kep-ma lirim-uyl lekim-o
these Kukapu and Aluwu banks [the border between Tilka and Tea-Dena] still remain

tara, kunu-karapi-kin-o
oh ancestor, with a shield of nothofagus beach wood

mara pera-kin-o
with a white mara *leaf [worn on head when fighting]*

ya yi-ma tepa ebab sirim tara-ni tirim
these men [the Kopia-Kubuka] prevailed, my ancestor did so [i.e., the Tilka helped them fight the Tea-Dena, Epola-Alya, et al]

[during the above line, he drops the *el ung* intonation. He pauses for 2 sec. before the next line, then starts in *el ung* again, as follows]

tara tirim-uyl kinya meri yi-yl-o
that's what my ancestor did - now this man down there [Tea-Dena]

kolya-yl yi waipi tep, peki turum-uyl tara-ni turum-o
the man from this place, I doing [here he mispeaks himself - starts to use the 'segmentary' first person, then switches to third person] stripped the place and destroyed it

kinya molo
but not now

eni yi-ma
you (pl) men

[inaudible for 5 seconds, as others interject]

1685 kang na-nga ung-uyl *brukim* tekimili
boy, you (pl) are cutting off my speech

[inaudible remark by another man]

meri yi-ma-ni ku *moni* sang-o
let these men give money

ya *lo* tek peangi el molo
making law, may you (pl) all live, not fighting

[during the next line, speaker lets the el ung *intonation trail off]*

i nyib ya na yi sika yi *ten*-ayl-nga
is it true what I say, I am only ten [i.e., there are only ten of us Tilka men]

pi el-ayl ui na-n ya na-nga lapa-yl-ma-ni ya yi-ma mek adalymel-alyi
so, before, I, my fore-fathers looked after the men here [Kopia-Kubuka]

1690 el-ayl lyiring ilyi
they took on the fight

ekepu ya nu korup olka nyik pilyingi
don't think I'll come looking for you (sg)

el kosing tok wi tolkumela-kin ku *moni*-ma naa lyilykuna
if they [Kopia-Kubuka] come and ask me to fight you (sg) will not get the money [i.e., I will help them instead of you, so you won't get any money]

ya meri tara tirim-na el-ayl nanu telka el-ayl nyikimil-alyi
over there [Tea-Dena] where my ancestors fought I should fight, they say

ya na yi ada-ma kuluring-ilyi na kulurudu-na-i
did I die when my ancestors did? [i.e., no, so I could have fought against them again with Kopia-Kubuka, had they asked me to]

1695 ekepu eni ung-iyl ku lyik mek pukumil-alyi, na pe yab on lyirid-iyl
now you (pl) came and are taking the money, I took the 'corpses' [i.e., helped carry away the injured. cf. remarks above by Tilka Rabi]

lo tep lyibu makur-nga-ko lyikir
making law, I'll take it; it is right that I do so

nu-nga *laik*-na nu-nga el nyikin pilyin lyin kanapa
it's up to you (sg), if you (sg) think it's your fight and want to take it up

pe ya yi mare naa pelymeli
here are there no men living? [i.e., no, there are many]

ya ui-ko nyimul-alyi
will we [Tilka and Kopia-Kubuka] tell you (sg) to come again?

1700 pe aku-na ya i ya naa lyiksunsin-lum pe
if you (sg) don't listen [and come again] and you (sg) whisper

ya nela kolya-lyi kopia-kubuka-nga kung ab-ma mel-ma nosinsip molyo
up there I look after Kopia-Kubuka pigs, women, and property

laka lep na nanu ne kalyipa gom-ma-nga pubu-kiyl
leaving [you] here I myself will go among the casuarina leaves [i.e., live among the Kulka, abandoning you to the Tea-Dena]

ne kolya-yl nosinsup pubu
I will leave that place [Tilka territory] for you and go

eni-ni tengi-yl tengi-ko kalya-yl
you (pl) will do it [fight, instead of me]

1705 pe na mel wanayl-ko nyib pep moly-alyi
I am a thing of value

pep moly-ayl el tara kunu karapi-kin no kep-ma-nga lyirim
I am, my ancestors took the shield [fought] along the river embankments

kopia-kubuka tepa ebab siba-lyi na ya moly-ayl
Kopia-Kubuka will fight and win; I'm here [to help them]

eni wilyala ilyi-nga nabina ongi e
why will you (pl) [Laulku] come?

i-me-ka ya midipu kujilyi-nga ya manya kapu el tim ilyi-nga
down below Midipu Kujilyi fought 'for things' [which is why I didn't help him this time]

1710 manya eni yi-ma sing-ayl na yi-ma-nga ku kina sikim-ayl nobu
below they are giving to the men, they give their money and I will take it

el abiyl molup i teb-ayl
I will hold the fight

ya yi-yl el numan sikimil nyib pilyikir
you (pl) men [Laulku] like to fight, I think

i-na el-ayl nunu mek pui, okun tensan ui
if you (sg) want to come and take the fight away, then come on and fight (sg) for them

LAULKU NUI (*in* el ung)

ya pilyikimili-o
listen (pl) here!

el naa nyai-o
don't talk (pl) about fighting

gavman lo kani-yl gi nyikim-o
the government law is tightening up on it

ui ting kanu-ma kapola ting-o
what they did before was o.k.

kinye *gavman lo* kani-yl gi nyi-pekim-a
but now the government law is stopping it

gi nyiba pekim-o
it's tightening up on it

eni yi mare kolungi pungi-lum
and if some of you (pl) go to die [of old age in jail]

pilyik kongunsuk el-nga teman tok pilyik piai-o
live (pl) mindful of the fight stories they tell

we-lum *gavman lo* gi nyiba pekim-o
otherwise, government law will tighten up

altepa ku *moni*-ma sikin-lum-o
you (sg) may give me money again

na tawa mel sikin-o
you (sg) give me a last meal

nob pukur-o
I take it and go

pe kinye makayl pansip puduyl-ni
now I am not putting makayl *[said by one exegete to really mean he* will *do so]*

kung por tobu nyibu ya
will I say I'll roast and give pig hindquarters?

pengi tobu nyibu ya
will I kill and give a [pig] head?

kung kolya-ma kula-boka silkuna
you (sg) would give boka *cane grass [i.e. rubbish things; this type of cane grass is not eaten by humans, only by pigs]*

nob pukur-kin-a
I'll 'eat' it and go

nob ku anum-uyl pim-lum-a
I'll 'eat' it; there's a lot of money

ung anum-uyl pilyikin molku-kin meri ui tokun-ayl-a
you (sg) know big speechs [for recruiting allies] and you (sg) shout them out

walu-walu ul ilyi tekin-lum opayl moluni opayl moluni
if you (sg) try your best at this, you (sg) will live tomorrow and the day after

ob lyip nobu-ko midi-a
I will come and 'eat' [compensation payment]

na-d kur mare monsikin naa nyi-a
don't hold (sg) any grudge against me

mem-ayl *baim* tekin
you (sg) are paying for the blood [of wounded allies]

KUBUKA TEPRA

lku-d okum ya suba-yl pilyikin-i
it's coming home, Shorty [Tilka Dop], do you (sg) hear it? [i.e., about how

Laulku should give to Tilka in the future: this is something we'll discuss in private]

nu ku *ten* kalya-ko nunu pilyi-o
you (sg) think about that ten kina

nu na kalya ku ten kolsi kalya naa pim nyik pilyin-iyl
don't think (sg) that I don't have ten [i.e., that I don't have enough to give to Tilka]

na pilyirid-iyl kanarud-ilyi, ya kani-ti on-te li naa lid-iyl
I heard and I saw, there was no body of me [i.e., no Kopia-Kubuka were killed]

nu tilupu kanul okun na-nga bulkud okun molurun kanap-kin
seeing you (sg) are the only one you (sg) came behind me [supported me. i.e., the other Kulka sided with Tea-Dena]

kanap kalya-yl na mong ang-nsily-ayl-nsikir
I look and use my eyes for seeing that

nu yi awilyi kalya-ma-kin pek adakun-ayl
you (sg), a big man, you (sg) live and go about

awilyi nu nani, ma mekin un-lum
if they give you (sg) a lot, you (sg) eat it and bring me some

olto-lu nabi-nyib-lyanga
we two will say 'I will eat it'

kanu-mel olto kanu-ma olto-lu nolybulu-o
in that way, we two [Kubuka and Tilka] will use it up ourselves

adi *ten*-la nanu tep-lyanga na tekir-i
and now I will give this ten [i.e., small amount] myself

adi *faiv* sin kani-sil lyip tep-lyanga kelip alu olto-lu nabiyl
this five [i.e., small amount] that you (sg) gave me I leave aside for you and me to use [after giving compensation to Laulku]

nyib top olkud sukud lyikir-o
I put it inside in front

pe paike na nabiltiyl nyikin ya molkuna-ja tekumul mel
if all of you (sg) [Tilka] had helped me, as we are doing/giving

paun-ur-ko silka-lyi
I would also give (them) a pound

pe te mol kani
but there was none

kani-yl nu tilupu kani-yl adi *paun* tilupu aki-yl nunu nui-o
but only yourself (sg), so that single pound you use yourself (sg)

[73 seconds of inaudible speech by Kopia Waria, Kopia Pigin, Palimi Wari]

TILKA DOP

na ya ku kina lyikir ilyi el-te tep tidu-na singi nyik pilyingi
I take this money, don't think they'll give this money (because) I fought

kang yi-ma sike kubikulyuwa lyik ora-nsik
the other fellows [Kopia-Kubuka] saw their faces

kang mare meri wiji-nsik tiring
some [of my] men helped down there [the Tea-Dena]

na midi ya suku-na molup-kin mol mel nyirid
but only myself, being in the middle, I said not to

na-nga yi tal kalya ya molybel-ayl, walsi-pilyi
my two men [Kopia Waria and Korowa] are here, ask them

na-nga ab malpilyi, na Kopia-Kubuka ab mal-te kep mol-ko
my father's sister's sons, I'm not the son of a Kopia-Kubuka woman [but my father's sister married here]

epola-alya ab kusika-midipu ab mal-te kep mol-ko
nor of an Epola-Alya or Kusika-Midipu woman

kungunuka ab mal yi lupu-yl-nga
I'm a son of a Kungunuka woman [i.e., of a woman whose talapi *is not allied on either side of this fight]*

ya yi-ke dena ab malpilyi yi ausiyl moluring
there were many sons of Dena women [among the Tilka]

na-n pup el mol nyib el *lo* pansip
I went and said no [to the fight] and put a stop to it

ne kang yi-ke pungi pansik tiring-kin el abolup el mol nyib
when the fellows were getting ready to go, I held the fight, saying no

ya kang-yi-ma el monsik tiring ilyi-nga sikimil-kiyl
some fellows here [Laulku] were wounded and that's why you (pl) are giving

ya kalya pilyik na-ni el-ir tep tid i nyik pilyingi, naa pilyai-o
you (pl) may think that I fought, but do not think so

i ekepu *mak* ilyi-nga medipulu nyikir
what I'm saying is the exact truth

ya meri yi-ma-n pilyik
the men down there [in Tea-Dena country] hearing

[9 seconds inaudible]

KUBUKA TEPRA

aki-yl-o
as for that one

ya ul ilyi kujilyi nani
Kujilyi, you (sg) talk

ya nu ku *ten* aki-o
this small amount of yours (sg) [given to Dop]

ul olto-nga-yl-o
it's our (du) affair

mel-ma paika paika bon-ayl naa nosinsubu-kiyl-o
I won't blame everything on [you]

bon-ayl naa nosibu tekir-o
I won't lay the load on [you]

ya na kapiyl molurum-ko-yl
even though there were injuries

mel yunu kanapa lyirim-uyl
the thing [i.e. arrow] went by itself 'found its own way'

pi yu-ni mong kadi pansibul-alyi yu kuduyl *kampani* mel molym-i
we both look at him [Kujilyi], is he [i.e., he isn't] like a 'company' [so he can't give us much money]

na midi nanu pubu nyib tekir-alyi
I wanted to go myself [to Kujilyi]

ya wi ya yi awilyi-yl sip-lyanga nu tep yadu modukur-o
I give the money to the big [Laulku] men and then to you(sg) [Tilka]

yu-nga kep na-nga-kep pea ul ilyi-nga we ung-iyl ya we ola nosik molurun
it's for him [Laulku] and me up there together, talking for nothing, you (sg) [Laulku] held it

kani-yl numana sirimul ul ilyi-nga
we were happy about this [i.e., the fight is mainly an affair of Laulku and Kopia-Kubuka, but we are happy for Tilka Dop to talk about it without fighting]

ekepu nunu bon-ayl ya yi-yl-kin naa pilyi-o
now don't feel (sg) angry [at Laulku's getting more money. cf. remark above by Tilka Alko about Laulku staying out next time with this man]

nanu pubu tekir
I myself will go [to Kujilyi]

pudu nu top yadu modukur-o
having given to you (sg), I will get it back [from Kujilyi]

[the following line is addressed to Kujilyi, who had been talking to someone else instead of listening]

kang kujilyi
Kujilyi!

nu bon-ayl ya yi-yl-kin naa pilyi-o
don't blame (sg) this man [the Laulku]

adi nu topa yadu modukum
they [the Laulku] are sending you (sg) back [because we've already paid them]

ti lepa nyim-lum aki-yl yuyu sikir-o
if there's any [money] left, then I give to him [Tilka]

ya i pena-na wedu lyikir
I get it out in public [and give it]

boni i-ke altepa yi-ke ul-ur pim nyik altekin boni-ti naa pilyi
don't think (sg) there's still something wrong [i.e., you can see that we're paying our allies properly]

[in following line, addressee shifts back to Laulku]

nanu pubu-d pansip top yadu modukur ilyi pora-kiyl-o
I want to go myself [to Kujilyi] I send [you] back, that's all

[*20 sec. of inaudible multiple overlapping speech, including remarks such as* **kopia kubuka-o**, *'Kopia-Kubuka!' Alya Keap begins speaking but takes a while to gain the floor. His first audible words are the following*]

ALYA KEAP

ku *moni*-iyl-o
this money

ku *mon*-ayl midi tekin kupulanum ilyi-o
what you (sg) are doing is giving money

pi na-kin ok ung ńyini kep kupulanum ilyi na pilyip kuni naa mel tekir
even if you (sg) come and talk to me, I don't understand this way [i.e., I don't understand how you got so much money, and I don't know how I can repay you]

ilyi pe ya ekepu el ilyi eni kubilek nanu top sirid ilyi-o
I gave this fight to you (pl) in the first place

ui yi ada-ma tok oma-ma pula tok aboluring-o
before, the old men [our ancestors] fought like frogs and fish

lui *nit* pep-o
the ax cut scars

ul ime tirim ilyi-o
they did like this

ekepu *gavman lo* mel kani-yl-n-o
but now [there is] government law

tep pulka kani-yl-ni na molkur-iyl
I would fight again, but I'll stay [and not fight again, because the law is here]

ne kani tapu-na molumul-kin-o
we were down there at the road [near Kusika-Midipu, Epola-Alya]

pe el kani-yl medi tola wanaka tea dena-sil elti-li lyingl-o
then the Tola-Wanaka and Tea-Dena took on the fight together [against us]

ya kopia-kubuka epola-alya kusika-midipu-ma yadu lyim
and the Kopia-Kubuka, Epola-Alya and Kusika-Midipu are together

el akisipa timul, ya wiyl-ola kakuyl yi nyikimil i-ma
we fought like that, up there they are talking about some Kaugel men

i-ma yi lupu-ma aima bi naa liai-o
they are 'different' people, don't call (pl) their names

ya meri awa yi mare okum nyikimil aku-ma bi naa liai-o
they say some of those Awa men [i.e. from west Kambia] are coming down there, don't call (pl) their names

kakuyl mare ongi nyikimil aku-ma bi naa liai
they say some Kaugel men will come, don't call their names

olyo-nga apa-pel torupalyi-ma kanu-ma molymeli
our uncles, cousins and in-laws are there [in Kaugel area]

tapu-na midi-kiyl
this is the only way

isipa nyilsik pai-o
go and say (pl) this [i.e., not to call out the names of our allies, so our enemies won't hear and attack them]

el meam el tep molyo-kiyl-o
I am fighting the Meam fight
ekepu ku *mon*-ayl sikim-lum-o
now he is giving money
ku anum-uyl tekin-lum-o
you (sg) are giving a lot of money
kakuna monsikin-o
you (sg) are giving a large amount
ku *mon*-ayl tekin kakuna monsikin-o
you (sg) give a great deal of money
[9 seconds inaudible]

KOPIA KOMI
olyo-nga kola lku-na-o
our mourning house
wal pakuyl-ma mudu-kilai nyikir-o
leave (pl) (European) clothes, I say
[some cross-talk, after which Komi continues]
wal pakuyl mudu-kilai i kalya nyikir-kiyl-o
leave your (pl) (European) clothes, that's what I say
oba ya yi-ma ekepu ku *moni* ku *tausen*-ilyi tekumul ilyi
now we are giving our money - one thousand kina
olyo-nga kangi-na ku-yl medipulu pora nyikim-o
on our skins money is finished
olyo-nga yi kamukamu kani-yl ola we lekim, ulyi nyiring-iyl
our friend forever [Poika Wangi] is just lying up there, we'll put on mud
aima pumulu wal mudu-kilai, i nyikir
we'll really go, leave your (pl) clothes, I say
olyo-nga kang-te-n naa kanak we molungi
don't let even one of us stay back

PALIMI LKURAYA (interjects)
kewa talap mol
let's not imitate Europeans

KOPIA KOMI
kewa talap kep mol, aima wal pakuyl mudu-kelkuk
not imitating Europeans, leaving your (pl) (European) clothes
we pula-bal tek ultuku pe aima ipulamui ui top pena mudukumul-kin-i
just wearing cordyline and loin cloth, and then early in the morning [we'll be on our way to the mourning rite at Peadu]

KUBUKA TEPRA
kupulanum ilyi nyik nyai
tell (pl) us which road

KOPIA KOMI
kupulanum ilyi-nga
about the road
[20 sec. of cross-talk by Kopia Pigin, Kowa, and Komi, shouting about which road to take]
ku kina pim-iyl kujilyi nyikim kalya mel wai i nyikir-kiyl
I say those who have money, come (pl) as Kujilyi says [on the highway]
i ne nekeda pai *kar* pul-ma naa pilyipa yu-nga el-ung-wa nyikim
go over there, the car owners not knowing talk their el-ung *[about how we can ride with him for free]*
nyilym kanuwa nyikim ku pim yi-yl puk-lyanga
the way they do, they talk like that, those men who have money go along
wilyala *get* tilu-na manya manya tiang olyo ya bo kupula pumulu-yl
and let them get down at that one gate up there [the turn-off to Oamul], we'll

go on the bush track
pup wi kupula tilupu-na pup meri-la molup-lyanga ku-yl kanu-na yad siring tangum-lum
we'll go and stay in one place, where the swampy bush is, if day breaks
aki-sik aima medipulu wai
come (pl) right to that place [whence we'll walk into Peadu en masse]

MIDIPU KUJILYI
mak-na pekim-ayl
that's exactly right [lit: 'on the mark']

KOPIA KOMI
o
yes

MIDIPU KUJILYI
aku-na peba nyikin pora-nsikin-ayl
you (sg) say that's how it will be, and with that you (sg) finish speaking

KOPIA KOMI
aku-na pipiyl
let it be so
oba na midi ya yi on naa kanud
I myself did not see the body [of Poika Wangi]
ya ku kina ilyi-nga molud
I stayed for this payment
yi on-ayl naa kanud wi adi anginsing-lum
I didn't see the body, they're said to have buried it up there
ung eke mel mare tung adi-lyi lelym nyib pilyikir
but I think that that is bent talk and that it [the body] is still there
[in a sobbing voice]
adi kulum-lum a
he died back there (out of our sight)
eni yi kis mareeee
you (sg) 'bad' men
na-nga yi-yl on naa kanakur iiii
I have not seen my man's body eeeee [weeps]
kola lku nyiring-iyl pamiyl kanai iiii
you (pl) said 'mourning house' [and didn't mention the body] let us go and you (pl) see [if the body is still there]
ku puku toba nyilymeli
they say 'the cliff will break' [a saying of Poika Wangi, said by exegetes to mean 'if you Kopia-Kubuka fight, we Poika-Palimi will all come to help; there will be so many of us that the Tambul Range will burst as we rush through']
kani-yl yi nai-d nyilymeli
to whom do they say this?
na-nga ana kola lku-na pamiyl kanaiii-a
my brother, let us go to the mourning house, you (pl) look! eeee
ekepu molym kanumel
now it is there

[From here to the end of the tape -- about 13 minutes -- is all about the funeral arrangements for Poika Wangi. There is no *el ung*. Komi finishes his speech saying he will take his money to the funeral because there is none left after this compensation payment. Then there is a long stretch of cross-talk. Kopia Yako says the Kopia-Kubuka must either come tomorrow early, or tonight by torch-light. He has received a message from a Poika saying there are two pigs left to be given to Kopia-Kubuka, but they must come soon to get them. More cross-talk. Yako adds there is no car to pick us up, so we must go by bush road. Unya says Komi is crying because our coffee is finished, so we have no money to take to the funeral. Then he asks Komi whether the No

Pengi ('Headwater') Kopia have money to bring, as their coffee comes later in the year. He says everybody should go to the funeral. Kujilyi says he had wanted to ask Joe Leahy if he could provide free rides, but now it's too late to ask. So Kopia-Kubuka should offer to buy fuel for Midipu Pana's car and Midipu Au's car. Those who go by car will not be able to get clay (with which to daub themselves for mourning), so those who walk should get it for them. More cross-talk. Then Panguwa starts some speeches, says he will leave for Oamul tonight. He calls on all No Pengi men to go with him.]

Appendix B: Grammatical sketch of Bo Ung, Ku Waru dialect

B.1 Introduction

The following brief grammatical outline is provided to help the reader interested in examining the lines of Ku Waru text in Appendix A and Chapter 7. Ideally, those texts would include a third line of morpheme-by-morpheme glosses throughout, but length restrictions preclude that here. This outline is intended to facilitate the reader's efforts to identify noun and verb endings, and basic construction types at phrase and clause levels. Where possible, verb inflections are summarily presented as paradigms in tables. There is brief discussion of the meaning and functions of some categories of the noun and verb (especially the latter) where these would otherwise be particularly difficult to infer from the category labels alone. We include an inventory of Ku Waru phonemes, but only the briefest indications concerning pronunciation. Despite all its limitations, this outline should make the recognition of morphemes and construction types possible for the reader who wishes to use it as an aid in working through the texts included in this book.

While most of New Guinea's 700-1000 languages are spoken by fewer than 2000 people each, most of the 250,000 people in the Western Highlands Province speak dialects belonging to a single dialect continuum, which ranges east at least as far as Kujip, north to Ruti, west to the Kaugel Valley, and south to Ialibu in the Southern Highlands Province (see Map 1). People who live at extreme ends of the continuum cannot generally understand each other unless they have had enough exposure to become bi-dialectal. In the modern context, opportunities for such exposure have greatly increased. Thus, a higher proportion of young men at Kailge can both understand and speak a reasonable approximation of the Mt. Hagen dialect (Melpa), than can old men, whose knowledge of Melpa tends to be a more passive 'hearing knowledge'. In 1983, we had the opportunity to observe the acquisition of a hearing knowledge of a Nebilyer dialect by a young man from Kumai, near Ruti, a Melpa-speaking area far to the north of Mt. Hagen town, where little is known about the Nebilyer Valley. We had visited him at Kumai, collecting data on his dialect. He later returned our visit, and when he first arrived at Kailge, he was able to understand almost nothing that was said in our local dialect. Within a few days, however, he had learned enough to be able to converse freely with people who addressed him in Ku Waru. His language learning was no doubt greatly facilitated by the fact that almost everyone at Kailge can understand his dialect (which is very similar to the Mt. Hagen one), even though he could not at first understand theirs.

This provides some indication of the similarity of the dialects in linguistic-structural terms, and degree of mutual intelligibility even of geographically fairly distant ones. *A fortiori*, within the greater continuum native-speakers of any one dialect are generally also able to understand all of the adjacent or nearby dialects. Thus, most native speakers (especially adult male ones) of Nebilyer dialects can understand both the Kaugel and Melpa dialects, whereas far fewer native speakers of Kaugel dialects can understand Melpa.

The dialect we describe here is the one spoken by people who have grown up at Kailge (see Map 1). It is known in the Nebilyer Valley as Kulyur or Ku

Waru, which means 'steep stone' or 'cliff' (see section 2.1). Though most of the speeches in our transcripts are in what would be classified as Ku Waru, the transcripts also include some lexical and grammatical variant forms associated with other nearby dialects. Rather than trying to describe this variation systematically, we will limit this account almost entirely to Ku Waru proper (as defined above), noting in passing some of the more important points of difference in other dialects.

B.2 Phonology and phonetics

The phonemes we recognize for the Ku Waru dialect are as follows:

CONSONANTS

	LABIAL	APICO-ALVEOLAR	PALATAL	VELAR
PLAIN STOP	p	t	s [s ts]	k
PRENASALIZED STOP	b [mb]	d [nd]	j [ns ɲɟ]	g [ŋg]
NASAL	m	n	ny, yn [ɲ]	ng [ŋ]
CONTINUANT	w	r	y	

	RETRO-FLEX TAP	APICO-ALVEOLAR	PALATAL	VELARIZED
LATERAL	rlt [ḷṭ]	*l*	ly, yl [ʎ]	l [g̯l, k̯l]

VOWELS

	FRONT		BACK
HIGH	i		u
MID	e		o
LOW		a	

The phonetic symbols in square brackets give a rough approximation of how the phonemes (or their major allophones) are pronounced, while the unbracketed characters are the ones we use in our practical orthography. The digraphs **ny** and **ly** in this orthography represent the same phonemes as **yn** and **yl** respectively. The latter spellings are used at the end of words, to prevent the y from being interpreted as a separate vowel, as in English *many*, *Polly*.

The difference between apico-alveolar and palatal stops is phonemic only in word-initial position, being conditioned elsewhere by following vowels. No such distinction is phonemic in the neighboring Kaugel or Meam dialects. In Meam, words which in Ku Waru have an s are pronounced with **t**. Where such Meam variants occur in the transcripts, they have been spelled accordingly with **t**.

The spelling system used here was chosen partly for optimal compatibility with that used by the Summer Institute of Linguistics for the Kaugel dialect. Since it has been developed to fit the phonemic patterns of these languages rather than English, many of the sounds are spelled with letters that have quite different typical phonetic values in English. Among the most important differences are the following.

From the English speaker's standpoint, the letters **b**, **d**, **j**, and **g**, even at the beginning of a word, must be read as though they had nasal sounds in front of them: **m**, **n**, **ny**, and **ng** respectively. At the end of a word, they sound like English **mp**, **nd**, **ns**, and **ngk** respectively. (In other words, the phonemic opposition in the stop consonants is between a pre-nasalized and a non-prenasalized or plain series, rather than voiced vs voiceless). The only exceptions to this in our texts are in introduced words from Tok Pisin and English, where **b**, **d**, and **g**, and **mb**, **nd**, **ng** are used as in the standard orthographies of those languages. This is in fact only a partial exception, because older Ku Waru people who speak little or no Tok Pisin actually do pronounce etymological **b**, **d**, and **g** in such words as **mb**, **nd**, and **ŋg** ([mbikpela] 'big', [ndok] 'dog', [ŋgod] 'God', etc.) In any case, words borrowed from these languages are always italicized in our texts, to signal the shift in spelling conventions.

The closest English approximation to the velarized lateral phoneme **l** in word initial or medial position is the sequence **gl**, as in *gloss* or *ugly*. In word-final position it sounds more like the **kl** of *klutz*. In all positions however, a closer approximation to the Ku Waru pronunciations can be made by trying to pronounce the **g** and **l** (or **k** and **l**) simultaneously, as the velar and lateral closures for these sounds are co-articulated rather than successive. When this lateral phoneme **l** occurs before **k**, it is not pronounced with a full, co-articulated velar stop, but is still noticeably velarized, i.e., with approximation between the velum, and base of the tongue.

The palatal lateral is roughly as in Spanish *caballero*, or English 'Wil<u>l</u> <u>y</u>ou?'. The word-final, voiceless version is like the Welsh **ll**, as in *Llanelly*.

The retroflex tap **rlt** occurs in only a small number of words (e.g., *Parlt* (women's name, *kera korlta* 'chicken') and may have come into the language through borrowing from the Enga language to the west, in which the sound is far more frequent.

The apico-alveolar ***l*** (which sounds similar to the clear English ***l*** of *Polly*) occurs only in borrowings from English and Tok Pisin, such as *lotu* 'church' or *pala*, 'to file'. Such words are thoroughly assimilated into the vocabulary of non-Tok Pisin speakers, but we always italicize them when they occur in Ku Waru texts to mark them as borrowings, spelled as per standard Tok Pisin orthography. This should assure that the ***l*** in *pala*, for example, will not be read as a velarized one.

Y and **r** are pronounced much as in British English, as is **w** except when it occurs before the front vowels, **i** and **e**. In that case it is pronounced with the lips spread rather than rounded.

Each of the five vowels has a number of allophones (variant pronunciations), much as in the Kaugel dialect described by Blowers (*Pacific Linguistics* Series A, No. 26). As in Kaugel, some word-final vowels in Ku Waru are voiceless when following stop consonants. In Ku Waru, this devoicing occurs only with high vowels **i** and **u**. For example, the words *pudi* 'wingbean' and *pudu* 'to reciprocate', are often pronounced as [puntḭ] and [puntṵ] respectively.

The high front vowel **i** is also lost as a phonetic syllable nucleus in final syllables when following consonants *other* than stops. If it is an accented vowel (see B.2.1 below) its underlying presence in such environments is sometimes evident from the absence of any accented vowel elsewhere in the word, and the 'transfer' of the accent (pitch rise) to the non-occlusive consonant (e.g., *pengl* 'head', with inherently accented final vowel, is often pronounced [peŋ̑]).

B.2.1 Accent

Ku Waru can best be described as having a pitch accent system, like Japanese. To a much greater extent than in English, the pitch of the voice in Ku Waru rises and falls independently of vowel length and apparent energy level. Thus, whereas stressed syllables in English usually carry the highest pitch within the word, there are minimal pairs in Ku Waru which differ **only** in pitch, and have what sounds to the English ear like identical 'stress' patterns. For example, the words *làpa* 'father', and (*kera*) *lapà* 'feather headdress' both sound to the Anglophone ear as though they were stressed on the first syllable, with pitch peaks on the first and second respectively. But we would not describe Ku Waru as a 'tone language', for (summarily-stated), unlike in true 'tone languages' such as Chinese, pitch in Ku Waru is not contrastive at the level of the syllable or mora, but at the level of the word. We have not marked accent in Appendix A, an omission which we think is justified here, given the overall aims of the present work. And there are two regularities of its occurrence which make its absence from the text less critical than might otherwise be the case. First, there is a general regularity in the position of the pitch peak: in a very high proportion of words, it occurs on the final syllable. And second, pitch accent has a very low functional yield: there are few pairs like the one illustrated above, in which the difference between two words consists **only** in a difference in placement of the accent. In the paradigms below, we have marked accent only where it does **not** occur on the final syllable, and this makes evident some crucial, minimal differences between forms of the verb.

B.3 Words and phrases

B.3.1 Pronouns

In common with most highland languages, Ku Waru has a three-term person system in the singular, and a two-term (i.e., two-person) system in the non-singular categories. This is evident in the free-standing pronouns, which are as follows.

	Singular	Dual	Plural
First Person	na `I`	olto `we two`	olyo `we`
Second Person	nu `you`(sg)	elti `you two` or `they two`	eni `you`(pl)
Third Person	yu `he`/`she`		

The glosses given for the singular and dual pronouns here are for their 'everyday' uses, rather than their 'segmentary' ones. For the latter, see section 5.2, where the significance of the disparity between the occurrence of singular or dual marking, versus the possibilities of interpretation of these forms as making reference to segmentary groupings, or *talapi*, is explained in full.

The three-term singular versus two-term non-singular system is also evident in the marking of person on the verb, as we shall see below.

B.3.2 The verb

For someone who is not a native speaker of a Papuan language, by far the most difficult (and most important) thing to master about the grammar of Ku Waru is the technique of building up a wide range of meanings from complex, more-or-less idiomatic combinations of a small basic stock of verbal and adverbial roots. These elements combine with each other and with adjunct nominal elements to do the work done in other languages by much larger stocks of mono-lexemic verbal elements. For instance, where the English speaker says 'He took the pig', the Ku Waru speaker gets along without a word for 'take', by saying *Kung-uyl lyipa meba pum*, literally 'Getting the pig and carrying it, he went'. Many other examples of Ku Waru compositional verbal expression are found in Appendix D. Each compositional meaning is associated not merely with the combination of roots listed, but with the roots in that particular order only. Thus for example, while *nyi- pilyi-* ('say-hear') means 'understand', the combination of the above two roots in the opposite order, *pilyi- nyi-*, means not 'understand' but 'be aware of', 'speak informedly'.

This verbal-compositional method is also used to formulate spatio-temporal relations of a kind which in other languages are case-marked in the noun phrase or with affixes or other relational elements. Thus, to expand on our earlier example, where the English speaker says 'He took the pig from Kailge to Palimung', the Ku Waru speaker says *Kung-uyl Palimung molupa lyipa meba Kailge-d pum*, 'Having been (at) Palimung, and gotten the pig, carrying it, he went to Kailge'.

This compositional technique is morphologically facilitated in Ku Waru by a distinction between what Papuanists generally call *medial* vs *final* forms of the verb. As in other Papuan languages, sentences in Ku Waru almost always end with a verb, the subject and object (if there is one) coming before. Some forms of the verb can occur **only** at the end of a clause or sentence, and others only in 'medial' position, i.e., in combination with a final verb (which they precede). The usual Papuan distinction between final and medial forms is further complicated in Ku Waru by the fact that some forms of the verb can appear in both positions. Those forms which can occur only finally inflect for person, number, tense, mood, and aspect, while the forms which can only appear medially -- which we call *non-final* -- inflect (i.e. vary in form) only for person and (optionally) number, and agree (notionally) in person, number, mood, and tense with the final verb with which they occur. The forms which can appear both medially and finally -- which we call the *chameleon* classes -- inflect for person, number, and for tense/mode/aspect categories which differ in value depending on whether the form in question is occurring medially or finally. The members of these different classes -- final, non-final and chameleon categories of the verb -- are discussed B.3.2.2., B.3.2.3., and B.3.2.4 respectively.

B.3.2.1 *Verb roots*

By and large, the distinctions between final, non-final, and chameleon verb forms apply only to Ku Waru verb inflection classes, not to verb **roots**. Almost all of the roots can be inflected so as to appear medially or finally. The only exceptions of which we are aware are a small number of roots which seem to appear only with non-final inflection. All are semantically adverb-like, e.g. *alte-* 'do again', *lak-* 'do vigorously'. As far as we know, there are no roots which can only occur in final (or chameleon) form.

All inflected verb forms consist of a root (the forms in the glossary ending with a hyphen: *te-* 'to do', *o-* 'to come', etc.) with following suffix(es). The exact form of each root and suffix varies somewhat depending on what other elements they are combining with. We will not try to account for all this variation exhaustively here, but will instead simply exemplify the form and function of each verbal category with reference to a verb root with back root vowel, *pu-* 'to go', and in some instances also, with reference to a second root *nyi-* 'to say' with front root vowel. Where forms of *nyi-* are not included, it may be assumed that the endings are the same as the corresponding ones for *pu-*. The forms taken by the inflectional suffixes on other roots are generally similar enough to those shown to be easily recognizable as such. Roots ending in a consonant add a high vowel before any consonant-initial suffix (except for roots roots ending in **-l-** or **-ng-** when followed by suffixes beginning with **-k**). If the last vowel in the root is **i** or **e**, the added vowel is **i**; if **u** or **o**, it is **u** ; if **a**, it is **a** or **u**. If the roots ends in a mid vowel (**e** or **o**), it changes to the corresponding high vowel (**i** or **u** respectively) in the perfective and remote past tenses, e.g. */te- m/* ➤ *tim* '(s)he did'; */o- m/* ➤ *um* '(s)he came'.

Rather than squeezing all the illustrative forms into one chart, we will divide them up into the three sets: final only, non-final, and chameleon. This division, made initially on purely distributional grounds (i.e., according to where the verb can occur within the clause) also corresponds to some basic semantic oppositions among Ku Waru verbal categories, in that the final class includes all the indicative mode forms, while the chameleon class forms all signal various non-indicative modes when occurring sentence-finally.

B.3.2.2 *Final verbs*

Final Forms of the Verbs *pu-* 'go' and *nyi-* 'say'

	Imperative /Hortative	Present Progressive	Perfective	Remote Past	Habitual
1sg	---	pukur nyikir	pud nyid	purud nyirid	pulyo nyilyo
2sg	pa nya	pukun nyikin	pun nyin	purun nyirin	pulto nyilto
3sg	---	pukum nyikim	pum nyim	purum nyirim	pulym nyilym
1du	pảbul nyảbul	pukủbul nyikỉbul	pủbul nyỉbul	purủbul nyirỉbul	pulybulu nyilybulu
2/3du	payl nyayl	pukủbil nyikỉbil	pungl nyingl	puringl nyiringl	pulybeli nyilybeli
1pl	pảmul nyảmul	pukủmul nyikỉmul	pủmul nyỉmul	purủmul nyirỉmul	pulymulu nyilymulu
2/3pl	pai nyai	pukủmil nyikỉmil	pung nying	puring nyiring	pulymeli nyilymeli

We now briefly characterize the semantics of the forms, and exemplify them.

The imperative forms are the basic 'directive' forms of the verb (though by no means the only ones: cf. remarks on the perfective below, and B.3.2.4., B.4.3.). The hortative forms are typically used to mean 'let's do it now', let's really do it', as opposed to the first person non-singular optative forms (see B.3.2.4.3 below), which are used for less urgent proposals.

Aside from the imperative/hortative series, whose meaning would seem to require that they be able to comprise a complete clause or sentence, all of these 'final-only' series are of the indicative mode. That is, they refer to actions, processes and events to which the speaker is attesting without epistemic or deontic qualification. Moreover, these four series (i.e., the columns 2-5 in the chart above) comprise all the indicative forms of the Ku Waru verb.

The four series differ in tense and aspect. The *present progressive* is generally used for characterizing actions/processes as ongoing at the time of the speech event, e.g.,

nu	tena	pukun
you	where	go-PPr-2sg

Where are you going?

Sometimes these verbs (much like the English progressive forms with which we have translated them) are also used for actions which are not actually ongoing at the time of speaking, but about to be. For example, a common way of taking leave from a conversation is to say, while still sitting down,

na	pukur
I	go-PPr-1sg

I'm going.

By contrast, the perfective is used to characterize actions/processes as completed, e.g.,

nu	tena	pun
you	where	go-Prf-2sg

Where did you go? or Where have you been?

While these perfective forms are generally used with a 'past tense' value, this is not invariably so. Thus, in answer to the question 'Where are you going' (*nu tena pukun*), one often hears from someone who wants to stay and strike up a conversation:

na	ya	molud
I	here	be/stay-Prf-1sg

While normally glossable as 'I have been here' or 'I have stayed here', the utterance in this context must be glossed and further understood as something like 'I'm here' (to stay, i.e., I have been here up until your arrival, and do not intend to go now that you have come). Another example of this kind is:

po	naa	pim
sugar	not	be-Prf-3sg

The sense of this can approximated by the awkward gloss 'Sugar hasn't finished being there' (or, 'is not there sufficiently', where the notion of sufficiency or aspectual 'perfection' is what is here conveyed by the perfective, further negated. This was jokingly said by a Ku Waru friend of ours after he tasted a cup of coffee into which we had put 10 spoonfuls of sugar, after he had complained that five was not enough!).

Another common non-past use of perfective forms is as a strong form of command or exhortation, e.g.,

ola molun pumul
up be/stand-Prf-2sg go-Prf-2/3pl
Stand up!!! Let's go!!!

As far as we know, this usage is limited to first person non-singular and second person forms of the verb, i.e. just those person categories which are also represented in the hortative/imperative series.

Another non-past use of the perfective is in the protasis (i.e., the 'if clause') in a (non-counterfactual) conditional construction, where it takes the subordinating marker *-lum* (which in these contexts can be glossed as 'if') e.g.,

na pud-lum nu na lubiyl ui
I go-Prf-1sg-if you me following come
If I go, you follow me.

kalunsab na-nga po kani makunsun-lum
cook-Ben-Opt-1sg I-Gen sugar cane that tie up-Ben-Prf-2sg-if
I'll cook for you if you tie up my sugar cane for me.

As can be seen from the second example, the perfective category in this context does not even have a relative tense value, signaling a time relationship between two reported events: nothing is specified by this sentence about which of the two favors must be done first. Rather, the perfective here seems to signal something about the logical status of the action it describes in relation to that of the apodosis (the 'then' clause), a relationship that could be glossed 'x given that y'.

In those clauses where the perfective is used to describe past events (which is by far its most frequent use), it has the value of a 'recent past' tense. The action described may have extended over many days, but this form of the verb is usually used only if the action has assertedly been completed on the same day as the time of speaking or the day before.

In this respect, the perfective contrasts with the remote past tense, which is only used in reference to actions, processes, and events which assertedly took place 'before yesterday', e.g.,

ya mongu mel-we kolsi pirim
here trouble small a little bit be/lie-RP-3sg
There was a bit of trouble here. (Appendix A, line 2: reference to fighting which had happened nine months before)

ui tara-ma-n sumuyl tiring
before ancestors-Col-Erg kina shell(s) do-RP-3pl
Our ancestors used to transact with kina shells.

Many more examples of the remote past tense can be found in Appendix A, especially in the *el ung* speeches, which so frequently concern events of the distant past. Throughout the transcript, the events of September 1982 are referred to in the remote past, while the various transactions in which the money was raised for the compensation payment (most of which took place on the morning of the same day or the day before) are generally referred to in the perfective.

The habitual forms are generally used for actions/processes which are asserted to be regular occurrences, habits, or states of affairs, e.g.,

kewa talym
foreigner/European imitate-Hab-3sg
He imitates Europeans (wears trousers, lives on wages, etc.)

olyo-nga uj lu-n sulymulu
we-Gen wood ax-Ins split-Hab-1pl
We split our wood with axes.

Habitual forms are also used in a related, weaker 'durative' sense to assert merely that the action, process, or state is of longstanding, e.g.,

ekepu	ya	kim	imi	tuyl-te	ilyi	ya	pelym
now	here	vegetable	mould	strike-Ppl-one	that	here	be-Hab-3sg

There is this one 'rotten vegetable' remaining (from Appendix A, line 641; cf. section 6.2.3.)

ilyi	waria	yuyu	abolupa	molym
that		he himself	hold-NF-3sg	be-Hab-3sg

That's something that Waria himself is holding (Appendix A, line 215)

Whether in its habitual meaning or its merely durative one, this form of the verb is used only when the process, action or state it describes is assertedly still ongoing at the time of speaking. (In that respect it is more strictly a present tense category than the present progressive). In the (remote) past tense, the distinction between perfective and habitual/durative is neutralized (i.e., disappears). Consider for example:

olyo-nga	langi-ma	olyo-nga	tara-ma-n	bo
we-Gen	food-Col	we-Gen	ancestor-Col-Erg	plant

tok	tiring	i	tep	molymolu
strike/do-NF-2/3pl	do-RP-2/3pl	this	do-NF-1	stay-Hab-1pl

In the same way as our ancestors planted foods, so we still do.

From the parallel which is being drawn here, it clear that the ancestors **habitually** or customarily planted food in the same way we do. But it is only when referring to the present, in the second clause, that the 'habitual' nature of the action is explicitly marked by the form of the verb. (See also the second example sentence in the discussion of remote past above, which also clearly refers to a notionally habitual activity).

B.3.2.3 *Non-final verbs*

Non-Final forms of the Verbs
pu- 'go' and *nyi-* 'say'

1sg	pup	nyib
2sg	pủk(un)	nyɨk(in)
3sg	pủpa	nyɨba
1du	pủp(ul)	nyɨb(ul)
2/3du	pu(ku)l	nyi(ku)l
1pl	pủp(un)	nyɨb(un)
2/3pl	puk	nyik

Besides the root *nyi-*, there are only two others which take the non-final suffix variants shown in the second column, viz. *o-* 'come', and *no-* 'consume'.

The 1du variant ending exemplified by *pupul/nyibul*, cognate to Kaugel *pupulu* , is at Kailge used most consistently by people with Kaugel-side connections (periods of residence there, etc.). Others use it more variably. The 2sg and 1pl forms *pukun/nyikin* and *pupun/nyibun* are standard in the Meam dialect and also variably used at Kailge - *pukun/nyikin* very frequently, and *pupun/nyibun* much less so.

As can be seen from the chart, these non-final verbs convey less about person/number than do the final verbs. This is true especially of the first person forms, the most frequent variants of which lack any specification of number. This may be related to the fact that the subject of each non-final verb is almost always the same as that of the first final verb which follows it (and all intervening verbs), so that the number of the subject is always fully specified at least once within the clause.

A similar linkage holds for temporal and modal values. The non-final verbs are not themselves marked for tense, but the actions, states, or relations described by them have assertedly taken place before or concurrently with that described by the final verb. Similarly, non-final verbs carry no modal specification independent of that of the final verb.

B.3.2.4 *Chameleon verb classes*

Chameleon Forms of the Verb *pu-* 'go'

	Future/ Imminent	Subjunctive/ Switch Reference 1	Optative/ Switch Reference 2
1sg	pubu	pulka	pab
2sg	puni	pulkuna	pån(i)
3sg	puba	pulka	půpiyl
1du	pubulu	pulkubula	påbiyl
2/3du	pungli	pulkubela	pangl
1pl	pumulu	pulkumula	påmiyl
2/3pl	pungi	pulkumela	pang

Each of these forms of the verb occurs both medially and finally, in different, though related, senses. We will now briefly describe and exemplify these for each series.

B.3.2.4.1 *Future/imminent*

The Future/Imminent when occurring finally is a straightforward future tense, e.g.,

na	ekepu	penga	lku	kolya	pubu
I	today	later	house	place	go-Fut-1sg

Later today I'll go home.

ab	keyn-nga	*kot*	kongun	*tunde*	tingi
woman	-Gen		day	Tuesday	do-Fut-2/3pl

They're going to hold Keyn's court case on Tuesday.

When occurring medially, the future/imminent form combines with a following verb to specify that the action/process/event referred to by the first verb is imminent in view of that referred to by the second. If the subject of the verbs is sentient, the usual sense is that he or she performed the action referred to by the second verb with the **intention** of thereby (or thereafter) performing the first. An example is:

nu	tena	puni	pukun
you	where	go-Imt-2sg	go-PPr-2sg

The Ku Waru expression is hard to translate, but the sense is something like: You are going with the intention of going where? Where are you on your way to?

Another example, with a perfective final verb, is:

nu	nabolka	ul	tini	un
you	what	affair	do-Imt-2sg	come-Prf-2sg

What business have you come to transact?

While any verb may occur as the second one in such a sequence, the verb *te-* 'do' is by far the most frequent, especially when the subject of the clause is non-sentient. The idea conveyed by such clauses is a weaker version of the above, in that the actions/processes referred to by the two verbs are not portrayed as distinct from one another. Rather, this is a kind of generalized **immediate future** construction, which can usually be glossed by English 'be about to', e.g.,

lo oba tekim
rain come-Imt do-PPr-3sg
The rain is about to come. (It's about to rain.)

When the subject is sentient, there is usually a further implication that the action/process is one he/she *intends* to perform, e.g.,

na lku kolya yad pubu tekir
I house place return go-Imt-1sg do-PPr-1sg
I am about to (or I intend to) go back home

kang-ayl ab lyiba tim
boy-Def woman get-Imt-3sg do-Prf-3sg
The boy was about to (or intended to) take a wife.

B.3.2.4.2 *Subjunctive/switch reference 1*

When occurring in final position, these forms convey a wide range of modal qualifications, being variously glossable as 'might (have) X', 'could (have) X' or 'should (have) X' where X is the action/process/state predicated by the verb so marked, e.g.,

na yi nuim molka pi naa molkur
I big man be-Sjv-1sg but not be-PPr-1sg
I could have been a big man, but I'm not.

nu-ni na mel-ti silkuna
you-Erg me thing-S/I give-Sjv-2sg
You should (have) give(n) me something.

Note that tense is not explicitly marked on these forms: time values must be inferred from context.

In the Ku Waru dialect proper, the main context in which these subjunctive forms occur medially is in the counterfactual conditional construction, where they are paired with another subjunctive verb as the final verb. The medial subjunctive verb in this context takes the postposition *-ja* which in this context can be glossed as 'if'. Examples are:

nu tela-d pulkuna-ja na peya pulkubula
you Tela-Dat go-Sjv-2sg-if I together go-Sjv-1du
If you had gone to Tela I would have gone with you.

yi korupa pulka-ja kung yupuk naa silka
man poor be-Sjv-1/3sg-if pig three not give-Sjv-1/3sg
If he had been a poor man he wouldn't have given three pigs.

Note that the first of these two examples differs from all of the previous examples of medial or non-final verbs in that the subject of the medial verb is not the same as that of the final verb. The possibility of such non-agreement is a general feature of this class of verb forms when used medially, both in this formally distinct counter-factual construction and elsewhere. Outside of this particular construction, these medial verbs lose their subjunctive meaning, but generally signal the possibility of a switch of subject in the following verb. Like the non-final verbs treated above, these Switch Reference 1 verbs agree with the following verb in tense and mode, and signal that the specified action took place before or simultaneously with the action specified by the final verb. For example:

tripela nyilkuna na-n *tupela* nyikir
three say-SR1-2sg I-Erg two say-PPr-1sg
You say three and I say two. (Merlan and Rumsey 1986: line 701)

For another example see Appendix A, line 732.

B.3.2.4.3 *Optative/Switch-Reference 2*

These forms when used in final position either convey a wish or proposal on the part of the speaker, or attribute one to the addressee. For example,

ilyi	opayl	pudu	tangl
that	tomorrow	reply	hit/do-Opt-2du

Tomorrow those two can reply to it [i.e., the speaker proposes that they do so] (from Appendix A, line 224).

na-nga	mai	aprali	tek	lying-lum	na	tena	pab
me-Gen	soil	seize	do-NF-2/3pl	take-Prf-2/3pl-if	I	where	go-Opt-1sg

If they take my land, where I am supposed to go [i.e. where do you propose that I go?]

olyo	no	kalap	meb	ob	namiyl
we	water	boil-NF-1	carry-NF-1	come-NF1	consume-Opt-1pl

Let's boil some water, bring it and drink it.

Verbs of the same form as these optatives occur medially in a very different function. As with the Sjv/SR1 series (but unlike the non-final verbs), the subject of these verbs in medial position regularly differs from that of the final verb with which they are in construction. And here again, Opt/SR2 forms lose their modal specification when used medially. Instead, they take on a temporal/aspectual meaning, signaling that the action/process/state specified by the medial verb is one which is predicated for a time period which is longer than that of the final verb, but encompasses it (rather than preceding it or being exactly the same time, as with SR1 verbs). Examples are:

pupa	molupiyl	kolya	tangurum
go-NF-3sg	remain-SR2-3sg	place	daybreak-RP-3sg

He kept on going and as he was doing so, day broke.

na	naa	molab	tiring
I	not	be-SR2-1sg	do-3pl-RP

They did it before I was born (lit.: I didn't exist; they did it).

B.3.2.5 *Negation*

Verbs are negated by adding the particle *naa* before them, e.g.,

na	naa	pilyikir
I	not	hear/understand-PPr-1sg

I don't understand.

naa	pupiyl
not	go-Opt-3sg

She (or he) shouldn't go./Don't let her (or him) go.

lo	naa	toba
rain	not	strike-Fut-3sg

It's not going to rain.

naa	lyip	meb	pumulu
not	get-NF-1	carry/bear-NF-1	go-Fut-1pl

We will not take it.

B.3.2.6 *Causative/benefactive verbs*

Any of the forms of the Ku Waru verb discussed above may be transformed into a causative/benefactive verb by adding *-nsi-* immediately after the root. If the root ends in l, the l is dropped.

In the benefactive uses of this marker, it signals that there is someone for whom the action/process/state is asserted to have been performed or brought about, or whom it in some way concerns. The beneficiary may or may not be explicitly identified within the same clause where the benefactive verb occurs, but if it is, it is regularly marked by the genitive postposition *-nga*. For example,

na *leda*-ti yab-ma-nga tonsikir
I letter-S/I person-Col-Gen strike/do-Ben-PPr-3sg
I am writing a letter for some people.

Compare:

na *leda*-ti tokur
I letter-S/I strike/do-PPr-1sg
I am writing a letter.

na-ni nu-nga ekepu buri mensibu
I-Erg you-Gen today sweep bear/do-Ben-Fut-3sg
Today I'll sweep for you.

Compare:

na ekepu buri mebu
I today sweep bear/do-Fut-1sg
Today I'll sweep.

na-nga nabina nyinsikimil
I-Gen why speak-Ben-PPr-2/3pl
Why are they talking about me?

Compare:

nabina ung nyikimil
why word speak-PPr-3sg
Why are they talking?

A suffix of the same form, *-nsi-*, is used to form causative verbs, e.g.,

na kib *su* monsikir
I foot shoe be-Csv-PPr-1sg
I am putting on shoes (lit.: causing shoes to be [on my feet]).

Compare:

kib *su* kib-na molym
foot shoe foot-Loc be-Hab-3sg
Shoes are on my feet.

na *trausis*-na pensip molyo
I trousers-Loc lie/be-Csv-NF-1 stand/be-Hab-1sg
I have it put it in my pocket. (literally: I am (here), having caused it to lie (concealed) in my trousers).

Compare:

trausis-na pelym
trousers-Loc lie/be-Hab-3sg
It's in my pocket.

na ekepu yi-ti wai top monsud,
I today man-S/I arrange do-NF-1sg-Prf be there-Csv-1sg-Prf
molym
be there-Hab-3sg
I arranged for a man to be there (lit.: arranging, caused him to be there); he is there.

Though identical in form, the causative and benefactive suffixes are functionally distinct, and sometimes even occur together on the same verb, e.g.,

olyo nu-nga ginsinsimulu
we you-Gen tight-*nsi-nsi*-1pl-Fut
We will tighten it for you.

B.3.2.7 *Participles*

Any Ku Waru verb root may be made into a noun by adding the suffix *-yl*. If the root ends in a mid vowel, *o* or *e*, it is raised to the corresponding high vowel, *u* or *i* respectively. If the root ends in a consonant, it adds a vowel as in B.3.2.1 above.

From the Anglocentric viewpoint, these verbal nouns have a broad range of functions, including:

Agent Nouns, e.g.,

lopa marsupial	/no-yl/ consume-Ppl	-->	lopa marsupial	nuyl eater (/eaten)
ukulu	/pe-yl/ sleep-Ppl	-->	ukulu one who sleeps (i.e., lives) near the Ukulu (River).	piyl
	/kan-yl/ see-Ppl	-->	kanuyl one who sees/ has seen	

Patient Nouns/Passive Participles, e.g.,

abu-n woman-Erg	/me-yl/ carry/bear-Ppl	-->	abun miyl one borne by a women (into the segmentary unit)

Abstract Verbal Nouns/Deverbal Adjectives, e.g.,

pangi be soft	/te-yl/ do-Ppl	-->	pangi tiyl soft, softness
koma be damp	/le-yl/ do/be-Ppl	-->	koma liyl damp, dampness

B.3.3 Noun phrases and postpositions

One of the most frequently-occurring types of multi-word noun phrase (NP) in Ku Waru is one in which a generic term is followed by more specific one within the genus. Women's names, for instance, more often than not are preceded by the generic *ab* 'woman'. Other common generics in such compound NPs include: *uj* 'tree' (*uj kalyipa* 'casuarina tree', *uj langilya* 'black palm', etc.); *lopa* 'marsupial' (*lopa alsu* 'tree kangaroo', etc.); *kera* 'medium-to-large winged creature' (including moths, bats, and all birds, but not small flying insects), *no* 'drinkable liquid other than milk', etc. Men's names are often preceded by segmentary group/category names as their relevant generic (cf. A Strathern 1971:15). Upper and lower level segmentary names themselves enter into generic specific compounds, which sometimes show more than two constituents: Kopia\Tolab\Supub, etc.

The relation between generic and specific terms in these compounds is one instance of what Joseph Greenberg (in *Universals in Language*) calls 'modifier-modified' relations. That the 'modified' should always come first in such compounds agrees with Greenberg's generalization (ibid) that this ordering is found in languages in which the verb comes last in the clause. The same ordering is also found in other types of modifier-modified NPs in Ku Waru. Examples are:

yi kayi we
man good very
very good man

Compare:

kayi we 'very good'; yi kayi 'good man'

kung kapo tal
pig fat two
two fat pigs

Compare:

kung tal, 'two pigs'; kung kapo 'fat pig'

B.3.3.1 *Case postpositions*

In the first of the previous two examples immediately above, the last element modifies the second, the two together modifying the first. In the second example, the last element modifies a complex comprising the first two. The marking of case relations in Ku Waru is done largely with elements of the latter sort. That is, instead of word-level case suffixes as in Latin or German (or prepositions as in English), Ku Waru has case *postpositions*, which occur only on the last word within the noun phrase which they modify. These are listed below. For examples of each use, see the transcript lines indicated after the glosses, all from Appendix A (where all postpositions identifiable as such by preceding hyphens).

Ergative/Instrumental *-n(i)*
'by the agency of' (cf. B.4.1. below), e.g., lines 315, 779, 1199, 1310, 1582, 1652, 1680
'by means of', e.g., lines 1528, 1533, 1534, 1649
also used for the subject of verbs of speaking, e.g., lines 417, 651, 652, 728, 1015, 1302

Genitive *-nga*
'belonging to', 'in relation to (e.g., kinsmen)', 'for' e.g., lines 65, 66, 79, 101, 105, 129, 132, 155, 176
'concerned with', 'about', e.g., lines 6, 29, 79, 92, 207, 218, 220, 237, 305
'for the benefit of', 'affecting' (with benefactive verbs: see B.3.2.6 above)

Dative *-d*
'to, towards', e.g., lines 551, 737, 1324, 1735, 1737
'addressed to', (i.e., person spoken to) e.g., lines 652, 1482, 1848

Locative *-na*
'in, at, on', e.g., lines 63, 66, 83, 144, 196, 456, 468, 505, 565

Comitative *-kin*
'with', 'accompanied by', e.g., lines 106, 323, 637, 896, 987, 1098, 1138, 1211
'and' (in coordinate NPs of the form NP_1*-kin* NP_2*-kin*), e.g., lines 322, 446, 505, 512, 513, 696, 765, 1467
'at the time of', e.g., lines 1144, 1414; cf also B.4.2.2. below

B.3.3.2 *Other postpositions*

Some other grammatical meanings are conveyed by postpositions as well. These include the following.

B.3.3.2.1 *Collective postposition -ma*

This is the nearest thing in Ku Waru to a plural number marker within the noun phrase (NP). On NPs referring to animate beings and most other sorts of countable objects, it specifies that there is more than one of them (and almost always more than two), and hence generally takes a plural-marked verb when functioning as its subject (but cf. section 5.1.1). An example is:

kang kel-ma ai lelymeli
boy small-Col grow be/do-Hab-2/3pl
Small boys grow up.

For further examples, see Appendix A, lines 69, 283, 288, 292, 348, 560, 735, 805; cf. also section 5.1.1 .

On other NPs referring to inanimate things, *-ma* is used to denote what we might think of as a plurality of objects, but with singular verb agreement, e.g.,

mel-ma	bulibali	nyirim
thing-Col	destroyed	be-RP-3sg

Things were destroyed.

ne-d	*ka*	*na*	mel-ma	lekim
over there	car	and	thing-Col	be-PPr-3sg

Over there [at Palimung] there is [they have] a car and things.

ya	luip kalipa	kep-ma	lirim,	lekim
here		embankment-Col	be-RP-3sg	be-Prog-3sg

These embankments of the Luip and Kalipa were here and still remain.

B.3.3.2.2 *Dual (salient pair) postposition -sil*

The most generally applicable gloss for this postposition is 'pair consisting of', e.g.: *abu-sil* 'pair of women'; *yi sub sul-sil* (man short tall - *sil*) 'a short man and a tall one', or 'a pair of men, one short and the other tall'; *mulu ma-sil* (sky ground *-sil*), 'heaven and earth'. As with the collective postposition, subject NPs marked with Dual marker *-sil* sometimes take agreeing verbs (i.e. dual-subject ones), and sometimes singular ones. For example:

i	ku	*handet*	ilyi	unya tepra-sil-n	tingl	ku-yl
this	money	hundred	this	Unya Tepra-Du-Erg	do-Du-Prf	money-Def

This hundred is what (the pair of men called) Unya and Tepra gave. (Appendix A, line 697).

But:

el	turum-uyl	topa-kin	epola alya-sil	lyirim
fight	hit-RP-3sg-Def	hit-RP-3sg-Com	Epola-Alya-Du	get-RP-3sg

When there was fighting, the Epola and Alya [tribes] took it up.

For more examples of each kind, see Appendix A, lines 415, 697, 700, 1222, 1456. Note that in none of these examples does the use of *-sil* add any extra information about number per se. For in each of them, we already know that two entities are being referred to, since both of them are named within the NP. Though especially common in segmentary contexts (see section 5.1.1), these bipartite compound NPs are perhaps the most usual place where one finds the dual marker *-sil* in general. What it seems to signify in such cases is not just that there are two entities, but that they are **paired** entities: social identities which are closely identified with each other, or taxonomic categories which share some salient semantic feature (cf. section 5.7).

B.3.3.2.3 *Definite marker -yl /-iyl /-uyl /-ayl*

This postposition marks a noun phrase as definite, i.e., one whose reference is being treated as presupposed or 'recoverable' from context. It can usually be glossed as 'the'. The allomorph (variant form) *-yl* occurs after vowels, and *-iyl / -uyl* after consonants. The allomorph *-ayl* occurs after both consonants and accented vowels. In the latter environment, it displaces the final vowel, e.g.,

moni ('money') + ayl --> *mon*ayl

meri ('down there') + ayl --> merayl

For examples of definite marking with *-yl /-iyl /-uyl /-ayl* , see Appendix A, lines 50, 93, 164, 165, 202, 302, 303, 361, 365, 373, 487, 572.

B.3.3.2.4 *Singular /indefinite -ti /-te*

This postposition generally has the opposite meaning to the definite one: i.e., it marks the noun as one whose reference is assumed not to be known. It can thus usually be glossed as 'a', 'an' (see Appendix A, lines 67, 70, 71, 248, 1630, 1632, 1790). Unlike in English, a noun in Ku Waru need not be marked as either definite or indefinite: it may occur without either postposition, in which case it is unspecified for definiteness. This being a three-term system rather than a two-term one, the 'indefinite' marker has a somewhat different range of functions than English *a /an /some*. It is, for instance, sometimes used to mean 'a different one from what you think'. i.e., presupposing not only that the addressee does not know the referent, but that she mistakenly thinks she does know it (see, e.g., Appendix A, lines 175, 381, 618).

B.4 Syntax

B.4.1 Basic clause types

In English and many other languages (e.g., most Australian Aboriginal ones), there is a fundamental division between intransitive verbs and transitive ones, and a more-or-less clear cut distinction between corresponding clause types: intransitive ones, involving a single core syntactic case role, and transitive ones involving two, one for the Agent of the action and one for the undergoer or 'Patient'. The basic clause types in Ku Waru are not amenable to any such binary classification, because most Ku Waru verbs can occur in construction with either one or two NPs in core syntactic case roles. Nor does the distribution of syntactic case-marked NPs provide evidence for a binary transitive-intransitive distinction.

The two core syntactic cases in Ku Waru are ergative, marked (optionally in most contexts) by the postposition *-n(i)* (see section B.3.3.1.), and absolutive, marked by zero (i.e., by the absence of a case postposition). A clause may contain one absolutive NP in construction with the verb (i.e., one 'argument') or two. In the former case, the verb may or may not agree in person/number with the NP. Where there are two absolutive NPs in construction with the verb, it always agrees with one of them. Alternatively, the clause may contain one ergative NP argument and one absolutive, the verb agreeing with one or the other.

Which clauses then are transitive and which intransitive? In Ku Waru this is best regarded as a matter of degree (as per Hopper and Thompson in *Language* 56:251-99). Instead of a binary distinction, we can posit for Ku Waru a transitivity scale which has at least five distinct steps. These can be established, not by ranking the verbs themselves for transitivity, but by asking, for each clause: 1) how many NPs are there in core syntactic case roles? (i.e., those whose primary function is to indicate the nature of the relation between its NP and the verb within the clause); 2) for what roles are they marked?; 3) with which, if any of the NPs does the verb agree?

According to these criteria, we can distinguish among at least the five clause types listed below. These formulae represent the clause types in their most fully explicit form, as they occur in isolated, elicited clauses or sentences. In longer texts, any of these NP argument types may be deleted from the clause when its reference is clear from the linguistic context, as is amply illustrated in Appendix A. The ergative case postposition is also optional, at least in clause type V. In textual examples where it is absent from clauses of this type, informants readily restore it in what they treat as equivalent repetitions of the same sentence.

The connecting line below each clause shows which NP the verb agrees with. In the two-argument clause-types, the two NPs are shown in the order in which they normally (but not invariably) occur.

```
TYPE I     NP-Abs    V (always third person - no agreement)

TYPE II    NP-Abs              V
           └───────────────────┘

TYPE III   NP-Abs    NP-Abs    V
                     └─────────┘

TYPE IV    NP-Abs    NP-Erg    V
           └───────────────────┘

TYPE V     NP-Erg    NP-Abs    V
           └───────────────────┘
```

Each of these major clause types has its own characteristic (if not invariant) meanings, which we will now briefly discuss and exemplify. Within some of the types it is possible to make further distinctions among sub-types, as we shall see.

In Type I clauses, the entity referred to by the Absolutive NP, if animate, is one which undergoes the action against its will or with no control over it, e.g.,

nu	siyl	topa	toba
you	slip	hit/do-NF-3sg	hit/do-Fut-3sg

You will slip and fall.

olyo	korupa	pukum
we	poor	go-3Sg Pres

We (pl) are poor.

Type II clauses are used for many of the same sorts of actions/processes/states as are intransitive verbs in English. Some simple examples are:

ab	dau	taiki	tepa	pulym		na	kolkur
woman	Dau	always	do-NF-3sg	go-Hab-3sg		I	die-PPr-1sg

[The woman called] Dau always goes. — I am dying.

Type II clauses may include any of a number of different verbs which we generally gloss in these contexts as 'be' 'exist' or 'be there'. Such one or two word glosses are quite inadequate to show these verbs' full contribution to the meaning of the clause, partly because it would require lengthier glosses to convey the relevant distinctions among ways of 'being' and partly because these verbs function as 'classificatory verbs' (as per Lang 1975, in *Pacific Linguistics* Series B, No.39), the choice among which is in part conditioned by the nature of the verb's subject. The Ku Waru existential verb roots include: *mol*-, used of liquids, certain other inanimate objects (e.g., shoes) and all living things (including plants); *pe*-, used of almost any kind of animate or inanimate object, generally only if it is lying flat, or is latent or concealed; *le*-, used only of inanimate objects, in a wide variety of states and positions, though often with the idea that they have been put in place; *angalyi*-, used mainly for certain body parts (primarily, but not exclusively, the appendages) and certain kinds of human artifacts, e.g., *lku* 'house'.

Type II clauses are also used in Ku Waru for attributing qualities, such as would generally be done in English with adjectives, e.g.,

kolya	su	lekim
place	smooth	be-PPr-3sg

The place is smooth.

don-nga	lku	si	nyim
Don-Gen	house	crowdedness	be/say-Prf-3sg

Don's house was crowded.

The penultimate word in each of these sentences has been translated (however awkwardly) as an abstract noun because none of these words can function attributively within a noun phrase. In order for them to be used that way, the verb itself has to be changed to a participle or otherwise embedded within the NP, e.g.,

uj	koma	liyl		mel	boni	tiyl
wood	dampness	be-Ppl		thing	heaviness	do-Ppl

damp wood — heavy thing

The Type III clause can perhaps be understood as a composite of types I and II, for it involves two absolutive NP arguments, one of which is semantically similar to the one in Type I and the other to the one in Type II. Furthermore, the argument with which the verb does **not** agree in Type III is just the one which is

semantically similar to the sole argument in Type I (which also fails to control verb agreement): similar in that the NPs which occur in that syntactic position often refer to notional 'patients' upon whom the action or process impinges, usually without their being able to control it. (While not all Type III clauses have such a patient, in those that do it is never the NP that controls verb agreement). Examples are:

na	pipiyl	tekim
I-Abs	shame-Abs	do-PPr-3sg

I feel ashamed.

olyo	tai	um
we-Abs	laughter-Abs	come-Prf-3sg

We burst out laughing.

Another very frequently occurring sub-type of the Type III clause is the possessive clause. This subtype is closely related to the existential clause subtype of Type II exemplified above. In common with many other languages, Ku Waru has no verb for 'to have'. Instead of predicating possession by placing the 'possessor' NP in transitive subject position, in Ku Waru it is done by making the 'possessed' NP the subject of an intransitive verb of 'being'. This much is true of many languages, but in most such languages, the 'possessor' NP is placed in some oblique case such as the dative, whereas in Ku Waru it usually goes into the absolutive, as the secondary argument in a type III clause. As far we know, any existential clause of Type II with one of the four classificatory verbs discussed above can be expanded into a possessive clause of Type III. Examples are:

na	no	*bia*	naa	molym
I	liquid	beer	not	be-Hab-3sg

I have no beer.

olyo	kim	imi	tuyl-te	pirim
we	vegetable	mould	hit-Ppl-one	sleep/lie-RP-3sg

We have long had this one mouldy vegetable.

Type IV is most closely related to types II and V. It involves an Absolutive NP which is usually a semantic patient, and an Ergative NP which is an agent. The latter is often an abstract noun. Examples are:

na	engl-n	kolkur
I	hunger-Erg	die-PPr-1sg

I'm famished (lit: 'dying of hunger').

na	uru-n	*spak*	tekir
I	sleep-Erg	be inebriated	do-PPr-1sg

I'm drunk with sleepiness (i.e., stupefied from lack of sleep).

Type V clauses in their full form also involve an ergative NP and an absolutive one, but are distinct from type IV in that the verb agrees with the ergative NP rather than with the absolutive. Semantically, Type V clauses tend to be of the sort which are most commonly coded as highly transitive clauses in many other languages -- i.e., with human or higher animate agents who have a high degree of control the action, and patients who/which do not (Hopper and Thompson in *Language* 56:251-99). Examples are:

koi-ni	no	*bia*	nolym
Koi-Erg	water	beer	consume-Hab-3sg

Koi drinks beer.

na-ni	kera	laima-yl	tud
he-Erg	bird	cassowary-Def	hit(kill)-Prf-1sg

I killed the cassowary.

B.4.2 Syntactic linkage

There are in Ku Waru a wide variety of formal devices for specifying the relationship between some predicate or proposition and something which follows it. The main ones are as follows.

B.4.2.1 *Relative clauses*

What we call the *relative* clause in Ku Waru is formally identical to the independent clause types I - V above, but occurs with an immediately following NP, which it modifies. If the modified NP is not the first element in the 'higher' clause, then the relative clause intervenes between the initial material and the NP. Examples are:

eni	ab	siring	yi	kamu-kamu-yi-ka-ko	molymeli
you	woman	give-2/3pl-RP	man	close kinsmen-Col-and	be-Hab-2/3pl

You who gave the woman and are her close relations, are here.

ilyi	yunu	puba	yi-yl	nyikim
this one	he himself	go-Fut-3sg	man-Def	speak-PPr-3sg

The man who is himself about to leave is talking.

pe	tokumil	kang-ma
but	hit-PPr-3sg	boy-Col

But as for the boys who got shot [lit: (whom) they shot]...

For further examples, see Appendix A, lines 143-4, 666, 1019, 1177, 1227, 1460, 1639, 1641, 1660, 1829.

B.4.2.2 *Other syntactic linkage types*

In addition to the morphologically unmarked relative clause, many other kinds of hypotactic or paratactic linkage in Ku Waru are formally indicated by clitic elements on the verb. Some of these occur only on final verbs, some only on non-final, and some on both. The morphemes which are used in this way include all the case postpositions, whose meanings in this context bear interesting relationships to their meanings as case markers. These will now be discussed and exemplified.

Ergative/instrumental *-n(i)* as a clause marker is quite rare, but does occur, signaling an efficient cause-effect relationship, e.g.,

koi-n	tim-n	gai-yl	okum
-Erg	do-Prf-3sg-Erg	sweet potatoes-Def	come-PPr-3sg

Koi made the sweet potatoes grow [or, more literally: because of what Koi did, the sweet potatoes are coming].

More often, the causal clause (or sentence) is indexed by an anaphoric pro-form, which itself takes the ergative marker, e.g.,

kung-n	num	kani-yl-ni	koi	kuru	tokum
pig-Erg	bite-Prf-3sg	that-Def-Erg		sickness	hit-PPr-3sg

A pig bit him; because of that, Koi is sick.

Comitative *-kin* occurs very frequently on final and non-final verbs, where it is generally glossed by informants as 'when', e.g.,

ku	*handet*	aku-ma	tep-kin
money	hundreds	those-Col	do-NF-1-Com

when we count how many hundred there are... (Appendix A, line 26)

ekepu eni ul ilyi tek tek poransing-kin
now you matter this do-NF-2/3pl finish-Prf-2/3pl-Com
...and now when you've finished with this matter...

For further examples see Appendix A, lines 26, 81, 130, 174, 196, 283, 382, 389.

Dative *-d* occurs on future/intentional (medial-cum-final) verbs, entailing that the action described by that clause happens just before, or is imminent in the action or state of affairs described by the following clause, e.g.,

olyo-nga lku takumulu-d ka kodup lku takulymulu
we-Gen house build-Imt-1pl-Dat vine pull house build-Hab-1pl
When we're about to build a house, we pull (i.e. gather) vines and (then) build the house.

kolya tanguba-d mun lekim
place be day-Imt-3sg-Dat twilight be-PPr-3sg
When it's about to become day, there's twilight.

Locative *-na* occurs on final verbs of clauses with a range of different logical links to the following clause. One thing such clause sequences have in common is that they differ in subject, so that *-na* functions, inter alia, as a kind of paratactic switch-reference marker. Examples are:

yi lupu-ma pilyangi-na pe olyo pilyip teamiyl
man other-Col hear-Hrt-2/3pl-Loc and we hear-NF-1 do-Opt-1pl
Let the others hear and let us listen (Appendix A, line 287-8).

naa nyim-na nyikir
not say-Prf-3sg-Loc say-PPr-1sg
Since he didn't say it, I'm saying it (Appendix A, line 1321)

(Compare: naa nyim nyikir, ' I'm saying "he didn't say it" ')

For further examples, see transcript lines 35, 188, 577, 620, 661, 671, 759, 840, 1092, 1127, 1164, 1245, 1340, 1693, 1754.

Genitive *-nga* occurs on final verbs. Just as the genitive on NPs can mean 'concerning', 'about', so the genitive on verbs or clauses can mean 'concerning the fact that'. An example is:

i tepa pelym peba-nga
thus do-NF-3sg remain-Hab-3sg remain-Fut-3sg-Gen
Concerning the fact that it has always been that way and will remain so,

mol nyik telymeli
no say-NF-2/3pl do-Hab-3sg
they say no [i.e., they deny it] (Appendix A, lines 85-6).

The above example is unusual in that *-nga* is affixed directly to the final verb of the first clause (or sentence). Far more frequently, *-nga* occurs on verbs with an intervening definite marker *-yl/-iyl* or emphatic marker *-ayl*. An example is:

yab-ma ung-iyl-nga na numan tekim
people-Col come-Def-Gen I mind do-PPr-3sg (*numan te-*'to please')
I'm pleased that the people came.

In addition to the five nominal case postpositions treated above, other morphemes which occur on the final verb as linkage markers include:

-kiyl (on final verbs only) 'because', 'since, 'and', e.g.,

yi-yl	yunga	kung-iyl	wa	tung-kiyl
man-Def	his	pig-Def	steal	do-Prf-2/3pl-because

populu	monsum
anger	be-Csv-Prf-3sg

He is angry because they stole his pig.

-lyanga (on non-final verbs only) 'after', e.g.,

aki-yl	lyip	kuni	tep-lyanga	pamiyl
this-Def	get-NF-1	straight	do-NF-1-after	go-Opt-2/3pl

Once we have straightened this out, let's go.

-ja (after a Sjv/SR1 verb, followed by a clause with another such verb) 'if' (in counterfactual sense only). For examples see B.3.2.4.2 above.

-lum (after Perfective final verb) 'if' (in non-counter-factual sense only), e.g.,

poj	mare	molum-lum	pilyip	nyibu
mistake	some	be-3sg-Prf-if	hear-NF-1	speak-Fut-1

If there's any mistake, I'll speak up when I hear it.

B.4.2.3 *Clause-initial linkage particles*

In addition to the verbal clitic morphemes discussed above, there are two conjunctive morphemes which occur clause (or sentence) initially rather than on the verb. These are *mola* 'or' (which also occurs between NPs) and *pe* 'but', 'so', 'and'. See Appendix A, line 53 for an example of the former, and lines 49, 69, 76, 650, 671, 755, 788 for the latter.

B.4.3 Reported speech and jussive verbs

The verb *nyi-* 'to say', is used very often in Ku Waru, both in final and non-final forms. Its subject NP (if any) is (optionally) marked with the ergative *-n(i)*. For an object, it may take a noun such as *ung* 'word(s)', 'speech', an anaphoric pronoun, or an indefinitely long stretch of reported speech. The verb *nyi-* is not obligatory in such contexts: sometimes the reported speech has no explicit framing verb or clause. The framing material may consist solely of an ergative-marked noun or pronoun, e.g.,

abayl-n	mol,	kangabola	kang-yiyl-nga
woman-Def-Erg	no	child	man-Gen

kang-yiyl-n	kangabola	na-nga	mol
man-Erg	child	I-Gen	no

The woman says 'no, the child is the man's'; the young man says 'the child is not mine'. (Rumsey and Merlan 1986:line 368-9)

In the more usual case where an explicit framing verb does occur, it almost always comes **after** the framed material. For examples, and further details concerning reported speech, see section 5.8 (cf. also Appendix D). As is clear from those examples, and others the reader may glean from Appendix A, almost all reported speech (cum reported mentation) in Ku Waru is constructed in 'direct discourse'. That is, the indexical categories of person, tense, spatial deixis, etc. are nearly always specified from the point of view of the reported speech situation rather than the reporting one. The exceptions to this are, in general, beyond the scope of this brief description. There is just one grammatically regular one which is common enough to call for some discussion here. Consider first the way of reporting commands which have been made to a non-singular addressee, e.g.,

lku-d	pai	nyim
house-Dat	go-2pl-Imp	say-Prf-3sg

He told them to go to the house.

lku-d	payl	nyim
house-Dat	go-2du-Imp	say-Prf-3sg

He told the two to go to the house.

Though we have glossed them with English jussive constructions, the Ku Waru sentences are identical in form to direct quotation, i.e. ' "Go", he said to them', etc. There is no other, less quotation-like way of formulating them in Ku Waru. However, there is what we could call a distinct jussive construction in Ku Waru when the addressee of the original command was singular rather than plural or dual. This construction makes use of a distinct form of the verb, which is identical to the participial form (see section B.3.2.7.) except that it ends in -i rather than -yl. Examples are:

lku-d	pui	nyim
house-Dat	go-Jus	say-Prf-3sg

He said to go to the house.

ola	molui	nyim
up	be-Jus	say-Prf-3sg

He said to stand up.

Sentences such as these are only a partial exception to the general Ku Waru tendency to favor 'direct' discourse, for the 'jussive' forms of the verb are also used by themselves as directive forms for singular addressees, as a kind of milder alternative to the imperative form, e.g. *lku-d pui* '(Please) go to the house'.

Appendix C: The conduct of warfare

By itself, our first-hand experience of Nebilyer warfare affords little basis for generalization, since it is limited to one battle. But since it is rare to find any first-hand accounts in the anthropological literature on New Guinea warfare, it seems worthwhile for us to report on the battle in some detail. This should provide a useful supplement to other accounts such Meggitt (1977) and Koch (1974, *War and Peace in Jalema*). As it turns out, our experience largely corroborates those descriptions, and also provides some new evidence bearing upon the relationship between oratory, warfare, and exchange.

The battle took place on January 6, 1986. It was fought as an episode in hostilities between two regional tribe-pairs, here called Peraka-Parka and Musika-Malka, which at that time had been going on for about two years. This battle took place on the north slopes of a ridge which lies between Musika-Malka country to the south and Peraka-Parka country to the north. Except for one large eucalyptus tree at its crest, the ridge is covered by kunai grass (see Plate 9). Early on the morning of the fighting, and several times throughout the day, that grass was fired, partly in order to increase visibility across the battlefield and remove potential hiding places. The ridge is clearly visible from a neighboring area dense in homesteads some three kilometers to the north, and seeing it fired, people there correctly surmised that there would be fighting on that day (notwithstanding an earlier report that it was to start on another day). A party of men (including Alan) set out to watch, and arrived on the scene at 11.30 a.m. By then the fighting had been going on for some time, and two men of Peraka-Parka had been wounded and had left the battlefield.

The two sides were ranged against each other along opposing fronts approximately 300 meters long and 100 meters apart. Combatants from Musika-Malka generally occupied the upper, southerly portion of the ridge, advancing and retreating across the first hundred meters to the north. Behind them, the crest of the ridge was lined with spectators (see Plate 9).

The Peraka-Parka, further to the north, occupied lower ground for the duration of the battle. This would seem to have put them at an obvious disadvantage, but none of the observers remarked upon this, or placed much importance on it when Alan asked about it. For by far the greater part of the six hours during which he watched, there was little or no fighting going on. The combatants simply stood still, out of arrow range from the opposing side, or shifted around behind the battle line, sometimes shouting at each other, but mostly being fairly quiet (cf. loc. cit., p.78 for a similar pattern among the Jalema). There was apparently little or no centralized tactical co-ordination on either side. At intervals of between thirty and ninety minutes, one or two men would advance, usually behind a shield, of which there were two or three per side. Other men on either side of them along the line would then move along with them, slightly behind, so as to form a sort of wedge. Generally, it was only when such movement took place that the combatants came within arrow range of each other. This usually happened at only one spot at a time, always within the eastern half of the front, where the ridge face was less steep. On the western half, none of the men ever advanced. Their presence seemed to serve mainly to prevent either side from outflanking the other at that end of the front. None of the offensive wedges on the eastern half moved sharply enough to risk being outflanked, and care seemed to be taken to avoid it.

Whenever there was offensive action, the advancing side set up a cry of [i:: i:: i:: ...]. The men advancing, those near them to the left and right, and anyone in danger of coming within arrow range on the opposing side, began a kind of weaving, bobbing, dance-like movement the purpose of which is said to be to make oneself a more difficult target; also to transfix the opposing side, distracting their attention from on-coming arrows. (Bird of Paradise feathers are attached to the top of the shields for the same reason.)

During one of the relatively quiet periods on the battlefield, orators from the Peraka-Parka side shouted taunts and insults from behind the line. These were delivered in exactly the same *el ung* prosodic style which is used at public exchange events (see section 5.3 for details). The only way in which the delivery of these speeches differed from that of *el ung* at exchange events was that the orators in this case stood in one place rather than striding back and forth. This is probably related to the fact that the addressed audience for these insults was located several hundred meters away, from where the striding, if visible at all, would not have had the same visual impact which it has at exchange events, where the addressed audience usually surrounds the striding orator.

Alan did not have a tape recorder with him at the battle to record any of this *el ung*, but one of the men who was present at the battle later recorded a reenacted version of one of the speeches, complete with *el ung* intonation. His version of the speech closely follows what Alan heard of the original. The complete text (with pseudonyms for all proper names) is as follows:

parka robi el ung nyiba, i nyim
speaking 'fight talk', Parka Robi said this:

nu yi korupa kapo we-ooo
you (sg) are a poor, poor man

ab tilyipu tokun kapo kapo-o
even though you have [lit. 'strike' [ie. copulate with]] many wives

kera lapa we tuyl
a man who puts on a borrowed wig

tauwu kilsa tekin
scraping a banana [to roast, instead of roasting a pig]

kera lapa we tuyl
one who puts on a borrowed wig

nu yi korupa korupa kupu kupu we
you (sg) are a poor, poor, utterly poor man

marai singi manya tuyl-o
your calves are never well-oiled

bulu kiulu muluyl yi-yl-o
you're a man with a dirty back

musika pulka ung muna sing*
they insulted Musika Pulka

mulu piyl, kului-o
short winded one, may you (sg) die

malka kajip *kopi* lensan
you (sg) can go pick coffee for Malka Kajip

emina-yl *kopi* tauwu kili lipiyl
your wives can gather the coffee pits left by birds [after they have eaten the ripe husks]

pulka nu kanakun molan
Pulka you (sg) can sit and watch

* In this line, the reenactor of the oratory has temporarily stepped out of that role and resumed that of the reporting spectator in order to tell us to whom Robi's insult was addressed.

nu ola-d ola-d sikin kanakun molan-o
you (sg) can keep looking up [like a child looking up at adults to beg food from them]

neka sul malka kajip neka ikepa moki tipiyl-o
Malka Kajip can pick his long red pandanus cone and give it to you [in return for your labor]

ya koib kolsi okun muna pilyini
don't think you (sg) are going to come here to Koib any more

puni pani nyibu tekir-o
you (sg) can go for good, I say

musika nu aima malka-kin-nga kongun kedimad tensikin ola-d ola-d kanakun molan-o
Musika, you (sg) can be a laborer for Malka and look up to him [i.e., one talapi *of the tribe-pair for the other]*

puni pani nyibu tekir-o
you (sg) can go for good, I say

kera kusal-ti rere nyikin molurun
you (sg) were crowing like a kusal *bird [over your having killed so many of us Peraka-Parka]*

kani-yl ekepu naa molyn ilyi-ko
but you (sg) are not doing that any more

ekepu nu kara pukun-o
now you (sg) are being obstreperous

pui-o
go (sg) away

eni ya mol nying ung mada nyai*
you (sg) [Peraka-Parka] don't speak, you (sg) have said enough

ung kis lekim i nyimul
our speeches are getting worse

ung nyilymeli-ma tongi, mol-o
those who speak like that [i.e., as I just spoke] will get killed, no!

* This line and the rest of the speech [as reenacted] was no longer addressed to the Musika-Malka on the distant ridge, but to the nearby Peraka-Parka tribesmen and other spectators on their side of the line.

Appendix D: Ku Waru Metalinguistic Expressions

Examples of Ku Waru metalinguistic expressions are listed below (cf. section 5.8). In order to allow the uses of these expressions to be examined in context, the examples have been taken from Appendix A and from Merlan and Rumsey (1986). Line numbers preceded by M are in the latter publication, others in Appendix A of this volume. Italicized words within these expressions are borrowings from Tok Pisin or English (cf. section B.2).

D.1 Nominal expressions for kinds of *ung/ing* 'talk, word, language, topic'

bo ung 'traditional talk' M10, M62, M185, M1417 (cf. section 6.2.7)

el ung 'fight talk' 576, 1094, 1105, 1285 (cf. section 5.3) ; sometimes used more generally for oratory or speech making, as in M1412

kodu ung, kodu tiyl ung 'talk to elicit sympathy or compassion' (from *kodu te-* 'be sorry (for)), 1694

mani ung 'warning, advice'

sika ung/ing sika 'true talk' 158, 168, 1485

ung ausipe 'a large (amount of) talk' 1083, 1225

ung *bamp* 'provocative talk', 'harrassment' (from Tok Pisin *bamp*, 'bump') M1552, cf. 1147

ung boni 'heavy talk', i.e. complaint, grudge, grievance M1410

ung eke 'bent speech' 1842 (cf. section 5.4)

ung gol 'deceitful talk', 'lie', 'trick' 160

ung kapola 'sufficient talk, talk that gets to the point' 1585

ung kayi we 'very good talk' 1672

ung kolsi, ung laya kolsi 'small amount of talk', 'very small amount of talk' 673, 1608

ung kuni 'straight talk' (cf. *ung eke*)

ung lapa [lit. 'father (of the) word/talk'] 'meaning, reason, intent'

ung lawa 'wrong talk' 'mistaken talk' 1307

ung mel kis 'bad-thing word' (*mel kis* 'bad thing' is a common euphemism for female and male genitalia) 1280

ung manya / manya ung 'low talk' i.e., sitting rather than standing, and in a low voice rather than projected for an audience 290, 124 cf. 695

ung mong 'topic', 'matter', 'meaning' (lit.: 'point of the word(s)) M298-9

ung mura 'cross words', 'argument' M37 (used with the verb *si-* 'give' rather than with *nyi-* 'say')

ung *namba ten* 'number ten talk' i.e., the best possible talk; talk which says exactly what one wants to hear 1673

ung para 'public talk' 1564 Compare *para nyi-* below. *para* literally means 'level': *ung para* is both speech which occurs on a level place (the *makayl pena* 'ceremonial exchange grounds' being some of the *only* level places in the the Ku Waru area) and speech which is typically subject to being 'levelled off' (*para nyi-*).

ung pengi 'head word' i.e. the main point, or most important part of a speech. 156, 161, 207

ung pipkau 'obstreperous, obstructive, or otherwise uncooperative talk' 1552

ung *promis* 'promise' 178

ung tumja 'thick talk' i.e., turgid, exaggerated, or overly lengthy talk 1105, 1225

ung urip 'casual conversation'

we ung 'worthless talk, talk for nothing'

we leba ung 'talk which will have been for nothing' 1495, 1498

yabu moluyl-na ing 'public talk ' (lit: 'talk where there are people') M71

D.2 Verbal expressions for ways of talking

Most of these expressions are verbal-compositional ones, where the meaning is specific to a particular combination of roots in a particular order (cf. section B.3.2). In order to give some indication of how these meanings are constructed, 'literal' glosses for the root combinations are provided in square brackets, listing individual glosses for each verb root, based on their most common glosses when each is used in isolation. This provides only a rough approximation of how the compositional meanings are built up, partly because they are more or less idiomatic (ibid) and partly because most of the roots have a range of other meanings as well. For more information about these, see the Glossary.

age nyi- 'to thank' (frequently used as explicit performative verb)
kaip nyi- 'to praise' (see section 7.1 for use as explicit performative)
kel- nyi- [leave-talk] 'finish talking, refrain from mentioning' 1362
kod- nyi- [pull-say] 'talk about' M298, M311
(ung) **kolumu te-** 'to interrupt (lit.: cut off) another's speech' 1114, M12
(ung) **wed lyi- nyi-** [away take-say] 'gossip, blab the news around' 1237
mili le- me- ad- 'carry the marsupial trap around': idiom for 'spread the news around' 1233
mod- nyi- [send - say] 'send the word, send a message, say it out' 991
nyi- kins- (/kis-ns/ [speak-bad-causative] 'speak badly', 'say wrongly'
nyi- kunu to- 'close the discussion' (lit.: speaking, close the door)
nyi- mons- (/mol-ns-/) [speak-stand-causative] 'raise (a subject) for discussion)' 618, 621
nyi- mod- [say-send]' '(verbally) resolve, dispose of' 1433, 'report' M219, M783
nyi- nosi- [say-put] 'decide' M822
nyi- pans- [say-put] 'tell, convey to' 1422
nyi- pora-ns- [speak-finish-cause] 'finish talking' 1236
nyi- si- [talk-give] 'tell, convey (a message) to' 680, 719
nyi- tada le- [talk-drop-put] 'conclude' 113
nyi- tubul- [speak-seek] 'talk back and forth with no resolution' M370
ol to- (nyi-) 'to whisper', 'talk privately' 615, 623, 631, M1528
para nyi- 'talk back and forth' (lit.: 'talk level') 1094
(ung) **pensi-** [lie-causative] 'interject'
pilyi- nyi- [hear-say] 'speak informedly', 'take into consideration' 870, 1076
(ung) **suku nyi-** interject (lit.: 'speak into') M279
sika nyi- 'speak truly' M787, M865
temani to- 'tell a story' M836
tubul- nyi- [seek-speak] 'discuss, try to resolve' M17
walsi- 'ask', 'ask for' M211-3, M501, M514, M1006, M1007, M1478, M1581, M1610, M1636
walsi- pilyi- [request-hear] 'ask about'

D.3 Other expressions used to characterize speech

In addition to the above expressions which refer specifically to *verbal* (or mental) acts, there are other, more general descriptors for acts, of which the verbal varieties are contextual subtypes. Some of these are listed below. Most or all of these expressions *can* be further specified as referring explicitly to verbal action, by adding the appropriate non-final form of the verb *nyi-* (e.g., *nyi- suku mod-*, 'speaking, throw in') or the noun *ung* 'speech', 'word(s)',etc. (e.g., *ung* resis *to-* 'to do speech-races').

aji mod- 'to relay' (lit.: 'to throw back')
gol to- 'to deceive' (usually verbally, i.e., to lie) M449, M788, M865
kuni te- 'to straighten out, to speak directly' (lit.: straight-do) M436, M1566, M1580, M1647
lubur- te- 'to repeat' or, also, in the case of speech: 'to summarize' M117, M158
pudu to- 'to reciprocate' 620, M1054, M1402 (also used of wealth objects)
resis **to-** 'to contest', 'to debate' (from Tok Pisin *resis*, itself from English *races*) M1517
suku mod- 'to contribute' (lit.: 'throw in') M260, M617, M1402
wed mod- 'throw it away, say it out' M261

D.4 Expressions describing effects of speech

Finally, we will list a few of the expressions which specify what we might call 'addressee effects', i.e., effects of the utterance upon the hearer or addressee.

kum si- 'not hear, not understand, be deaf' M1166 (with **t** in place of **s**; Meam dialect variant)

nyi- pilyi- [say-hear] 'think, believe' 383, 476, 507, 524, 679, 731, 736, 789; many other examples in Appendix A; cf. Chapter 6, note 24.

pilyi- 'hear', 'think', 'understand' 41, 69, 104, 135, 136, 140, 152

pilyi- lyi- [hear-take] 'understand, take to heart'

pilyi- sud- [hear - be perplexed] 'be confused', 'to hear and not know what to do', A1591 (with **t** in place of **s**; Meam dialect variant)

Notes

1 INTRODUCTION

1 Whether or not to call such assumptions 'theory' is in our opinion a matter of degree, depending on the extent to which one sets about systematically trying to make them (i) explicit; and (ii) consistent with each other and with what they are about.

2 A propos of the present example, it is relevant to note that among expatriates, even those with long and intimate contact with Highlanders, it is rare to find anyone who is aware of sub-divisions within their 'tribes'. Names of 'tribes' themselves are widely known, and, for larger tribes, some of the names of internal sub-divisions are sometimes known, but rarely the superordinate–subordinate relations among names.

3 This is not to say that general concepts are derived by induction from particular experiences: the relationship is a dialectical one, since experience is also partially determined by the concepts one brings to it (as we have argued above).

4 This is not to say that New Guineans are backward-looking. On the contrary, we often had trouble trying to get our informants to focus on past events, as they were generally more interested in the present, and even more so in the future. It is just that the only run of 'cases' they can adduce is from the more or less distant past.

5 It might be claimed that anthropologists were not so much unwilling to focus on the content of the speeches as unable to do so, given the limits of their understanding of the languages in question (cf. e.g. Salisbury 1962; Gell 1975; Barth 1975). But we maintain that if the contents of the speeches had been allowed an important theoretical position in their studies, they could accordingly have given more attention to language-learning, (just as anthropologists have mastered other diverse techniques such as calorie-counting and carbon-14 dating).

6 It is interesting to note the way in which anthropologists studying disputes have similarly ignored the detail of what was actually said, and thus avoided dealing with the fact that they are usually not 'about' just one issue but are speech events in which many claims and counter-claims are raised (cf. Goldman 1983).

7 Although 'objectivist' models have sometimes stripped exchange practice of its inherently dynamic or diachronic character (Bourdieu 1977:3–15), and reduced it to a static analog, nothing in the concept of exchange itself requires this.

8 Meggitt's spelling is *Te*, the more recent one used by Feil, *tee*.

9 Elsewhere in the book, Feil (1984:21) remarks that 'The *tee* system works identically among both Tombema and Mae'.

10 Exactly how similar they are remains an open question. Feil treats Mae and Tombema *tee* as very similar or identical (see previous paragraph and previous footnote), while others have stressed the differences (Lederman 1986c, Rubel 1987).

One must also bear in mind the different times at which Meggitt and Feil began their fieldwork: the former in 1955, five years after pacification, and the latter in 1974, almost a generation later (but before the recent resurgence of warfare in the area). However, the point of our present exegesis is not to arbitrate between these two accounts on empirical grounds, or resolve the differences as empirical ones between Mae and Tombema. Rather, we seek to expose some fundamental difficulties with the way both accounts pose the question of who conducts exchange.

11 Compare Stoljar (1973:189) who argues that 'the existence of a committable common fund' is *the* major defining attribute of the 'corporation' in the English common law tradition (from which social anthropological notions of the 'corporate person' are largely derived).

12 The smaller 'initiatory' gifts which precede the main payments are not ordered by clan in this way.

13 To say this is not to deny that these various aspects of corporateness can be closely linked in practice. For example, as Neil Maclean points out (p.c.), part of the work of representing an entity as 'corporate' consists in representing it as synchronized – as, for example, in the tightly choreographed marching and line dancing of fellow clansmen at a (Hagen/Nebilyer) *moka* exchange event. This does not undercut the utility of distinguishing among these criteria *in principle*. On the contrary, it is only then that we can investigate the extent of their interrelatedness as an open, empirical question.

14 'Preparations for the parade involve readying sugarcane and sweet potatoes for guests, renting feather headdresses, buying tree oil and accumulating pearl shells to be used as body decorations and as gifts for invited paraders, organizing invitations, and preparing the parade grounds. It is, in other words, a large mobilization of wealth and energy . . . their final *sai pombe* was estimated to have "cost" the Senkere community . . . approximately US$29,000' (Lederman 1980:483).

15 We have repeatedly placed this word in quotation marks because the word (which we have taken from Meggitt's (1974) account of *te*) tends to imply just the sort of split we want to avoid between 'what's really going on' vs. ways of talking about it. Elsewhere we will use the words 'signification' or '(semiotic) construction' with the hope that they do not carry that implication (or at least not to the same extent).

2 THE SETTING

1 This sort of dramatic declaration was not unique. See Connolly and Anderson (1987:264–5, 267) for an account of people slightly closer to Mt Hagen town burning their shields and weapons, declaring the end of the era of warfare (and also further reference to this in section 9.3).

2 Throughout this volume, superordinate-subordinate relations of this kind are indicated by a left-to-right oblique stroke, e.g. Kopia\Kabika = the Kabika segment of Kopia, etc. Coordinate relations are indicated by a hyphen, Kopia-Kubuka, etc.

3 SOME ASPECTS OF KU WARU SEGMENTARY SOCIALITY

1 Compare Deleuze and Guattari (1987:208–231), who distinguish among several different types of 'segmentarity', their central metaphor for which is not the tree, but the rhizome.

2 Compare Fortes (1979:x): 'When we talk about descent, descent group, lineage, segmentation . . . are referring to variables that are not completely isomorphous with one another. We can have descent, or filiation, operating without descent groups; we can have lineage systems without segmentation, or segmentation without descent groups or lineage systems'.

3 For discussion and pictures of dance formations used at exchange events in the Nebilyer Valley, see Strathern and Strathern (1971). For battlefield tactics, see Appendix C below.

4 See M. Strathern (1972a), A. Strathern (1971) for discussion of the pattern and degree of male-female residential segregation.

5 Our allusion here is to A. Strathern's (1972) distinction between principles of group recruitment and those of group identity: he claimed that, among the Melpa, 'descent' was irrelevant to the former, but operative in the latter.

6 Similar patterns are evident for the neighboring Melpa area in the ethnography of M. and A. Strathern, who also note wide variability in the size of 'tribes', and acknowledge the difficulties this poses for their early attempts to develop a typology of segmentary levels (A. Strathern 1971:17–8).

7 For an interesting account of Ulka segmentary structure by an Ulka man, see Nakinch (1977). (The usual local spelling is Ulga.)

8 See Merlan and Rumsey (1986) for further discussion and for an extended example of the way in which this conception ideology is deployed in Ku Waru social life – there in a dispute concerning the paternity of a yet-unborn child. The article includes a lengthy verbatim transcript of the dispute, which provides much fuller evidence than we can include here, both of the 'matter of fact' status of the basic assumptions within this ideology, and of some ways in which its implications are resisted or contested in practice.

9 This may not be true of the neighboring Hageners. A. Strathern (1972:10–11) describes a Melpa notion of *ndating,* which is passed on from father to son, and which accounts for aspects of a man's personality and appearance. But he comments that 'Hageners' notions about *ndating* are not entirely clear, and they cannot be regarded as saliently expressed dogmas. Most informants speak only of a father's "grease" (*kopong,* semen) and equate this with the "grease" of his group'.

10 Cf. Watson (1983, Ch.7), who has provided valuable distinctions for this discussion, and A. Strathern (1973:33) who suggests that 'the concept of "food" may be an important mediator between the concepts of identity through locality and identity through descent'.

11 This is borne out by at least two aspects of Ku Waru egocentric relationship terminology. First, the kinship terminology used by Nebilyer people, in common with many other Highland peoples (see papers in Cook and O'Brien 1980), is of the Iroquois type, in that all distinctions between patrilateral and matrilateral kinsmen are neutralized in ego's children's generation and below. As Feil (1978c) has pointed out, this facilitates the assimilation of non-agnatic cognates into 'agnatic' segmentary groups within two generations from the point of matrifiliative linkage. Of course, it is not just any non-agnatic cognates who get assimilated in this way, but in particular those who live and eat together, and hence share the *kopong* of common ground, over and above whatever they may share through common ancestry. The second way in which Nebilyer relationship terminology is congruent with the local ideology of human reproduction involves a kind of egocentric personal reference system which is not based on 'genealogical' connection, but *solely* on the relations of consubstantiality which arise from what we (following Watson 1983) have called 'post-natal influences', i.e. 'food name' relationships, which are contracted between people who have shared food together, as described in A. Strathern (1977a) (cf. section 9.1.3).

12 One of the two largest tribes in the Hagen-Nebilyer area, numbering over 7000 people, who occupy a contiguous region extending from the western outskirts of Mt

Hagen town, west to the Tambul foothills north of Kailge, (see Map 2), where this man had lived.

13 See section 7.2.2 for details concerning the staging of group entries at such occasions.

14 By January of 1986, 4 Kopia (and 11 Kubuka) men had taken land in the area where it was offered, though most did not move completely, but divided their time between Kailge and the settlement block.

15 This description is perhaps in need of some qualification. As shown on Map 3, the Palimi land at Ibumuyl is bounded by Kopia land to the east and north, and Kubuka to the south. To the west is the densely forested hinterland extending up the eastern slopes of the Tambul Range. As far as we know, it is a moot question how far up the slopes the Palimi land extends, or whether it is bounded on the west by a stretch of forest which is in principle exclusively Kopia.

16 We do not mean to imply that Wagner is wrong about the Daribi in this respect. There are no doubt large differences in the role of segmentary structures within various parts of the Highlands. See, for example A. Strathern (1984), Lederman (1986a), Rumsey (1986:292), Merlan (1988), and section 4.2 below.

17 Compare M. Strathern (1985MS:39) on 'groups' and wealth exchange among the Melpa: '. . . insofar as these exchanges contribute to men's descriptions (representations) of a collective life as involving conflict with like groups, they also contribute to armed and lethal confrontations . . . The cost is enormous.'

4 CEREMONIAL EXCHANGE AND MARRIAGE

1 There has been some indeterminacy during the past 40 years over whether the Palimi *talapi* as such has been an agent in these transactions, as we shall see.

2 This had happened throughout most of the Western Highlands Province by the 1970s, mainly as a result of the flood of pearl shells which were brought into the area by European colonists to exchange for local goods and labor (see Hughes 1978, also sections 2.2, 9.3).

3 Compare Feil (1984:72): 'Tombema do not even speak as though groups are responsible [for making *tee* payments]'.

4 *Makayl* differs in this respect from most forms of inter-*talapi* compensation in this area, especially when the latter is paid in cash, as in the events discussed in Chapters 4 and 5. In these kinds of transaction, contributions are publicly identified as coming from particular individuals (or small cohorts), but they are often given *en masse* to the recipient group, who are at liberty to divide them up as they choose.

5 This is apparently also true of the Melpa *moka*, as described by A. Strathern (1971, 1979a). During the course of a *moka* presentation, there are two distinct 'showings' of the items to be given: the first a series of 'private displays and discussions [between individual exchange partners] at all the homesteads involved in the *moka*' (A. Strathern 1971:117); and the second a 'concerted "showing" of gifts at the ceremonial ground' [at which the inter-group aspect of the transaction is in focus] (ibid; cf. A. Strathern 1979a).

6 In this respect, the Ku Waru people are intermediate between the Melpa, for whom the extensive ethnography reports no cases of women *moka* transactors, and the Mendi people, of whom Lederman (1986a) reports that women quite frequently operate as exchange transactors within the sphere of *twem* (cf. section 2.1. regarding her distinction between *twem* and *sem onda* transactions). As for the Enga *tee*, Feil (1978a, 1978b, 1984) reports that women sometimes transact, but only under special circumstances, such as the case of a recently-widowed woman who acted on her late husband's behalf.

7 They differ strongly in this respect from the Enga, among whom such consortia are

unheard of (Feil, pers. comm.) (Cf. Feil 1984, where all listed *tee* transactors are individual men.) The Melpa are apparently more like the Nebilyer people in this respect. In the one table where A. Strathern lists all interpersonal transactions which make up one of his inter-clan ones, two of the nine interpersonal transactions involve pairs of men, one as donor and the other as recipient (A. Strathern 1971:139). The donor pair are parallel cousins (FBS-FBS). No relationship is shown for the recipient pair.

8 Compare Feil (1978c) for some interesting similarities and differences between this pattern and the one he observed among the Tombema Enga. There too, people often choose to exchange with partners who live close by. But since among the Tombema *everyone* who exchanges must be an affine or matrilateral kinsman, people go to great lengths to rationalize their partnerships with co-residents (including co-clansmen) in those terms.

9 This is, of course, the classic role of the big-man in exchange systems such as the Melpa *moka*, for which see A. Strathern, whose book on the subject (1971) is aptly subtitled *Big men and ceremonial exchange* . . . Apparently no such role is attributed to big-men among the Tombema Enga. This seems to be related to the fact that, unlike the *moka* or *makayl*, the *tee* follows a constant serial order of clan-to-clan (and even (sub-clan to sub-clan) transactions. Since they do not have to be constantly created anew, the inter-group nexus are not treated as an 'achievement' in the way they are among Melpa and Ku Waru people (cf. Merlan 1988).

10 We are speaking here only of the inter-*talapi* aspect of this payment. Some of the interpersonal transactions which it comprised were made to Poika, and some of the wealth given to Palimi people was no doubt passed on to Poika.

11 Kalya's father's mother is said to have been a Kopia woman, but he has no known genealogical (or affinal) links to the Kopia\Galka.

12 But compare e.g. A. Strathern (1971:144–5) on Melpa, and Feil (1984:103) on Tombema Enga, for the considerable extent to which *moka* partners may be considered 'unrelated' to each other, versus complete relatedness recorded between partners by Feil.

13 We knew fairly well the single Kailge-area Palimi woman married to a Dena. Her mother was the sister of a recognized Kopia\Tolab big-man. During a period of conflict between Kopia-Kubuka and Tea-Dena she returned to Kailge, but during this time also regarded herself as one of the few Kailge people who could walk back and forth between Kopola and Kailge in relative safety.

14 Goodenough (1953) observed that Enga he spoke with claimed a determining relationship of the opposite kind. When he asked if they could marry people of certain other groupings, his informants replied, 'Yes! We fight!'

15 The Wola are closest and most similar to, indeed overlapping with, the people of the Mendi area, since described by Lederman (1986a), and earlier by Ryan (1959, 1961). Sillitoe's emphasis on individuals as transactors, and his denial of any collective perspective, differs rather strikingly from the other two authors.

5 SOME LINGUISTIC STRUCTURES OF SEGMENTARY POLITICS

1 Some examples are also drawn from a lengthy dispute, the transcript of which is published in Merlan and Rumsey (1986).

2 The most literal or ordinary sense of this word is 'boy' (as opposed to *yi* 'man'). But *kang* is also used by men for males of all ages, with connotations of camaraderie.

3 For examples of tribal and lower-level segmentary labels used in relation to the distribution of money see Appendix A, lines 10, 27, 205, 263, 306, 310, 312–3, 320,

325, 335, 500, 501; and in the context of the identification of persons (including the wounded) see 586, 594, 633, 634, 643, 645, 650, 735, 1363, 1364, 1365, 1368, 1369, 1571.

4 This usage is also attested in published transcripts of oratory among the Huli of the Southern Highlands (Goldman 1983:134, line 294) and the Melpa (A. Strathern 1975:199). It has also been reported among the Enga (Larson 1970), and among the Iqwaye, an Angan people on the southern fringe of the eastern Highlands (Jadran Mimica, pers.comm.). As far as we know, the only Highland ethnographer to have written about it in more than a passing reference until now (cf. also Rumsey 1986:289–90) has been H. Strauss (1962:296–7; 370–71).

5 'Die Sprecher identifizieren sich also mit ihrer Gruppe' (Strauss 1962:296).

6 This also true of Melpa and Huli. For examples, see references in n.4 above.

7 Compare Silverstein's (1976) treatment of 'the pronouns of power and solidarity' as implementing two distinct indexical functions, one of them referential, the other not. We have placed the word 'referent' in scare quotes here to indicate that these are the terms in which Silverstein would presumably see the data in question, and apply his analytical criteria to them. We ourselves have some doubts about the feasibility of this distinction, at least for the present case. For it would seem to require recourse to a 'real world' of presumed extra-linguistic 'objects' in which, e.g. the truth value of *kopia-ma-n payl tiring* 'All the Kopia did it' is the same as that of *kopia-n tirim* 'Kopia did it' (with 3sg.SP subject as opposed to 3pl.) Such a rarefied world of 'pure reference' is, it seems to us, of little use for understanding what goes on in this one, for reasons which should become clear in Chapters 6 and 7 below (cf. Austin 1975:145-6; Silverstein 1976).

8 Phonetically, there is considerable variation in the length of these vowels. Since our transcripts are phonemic ones, and vowel length is generally not distinctive in this dialect (cf. Appendix B.2), we have generally not shown it on the *el ung* markers −o and −a. They are always clearly discernible as such (and can be interpreted as having phonetically lengthened vowels in the transcripts), since they always come at the end of an orthographic line, and since there are no other post-positional morphemes −a or −o in the language.

9 For a sample of *el ung* showing pause lengths, see Appendix A, lines 1029–60. The presence of these pauses, and other prosodic markers discussed above, makes it possible to transcribe *el ung* speeches in such a way as to allow each line of transcript to show an actual, clearly bounded prosodic unit, a procedure which is not possible elsewhere in the transcript, where, unfortunately, the placing of line breaks is determined mainly by the exogenous criterion of what it is possible to gloss in a single, grammatically self-sufficient line of English.

10 In the one occasion where we heard *el ung*-style prosody being used in warfare, these paralinguistic features were absent. See Appendix C for discussion.

11 Marie Reay – whose (1959:117–120) account of a similar oratorical style among the Kuma is still one of the few for any Highlands people – describes a pattern whereby each line of oratory 'corresponds in time to a set of paces in one direction' (Reay 1959:118) and the rhetorical parallelism of paired, successive lines is therefore matched by a single back-and-forth circuit. While there is in the Nebilyer a rough correlation between the average duration of an *el ung* line and that of a line of striding, and rich use of rhetorical parallelism (see below), it is by no means such that each of the former is always spoken during one of the latter. There is at least a kind of ideal fit between the two, whereby the *general form* of the striding corresponds to aspects of the rhetorical structure. There may also be a *tendency* toward the kind of correspondence Reay claims for Wahgi, i.e. between oratorical lines and periods of striding in one direction, such that deviations from this unmarked, 'default condition' can themselves be used in rhetorically significant ways (cf. Halliday 1985:274–81 on the relation between the clause and the tone group in English). A rigorous investigation of these matters would require better data than we yet have on the physical

movements of orators as they speak – ideally a full visual record on film or video tape.

12 Ideally, we would like to have played these passages to a number of informants to see how they categorized them, as we did for the tropes of *ung eke* (see below). Unfortunately, we did not notice how many passages were *phonetically* intermediate in these respects until after leaving the field, so this has not been possible.

13 A corresponding expression *wö-mbo* ('men') is used at the opening of *el ik* speeches by Melpa orators (cf. A. Strathern 1975:199). Goldman (p.c.) reports a similar usage among the Huli.

14 One such context is in disputes, where it is regularly used in speeches by (would-be) mediators to pose binary options to the disputants, just as in Goldman's (1983:45–53) interesting discussion of the use of 'gambits' among the Huli of the Southern Highlands.

15 Their use in this context bears an interesting similarity in form/function to the use of the rhyming couplet (a kind of parallel structure) at the end of the classical sonnet. Compare also Shakespeare's use of the couplet within his plays at the end of an act or scene (e.g. *Othello*, acts I, II, IV, V; *Hamlet*, act II, act V scene I; *A Midsummer Night's Dream*, act II scene I, act V).

16 Cf. Kurylowicz 1964 on the relatively greater functional markedness of non-singular number categories in language generally.

17 For purposes of this tabulation, any single sequence of non-final verb(s) + final verb counts as one textual instance since the person marking on the former is governed by the latter (Appendix B.3.2.3).

18 One would expect the difference in frequency of plural forms to be even greater comparing the *el ung* with ordinary Ku Waru used in other contexts (e.g. in casual conversation among women). On the other hand, the ratio within *el ung* may be somewhat lower than indicated by this tabulation, since the transcript lines of *el ung* are generally somewhat shorter than the others. But it must also be considered that the tendency toward long chains of non-final verbs (which count as a single 'reference') is less great in *el ung*. In any case, the difference in line length is nowhere near 3.3 to 1.

19 Note that the term for this genre is therefore an instance of itself: a metaphor, which is, moreover, strikingly similar to the trope involved in the Greek term 'trope', as A. Strathern (1975:190) points out.

20 In order to get an idea how widely used are some of these tropes, we included among our informants Andrew Strathern, who has long experience and thorough knowledge of oratory in the Hagen/Dei Council area. He had not been present at any of the events represented.

21 Not everyone was asked all these questions, or in this order. Few of our informants would have stood for such a mechanical procedure. Nor was it necessary: given the intense interest these matters provoke, once the tape was played or the passage read aloud, most of the informants volunteered opinions about these and other matters before being asked.

22 Typical ways of evoking a single image may differ regionally within the greater Hagen/Nebilyer area. For instance, Andrew Strathern (pers. comm.) reports that he has heard this particular trope formulated in Melpa with reference to *ɸngimb* 'kunai grass' (= Nebilyer *angubu*), but not *sirku* (= Melpa *titik*).

23 As can be seen from the sample which we have discussed above, most of the tropes which Nebilyer people classify as *ung eke* are what Western semioticians would call metaphors. At least some, though, are varieties of metonym. We have not gone into this, as our main concern here is with what characterizes *ung eke* as such, rather than with trying to classify its tropes according to such exogenous distinctions. But to provide minimal evidence that not all of the tropes are metaphorical, we will here briefly point out some examples of metonymic ones. Kujilyi's figure of mistaking rain for shine and vice versa, (lines 211–2) can be taken as a kind of synecdoche (a

species of metonym). If the point is that the person referred to is prone to become confused, then it is made by citing a specific instance of a more general phenomenon. (This same figure could presumably also be used in such a way as to entail a homology: rain is to sunshine as x is to y, where x and y are another pair of (opposite) things which this person, it is asserted, confuses. In that case the figure would be functioning metaphorically as well as metonymically – homology being a metaphoric relation of resemblance between two lower-order relations. But no such homology was clearly evinced by any of the exegetical remarks of our informants, who instead tended to understand this trope as referring to a specific instance of a more general tendency to confuse things.) The figures referring to grasses on the battlefield (discussed at the beginning of this section) present a more complicated case. The image is a metaphorical one insofar as the battlefield dangers include getting pierced by a spear. But it is also metonymic insofar as the hardships include the quite literal one of sharp grasses in the open field, which becomes a synecdochic figure for the other dangers as well. It is also relevant to note that the shafts of the arrows are themselves made of a kind of cane grass, *kamaya,* which means that references to that particular kind of grass (line 943) as a battlefield danger can both be taken literally (insofar as *kamaya* stumps can pierce the feet), and as a synecdochic figure for 'arrows'. References to other kinds of grasses within these figures can be taken as evoking 'arrow' by a kind of double movement: first, either a synecdochic movement from a particular grass to grasses in general, or a metaphoric movement from one grass to another; and second, a metonymic (synecdochic) movement from part (arrow shaft) to whole (arrow, or bow-and-arrow, which are jointly referred to by a single lexeme *el,* which is also the word for 'fight').

24 Compare Bloch (1975) (the widely-cited introductory chapter to the work in which Strathern's paper appears), who claims that 'arrow talk', 'veiled speech', and 'straight talk' are distinct codes which may be ranked on a single scale of 'formality', as follows:

> . . . the most formal code 'arrow talk' [= Nebilyer *el ung*] is the code of confrontation from status. The next most formal code, 'veiled talk' [*ung eke*], handles the traditional authority of the leaders when they are not faced by rivals of equal status, while 'straight talk', the least formalised, is used for practical politics (1975:26).

25 Contra Bloch's (1975:26) formulation above; this is also true of the examples discussed in A. Strathern (1975): while most of the 'veiled speech' figures discussed by Strathern occurred in non-oratorical contexts, the 'arrow talk' (*el ik/el ung*) speech which is given at the end of the article contains at least one instance of *ik ek,* in lines 62–4: 'Koma man of Nggaluwa, say to me / "You walk about on the leaves of the pandanus fruit" / Where men live you go hunting for marsupials, men say'. Strathern (loc.cit.:201) explains this as 'an image of how short of land [the speaker] is, he walks, about like a marsupial on the leaves of pandanus fruit trees'. There are many other examples of veiled speech within A. Strathern (1971, Appendix 7) in the first of the two *el ik* speeches given there, which Strathern says 'was greatly admired for the multiplicity of its veiled figurative references . . .' (loc. cit.:240).

26 A. Strathern refers to *el ik* orators 'ending each allusive phrase with a long, drawn out o-o-o-o' (1971:120). Incidentally, Strathern's formulation should not be taken to mean that those stretches of *el ik* which realize one complete allusion end in the added, *el ik*-marking vowel. Rather, *el ik,* in common with *el ung,* is delivered in well-bounded *prosodic* units, each of which is marked with that ending (as well as by a sudden drop in pitch).

27 It could be said that the determination of how many wounded must be compensated *is* argued out later in the event. While this is a subject of later discussion, it is clear that Tamalu does not direct the question to anyone, and does not intend that it be answered at this point.

28 The term *lopa* is nowadays applied to cats, which have become quite popular as pets in the Nebilyer, as elsewhere in the Highlands.

29 The speaker of the reported speech is specified by line 467, which comprises a kind of elliptical (verbless) framing clause (see Appendix B.4.3). In everyday speech, the noun phrase comprising such a clause would normally take the ergative postposition (ibid.). Since the line-terminating *el ung* vowel -a/-o replaces any other word-final vowel (section 5.2), it may be that line 467 should be analyzed as /-kin-ni-a/, with an 'underlying' ergative marker *-ni-* whose vowel is lost before the following one, and whose *-n-* merges with that of the comitative postposition (length of continuant consonants being non-distinctive in such environments). The line was in any case understood by informants as a framing clause (and is otherwise difficult to construe at all).

30 See Rumsey (1986) for a discussion of some of functions of ambiguous language at the event represented in Appendix A, including the (reported?) speech at lines 421–2, 424–5.

31 Compare Goldman (1983:28 ff.) and Feld and Schieffelin (MS. n.d.) who find such a distinction in the linguistic ideology of the Huli and Kaluli respectively, but also Wagner (1978:55) who denies it for the Daribi.

6 WARFARE COMPENSATION PAYMENT TO LAULKU: AN ANALYSIS

1 The speeches of Appendix A were recorded by Alan Rumsey on a Sony TCM 600 cassette recorder. Draft verbatim transcripts of these recordings, with interlinear glosses, were produced over the next several weeks by the authors, with invaluable assistance from our main Ku Waru linguistic informants Andrew Wai, Ambak Owa, and Simon Mek. In addition to helping us produce phonemic renderings of the Ku Waru, and English glosses, these informants (all of them then in their late teens) offered many valuable comments on them, including initial characterization of many passages as *el ung* and *ung eke* (cf. section 5.4). We later conferred with most of the men who had been principal speakers at the events, usually playing for them taped extracts of at least their own speeches, and eliciting comment from them. From those who were willing we elicited comment on the speeches of other big-men and functionaries, as well as general background to the event from their varying perspectives. Francesca Merlan also interviewed a range of women about their interpretations of portions of the transcript, including many by then recurrently identified as *ung eke*. After our return to Sydney in 1984, we produced a revised, computerized draft of the entire transcript. This was taken back to Kailge in January 1986 by Alan Rumsey, who rechecked the entire transcript and recorded extensive further commentary on it.

2 The parentheses are explained in section 6.2.6.

3 See, e.g. lines 34–5. Not all of the objections to use of *el ung* stem from Wangi's death specifically, but rather from the more general notion that *el ung* is replete with associations having to do with fighting and hostility (cf. Strathern 1975). The use of *el ung* is also condemned as incompatible with Christianity (line 1090), for reasons similar to those given by the Ilongot people of the Philippines concerning their *purung* 'oratory' (Rosaldo 1973).

4 For details see Appendix A. Interestingly, most of these were not segmentary names, but rather, identifications according to the names of leading men within the various sub-clans: *Lain bilong Tamalu*, etc. It is not clear how much of a consensus this might reflect about who was responsible for organizing the payments, since the writing on these signs was all done by a few boys, and most adults were probably unaware of what it said.

5 Though things work as if this were the case, we have never heard anyone refer to any such ordering as an explicit norm. Some remarks in the transcript (e.g. line 95) do seem implicitly to assume such a norm. We did not notice the pattern until analyzing our transcripts after leaving the field, so we were not able to question the participants about it.

6 See Goldman (1983:Ch.4) concerning a similar patterning among the Huli.

7 See Kujilyi's remarks at lines 95–8. Uyl is the leading big-man of the Alya tribe. As Kujilyi well knew, it would have been difficult or impossible for Uyl to have appeared at Kailge at this time, owing to a then-recent action against him for suspected poisoning (see Rumsey and Merlan 1986:86, fn.6). Alya, the man referred to in line 97 (whose name is not to be confused with that of the Alya tribe), is a big-man from Epola, as is Koluwa, who is referred to in line 98.

8 The Alya speaker during this segment is Alya Keap, who was presumably not present during the first half of the proceedings, on the Kailge display ground. He is not a major big-man, and would ordinarily not be expected to take a leading role in organizing exchange transactions on the part of the Alya *talapi*. This task would normally fall upon Alya Uyl (as in line 95), who is absent for reasons discussed in n.7 above. By his use of segmentary first person in line 1795, Keap acknowledges the status of Epola-Alya as *el pul* 'owners of the fight', but denies his own ability to organize a compensation payment to Kopia-Kubuka which will be adequate to reward them for their present effort.

9 It is interesting to note in this connection that when Francesca Merlan, at the display ground, inquired of one of her Kopia friends concerning the identity of a certain Laulku man whom she did not recognize, he was identified not as a Laulku, but as the affine of a certain Kopia man. In retrospect, it would have been useful to have found out how many of the Mujika-Laulku at the display ground (as opposed to those who waited at the school ground) were affinally or matrilaterally related to Kopia-Kubuka.

10 This is explicitly contested in lines 838–40 by the treasurer of the school's Board of Management, who gives the first speech after the shift to the school ground. But he is overruled in lines 863–8 by his fellow Kubuka ('brother'), Tamalu, who assures him that the payment will not be held up by a lot of talk. Note the assumption behind this promise (which, by the way, proves impossible to keep), that what is out of keeping with the new order is not the paying of compensation in itself, but the use of elaborate oratory in conjunction with it (cf. Rosaldo 1973 for a similar argument among the Ilongot).

11 There is one point in the last speech on the transcript (by Kubuka Komi) where these two topics are brought together, by the quotation of a well-known saying of Poika Wangi's, to the effect that the Poika could always be relied upon to come to the aid of the Kopia-Kubuka in wartime (line 1847). Thus the obligation to mourn his death arises from a relationship of the same kind as that which is being sealed by the events of the day.

12 See Keenan and Schieffelin (1976) for an interesting empirical account of the way in which topics are dialogically negotiated in conversations. Cf. also Brown and Yule (1983:68–124) for fuller treatment of this notion than we can give here.

13 This must be qualified in that typical classification of men which obtains throughout this area (cf. A. Strathern 1971:187–8), and locates 'big-men' and 'rubbish men' as opposites, is a sliding, impressionistic and somewhat context-conditional one as applied to any particular man. Nevertheless, the major speakers include men who are generally considered among the most eminent locally, as is also reflected in the fact that many of them hold governmental commissions: Kujilyi was both Midipu councillor and a magistrate at the time, Unya a magistrate, and both Noma and Dop were councillors.

14 As observed in section 3.1.3, this cluster of three tribes is unusual in this area, where pairing is the rule. In fact, no local people refer to these allies by using the three terms

together as we do. The relevant alliances are generally referred to as Epola-Alya on the one hand, and Alya-Lalka on the other, so that Alya is variably paired with one and the other.

15 Alya here is a man's name, in form the same as that of the tribe with which his is paired.

16 These links are overall denser in the case of the upper Kopia, of whom Kupena is one, than the lower Kopia; but they are fairly strong for both, as indicated for instance by marriage data (see Tables 4–6, 4–7).

17 In private conversations, Kopia-Kubuka informants stressed that these Poika men had not been invited into the fight by the Kopia-Kubuka, but had come according to their own minds (*eneni-nga numan*).

18 The image is coordinated with his ticking off those people and segmentary units of concern to him on his hand, extending each finger of a clenched fist from pinkie towards thumb, the hand outstretched with palm upturned (cf. A. Strathern 1977b).

19 Though Tamalu does not cite any *talapi* names (cf. section 5.1.3), interpreters of the transcript surmised that he had in mind Mujika, Tilka, Palimi, Poika, and Laulku as his 'thumb'.

20 We did not do a full census of Tilka, but gathered information on internal Tilka segmentation. Working from the 1982 Principal Roll of Electors (see References), we believe the Tilka do not exceed 200 persons.

21 To the best of our understanding this amount was fifty kina.

22 The money, tacked on display boards, was counted and discussed at Kailge, but not actually taken off the boards and handed out until later, at the school-ground. See section 6.1.

23 Note the non-use of SP in this context, where Tilka is not being represented as a segmentary transactor.

24 The grammatical construction [proposition, *nyi- pilyi-* 'X thinks'] (and often, but not invariably, with yes-no clitic *-i* (see section 5.6), does X think?') is interpreted to mean that the supposition is incorrect. This may be in keeping with the idea that the *numan* of others is not knowable (see section 9.1).

25 As this book goes to press, a letter (dated 30 November 1989) from one of our main assistants at Kailge informs us that Mujika and Laulku will indeed be making a *makayl* payment of live pigs to Kopia in 1990.

7 COMPENSATION AND THE KULKA WOMEN'S CLUB

1 See section 3.1.3 regarding the indigenous paired-pair conceptualization of the internal structure of this alliance. Our five-term way of referring to it is strictly for ease of presentation, and does not follow indigenous practice.

2 Owing to commitments in Australia (where we returned for six months in 1982 to work on an Aboriginal land claim case), we were not present at Kailge during the Marsupial Road War. Our knowledge of what transpired is based on accounts given after we returned to Kailge on November 23, 1982, some two and a half months after the fighting.

3 This is dictated both by fieldwork constraints and publication limits. Though we did record the entire event on tape, our remaining fieldwork time after the event was not sufficient to transcribe it all verbatim. Instead, we first worked through the entire tape with informants and produced abstracts of the contents of each speech. Based upon these, we chose what seemed to be the most important speeches for our purposes, and transcribed those verbatim. This resulted in notebook-draft transcript for about two-thirds of the tape. As it was not feasible to include in this volume even a sizable portion of both that transcript and the one of the Kailge event, it was

decided to include the complete one of the latter in Appendix A, and to handle the former in the manner described below.

4 The Kailge club participated in this fete with great excitement. Though they eventually contented themselves with just decorating and dancing, their initial ideas for a novel and, they hoped, money-making project were rather alarming to Francesca Merlan. Since she was learning net-bag-making, and was by this time able to speak Ku Waru reasonably well, members of the club proposed that she be exhibited doing both these things. They would build a house for her in the Kumaku club compound, to which they could charge admission. In discussion of this matter, several club women did concede that it might be rather taxing – but, they said, think of the returns it would yield! If they were going to decorate and display, why could not Francesca? And, they pointed out, there were so many people in the area that there was little other opportunity for many of them to meet us.

5 Rostering of speakers is done at many gatherings like this one, and was also attempted at the women's club meetings, usually with only temporary success. People see this, and/or requesting permission to speak by raising of hands (as also happened at club meetings) as deriving from the European-introduced practices of social regulation, but generally thoroughly endorse them (without necessarily following them).

6 *Kapa* derives from English 'copper', and is used to refer to a structure with metal roofing. It is a point of pride to have in one's area or community a *haus kapa*.

7 One person suggested this was meant to stand for 'shield'.

8 In our experience this sort of regrouping for joint entry occurred frequently, not just before compensation events, but at almost any sort of public event attended at a distant display ground by a sizable contingent of men of common 'other' segmentary identity.

9 See Chapter 6, n.24, where the construction 'you think thus', implying the opposite is correct, is discussed.

10 A vast over-estimate, or rhetorical exaggeration. There were perhaps five hundred people present on this occasion.

11 At least at Kailge, Dumu's money-handling activities were regarded with great resentment and hostility, since the Kailge women occasionally thought he was short-changing them in some matters where pooled funds were used.

12 When Alan Rumsey returned to the field for a visit in January 1986 he found that fighting had broken out within the alliance, and over the two years we had been gone, six deaths had occurred in the warfare.

13 See e.g. Merlan and Rumsey (1986:90) for Kujilyi's comments on decisiveness of European court talk.

14 It is thus ironic that dominant images of Kujilyi are of him as suppliant female, as described in section 6.2.1.

15 In the case of the Kailge club, the formation of club splinter-groups proceeded along segmentary lines in 1982–3 (cf. section 7.1). At first there was only one club group, but a second one formed which had as its core women married into the Kopia\ Kabika sub-segment, and some women married to Kubuka. This partly reflects residential-territorial arrangements (see Map 3). The political orientation of women as club members was clearly defined by segmentary politics (at lower as well as higher segmentary levels, see section 3.2.3).

8 THE EVENTS IN PERSPECTIVE

1 This understanding of the matter has some things in common with Wagner's (1974), notwithstanding his criticisms of British social anthropology (ibid.). Wagner (op.cit. p.106) says of Daribi social nomenclature that the names 'only group people in the

way that they separate them or distinguish them', in which respect they 'are very flexible' (op.cit. p.107), being used at various levels of inclusiveness in various contexts.

2 Compare Sahlins 1961. Evans-Pritchard (1940:135) himself saw structural relativity as 'one of the most fundamental characteristics . . . of all social groups'.

3 This is not to say that it is always clear in practice which of the two types any given relationship belongs to. That is precisely what is often contested. The point is rather that a relationship cannot in principle be of both kinds at once: this is why the matter must be contested – the tacit ground on which the contest proceeds.

4 It should not be concluded that this is true in other contexts. In discussions among fellow Kopia, for example, segmentary person would not ordinarily be used to refer to all Kopia (much less Kopia-Kubuka), and there is often explicit appeal to the grounds for concerted action by all Kopia. The latter often happened during, for example, preparations for prestations to other *talapi*, including the ones under discussion here.

5 A partial exception may be found in the line cited from Kulka Pokea in Chapter 7 (p. 183): 'I will carry the words of you two to Kopola', where *elti* 'you two' presumably refers to K-M-E-A-L and Kopia-Kubuka. But this may not be an exception at all, since the two segmentary actors in question have just made a joint payment to the Kulka women's club, for whom he presumes to speak (in first person singular SP), positioning himself (and the club) as a mediator between *all* the *talapi* who are represented at that day's event at Palimung and the opposing side, who will assemble a few days later at Kopola.

6 Compare Feil (1984b) who argues that this is true in particular of interpersonal exchange relationships, as *opposed to* the realm of 'intergroup' relations, which are potentially hostile. Lederman (1986b) makes a similar suggestion concerning *twem* relations (as opposed to *sem* ones) in Mendi.

7 Elsewhere Strathern says of these types of relations that they 'may be between the parts of a person or between two persons' (1986 MS-A:8).

8 Compare A. Strathern (1971:221): 'It is important that these [exchange] networks are built out of reciprocative partnerships. Each man has a number of partners and he can bring pressure to bear on them. But he can not bring pressure to bear so effectively and directly on *their* partners in turn. He exerts pressure only through his immediate partner.' Feil (1984a) makes similar observations regarding the Enga *tee*.

9 The distinction between these two kinds of pairing seems to have some things in common with one drawn by the Kaluli people between *wel* versus *su*, which Schieffelin (1980) glosses as 'same' versus 'equivalent'.

10 This also seems to have been the case before pacification in the Melpa area: 'Informants at Mbukl maintained that in the past no war payments were made to major enemies, only to minor enemies, with whom it was expected that peace could be made and who might be one's allies in a different sequence of fights later' (A. Strathern 1971:90). Meggitt (1977) says the same about the Mae Enga.

11 This way of describing the matter is probably in any case appropriate only for non-lethal 'blows'. Ku Waru people do talk in terms of 'paying for new blood', etc. in the case of injuries, but they do not generally talk of paying for, or exchanging objects for, a human life. Where the injuries have been fatal, the payment is said to be compensation, not for the man's life itself, but for the grief and anger of the bereaved: 'We paid them to make them feel better'. Similarly, Strathern's informants stressed that 'the aim of compensation is not to make a standard, exact payment for a death, but to make a payment large enough to soothe the anger of the bereaved' (A. Strathern 1971:96; cf. p.90).

12 This is not to say that every adult male member of those units joins in the fighting, or that no one else does. Here we are talking about matters of socially-constructed (and contested) *talapi*-level agency, a matter which we as analysts would not be able to

determine by a simple head count on the battlefield (cf. Ch.6–7, and section 8.3 below).

13 Separate relations of oppositional parity *may* obtain among some of the units on one side, who may be 'minor enemies' (as above), but that is an incidental complication. It does, however, show that oppositional parity is not exclusive, the way compositional parity is. In that respect it is more like serial parity (cf. above).

14 Note that this form of parity differs from all the others in that it holds among 'actors' which are *not* of the same order: the government and everybody else. As Neil Maclean (p.c.) observed to us, this is why the government is able to *be* a universal partner – i.e., that it has the wherewithal to dominate the political field. So in contrast to all the other kinds of relationship being modeled here it is not at all clear that there can actually *be* a relation of parity among the actors in this one, or what that would even mean. We use the term *universal parity* not as a sociologically defensible description of the relevant power relationship, but to capture the way in which these relationships are indigenously formulated (misrecognized?) by actors such as the Kulka women's club (cf. M. Strathern 1985b).

15 The Strathern corpus has anticipated these as well. A. Strathern (1979a) refers specifically to oratory, but Strathern and Strathern (1971) includes extensive discussion of the social-political uses of body decoration at exchange events. The work of O'Hanlon (1983) in the nearby Wahgi area has also been most revealing in this respect.

16 It is less well known that the 'conversion' can work in the other direction: from agnatic to affinal status, in order to 'straighten the way' for exchange. See Feil (1978c) for an excellent account of the way this works among the Tombema Enga.

17 In fairness we must add that Gewertz does allow for one kind of ambiguity which objects may have, which is that they may be 'willfully shorn of meaning', i.e. treated as though they were *mere* objects, rather than items of meaningful transaction (ibid.). But this is not the sort of ambiguity we are talking about here. In fact, that is one sort of ambiguity which probably would *not* have been possible in any of the transactions discussed here. For while Ku Waru people might in some contexts speak of money as 'just money' (or, far less plausibly, 'just colored pieces of paper'), we cannot imagine their ever speaking (or otherwise acting) that way about money plastered on a decorated display board standing up in a *makayl pena* 'ceremonial exchange ground', at an event the announced purpose of which is to present a compensation payment.

18 Nor does speech play a similar, or equally central part in all Highland exchange systems. For example, regarding the Wiru (Pangia, Southern Highlands), A. Strathern reports that ' . . . in striking contrast to the invariable pattern of events at a Hagen *moka*, no formal speeches are made. Chief recipients and secondary ones may also come from rival or hostile groups. They keep well apart and, again, do not exchange words. There is a definite convention of silence here.' Describing the confused forward rush in which pork-leg prestations are finally made to recipients in a body, he further observes that 'The effect is very far removed from that of the public speech-making at the conclusion of a *moka*, when all the emphasis is on corporate statements about relations between groups and there is much stress on people forming an audience and listening properly. At Wiru pig-kills no audience or set of spectators as such gathers at all. Recipients appear as men of a certain village and are noted as such. But the donors interact individually with their chosen partners and no verbal statements at a group level appear to be made at all' (1978:79–80). Needless to say, the contrast with Nebilyer exchange events, such as those analyzed above, is equally striking. Unfortunately, we do not have room to take up the implications of this contrast here, as it would demand a detailed comparison between Wiru and (Hagen/)Nebilyer segmentary sociality and exchange. See however, A. Strathern (ibid.; 1984) for interesting attempts along those lines.

19 Nebilyer people distinguish sharply between what goes on on the *pena* (display

ground) and in the *lku kolya* (house area) and do not expect the latter to be openly accessible to outsiders. But what is said in speeches on the *pena* – especially at inter-*talapi* exchange events – is expected to be widely heard or reported, and closely scrutinized by all and sundry. Thus, our recording, transcription, and close analysis of such speeches was considered entirely proper, whereas no such approval would have been given for the public disclosure and scrutiny of transcripts of 'in-house' discussions or other private conversations.

9 PERSPECTIVES ON 'EVENT'

1 In saying this we do not ignore work in 'ethnography of speaking', but find that it tends not to treat speech as social action in any way that might make it more relevant to our concerns. Following Hymes (1974), 'speech' is taken as the substantive focus of this approach, especially its range of varieties in different societies. But this tends to have the consequence in practice that speech is treated as separable from other dimensions of social life. For example, in the first book-length ethnography of speaking within a particular society, the Kuna, Sherzer (1983:11) justifies his central focus on language and speech by saying that they 'have a patterning of their own, as do social organization, politics, religion, economics, and law ...' This begs all the questions of relations among forms of social action that we would want to investigate. Just as linguists had earlier struggled to achieve for their field the status of an autonomous science, Sherzer (like ethnographers of speaking generally) locates his subject matter as a third one between 'language' per se and 'culture', rather than treating speech as one of the moments of social action. Thus, within the general approach (and despite Hymes' (1974:196) warnings against such separation), ways of speaking are often described as structural types at rest, as it were, apart from treatment of their use as part of social action.

2 Indeed, it can be said that the rise of a separate subject matter of linguistic pragmatics is the consequence of the maintenance within mainstream linguistic theories of the Saussurean dichotomies of *langue* and *parole*, synchrony and diachrony, social and individual, system and event, formal and substantive.

3 M. and A. Strathern use the term 'Hageners' to include both the Melpa and the Nebilyer Valley people, whom the Melpa call Temboka (M. Strathern 1972a: 1–2).

4 In local language people say of such obstructions *mi tum* 's/he tabooed it', where *mi* is also the word for 'divination substance' (see Strauss 1962:206–79, A. Strathern 1971:87). This is commonly used today to express proclamation of a strong ban upon actions or objects which have seriously affected individual or wider interests.

5 Note the nearly identical Melpa and Ku Waru forms of this word.

6 Cf. Sahlins (1968) on the contingent evaluation of action, varying with social distance among those involved, as a general characteristic of 'tribal' sociality; and our comments on theft and deception above.

7 *We* is also used as the equivalent of 'free, for no return', as in the scrawled notices on Kailge trade stores *we mol* 'not free'. The English gloss 'for nothing' covers both senses.

8 This unverifiability is limited by the fact that to some extent the body is the mirror of the *numan*, providing the only direct evidence of internal dispositions. See section 9.1.4.

9 In Ku Waru (as in Melpa) there is a noun, *mel*, which lexicalizes the general notion of 'thing, object'. One of its commonest senses – perhaps the prototypical one – is that of 'things of especial value', as in phrases like *ab mel-ma* 'bridewealth' (lit. 'woman things'). This contrasts strikingly, for example, with many Australian indigenous languages, in which there is no such generic noun. The Hagen/Nebilyer *mel* is also

used as nominal and verbal modifier, in the first instance to mean 'like, similar to' (e.g. *owa mel-te* 'a thing/ something like a dog', and in the second 'in the manner of' (*el tiring mel* 'they were sort of fighting/(what) they were doing (was) like fighting'). That is, an apparent substantive ('thing') here provides a way of expressing a standard of comparison.

10 But cf. Hocart (1933) on the lack of differentiation in Melanesian society between 'religion' and 'business'.

11 See also M. Strathern (1985a:121) for a similar remark about the ambiguity of wealth transaction in Hagen.

12 When some collectors from the Museum of Brussels came through the Nebilyer Valley in 1982 it became clear that some men had preserved one or two of their really outstanding shells, but it also became apparent that very few shells had been saved. Our Councillor sold a particularly fine one to them for forty kina. He was happy to sell and delighted with the hard bargain he drove. Other men regretted not having kept any. Pearl shell is still used as an everyday ornament, shaped as a half-moon and slung around the neck on a string.

13 It was decided that food exchanges would be made in the first instance, but that later transactions might involve predominantly pigs and money – an indication of an escalating scale of values.

14 Of course we would stress that researchers have the choice of placing themselves in this situation.

15 We owe the formulation of this point to a recent paper, (M. Strathern, in press), reading of which has helped us to focus parts of this discussion. This is not to say Strathern would necessarily endorse the discussion in this form.

16 The fact that a person's name is given in commemoration of a specific event or circumstance does not mean that names themselves are unique. The boy Pai whose name is discussed here was sometimes known as Kaylke Pai to distinguish him from another boy, Walyo Pai, who lived at Walyo, up the slope from Kailge. Unfortunately we never asked about the naming of Walyo Pai. What is significant is that the circumstances commemorated by each name-giving are particular ones, not that the form of the name necessarily be unique.

17 It is clear, however, that certain kinds of contingencies are more salient than others as sources of names, and further, that gender dichotomy is important in the selection, viz. the number of males mentioned above whose names allude to specific episodes of fighting.

18 We are impressed by a striking contrast with (our experience of) Australian Aboriginal people, who seem to express nothing similar to this notion of 'boredom', despite a life-style which outsiders might judge to be characterized by inactivity, a relative lack of observable events or anything happening for long periods of time. Valued actional styles tend to be almost the antithesis of the urgent, competitive Nebilyer style. Some younger, English-speaking Aboriginal people we know make use of the English word 'bored' to describe their disposition, in striking contrast to their elders' usage in English and in indigenous languages, which seem to have no equivalent.

19 Of course parallelism need not be *limited* to pairing; it may, in Jakobson's (1966:399) terms, consist of 'recurrent returns' of a variety of kinds. But the parallelism of pairs is pervasive in our Nebilyer material. See also Fox 1988.

20 In rhetorical parallelisms like *koyik nun-lum/kalk nun-lum*, note how the compositional (as opposed to lexicalizing) method of building up verbal meanings (see Appendix B, Appendix D) is taken up and enhances the possibility of formal similarity of portions of lines. Generally, the compositional building of verbal meanings, involving as it does possibilities of multiple pairings of verb roots with others, exemplifies pairing as a linguistic structural resource which appears to have many features in common with other kinds of pairing discussed in section 5.7.

21 Goldman (1983:154–5, 171 ff.) describes as a feature of Huli mediators' talk the

posing of binary options, but notes they do not pose specific 'directives to action'. He regards this as their detaching themselves from 'repercussions attendant on party or issue polarization' (1983:155). There is no doubt an element of this in the kind of non-directive apodosis we describe here for the Nebilyer; see also A. Strathern (1975), who argues that points made obliquely will not provoke violent reactions. While this may be, our investigations indicate that points made obliquely are not universally taken in exactly the same way.

22 By way of contrast, in dual (moiety) classifications such as are found in Aboriginal Australia, if we know that e.g. turkey and brolga are of different moieties, and that turkey and owlet nightjar are of the same, then we can infer that owlet nightjar and brolga are of different moieties.

23 Once again, M. Strathern (1972b) seems to have anticipated this form of 'invention' by juxtaposition and refraction in her discussion of Hageners' relation to the court system. There, she argued that the institution of a village court system, proposed prior to Independence, would be well received, because Hageners did not see relations of power as completely imposed from without, but rather as resources in which they could and would participate. But lest the reader think that the form of 'invention' we have described is general to the 'Highlands' (and also, independent of specific colonial histories), we would point to examples which seem rather different in character, such as Clark's (1988) discussion of the Wiru (Pangia, Southern Highlands) sense of radical disjunction between the pre-colonial past in which people say they were 'wild pigs', and the present in which people seem to value most highly not a sense of their own vitality and participation in shaping events, but the possibility of becoming 'tame' and 'domesticated' like Europeans.

24 In the present ethnographic context, an especially notable example of this separation is in the work of Roy Wagner. He has provided some of the most subtle and powerful ways of thinking about various forms of Melanesian social life (and our debt to him will have been readily apparent above) but he says of his approach that it 'eschews the practical and normative issues of how meaning is linked to social action' (Wagner 1986b:123). In this respect, Wagner's position is all too compatible with that of Feil and Meggitt, in that it reproduces the same divide (albeit from the other side) between the study of social action and of 'meaning'. An even starker disjunction between the two is implied by Wagner's characterization of meaning as 'a specialized form of perception . . . [which] remains as purely personal as the sense you or I make individually of a certain color or sound . . .'. (1988:x–xi). Wagner's model of culture does have something like an actional dimension, insofar as these 'personal perceptions' are 'expanded into larger cultural forms' by a process which Wagner calls 'obviation' (1988:xi, 1978, 1986b); but in practice he locates this process in more or less *stereotypic* actions or products (e.g. a given Daribi myth or ritual) rather than in concrete historical contexts (a given recitation of the myth or performance of the ritual by a particular actor in this or that set of circumstances). In this respect Wagner's notion of obviation, for all his disclaimers, resembles Lévi-Strauss' notion of the resolution of basic contradictions as the functional dynamic of myth, insofar as the contradictions turn out to be of a highly abstract and general order, and their 'resolution' a property of the myth as type, rather than as performance in context.

Glossary

The following glossary includes all Ku Waru and Tok Pisin (Neo-Melanesian Pidgin) words which occur in the text of Chapters 1 to 9, and all Ku Waru words which occur more than twice in App A. For other Ku Waru expressions in App A which characterize speech, see App D. For other Tok Pisin words used in App A, see the interlinear glosses, also Mihalic (1971). Tok Pisin words in italics below.

ab	woman
ab *klap*	women's club
ab kuime	bridewealth
ab kunana	courting song
ab lku	woman's house
abol-	hold, grasp
abola	girl
abu	woman
abu-n miyl	'woman-borne', i.e. identified with the *talapi* via one's mother (matrifiliation)
ad-	wander, go about
ada	old man
adi	that, yonder, not visible
ag (ik)e nyi-	thank, give thanks
aima	really
aj	back (that way, away)
aji	back
aki	this one
aki si-	do thus
ak-	extract, give compensation
alte-	do again
amamas	happiness, pride
ang	same-sex sibling (vocative)
angalyi-	stand, be (standing) in a place
angubu	thatch, kunai grass (*Imperata Arundinacea*)
ansipe	far
apa	uncle
ausiyl	a large amount of, too many
awilyi	big
ayl	tail
-ayl	definite, (see App B.3.3.2.3.)
bagarap	to be damaged
bal	apron, loincloth, netbag type
bamp	see ung *bamp* in App D
berlto-	count
bilyipa	brother-in-law
bisnis	business, trade
bo	seedling, cutting
bo	indigenous, autochthonous
bo ul	customary matter
bo ung	native language or way of speaking

boni	heavy; injury, grievance
bonunga	yesterday
brukim	to break
bulkud	back side, on the back
bulu-mingi	back bone, spine
dowa	eagle
ekepu	today, now
el parka yi	major enemy
el pul	fight source
el ung	fight talk (see section 5.3)
elti	you two
eltili	you two yourselves
ena	sun
eneni	you yourselves, they themselves
engl	hunger
eni	you pl, they
ga(i)	sweet potato
gavman	government
gol to-	deceive
gom	leaf
gris	nutritive substance; (see section 3.1.2)
handet	hundred
haus kapa	metal-roofed building
-i	yes-no question; (see section 5.6)
i-me	these
idi	there, that
ilyi	this
ing	word, language, speech
-ir	one, an (singular/ indefinite)
isi-	do thus
-iyl	definite (see App B.3.3.2.3.)
-ja	interrogative marker, conditional marker
ka	rope, connection, road
kabu	worm
kadi	real, genuine
kakuna	a large amount of wealth

kala- lyi-	breed, procreate
kalya to-	to poke
kalyipa	casuarina tree
kamaya	cane grass species
kan-	to look at, see
kang(a)	boy, lad
kange	fairy tale
kangi	skin, body
kani (-yl/-lyi)	this, that, seen one, known one
kansil	village councillor
kanu	that, seen i.e. known to speaker/ addressee
kanuwa	that
kapis	cabbage
kapiyl	accident, wound
kapola	o.k., all right
kapu	poor, rubbish, dry
kare	some, more
kaspis	potato
kayi	good
ke nyi-	make noise
keap	*kiap*, patrol officer, official
kedemadi yi	retainer
kel	little
kel-	to leave, to lose
keli	edge
kep	or, even
kepa	type of arboreal marsupial
kera	bird
kewa	foreign, European, modern
kewa nui	cannibal
ki	hand, arm
kiap	patrol officer
kibolu	stick, club
kik	ashes
-kil	some, a group (paucal)
-kilyi	see *-kiyl*
kim	vegetables
kina	unit of New Guinea currency, gold-lipped pearl shell
kinya	now, today
kirip	corner, nook

kiripul	door step, dooryard
kis	bad
-kiyl	because, since, and
kob	first (born); common as segmentary label
kol-	die
kolipa	father-in-law, wife's parents
kolsi	liittle, small, a bit
kolya	place, region
kolya pul	owner, lit. 'place base'
koma	wet
kompensesen	compensation
kona	new, raw
kongun	work, day
konguns-	consider (*lyi- konguns-*)
kopong	nutritive substance, see *gris*
kopsi-	cut
kor	already, finished
kor-	look for, search
kot	court
ku	stone, money
ku *lep*	leftover money
ku *moni*	money
ku waru	'steep stone', i.e. cliff
kubi	nose, hill
kubi le-	lead, go first
kuda	region, place, side
kudanga	side, over there, that
kuduyl	red European, caucasian
kul-	die
kuluyl	black storm clouds
kulysi-	put posts on plants (for support)
kum	ear
kung	pig
kung pala	pig fence
kung pengi	pig's head, initiatory payment (see section 4.1)
kung por	return payment, pig's hindquarter (see section 4.1)
kuni	straight
kunu	door, shield
kunutapiya	shield
kupari	insane
kupena	poison
kupsi-	cut, carve
kupula	path, passage way
kupulanum	road, way (lit. mother path)
kuruwi	bird of paradise species
kuskus	secretary, clerk
kuyi-	bake
lain	line, social grouping
langi	food
langi mong	choice food
lawa	wrong, fault, mistake
le	excrement, excretion
le-	put, place, be in a place
lku	house
lku tapa	men's house (see section 3.1.2)
lo	law
lopa	marsupial
lopa ka el	Marsupial Road War (see section 3.2.2)
lu	ax
-lum	conditional, if, perhaps
lupu	different, other
lyi-	to get, take
-ma	collective number (see App B.3.3.2.1)
mada	enough
madu	downwards
ma(i)	ground, soil
makayl	ceremonial exchange
makayl pena	display ground
mak	mark, limit, extent, kind
maku to-	to tie up, bundle
manya	down, down low
mara	forest tree species
marlti	dance, line dance
matres	magistrate
me-	carry, bear
medepa	in the middle
medi	downwards, afterward

medipulu self, itself
mel thing, valuable (see section 9.1.1)
memi blood
meri, mere down, that, that one down there
mim te- create, fix
mini-wal fright
miyl carried, borne (as in abu-n miyl)
modu- to send
moka ceremonial exchange
mokabu compensation for injury
moki te- distribute, share
mol no
mol- be at a place, exist, live
molo or
mong eye, center point, trouble
moni money
mons- put in a place, care for
mulu breath, mountain, sky
na and
na I
naa not
nabina why
nabisiyl how many
nabisipa how many, how
nabitiyl how many (Meam dialect)
nabolka what
nai who
nambawan first, best
nanu I myself
nar where
ne(la) over there
nedu over that way
nekeda over that way
-nga genitive (see App B.3.3.1)
-ni ergative/instrumental (see App B.3.3.1)
no water, creek, river
no- drink, eat, consume
nok- to wait for, look after
nos(i)- put
-nsi- causative/benefactive (see App B.3.2.6)
nu you (singular)
nunu you yourself
numan mind, intention, will
nyi- say
nyi- pilyi- believe, think
o- come
oba or, and, (lit., 'coming')
obil bone
oi boundary
ola up, on top
olad(u) up, upward
olto we two (you and I, he/she and I)
olyo we
olyolyo we ourselves
opayl tomorrow
opis office
owa dog
pabu thumb
pai pet
pait fight
paka to- cover, wear
pakuyl covering, worn (as in *wal pakuyl*, 'shirt', 'European clothing')
pansi- put, place at rest
papu well, well done
parka bird of paradise species
pawa power, strength, determination
payl all, everything
pe- to live, lie down, to sleep
pel cousin
pela boar
pelipa cousin
pena outside, display ground, public space
penga later
pengi head
pensi- (*pe-nsi-*) let live, provide with a home

pikuyl	people, population
pilis	village
pilyi-	listen, think
pipi	lid of pot
pipilyika	confederation, cooperation
pipiyl	shame
plak	flag
pol	bridge, plank, platform, flat surface
polu to-	ripen
popolu	anger, resentment
por	behind, bottom, arse, back
pora	finished, finish
porltap	chicken
pren	friend
pu-	go
pudu	debt, residue, return
pul	root, base, cause
pul yab	owners (base people)
pula	arse-grass, rear-end covering
punya	garden, year
puruyl	rotten
rais	rice
senis	change
si-	give
sika (sike)	true, sure, certain(ly), yes
-sil	salient pair (see App B.3.3.2.2.; section 5.7)
simiji	center beam of house
sirku	sharp grass
suba	superb bird of paradise
suku(d(u))	inside
sumuyl	gold-lipped pearl shell, woman's name
suril	flea
sur-	peck, make holes in
surub	short
tai te-	laugh
takan	quiet
takis	tax
tal	two
talapi	segmentary identity (see section 3.1.1)
talko	day before yesterday
tambu	taboo
tami (taim)	bailer shell
tapa	men's house (see section 3.1.2)
tapor	spade
tapu to-	go around together
tara	ancestor, father
tausen	thousand
tauwu	banana
-te	one, a (indefinite; see App B.3.3.2.4)
te-	do, make, transact
tensi-	(*te-nsi-*) do for
temal	omen
tenga	different
tepi	fire
terile-	sum, add together
ti-	give (Meam dialect; cf. *si-*)
tika	sure, certain(ly), yes (Meam dialect; cf. *sika*)
tilu	only one
tilupu	one, single
to-	hit, kill
todul	strong, strength
toksave	information, advice
tom yaya kange	chanted story genre
torupalyi	fathers-in-law
trik	deceive
tud-	be stumped (Meam dialect)
tultul	appointed village assistant officer under Australian Administration
uj(i)	tree, wood
ul(u)	affair, matter
ultuku	tomorrow
ulyi	clay, mud
ung	word, language, speech
ung eke	'bent speech', trope; (see section 5.4)
ung kuni	'straight speech'; (see section 5.4)

ung lapa	See App D
ung mong	See App D
ung urip	See App D
uru pe-	sleep
-uyl	definite (see App B.3.3.2.3)
waku to-	leave, let lose
wal	netbag
walsi-	ask
walu	young
wanap ka	initiatory payment (see section 4.1)
wantok	compatriot
wantok sistem	favoritism, nepotism
wanya	hat, cap
we	(for) nothing, free
wedu	away, out
weli te-	make a mess
wenepu	young woman
wiji	up there
wijuyl	up
wilyala	up there
wilyi	up, there
witnis	witness
ya	here, forth
yab(u)	people (/*yi-ab*/, lit: man-woman)
yad(u)	this way, to here
yi	man
yi nuim	big-man
yi obil	initiatory payment (see section 4.1)
yi pengi	main payment (see section 4.1)
yi-yl-n miyl	man-borne, i.e., identified with the *talapi* via one's father (patrifiliation)
-yl	definite (see App B.3.3.2.3)
yu	he, she
yunu, yuyu	he himself, she herself

References

Aarsleff, H. 1983. *From Locke to Saussure: Essays on the study of language and intellectual history*. Minneapolis: University of Minnesota Press.

Austin, J. L. 1975. *How to do things with words.* Cambridge, Mass.: Harvard University Press. (Second edition).

Bakhtin, M. M. 1981. *The dialogic imagination: Four essays,* M. Holquist, ed. Austin: University of Texas Press.

1986. *Speech genres and other late essays.* C. Emerson and M. Holquist eds. Austin: University of Texas Press.

Barnes, J. 1962. 'African models in the New Guinea Highlands'. *Man* 62: 5–9.

Barth, F. 1966. *Models of social organization*. London: Royal Anthropological Institute, Occasional Paper No. 23.

1975. *Ritual and knowledge among the Baktaman of New Guinea*. New Haven: Yale University Press.

Barthes, R. 1982 'Le discours de l'histoire'. *Poétique*. 49: 13–21.

Benveniste, É. 1969. 'Sémiologie de la langue'. *Semïotica* 1: 3–12, 127–35. The Hague: Mouton.

1971 [1946]. 'Relationships of person in the verb'. In *Problems in general linguistics*. Miami Linguistics Series No. 8, 195–204. Coral Gables: University of Miami Press.

Berndt, R. 1964. 'Warfare in the New Guinea Highlands'. *American Anthropologist* 66: 183–203.

Black, M. 1962. *Models and metaphors: Studies in language and philosophy*. Ithaca, N. Y.: Cornell University Press.

Bloch, M., (ed). 1975. *Political language and oratory in traditional society*. London: Academic Press. (Also 'Introduction' in same volume, pp. 1–28).

1977. 'The past and present in the present'. *Man* 12: 278–92.

Boas, F. 1966 [1911]. 'Introduction' to *Handbook of American Indian languages*. BAE-B, Part I, pp. 1–83. Washington, D.C.: Smithsonian Institution.

Bourdieu, P. 1977. *Outline of a theory of practice.* (Trans. R. Nice). Cambridge: Cambridge University Press.

Brandewie, E. 1981. *Contrast and context in New Guinea culture: The case of the Mbowamb of the central highlands*. St. Augustin, West Germany: Studia Instituti Anthropos, v. 39.

Brown, D. J. J. 1980. 'The structuring of Polopa kinship and affinity'. *Oceania* 50: 297–331.

Brown, G. and G. Yule 1983. *Discourse analysis.* In Cambridge Textbooks in Linguistics, pp. 68–124. Cambridge: Cambridge University Press.

Brown, P. 1962. 'Non-agnates among the patrilineal Chimbu'. *Journal of the Polynesian Society* 71: 57–69.

Bulmer, R. 1960. 'Leadership and social structure among the Kyaka people of the Western Highlands District of New Guinea'. Unpublished Ph.D. thesis. Canberra: Australian National University.

Chomsky, N. 1965. *Aspects of the theory of syntax.* Cambridge, Mass.: MIT Press.

Clark, J. 1988. 'Kaun and Kogono: Cargo cults and development in Karavar and Pangia'. *Oceania* 59: 38–56.

Connolly, B. and Anderson, R. 1987. *First contact: New Guinea's Highlanders encounter the outside world.* New York: Viking Penguin.

Cook, E. A. and O'Brien, D., eds. 1980. *Blood and semen: Kinship systems of Highland New Guinea.* Ann Arbor: University of Michigan Press.

de Lepervanche, M. 1967–8. 'Descent, residence and leadership in the New Guinea Highlands'. *Oceania* 37: 134–58, 38: 164–89.

Deleuze, G. and F. Guattari 1987. *A thousand plateaus: Capitalism and schizophrenia.* (Trans. B. Massumi). Minneapolis: University of Minnesota Press.

Derrida, J. 1976. *Of grammatology.* Baltimore: Johns Hopkins University Press.

Dresch, P. 1986. 'The significance of the course events take in segmentary systems'. *American Ethnologist* 13(2): 309–24.

Dumont, L. 1970 [1966]. *Homo hierarchicus.* Chicago: University of Chicago Press.

Durkheim, E. and Mauss, M. 1963 [1901–2]. *Primitive classification.* London: Cohen and West.

Durkheim, E. 1964 [1893]. *The division of labor in society.* New York: The Free Press of Glencoe.

Evans-Pritchard, E. E. 1940. *The Nuer: A description of the modes of livelihood and political institutions of a Nilotic people.* New York and Oxford: Oxford University Press.

Feil, D. K. 1978a. 'Women and men in the Enga *Tee*'. *American Ethnologist* 5: 263–79.

1978b. 'Enga women in the *Tee* exchange'. *Mankind* 11: 220–30.

1978c. 'Straightening the way: An Enga kinship conundrum'. *Man* (n.s.) 13: 380–401.

1979. 'From negotiability to responsibility: A change in Tombema-Enga homicide compensation'. *Human Organization* 38: 356–66.

1980a. 'Symmetry and complementarity: Patterns of competition and exchange in the Enga *Tee*'. *Oceania* 51: 20–39.

1980b. 'When a group of women take a wife: Generalized exchange and restricted marriage in the New Guinea Highlands'. *Mankind* 12: 286–99.

1981. 'The bride in bridewealth: A case from the New Guinean Highlands'. *Ethnology* 20: 63–75.

1984a. *Ways of exchange: The Enga Tee of Papua New Guinea.* St. Lucia: University of Queensland.

1984b. 'Beyond patriliny in the New Guinea Highlands'. *Man* (n.s.) 19(1): 50–76.

Feld, S. and Schieffelin, B. MS. 'Hard words: A functional basis for Kaluli discourse'. Unpublished typescript.

Finney, B. 1973. *Big men and business: Entrepreneurship and economic growth in the New Guinea Highlands.* Canberra: Australian National University Press.

Fitzpatrick, P. 1980. *Law and state in Papua New Guinea.* London and New York: Academic Press.

Forge, A. 1972. 'The golden fleece'. *Man* (n.s.) 7: 527–40.

Fortes, M. 1953. 'The structure of unilineal descent groups'. *American Anthropologist* 55: 17–41.

1979. 'Preface'. In L. Holy ed. *Segmentary lineage systems reconsidered.* Belfast Queen's University: The Queen's University Papers in Social Anthopology 4.

Fox, J. J. 1974. 'Our ancestors spoke in pairs: Rotinese views of language, dialect, and code'. In R. Bauman and J. Sherzer, eds., *Explorations in the ethnography of speaking,* pp. 65–85. Cambridge: Cambridge University Press.

Fox, J. J., ed. 1988. *To speak in pairs: Essays on the ritual languages of eastern Indonesia.* Cambridge Studies in Oral and Literate Culture. Cambridge: Cambridge University Press.

Geertz, C. 1973. *The interpretation of cultures.* New York: Basic Books.

Gell, A. 1975. *Metamorphosis of the cassowaries: Umeda society, language and ritual.* London: Athlone Press.

Gewertz, D. 1984. 'Of symbolic anchors and sago soup: The rhetoric of exchange among the Chambri of Papua New Guinea'. In D. L. Brenneis and F. R. Myers, eds., *Dangerous words: Language and politics in the Pacific,* pp. 192–213. New York and London: New York University Press.

Giddens, A. 1979. *Central problems in social theory: Action, structure and contradiction in social analysis.* Hong Kong: The Macmillan Press Ltd.

1984. *The constitution of society: Outline of the theory of structuration.* Oxford: Polity Press.

Gitlow, R. 1947. *Economics of the Mount Hagen Tribes, New Guinea.* Seattle: University of Washington Press.

Glasse, R. M. 1968. *The Huli of Papua: A cognatic descent system.* Paris: Mouton.

Goldman, L. 1983. *Talk never dies: The language of Huli disputes.* London and New York: Tavistock.

Goodenough, W. 1953. 'Ethnographic notes on the Mae people of New Guinea's western Highlands'. *Southwestern Journal of Anthropology* 9: 29–44.

Gordon, R. J. and Meggitt, M. J. 1985. *Law and order in the New Guinea highlands: Encounters with Enga.* Hanover: published for University of Vermont by University Press of New England.

Gregory, C. A. 1987. Review of R. Lederman, *What gifts engender. Man* 22: 759–60.

Habermas, J. 1984. *The theory of communicative action, Vol. 1: Reason and the rationalization of society.* Boston: Beacon Press.

Halliday, M. A. K. 1985. *An introduction to functional grammar.* London: Edward Arnold.

Hallpike, C. 1977. *Bloodshed and vengeance in the Papua mountains: The generation of conflict in Tauade society.* Oxford: Clarendon Press.

Hocart, A. M. 1933. *The progress of man.* London: Methuen.

Hogbin, I. and Wedgwood, C. 1953. 'Local grouping in Melanesia'. *Oceania* 23(4): 241–76.

Hughes, I. 1978. 'Good money and bad: Inflation and devaluation in the colonial process'. *Mankind* 11: 308–18.

Hymes, D. 1974 [1962]. 'The ethnography of speaking'. In B. Blount, ed., *Language, culture and society: A book of readings,* pp. 189–223. Cambridge, Mass. Winthrop Publishers.

Irvine, J. 1979. 'Formality and informality in communicative events'. *American Anthropologist* 81: 773–90.

Jakobson, R. 1966. 'Grammatical parallelism and its Russian facet'. *Language* 42(2): 399–429.

1971 [1957]. 'Shifters, verbal categories, and the Russian verb'. In *Selected writings,* vol. 2, pp. 130–47. The Hague: Mouton.

Jorgensen, D. 1981. 'Taro and arrows: Order, entropy and religion among the Telefolmin'. Unpublished Ph.D. thesis, University of British Columbia.

Josephides, L. 1985. *The production of inequality: Gender and exchange among the Kewa.* London: Tavistock.

Keenan, E. O. and Schieffelin, B. 1976. 'Topic as a discourse notion: A study of topic in the conversation of children and adults'. In C. Li, ed., *Subject and topic,* pp. 335–84. New York: Academic Press.

Keesing, R. 1975. *Kin groups and social structure.* New York: Holt, Rinehart and Winston.

Kelly, R. 1977. *Etoro social structure*. Ann Arbor: University of Michigan Press.

Kurylowicz, J. 1964. *The inflectional categories of Indo-European*. Heidelberg: Winter.

Lakoff, G. 1987. *Women, fire and dangerous things: What categories reveal about the mind*. Chicago: University of Chicago Press.

Lancy, D. F. and Strathern, A. J. 1981 '"Making twos": Pairing as an alternative to the taxonomic mode of representation'. *American Anthropologist* 83: 773–95.

Langlas, C. M. 1974. 'Foi land use, prestige economics and residence: A processual analysis'. Unpublished Ph.D. thesis. Honolulu: University of Hawaii.

Langness, L. L. 1964. 'Some problems in the conceptualization of Highlands social structures'. In J. B. Watson, ed., *New Guinea: The Central Highlands. American Anthropologist 66, Special Publication No. 4*, 162–82.

Larson, J. E. 1970. 'The dynamics of Enga persuasive speech'. Wapenamanda, New Guinea: Kristen Press.

Lawrence, P. 1964. *Road belong cargo*. Melbourne: Manchester and Melbourne University Presses.

1984. *The Garia: An ethnography of a traditional cosmic system in Papua New Guinea*. Melbourne: Melbourne University Press.

Lederman, R. 1980. 'Who speaks here? Formality and the politics of gender in Mendi, Highland Papua New Guinea'. *Journal of the Polynesian Society* 89: 479–98.

1986a. *What gifts engender: Social relations and politics in Mendi, Highland Papua New Guinea*. Cambridge: Cambridge University Press.

1986b. 'Changing times in Mendi: Notes towards writing Highlands history'. *Ethnohistory* 33(1).

1986c. Review of Feil *Ways of Exchange*. *Oceania* 57: 63–4.

Lévi-Strauss, C. 1963. *Structural anthropology*. (Trans. C. Jacobson and B. G. Schoepf) New York: Basic Books.

1966. *The savage mind*. Chicago: University of Chicago Press.

1969. *The Elementary Structures of Kinship*. Boston: Beacon Press.

Maclean, N. 1985. 'Understanding Maring marriage: A question of the analytic utility of the domestic mode of production'. In D. Gardner and N. Modjeska, eds., *Recent studies in the political economy of Papua New Guinea societies*. Sydney: Special Issue No. 4, *Mankind*.

Malinowski, B. 1922. *Argonauts of the Western Pacific*. London: Routledge and Kegan Paul.

1949 [1923]. 'The problem of meaning in primitive languages'. In C. K. Ogden and I. A. Richards, eds., *The meaning of meaning*, pp. 296–336. International Library of Psychology, Philosophy, and Scientific Method. London: Routledge and Kegan Paul.

Mauss, M. 1954 [1925]. *The gift: Forms and functions of exchange in archaic societies*. (Trans. I. Cunnison). London: Cohen and West.

Meggitt, M. 1964. 'Male-female relationships in the Highlands of Australian New Guinea'. *American Anthropologist* 66: 204–24.

1965. *The lineage system of the Mae-Enga*. Edinburgh: Oliver and Boyd.

1971. 'The pattern of leadership among the Mae-Enga of New Guinea'. In R. M. Berndt and P. Lawrence, eds., *Politics in New Guinea*, pp. 191–206. Nedlands: University of Western Australia Press.

1974. 'Pigs are our hearts'. *Oceania* 44: 165–203.

1977. *Blood is their argument*. Palo Alto: Mayfield.

Meigs, A. 1984. *Food, sex and pollution: A New Guinea religion*. New Brunswick, N. J.: Rutgers University Press.

Merlan, F. 1988. 'Marriage and the constitution of exchange relations in the Highlands of Papua New Guinea: A comparative study'. *Journal of the Polynesian Society* 97(4): 409–33.

1989. 'Turning the talk, Ku Waru "bent speech" as social action'. In *Proceedings of the Chicago Linguistic Society, 1989 Parasession on Language in Context*. Chicago: Chicago Linguistic Society.

Merlan, F. and Rumsey, A. 1986. 'A marriage dispute in the Nebilyer Valley, Western Highlands Province, Papua New Guinea'. *Pacific Linguistics* Series A-74, 69–180.

Milhalic, F. 1971. *The Jacaranda dictionary and grammar of Melanesian Pidgin*. Milton, Queensland: Jacaranda Press.

Nadel, S. F. 1957. *The theory of social structure*. London: Cohen and West.

Nakinch, T. 1977. 'The origin and formation of the Ulga and Upuka people in the Nebilyer area of Mt Hagen, W. H. P.' Occasional Paper, Institute of Applied Social and Economic Research, Boroko, P.N.G.

National Parliament. 1982. 'Principal Roll of Electors'. Electorate of Tambul-Nebilyer. Port Moresby, Papua New Guinea. Government Printer.

O'Hanlon, M. 1983. 'Handsome is as handsome does: Display and betrayal in the Wahgi'. *Oceania* 53: 317–33.

Ortner, S. 1984. 'Theory in anthropology since the 'sixties'. *Comparative Studies in Society and History* 26: 126–66.

Patrol Reports. 1950/51. AS 13/26 item 148. Kaugel River Valley patrol, no.1of 50/51. (ADO A. Timperley, PO B. Corrigan). Canberra: Australian Archives.

1955. AS 13/26, No. 4 of 1955. Kaugel Valley. Canberra: Australian Archives.

Peirce, C. S. S. 1960. *Collected papers* C. Hartshorne, P. Weiss and A. Burks, eds. Cambridge, Mass.: Harvard University Press. 8 vols.

Popper, K. 1959. *The logic of scientific discovery*. London: Hutchinson.

Pouwer, J. 1960. 'Loosely structured societies in Netherlands New Guinea'. *Bijdragen tot de Taal-Land-en Volkenkunde* 116: 109–18.

Radcliffe-Brown, A. R. 1965 *Structure and function in primitive society*. New York: Free Press.

Read, K. E. 1959. 'Leadership and consensus in a New Guinea society'. *American Anthropologist* 64: 425–36.

Reay, M. 1959. *The Kuma: Freedom and conformity in the New Guinea Highlands*. Melbourne: Melbourne University Press.

Rosaldo, M. Z. 1973. 'I have nothing to hide: The language of Ilongot oratory'. *Language in Society* 2: 193–223.

Ross, W. A. 1936. 'Ethnological notes on Mt Hagen Tribes (Mandated Territory of New Guinea)'. *Anthropos* 31: 341–63.

1969. 'The Catholic mission in the western Highlands'. In *The history of Melanesia*, Second Waigani Seminar, pp. 319–27. University of Papua and New Guinea, with the Australian National University.

Rubel, P. 1987. Review of D. K. Feil *Ways of exchange. American Ethnologist* 14(3): 591–3.

Rubel, P. and A. Rosman 1978. *Your own pigs you may not eat: A comparative study of New Guinea societies.* Chicago: University of Chicago Press.

Rumsey, A. 1986. 'Oratory and the politics of metaphor in the New Guinea Highlands'. In T. Threadgold, E. A. Grosz, G. Kress and M. A. K. Halliday, eds., *Semiotics, ideology, language,* pp. 283–96. Sydney: Sydney Association for Studies in Society and Culture.

1989. 'Grammatical person and social agency in New Guinea Highland exchange systems.' In *Proceedings of the Chicago Linguistic Society, 1989 Parasession on Language in Context*. Chicago: Chicago Linguistic Society.

1990 'Wording, meaning and linguistic ideology'. *American Anthropologist,* 92(2):346–61.

Ryan, D'A. 1959. 'Clan formation in the Mendi Valley'. *Oceania* 29: 257–90.

1961. 'Gift exchange in the Mendi Valley'. Unpublished Ph.D. thesis. University of Sydney.

Sacks, H., Schegloff, E. A. and Jefferson, G. 1974. 'A simplest systematics for the organization of turn-taking in conversation'. *Language* 50(4): 696–735.

Sahlins, M. D. 1961. 'The segmentary lineage: An organization of predatory expansion. *American Anthropologist* 63: 322–45.

1963. 'Poor man, rich man, big man, chief'. *Comparative Studies in Society and History* 5: 285–303.

1965. 'On the ideology and composition of descent groups'. *Man* 65: 104–7.

1968. *Tribesmen*. Englewood Cliffs, N.J.: Prentice-Hall.

1972. *Stone age economics*. Chicago: Aldine.

1981. *Historical metaphors and mythical realities: Structure in the early history of the Sandwich Islands Kingdom*. Association for the Study of Anthropology in Oceania, Special Publication No. 1. Ann Arbor: University of Michigan Press.

1985. *Islands of history*. Chicago: University of Chicago.

Salisbury, R. 1962. *From stone to steel*. Melbourne: Melbourne University Press.

Sapir, E. 1949. 'The unconscious patterning of behavior in society'. In D. Mandelbaum, ed., *Selected writings of Edward Sapir*, pp. 544–59. Berkeley and Los Angeles: University of California Press.

Scheffler, H. 1964. 'Descent concepts and descent groups: The Maori case'. *Journal of the Polynesian Society* 73: 126–33.

1985. 'Filiation and affiliation'. *Man* (n.s.) 20: 1–21.

Schieffelin, E. 1976. *The sorrow of the lonely and the burning of the dancers*. New York: St Martin's.

1980. 'Reciprocity and the construction of reality'. *Man* 15(3): 502–17.

Schwimmer, E. 1973. *Exchange in the social structure of the Orokaiva*. London: C. Hurst and Co.

1974. 'Objects of mediation: Myth and praxis.' In I. Rossi, ed., *The unconscious in culture: The structuralism of Claude Lévi-Strauss in perspective*. New York: E. P. Dutton and Co.

Sexton, L. D. 1982. '"Wok Meri": A women's savings and exchange system in Highland Papua New Guinea'. *Oceania* 52: 167–98.

1984. 'Pigs, pearlshells and "women's work": Collective response to socio-economic change in Highland Papua New Guinea'. In D. O'Brien and S. Tiffany, eds., *The value of the devalued: Perspectives on women from the Pacific*. Berkeley: University of California Press.

Sherzer, J. 1983. *Kuna ways of speaking: An ethnographic perspective*. Austin: University of Texas Press.

Sillitoe, P. 1979. *Give and take: Exchange in Wola society*. Canberra and London: Australian National University Press.

Silverstein, M. 1976. 'Shifters, linguistic categories, and cultural description'. In K. Basso and H. Selby, eds., *Meaning in anthropology*, pp. 11–56. Albuquerque: University of New Mexico Press.

1979. 'Language structure and linguistic ideology'. In P. R. Clyne, W. F. Hanks and C. L. Hofbauer, eds., *The elements: A parasession on linguistic units and levels*, pp. 193–247. Chicago: Chicago Linguistic Society.

1981. 'The limits of awareness'. *Sociolinguistic Working Paper No. 84*. Austin, Texas: Southwest Educational Development Laboratory.

Sinclair, J. 1971. *The Highlanders*. Milton, Queensland: Jacaranda Press.

Smith, M. G. 1956. 'On segmentary lineage systems'. *Journal of the Royal Anthropological Institute* 86: 39–79.

Sorensen, E. R. 1972. 'Socio-ecological change among the Fore of New Guinea'. *Current Anthropology* 13 (3–4), June-October.

Stoljar, S. J. 1973. *Groups and entities*. Canberra: Australia National University Press.

Strathern, A. (A. J.) 1971. *The rope of moka: Big men and ceremonial exchange in Mt Hagen, New Guinea*. Cambridge: Cambridge University Press.

1972. *One father, one blood*. London: Tavistock.
1973. 'Kinship, descent and locality: some New Guinea examples'. In J. Goody, ed., *The Character of Kinship*. Cambridge: Cambridge University Press.
1975. 'Veiled speech in Mt Hagen'. In. M. Bloch, ed., *Political language and oratory in traditional society*, pp.185–203. London, New York and San Francisco: Academic Press.
1977a. 'Melpa food-names as an expression of ideas on identity and substance'. *Journal of the Polynesian Society* 86: 503–11.
1977b. 'Mathematics in the moka'. *Papua New Guinea Journal of Education* 13(1): 16–20.
1978. '"Finance and production" revisited: In pursuit of a comparison'. *Research in Economic Anthropology* 1: 73–104.
1979a. '"It's his affair": A note on the individual and the group in New Guinea Highlands societies'. *Canberra Anthropology* 2(1): 98–113.
1979b. *Ongka: A self-account by a New Guinea big-man*. [Trans. A. J. Strathern]. London: Duckworth.
1981. '"Noman": Representations of identity in Mount Hagen'. In L. Holy and M. Stuchlik, eds., *The structure of folk models*, pp.281–303. New York: Academic Press.
1982. 'The division of labor and processes of social change in Mt Hagen'. *American Ethnologist* 9: 291–319.
1984. *A line of power*. London: Tavistock.
Strathern, M. (A. M.) 1968. 'Popokl: The question of morality'. *Mankind* 6: 553–62.
1972a. *Women in between: Female roles in a male world*. London and New York: Seminar (Academic) Press.
1972b. *Official and unofficial courts*. New Guinea Research Bulletin No. 47. Canberra: The Australian National University.
1975. *No money on our skins: Hagen migrants in Port Moresby*. New Guinea Research Bulletin 61. Canberra: Australian National University.
1979. 'The self in self-decoration'. *Oceania* 49: 241–57.
1985a. 'Discovering "social control"'. *Journal of Law and Society* 12(2): 111–34.
1985b. 'John Locke's servant and the *hausboi* from Hagen: some thoughts on domestic labour'. *Critical Philosophy*. 2: 21–48.
1985 MS. 'The mediation of emotions'. Written for *Conflict and control in the New Guinea Highlands*, W. E. Wormsley, ed.
1986 MS-A. 'Increment and androgyny: Reflections on recent developments in the anthropology of Papua New Guinea'. Prepared for The Dialectic of Gender in the Southern Lowlands, at session convened by the Centre for Australian and Oceanic Studies, Catholic University, Nijmegen, The Netherlands.
1986 MS-B. 'Dual models and multiple person: Gender in Melanesia'. Notes for AAA 1986 Meetings, session on Melanesian Ethnography in the Production of Anthropological Theory.
1987. 'Producing difference: Connections and disconnections in two New Guinea Highland kinship systems'. In J. Collier and S. Yanagisako, eds., *Gender and Kinship*. Stanford: Stanford University Press.
1988. *The gender of the gift: Problems with women and problems with society in Melanesia*. Berkeley and Los Angeles: University of California Press.
in press. 'Artefacts of history: events and the interpretation of images'. In J. Siikala, ed., *Culture and History in the Pacific*. Helsinki: Transactions of the Finnish Anthropological Society.
Strathern, A. and M. (A. J. and A. M.) 1968. 'Marsupials and magic: A study of spell symbolism among the Mbowamb'. In E. R. Leach, (ed.), *Dialectic in Practical Religion*. Cambridge Papers in Social Anthropology, pp.179–202.
1971. *Self-decoration in Mount Hagen*. London: Duckworth.

Strauss, H. MS. 'Grammatik der Melpa-Sprache'. Deposited with Department of Linguistics, Research School of Pacific Studies, Australian National University, Canberra.

Strauss, H. [with H. Tischner]. 1962. *Die Mi-Kultur der Hagenbergstaemme*. Hamburg: Cram, de Gruyter.

Taylor, J. L. 1933. James L. Taylor diary and Mount Hagen patrol report. AS 13/26 Q836/3, part 2 (56).

Turton, D. 1979. 'A journey made us'. In L. Holy, ed., *Segmentary lineage systems revisited*. Belfast, Queen's University: The Queen's Papers in Social Anthropology 4.

Tyler, S. A., ed., 1969. *Cognitive anthropology*. New York: Holt, Rinehart and Winston.

Vicedom, G. F. and H. Tischner 1943–8. *Die Mbowamb: Die Kultur der Hagenberg-Staemme in Oestlichen Zentral Neu-Guinea*. 3 vols. Hamburg: Friederichsen, de Gruyter.

Wagner, R. 1967. *The curse of Souw: Principles of Daribi clan formation and alliance*. Chicago: University of Chicago Press.

1974. 'Are there social groups in the New Guinea Highlands?' In M. J. Leaf, ed., *Frontiers of anthropology*, pp.95–121. New York: Van Nostrand Co.

1975. *The invention of culture*. Englewood Cliffs, N.J.: Prentice-Hall.

1978. *Lethal speech: Daribi myth as symbolic obviation*. Ithaca and London: Cornell University Press.

1986a. *Asiwinarong: Ethos, image, and social power among the Usen Barok of New Ireland*. Princeton: Princeton University Press.

1986b. *Symbols that stand for themselves*. Chicago: University of Chicago Press.

1988. 'Foreword' to *The heart of the pearlshell*, J. F. Weiner (pp. ix–xii). Berkeley: University of California Press.

Warry, W. 1985. 'Politics of a new order: The Kafaina movement'. In *Women in politics in Papua New Guinea*. Department of Political and Social Change, Australian National University Working Paper No. 6.

Watson, J. B. 1983. *Tairora culture: Contingency and pragmatism*. Seattle and London: University of Washington Press.

Weber, M. 1958 [1905]. *The Protestant ethic and the spirit of capitalism*. (Trans. T. Parsons). New York: C. Scribner's Sons.

Weiner, A. 1976. *Women of value, men of renown: New perspectives in Trobriand exchange*. Austin: University of Texas Press.

Weiner, J. F. 1982. 'Substance, siblingship and exchange: Aspects of social structure in New Guinea'. *Social Analysis* 11: 3–34.

1985. 'Affinity and cross-cousin terminology among the Foi'. *Social Analysis* 17: 93–112.

1988. *The heart of the pearlshell: The mythological dimension of Foi sociality*. Berkeley: University of California Press.

Whorf, B. L. 1956. *Language, thought and reality: Selected writings of Benjamin Lee Whorf*. J. B. Carroll, ed. New York: Wiley.

Young, M. 1971 *Fighting with food: Leadership, values and social control in a Massim society*. Cambridge: Cambridge University Press.

Index

ab kuime, *see* bridewealth
abu lku, *see* woman's house
action, *see* social action
addressees of speech, 127
address, forms of, 90–1, 96–7
affinal links and exchange transactions, 64–5, 81–2
African-derived theory of segmentary lineage structure, 36
agency and social action, 89–90, 242–4
agents, identifying in oratory, 91–5
agnation, 3
  agnatic affiliations, 10
alliances,
  and participation in war, 139
  as topics of talk, 136–8
  of Kopia, 48–50
allies, exchange between in Nebilyer, *see* *makayl*
Alya, 38
apical ancestors, *see* descent theory
appearance, social significance of, 233–5
Araim Kopia, 45–8

Bakhtin, M., 118
'base-man', 44
'bent speech', *see ung eke*
Benveniste, E., 220
big-men,
  as topics of talk, 130
  role in segmentation, 135–6
binarism, 209
bisnis, 29
  and women's intervention, 212
  clubs, 158–60
Bloch, M., 110
bo ul, 29–30
bodily substance, 42–3
Bourdieu, P., 215
bridewealth, 71–5
brother pair, 37–8
Bulmer, R., 83–5
business ventures, 27–8

cash, and marriage arrangements, 71, 74, 81
cash crops, 26–7
Catholic Church, 23–4
ceremonial exchange,
  see exchange, *makayl*
change,
  social action and, 241–2
  theorization about, 188–90
coffee,
  as a cash crop, 26–7
  cultivation, 26, 27–8
color, imagery, 106–7, 228
compensation payments, 123, 125
  and *gavman lo*, 127
  first round, analysis, 122–55
  for disequilibrium, 235
  inter-*talapi*, 143
  return payments, analysis, 156–8
  women's participation, 157, 169–87
complementary opposition, 3
  examples, 50, 52
compositional parity, 40, 206, 207–8
concealment, 224–6
concrete instances, *see* tokens
consortia and exchange, 63–4
contingent juxtaposition, 236–8
corporate action, 11–16
  and exchange, 63
  criteria for, 12
corporate nature of *talapi*, 40–1
court system, village, *see kot*
crops, 20, 26–7
currency, pearl shell, 26, 27, 229
  see also money

deceit, 225, 226
demography, Kailge area, 20–3
Dena *ab* Kopil, speech at Kopola, 185–6, 194
descent theory, 8, 10
  and *talapi*, 36–7
  see also segmentary lineage theory
devaluation of kina shell currency, 26, 27, 229
'development', 23–8
difference,
  and exchange, 200–10
  see also sameness/difference
differentiation, orders of, 199–201
direct compensation, 84
disequilibrium, effect of, 235
domestic organization, 67, 69–70
donor/recipient relationships, 63–5
dual organization, 205, 208–9
dual number, grammar of, 95–6
Durkheim, E., on segmentation, 35

economic factors of marriage patterns, 80–1
economic life, 26–7
el pul, *see* fight source
el ung, 88, 98–102
  at Kailge, 127, 128
  binarism, 209
  prosodic features, 98–9
  relation to *ung eke*, 109–10
  situations limiting, 124
  topics of, 136–8
  use of, 154
    by women, 186–7
enemies,
  and inter-*talapi* relations, 207–8
  intermarriage with, 83–4
  of Kopia, 48–50
Enga, 10–14
  and marriage patterns, 83–5
Epola, 38
Epola-Alya(-Lalka) relations with Kopia-Kubuka, 136–9
equivalence in exchange, 204–5
ethnographic sources, 30–1
ethnohistory of Kopia *talapi*, 45–8
European advent, New Guineans' attitude, 189
Europeans,
  as events, 231
  exploration of Mt Hagen area, 23–7
  influences, 22–8
Evans-Pritchard, E. E., 199

events,
  and structure, 214–20
  anthropology of, 1–7
  concept of; 221–2, 239–40
  contemporary, 236–8
  latent aspects, 30
  ordering of speakers, 126–7, 161–2, 167
  participation, 126
  persons as, 230–1
  public nature of, 31–2
  relation of kinds, 236–8
  significance of talk at, 88–9
  spatial aspects, 125–6
  theorization, 188–90
exchange,
  analysis of Kopia, 57–67
  and marriage, 67–74, 81–7
  and structure, 200–10
  and warfare, 206–7
  basis for conducting, 14
  cycles of payments, 58–9
  external Kopia, 59–65
  implications of language use, 218–20
  internal, 66
  persons effecting, *see* agency
  related events, 123–5
  segmentary difference, 200–1, 204, 207
  significance of food, 231–3
  talk, 120–1
  theories of, 3, 8–17
  types of, 82, 216–17
exchange events,
  first round, 123–8
  nature of, 218–19
  return, 156–8, 160–84, 185–7
  significance of site, 127, 164–7
exchange-mediated difference, 207
exchange relationships and pairing, 204–9
exchange transactions, *see* transactions

favoritism, *see wantok sistem*
Feil, D. K.,
  on exchange systems, 10–14, 243
  on basis of exchange, 68
fellowship activities, 32
female imagery in *ung eke*, 104
fight plans, future, 152–5
fight source,
  identification, 133–4, 157, 161, 162, 177
  Kopia as, 60
figurative speech, *see ung eke*
flag, use at events, 156, 169, 170, 183, 185
focused speech, 125
food, significance of, 231–3

Galka segment, 46
garden plots, 44
gavman, 211–13
gavman lo, 28–9
  and compensation payments, 127
  and future *talapi* relations, 152–5
  attitudes to, 195–7
  influence of, 178, 180, 183
gender and naming practices, 236
genealogical aspects of exchange, 64–5
geography, Kailge area, 20–3
Gewertz, D., 218–19
Goldman, L., 223
'government law', *see gavman lo*
governmental influences, 22
group identity, 9

heteroglossia, 118–9
hierarchichal structure, 35, 38–40
  see also compositional parity
  and *talapi*, 38–40
Hymes, D., 364 note 1

Ibumuyl area, *talapi*, 52–3
identity, social, *see* social identities
imagery, in *ung eke*, 102–4, 105–9
immigrants, acceptance of, 42
  examples, 52–3
'in-betweenness' of women,
  see women, intermediary status
individuals and exchange, 10–16, 63–4
instances, concrete, *see* tokens
interpersonal exchange, 61–5
interpersonal relationships,
  and pairing, 204
  and segmentation, 201–2
interpretation of tropes, 103–9
inter-*talapi* events, linguistic devices, 88–9
inter-*talapi* marriage, 75–80
inter-*talapi* relations, 136–44
  and exchange, 61–5, 199–210
  and language use, 217–18
  and pairing, 204–9
  and warfare, 207
  in future, 152–5
  speeches about, 167–9
intra-*talapi* exchange, 66
intra-*talapi* marriage, 75, 77–8

Josephides, L., 68

Kabika segment, 46
Kailge area, 20–3
  Kopia *talapi* within, 45–52
  Palimi segments, 52–5
Kaja segment, 46
Kakuyl, 22–3
kewa, 29–30
kiap,
  intervention in warfare, 190–1
  speech by one at Palimung, 179–80
Kidi segment, 46
kina shell currency, *see* currency, pearl shell
Kodu, speech at Palimung, 170–1, 193
Kopia *talapi*, 45–8
  external relations, 48–50
  internal opposition, 50–2
  internal structure and ethnohistory, 45–8
Kopia-Kubuka,
  alliance, 50, 141–4
  external exchange, 59–65
  relations with,
    Epola-Alya(-Lalka), 136–9
    Mujika, 147–52
    Poika-Palimi, 139
    Tilka, 145–6
Kopia/Tolab, contributions to *makayl*, 61–2
Kopil segment, 46
Kopil (Dena *ab*), *see* Dena *ab* Kopil
Kopola payment event, 185–7
kopong, 42–3
kot, 29
Ku Waru people, language, 22, Appendix B
Kubuka,
  exchange involvement, 59–61
  relations with,
    Kopia, 141–4
    Laulku, 141–2, 142–3
  see also Kopia-Kubuka
Kujilyi,
  as topic of talk, 131–5
  role in compensation event, 130–5
  speech at Palimung, 172–6
Kulka women's club, *see* women's club
Kupena segment, 46
Kusika, 38

Lalka, 38
Lama, 21
Lancy, D. F. and A. J. Strathern, 114–15
land,
  and *talapi*, 44–5
  relation to kinship, 42–3
land use and social groupings, 44
language philosophy, 222

Laulku,
  compensation to, 122–55
  relations with Kubuka, 141–2, 142–3
law and order, European, *see gavman lo*
Lederman, R., 14–16, 39, 68
Lévi-Strauss, C.,
  on dual organization, 205
  on reciprocity, 208–9
linguistic indexes, 97–8
lku tapa, *see* men's house

Maclean, N., 351 note 13, 363 note 14
makayl,
  and *talapi* structure, 38
  distribution of objects, 61
  external, 59–65
  phases of cycle, 58–9
  structure and history, 57–67
makayl partners and intermarriage, 82–4
makayl relationship, 58–9
male imagery in *ung eke*, 103–4
male social prominence, features of, 32–3
Malinowski, B., 9–10, 89, 222
marital destination, influencing factors, 20
markets, use of, 28
marriage, 18, 67–87
  patterns, 69, 74–87
  prohibitions against, 75
Marsupial Road War, 1–7, 48
  background, 49–50
  compensation payments, 122–3, 156–7
  fight source, 133–4
  Sibeka sweet potato garden battle, 1, 49–50
  women's intervention, 1, 156
matrifiliation, 69–70
matrilateral links and exchange transactions, 64–5, 81–2
Meam people, 21, 22
meetings of women's clubs, 159–60
Meggitt, M., 10–14, 39, 83–5, 135–6, 243
Melpa people, 21–2
  ethnographic studies of, 30–1
men, marriage, 75–7
Mendi, 14–16, 39
men's house, 37
  groupings in Kopia *talapi*, 46
  occupants, 71
Midipu, 38
Mijiyl, speech at Palimung, 171–2, 193
missionaries, 23–4
money, 27
  and women's clubs, 158, 159
  see also bisnis; currency
mortuary payments, 82
motivation, and corporate action, 12–13, 14
Mt Hagen town, as administration centre, 21–2
Mujika,
  relations with Kopia-Kubuka, 147–52
  role in warfare, 147–52

names,
  forms, 91–3
  relation between place and group, 41–2
  segmentary, *see* segmentary names
  use in public oratory, 93–5
Nebilyer Valley peoples, 20–3
Neka, speech at Palimung, 180–1, 193–4
neutral tribes, 126
  payments, 144–7
New Guineans' assessment of European advent, 189
Noma,
  speeches at Palimung, 77
  speech at Kailge, 161–3
novelty,
  and disequilibrium, 235
  in events, 231
  in exchange objects, 230
numan, 226–8
number categories, grammar and, 95–8

objects, significance in exchange, 218–20, 228–30
oppositional parity, 40, 208
oratory,
  and agency, 91
  styles of, 98–113, 116–21
  types used, 133
  see also talk
order, European style, *see kewa*
order, indigenous, *see bo ul*
order of speakers, 126–7, 161–2, 167
ownership of land, 44

paired *talapi*, name forms, 91–3
pairing, 113–16
  and exchange relationships, 62–3, 204–9
  and intermarriage, 82–4
  and structure, 215–16
  examples, 140
  meaning of, 241–2
pairs of brothers, *see* brother pairs
Palimi segments,
  co-resident with Kopia, 52–5
  internal opposition, 54–5
  relationship with Kopia-Kubuka, 139–41

Palimung compensation event, 163–84
Palimung trade-store, 27–8
Palimung-Yubika area, *talapi*, 38–9
parallelism, 99–100
parity,
  and structure, 215–16
  and exchange, 205–9
partnership, *makayl*, see *makayl* partners
payback, 59
payments,
  analysis of payment events, 122–97
  initiatory, 123
  return, 156–7, 180, 182
  types of, 82
  women's, 212
  see also transactions
pearl shell, *see* currency, money
performative structure, 188, 189
personal names, use in public domain, 94
persons as events, 230–1
place names, 41–2
place-titles and oratory, 91, 94
plural number,
  grammar of, 95–6
  use in *el ung*, 101
Poika, relationship with Kopia-Kubuka, 139–41
Poika-Palimi exchange involvement, 59–61
Pokea speech at Palimung, 169–70, 183–4
prescriptive structure, 188, 189
prestation ground,
  change of, 127–8
  implication of site, 127, 164–7
  Kailge, 125, 127
prostitute, image of, 132–3
public domain, events held in, 31–2
public speaking, importance of, 31–3

questions, rhetorical, *see* rhetorical questions

recipient/donor relationships, *see* donor/recipient relationships
recruitment for war, 208
  and exchange, 59–61
  inter-*talapi*, 143
reference,
  forms of, 90–3, 111
  to segment identities, 93–4
reflexive nature of public talk, 116–20
regional marriage patterning, 69, 75–87
relation between structure and history, 3–8
relationships, ways of making, *see* structuring structures
religious conversion, 24
religious gathering, *see also* fellowship activities
reparation, 84, *see* compensation
reported speech, 116–20
representation, and groups, 13–14, 16
reproduction, 42–3
revelation of objects, 228–30
rhetorical devices in *el ung*, 99–100
rhetorical questions, 11–13
roads, Nebilyer Valley, 20–1
Rubel, P. and A. Rosman, 205

Sahlins, M. D., 8, 188–90
sameness of *talapi*,
  and segmentary sociality, 200–1, 207
sameness/difference, 199–201, 217–18
segmentary difference, 199–201
segmentary lineage theory, 3, 8–9, 36
  see also descent theory
segmentary groups, 9, 40–1
  and territories, 44–5
segmentary names, 91–5
  and oratory, 91
  context of non-use, 94–5
  context of use, 93–4
segmentary nature of *talapi*, 35–6
segmentary order, 29–30, 199–210
  and *gavman*, 211–12
  effect of women's action, 210, 213–14
segmentary person, 96
  grammar of, 95–8
  interpretation of, 110–11
  non-use of, 193
  use in *el ung*, 100
segmentary relationships,
  and exchange, 200–10
segmentation, 2, 35–6
  and exchange theory, 8–17
  and marriage, 75, 75–80
  and structure, 198–200
  internal opposition, examples, 50–2, 54–5
  levels of, 214
  of Kopia *talapi*, 45–8
  role of big-men, 135–6
  structural analysis examples, 44–5,
sem, 14, 15
serial parity, 40, 205, 206
Sibeka gardens, use of, 21
Sibeka sweet potato garden battle, *see* Marsupial Road War
siblingship, 43, 201, 217
Silverstein, M., 97
singular number, grammar of, 95–6

social action,
  agency and, 89–90
  disposition to, 238–9
  elements of, 221–4
  future options, 241
  juxtaposition with meaning, 239–44
  reasons for, 227–8
  significant effects and, 224–35
  talk and, 119–21
social differentiation, *see* segmentation
social identities, 215–16
  corporate, 40–1
  name forms, 91–5
  use of segmentary person, 95–8
social significance of,
  action, 224–8
  food, 231–3
  objects, 228–30
  the body, 233–5
socio-economics and marriage patterns, 80–1
sociopolitical grouping and marriage patterns, 80
source of fight, *see* fight source
speakers,
  competition among, 125–6
  orientation in *ung eke*, 104–5
  self-identification, 193
speech making,
  actions during, 99
  at Palimung, 165–84
  forms used by women, 193–5
  imagery in, 102–9
  phases, 128
  preliminary, 125, 160–3
  reflexive content, 116–20
  styles of, 32
  topical analysis, 129–55
Strathern, A. J., 9, 31, 86–7, 88, 216
  and D. F. Lancey, 114–15
Strathern, Marilyn, 5, 31, 67–8, 70, 74–5, 155, 187–90, 203–4, 206, 213, 223–4, 225–7, 366 note 23
Strauss, Hermann, 96, 114
structural analysis, 198–210
  and events, 3–4, 6
  of Kopia *talapi*, 45–8
structural relativity, 199–200
structural types,
  talapi as, 34–44
structure,
  African-derived theory of, 36
  and event, 214–20
  theorization, 188–90
  and *talapi*, 36–7
  segmentary, *see* segmentation
'structuring structures', 215–16
synchronized action of groups, 13

talapi, 2, 34–40
  alliances, 4
  delineation, 38–40
  future relations, 152–5
  meaning of, 36
  Nebilyer, structure and history, 45–55
  structural analysis, 34–45
talk,
  as social action, 119–21, 222–4
  fight, *see el ung*
  reflexive nature, 116–20
  relationship to intention, 222–3, 225
  understanding, 120–1
tapa lku, see lku tapa
Tea-Dena relations with Kopia, 48
tee exchange, 84, 85–6
temal, 228
'Temboka', 22
territorial nature of *talapi*, 41–5
theft, 225–6
Tilka,
  payment received, 144–7
  relations with Kopia-Kubuka, 145–6
  role in warfare, 144–7
titles, reference use, 94
tokens, and events, 4
Tola *talapi*, relations with Kopia, 48
Tolab segment, 46, 47
topics of speeches, 129–55
topics of *ung eke*, 102–9
transactional relationships, 201–2
transactions, 58–9,
  examples, 60–2
  individual transactions, 10–16
  interpersonal, 61–5
  inter-*talapi*, 61–5
  sequence, 60, 123
transactors, nature of, 10–16, 214–15
tribal allies, *see* alliances
tribe-pairs, 39
tropes, 102
  examples, 103–9
  see also ung eke
twem, 14, 15
types *see* structural types

Ukulupiyl segment, 46
Ulka, 38–9
ung eke, 102–9

relation to *el ung*, 109–10
significance in social action, 240–1
universal parity, 212, 213
Uwa, accident, 124–5

valuation of objects, 229–30

Wagner, R., 3, 9, 40, 56, 187–8, 203, 221, 243–4
Waipiyl segment, 46
Wanaka *talapi*, relations with Kopia, 48
Wangi, death, 123–4
wantok sistem, 29
war talk, *see el ung*
warfare,
and exchange, 5, 57–8, 59, 206–7
imagery denoting, 107
intervention in, 190–7
participation in, 139
plans for future, 152–5
relation to segmentary difference, 207
women's attitude to, 194, 197
warfare compensation, *see* compensation payments
wealth objects,
distribution, 61
significance in exchange, 218–20, 228–30
Weiner, J., 203
Wiyal Kopia, 45–8
woman's house, 37
occupants, 70
women,
actions, 1, 6, 191–7
implications of, 187
as donors, 156
as intermediaries, 191–2, 194–5, 197
as recipients of compensation, 180, 184, 187
as transactors, 62, 192–3
intermediary status, 181–2, 184, 185–7, 213–14
intervention in warfare, 191–7
marriage, 67–74
participation in compensation, 156–87
women's club (Kulka), 156–7, 169–72
acceptance at events, 169–70, 181–3, 185
as transactor, 210–14
women's clubs, 158–60, 191–7
activities, 160
women's speeches, 170–2, 180–1, 185–6, 193–5

yi pengi, 58, 60